Europe For Dummies
5th Edition

D0439701

A List of Handy Foreign-Language Words and Phrases

English	French	Italian	German	Spanish
My name is . . .	**Je m'appelle . . .** (zhuh mah-*pell*)	**Mi chiamo . . .** (me key-*ah*-mo)	**Ich heisse . . .** (eek *high*-suh)	**Me llamo . . .** (male)/ **Me llama . . .** (female) (may *yah*-moe/*yah*-mah)
Thank you	**Merci** (mair-*see*)	**Grazie** (*grat*-tzee-yay)	**Danke** (*dahn*-kah)	**Gracias** (*grah*-thee-yahs)
Please	**S'il vous plaît** (seel-vou-*play*)	**Per favore** (pair fa-*vohr*-ray)	**Bitte** (*bih*-tuh)	**Por favor** (por fah-*bohr*)
Yes/No	**Oui/Non** (wee/no)	**Si/No** (see/no)	**Ja/Nein** (yah/nine)	**Si/No** (see/no)
Do you speak English?	**Parlez-vous anglais?** (par-lay-*vou* on-glay)	**Parla Inglese?** (par-la een-glay-zay)	**Sprechen Sie Englisch?** (zprek-can zee een-glish)	**Habla usted inglés?** (ah-blah oo-sted een-glais)
Good day	**Bonjour** (bohn-*szourh*)	**Buon giorno** (bwohn jour-noh)	**Guten tag** (*goo*-tehn tahg)	**Buenos días** (*bway*-nohs *dee*-hs)
Goodbye	**Au revoir** (oh-ruh-*vwah*)	**Arrivederci** (ah-ree-vah-*dair*-chee)	**Auf wiedersehen** (owf *vee*-dair-zay-yen)	**Adiós** (ah-dee-yohs)
Excuse me	**Pardon** (pah-*rdohn*)	**Scusi** (*skoo*-zee)	**Entschuldigung, bitte** (ent-*shool*-dee-gung *bih*-tuh)	**Perdóneme** (pair-*dohn*-eh-meh)
I'm sorry	**Je suis desolée** (zhuh swee day-zoh-*lay*)	**Mi dispiace** (mee dees-pee-*yat*-chay)	**Es tut mir leid** (ehs toot meer lyd)	**Lo siento** (lo see-*yen*-toh)
How much is it?	**Combien coûte?** (coam-bee-*yehn* koot)	**Quanto costa?** (*kwan*-toh coast-ah)	**Wieviel kostet es?** (*vee*-feel *koh*-steht es)	**Cuánto cuesta?** (*kwan*-toh *kway*-stah)
1/2/3	**un** (uhn)/ **deux** (douh)/ **trois** (twah)	**uno** (*oo*-no)/ **due** (*doo*-way)/ **tre** (tray)	**eins** (eye'nz)/ **zwei** (zv'eye)/ **drei** (dr'eye)	**uno** (*oo*-noh)/ **dos** (dohs)/ **tres** (trays)

A List of Handy Foreign-Language Words and Phrases

English	French	Italian	German	Spanish
Where is the bathroom?	**Où est la toilette?** (ou *eh* lah twah-*let*)	**Dov'é il bagno?** (doh-*vay* eel *bahn*-yoh)	**Wo ist die toilette?** (voh eest dee toy-*leht*-tah)	**Dónde está el servicio/ el baño?** (*dohn*-day eh-*stah* el sair-bee-thee-yo/el *bahn*-yoh)
I would like this/that	**Je voudrais ce/ça** (zhuh vou-*dray* suh/sah)	**Vorrei questo/quello** (voar-*ray* kway-sto/ kwel-loh)	**Ich möchte dieses/das** (eek mowk-tah dee-zes/dahs)	**Quisiera éste/ese** (kee-see-*yair*-ah *eh*-stay/ *eh*-seh)
... a double room for X nights	**une chambre pour deux pour X soirs** (oou-n *shaum*-bra pour douh pour X swa)	**una doppia per X notte** (ooh-nah *dope*-pee-ya pair X *noh*-tay)	**ein Doppelzimmer für X nachts** (eye-n *doh*-pel-tzim-merr fear X nahkts)	**una habitacióndoble por X noches** (oo-nah ah-bee-ta-thee-*yon* doh-blay poar X *noh*-chays)
with/without bath	**avec** (ah-*vek*)/ **sans** (sahn) **bain** (baahn)	**con** (/coan)/ **senza** (*sen*-zah) **bagno** (*bahn*-yoh)	**mit** (miht)/ **ohne** (oh-nuh) **bad** (baad)	**con** (cohn)/ **sin** (seen) **baño** (*bah*-nyoh)
Check, please	**La conte, s'il vous plaît** (lah kohnt-ah seel-vou-play)	**Il conto, per favore** (eel *coan*-toh, pair fah-voar-ay)	**Die Rechnung, bitte** (dee rek-noong bit-tuh)	**La cuenta, por favor** (lah kwain-tah por fah-bohr)
Is service included?	**Le service est-il compris?** (luh sair-*vees* eh-teal coam-pree)	**É incluso il servizio?** (ey een-clou-so eel sair-veet-zee-yo)	**Ist die Bedienung inbegriffen?** (ihst dee beh-dee-nung in-beh-grih-fen)	**Está el servicio incluido?** (eh-stah el sair-bee-thee-yo een-clu-*wee*-doh)

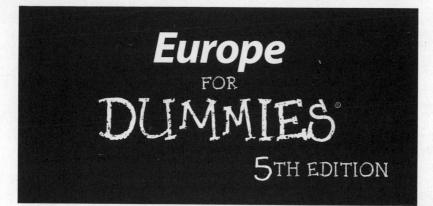

Europe
FOR
DUMMIES®
5TH EDITION

WILEY

Wiley Publishing, Inc.

Europe For Dummies®, 5th Edition

Published by
Wiley Publishing, Inc.
111 River St.
Hoboken, NJ 07030-5774
www.wiley.com

For general information on our other products and services, please contact our Customer Care Department within the U.S. at 800-762-2974, outside the U.S. at 317-572-3993, or fax 317-572-4002.

For technical support, please visit www.wiley.com/techsupport.

Wiley also publishes its books in a variety of electronic formats. Some content that appears in print may not be available in electronic books.

ISBN: 978-0-470-34545-0

Manufactured in the United States of America

10 9 8 7 6 5 4 3 2 1

WILEY

About the Authors

Donald Olson (Chapters 1–11 and 15) is a novelist, playwright, and travel writer. His newest novel, *Confessions of a Pregnant Princess*, was published in 2005 under the pen name Swan Adamson. His travel stories have appeared in *The New York Times, Travel & Leisure, Sunset, National Geographic* books, and many other publications. His guidebooks *London For Dummies, Frommer's Best Day Trips from London, Frommer's Irreverent London, Germany For Dummies,* and *Frommer's Vancouver & Victoria* are all published by Wiley. He also writes *England For Dummies,* which won a 2002 Lowell Thomas Travel Writing Award for best guidebook.

Liz Albertson (Chapter 12) worked as an editor for Frommer's Travel Guides for four years before making the leap to the other side of the computer as the author of *Ireland For Dummies.* When she isn't researching and writing, Liz spends much of her time in Ireland sitting in on traditional music sessions, fiddle in hand. She currently teaches fifth and sixth grade in New Haven, Connecticut.

Cheryl A. Pientka (Chapter 13) is a freelance journalist and a literary scout. She is the author of *Paris For Dummies* and co-author of *France For Dummies.* A graduate of Columbia University Graduate School of Journalism and the University of Delaware, she lives in New York when she can't be in Paris.

George McDonald (Chapter 14) is a former deputy editor of and currently contributing writer for *Holland Herald,* the in-flight magazine for KLM Royal Dutch Airlines. He has written extensively about Amsterdam and the Netherlands for international magazines and travel books such as *Frommer's Belgium, Holland & Luxembourg* and *Frommer's Europe.*

Darwin Porter and **Danforth Prince** (Chapters 16 and 17) have written numerous best-selling Frommer's guides and are co-authors of *Frommer's Europe.* Porter is a former bureau chief for the *Miami Herald,* and Prince, who began writing with Porter in 1982, worked for the Paris bureau of the *New York Times.*

Hana Mastrini (Chapter 18) is a native of the western Czech spa town of Karlovy Vary who became a veteran of the "Velvet Revolution" as a student in Prague in 1989. She is the author of *Frommer's Prague & the Best of the Czech Republic* and co-author of *Frommer's Europe* and *Frommer's Europe by Rail.*

Bruce Murphy and **Alessandra de Rosa** (Chapters 19–21) are part-time residents of Rome. Murphy's work has appeared in magazines ranging from *Cruising World* to *Critical Inquiry.* An avid traveler since her first cross-Europe trip at the age of 2, de Rosa was born in Rome and has lived and worked in Rome, Paris, and New York City. They are the authors of *Italy For Dummies* and *Rome For Dummies.*

Neil Schlecht (Chapters 22 and 23) is a writer and cycling aficionado who has lived in Spain, Brazil, and Ecuador. He has worked in Spain as an English teacher, a consultant on social and economic development projects for the European Union, and as a contributing writer for a Spanish art and antiques magazine. He is the author of a dozen travel guides, including *Spain For Dummies.*

Vancouver-born **Tania Kollias** (Chapter 24) longed to travel since a teen trip to England to meet the relatives, and used a Frommer's guide for her first solo journey to Europe. A degree, four continents, and many journals later, she now lives in her father's native Athens, Greece, where she wrote the country's first comprehensive listings book for expats, edited the *Now in Athens* monthly for the 2004 Olympics, and still works as a journalist and writer. She travels in and out of Greece whenever she gets the chance.

Publisher's Acknowledgments

We're proud of this book; please send us your comments through our Dummies online registration form located at www.dummies.com/register/.

Some of the people who helped bring this book to market include the following:

Editorial

Editors: Michael Kelly, Development Editor; Ian Skinnari, Project Editor; Erin Amick, Production Editor

Copy Editor: Elizabeth Kuball

Cartographer: Guy Ruggiero

Editorial Assistant: Jessica Langan-Peck

Senior Photo Editor: Richard Fox

Cover Photos:
Front: © David C. Tomlinson/ Getty Images
Back: © Richard Broadwell/ Alamy Images

Cartoons: Rich Tennant (www.the5thwave.com)

Composition Services

Project Coordinator: Kristie Rees

Layout and Graphics: Melissa K. Jester, Stephanie D. Jumper

Proofreaders: Cara Buitron

Indexer: Silvoskey Indexing Services

Publishing and Editorial for Consumer Dummies

Diane Graves Steele, Vice President and Publisher, Consumer Dummies

Kristin Ferguson-Wagstaffe, Product Development Director, Consumer Dummies

Kelly Regan, Editorial Director, Travel

Publishing for Technology Dummies

Andy Cummings, Vice President and Publisher, Dummies Technology/ General User

Composition Services

Debbie Stailey, Director of Composition Services

Contents at a Glance

Maps at a Glance

Table of Contents

Introduction

● ●

*F*inally, you're taking that long-awaited trip to Europe. Congratulations! You're about to embark on a great adventure, and in addition to the excitement, you may feel a bit overwhelmed. You have lots of plans to make: where to stay, where to dine, how long to remain in each country, how to travel from place to place, and which attractions to see — but we're here to help you every step of the way. You already took a step in the right direction by buying *Europe For Dummies,* 5th Edition!

About This Book

You have in your possession a reference tool, not a guidebook that you have to read from cover to cover. Open up this book to any chapter to find the answers on how to make your European travel dreams come true. You *can* read *Europe For Dummies* from start to finish if you want, but if you're already familiar with some aspects of international travel, feel free to skip over the first two parts and jump right into the destination descriptions.

This is a selective guidebook to Europe. Our goal throughout is to give you a really good selection of each country's highlights. That means we exclude places that other, more exhaustive guidebooks routinely include. Brussels, Copenhagen, and Lisbon are important cities, but from the perspective of the first-time visitor to Europe, they can't compete with London, Paris, and Madrid. In addition, so much is really worth seeing in Europe that you don't need to waste your time with the second-rate, the overrated, or the boring.

Please be advised that travel information is subject to change at any time — and this is especially true of prices. We, therefore, suggest that you write or call ahead for confirmation when making your travel plans. The authors, editors, and publisher cannot be held responsible for the experiences of readers while traveling. Your safety is important to us, however, so we encourage you to stay alert and be aware of your surroundings. Keep a close eye on cameras, purses, and wallets, all favorite targets of thieves and pickpockets.

Conventions Used in This Book

If you've ever tried to extract some information from a guidebook and felt that you needed training in hieroglyphics to interpret all the different symbols, we're happy to report that you won't have that problem with user-friendly *Europe For Dummies.* The use of symbols and abbreviations is kept to a minimum.

The few conventions that we do use include the following:

- **Abbreviations for credit cards:** AE (American Express), DC (Diners Club), MC (MasterCard), and V (Visa).

- **Two prices for everything:** First in the local currency, which often is the euro (€), followed by the U.S. dollar equivalent. These dollar conversions were calculated using the exchange rate listed in each destination chapter and were accurate at press time.

  Exchange rates can and will fluctuate, and the rate probably will not be the same when you visit. However, because the fluctuations tend to stay within around 10 percent to 20 percent, our conversions give you a fair idea about how much you'll pay (assuming the price itself doesn't go up, of course). But be aware that money markets worldwide have been volatile, to say the least, and that the U.S. dollar has been trading low against the euro.

- **Dollar-sign ratings for all hotels and restaurants:** The number of signs indicates the range of costs for one night in a double-occupancy hotel room or for a meal at a restaurant (excluding alcohol), from $ (budget) to $$$$$ (splurge). Because of the number of countries covered in this book, these ratings are relative, applied on a city-by-city basis. So a $ hotel in pricey London may be a quirky bed-and-breakfast with shared bathrooms; but a $ hotel in far-cheaper Athens may well be a centrally located mid-scale hotel. The same goes for restaurants: At a rustic $$$$ joint in Madrid, you may get a delicious, stick-to-your-ribs stew for about $30; but a $$$$ restaurant in Paris dishes up fancy, haute-cuisine dishes that can cost as much as $85 per course.

- **Two categories for hotels:** Our personal favorites (the "tops") and those that don't quite make our preferred list but still get our hearty seal of approval (the "runners-up"). Don't be shy about considering those in the second category if you're unable to get a room at one of our favorites or if your preferences differ from ours. The amenities that the runner-up hotels offer and the services that they provide make all of them good choices to consider as you determine where to rest your head at night.

- **Cross-references to maps:** For those hotels, restaurants, and attractions that are plotted on a map, a page reference is provided in the listing information. If a hotel, restaurant, or attraction is outside the city limits or in an out-of-the-way area, it may not be mapped.

Foolish Assumptions

As we wrote this book, we made some assumptions about you and what your needs may be as a traveler. Here's what we assumed about you:

- ✔ You may be an inexperienced traveler looking for guidance when determining whether to take a trip to Europe and how to plan for it.

- ✔ You may be an experienced traveler, but you don't have a lot of time to devote to trip planning or you don't have a lot of time to spend in Europe when you get there. You want expert advice on how to maximize your time and enjoy a hassle-free trip.

- ✔ You're not looking for a book that provides all the information available about Europe or that lists every hotel, restaurant, or attraction available to you. Instead, you're looking for a book that focuses on the places that will give you the best or most memorable experience in Europe.

If you fit any of these criteria, then *Europe For Dummies* gives you the information you're looking for.

How This Book Is Organized

We divide *Europe For Dummies* into six parts. The first two parts cover planning and travel skills. The next three parts divide Europe into three regions; you get the lowdown on 15 of Europe's most popular destinations, with each chapter organized as a mini-guidebook. You find the information you need to conquer each city: how to get around, local customs, the best hotels and restaurants for every budget, out-of-the-way gems, noteworthy day trips, and more, all with little in the way of historical background. We even recommend how much time to spend at each major attraction. The last part includes some fun top-ten lists as well as an appendix packed with helpful travel info you can use on the go.

Part I: Introducing Europe

This part covers where to go, how to link it all together, and how to budget for your dream trip. We give you our picks of the best destinations and sights and our recommendations for the most fun-packed itineraries to fit your interests and vacation schedule.

Part II: Planning Your Trip to Europe

If you're looking for a deal (and isn't everybody?), read on. This part reveals the tricks of the trade for finding the best prices on plane tickets, rail passes, and car rentals. We help you find the best hotel in any price range and share budgeting tricks so that you can travel Europe without breaking the bank. We discuss tips for students, seniors, families, travelers with disabilities, and gay and lesbian travelers. Then we guide you through applying for passports; making reservations; dealing with trip insurance, health issues, and Customs; and figuring out how to keep in touch while traveling. We do everything but pack your bag!

Part III: The British Isles

First, we help you discover **London** and make side trips in England to **Bath, Salisbury** and **Stonehenge,** and **Oxford.** Then we direct you north to **Edinburgh** and other Scottish highlights such as **Loch Ness, Inverness,** and **Glasgow.** Finally, we take you across the waters to **Dublin** and the best of **Ireland's countryside,** from the Wicklow Mountains to the Ring of Kerry.

Part IV: Central Europe

Many adventures await you in Central Europe. From the much-loved and ever-popular city of **Paris,** we take you to the palace at **Versailles** and the Gothic cathedral at **Chartres.** After cruising **Amsterdam's** famous canals, we help you explore the Dutch tulip fields in **Haarlem** and enjoy the **Hoge Veluwe Park** with its Kröller-Müller Museum. In Germany, we bring you to **Munich** and **Bavaria,** where you can drink beer with oompah bands and explore **Neuschwanstein,** the ultimate Romantic castle.

You raise a glass (of coffee) to the Hapsburgs in genteel **Vienna** before heading to **Innsbruck** in the **Austrian Alps.** Finally, you head to the magical baroque cityscape of **Prague** in the Czech Republic.

Part V: Mediterranean Europe

The bright Mediterranean basin has been home to Europe's great civilizations. From the multilayered city of **Rome,** we direct you to **Naples** and the ancient ruins of **Herculaneum** and **Pompeii,** each just a day trip away. Then you journey to **Florence,** the city of the Renaissance, and the nearby Tuscan towns of **Pisa, Siena,** and **San Gimignano,** which help bring the Middle Ages back to life. We round out our Italian tour with the canal city of **Venice,** one of the most beautiful and unusual cities on Earth.

Next we take you to Spain. You start in **Madrid,** which houses great museums and tapas bars, and the nearby towns of **Toledo** and **Segovia,** medieval gems that provide respite from big-city sightseeing. Then you visit the great city of **Barcelona,** with its *modernismo* architecture and Gothic quarter.

Finally, to **Athens** we go, pointing out the ancient ruins and best hotels and restaurants in a metropolis that underwent a major upgrade for the 2004 Olympic Summer Games. From Athens, we guide you to further antiquities in **Delphi** and then on to the Greek island villa of **Santoríni.**

Part VI: The Part of Tens

We fill this part with ten of Europe's must-see sights — and ten over-rated ones — as well as advice on ten ways to break out of the tourist mold.

In the back of this book, we include an appendix — your Quick Concierge — containing handy information such as average rail times between different European cities, clothing size conversions, and contact information for various tourism agencies. You can find the Quick Concierge easily because it's printed on yellow paper.

Icons Used in This Book

Throughout this book, helpful little icons highlight particularly useful information. Here's what each icon means.

 This icon highlights money-saving tips and/or great deals.

 This icon highlights the best a destination has to offer in the categories we discuss in Chapter 1.

 This icon gives you a heads-up on annoying or potentially dangerous situations such as tourist traps, unsafe neighborhoods, rip-offs, and other things to beware of.

 This icon, in addition to flagging tips and resources of special interest to families, points out the most child-friendly hotels, restaurants, and attractions.

 This icon is a catchall for any special hint, tip, or bit of insider's advice that helps make your trip run more smoothly.

 Sometimes a great hotel, restaurant, or sight may require a bit of effort to get to. We let you in on these secret little finds with this icon. We also use this to peg any resource that's particularly useful and worth the time to seek out.

Where to Go from Here

To Europe, of course! Think of us as your advance scouts. These pages are chock-full of insider tips, hints, advice, secrets, and strategies that we collected while crisscrossing the British Isles and the Continent. We explored, we took notes, and we made mistakes — and learned from them — so that you don't have to make the same errors, even if you're a first-time traveler.

From here, you depart on your big European adventure. Keep in mind that Europe is not a giant museum from the past, but a living and vital culture. If you open yourself to all its possibilities — new friends, experiences, sights, and sounds — you're bound to have a vacation that will stay with you long after you return.

Bon voyage!

Part I
Introducing Europe

"He had it made after our trip to Italy. I give you Fontana di Clifford."

In this part . . .

What comes to mind when you're looking at a map of Europe? So many beautiful countries, so many glamorous cities, and so many possible itineraries. Before you jump on that plane, you need a travel plan that allows you to visit as many of the places on your wish list as possible. This part guides you through the necessary steps that you need to take in order to build your ideal travel plan. In these chapters, we introduce you to Europe, help you decide when and where to go, and give you five great itineraries.

Chapter 1

Discovering the Best of Europe

- -

In This Chapter

▶ Finding the best museums, historic sights, food, and architecture

▶ Discarding misconceptions before you go

▶ Traveling to the most intriguing cities and attractions

- -

*E*urope offers a roster of the world's most exciting cities, romantic landscapes, outstanding museums, historic sights, culinary creations, and architectural wonders. In this book, we guide you to the best of the best.

In order to make your trip as smooth and hassle-free as possible, you need to start planning a few months before you leave. You'll be dealing with things such as passports (see Chapter 9), rail passes (see Chapter 6), plane tickets (see Chapter 5), and foreign currencies (see Chapter 4). But for now, just sit back and dream of the possibilities.

You can sail past time-washed palaces and grandiose churches on Venice's Grand Canal for the price of a bus ticket. You can splurge on a five-star meal or people-watch from a sidewalk cafe in Paris. You can wander through the Tower of London, ground zero for so much English history over the last 900 years. Or you can drain creamy mugs of Guinness while clapping along to traditional Celtic music on a pub crawl through Dublin.

You may want to gaze in stupefied wonder at the famed scene of *God Creating Adam* on Michelangelo's Sistine Chapel ceiling in Rome. Or you may linger over breakfast in a revolving restaurant atop Switzerland's Schilthorn Mountain, surrounded by snow-covered peaks and glacier-filled valleys. How about a picnic lunch on the Greek island of Santoríni, hundreds of feet above the Mediterranean amid the ruins of a Mycenaean city?

Europe, with all its bewitching and unforgettable sights, is yours to discover, experience, and enjoy. To get you started on your European adventures, this chapter gives you a selection of what we consider to be the "best of the best" choices. The highlights in this chapter are also tagged with the Best of the Best icon in the destination chapters of this book.

Europe

The Top Museums

Europe is home to some of the world's greatest museums, displaying a cultural kaleidoscope of Western and worldwide art and artifacts, dating from prehistoric times to the present day. Classical busts, Renaissance paintings and sculptures, Impressionist landscapes, Cubist portraits, contemporary installations — in the museums of Europe, you'll find incredible riches from every epoch and in every style.

- **The Louvre (Paris):** Our short list has to start with the **Louvre** (see Chapter 13), one of those great treasure-trove museums that dazzles with ancient sculptures (including that armless beauty *Venus de Milo*), Egyptian mummies and medieval artifacts, and some true icons of Renaissance art, including da Vinci's *Mona Lisa* and Delacroix's ultra-French *Liberty Leading the People*.

- **Musée d'Orsay (Paris):** After exhausting yourself at the Louvre, you can cross the Seine River to visit an old train station that's been transformed into the **Musée d'Orsay** (see Chapter 13). This museum picks up the thread of French art where the Louvre leaves off, highlighting the best from the Romantic period onward, including the world's greatest collection of crowd-pleasing Impressionists such as Manet, Monet, Degas, Cézanne, Renoir, Gauguin, van Gogh, Seurat, and more.

- **The Vatican Museums (Rome):** One of Europe's greatest collections, the **Vatican Museums** (see Chapter 19) inspire at every turn. The Vatican's Painting Gallery houses Raphael's *Transfiguration* and Caravaggio's *Deposition.* The antiquities collections preserve some of the world's greatest examples of ancient Greek, Egyptian, Etruscan, and Roman sculpture. This is where you find the former private papal apartments, frescoed by Pinturicchio and Raphael, and, of course, the perennially awe-inspiring Sistine Chapel, with its ceiling frescoed by Michelangelo.

- **The British Museum (London):** You can get up close and personal with artifacts from the dawn of human history at London's renowned (and admission-free) **British Museum** (see Chapter 10). Fabulous examples from every epoch of the ancient European, Mediterranean, or Middle Eastern worlds are on view: Celtic treasure hordes; the Parthenon Sculptures of Greece; remains of Assyrian palaces; the Rosetta stone, which helped archaeologists crack the language of hieroglyphics; intricately decorated Greek vases; and superb examples of Egyptian mummies. And that's just the beginning.

- **Museo Nacional del Prado (Madrid):** In the **Prado** (see Chapter 22), you get to enjoy masterworks by the greats of Spanish art — courtly and insightful works by Velázquez, dark and tragic images by Goya, elongated and uniquely colorful canvases by El Greco, and nightmarishly surreal paintings by Hieronymus Bosch.

✔ **The Galleria degli Uffizi (Florence):** Take a stroll through the
  Galleria degli Uffizi (Uffizi Galleries; see Chapter 20), a veritable
  textbook on the development of Italian painting during the
  Renaissance. Compared to the great museums of other cities, the
  Uffizi is small, but it houses an embarrassment of riches, from earlier works by Giotto, Fra Angelico, and Botticelli (the goddess-on-a-
  half-shell *Birth of Venus* and flower-filled *Primavera* both hang here)
  through the height of the Renaissance, represented by da Vinci,
  Raphael, and Michelangelo.

✔ **The Deutsches Museum (Munich):** Overloaded on art and ancient
  relics? Head to the **Deutsches Museum** (see Chapter 15), one of the
  world's greatest science and technology museums. Here you'll find
  fleets of early Mercedes, eye-popping electrical demonstrations, a
  hangar full of historic aircraft, lab benches where famous experiments in nuclear physics took place, and giant machines used to
  dig tunnels under the Alps. This informative and often hands-on
  museum is a delight for all ages.

The Top Historic Sights

Europe is the wellspring of Western culture, a living textbook of human
history. Europeans think in terms of centuries and millennia, not
decades. Americans may speak of the '60s; Italians just as breezily refer
to *il seicento* (the 1600s). Europe allows you to dip into history at just
about any point. You're surrounded by it in every city you visit.

✔ **Best Greek and Roman ruins:** You can see remnants of the ancient
  Greek and Roman empires and the remains of massive temples
  some 1,500 to 3,000 years old at the **Acropolis** or **Ancient Agora** in
  Athens and at **Delphi** (see Chapter 24). In Rome, you can wander
  through the **Roman Forum** and explore the ultimate sports arena of
  the ancient world, the **Colosseum** (see Chapter 19).

✔ **Best prehistoric sites:** Prehistoric standouts include the brooding
  standing stones of **Stonehenge** (see Chapter 10), in England; the
  ruins of the ancient Minoan city of **Akrotíri** (see Chapter 24), on
  the Greek island of Santoríni; the Stone Age passage tomb of
  Newgrange (see Chapter 12), in Ireland; and remnants of the earliest settlements of what is now Paris, excavated under the square in
  front of **Notre-Dame Cathedral** (see Chapter 13).

✔ **Best castles:** You'll find castles and fortified structures from
  the Dark Ages and Middle Ages (from A.D. 500 to 1500) strewn
  across Europe. Pride of place goes to the **Tower of London** (see
  Chapter 10), with its bloody legends and famed crown jewels;
  Edinburgh Castle (see Chapter 11), glowering atop a volcanic hill
  in the center of the city; and **Pražský Hrad** (Prague Castle; see
  Chapter 18), with its soaring cathedral and half-timbered lane of old
  alchemists' shops.

✔ **Best medieval neighborhoods:** The medieval era saw the development of now-major cities throughout Europe, leaving behind a legacy of fascinating cobblestone medieval quarters such as the **Altstadt** of Bern (see Chapter 17), the **Staré Město** in Prague (see Chapter 18), **Trastevere** in Rome (see Chapter 19), and the **Barri Gòtic** in Barcelona (see Chapter 23).

✔ **Best hill towns:** Tiny hill towns and hamlets sprang up between A.D. 500 and 1500, and this book describes the best of them, including **Chartres** in France (see Chapter 13), **Innsbruck** in Austria (see Chapter 16), the Tuscan hill towns of **Siena** and **San Gimignano** (both in Chapter 20), and Spain's time capsules of **Toledo** and **Segovia** (both in Chapter 22).

The Top Culinary Delights

European cuisine runs the gamut from stick-to-your-ribs *rösti* (deluxe hash browns spiked with ham and eggs) of the Swiss Alps to France's traditional *coq au vin* (chicken braised in red wine, with onions and mushrooms). Mix in the fabulous **pastas** of Italy, the dozens of types of **sausage** in Prague and Munich, and the incredible yet unknown **cheeses** of Ireland, and you're in for a festive feast every day of your European journey.

✔ **Best Mediterranean meals:** The cooking of Italy (see Chapters 19–21) goes far beyond **pasta,** which is merely considered a *primo,* or first course. For your *secondo,* or second course, you can sample Adriatic **fish** in a Venetian trattoria patronized by local gondoliers, dig into a mighty *bistecca fiorentina* (an oversize T-bone brushed with olive oil and cracked pepper and then grilled) in Florence, or dine on *saltimbocca* (wine-cooked veal layered with sage and prosciutto) in a Roman restaurant located in the ruins of an ancient theater.

A night out in Madrid (see Chapter 22), where dinner starts at 10 p.m., may mean a traditional **roast suckling pig** in a restaurant unchanged since the days when Hemingway was a regular, or a giant Valencian *paella* (rice tossed with a seafood medley) to share with everyone at the table under the wood beams of a country-style inn. Meanwhile, Barcelona (see Chapter 23) has become one of Europe's hottest dining destinations, with fresh seafood right out of the Mediterranean and highly imaginative takes on Catalan cooking.

✔ **Best British meals:** England (see Chapter 10) once had a reputation for serving the worst food in Europe. Traditional favorites still include **shepherd's pie** (ground lamb capped by mashed potatoes), **fish and chips,** and **bangers and mash** (sausages and mashed potatoes). But, oh, how times have changed. Much to Paris's chagrin, London now enjoys the **hottest restaurant scene** in Europe, and its celebrity chefs and designer dining spots surf the crest of modern cooking trends and serve the hippest fusion cuisines. Even the old traditional dishes taste better now that they've been "rediscovered."

✔ **Best bets for a sweet tooth:** French and Italian pastries are divine, but you can also sate your sweet tooth in Vienna (see Chapter 16), home of the **Sachertorte,** the original Death by Chocolate. And what better way to cap off a night of clubbing in Madrid than to join the locals for *churros y chocolada* (fried dough strips you dip in thick hot chocolate) as the sun rises? Don't worry: You'll do so much walking on your trip that you probably won't gain too much weight . . . assuming of course you don't discover the *gelato* (super-rich ice cream) of Florence (see Chapter 20) or **sticky toffee puddings** in England (see Chapter 10).

✔ **Best beer and wine:** You can savor some of the finest wines in the world in France, Italy, and Spain, or take a swig from a liter-sized mug of beer in Germany. But did you know that **Eastern European beers** are finally getting the recognition they deserve in Prague (see Chapter 18)? And rightly so, because all Pilseners, and what became Budweiser, originally hail from the Czech Republic. And how about the *heuriger* in Vienna (see Chapter 16)? These small, family-run wine estates serve up their white wines accompanied by simple, hearty Austrian dishes.

The Architectural Highlights

Europe's famous cathedrals, palaces, and castles draw visitors from around the globe. You can enjoy the sight of devilish gargoyles and marvel at the ancient rose windows in Paris's **Cathédrale de Notre-Dame** (see Chapter 13), gape at Michelangelo's *Pietà* sculpture and Bernini's towering altar canopy in Rome's **St. Peter's Basilica** (see Chapter 19), and admire magnificent creations of medieval masonry and Renaissance engineering everywhere in between.

✔ **Chartres Cathedral (beyond Paris): Chartres Cathedral** (see Chapter 13) is a study in formal Gothic, from its 27,000 square feet of stained glass to its soaring spires and flying buttresses.

✔ **Westminster Abbey (London):** Britain's most revered church, **Westminster Abbey** (see Chapter 10) has been the site of coronations and the final resting place of kings and queens for some eight centuries.

✔ **St. Mark's Basilica (Venice):** The multiple domes, rounded archways, and glittering mosaics of **St. Mark's Basilica** (see Chapter 21) hint at how this great trading power of the Middle Ages sat at the crossroads of Eastern and Western cultures; it's as much Byzantine as it is European.

✔ **The Duomo (Florence):** When the Renaissance genius Brunelleschi invented a noble dome to cap **Florence's Duomo** (see Chapter 20), Europe's architectural landscape changed forever. For the first time since antiquity, domes started sprouting up all over Europe. Visit Florence's original, and you can clamber up narrow staircases between the dome's onion layers to see just how Brunelleschi performed his engineering feat — and get a sweeping panorama of the city from the top.

✔ **Residenz Palace and Schloss Nymphenburg (Munich):** In the 17th and 18th centuries, powerful kings governing much of Europe claimed they ruled by divine right and built palaces to prove it. The Bavarian Wittelsbach dynasty ruled for 738 years from Munich's **Residenz Palace** and the pleasure palace outside town, **Schloss Nymphenburg** (see Chapter 15).

✔ **Hofburg Palace (Vienna):** The Hapsburg emperors set up housekeeping in the sprawling **Hofburg Palace** (see Chapter 16), where the chapel is now home to a singing group known as the Vienna Boys' Choir, and where museums showcase everything from classical statuary and musical instruments to medieval weaponry and the imperial treasury.

✔ **Buckingham Palace (London):** You can line up to watch the Changing of the Guard at **Buckingham Palace** (see Chapter 10), and even tour the royal staterooms in August and September, when Her Majesty Elizabeth II isn't at home.

✔ **Versailles (beyond Paris):** A short train ride from downtown Paris brings you to the palace to end all palaces, **Versailles** (see Chapter 13), where Louis XIV held court, Marie Antoinette kept dangerously out of touch with her subjects (who were brewing revolution back in Paris), and the Treaty of Versailles ending World War I was signed.

✔ **Neuschwanstein (beyond Munich):** Tourists aren't the only ones looking to recapture a romantic, idealized past. Mad King Ludwig II of Bavaria was so enamored with his country's fairy-tale image that he decided to build **Neuschwanstein** (see Chapter 15) in the foothills of the Alps south of Munich. This fanciful 19th-century version of what Ludwig thought a medieval castle *should* look like is a festival of turrets and snapping banners that later inspired Uncle Walt's Cinderella Castle in Disneyland.

✔ **La Sagrada Família** and **La Pedrera (Barcelona):** Lest you think architectural innovations are all relics of the distant past, head to Barcelona (see Chapter 23), where one of the greatest architects of the early 20th century, Antoni Gaudí, used his own unique riff on Art Nouveau to design everything from surreal apartment buildings, such as **La Pedrera,** to the wild, futuristic church, **La Sagrada Família,** still under construction.

Chapter 2

Deciding When and Where to Go

*T*his chapter takes you through the pros and cons of traveling to Europe at different times of the year. You also find a rundown of the most popular festivals, as well as some strategies for staving off sightseeing overload.

Going Everywhere You Want to Go

Europe is loaded with desirable destinations and discoveries. Narrowing our coverage was tough, but a guidebook only contains so many pages, and you only have so much time in your vacation schedule. Keeping that in mind, we present the must-see destinations and the best of all possible side trips to give you a wide-ranging picture of all that Europe has to offer.

The splendor of the British Isles

The best place to start is **London** (see Chapter 10), the history-drenched capital of the United Kingdom. From the medieval Tower of London to the neo-Gothic Houses of Parliament and the up-to-the-second Tate Modern, London offers a wealth of sightseeing possibilities.

It vies with New York as the hotbed of English-language theater, and its museums cover everything from Old Masters (National Gallery) and decorative arts (the Victoria & Albert Museum) to naval history (Greenwich's Maritime Museum) and contemporary art (Tate Modern). The city contains the pomp and ceremony associated with the royal family and the bump and grind of the trendiest neighborhoods and nightclubs. You can dine on everything from pub grub to Indian fare to modern British cuisine.

Easy day trips from London include the Georgian splendors and Roman ruins of **Bath,** the mysterious prehistoric stone circle of **Stonehenge,** the Gothic cathedral of **Salisbury,** and the busy streets and quiet quads of **Oxford,** one of the world's pre-eminent university towns.

Edinburgh (see Chapter 11), the capital of Scotland, is a dynamic international destination whose old city is presided over by an impressive castle and whose Georgian New Town is a grid of genteel streets for shopping and dining. You can haunt the pubs once frequented by local son Robert Louis Stevenson, find out about Scottish Impressionism at the National Gallery, visit the royal yacht *Britannia,* and stroll the Royal Mile in search of tartan scarves and memorable attractions (from a whisky tour to royal Holyrood Palace).

From bustling Edinburgh, you can make a day trip to **Inverness** and search for the Loch Ness Monster from the ruins of Urquhart Castle, or head down to happening **Glasgow,** an industrial city revitalizing itself as a cultural center.

Although a visit to the Irish capital of **Dublin** (see Chapter 12) has its charms, such as admiring the Book of Kells at Trinity College, exploring Celtic history at the Archaeological Museum, following in the footsteps of James Joyce and other Irish scribes, and pub-crawling through Temple Bar, the best way to enjoy Ireland is to rent a car and drive through the Irish countryside.

To that end, we offer plenty of coverage of the passage tomb at **Newgrange,** the Celtic crosses and windswept heaths of the **Wicklow Mountains** and **Glendalough,** and the fishing villages and ancient sites of the **Ring of Kerry** and **Dingle Peninsula.**

The heart of the Continent

Many people consider chic, glamorous **Paris** (see Chapter 13) the capital of European sightseeing. From viewing the masterpieces in the Louvre and the Impressionists collection of the Musée d'Orsay to climbing the Eiffel Tower, cruising the Seine, or simply whiling the day away at a cafe in the St-Germain-de-Pres or Marais neighborhoods, Paris has enough to keep you busy for a lifetime. In Parisian bistros and brasseries, you can sample everything from the finest 5-star cuisine in town to cheaper fixed-price menus.

But do take the time to day-trip from Paris to **Versailles,** one of the "royalest" royal residences in Europe, or to **Chartres,** one of the world's great Gothic cathedrals, famed for its exquisite stained glass.

Amsterdam (see Chapter 14) is as famed for its canals lined by charming 17th-century town houses as it is for its social and cross-cultural tolerance, with examples ranging from the libidinous (the red-light district and "smoking" cafes) to the heroic (the Dutch house where Anne Frank and her family hid during the Nazi occupation). This unique Dutch city was home to artistic giants such as Rembrandt and van Gogh, whose works are showcased in Amsterdam's fabulous museums. Food-wise, you can enjoy an Indonesian feast in the Leidseplein district, fresh herring from an outdoor stall, and local beers and gin.

Nearby, you can sample a less hectic Dutch way of life in the smaller city of **Haarlem** or tour tulip gardens, windmills, and re-created villages in the countryside. You can also ride bikes for free in **Hoge Veluwe National Park,** with its stunning Kröller-Müller Museum dedicated to van Gogh and other modern-era artists.

The pulsing heart of life-loving Bavaria is **Munich** (see Chapter 15), a cultural powerhouse packed with a bevy of fine museums and two outstanding baroque palaces, and host to Oktoberfest, the biggest beer party in the world. You can munch on bratwurst and pretzels in beer halls and stroll the old center and expansive Englischer Garten city park, or visit the Pinakothek art galleries to feast on masterpieces from Germany and elsewhere throughout Europe.

Half the fun of Munich is traveling out of town to visit **Neuschwanstein,** the ornate fairy-tale castle of Mad King Ludwig. The darker side of history is here, too. Just outside Munich, the town where the Nazi Party got its start, you can tour the sobering concentration camp at **Dachau.**

Over the Alps in **Austria** (see Chapter 16), you can visit **Vienna,** a city that was once capital of the giant Austro-Hungarian Empire and still retains its refined architectural and artistic grandeur. Steep yourself in this heritage by climbing the cathedral towers, sipping coffee at a famous cafe, admiring the masterpieces of the Kunsthistoriches Museum, or taking in a performance at the renowned Vienna State Opera house — Vienna is, after all, one of the great music centers of Europe, where Mozart, Johann Strauss, and other famous composers made their careers. Another popular Austrian destination is **Innsbruck,** a lovely little town tucked away in the heart of the Austrian Alps.

After a visit to the Swiss capital of **Bern** (see Chapter 17), where you can admire hometown boy Paul Klee's masterpieces, see where Einstein came up with $E=mc^2$, feed the town mascots at the Bear Pits, and float down the river with the locals, you can delve into the heart of the **Swiss Alps,** the Bernese Oberland region around the towering Jungfrau peak. Here, small resort towns and Alpine villages cling to the sides of the mighty Lauterbrunnen and Grindelwald valleys, surrounded by glaciers and ribbon-thin waterfalls, accessible by scenic railways, cable cars, and miles of hiking and skiing trails.

Finally, take a foray into Eastern Europe to see how the medieval and baroque city of **Prague** (see Chapter 18), once stifled behind the Iron Curtain, has come roaring back to life and become one of Europe's most popular destinations. This dreamy city of church spires, castles, and ancient streets is one of the world's top centers for sampling beer and classical music. You find a plethora of concerts every night and in every venue imaginable — from symphonies playing in grand halls to street trios improvising under a medieval bridge abutment.

The charms of the Mediterranean

Rome (see Chapter 19), once the most powerful city in the Western world, brims with famous sites, from the ancient Forum and Colosseum to massive St. Peter's Cathedral. Dozens of museums house everything from ancient Roman statues, frescoes, and mosaics to Renaissance masterpieces. One of the city's greatest treasures is Michelangelo's magnificent ceiling in the Sistine Chapel. The cityscape itself is a joy to wander, a tangle of ancient streets and Renaissance-era boulevards punctuated by public squares sporting baroque fountains (such as famed Trevi Fountain), Renaissance sculpture, and Egyptian obelisks.

From Rome you can easily day trip to **Tivoli,** where the atmospheric ruins of Hadrian's villa and the famed gardens of the Villa d'Este provide enchanting diversions, or take the subway to **Ostia Antica,** the ancient port of Rome.

Florence (see Chapter 20), birthplace of the Renaissance, is loaded with a lifetime's worth of world-class museums and churches designed or decorated by some of the greatest names in Italian art. Here you find Michelangelo's towering *David,* Botticelli's sublime *Birth of Venus,* Leonardo's moving *Annunciation,* and other artistic icons. Florence is also a great place to dine on succulent Tuscan fare, sample fine Italian wines, and wander old neighborhoods known to Dante.

Florence is the capital of **Tuscany,** one of Europe's most popular regions. In this fabled and sublimely beautiful land, the tower of **Pisa** leans, wineries turn ripe grapes into Brunellos and Chiantis, and hill towns such as **Siena** and **San Gimignano** bring the Middle Ages to life with their forbidding stone towers and finely decorated churches.

Venice (see Chapter 21) floats like a dream on its lagoon, with ornate palaces and tiny footbridges spanning a network of canals. The only modes of transportation here are boats and your own two legs. The interior of St. Mark's Cathedral glitters with golden mosaics, and the works of great Venetian artists, such as Titian, Tintoretto, and Veronese, adorn the walls of the Accademia Gallery and Doge's Palace.

After feasting on Venice's seafood specialties, take the public ferry to explore the outlying islands of **Murano** (where Venetian glass blowing was invented), **Burano** (a colorful fishing village), and **Torcello** (an undeveloped island hiding another gorgeously mosaicked church). And consider setting aside a day on the Veneto mainland to see the Giotto frescoes in **Padova** (Padua).

The lively Spanish capital of **Madrid** (see Chapter 22) is renowned for its museum collections, from the masterworks in the Museo Nacional del Prado to Picasso's *Guernica* in the Reina Sofia. Tour the Royal Palace, take in a professional bullfight, or roam from bar to bar sampling tapas before indulging in a hearty 10 p.m. dinner and resting up to catch a flamenco show or party in the clubs until dawn.

From Madrid, you can easily explore the medieval capital of **Toledo,** the kingly monastery at El Escorial (both boasting many El Greco paintings), and the impressive Roman aqueduct and Gothic cathedral of **Segovia.**

Barcelona (see Chapter 23), the sophisticated capital of Spain's Catalonia region, invites you to explore its picturesque Gothic quarter (Barri Gòtic), ramble down Las Ramblas (one of Europe's liveliest pedestrian promenades), hang out at the beach (along the city's revitalized waterfront), and take in the works of local early 20th-century greats Picasso and Miró (each of whom has a museum dedicated to his work). Barcelona is perhaps most famous for Gaudí, whose *modernista* architecture is the stuff of singular town houses, a funky city park, and the only great European cathedral still being built, his Sagrada Família.

Last, but certainly not least, head off to the heart of the Mediterranean, the ancient Greek capital of **Athens** (see Chapter 24), a sprawling modern city with the ruins of the 2,500-year-old Parthenon looming over it from atop the Acropolis Hill. Packed around the *tavérnas* and enticing shops lie other enduring reminders of Greece's Golden Age, such as the Temple of the Olympian Zeus and the Temple of the Winds. The city's archaeological museums highlight not only remnants from the Classical Age but also statues from the Cycladic era and earlier ages.

The possibilities for side trips from Athens are extraordinary. Visit the romantic ruins of **Delphi,** where the ancient world's premier oracles advised kings and commoners alike. Or take off for the island of **Santoríni,** a haven for sun-worshippers, with its beaches, white wine, summer nightlife, and Minoan and Mycenaean ruins.

The Secret of the Seasons

Although it's harder than ever to predict weather with any degree of accuracy, Europe in general experiences few seasonal surprises. The weather in Europe is roughly similar to that of the northeastern United States. You may run into a warm, breezy day in December in Sicily, or a cold snap in summer in Scotland, and you'll probably hear reports of unseasonably "weird weather" from England to the Czech Republic.

Europe tends to be slightly wetter than the United States in autumn, winter, and spring, and drier in summer. Rain is a year-round occurrence in England, and the peaks of the Alps never lose all their snow.

Be prepared for all varieties of weather by packing clothes that you can layer, long underwear, a folding pocket umbrella, and lightweight clothes for warmer days.

Spring is great because . . .

✔ During this *shoulder season* (between low and high seasons), the weather tends to be pleasantly mild, but unpredictable. Temperatures may still be cool enough for skiing in the Alps but already warm enough to sit outside at a sidewalk cafe in Paris or Rome. European springs can be notoriously fickle, though; be prepared for rain, cold spells, sudden heat waves, and/or perfect weather.

✔ Airlines usually offer more reasonable rates than in summer.

✔ Europe is neither too crowded nor too solitary.

✔ Tulips bloom in Holland and the great gardens of England and throughout Europe are perking up.

But keep in mind . . .

✔ Shoulder season is becoming ever more popular (read: crowded) as frequent travelers tire of the summer hordes and take advantage of airlines' reduced rates.

✔ The off-season often runs October to Easter, so in early spring, some things may still be closed — from hotels and attractions to rural tourism destinations such as vineyards or farms.

Summer is great because . . .

✔ All the services that cater to tourists open their welcoming arms — this is the height of the tourist season, with the exception of ski resorts. Early summer, especially June and July, is the most popular time to visit Europe.

✔ Colorful folk festivals, open-air music, and theatrical performances abound in summer.

✔ Attractions are made even more attractive by evening illumination or sound-and-light shows and special performances.

But keep in mind . . .

✔ In summertime, Europe can feel like one giant bus tour. In fact, the crowds are the season's biggest drawback.

✔ The prices are the highest of the year — especially for airfares and hotels.

✔ Popular museums and attractions have long lines. You may have to wait for hours to get inside at peak times.

✔ The temperatures really heat up across Europe in August, especially during the second half of the month, and air-conditioning is not always available. Europeans go to the beaches, leaving the sweating cities to the tourists.

✔ In southern Europe, the heat can be intense all summer long.

Fall is great because . . .

✔ The bulk of the tourists have left.

✔ Crops ripen, and wine and harvest festivals celebrate the season.

✔ As in spring, the fall shoulder season brings reasonable rates on airlines and some hotel bargains.

✔ The opera and concert seasons for Europe's best companies and grand performance halls tend to begin in mid- to late fall.

 But keep in mind . . .

✔ The weather can turn on you suddenly, with lots of drizzle, and the occasional wintery cold snap.

✔ Some tourist facilities — hotels, restaurants, and a few sights — close for the season in October and November.

✔ Tourism is increasing at this time of year as visitors try to escape the crowds of summer.

Winter is great because . . .

✔ During low season (from mid- or late Nov through Easter, excluding Christmas week), hotel and travel expenses drop and you often have entire churches, museums, or even small towns to yourself.

✔ Christmas in Paris — or Rome or London or Munich or Madrid or Venice — can be beautiful and an experience to remember.

✔ You haven't really skied until you've been to the Swiss Alps and gone downhill for more than an hour without ever having to wait for a lift.

 But keep in mind . . .

✔ You may not want to spend your vacation bundled up, shielding yourself from the cold.

✔ Tourism destinations tend to freshen up during this period of calm. Museums review and reorganize their exhibits; churches and monuments undergo restorations or cleanings; and local transportation, tourist offices, and shops shorten their hours, while some restaurants and hotels close for a week or even a month.

✔ Some of the most popular destinations, such as islands, smaller tourism-based cities, and spas, close up almost entirely.

Europe's Calendar of Events

A great way to tour is to plan an entire vacation around a single large festival or seasonal celebration. You can witness a slice of European life that most tourists never get to see. Celebrate the festival with the locals and take tons of pictures, and you'll return home with some unforgettable memories.

Book your accommodations as soon as possible if your plans include traveling to a location where a major festival or other cultural event is taking place. Attendees snatch up accommodations quickly at festival time, sometimes months in advance. For big festivals in smaller places, such as the Palio in Siena, Italy, all the hotels within the town walls may be sold out over a year in advance. If necessary, book a room in a neighboring town.

What follows is a subjective list of the top festivals in Europe. Specific country guidebooks, such as those published by **Frommer's** (Wiley Publishing, Inc.), list many, many more festivals. For exact dates or more information, contact the local tourist offices (see the "Fast Facts" sections of Chapters 10 through 24 for listings) or visit the event Web site.

✔ **Carnevale,** Venice, Italy (and many other cities throughout Europe): Carnevale is a feast of food and wine and a raucous celebration of spring — a true pagan holdover grafted onto the week preceding Christian Lent. Carnevale turns the world upside down: Those of modest means hobnob with (or lampoon) the elite and those in power, and everyone has a roaring good time. The most famous celebration in Europe is Venice's Carnevale, a series of elegant-yet-tipsy masked balls harking back to the 18th century, but you'll find celebrations throughout Europe, including Munich and Madrid. Carnevale starts a week or two before Ash Wednesday (usually in late Feb) and culminates on the final Tuesday, called "Fat Tuesday" (*Mardi Gras* in French). Fat Tuesday immediately precedes the sober period of Lent.

✔ **Easter,** throughout Europe: In London, you can see multicolored floats parade around Battersea Park. In Florence, you can watch an ox-drawn cart stuffed with fireworks explode in front of the cathedral. In Rome, the Pope makes a special appearance on his balcony. Celebrations vary widely between Good Friday and Easter Monday.

✔ **Palio,** Siena, Italy: One of the highlights of the Italian summer is this breakneck, bareback, anything-goes horse race around the sloping, dirt-covered main piazza of medieval Siena (www.paliosiena.com). Even a horse that's thrown its rider can take the prize, and whips are used as much on competing riders as on the horses. The parties held before and after the horse race are street feasts to behold, no matter who wins. The horse race occurs twice each summer, July 2 and August 16.

✔ **Running of the Bulls,** Pamplona, Spain: One of the more dangerous festivals you can see is this one, where courageous fools dressed in white, with red kerchiefs, run through the narrow streets of Pamplona chased by enraged bulls (www.sanfermin.com). This wild event ends when the bulls chase the last runners into the harbor — after forcing most of them to jump the fences for safety. After that, all involved drink wine, set off fireworks, and, of course, attend the many bullfights. You can experience the Running of the Bulls vicariously by reading Hemingway's *The Sun Also Rises,* or see it yourself from July 6 to 14.

✔ **Bastille Day,** Paris, France: France celebrates its nation's birthday with street fairs, parades, feasts, and pageants, starting with a procession along the Champs-Elysées and ending with fireworks over Montmartre. Bastille Day is July 14.

✔ **Edinburgh International Festival** and **Fringe Festival,** Edinburgh, Scotland: One of Europe's premier cultural extravaganzas, the festival features art, dance, films, plays, and music of some of the world's top creative talents and performers. The traditional bagpipes-and-kilt Military Tattoo at Edinburgh Castle is the festival's highlight. The **Edinburgh International Festival** (www.eif.co.uk) takes place over three weeks in August. The **Fringe Festival** (www.edfringe.com), also held in August, started off as a small, experimental offshoot to the main festival, but it has exploded in popularity and now hosts more than 1,500 shows and events. Either way, August is a fantastic time to be in Edinburgh.

✔ **Bloemencorso,** Amsterdam, the Netherlands: This major flower festival takes place in a country obsessed with blooms. The event begins with a colorful parade of floral floats in the nearby flower market town of Aalsmeer and ends in Amsterdam on the Dam Square. And get this — tulips are not included (it's too late in the season for them). The festival (www.bloemencorsoaalsmeer.nl) takes place on the first Saturday in September.

✔ **Oktoberfest,** Munich, Germany: *Wilkommen* to the world's biggest keg party! This festival attracts tens of thousands of revelers who listen to brass oompah bands, feast on roasted ox and sausages, and sit under giant tents drinking liter-size mugs of beer. Oktoberfest (www.oktoberfest.de) actually begins in mid-September. The first weekend in October is the final flourish.

✔ **Christmas,** throughout Europe: You can enjoy the Christmas fun and festivities anywhere in Europe from a few weeks before the holiday until January 6 (the Epiphany). Squares and piazzas across the Continent are set up with Christmas markets, where you can buy handcrafted items and traditional holiday foods, and in some countries *crèches* (Nativity scenes) are displayed in public squares and church chapels. Trafalgar Square in London is decorated with a giant Norwegian spruce, and holiday concerts ring out in churches and concert halls all over Europe. On Christmas Eve, you can go to Oberndorf, north of Salzburg, Austria, to sing "Silent Night" in the town where the song was written. Or you can receive a blessing from the pope at noon on Christmas Day, when he leans out his window in Rome to give a Mass blessing, broadcast around the world.

Tips for Successful Trip Planning

When planning your trip — both the whole trip and the daily schedule — make sure to leave room for downtime, changing plans, and spontaneity:

✔ **Make time for relaxation.** For every seven days of rigorous sight-seeing, plan at least one day for doing little or nothing.

✔ **Mentally prepare yourself for those inevitable changes in your plans.** You never know when circumstances will cause you to miss a train, for example. Try to rethink your altered situation in order to make the most of your revised circumstances.

✔ **Be spontaneous.** Take advantage of unexpected opportunities, such as day trips or festivals, and don't hesitate to spend more or less time in a place after you get to know it.

Travelers who return to Europe for a second or third visit often plan their itineraries in a way that allows them to enjoy a more leisurely pace away from the crowds and pressures of the big cities. But on your first visit, your goal may be to visit as many major cities and sights as possible, and the whirlwind tour is still the best way to do that. After you've seen the "must-sees," you can return as an experienced European traveler to explore lesser-known attractions and other interesting areas in greater depth.

Seeing it all without going nuts

The idea of planning a large-scale trip can seem overwhelming — so much history and culture, so little time! Here are six ways to maximize your time and still see as much as possible:

✔ **Don't duplicate types of sights.** You know that many sights in Europe are unique and worth seeing in their own right. But let's face it: Visiting *every* church in Rome or *every* museum in London can be wearying or even boring. Pick one or two examples of each and move on.

✔ **Stay centrally located.** On your first trip, use your limited time to see as much of Europe as you can, instead of taking days to travel to a peripheral corner. Consider skipping some of the more geographically remote countries, such as Norway, Sweden, Portugal, Spain, and Greece, because — unless you take advantage of no-frills airlines — traveling to them takes a long time. See Parts III through V to help you choose destinations that keep this idea in mind.

✔ **Select side trips prudently.** We highly recommend day trips because they add variety to your city sightseeing. But pick your excursions wisely, and make sure these trips don't take time away from the major city you're visiting. If you're in Florence for just one day, don't plan to visit Pisa as well, because you'll end up seeing neither. Unless you hook up with a time-specific escorted tour, reserve a full day to see any destination that's more than a city-bus ride away.

✔ **Go your separate ways.** If you plan six days in London to accommodate the sightseeing wishes of each member of the family, you're wasting time unnecessarily. You don't have to tour Europe as Siamese triplets. Your partner can spend a few more hours in the British Museum, your kids can ride the British Airways London Eye, and you can check out Shakespeare's Globe Theatre. That way you all spend a single afternoon doing what otherwise would have taken a day and a half.

✔ **Practice extreme time-saving techniques.** No matter how pretty the countryside, you can save a lot of precious vacation time by taking night trains between major cities. That way, you won't have to use a whole day just getting from Point A to Point B. This may not be the most comfortable way to spend the night, but because you arrive at your destination so early, it's a strategy that allows you to visit a museum before the crowds arrive (you can always take a siesta later).

✔ **Keep in mind that you'll probably come back.** Assume it. Europe still has a lot left to see, no matter how much you pack in. Europe will wait for you.

Staying sane on the museum trail

For many travelers, Europe is synonymous with history and art, and you may feel like you've seen it all by the time your vacation is over. These hints can help you get the most out of your visits to the great museums without overloading your brain:

✔ **Plan to go to big museums twice.** Spread the visit over two or three days, if you have the time and inclination, because some museums are just too big to get through in one day. Consider this strategy for the Louvre, Prado, Vatican Museums, British Museum, Uffizi, and National Gallery (London).

✔ **Split up.** Nothing is as subjective as taste in art. You and your companions don't have to stick together in museums and spend all your time looking at the same paintings. You can each go through at your own pace and peruse your own pleasures. This strategy also gives you and your companions some time apart. (Even the closest of friends and family can get on each other's nerves.)

✔ **Take advantage of the audio tour.** Audio tours in museums are easy and fun and can add immeasurably to your enjoyment of a work of art or a historic site. Nowadays, most audio tours are digital, and you go at your own pace. The exhibited works have numbers next to them, which you just punch into the wand's keypad. It then gives you the facts and background of the work, artist, era, and so on. This way, you get the lowdown on the works that most intrigue you.

✔ **Do the guided-tour thing.** Museum tours are led by experts who explain the background and significance of the most important works and can answer your questions. In huge museums, they guide you directly to masterworks you'd otherwise have to find on your own.

✔ **Do your homework.** The art and artifacts will be much more engaging and interesting if you know something about what you're looking at. Whether you skim your guidebook for the information or take a class in art history before your trip, a little brushing up on European artists and movements will enrich any museum-going experience.

✔ **Keep the museum hours in mind.** To avoid disappointment, it's always a good idea to verify a museum's opening days and hours before your visit. Many of the big museums stay open until 7 or 8 p.m. on one or two evenings a week, and in summer, some of them stay open as late as 10 p.m. or even midnight. This is a great time to visit because the galleries are less crowded, and you can visit another must-see site during the day.

✔ **Concentrate on the masterpieces.** Even a moderate-size museum can overwhelm you if you don't pace yourself. Don't feel obligated to see every work on display. Many museums include a list of the masterpieces on their floor plans, and you can skip entire wings of less important works.

Dealing with cultural overload

While visiting Florence, the French writer Stendhal was so overwhelmed by the aesthetic beauty of the Renaissance — and so exhausted by trying to see absolutely everything — that he collapsed. Stendhal's case is an extreme one, perhaps, but he's not the last one to break down from too much Europe.

Even if you don't faint in the piazza, after a few days or weeks of full-steam-ahead sightseeing, you may feel unaccountably tired or irritable, catch a cold, or just stop caring whether you see another church or painting in your life. When the idea of visiting the Louvre makes you groan and want to take a nap, it's time to recharge your mental batteries.

Check out these hints for remedying traveler's burnout:

✔ **Just because something is famous, don't feel obligated to do or see it.** If you're going to wear yourself out, do it on the stuff you love. Skip what doesn't interest you and limit yourself to those attractions that you *really* want to see.

✔ **Pace yourself.** Don't feel obligated to race around like a marathon runner when you're soaking up the variety of Europe's cultural offerings. Schedule rest periods. Leave room to picnic, to dip your hands in a fountain, and to stop and smell the cappuccino. Don't pack too much into your overall trip itinerary or your daily sightseeing agenda.

✔ **Put variety into your sightseeing.** Visit a church, ruin, or museum, and then relax in a cafe or in a park before hitting your next site. Don't visit one big museum after another. Give other areas of your brain a workout so that your trip doesn't blur into one large, colorful mirage of Gothic cathedrals and Old Masters.

✔ **Do the siesta thing.** In Mediterranean countries, many businesses close in the early afternoon (the hottest part of the day), so why not do as the locals do and take a nap? It can do you a world of good, both physically and mentally. After you're awake and refreshed, you can return to your sightseeing.

✔ **Take a break when the sightseeing starts getting to you.** Whatever it takes to bring your cultural appreciation back from the brink, do it. Take a day to get off the beaten path. Go shopping. Go to a soccer match. Above all, stop trying to rack up sightseeing points. Sit down with a coffee or a glass of wine and write postcards. After describing your unforgettable experiences to your friends back home, chances are you'll be psyched to get back on the sightseeing trail.

How to Schedule Your Time

Table 2-1 gives you an idea of the minimum amount of time that's needed to "see" Europe's major cities. This schedule allows time to settle in, visit the major sights, get a taste for the place, and maybe go on one day trip.

Table 2-1	How Much Time to Spend in Each City
City	**Amount of Time**
Amsterdam	2–3 days
Athens	2 days

(continued)

Table 2-1 *(continued)*

City	Amount of Time
Barcelona	2–3 days
Bern/Alps	1–3 days
Dublin	1–2 days
Edinburgh	1–2 days
Florence	2–3 days
London	3–4 days
Madrid	2–3 days
Munich	2 days
Paris	3–4 days
Prague	2–3 days
Rome	3–4 days
Venice	2–3 days
Vienna	1–3 days

Remember to add on at least one extra day for each overnight side trip you want to take. Also, try to stay longer in some of the major cities, such as London, Paris, or Rome — you won't run out of things to do.

Chapter 3

Presenting Five Great Itineraries

In This Chapter
- ▶ Seeing the best of Europe in two weeks
- ▶ Experiencing Europe on the three-week Grand Tour
- ▶ Discovering the best art in two weeks
- ▶ Spending a romantic week with your lover
- ▶ Bringing the kids for a week of fun for ages 5 to 105

*B*efore you start gathering information on specific destinations or checking on airfares, you need to piece together a skeleton itinerary for your trip to Europe. Choosing all the places you want to visit is the easy part. Figuring out which of them you have time to see takes some work. To ease the burden, we present five possible itineraries in this chapter.

We've fit most of these tours into a one- or two-week timeframe, because so many of us get just one or two precious weeks of vacation. We also include a three-week whirlwind extravaganza in case you can carve out a few extra days.

These itineraries assume two extra weekend "freebie" days. Many flights to Europe from North America leave in the evening, so if you can get a Europe-bound flight on Friday night, you have all day Saturday in Europe as well. If you fly back home on the last Sunday of your trip, all of a sudden, your "week" is nine days long. Traveling like this, you have to disregard jet lag, which typically throws a wrench into the schedules of transatlantic travelers after they arrive in Europe. Keep in mind that opening hours vary from season to season. Because summer is the most popular travel time, we've arranged these itineraries assuming summer schedules. You may have to tweak them if you're visiting in the off season or if one of the days you happen to be in a particular European town falls on a Sunday, a Monday, or another day when some sights may be closed.

Occasionally, we include specific train times and schedules, but remember that this is just to get you thinking about how to schedule your time. Rail and airline timetables can and will change regularly, so always check the current schedules. (Chapter 6 shows you how to do just that.)

The Everything-but-the-Kitchen-Sink-in-Two-Weeks Tour

If you're determined to see as much as you can on your trip, here's one way to do it. But rest up first because you'll be on the go nonstop and won't have time for jet lag.

Take an overnight plane that lands early in **London** (see Chapter 10). Spend **Days 1 through 4** as outlined in the itineraries we recommend in Chapter 10, using the extra, fourth day to take in whichever side trip most intrigues you: **Oxford, Bath,** or **Stonehenge.** This itinerary gets in the greatest sights and experiences of London, from the National Gallery and British Museum to the Tower of London and Westminster Abbey; from shopping at Harrods to joining a London Walks tour and taking in a Shakespeare play at the Globe.

On **Day 5,** take the earliest Eurostar train through the Channel Tunnel to **Paris** (see Chapter 13). Get settled in your hotel, have lunch, and head to the Musée Rodin. Then, suspend your sightseeing until the next day and instead enjoy the late afternoon people-watching in a classic French cafe followed by a sunset cruise on the Seine.

Spend **Days 6 through 8** as outlined in Chapter 13 (the "If you have three days" suggested itinerary), marveling at Notre-Dame and Sainte-Chapelle, perusing the art treasures of the Louvre and Musée d'Orsay, and climbing the Eiffel Tower.

Leave plenty of time to stroll through the chic Marais quarter, along the banks of the Seine River, and around bohemian-turned-touristy (but still fun) Montmartre. Plan a day at the extravagant Versailles, the palace to end all palaces. Treat yourself to at least one first-class dinner to celebrate your arrival in one of the world capitals of cuisine.

On the morning of **Day 8,** get up early and head to the Gare de Lyon train station to reserve a couchette for that night's train to Venice, leaving around 7 or 8 p.m. You can also store your bags at the station so that you don't have to lug them around during your final day in Paris.

Train stations make excellent way stations for your luggage when visiting a city for a short time. Most train stations around Europe have lockers or a luggage storage office where you can leave your heaviest bags for around $10 a day.

When you arrive in **Venice** (see Chapter 21) on **Day 9,** check out the next morning's schedule for trains to Florence and leave your bags in the lockers; you can live out of your backpack or carryall for this one day.

Then dive (well, not literally) into the city of canals. Cruise the Grand Canal on the *vaporetto* (public ferry) to one of Europe's most beautiful and historic squares, Piazza San Marco. Tour the glittering mosaic-filled St. Mark's cathedral and ride the elevator to the bell tower for sweeping views across the city and its canals.

Tour the Palazzo Ducale (Doge's Palace) for a behind-the-scenes look at Venetian history and intrigue. Have a snack on your way to check into your hotel in the early afternoon, and then visit the masterpieces of the Accademia in the midafternoon. Take a gondola ride before dinner and wander the quiet, romantic streets after your meal. Try to get to bed at a reasonable hour because you'll have to get up early.

On the morning of **Day 10,** head to the train station at least 90 minutes before your train departs (this allows time for the slow public ferry to get there). Retrieve your bags, take the first morning train you can to **Florence** (see Chapter 20), and drop your bags at your hotel.

Have a lunch on the go so that you leave plenty of time to see the Duomo (cathedral), climbing its ingenious and noble dome to get a city panorama, and marveling at the mosaics inside the adjacent baptistery. By 3 p.m., make your way to the world's premier museum of the Renaissance, the Uffizi Galleries (it's best to reserve your admission ticket beforehand). Have a Tuscan feast at Trattoria Garga before bed.

Be in line at the Accademia on **Day 11** when it opens so that you can see Michelangelo's *David* before the crowds arrive. If you don't linger too long, you'll have time to swing by the church of Santa Maria Novella before lunch for a look at its Renaissance frescoes. (A young apprentice named Michelangelo helped out on the Ghirlandaio fresco cycle.)

After lunch, while the city is shut down for the midday *riposo* (rest), make your way over to the Giotto frescoes in Santa Croce church, the final resting place of Michelangelo, Galileo, and Machiavelli. On your way back to the heart of town, stop by Vivoli for their excellent gelato.

Cross the shop-lined medieval bridge called Ponte Vecchio to get to Oltrarno, the artisan's quarter, and the Medicis' grand Pitti Palace, where the painting galleries will keep you occupied until closing time at 7 p.m. Oltrarno is full of good, homey restaurants where you can kick back, toast your 36 hours in Florence, and plan your return.

Get up extra early on **Day 12** to catch the 7:30 a.m. train to **Rome** (see Chapter 19), which pulls in around 9:15 a.m. Spend **Days 12 through 14** as outlined in Chapter 20 in the "If you have three days" section. See the glories of ancient Rome at the Forum, Colosseum, and Pantheon, and the riches of the capital of Christendom at St. Peter's.

In addition to the superlative Vatican Museums, make time while in Rome for two additional world-class museums: the Capitoline Museums and the gorgeous Galleria Borghese (reserve your admission at the Borghese before you leave home).

Spend **Day 15,** your last full day in Europe, at **Tivoli,** a nearby hill town full of palaces, gardens, and the haunting ruins of Emperor Hadrian's villa. Return to Rome in time for dinner and then make your way to the famous Trevi Fountain. It's tradition to toss a coin into the water to ensure that one day you'll return to the Eternal City.

Most flights from Rome back to North America leave either in the morning or early afternoon. Either way, **Day 16** is a wash; spend the morning getting to the airport and the day in the air.

The Three-Week Grand Tour of Europe

Slightly less intense than the two-week tour outlined in the preceding section, this itinerary allows a little leisure time to get out and enjoy the countryside, with a few scenic drives and mountain hikes thrown in for good measure.

Days 1 through 4 are the same as those in the preceding "Everything-but-the-Kitchen-Sink-in-Two-Weeks" trip — you start in **London** (see Chapter 10).

On the morning of **Day 5,** take an early flight to **Amsterdam** (see Chapter 14). You can usually get a cheap fare with easyJet (www.easyjet.com). After you settle in, spend **Days 5 and 6** as described in Chapter 14 in the "If you have two days" section — relaxing with a canal cruise and imagining life in all those narrow, gabled, 17th-century town houses.

Continue with that two-day itinerary, enjoying the masterpieces in the Rijksmuseum and the Van Gogh Museum, a bike ride, an Indonesian feast in the hopping Leidseplein neighborhood, and a sobering tour of the Anne Frank House. Dine early on the evening of **Day 6,** because you need to catch the overnight train to Munich, which leaves around 7:30 p.m.

First thing to do when you arrive in **Munich** (see Chapter 15) is pause at the train station to book an overnight couchette to Venice for the next evening. Spend **Days 7 and 8** in Munich as in our recommended suggested itineraries in Chapter 15. The overnight train to Venice leaves very late (around 11:30 p.m.), so after dinner on the evening of **Day 8,** bide your remaining time in Munich in true Bavarian style at the Augustinerkeller beer hall, 5 long blocks from the train station.

When you get to **Venice** (see Chapter 21), check into your hotel, and then head to the center of town. Spend **Day 9** enjoying the three major sights: St. Mark's Cathedral, the Doge's Palace, and the Accademia

Gallery. Spend **Day 10** visiting the outlying islands of the Venetian lagoon with their glass- and lace-making traditions, fishing villages, and glittering church mosaics.

For **Day 11,** spend the morning in the museums, especially the Peggy Guggenheim, and then the early afternoon simply wandering through Venice's enchanting back alleys. Be sure to leave yourself plenty of time to hop on a late-afternoon train to **Florence** (see Chapter 20), arriving in time to check into your hotel and find a late (around 10 p.m.) dinner.

For **Days 12 through 14,** visit Michelangelo's *David,* the Uffizi Galleries, the Pitti Palace museums, Fra' Angelico's frescoes in San Marco monastery, the Medici Tombs, the cathedral and its dome, Bargello sculpture gallery, and the shop-lined Ponte Vecchio spanning the Arno River.

Starting with an early morning train to **Rome** (see Chapter 19), spend **Days 15 through 18** exactly as Days 12 through 15 in the preceding section, with one addition: On the morning of **Day 18,** head to the train station to check your bags and to book a couchette for the overnight train to Paris before heading out to Tivoli for the day. Leave Tivoli by 4 p.m. at the latest so that you'll be back in Rome by 5 p.m. — enough time to pick up some picnic supplies for dinner on the train. The Paris train leaves around 7:30 p.m.

Spend **Days 19 through 22** in **Paris** (see Chapter 13), following the schedule for Days 5 through 8 under the two-week itinerary in the preceding section.

Most flights from Paris back to North America leave in the morning or early afternoon, so spend the morning of **Day 23** getting to the airport and spend the day flying home.

Two Weeks in Europe for Lovers of Art

For this trip, you can work out the daily sightseeing schedules on your own. Most of the cities in this suggested itinerary have two-and-a-half days of sightseeing time budgeted, which gives you enough time to check out the masterpieces in the major museums.

Head to **London** (see Chapter 10) for **Days 1 through 3.** Your first order of business should definitely be the medieval, Renaissance, and baroque masterpieces of the National Gallery. The other great art collection is the Tate Gallery, now divided between two buildings, one on each side of the Thames: The Tate Britain covers the British greats, and the Tate Modern, a vast space in Southwark, concentrates on international art in the 19th and 20th centuries (from Impressionism to contemporary works), with stellar temporary exhibits.

While at the National Gallery, you may also want to nip around the corner to the National Portrait Gallery (same building, different entrance). Although the collection exists more for the cultural importance of its subjects, some artistically fine portraits reside here as well (especially by Holbein, Reynolds, and Warhol).

No museum buff should miss the British Museum, with its outstanding antiquities collections (including the Parthenon sculptures), or the Victoria & Albert Museum, which has London's best sculpture collection (including Donatello, Giambologna, and Bernini) in addition to miles of decorative arts.

On the morning of **Day 4,** catch a Eurostar train to **Paris** (see Chapter 13). Spend **Days 4 through 6** in the City of Light, exploring the treasures of the Louvre over a full day. Fans of Impressionism and French art in general should devote at least two-thirds of a day to the Musée d'Orsay.

Paris has so many smaller art museums that choosing from among them can be difficult, and squeezing them all in during your visit can be nearly impossible. Entire museums are devoted to single artists (such as Rodin and Picasso), and others are devoted to eras (such as the incomparable modern collection at Centre Pompidou). One of our favorite Paris art treasures is Monet's 360-degree *Waterlilies* in specially built basement rooms of the Orangerie, off Place de la Concorde. At the end of **Day 6,** hop on the overnight train to Florence.

Days 7 through 9 are for **Florence** (see Chapter 20). Reserve one entire day for the Uffizi Galleries and its masterpieces of Renaissance art. The Pitti Palace's Galleria Palatina covers the High Renaissance and baroque eras. Michelangelo's *David* and his unfinished *Slaves* in the Accademia are a must, while Donatello reigns supreme at the Bargello sculpture museum. A veritable who's who of Italian greats were responsible for the rich decorations in Florence's churches, so visit as many of them as you can.

Then you can see Brunelleschi's magnificent architecture: the Duomo, Santo Spirito, and the Pazzi chapel at Santa Croce. Florence is one place where you'll definitely run out of time long before you run out of art.

Days 10 through 12 find you in **Rome** (see Chapter 19). Take the morning train here from Florence on **Day 10** and start exploring the baroque period with Bernini's giant sculptures adorning the fountains in Piazza Navona and on display in the recently restored and utterly glorious Galleria Borghese.

The Vatican Museums (home to the Raphael Rooms, the Pinacoteca painting gallery, and Michelangelo's Sistine Chapel) require at least two-thirds of a day. The Capitoline Museums split their collections between ancient sculpture and mosaics and Renaissance and baroque painting.

Rome's churches are filled with art, from Filippino Lippi's frescoes in Santa Maria Sopra Minerva (where you also find Michelangelo's *Risen Christ*) to the Caravaggios in Santa Maria del Popolo and Michelangelo's *Moses* in San Pietro in Vincoli. Again, you're unlikely to run out of art to ogle in your three days here.

On the evening of **Day 12,** get on the overnight train for the long haul to Barcelona. If you don't like those overnight trains, wait for the 8:55 a.m. train, although you'll have to adjust the rest of your itinerary to accommodate the 5½-hour trip. Volareweb.com (www.volareweb.com) sells cheap, no-frills flights to Barcelona.

Spend **Day 13** in the Catalonian capital of **Barcelona** (see Chapter 23). You should definitely take in the intriguing early Picasso works at the museum dedicated to this hometown hero and make a survey of Antoni Gaudí's sinuous and surprising architecture. At the end of the day, board the overnight train to Madrid.

Plunge into the myriad museums of **Madrid** (see Chapter 22) on **Days 14 and 15.** Spain is the land of Picasso, Velázquez, Goya, El Greco (by adoption), Murillo, and Ribera. You have a day to devote to the Museo del Prado and another day to split between the Reina Sofía Museum (home of Picasso's *Guernica*), the Thyssen-Bornemisza Museum, and — if you can stand any more art at this point — the Monasterio de las Descalzas Reales.

Day 16 is your day to travel home.

A Week of Romance, European Style

Nothing kills a romantic mood faster than dashing hurriedly from place to place, so we leave the daily scheduling for this tour up to you.

The mere mention of **Paris** (see Chapter 13) conjures up romantic images, so it's a great place to begin. Spend **Days 1 through 3** enjoying Paris's famed museums — the Musée d'Orsay has both French Romantic-era painters and loads of those lovable Impressionists.

But take time to enjoy the finer points of Parisian life. Linger at cafe tables, spend an evening strolling Montmartre, have long meals at fine restaurants and cozy bistros, explore Paris's gorgeous parks, take a dinner cruise along the Seine, and ascend the Eiffel Tower one evening for a panorama of Paris, City of Light.

Indulge in the romance of yesteryear by spending a day at Versailles, the palace to end all palaces. On the evening of **Day 3,** board the overnight train or a late-evening flight on no-frills SmartWings (www.smartwings.com) to Prague.

Prague (see Chapter 18), your focus for **Days 4 and 5,** is a city of baroque palaces, mighty fortresses, delicious beers, hidden gardens, and classical street musicians who play a mean Dvořák. Spend an afternoon delving into Prague's rich Jewish heritage at its synagogues and museums. Take a sunset stroll across the statue-lined Charles Bridge.

Spend a day (or at least a morning) exploring Prague Castle, both to appreciate its soaring Gothic cathedral and to see how a fortress-city of the Middle Ages looked and worked. Whatever else you do, try to fit in as many of Prague's delightful evening concerts as you can.

At the end of **Day 5,** hop an overnight train to **Venice** (see Chapter 21) for **Days 6 through 8.** La Serenissima — "The Most Serene" city of canals, palaces, Byzantine mosaics, and delicate blown glass — makes a romantic out of everyone. This extraordinarily atmospheric and secretive, sensual city has always been a haven for lovers, so we leave you to your own devices in exploring.

Don't pass up a ride in a traditional gondola (despite the outrageous prices). Make sure you have a couple of long, drawn-out Italian feasts by candlelight, a cruise down the majestic sweep of the Grand Canal, and some moonlit strolls through the narrow, winding alleys and over the countless canals.

To round out your romantic adventures in Venice, set aside one full day to explore the smaller fishing, glass-blowing, and lace-making islands in the Venetian lagoon.

You'll most likely have to fly home from (or at least connect through) Milan, so leave all of **Day 9** free for the return trip. Allow at least 90 minutes from the time you leave your Venice hotel to get to the train station (either to take the train to Milan in 2½–3½ hours, or to catch the shuttle to the Venice airport in 20 minutes).

A Week in Europe That the Kids Will Love

When planning your family itinerary, leave plenty of time for the kids to rest, and remember that most kids' ability to appreciate even the finest art and coolest palaces wears out quickly. *You* may want to spend five hours in the Louvre, but the tykes will be lucky to last two. Take Europe at their pace so that you can all get something out of it and have a fantastic, rewarding, and (*shh!* don't tell) educational time.

For this trip, fly into London and out of Rome. Your overnight plane lands early on **Day 1** in **London** (see Chapter 10). Check into your hotel, and then head for the British Airways London Eye, a giant observation wheel that offers a thrilling overview of the city. From there, head across the Thames to see the Houses of Parliament with the giant Clock Tower holding the bell called Big Ben. At nearby Westminster Abbey, you can see the tombs of great poets, explorers, kings, and queens.

After lunch, cross St. James's Park to peer through the gates at Buckingham Palace, the residence of the queen of England, before making your way to the Tower of London, where the Yeoman Warders (or Beefeater Guards) give some of the most entertaining tours in all of Europe, turning a millennium of dry history into juicy tales of intrigue. The Crown Jewels glitter as brightly as the armor and battle-axe blades on display in the armory-and-torture-device museum.

Start off **Day 2** with a cruise down the Thames to **Greenwich,** which still retains a bit of its village ambience and is home to a bevy of exciting sights. Start with a peek at the *Cutty Sark,* the most famous of the multi-sailed clipper ships, now being restored after a big fire in 2007. Then make your way to the National Maritime Museum, where you'll see ship models and find out about the famed Royal British Navy in the days when the sun never set on the British Empire. At the nearby (within walking distance) Old Royal Observatory, the kids can walk down the *prime meridian* (the line that separates Earth's two hemispheres), have fun jumping from one to the other, and set their watches at the source from which all the world's clocks get their reading: Greenwich mean time.

Take a boat from Greenwich back to London and spend the late afternoon relaxing. In the evening, get cultural. See a big splashy musical, such as *Phantom of the Opera,* a cutting-edge play in the West End, or Shakespeare performed in the Globe Theatre.

Reserve **Day 3** for a day trip to **Salisbury,** with its towering Gothic cathedral, and evocative **Stonehenge,** where imaginations can run wild speculating on the mysteries of this evocative site.

From London, take the earliest Eurostar train through the Channel Tunnel to Paris (see Chapter 13) on **Day 4.** Get settled in your hotel, have lunch, and head to Notre-Dame, which you can make even more interesting if you take the time to clamber up the North Tower so that the kids can examine those famed gargoyles up close. On a sunny day, even the most jaded of teenagers can't help but be impressed by the delicate spectacle of light and color through Sainte-Chapelle's stained-glass windows.

Spend at least two hours in the Louvre to see the *Mona Lisa* and other artistic treasures. From here, it's off to the Eiffel Tower.

In the morning of **Day 5,** take your bags to the Gare de Lyon train station and leave them in lockers so that you can catch that evening's overnight train to Rome (it leaves around 7:30 p.m.).

Then take the RER (light-rail train) out to **Versailles,** the biggest, most impressive palace in all of Europe. Even all this lavishness gets pretty boring pretty quickly for the kids, so just take a quick tour of the highlights. A less educational alternative to a day at Versailles is a day at Disneyland Paris. Be back in Paris in plenty of time to shop for picnic supplies for dinner on the train and be at the station by 7 p.m.

Your train pulls into **Rome** (see Chapter 19) on **Day 6** around 10 a.m. Check into your hotel, splash some water on your faces, and head off to the Markets of Trajan, where the kids can wander down an ancient Roman street and explore the empty shops pigeonholing the remarkably intact ruins of the world's first multilevel shopping mall.

Truth be told, this section of the Imperial Fori is a bit more impressively intact than the far more famous Roman Forum across the street, but you'll still want to wander through that seat of Roman Imperial power.

You can walk from the Roman Forum to the massive Colosseum, where the kids can clamber around and imagine tournaments of wild beasts and gladiator fights.

If you finish with the Forum and Colosseum by 2 p.m., you have enough time to visit one or two catacombs along the Appian Way. The littlest kids may be afraid, but most will get a thrill out of wandering miles of spooky underground tunnels lined with the open-niche tombs of ancient Christians. The best catacomb to visit is the Catacombe di San Domitilla.

On **Day 7,** head across the Tiber to St. Peter's Basilica and the adjacent Vatican Museums. The sheer size of St. Peter's is inspiring to anyone, especially if you tour the subcrypt of papal tombs and climb the dome. Impress the kids by pointing out that Michelangelo carved his *Pietà* sculpture when he was just 19 years old.

Then walk around the wall to the Vatican Museums, home to ancient sculptures, the Raphael Rooms, and of course, the sublime Sistine Chapel frescoed by Michelangelo.

From there, head over to the Spanish Steps in time for the *passeggiata,* a see-and-be-seen stroll in the surrounding streets. And before you head to bed for the night, stop by the Trevi Fountain (best after dark) so that everyone can toss in a coin to ensure a return to the Eternal City.

Spend **Day 8** on a day trip to **Ostia Antica,** ancient Rome's port. It's an Imperial-era ghost town of crumbling temples, weed-filled shops, mosaic-floored houses, dusty squares, cavernous baths, and paved streets deeply rutted by cart wheels — on par with Pompeii, but without the hordes of tourists and just a Metro ride away from downtown Rome.

Most flights from Rome leave in the early afternoon, so plan on spending **Day 9** just getting packed and to the airport two hours before your flight.

Part II
Planning Your Trip to Europe

The 5th Wave   By Rich Tennant

ATTENZIONE!

"It says, children are forbidden from running, touching objects, or appearing bored during the tour."

In this part . . .

*H*ere we get down to the nitty-gritty of trip planning. In the following chapters, you'll find indispensable information on everything from managing your money and shopping for plane tickets to choosing a tour operator and reserving a hotel room. We point out special resources available for travelers with particular needs — including students, seniors, families, and gays and lesbians — and make some experience-based suggestions on what to pack, how to get a passport, and how to take advantage of special rates for rental cars and rail passes. In short, we provide you with the practical advice and information you need to make your European dream vacation come true.

Chapter 4

Managing Your Money

. . . .

In This Chapter

▶ Getting a general idea of your trip's total cost
▶ Working out a budget
▶ Considering easy-to-overlook expenses and cost-cutting measures
▶ Deciding which is best for you: ATMs, credit cards, or traveler's checks
▶ Beating the exchange-rate game
▶ Understanding the value-added tax (VAT) and getting it back
▶ Keeping your money (and valuables) safe

. . . .

*T*his chapter addresses some essential money-related questions, such as, "Can I afford a trip to Europe?" and "What are the real expenses involved?"

If you're wondering approximately how much you should realistically budget for your trip, read on. In this chapter, you'll also find hints, tips, and secrets on how to trim your budget down to an amount you can actually afford.

After you have your budget planned out, you need to know how to handle your money when you get to Europe. As you travel, you have many payment options, including ATM cards, credit cards, traveler's checks, and local currency. This chapter weighs the benefits and annoyances of each method and shows you how to get the most out of your money. We share a bit about currency exchange rates, which have been drastically simplified with the advent of the euro, and explain the European version of a sales tax. At the end of the chapter, you'll find some safety tips for securing your money and yourself.

Planning Your Budget

You can make two different trips to the same city for the same amount of time and see all the same sights, but come out with a total bill that differs by thousands of dollars. This book shows you how to maintain the quality of your trip while stretching your dollars along the way.

Traveling frugally means looking for simple, clean, and comfortable hotels rather than those with minibars and spas; knowing when to splurge, when to skimp, and how to spot rip-offs; buying rail passes and museum cards instead of individual tickets; and enjoying meals in local bistros, cafes, and *trattorie* (family-run restaurants) rather than expensive restaurants.

Before you delve into the specific tips on saving money, plan out a rough trip budget. Your total cost depends greatly on your means and tastes. If you look through the listings in the destination chapters of this book, you can easily figure out what price level of hotel and restaurant appeals to you. Just plug the average cost for these accommodations into your expected daily expenses. As long as you round all dollar amounts up to allow for some padding, you should get a basic idea of your costs. As always, overestimating is wise. End your trip with some surprise leftover cash rather than a disastrous shortfall.

In addition to the prices listed later in this book, here are some general guidelines:

- ✔ **Long-distance transportation:** One of your biggest expenses will be transportation. International airfares vary dramatically, depending on the season and the carrier; the same is true of airfares within Europe. But a host of no-frills airlines now makes air travel on the Continent an inexpensive option (see Chapter 5 for ways to get the best deal). Traveling through Europe by train, however, is a lot more fun than flying, and money-saving rail passes are available to help you travel between regions or countries for less money. To save time and money, you may want to make your long trips at night, upgrading to a couchette (see Chapter 6 for options and prices). For short rail trips within Europe, it sometimes makes sense to pay for individual tickets when you arrive.

- ✔ **Local transportation:** Once you're in the city of your dreams, you need to get around. In some places, you can do all your sightseeing on foot. But in other, larger cities, you need to use some form of public transportation: subway, tram, bus, or taxi (if you want to splurge). Many cities offer inexpensive full-day transportation tickets that bring costs way down. Budget at least $15 a day for your local public transportation costs.

- ✔ **Lodging:** Hotel costs vary from country to country and depend on your personal tastes. In general, budget hotels and low-end B&Bs range in price from around $100 to $175 per double. If you're willing to stay in dormitory-like hostels, the rate drops to about $40 to $75 a night per person. For a first-class or luxury-grade hotel room, expect to pay anywhere from $250 to $300 and up for double occupancy. Keep in mind, though, that by shopping around, you can often find special deals that bring hotel prices way down. You'll find money-saving tips in Chapter 7.

- ✔ **Dining:** Sampling an area's local cuisine should play as large a role in your vacation as sightseeing does, so allow a generous budget for meals. For a simple lunch (not a sandwich at a takeaway shop), plan to spend $25 to $35 on average (more in London). If you want a big dinner every night, budget around $50 to $75 per person for a moderately priced restaurant and $75 and up per person to dine at a more upscale restaurant. Again, be aware that food prices will vary from country to country (the most expensive meals will definitely be in London and Paris).

You probably don't need to budget money for breakfast because most hotels offer breakfast with a room. If not, buying a small breakfast at a cafe costs about $10.

✔ **Attractions/shopping:** Museum hounds and sightseeing fanatics should figure enough cash into their budgets to cover the costs of admission. Don't be chintzy here. Estimate an average of $20 per sight ($25–$35 for biggies). Therefore, stopping at three major sights per day adds up to roughly $60 to $100. Budget at least $10 a day for postcards and other minor souvenirs, more if you're a chronic shopper.

All the big national museums in London are now free, and so are a few other major sites throughout Europe, such as the Roman Forum. Also, many cities sell museum passes that give you substantial savings on cultural attractions. You'll find more information about these savings in the "Shaving off sightseeing and shopping costs" section, later in this chapter.

Using the three-week grand tour from Chapter 3 as a sample (making one change: instead of flying home from Paris, on the last day you take a no-frills flight back to London and fly home from there), Table 4-1 presents an estimated per-person budget for two adults traveling together. We've averaged our prices on the "plus" side for this three-week trip (starting with calculating for 22 days to allow for an extra travel day). Single travelers booking a single room may be able to shave off a few dollars for lodging.

Airline fares, as you probably know, can fluctuate dramatically, and the value of the U.S. dollar against the European euro also affects prices. At press time, the dollar was very low against the euro, meaning prices in Europe were higher for American travelers.

Table 4-1	Expenses for a Three-Week Trip to Europe during High Season (Per Person)
Expense	*Cost*
Airfares, including taxes (round-trip NYC–London $600; London–Amsterdam $50; Paris–London $80)	$730
Eurail Selectpass Saver (four countries/five days)	$447

(continued)

Table 4-1 *(continued)*

Expense	Cost
Three nights in second-class train couchettes ($39 each; you can reserve a second-class couchette on a first-class pass)	$117
18 days of city transportation ($15 a day)	$270
19 nights in hotels ($100 per person per night, averaged from midrange hotel prices in this book)	$1,900
44 meals (22 lunches at $25, plus 22 dinners at $50; breakfast usually comes with hotel room)	$1,650
Sightseeing admissions ($60 a day for 18 days)	$1,080
Souvenirs, postcards, coffee, and miscellaneous stuff ($25 a day)	$550
TOTAL	**$6,744**

As Table 4-1 indicates, you can finance a thrilling three-week trip, which hits most of Europe's must-see sights, for under $7,000 per person. Yes, it looks like a lot of money, but the experience of traveling in Europe is priceless. If our rough average amount is too much, don't give up hope — the budget does have some leeway.

To trim more money from your budget, for example, you can cut out $117 by sleeping in unreserved compartments on overnight trains (the pull-out-seat kind) instead of couchettes. Buy a sandwich or a piece of pizza for lunches (around $10 a person) and keep your dinner costs down to $30 apiece, and your dining total shrinks from $1,650 to $880. Reduce your miscellaneous expenses to $10 a day by making your photos your postcards and skipping the souvenirs, and $550 is whittled down to $220.

Factoring in these adjustments, the new grand total comes to around $5,527 — still a great value for everything that you're getting. You can even manage a two-week trip to Europe for as little as $3,000, if you travel smart, go during the off-season, and keep your budget in mind. The next section presents some tips to help you do just that.

Keeping a Lid on Hidden Expenses

 No matter how carefully you plan a budget, it seems like you always end up shelling out for expenses that you didn't expect. The following is a list of common (yet completely avoidable) travel expenses, and ways to keep them from putting a dent in your vacation fund:

✔ **Find out what your rental covers.** When shopping for car rentals, always make sure you know what the quoted rate includes — and excludes. Some charges that the rental agent may or may not mention to you include airport pickup/drop-off surcharge, drop-off fee for renting in one city and dropping off in another, the collision damage waiver (CDW), local taxes, mileage (is it limited or unlimited?), and a tank of gas. See Chapter 6 for more information about renting a car.

✔ **Ask whether taxes are included.** In most of Europe, taxes are automatically included in the hotel rates. In some countries, however, hotels may quote you the prices before tax — usually the case in Spain (7 percent), sometimes in England (17.5 percent), and occasionally at expensive hotels in the Czech Republic (22 percent). Always ask to be sure.

✔ **Never place a phone call from a hotel room.** On long-distance calls, the markup is often 200 percent. Hotels may even charge for what should be free calls to the local AT&T, MCI, or Sprint calling-card number. Always use a pay phone or consider renting a cell-phone if you plan to make many calls (see Chapter 9).

✔ **Look before you tip.** Many restaurants include a service charge in your bill, so tipping another 15 percent is tossing your money out the window. Always ask if service is included. If not, tip about 15 percent, just like at home. If service is included, and you felt that your server did a good job, leave a bit extra on the table anyway (one euro, for example, or in England, a pound coin).

✔ **Watch out for high commission on exchange rates.** Find out the bank's commission fee or percentage before exchanging traveler's checks, or you could end up leaking a little extra cash each time you change money.

Cutting Costs — But Not the Fun

The following list just gives you a taste of all the budget strategies that exist. No doubt you'll encounter more ways to stretch your travel dollar.

Planning ahead for discounts

Airfare to Europe can make you blow your budget before you even leave home, but fear not — there are plenty of ways to save:

✔ **Go off-season.** If you can travel at non-peak times (Oct–May for most major cities and tourist centers), you'll find hotel rates up to 30 percent below the prices of peak months.

✔ **Travel midweek.** If you can travel on a Tuesday, Wednesday, or Thursday, you may find cheaper flights to your destination. When you ask about airfares, see if you can get a cheaper rate by flying on a different day. (For more tips on getting a good fare, see Chapter 5.)

✔ **Try a package tour.** For many destinations, you can book airfare, hotel, ground transportation, and even some sightseeing just by making one call to a travel agent, airline, or packager, for a price much less than if you put the trip together yourself. The savings can be amazing. (See Chapter 5 for more about package tours.)

✔ **Always ask for discount rates.** You may be pleasantly surprised to discover that you're eligible for discounts on sights, transportation, hotels, you name it. Members of automobile clubs, such as AAA and CAA, trade unions, or AARP; frequent fliers; teachers; students; families; and members of other groups sometimes get discounted rates on car rentals, plane tickets, and some chain-hotel rooms. Ask your company whether employees can use the corporate travel agent and corporate rates even for private vacations. You never know until you ask.

If your family emigrated from Europe, you may get another discount. Many ethnic travel agencies (usually found in major cities) specialize in getting forgotten sons and daughters rock-bottom rates when returning to the old country. It's worth looking into if you can find one near you.

Trimming transportation expenses

Getting to Europe uses up most of your transportation budget, but just getting from place to place can add up too. Here are a few ways to make the most of your remaining transportation dollars:

✔ **Reserve your rental car before you leave.** If you know you want to have a car for some or all of your trip, rent it through a major U.S. company before you leave, saving big bucks over the cost of renting on the spot in Europe (see Chapter 6 for details).

✔ **Don't rent a gas guzzler.** Renting a smaller car is cheaper, and you save on gas to boot. Unless you're traveling with kids and need lots of space, don't go beyond the economy size. For more about car rentals, see Chapter 6.

✔ **Invest in a rail pass.** Europe's extensive train system constitutes its greatest transportation asset. The train system's best value is its family of Eurail passes (see Chapter 6).

✔ **Buy a single- or multi-day transportation pass for local transportation needs.** Most big cities offer specially priced day or multiday tickets for their public transportation systems. These passes provide enormous savings over individual ticket prices and free you up from the need to always have the correct fare.

✔ **Walk a lot.** A good pair of walking shoes can save lots of money in taxis and other local transportation. As a bonus, you'll get to know your destination more intimately because you explore at a slower pace.

Lowering your lodging bill

Hotel costs in Europe can be sky-high, especially in big cities. If you don't relish the thought of paying big bucks for a swank room that you won't be spending much time in anyway, try some of the following tips:

- ✔ **Catch 20 winks on an overnight train for $39 (or maybe even free!).** Armed with your trusty rail pass, you can jump on an overnight train and fork over just $39 for a reserved bunk in a sleeping couchette. Or if you're feeling lucky, take your chances on finding an empty sitting compartment, slide down the seat back, and — *voilà!* — you have a bed for free. In the morning, you'll have reached your destination and saved yourself a night's hotel charge.

- ✔ **Leave the private plumbing at home; take a room without a bathroom.** You can get a hotel room that shares a bathroom down the hall for about two-thirds as much as you pay for a virtually identical room with its own plumbing.

- ✔ **Get a triple or cots, not two rooms, if you have kids.** At most European hotels, kids stay for free in a parent's room. At the worst, a hotel may charge a small fee ($15–$25) for the extra bed.

- ✔ **Rent a room instead of staying at a hotel.** At $40 to $80 a night, private rooms for rent beat out even the cheapest B&Bs or pensions. You also get the experience of staying in a European home, which no five-star hotel can give you for any price (see Chapter 7).

- ✔ **Give the ultracheap accommodations a try.** If sleeping near 150 roommates (mostly students) on a wooden floor under a big tent sounds appealing, you can spend a night in Munich for $15. Budget options abound in Europe, from hostels (beds from $40–$52) to convents ($40–$75) to extreme options such as Munich's aforementioned mega tent. See Chapter 7 for more details.

- ✔ **Opt for a double bed instead of two singles.** Fewer sheets for the hotel to wash equals savings for you. Though this twin-versus-double option is disappearing in many places, it still holds true in some countries.

- ✔ **Get out of town.** In many places, big savings are just a short drive, tram trip, or bus ride away. Hotels outside the historic center, in the next town over, or otherwise less conveniently located are great bargains.

- ✔ **Never allow the hotel to handle your laundry.** Unless you enjoy being taken to the cleaners, you can wash a few pieces of clothes in the sink each night, roll them in towels to sop up the dampness, and hang them on the radiator to dry — or even better, on the heated towel racks (an amenity even cheap places are installing). Or look for a laundry shop that washes and dries clothes based on weight (an average load costs $15). Most European cities have them; start looking near the local university.

✔ **Rent a room that doesn't include breakfast.** Often hotels charge an extra $15 to $20 a night when breakfast is included. You can sometimes get the same food for about $10 at a nearby cafe.

Digging for dining bargains

Don't worry, you won't have to go hungry or even eat bad food to keep dining costs to a minimum. You can find plenty of ways to eat well in Europe without breaking the bank:

✔ **Stuff yourself if your hotel room rate includes breakfast.** Don't be shy about loading up on the food that comes with your room.

✔ **Reserve a hotel room with a kitchenette.** Doing your own cooking and dishes may not be your idea of a vacation, but you can save money by not eating in restaurants three times a day. Even if you only make breakfast or cook the occasional dinner, you'll save in the long run.

✔ **Try expensive restaurants at lunch instead of dinner.** Lunch menus often offer many of the same dishes, but at a fraction of the dinnertime cost.

✔ **Lunch on pub grub in Britain and Ireland.** An authentic, yet cheap, meal in a British pub includes a sandwich and a sturdy pint of ale. If you don't want to go to a pub, you can easily find great sandwich bars and cheaper fast-food specialties throughout Britain and Ireland and in every country in Europe.

✔ **Order from fixed-price and tourist menus.** Fixed-price meals can be up to 30 percent cheaper than ordering the same dishes a la carte. Although the options on a fixed-price menu are limited, you can't beat the price.

✔ **Picnic often.** For about $15, you can buy food in a supermarket and dine like a king wherever you want — on a grassy patch in the city park, in your hotel room, or on the train.

Shaving off sightseeing and shopping costs

Some of the best sights in Europe are absolutely free, and you can often find ways to get a discounted rate on the rest:

✔ **Purchase a Paris Museum Pass.** The Paris Museum Pass gives you unlimited entry for four full days to virtually all Parisian museums and sights (the Eiffel Tower is the only major one not on the list) for only 45€ ($72). You can find similar passes in other cities that also include free travel on city buses and subways and other benefits.

✔ **Visit the free or near-free sights.** You can, for example, witness firsthand Paris cafe culture for the price of a cup of coffee (around 3.50€/$5.60) or cruise the Grand Canal in Venice for 6.50€ ($10) on the public *vaporetto* (water ferry). Other free sights and experiences include London's British Museum, Tate Gallery, and National Gallery;

Rome's Pantheon, Forum, and lively piazzas; and throughout Europe, most churches and cathedrals, church services where choirs sing, medieval quarters, sidewalk performers, baroque fountains, city parks, and street markets.

✔ **Take advantage of free or reduced-price museum days.** See the Vatican for free on the last Sunday of every month. You can uncover such policies at many other museums as well. The Louvre, for example, waives admission on the first Sunday of the month and is also almost half-price after 3 p.m. Check the museum's Web site for information about free days and hours of reduced admission, but remember that other people have the same idea — the museums will be most crowded during these free times.

✔ **Skip the souvenirs.** Your photographs and memories serve as the best mementos of your trip. Ten years down the road, you won't care about the T-shirts, key chains, *Bier* steins, and the like.

✔ **Use ATMs instead of traveler's checks.** If you're using traveler's checks, trade them *only* at a bank for local currency or you'll get a bad exchange rate. Also, exchange booths at major tourist attractions give the most miserable rates. Nowadays it makes more sense, and costs less, to withdraw money from European ATMs using your bank card. (See the following section for more information about traveler's checks and ATMs.)

Handling Money

You're the best judge of how much cash you feel comfortable carrying or what alternative form of currency is your favorite. That's not going to change much on your vacation. True, you'll probably be moving around more and incurring more expenses than you generally do (unless you happen to eat out every meal when you're at home), and you may let your mind slip into vacation gear and not be as vigilant about your safety as when you're in work mode. But those factors aside, the only type of payment that won't be quite as available to you away from home is your personal checkbook.

Using your ATM card

Nowadays you can saunter up to an ATM in virtually any city or small town in Europe and retrieve local cash, just as you would back home. Using the ATM is the fastest, easiest, and least expensive way to exchange money. When you use an ATM, you take advantage of the bank's bulk exchange rate (better than any rate you would get changing, say, traveler's checks at a bank), and the fees your home bank may charge you for using a nonproprietary ATM are usually less than a commission charge on a traveler's check would be.

Both the **Cirrus/Maestro** (☎ 800-424-7787; www.mastercard.com) and
PLUS (☎ 800-843-7587; www.visa.com) networks offer automated ATM
locators that list the banks in each country that will accept your card.
Look at the back of your bank card to see which network you're on, and
then call or check online for ATM locations at your destination. Or, as an
alternative, you can search for any machine that carries your network's
symbol. In Europe, nearly every bank ATM is on both systems.

Be sure you know your personal identification number (PIN) before you
leave home, and find out your daily withdrawal limit before you depart.
Also, keep in mind that many home banks impose a fee every time you
use your card at a different bank's ATM, and that fee can be higher for
international transactions (up to $5 or more) than for domestic ones
(where they're rarely more than $2).

Increased internationalism has essentially eliminated the worry that
your card's PIN needs special treatment to work abroad, but you should
still check with the issuing bank before you leave. Most European systems use four-digit PINs; six-digit ones sometimes won't work.

Charging ahead with credit cards

Credit cards are a safe way to carry money. They also provide a convenient record of your expenses, and they generally offer relatively good
exchange rates. You can also withdraw cash advances from your credit
cards at banks or ATMs, provided you know your PIN. If you've forgotten
yours, or didn't even know you had one, call the number on the back of
your credit card and ask the bank to send it to you. It usually takes five
to seven business days, though some banks will provide the number
over the phone if you tell them your mother's maiden name or some
other personal information.

Visa and **MasterCard** are almost universally accepted at European
hotels, restaurants, and shops. The majority of these places also take
American Express, although its high commissions and unhurried reim-
bursement process are leading more and more small businesses to deny
acceptance. The **Diners Club** card has always been more widely
accepted in the cities and at more expensive European establishments
than in smaller towns and budget joints, but its partnership with
MasterCard means that the card may soon be welcomed at establishments that take MasterCard.

Except in the most exclusive restaurants and hotels, most Europeans
have never heard of **Carte Blanche.** You rarely find a place that accepts
Discover, and gas station and department-store credit cards are worth-
less overseas. Leave all those at home. Likewise, when visiting smaller,
cheaper, family-run businesses, such as some inexpensive hotels and
restaurants, most rental rooms, and some neighborhood shops, you
may find that *all* your plastic is useless, even Visa. Therefore, never
rely solely on credit cards.

Chip and PIN: Credit cards European-style

Over the past few years, several European countries have moved away from the magnetic-stripe credit cards Americans use to a new system called "chip and PIN." As a result, some American travelers have had trouble using their credit cards, particularly in England and France. Although businesses that show the Visa or MasterCard logo all have the equipment to take U.S.-style swipe cards, some retailers believe that they can't take swipe cards that don't have PINs. In France, many self-service vendors, including gas stations and automatic ticket kiosks throughout the entire national rail network, will only operate with chip-and-PIN cards. So what should you do?

- **Get a four-digit PIN number from your credit cards' issuing banks before leaving the U.S.** Call the number on the back of each card and ask for one. Get the PIN for your credit cards (this isn't for your ATM card).

- **Keep an eye out for the right logos.** You want Visa and MasterCard, not Maestro, Visa Electron, or Carte Bleue.

- **Consider Amex.** American Express is accepted at fewer locations than Visa or MasterCard, but an Amex card will always work where the Amex logo is displayed.

- **Make sure you have enough cash.** As a last resort, you should be able to cover your purchases with cash.

When you use your credit cards overseas, you pay the premium interest rate (usually around 19 percent) on cash advances, not the low introductory rate that many credit cards offer. Likewise, with most cards, you start to accrue interest *immediately* when you make a cash advance (rather than at the end of the month and only if you don't pay up, as with purchases). If you use American Express, you can usually only obtain a cash advance from an American Express office.

Keep in mind that when you use your credit card for purchases abroad, most banks assess an additional 2 percent to 3 percent fee on top of the 1 percent fee charged by Visa, MasterCard, or American Express for currency conversion on credit charges. It's a sneaky way to add fees that are basically unwarranted. But because traveler's check exchange rates and service fees add up to about 6 percent per transaction, using credit cards may still be a better option for on-the-spot purchases.

Some credit card companies recommend that you notify them of any impending trip abroad so that they don't become suspicious when the card is used numerous times in a foreign destination and block your charges. Even if you don't call your credit card company in advance, you can always call the card's toll-free emergency number if a charge is refused (a good reason to carry the phone number with you). But perhaps the most important lesson here is to carry more than one card on your trip; a card may not work for any number of reasons, so having a backup is the smart way to go.

Cashing traveler's checks

These days, traveler's checks are less necessary because most towns and cities in Europe have 24-hour ATMs that allow you to withdraw cash as needed. However, keep in mind that you'll likely be charged an ATM withdrawal fee if the bank is not your own, so if you're withdrawing money every day, you may be better off with traveler's checks. Traveler's checks have a built-in safety factor, too: If you lose your traveler's checks, you haven't lost your money.

If you choose to carry traveler's checks, be sure to keep a record of their serial numbers separate from your checks, in the event that they're stolen or lost. You'll get a refund faster if you know the numbers.

You can buy traveler's checks at most banks. They're offered in denominations of $20, $50, $100, $500, and sometimes $1,000. Generally, you'll pay a service charge ranging from 1 percent to 4 percent. The most popular traveler's checks are offered by **American Express** (☎ 800-807-6233 or 800-221-7282 for card holders — the latter number accepts collect calls, offers service in several foreign languages, and exempts Amex gold and platinum cardholders from the 1 percent fee); **Visa** (☎ 800-732-1322); and **MasterCard** (☎ 800-223-9920).

American Express, Thomas Cook, Visa, and **MasterCard** offer **foreign currency traveler's checks,** useful if you're traveling to one country or to the euro zone; they're accepted at locations where dollar checks may not be.

Take your traveler's checks (along with your passport for identification) to any bank or exchange booth in Europe, and they'll change the checks for the equivalent amount of local currency, minus exchange-rate fees. (You can find more about shopping for exchange rates in the following section.) Keep in mind that without a passport or appropriate bank identification, you won't be able to cash them.

Paying for a hotel room, shop purchase, or meal directly with a traveler's check drawn on U.S. or nonlocal currency virtually ensures that you get the worst possible exchange rate. Exchange your traveler's checks for local cash at a bank or the American Express office.

Exchanging Money at the Best Rate

Make sure that you do some research before you change your cash, or you risk getting ripped off. Exchange rates are the best and easiest way small-time financiers can take advantage of inattentive tourists.

Shop around for the best exchange rate. If you do, you often notice that exchange rates at banks right next door to each other can differ by 40 percent. The business section of major newspapers (and Europe's main English-language paper, the *International Herald Tribune*) lists the current rates for European currencies. The figures published are prime rates, so although you won't find a street price that's as attractive, they're good guides to follow when shopping for rates.

In the "Fast Facts" section of each destination chapter in this book, we give you the exchange rate for that country. Although currency conversions in this guide are accurate as of this writing, European exchange rates fluctuate constantly. For up-to-date rates, look in the business pages or travel section of any major newspaper, and check online at the **Oanda Currency Converter** (www.oanda.com).

Most banks and currency-exchange services display a chart of the current exchange rates that they offer, often in an outside window or inside at the international teller's window. Make sure that you look at the rate the bank buys, not sells, the currency that you need to exchange. When you compare the rates at different banks, look for the chart with the highest number in the buying-dollars column to find the best rate.

 Remember to factor in the commission, if any, when comparing rates. The commission can be a flat fee that equals a few dollars or a percentage (usually 2 percent to 6 percent) of the amount you exchange. (Banks display commission costs in the fine print at the bottom of the daily rate chart.) Occasionally, a slightly less attractive exchange rate coupled with a low or flat-fee commission can cost you less in the long run (depending on how much you exchange) than a great-looking rate with a whopping commission.

 You can also exchange money at commercial exchange booths (multilingually labeled as *change/cambio/wechsel*). The rates here are generally lousy and the commissions high, but they do keep longer hours than banks. Only use commercial exchange booths as a last resort if banks are closed and you can't access an ATM. Hotels and shops also offer terrible rates.

Buying Currency before You Leave

 Though the age of ATMs makes this less necessary, some people still purchase about $50 worth of local currency for each country that they'll visit even before they leave home. Doing so gets you from the airport or train station to the better exchange rates of a downtown bank. Likewise, this money can tide you over until you get your hands on some more, if you arrive in town late at night or on a bank holiday.

AAA offices in the United States sell ready-to-go packs of several currencies at relatively reasonable rates, although you can get better ones at any bank (call ahead — usually only banks' main downtown branches carry foreign cash). Shop around for the best rate, and ask the teller to give you small bills (close to $10 denominations) because you need the cash primarily to buy inexpensive items like maps, bus tickets, and maybe food.

One big merger: The euro

In 2002, most Western European nations finally did away with their francs, marks, pesetas, and lire and finalized the adoption of a single European currency called the *euro* (€). As of this writing, 1€ equals about $1.60, and conversions in this guide were calculated at this exchange rate.

Countries in this guide that use the euro include Austria, France, Germany, Greece, Ireland, Italy, the Netherlands, and Spain. The United Kingdom (which includes Scotland) and Switzerland have not adopted the euro, and the Czech Republic, which joined the European Union (EU) in May 2004, has yet to jump the appropriate economic hurdles to be able to join the more exclusive club of the single-currency zone.

Paying and Redeeming the VAT

Most purchases that you make in Europe have a built-in **value-added tax (VAT)** of approximately 17 percent to 33 percent, depending on the country. Theoretically, most European Union (EU) countries are supposed to adopt the same VAT tax across the board (especially the euro countries because, technically, they share a single economic system), but that's a convention still being worked out.

The VAT tax is the European version of a state sales tax, only it's already embedded in the price instead of tacked on at the register. The price tag on merchandise is the price you pay.

If non-European Union citizens spend more than a certain amount at any one store, they're entitled to some or all of the VAT via refund. This amount ranges from as low as £50 ($100) in England to 182€ ($291) in France; the minimum purchase amount varies from store to store. You can also avoid the VAT if you have your purchases shipped directly from the store, but the high cost of shipping generally offsets any savings on the taxes.

To receive a VAT refund, request a **VAT-refund invoice** from the cashier when you make your purchases, and take this invoice to the Customs office at the airport of the last EU country that you visit. Have all your VAT-refund invoices stamped before you leave Europe. After you've returned home, and within 90 days of your purchase, mail all your stamped invoices back to the stores, and they'll send you a refund check. This process usually takes from few weeks to a few months.

 Many shops now participate in the **Tax Free for Tourists** network (look for a sticker in the store window). Shops in this network issue a check along with your invoice. After Customs stamps the invoice, you can redeem it for cash directly at the Tax Free booth in the airport (usually near Customs or the duty-free shop), or you can mail it back to the store in the envelope provided within 60 days for your refund.

Avoiding Theft

Random, violent crime rates are still much lower in Europe than in the United States. On the whole, Europe's big cities are safer than U.S. cities. The two biggest things you need to worry about are pickpockets and the crazy traffic.

Stay safe by sticking to populated streets after dark, and know the locations of bad neighborhoods. Each destination chapter in this book includes discussions of neighborhoods, as well as sections on safety (under "Fast Facts"), which list the less savory parts of town.

If your wallet is missing and you didn't leave it in a restaurant or hotel, chances are that it's gone for good. If you heed the advice in Chapter 9 and keep all your important stuff in a money belt, all you've lost is a day's spending money (and a wallet).

Make two copies each of your itinerary, your plane tickets, and your vital information, including the information page of your passport, your driver's license, and your student or teacher's identity card. Also, include your traveler's check numbers, your credit card numbers (write the numbers backward to "code" them), and the phone numbers listed later in this chapter for the issuers of your bank cards, credit cards, and traveler's checks. (If you lose any of these items on the road, call those numbers collect to report your loss immediately.) Leave one copy of each of these items with a friend at home and carry the second copy with you in a safe place (separate from the originals) while you travel.

Hazard #1: The pickpocket

Pickpockets target tourists, especially Americans. Pickpockets know that American tourists often carry lots of money and expensive cameras. Make sure you're especially careful in crowded areas (buses, subways, train stations, and street markets) as well as most touristy areas (the Eiffel Tower, the Colosseum, and so on).

Don't tempt thieves. Leave your jewelry at home and don't flaunt your wallet or valuables. Follow these tips to theft-proof yourself:

- ✔ **Keep all valuables (plane tickets, rail passes, traveler's checks, passport, credit cards, driver's license, and so on) in a money belt and wear it at all times.** Keep only a day's spending money in your wallet (see Chapter 9 for more about this).

- ✔ **Carry your wallet in a secure place, such as a back pocket that buttons or in the front pocket of your jeans.** When riding buses, casually keep one hand in your pocket with your wallet.

- ✔ **Don't hang your purse strap off one shoulder where a thief can easily grab it.** Instead, hang your purse across your chest. If your purse has a flap, keep the flap and latch side against your body, not facing out where nimble fingers have easy access. When on the sidewalk, walk close to the wall instead of the curb, and keep your purse toward the wall. Also, beware of thieves who zip up on their scooters and snatch away purses.

✔ **Don't hang your purse or travel bag on the back of your chair in an outdoor cafe.** You may be so engrossed in people-watching that you don't see a fast-moving thief who's ready to snatch your bag and disappear into a crowd.

✔ **Don't leave your camera around your neck when you aren't using it.** Instead, stow your camera in a plain bag. (A camera bag announces, "Steal my camera" to thieves.)

✔ **Travel in a trench coat (good for warmth, rain, a makeshift blanket, and fitting into European crowds).** You can fit all your valuables inside your coat or pants pockets, and with the trench coat wrapped around you, you can feel pickpocket-proof.

Hazard #2: The scam artist

Each con artist uses his own specific tactics to rip you off. Here are some of the most common swindles:

✔ **In countries that count pocket change in increments of hundreds (not so much of a concern since the introduction of the euro), watch out for dishonest types who confuse new arrivals with all those zeros.** For example, some people will give you change for 1,000,000 Turkish lire when you paid with a 10,000,000 bill, unless you catch them. Until you're used to the money system, examine each bill carefully before you hand it over and make sure you show the receiver that you know what you're doing.

✔ **Waiters sometimes add unordered items to your tab, double the tax (allocating 15 percent for the state and 15 percent for the waiter), or simply shortchange you.**

✔ **A stranger may offer to help you exchange money, befriend you, and walk off with your wallet after hugging you goodbye.** Decline any stranger's offer for assistance and continue on your way.

✔ **Hotels may sneak in minibar, phone, or other charges.** So, if your bill is any higher than the rate (plus tax) you agreed upon multiplied by the number of nights you stayed, ask a manager to explain your bill.

✔ **Hotels charge obscenely high telephone rates, with markups anywhere from 150 to 400 percent — especially on long-distance calls, and it's perfectly legal.** In fact, hotels often charge you for the free local call to your calling-card company! Do your wallet a favor and pretend that the hotel phone doesn't exist. Use pay phones or the post office instead.

✔ **If your escort on a guided bus tour recommends a shop for buying local crafts or souvenirs, she may be getting a kickback from that store.** In return, the store charges heavily inflated prices for items. (In defense of tour guides, however, this kickback system is one of the only ways they can make a living, because they're notoriously underpaid — in part because companies unofficially expect them to take advantage of this option as an unlisted perk.)

Keeping valuables safe on trains

Here are some tips for keeping your stuff safe and secure on an overnight train:

✔ **Don't flaunt your valuables.**

✔ **Lock your door and make sure that everyone in the couchette understands the importance of keeping your door locked.** Conductors usually emphasize this point, but doing it yourself doesn't hurt either.

✔ **Reserve the top bunk.** Although the top bunk is hotter, it puts your goods above the easy reach of most thieves, and you can sleep with your head next to your bags.

✔ **Stow your bags in the luggage niche above the door.** If you strap or lock your bags to this railing, a thief can't easily tug them down and run off with them.

✔ **Turn your valuables into a pillow.** You may not experience the most comfortable sleep, but if you wrap your valuables in your clothes and put it in a sack, the discomfort is worth the reward.

✔ **Take special precautions when sleeping in unreserved sitting couchettes.**

Coping with a stolen wallet

If you lose your wallet, don't panic. If you follow the tips earlier in this section, you won't have more than a day's spending money in your wallet.

If you lose your **traveler's checks** and you remembered the all-important rule of writing down the check numbers and keeping them in a separate and safe place, you can easily replace them in any big European city. Just call the issuer of your checks for details (see "Cashing traveler's checks," earlier in this chapter, for telephone numbers).

If you lose **credit cards** or **ATM cards,** you'll need to cancel them immediately. Before you leave on your trip, create a list of the international customer-service numbers given on the back of each card. Keep the list in a safe spot (not with your cards). Note that these are special U.S. numbers set up explicitly for emergencies abroad. Go to any pay phone in Europe and dial an international operator to connect your collect call.

Your credit card company or insurer may require a police-report number or record of the loss. Check with your credit card company before you leave home to get the phone number to call (usually a collect call) to report a lost or stolen card.

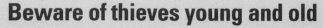

Beware of thieves young and old

As you make your way around Europe, be aware that you may encounter masterful thieves and pickpockets (although you won't realize it until you reach for your wallet and find it missing). Often, these thieves are Gypsies — easy to spot, in their colorful but ragged clothes. Although you may find them anywhere — especially around major tourist attractions — they're most prevalent in southern Europe.

The adults mainly beg for money and can be very pushy doing so. The ones you really need to watch out for, however, are the children. They'll swarm you while babbling and sometimes holding up bits of cardboard with messages scrawled on them to distract you, during which time they rifle your pockets faster than you can say "Stop!" If you're standing near a wall or in a metro tunnel, they'll even be so bold as to pin you against the wall with the cardboard message so as to fleece you more easily.

Although not physically dangerous, they're very adept at taking your stuff, and they're hard to catch. Keeping on the lookout is your best defense. If a group of scruffy-looking children approaches, forcefully yell, "No!", glare, and keep walking; if they persist, yell "Politz!" (which sounds close enough to "police" in any language). If they get near enough to touch you, push them away — don't hold back just because they're children.

Your credit card or ATM card issuer may be able to wire you a cash advance or issue an emergency replacement card in a day or two. In situations such as these, carrying traveler's checks, which are easily replaced, can save your entire vacation.

 An alternative to getting quick cash in an emergency is to have a friend wire you money. Reliable, international services include **Western Union** (☎ **800-CALL-CASH** [800-225-5227]; www.westernunion.com) and American Express's **MoneyGram** (☎ **800-666-3947**; www.moneygram.com), which allow someone back home to wire you money in an emergency in less than ten minutes.

When traveling abroad, you're a non-entity without your **passport.** If you lose your passport, go immediately to the nearest U.S. consulate. Make sure that you bring a photocopy of your passport's information pages (the two pages facing each other with your picture and vital information), passport-size photos (bring some with you), and any other form of identification that wasn't lost.

 Identity theft and fraud are potential complications of losing your wallet, especially if you've lost your driver's license along with your credit cards. Notify the major credit-reporting bureaus *immediately;* placing a fraud alert on your records may protect you against liability for criminal activity. The three major U.S. credit-reporting agencies are **Equifax**

(☎ **888-766-0008;** www.equifax.com), **Experian** (☎ **888-397-3742;** www.experian.com), and **TransUnion** (☎ **800-680-7289;** www.trans union.com). Finally, if you've lost all forms of photo ID, call your airline and explain the situation; they may allow you to board the plane if you have a copy of your passport or birth certificate and a copy of the police report you've filed.

Chapter 5

Getting to Europe

• •

In This Chapter

▶ Consulting a travel agent
▶ Considering package tours
▶ Choosing an escorted tour
▶ Arranging your own flights

• •

*J*ust thinking about your European vacation fills you with excitement. At last all those famous sights, scenes, and experiences you've been dreaming about are going to become reality. All that's left is to figure out how to get there.

Airline options are plentiful. To check out the offerings, you can tap a travel agent for assistance, call flight reservation desks on your own, or cruise the Internet for the best deals. Also, you can choose to set out on your European explorations with or without a professional guide.

Before you get down to the business of booking a flight, take time to wing your way through this chapter.

Seeking a Travel Agent's Advice

Word of mouth is the best way to find a qualified, reliable travel agent. Finding a cheap deal on airfare, accommodations, and a rental car is the least a good travel agent can do. A more helpful agent goes the extra mile to give you vacation value by considering comfort and expense.

Great agents can give advice on several travel issues, including how much time to spend in a particular destination and how to choose an economical and practical flight plan. They can also make reservations for competitively priced rental cars and find deals at better hotels.

To help your travel agent help you, do a little research before you sit down to talk; picking up this book is a great start. Read the destination chapters so that you'll have a general idea of where you want to stay and what you want to do. If you have access to the Internet, check prices on the Web to get a ballpark feel for prices (see "Booking your flight online," later in this chapter, for airline-shopping ideas).

When you have enough information in hand, pack up your notes and make an appointment to see a travel agent with experience in Europe. Agents rely on a variety of resources, so your arrangements are likely to cost less than if you seal the deal yourself. Plus, your agent can suggest alternatives if your first choice of hotels is unavailable, and issue airline tickets and hotel vouchers.

 The travel industry is built on commissions. When you book a vacation, your agent earns a paycheck from the airline, hotel, or tour company with which you're doing business. Some airlines and resorts started eliminating agents' commissions several years ago. Customers now have to make specific mention of certain hotels or airlines if they're interested in booking; otherwise, the agent may not bring them up as options. Bear in mind, too, that some travel agents now charge a fee for their services.

Exploring Package-Tour Possibilities

For lots of destinations, package tours can be a smart way to go. In many cases, a package tour that includes airfare, hotel, and transportation to and from the airport costs less than the hotel alone on a tour you book yourself. That's because packages are sold in bulk to tour operators, who resell them to the public.

Comparing packages

When dealing with packagers, keep in mind that differences exist among the available options — differences that may significantly affect your travel experience. Set side by side, one combo may top another in any of the following ways:

✔ Better class of hotels

✔ Same hotels for lower prices

✔ Accommodations and travel days (days of departure and return) may be limited or flexible

✔ Escorted and independent packages available — not one or the other only

✔ Option to add on just a few excursions or escorted day trips (also at discounted prices) without booking an entirely escorted tour

 Some packagers specialize in overpriced, international chain hotels. Spending time shopping around can yield rewards; don't hesitate to compare deals and details before you fork over your funds.

Hunting down the deals

You can find a tour package on your own. In fact, the information is right under your nose: Start by looking for packagers' advertisements in the travel section of your local Sunday paper. Also check national travel magazines such as *Arthur Frommer's Budget Travel, Travel + Leisure, National Geographic Traveler,* and *Condé Nast Traveler.*

Reputable packagers include these standouts:

- ✔ **American Express Vacations** (☎ 800-346-3607; www.american express.com/travel)
- ✔ **Euro Vacations** (☎ 877-471-3876; www.eurovacations.com)
- ✔ **Go-Today.com** (☎ 425-487-9632; www.go-today.com)
- ✔ **Liberty Travel** (☎ 888-271-1584; www.libertytravel.com)
- ✔ **Magical Holidays** (www.magicalholidays.com)

Airlines often package flights together with accommodations. When you check out the airline choices, look for one that offers both frequent service to your airport and frequent-flier miles.

The following airlines offer tour packages:

- ✔ **American Airlines Vacations** (☎ 800-321-2121; www.aavacations.com)
- ✔ **Continental Airlines Vacations** (☎ 888-898-9255; www.cool vacations.com)
- ✔ **Delta Vacations** (☎ 800-872-7786; www.deltavacations.com)
- ✔ **Northwest Airlines World Vacations** (☎ 800-800-1504; www.nwa worldvacations.com)
- ✔ **United Vacations** (☎ 888-854-3899; www.unitedvacations.com)
- ✔ **US Airways Vacations** (☎ 800-455-0123; www.usairways vacations.com)

Most European airlines offer competitive packages as well (see the Quick Concierge for their Web sites and toll-free numbers).

Several big **online travel agencies** — Expedia, Travelocity, Orbitz, Site59, and Lastminute.com — also do a brisk business in packages. If you're unsure about the pedigree of a smaller packager, check with the Better Business Bureau in the city where the company is based, or go online to www.bbb.org. If a packager won't tell you where it's based, don't book with it.

The biggest hotel chains and resorts sometimes offer packages, too. If you already know where you want to stay, call the hotel or resort and ask about land/air packages.

Joining an Escorted Tour

Many people love escorted tours. The tour company takes care of all the details and tells you what to expect at each leg of your journey. You know your costs up front, and you don't get many surprises. Escorted tours can take you to see the maximum number of sights in the minimum amount of time with the least amount of hassle.

 If you decide to go with an escorted tour, consider purchasing travel insurance, especially if the tour operator asks you to pay up front. But don't buy insurance from the tour operator! If the tour operator doesn't fulfill its obligation to provide you with the vacation you paid for, there's no reason to think that it will fulfill its insurance obligations, either. Get travel insurance through an independent agency. (We tell you more about the ins and outs of travel insurance in Chapter 9.)

When choosing an escorted tour, along with finding out whether you have to put down a deposit and when final payment is due, ask a few simple questions before you buy:

- ✔ **What is the cancellation policy?** Can the tour operator cancel the trip if it doesn't get enough people? How late can you cancel if you're unable to go? Do you get a refund if you cancel? What if the tour operator cancels?

- ✔ **How jam-packed is the schedule?** Does the tour schedule try to fit 25 hours into a 24-hour day, or does it give you ample time to relax by the pool or shop? If getting up at 7 a.m. every day and not returning to your hotel until 6 or 7 p.m. sounds like a grind, certain escorted tours may not be for you.

- ✔ **Can you opt out of certain activities?** Does the tour allow picking and choosing activities; or does the bus leave once a day, and you're out of luck if you're not onboard?

- ✔ **How large is the group?** The smaller the group, the less time you spend waiting for people to get on and off the bus. Tour operators may be evasive about this, because they may not know the exact size of the group until everybody has made reservations, but they should be able to give you a rough estimate.

- ✔ **Is there a minimum group size?** Some tours have a minimum group size and may cancel the tour if they don't book enough people. If a quota exists, find out what it is and how close they are to reaching it. Again, tour operators may be evasive in their answers, but the information may help you select a tour that's sure to happen.

- ✔ **What exactly is included?** Don't assume anything. You may have to pay to get yourself to and from the airport. A box lunch may be included in an excursion, but drinks may be extra. Beer may be included but not wine. Are all your meals planned in advance? Can you choose your entree at dinner, or does everybody get the same chicken cutlet?

Making Your Own Arrangements

So you want to plan the trip on your own? This section tells you all you need to know to research and book the perfect flight.

Booking your flight

With the introduction of *codesharing* — one carrier selling flights as its own on another carrier — customers now enjoy more travel options and an easier time making flight arrangements. Chances are, you can call your favorite airline and come up with a plan that flies you from just about anywhere in North America to just about anywhere in Europe.

Listed in the Quick Concierge are the phone numbers and Web sites for all the major North American and European airlines that offer direct flights from North America to Europe. In these days of airline alliances, widespread codesharing, and carrier consolidation, it hardly seems to matter which airline you call to make your booking. Chances are, their interlocking partnerships will ensure you can flit from your hometown to your European destination on any combination of carriers, foreign or domestic, and any one of them can arrange this for you.

Getting to Europe from the U.S., you may have to travel first to a hub, such as New York, Chicago, Minneapolis/St. Paul, Atlanta, Los Angeles, or San Francisco, in order to pick up a direct flight to your destination. To reach smaller European cities, you'll probably be routed through a major European hub such as London, Paris, or Frankfurt.

Shopping for the best airfare

Competition among the major U.S. and European airlines is unlike that of any other industry. Every airline offers virtually the same product (basically, a coach seat is a coach seat is a . . .), yet prices can vary by hundreds of dollars.

Business travelers who need the flexibility to buy their tickets at the last - minute and change their itineraries at a moment's notice — and who want to get home before the weekend — pay the premium rate, known as the *full fare*. But if you can book your ticket far in advance, stay over Saturday night, and are willing to travel midweek (Tues, Wed, or Thurs), you can qualify for the least expensive price — usually a fraction of the full fare. On most flights, even the shortest hops within the United States, the full fare is close to $1,000 or more, but a 7- or 14-day advance-purchase ticket may cost less than half that amount. Obviously, planning ahead pays.

The airlines also periodically hold sales in which they lower the prices on their most popular routes. These fares have advance-purchase requirements and date-of-travel restrictions, but you can't beat the prices. As you plan your vacation, keep your eyes open for these sales, which tend to take place in seasons of low travel volume — for Europe that's generally September 15 through June 14. You almost never see a sale around the peak summer-vacation months of July and August, or around Thanksgiving or Christmas, when many people fly regardless of the fare they have to pay — though this is less true if you can get a direct flight to Europe from your home airport (most folks travel domestically for the holidays). Often, flying into Europe's major cities (usually London and Paris) brings the price of a ticket down. Also, look into purchasing an *open-jaw* plane ticket, one that allows you to fly into one European city and depart from another — say, flying into London but out of Madrid on your way home. Open-jaw tickets can sometimes be a more expensive option, but it's a wonderful way to keep your itinerary flexible, and you don't have to backtrack to the first city on your trip.

Consolidators, also known as bucket shops, are great sources for international tickets. Start by looking in Sunday newspaper travel sections; U.S. travelers should focus on the *New York Times, Los Angeles Times,* and *Miami Herald.* For less-developed destinations, small travel agencies catering to immigrant communities in large cities often have the best deals.

Bucket-shop tickets are usually nonrefundable or rigged with stiff cancellation penalties, often as high as 50 percent to 75 percent of the ticket price, and some put you on charter airlines with questionable safety records.

Some reliable consolidators include:

- ✔ **Air Tickets Direct** (☎ 800-778-3447; www.airticketsdirect. com)

- ✔ **AutoEurope** (☎ 888-223-5555; www.autoeurope.com)

- ✔ **Cheap Tickets** (☎ 800-755-4333; www.cheaptickets.com)

- ✔ **Flights.com** (www.flights.com)

- ✔ **Lowestfare.com** (☎ 866-210-3289; www.lowestfare.com)

- ✔ **STA Travel** (☎ 800-781-4040; www.statravel.com)

Booking your flight online

The "big three" online travel agencies, **Expedia** (www.expedia.com), **Travelocity** (www.travelocity.com), and **Orbitz** (www.orbitz.com) sell most of the air tickets bought on the Internet. Canadian travelers should try www.expedia.ca and www.travelocity.ca. U.K. residents can go to www.expedia.co.uk, www.opodo.co.uk, or **Travelsupermarket** (☎ 0845-345-5708; www.travelsupermarket.com), a flight search engine that offers flight comparisons for the budget airlines whose seats often end up in bucket-shop sales. Meta search sites (which find and then direct you to airline and hotel Web sites for booking) include **Sidestep.com** and **Kayak.com** — the latter includes fares for budget carriers, such as JetBlue and Spirit, and the major airlines. **Site59.com** is a great source for last-minute flights and getaways. In addition, most **airlines** offer online-only fares that even their phone agents know nothing about.

Great **last-minute deals** are available through free weekly e-mail services provided directly by the airlines. Most of these deals are announced on Tuesday or Wednesday and must be purchased online. Most are only valid for travel that weekend, but some can be booked weeks or months in advance. Sign up for weekly e-mail alerts at airline Web sites or check megasites, such as **Smarter Living** (www.smarterliving.com), that compile comprehensive lists of last-minute specials. For last-minute trips in the U.S. and Europe, www.lastminute.com sometimes has better deals than the major-label sites.

Watch local newspapers for **promotional specials** or **fare wars,** when airlines lower prices on their most popular routes. Also, keep an eye on price fluctuations and deals at Web sites such as **Airfarewatchdog.com** and **Farecast.com.**

Frequent-flier membership doesn't cost a cent, but membership may entitle you to better seats, faster response to phone inquiries, prompter service if your luggage is stolen or your flight is canceled or delayed, or if you want to change your seat (especially after you've racked up some miles). And you don't have to fly to earn points; **frequent-flier credit cards** can earn you thousands of miles for doing your everyday shopping. With more than 70 mileage awards programs on the market, consumers have never had more options. Investigate the program details of your favorite airlines before you sink points into any one of them. Consider which airlines have hubs in the airport nearest you, and, of those carriers, which have the most advantageous alliances given your most common routes. To play the frequent-flier game to your best advantage, consult the community bulletin boards on **FlyerTalk** (www.flyertalk.com) or go to Randy Petersen's **Inside Flyer** (www.insideflyer.com). Petersen and friends review all the programs in detail and post regular updates on changes in policies and trends.

Chapter 6

Getting Around Europe

*T*raveling around Europe is part of the fun of a European vacation. Trains, planes, boats, buses, and rental cars make traveling from country to country fast and easy. But this is where a little basic knowledge can also help you to save hundreds of dollars. Choosing the right rail pass and knowing how to get the best travel deals from no-frills airlines and rental-car agencies can slash your travel budget in half. This chapter provides the ins and outs of traveling within Europe.

Flying Around Europe

Air travel within Europe makes sense only if you need to cover great distances in a limited amount of time. The good news is that with the advent of **no-frills airlines,** air travel in Europe is now an option even to those on the strictest of budgets.

Though train travel is always more fun, flying is something to consider if your train ride would take up most of a day, and if the plane ticket is actually cheaper than the train. Always remember, however, that train stations in European cities are usually right in the city center, close or easily accessible to hotels and attractions. If you arrive by plane, you have to consider the hassle of getting into the city from the airport, sometimes making the savings in time and money not really worth it.

You have three main choices for air travel within Europe:

  ✔ **Regular flights on major European carriers:** Although this is your best bet, it's also the most expensive option. You can call the airlines' toll-free numbers (see this book's Quick Concierge) before you leave for Europe to arrange these flights, or you can contact a travel agent or the airline's office in any European city.

✔ **Consolidator tickets:** Budget travel agencies across Europe, especially in London and Athens, sell cheap tickets from consolidators. Although these tickets aren't totally unreliable, they constitute the least-safe way to fly. Shady consolidators can go out of business overnight (always pay for these tickets with a credit card so that you can cancel payment if the consolidator goes bust), they have a higher rate of cancellation, and many of the airlines (often Middle Eastern and Asian carriers) follow lower safety standards than major North American and European carriers.

✔ **Small, no-frills airlines:** Over the past few years, Europe has developed a fabulous system of **no-frills airlines.** Modeled on American upstarts such as Southwest and JetBlue, dozens of these small carriers sell one-way tickets for destinations throughout Europe for well under $100. By keeping their overhead down — electronic ticketing (often via Web sites exclusively, no phone calls allowed), no meal service, and flights to and from major cities' secondary airports or smaller cities — these airlines are able to offer amazingly low fares.

The two big players in the no-frills business are **easyJet** (www.easy jet.com), which has hubs in London, Liverpool, Bristol, Manchester, Barcelona, Amsterdam, and Paris; and **Ryanair** (www.ryanair.com), which flies out of London, Glasgow, Dublin, Shannon, Bremen, Stockholm, Brussels, Milan, St. Tropez, and several other locations. The current short list of the most dependable among the other choices includes: **Virgin Express** in Brussels (www.virgin express.com); **Germanwings** (www.germanwings.com) and **Tuifly** (www.tuifly.com) in Germany; **Volare** (www.volareweb.com) in Italy; **Sterling** (www.sterlingticket.com) in Scandinavia; and **Air Europa** (www.air-europa.com) and **Spanair** (www.spanair.com) in Spain.

There are many more. Independent Web sites such as www.low costairlines.org keep track of the industry.

Taking the Train

Fast, efficient, convenient, and comfortable, trains rule European travel. As a rule, European trains run on time, are clean, and utilize a vast rail network that includes almost every major and minor city — all with the added bonus of watching all that scenery roll by.

For average travel times by rail between the destinations in this book, see this book's Quick Concierge.

Figuring out the basics of train travel

In North America, most folks hop in the car or book a plane ticket for long-distance travel, but in Europe, people still take the train. Though no-frills airlines (discussed earlier in this chapter) are now the best way to cover great distances between far-flung countries, the train is still king when it comes to exploring Europe. But before you ride the rails, you should know a few things.

Understanding train classifications

Europe offers several train classifications that range from local runs that stop at every tiny station to high-speed bullet trains (France's TGV; Italy's ETR; Pendolino, Spain's AVE), new international high-speed runs (Thalys from Paris to Brussels; Artesia from Paris to Turin and Milan; and from Barcelona to Madrid), and the **Eurostar** Channel Tunnel train between London, Paris, and Brussels. The popular **EC** (Eurocity), **IC** (Intercity — same as Eurocity, but doesn't cross an international border), and **EN** (Euronight) are other fast trains.

The **Eurostar** train (☎ **08705-186-186** in London, **0044-1235-617-575** in France and Belgium, **800-EUROSTAR** [800-387-6782] in the U.S.; www.euro star.com) runs through the Channel Tunnel and connects London's St. Pancras International Station with the Gare du Nord in Paris and Central Station in Brussels. Both trips take about three hours (plus or minus the one-hour time-zone difference). Because the old train-ferry-train route between Dover and Calais takes so much longer, Eurostar is an option worth considering.

Many high-speed trains throughout Europe require that you pay a supplement of around $15 to $25 in addition to your regular ticket price. If you buy point-to-point tickets, this supplement is included in the full price. If you travel with a rail pass, you won't have to pay this supplement.

Finding schedule and fare information

Contact **Rail Europe** (☎ **877-257-2887** in the U.S., 800-361-7245 in Canada; www.raileurope.com) to receive more information about train travel in Europe and to get online schedule information. Looking at Rail Europe's Web site is an easy way to get an idea of train schedules. You can also visit the Web sites of the individual national rail systems in Europe, which always have the latest schedules and prices (occasionally even in English).

Most train schedules and signs use native names for cities, not the English equivalent. For example, Athens is Athinai, Cologne is Köln, Copenhagen is København, Florence is Firenze, Lisbon is Lisboa, Munich is München, Naples is Napoli, Pamplona is often Iruñea, Prague is Praha, Venice is Venezia, Vienna is Wien, and so on.

Making reservations

Some of the speediest high-speed trains require reservations, including Eurostar (the Channel Tunnel train), TGV in France, Pendolino in Italy, and long-distance trains in Spain. And it's also a good idea to reserve a seat for any train travel during the crowded summer months and during holiday periods. If you don't, even if you have a rail pass, you may find yourself standing.

Europe's Primary Train Routes

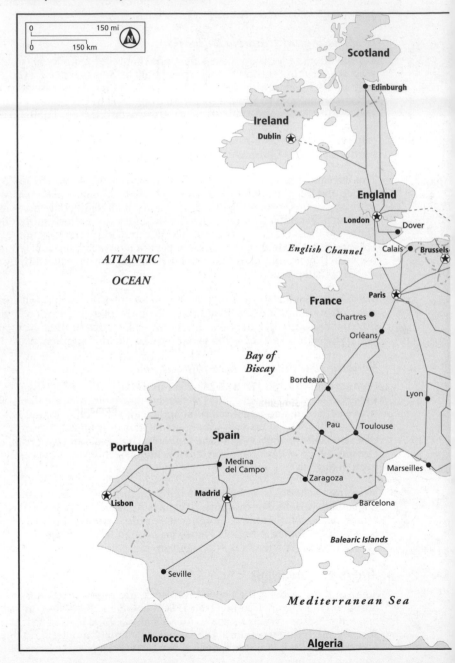

Layout of the train

Some European trains still have the old-fashioned seating configuration wherein each car has ten small compartments, with seats for six to eight people in second (or standard) class, and four to six people (in plushier chairs) in first class, with a corridor running alongside. Most European trains, however, have switched to modern "saloon" cars with seats running down both sides of an open aisle. *Note:* Many adult rail passes (see "Saving time and money with rail passes," later in this section) are for travel in first-class compartments — a lovely luxury.

You must reserve ahead of time, for a fee, any train marked with an *R* on the schedule — usually around $20. You can almost always reserve a seat within a few hours of the train's departure, but booking a few days in advance at the station assures that you have a seat. You must also reserve any **sleeping couchettes** or **sleeping berths** (see the next section, "Taking overnight trains," for more information).

 Unless you're on an extremely tight schedule, it's probably better not to buy or reserve individual train tickets before leaving home. Doing so locks you into a schedule that you may want to change once you're in Europe. The exceptions are the Eurostar and the Artesia train between Paris and major Italian cities; it's smart to reserve both before arriving in Europe. Remember, though, that if you're going to buy a money-saving rail pass, you need to do so before leaving home; see "Saving time and money with rail passes," later in this chapter.)

Traveling without a reserved seat on a regular train can become a problem in the summer and during holiday periods, when European trains are full. Without a reservation, you aren't guaranteed a seat, no matter what kind of rail pass you have. Many overnight trains now require you to make at least a seat reservation for around 5€ ($8), if not a couchette or sleeper (see earlier in this section).

 To find out if a seat is reserved, look on the partition outside individual train compartments; there you'll see a little plastic window with RESERVED on it for those seats that have been reserved. In newer trains, the RESERVED sign may be a computerized display above the seat. To save yourself the trouble of getting booted out later in your trip, check to make sure that you're occupying an unreserved seat before you claim it. If you have reserved a seat, no problem: You're assigned a specific seat in a specific train car.

Taking overnight trains

Go to bed in Paris, wake up in Rome. What could be more convenient? On an overnight train, not only do you get a cheap (if uncomfortable) bed for the night, but you also maximize your time and money.

On an overnight train, you have four sleeping choices:

✔ **Regular seats:** Use this as a last resort, because you won't get much sleep sitting up.

✔ **Fold-out seats:** In regular sitting compartments, you can often pull facing seat bottoms out toward each other, collapsing the seat backs. It's not a very comfortable way to nap, and the doors in these basic compartments don't lock.

✔ **Flip-down couchettes:** Sleeping couchettes (six per compartment in standard class; four or two per compartment in first class) are narrow, flip-down, shelflike bunks. In a couchette compartment, you can lock the door (make sure it's locked before you go to bed) and a conductor watches over the rail car and your passport, which he holds overnight for border crossings. For about 30€ ($48) per couchette, this option is one of the cheapest sleeping deals that you can find in Europe. Unless you reserve an entire compartment, prepare to share your room with strangers.

✔ **A sleeping-car berth:** Usually, sleeping-car berths are only a first-class option. For 40€ to 95€ ($64–$152), depending on distance traveled and how many bunks there are, you get a tiny room with two to four bunks and a private sink. Berths are a smidgen comfier than couchettes, but strangers may populate the other bunk if you're traveling alone.

Don't drink the water on the trains, not even to rinse your mouth. Use this water for hand-washing only. Trains, especially overnight trains, dehydrate you quickly, so make sure that you bring bottled water to sip and to rinse your mouth and toothbrush the next morning.

Saving time and money with rail passes

The *rail pass* — a single multi-use ticket that allows you unlimited travel for a certain number of days of travel within a set period of time — was the greatest value in European travel until no-frills airlines came along, and it remains the easiest and most economical way to get around Europe by train. If your trip is going to cover countless kilometers on the rails, a pass ends up costing you considerably less than buying individual train tickets once you arrive. A rail pass also gives you the freedom to hop on a train whenever you feel like it, making a day trip out of town cheap and easy. An extra bonus of the rail pass is that you don't have to wait in ticket lines, unless you want to reserve a seat (always a good idea).

The granddaddy of passes is the **Eurail** pass, now called the **Eurail Global Pass,** which covers 20 countries (most of Western Europe, except the U.K.). If you're taking a whirlwind, Europe-wide tour, this is your single best investment. The more modest but flexible **Selectpass** covers three to five contiguous countries for more focused trips. Just remember: Eurail passes must be purchased before you arrive in Europe.

These rail passes also include discounts on private rail lines (such as those in the Alps) and the Eurostar between London and Paris or Brussels, and give you discounts or free travel for ferry crossings (Italy to Greece) and some boat rides on rivers (Rhine, Mosel) and lakes (especially Swiss lakes).

Using a rail pass

From the date that you buy your rail pass, you have six months to begin using it. You have to validate your pass at a European train station the day you want to start using the pass. Validating your rail pass is the only time that you have to wait in a ticket line, unless you're reserving seats or couchettes or buying supplements. With consecutive-day, unlimited-use Eurail passes, you can just hop on trains at whim.

Rail passes are available in either **consecutive-day** or **flexipass** versions (in which you have two months to use, say, 10 or 15 days of train travel). Consecutive-day passes are best for those taking the train very frequently (every day or every couple of days) and covering a lot of ground. Flexipasses are for folks who want to range far and wide but take their time doing so.

The flexipass gives you a certain number of days (5–15) to travel within a two-month period from initial validation. Printed on your flexipass are a number of little boxes that correspond with the number of travel days you bought. Write the date in the next free box (in ink) every new day that you board a train. The conductor comes around, checking your ticket to make sure that you've put down the right date.

 What date do I write down for overnight trains, you ask? A Eurail day begins at 7 p.m. and runs 29 hours until the following midnight. In other words, when you board an overnight train after 7 p.m., write the next day's date in the box. Doing so clears you for that night and any traveling that you do the next day.

Eurail covers Austria, Belgium, Croatia, Czech Republic, Denmark, Finland, France, Germany, Greece, Hungary, Ireland, Italy, Luxembourg, the Netherlands, Norway, Portugal, Romania, Spain, Sweden, and Switzerland. *Note:* The United Kingdom (England, Scotland, Wales, and Northern Ireland) isn't included because U.K. countries use the BritRail pass (also available from Rail Europe).

Knowing your options

There are **saverpasses** for two to five people traveling together, and **rail/drive** passes that mix train days with car-rental days. If you're 25 or under, you can opt to buy a regular first-class pass or a less-expensive second-class **youth pass;** if you're 26 or over, only first-class passes are available. Passes for children 4 to 11 are half-price, and children 3 and under travel free. Seniors 60 and older qualify for special discounted passes.

The following prices that we list for the various rail passes are for 2008, but keep in mind that they rise each year:

✔ **Eurail Global Pass:** Consecutive-day Eurailpass, valid in every country participating in the Eurail network, $741 for 15 days; $968 for 21 days; $1,202 for one month; $1,607 for two months; or $2,094 for three months.

✔ **Eurail Global Pass Flexi:** Good for two months of travel, within which you can travel by train for 10 days (consecutive or not) for $881 or 15 days for $1,158.

✔ **Eurail Global Pass Saver:** Good for two to five people traveling together, it costs $632 per person for 15 days; $822 for 21 days; $1,020 for one month; $1,442 for two months; or $1,786 for three months.

✔ **Eurailpass Saver Flexi:** Good for two to five people traveling together, it costs $608 per person for 10 days within two months or $800 per person for 15 days within two months.

✔ **Eurail Global Pass Youth:** The second-class rail pass for travelers under age 26 costs $485 for 15 days; $628 for 21 days; $782 for one month; $1,104 for two months; or $1,364 for three months.

✔ **Eurail Global Pass Youth Flexi:** Only for travelers under age 26, allowing for 10 days of travel within two months for $574 or 15 days within two months for $754.

✔ **Eurail Selectpass:** For trips covering three to five contiguous Eurail countries connected by rail or ship. It's valid for two months, and cost varies according to the number of countries you plan to visit. A pass for **three countries** is $473 for five days, $522 for six days, $619 for eight days, and $717 for 10 days. A **four-country** pass costs $529 for five days, $578 for six days, $675 for eight days, and $771 for 10 days. A pass for **five countries** costs $583 for five days; $632 for six days; $731 for eight days; $825 for 10 days; and $1,047 for 15 days.

✔ **Eurail Selectpass Saver:** Same as the Eurail Selectpass (and slightly less expensive), but for two to five people traveling together. Per person, the **three-country** pass is $401 for five days, $445 for six days, $574 for eight days, and $607 for 10 days. A pass for **four countries** is $447 for five days, $492 for six days, $574 for eight days, and $654 for 10 days. A **five-country** pass is $494 for five days, $537 for six days, $619 for eight days, $700 for 10 days, and $890 for 15 days.

✔ **Eurail Selectpass Youth:** Good in second class, only for travelers 25 and under. Cost varies according to the number of countries you plan to visit, but all passes are valid for two months. For **three countries,** the per-person price is $307 for five days, $342 for six days, $401 for eight days, $464 for 10 days. A **four-country** pass costs, per person, $344 for five days, $375 for six days, $438 for eight days, and $489 for 10 days. A **five-country** pass is $379 for five days, $410 for six days, $473 for eight days, $534 for 10 days, and $680 for 15 days.

✔ **Eurail Select Pass Drive:** This pass offers the best of both worlds, mixing train travel and rental cars (through Hertz or Avis) for less money than it would cost to do them separately (and it's one of the only ways to get around the high daily car-rental rates in Europe when you rent for less than a week). A flexipass, it includes three, four, or five days of unlimited, first-class rail travel and two days of unlimited mileage car rental (through Avis or Hertz) within a two-month period. Prices (per person for one or two adults) vary with the class of the car and the number of adjoining (contiguous border) countries you'll be visiting (three, four, or five). For a **three-country** pass that includes three days of train travel and two days of car rental, the cost is: $321/$744 economy, $458/$778 compact, $476/$796 intermediate, $516/$836 automatic. You can add up to six extra car days ($52 each economy, $70 compact, $78 midsize, $98 small automatic). You have to reserve the first "car day" a week before leaving home but can make the other reservations as you go (subject to availability). If you have more than two adults in your group, the extra passengers get the car portion free but must buy the four-day rail pass.

There are also **national rail passes** of various kinds (flexi, consecutive, rail/drive, and so on) for each country, **dual country passes** (Eurail France–Italy or Eurail Switzerland–Austria, for example), and **regional passes** such as BritRail (covering Great Britain) and the European East Pass (good in Austria, the Czech Republic, Hungary, Poland, and Slovakia).

Purchasing your rail pass

You must buy passes for Eurail and its offshoots *before* you leave home. (You can purchase passes in some major European train stations, but you pay up to 50 percent more.) You can buy rail passes from most travel agents, but the largest supplier is **RailEurope** (☎ 877-257-2887 in the U.S., 800-361-7245 in Canada; www.raileurope.com), which also sells most national passes.

Passing on passes

Nifty as they are, rail passes aren't the wisest investment for every trip. If you're on an extended tour of Europe and plan to travel to several different countries by train, a Eurail pass is generally a good idea. However, if you're taking shorter, more focused trips, or if you plan to take only a couple of train rides over the course of your visit, a rail pass may end up costing more than buying point-to-point tickets after you arrive.

Is any pass right for you? The answer is different for every trip, so prepare to do some math. After you create an itinerary, you can estimate how much you think you'll spend on individual tickets by contacting

Rail Europe (☎ 877-257-2887 in the U.S., 800-361-7245 in Canada; www. raileurope.com) for prices. Choosing which pass is right for you can be tricky as well. For example, you have to travel at least 22 days (24 days with the youth pass) to make a two-month consecutive-day pass a better deal per trip than the 15-days-within-2-months flexipass. You have to decide if the extra days are worth it, depending on your travel plans and how much freedom you want to jump trains on a whim.

Navigating the train station

Like the trains themselves, European train stations are generally clean and user-friendly. They also offer good snack bars. Spending 20 minutes there when you first arrive in a city can help orient you and prepare you for your visit.

Most train stations are fairly safe, but because they're central clearing-houses for tourists, pickpockets flourish. Never abandon your bags, always pay attention, and don't become distracted by hotel touts offering rooms.

Here are a few suggestions for taking advantage of the train station's resources:

- **Hit the ATM.** Most stations have a bank or ATM where you can pick up some of the local currency.

- **Find the tourist-board kiosk.** Pick up whatever free info, maps, and brochures you need.

- **Visit a newsstand.** Unless the free map that you picked up from the tourist office is better (a rare thing), buy a map. Buy a phone card if you'll be in the country long enough to use it, purchase the local English-language information/events magazine, and buy a local transportation pass or individual tickets for the bus or subway.

- **Find the lockers.** If you want to dump your heaviest bag, find the lockers or the luggage storage office; the cost is generally about $10 a day. You'll definitely want to do this if you're only in town for a half-day visit, but even if you're spending the night, it's easier to go hotel hunting *without* your heaviest luggage.

- **Make some calls.** Find a phone and call around for a hotel, or use the station's hotel booking service. See Chapter 7 for more hotel advice. (You'll save a lot of precious time by reserving your hotel room before you arrive.)

In smaller towns, the tiny station bar may double as the ticket office. Most stations, however, have banks of ticket windows, and more and more of them have automated ticket machines. Try to figure out which window you need before getting in the invariably long lines. The bulk of windows are for purchasing regular tickets, and a few windows are for people who are only making seat reservations (if, for example, you have a Eurail pass but want to be assured of a seat or couchette).

Ticketing tips for public transport

Although most metros (subways) have turnstiles, other forms of public transportation (buses, trams, cable cars) in European cities sometimes operate on the honor system. As soon as you board, you're expected to punch your ticket in a little box on the bus. Make sure that you hold on to all tickets (metro, bus, or otherwise) for the duration of your ride, because spot inspectors board regularly or stop you in the metro tunnels. If they discover that you don't have a valid ticket, they fine you on the spot; fines range from $20 to $300. On the London Underground (subway), you need your ticket to get back out at the end of your journey.

Before you exit the train station, verify the options for your departure, and check train times for any day trips that you plan to make. You can then swing by the train station a day or two before you leave to buy your tickets and reserve seats or couchettes rather than wait until the last minute, when the lengthy ticket lines may thwart your plans.

The rail information desk — not to be confused with the city tourist board's desk (the two won't answer each other's questions) — usually has a long line and a harried staff. Use the do-it-yourself information sources as much as possible. Modern stations in big cities usually have computerized rail information kiosks and automatic, multilingual ticketing machines.

When the lines at the information desk are long, you can still access the information you need the old-fashioned way. Almost all stations (except some in Paris) have **schedule posters** that list the full timetables and regular track numbers for all trains that pass through the station. Arrivals are usually on a white poster and departures are on a yellow one. These posters show you the trains, their departure times, whether you need a reservation (usually marked by a prominent R), stops along the route, and the final destination for that train. Keep in mind that track assignments may change on a daily basis. In larger stations, check the electronically updated departure boards. You can then seek out a conductor on the indicated platform and say your destination in a questioning voice while pointing at the train-in-waiting for reconfirmation before boarding. After you're onboard, you may also want to triple-check with one of the other passengers.

Make sure that you get on the right *car*, and not just the right train. Individual train cars may split from the rest of the train down the line and join a different train headed to a different destination. Making sure that you're on the right car is especially important when taking a night train. (If you have a reserved spot, you don't have to worry.) Each car has its own destination placard on the side of the car, which may also list major stops en route. If you have a reserved seat, the ticket will tell you which car and seat is yours.

In many countries now, you *must* stamp your ticket in a little box — usually attached to a column at the beginning of each track — in order to validate it before boarding the train. Conductors are increasingly issuing fines for not validating the ticket, even to unknowing tourists who plead ignorance. This is not an issue, of course, if you're traveling with a rail pass.

Sailing to Your Destination by Ferry

A ferry trip may figure into your European travel plans, perhaps the traditional English Channel crossing from Dover, England, to Calais, France, or to Greece from Italy. Ferry travel is usually scenic and can be cheap, but it's also slow. For approximately double the money of a ferry, you can often take a *hydrofoil* (a sort of a ferry on steroids). A hydrofoil travels about twice as fast as the ferry, but you're stuck below deck for the entire trip and the noise level can be deafening.

Getting Around by Bus

Regional and long-haul bus service in Europe is efficient and inexpensive, but it's also the slowest mode of travel, taking two to four times as long as the train. But in some rural and more remote parts of Europe, buses are your best (perhaps only) option. If the bus makes a better connection for your itinerary (Florence to Siena, for example), take it. In some countries — especially Ireland, Greece, and parts of Spain — the bus network is better than the train service.

Driving in Europe

Although trains are great, a car is sometimes the best way to see Europe, or certain parts of it. A car gives you the freedom to explore scenic areas, head down any road you feel like, and visit vineyards, medieval hamlets, and fortified castles. With a car, you can make your own schedule and get away from the set time structures of trains. Using a car is the easiest way to explore any small region in depth.

But driving a car also has its downside. For example, you have to deal with aggressive drivers, navigate nerve-racking and confusing city traffic, try to understand road signs in different languages, and find and pay for parking whenever you stop. Likewise, you can't relax when you're behind the wheel, and the gasoline prices in Europe are usually at least double what they are in the U.S.

Obtaining an international driver's permit

If you plan to drive in Europe, you may want to bring along and carry, in addition to your regular driver's license, an *international driving permit*. This permit isn't required; it merely translates your data into several languages. The permit costs $15 from AAA (call ☎ 407-444-7000 to find the office nearest you, or visit www.aaa.com). You don't have to be an AAA member to get the pass, but if you are, ask for any free info and maps that they can send you to cover the European countries you'll be visiting.

Knowing when to rent a car

If you want to cover lots of ground, concentrate on the cities, or go solo, taking the train is better than renting a car. However, if you're exploring a single country or region, want to visit many small towns, and traveling in a party of three or more, renting a car makes economic sense. Splitting the cost of one car rental is cheaper than train tickets when you're traveling with a group, and renting a car allows you more flexibility if you're traveling with kids. Tuscany, Provence, southern Spain, and Ireland are among the most scenic and rewarding areas in Europe to explore by car.

Avoid renting and having a car in cities. It's stressful and exorbitantly expensive. Between hotel parking charges and garage and lot fees, you can expect to pay anywhere from $15 to $100 a day just to park. Save renting the car for exploring the countryside. Arrange to pick up your rental car the morning you leave the first city on your driving itinerary and to drop it off as soon as you pull into your final destination.

In areas where you want to visit the countryside, you can mix and match your modes of transportation. For example, you can take the train to Florence, and then spend two or three days driving through the vineyards and hill towns of Tuscany to Rome. Rail-and-drive passes (see "Figuring out the basics of train travel," earlier in this chapter) are an easy way to do this.

Saving time and money on rental cars

Car-rental rates vary even more than airline fares. The price depends on the size of the car, the length of time you keep it, where and when you pick it up and drop it off, where you take it, and a host of other factors. Asking a few key questions may save you hundreds of dollars.

Follow these tips to get the best deal on a rental car:

- ✔ **Arrange your rental before you leave home.** You can get the best rates on car rental if you rent ahead of time directly through a major international rental company. See the Quick Concierge for the numbers of the major rental companies, plus those that specialize in European travel.

- ✔ **Shop around.** You may think that the rental-car companies offer similar rates, but they don't. For the same three-day weekend, you may hear $50 from one company and $130 from another. The European specialists at **Auto Europe** (☎ 800-223-5555;

www.autoeurope.com) and **Europe By Car** (☎ 800-223-1516; www.europebycar.com) invariably offer the best rates. Make sure to find out what your rental rate includes — or *excludes* — such as a collision-damage waiver (CDW), taxes, mileage (you definitely want unlimited), and any other restrictions that may apply.

✔ **Shop online.** As with other aspects of planning your trip, using the Internet can make comparison-shopping for a car rental much easier. You can check rates at most of the major agencies' Web sites. Plus, all the major travel sites — **Travelocity** (www.travelocity.com), **Expedia** (www.expedia.com), **Orbitz** (www.orbitz.com), and **Smarter Living** (www.smarterliving.com), for example — have search engines that can dig up discounted car-rental rates. Just enter the car size you want, the pickup and return dates, and the location, and the server returns a price. You can even make the reservation through any of these sites.

✔ **Be flexible.** When giving the rental company your dates for pickup and delivery, inform them that you're open to other dates as well, if changing your dates means saving money. Picking up the car on Thursday instead of Friday, or keeping it over the weekend, may save you big bucks. You may also save money if you rent for a full week rather than two days. Finally, check whether the rate is cheaper if you pick up the car at a location in town instead of the airport.

✔ **Know your restrictions.** Most rental companies restrict where you can drive. With some companies, you must stay in the country of rental (usually only smaller, national outfits mandate this rule). Likewise, most don't allow you to take a car that you rented in England to Ireland or the Continent. Few let you drive from any Western European country into Eastern Europe, so if you're planning to drive to Prague, make sure that you make arrangements with the rental agency before you leave.

✔ **Check any age restrictions.** Many car-rental companies add on a fee for drivers 24 and under, while some don't rent to them at all. If you're 24 or under, research which companies will rent to you without a penalty.

✔ **Lease for longer periods of time.** Companies don't always remind you of the leasing option, but if you want a car for more than 17 days (up to six months), tell them that you want to short-term-lease the car (Auto Europe and Europe By Car both offer this option). Leasing a car gives you a brand-new car and *full* insurance coverage with no deductible. The minimum age for renting a car ranges from 18 to 27, but anyone 18 or over can usually lease a car.

✔ **Mention the ad.** If you see an advertised price in your local newspaper, be sure to ask for that specific rate; otherwise you may be charged the standard (higher) rate. Don't forget to mention membership in AAA, AARP, and trade unions. These memberships usually entitle you to discounts ranging from 5 percent to 30 percent.

✔ **Check your frequent-flier accounts.** Not only are your favorite airlines likely to have sent you discount coupons, but most car rentals add at least 500 miles to your account.

✔ **Consider a stick shift instead of an automatic.** You can save up to 40 percent on the price of car rental if you rent a stick-shift car instead of an automatic. As an added bonus, stick shifts are more fuel efficient and often give you better control on Europe's many narrow, windy, hilly roads and tight streets in ancient cities.

✔ **Look into coverage you may already have.** The *collision damage waiver* (CDW) basically allows you to total the car and not be held liable. Your credit card may cover the CDW if you use it to pay for the rental, so make sure that you check the terms of your credit card before purchasing the CDW. However, keep in mind that some rental agencies in Italy won't accept a credit card CDW for rentals; you must purchase it separately instead. Travel Guard (☎ 800-826-4919; www.travelguard.com) sells independent CDW coverage for a mere $7 a day — a sight better than the $10 to $20 per day that rental agencies tend to charge.

✔ **Carefully consider the other insurance options.** The car-rental companies also offer additional *liability insurance* (if you harm others in an accident), *personal accident insurance* (if you harm yourself or your passengers), and *personal effects insurance* (if your luggage is stolen from your car). Your insurance policy on your car at home probably covers most of these unlikely occurrences. However, if your own insurance doesn't cover you for rentals or if you don't have auto insurance, definitely consider the additional coverage (ask your car-rental agent for more information).

✔ **Remind the company that you've already paid.** Make sure that you know exactly what you paid for when you arranged your car rental. Many times, the car pickup offices in Europe overlook the fact that your credit card was already charged for the rental cost, and they try to double-charge you. Usually, you end up with one charge on your card from the European office for the first full tank of gas that it provides (which is almost never included in the original rental price).

✔ **Inspect the car before driving away.** If the rental agency doesn't know that something is wrong with the car you rented when you drive it off, it'll assume that you broke the car and charge you accordingly. If the car's condition doesn't match the inspection form that they want you to sign, point out the discrepancy. Otherwise, you're legally liable for the condition after you drive away. Make sure that all locks and doors work, check the various lights, and scan the entire car for dents, scratches, and fabric rips.

✔ **Check for repair and safety equipment.** Check the trunk to make sure that your rental car is equipped with a jack, inflated spare, snow chains (for winter driving), and a hazard triangle (most countries require that you hang this on your trunk if you're broken down on the side of the road). Likewise, check the glove compartment for a parking disk. (Ask the rental agency about the parking disk; they'll explain the country's honor-system parking lots, if the system applies.)

✔ **Gas up before you return the car.** When leaving the rental company, make sure the car has a full tank of gas so that you don't have to worry about dealing with local gas stations immediately. Also, make sure that you return the car with a full tank of gas. Similar to rental-company practices in North America, if you forget to fill up the car before you return it, the company will kindly fill it for you at obscenely jacked-up prices. Before you return the car, find a gas station and top off the tank.

Understanding European road rules

Except for driving on the left in Great Britain and Ireland, European road rules are similar enough to American ones that you can drive without further instruction. However, the following important differences do exist:

✔ **Watch out for aggressive drivers.** Most European drivers are much more aggressive than American drivers.

✔ **Don't cruise in the left lane.** You do *not* ride in the left lane on a four-lane highway; it's for passing only.

✔ **Help other drivers pass you.** If a vehicle comes up from behind and flashes its lights at you, it's signaling for you to slow down and drive more on the shoulder of the road, so it can pass you more easily.

✔ **Be aware of speed limits.** Except for parts of the German Autobahn, most highways list speed limits of approximately 100 to 135kmph (60–80 mph).

✔ **Remember to convert from kilometers.** European measurements relating to vehicles are in kilometers (distances and speed limits). For a rough conversion, remember that 1 kilometer equals 0.6 miles.

✔ **Watch out for gas prices.** Gas may look reasonably priced, but the price is per liter, and 3.8 liters equals 1 gallon, so multiply by 4 to guestimate the equivalent per-gallon price.

✔ **Buy a toll sticker.** Some countries, such as Austria and Switzerland, require highway stickers in lieu of paying tolls (or as a supplement to cheap tolls). If you rent a car within such a country, your car already has a sticker. But, if you're crossing a border, check at the crossing station to see whether you need to purchase a sticker on the spot for a nominal fee.

✔ **Drive defensively.** Assume that other drivers have a better idea of what they're doing than you, and take your hints from them.

Chapter 7

Booking Your Accommodations

Accommodations will probably eat up the biggest slice in your travel budget. But because you have so many options of where to stay, lodging is also an area in which you can save a lot of money. In Paris, for example, you can spend several hundred dollars on a lavish luxury hotel room, stay in a clean but simple two-star hotel down the street for around $100, or check into a hostel for about $40 per person per night. This chapter gives you the lowdown on the types of accommodations you'll encounter throughout Europe.

Understanding European Hotels

Hotels in Europe, with the exception of the great luxury hotels, tend to have fewer frills and features than hotels in the United States. For example, free cable television is standard at even the cheapest U.S. motel chains. In Europe, however, few inexpensive hotel rooms even have televisions.

Europe's more traditional hotels and *pensions* (smaller, family-run places) typically differ from American hotels in the following ways:

- **The appearance of the lobby rarely reflects the appearance of the rooms.** Never judge a European hotel by the front entry; expensive hotels sometimes invest heavily in the lobby but cut corners on the rooms, and cheaper hotels often have just a dingy desk in a hallway, but spotless accommodations upstairs.

- **"Double" beds are often two side-by-side twin beds made with a single sheet and blanket (or overlapping twin sheets).**

✔ **Hotels in old European buildings often don't have elevators.** If they do, the few elevators that are available are likely to be small and slow.

✔ **Floors are often covered with tile or linoleum instead of carpet.**

✔ **Bathrooms are vastly and surprisingly different from the American norm.** For more details, see the next section, "The bathroom: The big culture shock."

✔ **You can trust hotel staff to provide you with general information and pamphlets about sightseeing and attractions, but be wary of anything beyond that.** A restaurant recommended by an employee may be one owned by a relative or someone who has agreed to give the hotel a kickback. Usually the place is fine, but never count on a hotel to direct you to the best food in town. Hotel staff members may also offer to get you tickets for the theater or cultural shows, but tickets are usually cheaper from the box office or local tourism office.

The bathroom: The big culture shock

People who haven't traveled in Europe think that language, architecture, and food best illustrate the cultural differences between North America and the Continent. But for many newcomers traveling in Europe, the greatest culture shock is the bathroom. It all starts in your first cheap pension, when you find out that the only bathroom is down the hall and shared by everyone on the floor.

Although more and more European hotels are installing bathrooms in every room, in small, inexpensive pensions and B&Bs, this is not the case. If you simply can't bear the thought of sharing a bathroom, you'll have to pay extra for a private bathroom in your room. Except in luxury hotels, don't expect your bathroom to be large and glamorous. The bathrooms in many budget hotels are almost as small as those in airplanes.

Europeans usually refer to the bathroom itself simply as the *toilet*. You may also hear the term *wc* (short for the British euphemism "water closet"). A *bathroom* is where you take a bath.

See the section on electronics in Chapter 9 for information on what isn't safe to plug into European bathroom outlets. (Here's a hint: everything.)

The shower: Another new adventure

In some of the cheaper European hotels, the shower is a nozzle stuck in the bathroom wall with a drain in the floor and no shower curtain. You may have to remove the toilet paper from the bathroom to keep it dry while you drench the entire room with your shower. You won't encounter this phenomenon in most hotels; it's more prevalent in southern Italy and Greece.

Likewise, the least expensive hotels are generally not going to have full-size bathtubs, either. You may encounter half-tubs, in which you can sit but not stretch out. Your water source in some showers will be a flexible, wall-mounted hose with a spray nozzle attached to it.

That extra thing: Not a toilet

The extra porcelain fixture that looks like another toilet is called a *bidet* (bi-*day*). *Do not use the bidet as a toilet.* The water that jets up and out is meant to clean your private parts.

Finding the Best Room at the Best Rate

This section offers information and advice that helps you find the accommodations that meet your needs and your budget.

Comparing room rates and ratings

The hotels listed in this book are rated from $ to $$$$$. These ratings are not an official ranking system, nor do they reflect the overall quality of a hotel. Rather, these categories reflect the approximate price range of the recommended hotels related to their overall value. A ranking of $ indicates a budget hotel, $$ means a fairly cheap hotel, $$$ is applied to moderate hotels, $$$$ means more upscale accommodations, and $$$$$ is for a recommended splurge. These ratings are comparable only within the same city, meaning that a $ hotel in an expensive place like London may cost nearly the same as a $$$$ hotel in a far cheaper area such as Athens.

In addition to these categories, we include the hotel's actual rates, which should make finding something in your price range much easier. Of course, rates can and do go up regularly, so always check the hotel's Web site for current prices or verify them when you call to make your reservation.

The *rack rate* is the maximum rate a hotel charges for a room. It's the rate you get if you walk in off the street and ask for a room for the night. Sometimes these rates are posted on the back of your door or on a wall near the reception desk.

Hotels, of course, are more than happy to charge you the rack rate, but you can almost always do better. Perhaps the best way to avoid paying the rack rate is surprisingly simple: Just ask for a cheaper or discounted rate. You may be pleasantly surprised. You'll stand a better chance of receiving a lower rate if you're traveling in the off-season or if you're staying several days at that one hotel. If you're booking ahead, many hotels often run specials on their Web sites that clock in well below the official rack rates. The rates at the smallest, least expensive hotels, pensions, and B&Bs are usually not negotiable.

Room rates change with the season as occupancy rates rise and fall. But even within a given season, room prices are subject to change without notice, so the rates quoted in this book may be different from the rate you receive when you make your reservation. If you're thinking of booking a room at a major international chain, be sure to mention membership in AAA, AARP, frequent-flier programs, or any other corporate rewards programs. You never know when the affiliation may be worth a few dollars off your room rate.

Reserving a room through a large chain hotel's toll-free number may result in a lower rate than calling the hotel directly. On the other hand, the central reservations number may not know about discount rates at specific locations. Your best bet is to call both the local number and the toll-free number and see which one gives you a better deal.

Verify all hotel charges when you check in. You don't need to pay in advance (though occasionally, a budget hotel may require it), but make sure that you and the hotel clerk agree on the rate. Does it include breakfast, taxes, and showers? What are the phone rates? Do they charge even for you to dial your calling card's toll-free number? Also, be sure that the quoted rate is per room, not per person, as may be the case in resort-type coastal towns and islands.

In most European destinations, taxes are automatically included in the quoted rates. However, in some countries (often in Spain, where it's 7 percent; in England, where it's 17.5 percent; and in France, where it varies depending on the classification of the hotel), these local taxes are not included in the price quoted over the phone. Always ask, "Does that price include all taxes?"

When you check in, take one of the hotel's business cards. You'd be surprised at how many people forget their hotel's name or location after a long day of sightseeing. Many cards have a little map on the back. If you're clueless about where your hotel is, hop in a cab and show the driver the card with the hotel's address.

Making hotel reservations

Everyone goes about finding and reserving hotels differently, but you'll save yourself time and tons of hassle if you book your hotel rooms before you leave home. That way you don't have to make calls when you arrive or trudge from one hotel to the next before you find one that suits you. Booking in advance minimizes the stress and uncertainty when you arrive tired and in a strange place. If you're traveling with young children, you don't want to be fumbling for coins in the train station as you simultaneously try to reserve a room and keep the kids from running off for parts unknown.

If you're not planning to reserve your hotel rooms in advance, at least find out whether you'll be arriving in town during a festival or trade fair. If you are, the gala may be the highlight of your trip, but you could end up sleeping under the stars if you haven't booked a room well in advance (before you leave home).

If you want to reserve a room in a European hotel by fax or e-mail, use simple language in your communications and include the following information:

- ✔ Your name

- ✔ The number of people in your party

- ✔ What kind of room you want (Make sure you say "double with one bed with private bathroom" or "double with two beds and a shared bathroom," and specify "two adults, one child, in the same room.")

- ✔ The number of nights you want to stay.

- ✔ The date of the first night

To avoid confusion, always spell out the full name of the month — Europeans numerically abbreviate dates day/month/year, not month/day/year as Americans do (so "5/6/2009" would be read May 6 in the United States, but June 5 in Europe).

Always request that the hotel confirm your reservation with a follow-up fax or printable e-mail that includes all the details (number of people, room rate, nights you'll be staying, and so on). Most hotels do this without being asked, but always make sure. Bring the confirmation with you because it gives you printed proof that you've booked a room.

Using a hotel booking service

At the train station or the local tourism office in most European towns, you'll find a central hotel reservation service. To use the service, tell the people working there your price range and the part of the city you'd like to stay in, and they'll find you a room. In each city chapter in this book, we list hotel booking services at the beginning of the hotel section.

The advantages of hotel booking services are:

- ✔ **They do all the legwork for you.** Staff members speak English, so they can act as interpreters while calling hotels for you.

- ✔ **They're helpful when rooms are scarce.** If all the hotels are full, they can often find rooms in hotels that aren't listed in the guidebooks or other popular resources.

- ✔ **They know the hotels.** The best ones can find accommodations that perfectly match your needs and price range.

But booking services do have their drawbacks:

- ✔ **Contacting hotels directly is generally cheaper.** Booking services usually charge a nominal fee of $5 to $10. In many countries, hotels charge higher rates for bookings they receive through hotel booking services.

- ✔ **A tourism office booking-desk clerk offers no opinion about the hotels.** Agents just provide you a list to choose from that may include amenities and prices, but little else.

- ✔ **They may be biased.** A booking agency, especially a private one, may try to steer you to places on its "push list." Rather than an honest evaluation, its "advice" is frequently a sales pitch for the hotel itself.

In a few large cities — Prague and Rome come to mind — and on popular Greek islands, hotel reps may approach you as you step off the train or boat. Some are drumming up business for a perfectly respectable hotel or pension, but others may be out to fleece you. If an offer interests you, make sure that the rep pinpoints the exact location of the hotel on a map and get the price in writing before you go off with him. Pay close attention to any photos he shows you — a little photo retouching and some strategic furniture rearrangement can make a dismal cell look more like a palatial suite.

Surfing the Web for hotel deals

Shopping online for hotels is generally done one of two ways: by booking through the hotel's own Web site or through an independent booking agency (or a fare-service agency such as Priceline.com). It's best to shop around and compare the online sites because prices can vary considerably from site to site. Keep in mind that a hotel at the top of a site's listing may be there for no other reason than that it paid money to get the placement.

Of the major sites, **Expedia** (www.expedia.com) offers a long list of special deals and "virtual tours" or photos of available rooms so that you can see what you're paying for. **Travelocity** (www.travelocity.com) posts unvarnished customer reviews and ranks its properties according to the AAA rating system. **Hotels.com** is also reliable. An excellent free program, **TravelAxe** (www.travelaxe.net), can help you search multiple hotel sites at once — even ones you may never have heard of — and conveniently lists the total price of the room, including the taxes and service charges. Another booking site, **Travelweb** (www.travelweb.com), is partly owned by the hotels it represents (including the Hilton, Hyatt, and Starwood chains) and is plugged directly into the hotels' reservations systems. If you book your hotel online, it's a good idea to get a confirmation number and make a printout of any online booking transaction.

In the opaque Web site category, **Priceline.com** and **Hotwire.com** are even better for hotels than for airfares; with both, you're allowed to pick the neighborhood and quality level of your hotel before offering up your money. Priceline's hotel listings cover Europe, but it's generally better at getting five-star lodging for three-star prices than at finding anything at the bottom of the scale. On the downside, many hotels stick Priceline guests in their least desirable rooms. For both Priceline and Hotwire, you pay up front, and the fee is nonrefundable. *Note:* Some hotels do not provide loyalty-program credits or points or other frequent-guest amenities when you book a room through opaque online services.

One of the pluses of Web sites is that they often include virtual brochures, so you can see pictures of the rooms ahead of time. You can also usually get the latest hotel rates, plus any discounts the booking service may be able to secure (especially at pricier inns).

But hotel-booking Web sites also have some big minuses. Because most of them charge a fee to the hotels they list and the hotels themselves provide the write-ups and other info, you must take any descriptions or recommendations with a grain of salt. Travel guidebooks like this one provide unbiased recommendations, but most hotel-booking Web sites are just a new form of promotional material. Also, the bulk of the hotels that choose to be listed on these sites are high-end, business-oriented, owned by chains, or all of the above. The best small hotels in the historic city centers, mom-and-pop pensions, and outright cheap places are usually absent.

Some lodging sites specialize in a particular type of accommodation, such as bed-and-breakfasts (B&Bs), which you don't find on mainstream booking sites. Others offer weekend deals at chain properties, which cater to business travelers and have more empty rooms on weekends.

HotelChatter.com is a daily Webzine offering smart coverage and critiques of hotels worldwide. Go to **TripAdvisor.com** or **HotelShark.com** for helpful independent consumer reviews of hotels and resort properties.

Finding deals at the last minute

If you arrive at your destination with no hotel reservation, a guidebook like this can come in very handy. Before you get to town, study the hotel reviews and figure out which ones best fit your taste and budget. Then rank your top choices by writing 1, 2, 3, and so on in the book's margin. Prioritizing the hotels prepares you to move quickly to the next-best option if your first choice is full.

After your train pulls into the station, get some change or buy a phone card at a newsstand and start calling hotels to check for vacancies. This strategy gives you a head start on the many people who look for a room by marching out of the station with their bags and walking to the nearest hotel. If you're uncomfortable making the calls yourself, the train station or tourism office may have a hotel reservation service that can do this for you (see "Using a hotel booking service," earlier in this chapter).

Checking in at the chains

International chain hotels, which you can usually reserve from home, are sometimes located on the edge of town in the business or industrial district. They're huge, impersonal, and expensive, but you can count on a certain level of amenities and services.

There is one chain that does it a bit differently in Europe. By partnering with existing downtown hotels, **Best Western International** (☎ 800-528-1234; www.bestwestern.com) usually offers personality *and* location. Often a European Best Western is a local bastion of a hotel that's been a solid low-end-of-luxury choice in that city for decades, if not a century or more.

If you can't find a room this way, you can try wandering the streets checking each hotel you pass. The areas around city train stations usually are full of cheap hotels, but they're also often in bland — sometimes seedy — neighborhoods.

Hotels outside the center of town often have more rooms available and are cheaper than centrally located ones. You may be able to get a good deal in the next town over, but it won't be worth the trouble if it's more than a 30-minute train ride away.

To get the best price on the best room, follow these tips:

- ✔ **Compare different hotels.** Many people don't want to run from place to place, but if you have some time and are counting your pennies, it's worth a try. Don't assume that the first hotel you visit is the best. If you've called around and lodging seems in short supply, take a room where you can get it. But if rooms seem plentiful, tell the first hotel you stop in that you'll think about it and head to another one nearby.

- ✔ **Ask to see different rooms.** When you get to the hotel, don't feel obligated to take the first room you're shown. Ask to see some other ones. Open and close windows to see how well they block out noise. Check the rates posted on the room door (usually there by law) to make sure they match the rate you were quoted and the rate that's posted in the lobby. Ask whether some rooms are less expensive than others.

After you make your reservation, asking one or two more pointed questions can go a long way toward making sure you get the best room in the house. Always ask for a corner room. They're usually larger, quieter, and have more windows and light than standard rooms, and they don't always cost more. Also, ask if the hotel is renovating; if it is, request a room away from the renovation work. Inquire, too, about the location of the restaurants, bars, and discos in the hotel — all sources of annoying noise. And if you aren't happy with your room when you arrive, talk to the front desk. If they have another room, they should be happy to accommodate you, within reason.

 ✔ **Bargain.** The more empty rooms a hotel has to fill for the night, the better your chances of getting a lower price. If you're staying a single night during high season, you'll have to pay the going rate. But for off-season stays and for longer than three nights, ask for a discount. Many places have weekend discounts, too.

For more tips on saving money on hotel costs, see Chapter 4.

Discovering Other Options

The reviews in this book include standard hotels (along with a few traditional and charming family-run pensions), which are generally large and likely to have rooms available. But hotels aren't your only lodging option.

The most popular alternatives

Each country seems to have its own hotel alternatives, from Alpine hikers' shacks to rental villas in Tuscany. Here's a quick rundown on the most popular substitutes for the traditional hotel (for more information on each of these, check with the local tourism office):

✔ **B&Bs or pensions:** When Europeans go on vacation, they often stay at these small, family-run versions of hotels. If the hotels in town charge $150 for a double, a pension usually costs only $80 to $100. Upscale B&Bs can be found in larger cities such as London and Paris.

Some B&Bs require you to pay for breakfast or *half* or *full board* (meaning that one or all meals are included); private bathrooms are still rare (although this is changing); and the service is almost always genial and personable.

 ✔ **Private room rentals:** Even the cheapest B&B can't beat the price of renting a room in a private home, which can run as low as $40 to $60 for a double. This is a great option for single travelers because you don't pay the single-occupancy rate that most hotels charge.

The quality of the accommodations in rental rooms is less consistent than at standard hotels, but at worst you're stuck in a tiny, plain room. At best, you get comfortable furniture, a homey atmosphere, a home-cooked breakfast, and a feel for what it's like to be part of a European family.

✔ **Motels:** Europe has adopted this American form of modular innkeeping, but most travelers don't know this because — as in the United States — motels cluster around city outskirts at highway access points. If you're doing your travel by car and arriving late, these places are a great, cheap lodging option. They're completely devoid of character, but they're often real bargains. Some are even fully automated so you check yourself in and out.

✔ **Converted castles and other historic buildings:** These usually high-quality lodgings can be outrageously expensive, or they can be surprisingly cheap state-run operations. (Spain's *paradores* are the best example of the latter.)

✔ **Rental apartments or villas:** If you're planning a long stay in one location and want to feel like a temporary European, or if you have a large traveling party (a big family or two families traveling together), these options are the best.

Rental apartments or villas are easiest to book through a travel agent or rental consortium, such as **Barclay International Group** (☎ **800-845-6636;** www.barclayweb.com), but you can sometimes get better rates by contacting the owners directly (with addresses or phone numbers from newspaper travel sections, magazines, English-language magazines, and tourism boards).

✔ **Apartment or home swaps:** Some travelers beat the cost of European hotels by exchanging their home or apartment with Europeans for a specified period of time. There are no guarantees here; it's up to you to work out the details and take the risks. If this option intrigues you, check out the offerings on **craigslist** (www.craigslist.com); you may also find short-term apartment rentals there.

Hostels and other bargain options

If you're on a severely limited budget, or if you like hanging out with primarily youthful backpackers, you may want to stay in a hostel. They used to be called *youth hostels,* but the only ones that still follow the under-26-only rule are in southern Germany. Most hostels are now open as cheap digs for travelers of all ages, with nightly rates ranging from $25 to $50 per person.

Some are affiliated with the official hostel organization, Hostelling International (or IYH, as it's known abroad), which means they have to live up to a certain set of standards. Increasingly, private, unaffiliated hostels are opening up (often closer to the center of town than the official hostel), and although they may not have the IYH stamp of approval, in some cases they're actually nicer places.

In a hostel, you stay in beds or bunks in shared, dormlike rooms, though increasingly hostels are offering private rooms sleeping two to four people as well. You find anywhere from four to eight beds per room (the current trend) to as many as 100 beds in one big gymnasium-like space (this sort of arrangement is slowly disappearing); most hostels have a mix of different-size rooms at varying prices. Families can usually find hostels with four-bunk rooms. Many hostels separate the sexes into different rooms or floors and supply lockers for safe bag storage. Bathrooms are usually shared (but this, too, is changing as more private rooms are made available), breakfast is often included, and other cheap but school cafeteria-like meals may be available.

Hostels (especially the official IYH ones) are often far from the city center, occasionally on the outskirts of town, and they fill up with high-school students in the summer. Year-round, many seem to be little more than giant backpacker singles' bars — great for meeting your fellow travelers, but terrible for getting to know the local city and culture.

Almost all hostels impose evening curfews (usually between 10 p.m. and midnight), midday lockout periods, and length-of-stay limits (often a maximum of three days). You may only be able to make reservations weeks in advance by going online, one day ahead of time by calling, or not at all, in which case you'll need to show up early if you want a bed.

To stay in many "official" IYH hostels — or at least to get a discount — you must be a card-carrying member of **Hostelling International,** 8401 Colesville Rd., Suite 600, Silver Springs, MD 20910 (☎ **301-495-1240;** www.hiusa.org). Membership is free for children 17 and under, $28 per year for adults 18 to 54, and $18 for seniors 55 and older. You can also buy the card at many hostels abroad. You can find hostel listings on Hostelling International's Web site (www.hihostels.com) and at the private sites www.hostels.com and www.hostels.net.

Most hostels furnish a blanket but require you to have your own sleep-sack, which is basically a sleeping bag made out of a sheet. If you plan to stay in hostels on your trip, buy one (from Hostelling International) before you leave, or make one (fold a sheet in half and sew it closed across the bottom and halfway up the side). Some hostels sell sleep-sacks, and a few insist that you rent one of theirs.

In addition to hostels, several other options exist for low-budget lodging (ask for details at the tourism office):

- ✔ **Convents:** Especially in predominantly Catholic countries such as Italy, Spain, and France, staying in convents and other religious buildings enables you to save money and get an immaculate and safe room, no matter what your religious affiliation. Rooms in convents, available in many major cities and pilgrimage sites, cost as little as $15 and generally no more than $100 per night. Your room probably won't be any fancier than the cells that the nuns or monks occupy, but a few are quite posh. Many convents do give preference to visitors of their own denomination or from that religious order's country of origin.

- ✔ **University housing:** During the summer, when school is not in session, check with local universities to see whether any unused dorm rooms are for rent (at rates comparable to hostels). This tip is especially useful in London during the summer holidays.

✔ **Pod hotels:** Pod hotels originated in Japan, where space is at a premium, and they're now spreading through Europe. The concept is simple: You rent a private, podlike cabin that contains a bed, lighting, a toilet, and a sink, but little else (you may not even have a window). Pod hotels are a step up from hostels and cost a bit more, but they represent a new trend in inexpensive European hotels (cost is generally well under $100 per night); you'll be seeing more of them in European cities and airports. Yotel (www.yotel.com) in London and Qbic Hotel (www.qbichotel.nl) in Amsterdam are two examples.

✔ **Tent cities:** During the height of the summer season, some cities, including Munich, London, Paris, Venice, and Copenhagen, have hangarlike rooms or large tents for travelers on an extremely tight budget. For anywhere from $10 to $25, you get a floor mat and a blanket, more than 100 roommates, and a cup of tea in the morning. Most of the people at these giant slumber parties are students, but the tent cities are open to everyone. Essentially, this is one step above sleeping on a park bench (which, by the way, is dangerous, not recommended, and usually illegal).

If you use any type of shared-space lodging, such as hostels or tent cities, be very careful with your belongings. Always play it safe; leave your pack in the lockers (if you're staying in a hostel) or at the train station (if you're staying in another type of communal lodging). For safety tips on overnight trains, see Chapter 4.

Chapter 8

Catering to Special Travel Needs or Interests

● ●

In This Chapter

▶ Taking the family to Europe

▶ Traveling discounts for the senior set

▶ Accessing Europe for travelers with disabilities

▶ Getting out and about for gays and lesbians

● ●

*I*f you're headed to Europe with a particular interest or concern in mind, here is the place to look for information. This chapter has resource information and travel tips for families, seniors, gays and lesbians, and travelers with disabilities.

Traveling with the Brood: Advice for Families

If you have trouble getting your kids out of the house in the morning, dragging them thousands of miles away may seem like an insurmountable challenge. But family travel can be immensely rewarding, giving you new ways of seeing the world through younger pairs of eyes. Europeans expect to encounter traveling families, because that's how they travel. You're likely to run into caravanning European clans, including grandparents and babes in arms. Locals tend to love kids, especially in Mediterranean countries. Hotels and restaurants often give you an even warmer reception if you have a child in tow.

Your best bet for help with small children may be three- and four-star hotels. The baby sitters on call and a better infrastructure for helping visitors access the city and its services more than offset the hotels' higher costs.

Most museums and sights offer reduced prices or free admission for children under a certain age (anywhere from 6–18), and getting a cot in your hotel room won't cost you more than 30 percent extra, if that. Always ask about discounts on plane and train tickets for kids, too.

Frommer's family-friendly Europe

Here's a list of Frommer's European travel guides (all from Wiley Publishing) that will help you to plan a family-friendly European holiday:

- ✔ *Frommer's Brittany with Your Family*
- ✔ *Frommer's Croatia with Your Family*
- ✔ *Frommer's Devon & Cornwall with Your Family*
- ✔ *Frommer's Greek Islands with Your Family*
- ✔ *Frommer's Ireland with Your Family*
- ✔ *Frommer's London with Kids*
- ✔ *Frommer's Mediterranean Spain with Your Family*
- ✔ *Frommer's Normandy with Your Family*
- ✔ *Frommer's Northern Italy with Your Family*
- ✔ *Frommer's Provence & the Côte d'Azur with Your Family*
- ✔ *Frommer's Tuscany & Umbria with Your Family*

For a list of more family-friendly travel resources, visit www.frommers.com/planning.

A number of books that offer hints and tips on traveling with kids are available. *Take Your Kids to Europe: How to Travel Safely (and Sanely) in Europe with Your Children,* by Cynthia Harriman (Globe Pequot Press), offers practical advice based on the author's four-month trip with her hubby and two kids. Another worthwhile book is *Family Travel & Resorts,* by Pamela Lanier (Lanier Publishing International), which gives some good general advice that you can apply to travel in the United States, Europe, and elsewhere. You also may want to check out the reliable *Adventuring with Children: An Inspirational Guide to World Travel and the Outdoors,* by Nan Jeffrey (Avalon House), which includes specific advice on dealing with everyday family situations, especially those involving infants, which can become Herculean labors when you encounter them on the road.

You can find good family-oriented vacation advice on the Internet from such sites as the **Family Travel Forum** (www.familytravelforum.com), a comprehensive site that offers customized trip planning; **Family Travel Network** (www.familytravelnetwork.com), an award-winning site that offers travel features, deals, and tips; **TravelWithYourKids.com** (www.travelwithyourkids.com), another site with trip-planning tools; and **Family Travel Files.com** (www.thefamilytravelfiles.com), which offers an online magazine and a directory of off-the-beaten-path tours and tour operators for families. The highly regarded **Smithsonian Study Tours** has inaugurated a Family Adventures division (☎ 877-338-8687; www.si.edu/tsa/sst) that runs escorted educational and adventure trips specifically designed for the entire clan.

Making Age Work for You: Advice for Seniors

Seniors comprise a huge proportion of transatlantic travelers to Europe. In general, older travelers in good health won't encounter any major problems, but be aware that smaller, less expensive hotels, pensions, and B&Bs often do not have elevators or porters to carry your luggage. If climbing stairs or hauling suitcases is difficult, make sure your chosen hotel has an elevator (it may be called a *lift*) and porter service. If you're a senior traveling on an escorted tour, these issues are all taken care of for you. And just a reminder: Bring a good pair of walking shoes that will handle cobblestone streets.

If you're a senior citizen, you may be eligible for some terrific travel bargains. Members of **AARP** (formerly known as the American Association of Retired Persons), 601 E St. NW, Washington, DC 20049 (☎ **888-687-2277**; www.aarp.org), get discounts on hotels and car rentals. AARP offers members a wide range of benefits, including *AARP: The Magazine* and a monthly newsletter. You won't find as many AARP deals in Europe as you do in the United States, however; generally they're offered only by American chains operating in Europe. Anyone over 50 can join AARP.

Avis, Hertz, and National give an AARP discount (5–30 percent), and many rental dealers that specialize in Europe — Auto Europe, Kemwell, Europe By Car — offer rates 5 percent lower to seniors. For contact information, look under "Toll-free numbers and Web sites" in this book's Quick Concierge.

Make sure to ask about senior discounts when you book your flight. People over 60 or 65 also get reduced admission at theaters, museums, and other attractions in most European cities. Additionally, they can often get discount fares or cards on public transportation and national rail systems. Make sure to carry identification that proves your age.

Grand Circle/Overseas Adventure Travel, 347 Congress St., Boston, MA 02210 (☎ **800-959-0405**; www.gct.com), specializes in vacations for seniors (as do hundreds of travel agencies). The tour-bus style of most of these packages is not for everyone, however. If you're a senior who wants a more independent trip, you should probably consult a regular travel agent.

Many reliable agencies and organizations target the 50-plus market. Give **Elderhostel** (☎ 877-426-8056 or 617-426-8056; www.elderhostel.org) a ring if you want to try something more than the average guided tour or vacation. Foreign universities host these trips, and your days are filled with seminars, lectures, field trips, and sightseeing tours, all led by academic experts. You must be 55 and older to participate in Elderhostel (a spouse or companion of any age can accompany you), and the programs range from one to four weeks.

Road Scholar tours (☎ 800-466-7762; www.roadscholar.org), an off-shoot of Elderhostel, is aimed at giving adults (not just seniors) a tour that combines learning with travel. Resident experts — local professors and professionals — join the group for on-site talks, culture and language lessons, and field trips. There's freedom in the schedule, though, allowing you to do a fair amount of exploring on your own.

ElderTreks (☎ 800-741-7956; www.eldertreks.com) offers small-group tours to off-the-beaten-path or adventure-travel locations, restricted to travelers 50 and older.

Accessing Europe: Advice for Travelers with Disabilities

A disability shouldn't stop anybody from traveling to Europe. Although access remains an issue in some countries or regions, the major cities have made an effort in the past few years to accommodate people with disabilities. More options and resources are out there for the Europe-bound traveler with disabilities than ever before, including accessible train cars and public transportation. You'll find plenty of organizations to help you plan your trip and provide specific advice before you go.

Organizations that offer assistance or information to travelers with disabilities include **MossRehab** (☎ 215-456-9603; www.mossresourcenet.org), which provides a library of accessible-travel resources online; the **Society for Accessible Travel & Hospitality** (SATH; ☎ 212-447-7284; www.sath.org), which offers a wealth of travel resources for all types of disabilities and informed recommendations on destinations, access guides, travel agents, tour operators, vehicle rentals, and companion services; and the **American Foundation for the Blind** (AFB; ☎ 800-232-5463; www.afb.org), a referral resource for the blind or visually impaired that includes information on traveling with Seeing Eye dogs.

The worldwide organization known as **Mobility International**, P.O. Box 10767, Eugene, OR 97440 (☎ 541-343-1284 V/TTY; fax: 541-343-6812; www.miusa.org), promotes international disability rights, provides reference sheets on travel destinations, and hosts international exchanges for people with disabilities. Its *A World of Options* book lists information on everything from biking trips to scuba outfitters.

Many travel agencies offer customized tours and itineraries for travelers with disabilities. **Flying Wheels Travel** (☎ 507-451-5005; www.flyingwheelstravel.com) offers escorted tours and cruises that emphasize sports and private tours in minivans with lifts. **Access-Able Travel Source** (☎ 303-232-2979; www.access-able.com) offers extensive access information and advice for traveling around the world with disabilities. **Accessible Journeys** (☎ 800-846-4537 or 610-521-0339; www. accessiblejourneys.com) offers wheelchair travelers and their families and friends resources for travel.

Avis Rent A Car has an Avis Access program that offers such services as a dedicated 24-hour toll-free number (☎ 888-879-4273) for customers with special travel needs; special car features such as swivel seats, spinner knobs, and hand controls; and accessible bus service.

For more information specifically targeted to travelers with disabilities, check out the quarterly magazine *Emerging Horizons* ($16.95 per year, $21.95 outside the U.S.; www.emerginghorizons.com) and *Open World Magazine,* published by SATH ($13 per year, $21 outside the U.S.).

Following the Rainbow: Advice for Gay and Lesbian Travelers

Western Europe has led the way when it comes to same-sex issues (gay couples can be married in Holland and Spain, and civil union provisions exist in Denmark, England, and Germany). In terms of gay culture, you'll find large and active gay communities in all major European cities, especially London, Paris, and Amsterdam. Many cities have telephone help lines or walk-in offices for gays and lesbians; some Web research will help you locate them. In addition, most European cities host gay-pride events, including a huge yearly Europride festival that moves from city to city. Check the Web site www.europride.com for a list of cities and dates.

There is a level of sophistication and acceptance in Europe that has called to gays and lesbians for decades, and in general you won't encounter any problems. Hotels in the European Union, for example, cannot discriminate against same-sex couples. But do some research on the city or area you're planning to visit. As is usually the case, smaller, more traditional towns are often not as accepting.

Your best all-around resource is the **International Gay and Lesbian Travel Association** (IGLTA; ☎ 800-448-8550 or 954-776-2626; www. iglta.org), the trade association for the gay and lesbian travel industry. IGLTA offers an online directory of gay- and lesbian-friendly travel businesses; go to its Web site and click on Members.

Many agencies offer tours and travel itineraries specifically for gay and lesbian travelers. **Above and Beyond Tours** (☎ 800-397-2681; www. abovebeyondtours.com) is the exclusive gay and lesbian tour operator for United Airlines. **Now, Voyager** (☎ 800-255-6951; www.nowvoyager. com) is a well-known San Francisco–based gay-owned and -operated travel service. **Olivia Cruises & Resorts** (☎ 800-631-6277 or 510-655-0364; www.olivia.com) charters entire resorts and ships for exclusive lesbian vacations and offers smaller group experiences for both gay and lesbian travelers.

Look for gay-specific travel guides at your local travel bookstores, gay and lesbian bookstores, or online at **Giovanni's Room,** 1145 Pine St., Philadelphia, PA 19107 (☎ **215-923-2960;** www.giovannisroom.com) or **A Different Light Bookstore** (www.adlbooks.com). **Gay.com** (www.gay.com) offers guidebooks and travel resources for the global gay and lesbian scene. **StandOut Destinations** (www.standoutdestinations.com) gives a gay perspective to the travel experience, covering not only destinations but also gay-specific travel issues.

Chapter 9

Taking Care of the Remaining Details

*B*esides deciding on an itinerary and booking your flight, what else do you have to do? This chapter answers questions about obtaining or renewing a passport, deciding whether to purchase additional insurance, figuring out what to pack, and staying in touch while you're away from home.

Getting a Passport

A valid passport is the only legal form of identification accepted around the world; you can't cross an international border without it. Wherever you enter Europe, an official stamps your passport with a visa that is valid for 90 days within the same country. (If you plan to visit longer in any one country, you can get a specific visa by contacting any of the country's consulates in the United States before you leave, or any U.S. consulate when you're abroad.)

 Getting a passport is easy, but the process takes some time. For an up-to-date country-by-country listing of passport requirements around the world, go to the Web site of the U.S. State Department at `http://travel.state.gov` and start at "Country Specific Information."

Applying for a U.S. passport

If you're applying for a passport for the first time, follow these steps:

1. Complete a **passport application** in person at a U.S. passport office; a federal, state, or probate court; or a major post office. To find your regional passport office, check the **U.S. State Department** Web site (http://travel.state.gov/passport) or call the **National Passport Information Center** (☎ 877-487-2778) for automated information.

2. Present a **certified birth certificate** as proof of citizenship. (Bringing along your driver's license, state or military ID, or Social Security card is also a good idea.)

3. Submit **two identical passport-size photos,** measuring 2 × 2 inches. You often find businesses near a passport office that take these photos. *Note:* You can't use a strip from a photo-vending machine because the pictures aren't identical.

4. Pay a **fee.** For people 16 and over, a passport is valid for ten years and costs $97. For those 15 and under, a passport is valid for five years and costs $82. For expedited service, add $60 per passport application.

If you have a passport in your current name that was issued within the past 15 years (and you were over age 16 when it was issued), you can renew the passport by mail for $67.

Whether you're applying in person or by mail, you can download passport applications from the U.S. State Department Web site at http://travel.state.gov/passport. For general information, call the **National Passport Agency** (☎ 202-647-0518). To find your regional passport office, either check the U.S. State Department Web site or call the **National Passport Information Center** toll-free number (☎ 877-487-2778) for automated information.

 Allow plenty of time before your trip to apply for a passport; at press time, standard processing took four to six weeks; expedited service, which requires an additional fee, took two weeks. If you use the expedited service, it's also a good idea to arrange overnight delivery (for an extra charge) to send your passport application and receive your passport.

Applying for other passports

The following list offers more information for citizens of Australia, Canada, New Zealand, and the United Kingdom:

- **Australians** can pick up an application from your local post office or any branch of Passports Australia, but you must schedule an interview at the passport office to present your application materials. Call the **Australian Passport Information Service** (☎ 131-232), or visit the government Web site (www.passports.gov.au).

✔ **Canadians** can pick up applications at travel agencies throughout Canada or from the central **Passport Office,** Department of Foreign Affairs and International Trade, Ottawa, ON K1A 0G3 (☎ 800-567-6868; www.ppt.gc.ca). *Note:* Canadian children who travel must have their own passports.

✔ Residents of **Ireland** can apply for a ten-year passport at the **Passport Office,** Setanta Centre, Molesworth Street, Dublin 2 (☎ 01-671-1633; www.irlgov.ie/iveagh). Those under age 18 and over 65 must apply for a three-year passport. You can also apply at 1A South Mall, Cork (☎ 21-494-4700), or at most main post offices.

✔ **New Zealanders** can pick up a passport application at any New Zealand Passports Office or download it from their Web site. Contact the **Passports Office** at ☎ 0800-225-050 in New Zealand or 04-474-8100, or log on to www.passports.govt.nz.

✔ **United Kingdom** residents can pick up applications for a standard ten-year passport (five-year passport for children 15 and under) at passport offices, major post offices, or travel agencies. For information, contact the **United Kingdom Passport Service** (☎ 0870-521-0410; www.ukpa.gov.uk).

 When you receive your passport, make a photocopy of the first two pages and bring it with you; it'll come in handy if, for any reason, you need to replace a lost or stolen passport.

If you lose your passport while traveling, *immediately* find the nearest U.S. embassy or consulate. Bring any forms of identification so that they can process a new passport for you.

Always carry your passport with you, safely tucked away in your money belt or in a vest pocket that you can button. Take it out only when necessary, such as at the bank while changing traveler's checks, for the guards to verify when crossing borders, or for the train conductor on overnight journeys by couchette.

 European hotels customarily register all guests with the local police. When you check in to your hotel (particularly in southern Europe), the desk clerk may ask to keep your passport overnight (to fill out the paperwork when business is slow). To avoid having your passport get lost or misplaced, ask the desk clerk to fill out your paperwork while you wait, or arrange to pick it up in a few hours.

Playing It Safe with Travel and Medical Insurance

Three kinds of travel insurance are available: trip-cancellation insurance, medical insurance, and lost-luggage insurance. The cost of travel insurance varies widely, depending on the cost and length of your trip, your age and health, and the type of trip you're taking. You can get estimates from various providers through **InsureMyTrip.com**. Enter your trip cost and dates, your age, and other information, for prices from more than a dozen companies. Here is our advice on all three:

- ✔ **Trip-cancellation insurance** helps you get your money back if you have to back out of a trip, if you must go home early, or if your travel supplier goes bankrupt. Allowed reasons for cancellation can range from sickness to natural disasters to the U.S. State Department declaring your destination unsafe for travel.

  A good resource is **Travel Guard Alerts**, a list of travel suppliers considered high-risk by Travel Guard International (www.travel guard.com). Protect yourself further by paying for the insurance with a credit card — by law, you can get your money back on goods and services not received if you report the loss within 60 days after the charge is listed on your credit-card statement.

  Note: Many tour operators, particularly those offering trips to remote or high-risk areas, include insurance in the cost of the trip or can arrange insurance policies through a partnering provider, a convenient and often cost-effective way for the traveler to obtain insurance. Make sure the tour company is a reputable one, however. Some experts suggest that you avoid buying insurance from the tour or cruise company you're traveling with, saying you're better off buying from a third-party insurer than you are putting all your money in one place.

- ✔ If you have health coverage at home, buying **medical insurance** for your trip doesn't make sense for most travelers. For travel overseas, most health plans (including Medicare and Medicaid) do not provide coverage, and the ones that do often require you to pay for services up front and reimburse you only after you return home. Even if your plan does cover overseas treatment, most out-of-country hospitals make you pay your bills up front, and send you a refund only after you've returned home and filed the necessary paperwork with your insurance company. As a safety net, you may want to buy travel medical insurance, particularly if you're traveling to a remote or high-risk area where emergency evacuation is a possible scenario. If you require additional medical insurance, try **MEDEX Assistance** (☎ 410-453-6300; www.medexassist.com) or **Travel Assistance International** (☎ 800-821-2828; www.travel assistance.com).

- ✔ **Lost-luggage insurance** is not necessary for most travelers. On domestic flights, checked baggage is covered up to $2,500 per ticketed passenger. On international flights (including U.S. portions of international trips), baggage coverage is limited to approximately $9.07 per pound, up to approximately $635 per checked bag. If you plan to check items more valuable than the standard liability, find out if your valuables are covered by your homeowner's policy or get baggage insurance as part of your comprehensive travel-insurance package. Don't buy insurance at the airport — it's usually over-priced. Be sure to take any valuables or irreplaceable items with you in your carry-on luggage; many valuables (including books, money, and electronics) aren't covered by airline policies.

If your luggage is lost, immediately file a lost-luggage claim at the airport, detailing the luggage contents. For most airlines, you must report delayed, damaged, or lost baggage within four hours of arrival. The airlines are required to deliver luggage, once found, directly to your house or destination free of charge.

For more information, contact one of the following recommended insurers: **Access America** (☎ **866-807-3982;** www.accessamerica. com), **Travel Guard International** (☎ **800-826-4919;** www.travel guard.com), **Travel Insured International** (☎ **800-243-3174;** www. travelinsured.com), and **Travelex Insurance Services** (☎ **888-457-4602;** www.travelex-insurance.com).

Staying Healthy when You Travel

Getting sick on vacation is bad enough, but trying to find a doctor in a foreign country can add to the stress of being ill. Bring all your medications with you, as well as an extra prescription in case you run out. Ask your doctor to write out the generic, chemical form rather than a brand name to avoid any confusion at foreign pharmacies. And note that it's not always possible to bring a U.S. prescription into a European pharmacy to get it filled; in some countries, you'll have to find a licensed doctor to write the prescription for you.

Check with your health-insurance provider to find out the extent of your coverage outside your home area. For travel abroad, you may have to pay all medical costs up front and be reimbursed later. For information on purchasing additional medical insurance for your trip, see the preceding section.

Avoiding "economy-class syndrome"

Deep vein thrombosis or, as it's known in the world of flying, "economy-class syndrome" is a blood clot that develops in a deep vein. It's a potentially deadly condition that can be caused by sitting in cramped conditions — such as an airplane cabin — for too long. During a flight (especially a long-haul flight), get up, walk around, and stretch your legs every 60 to 90 minutes to keep your blood flowing. Other preventive measures include frequent flexing of the legs while sitting, drinking lots of water, and avoiding alcohol and sleeping pills. If you have a history of deep vein thrombosis, heart disease, or another condition that puts you at high risk, some experts recommend wearing compression stockings or taking anticoagulants when you fly; always ask your physician about the best course for you. Symptoms of deep vein thrombosis include leg pain or swelling, or even shortness of breath.

If you have a serious and/or chronic illness, talk to your doctor before leaving on a trip. For conditions such as epilepsy, diabetes, or heart problems, wear a **MedicAlert identification tag** (☎ 888-633-4298 or 209-669-2450 outside the U.S.; www.medicalert.org), which immediately alerts doctors to your condition and gives them access to your records through MedicAlert's 24-hour hot line. Contact the **International Association for Medical Assistance to Travelers (IAMAT; ☎ 716-754-4883** or, in Canada, 416-652-0137; www.iamat.org) for tips on travel and health concerns in the countries you're visiting, and lists of local, English-speaking doctors. The U.S. **Centers for Disease Control and Prevention** (☎ 800-311-3435; www.cdc.gov) provides up-to-date information on health hazards by region or country and offers tips on food safety. If you do get sick, ask the concierge at your hotel to recommend a local doctor — even his own doctor, if necessary — or contact the local U.S. embassy for a list of English-speaking doctors. If a situation requiring emergency medical assistance arises while you're traveling, call for an ambulance; emergency numbers are listed in the "Fast Facts" section at the end of each destination chapter in this book.

Dealing with European Healthcare

Europeans often rely on their local pharmacist to treat their ailments. So even if you don't speak the language, just walk up to the counter, groan, and point to whatever hurts.

If your condition requires further medical attention, you can visit any European hospital. (Don't worry: Most hospitals have English-speaking doctors.) Many European countries practice semi- or fully socialized medicine, so they may send you on your way with a prescription and a small medical bill.

If you must pay for healthcare, especially overnight care or other costly procedures, most health-insurance plans and HMOs foot some of the bill. Many plans require you to pay the expenses up front but reimburse you when you get back. (Save your hospital receipt; you need it to fill out claim forms.) Members of **Blue Cross/Blue Shield** can use their cards at certain hospitals in most major cities worldwide, which means lower out-of-pocket costs. For more information, call ☎ **800-810-BLUE** (800-810-2583) or go to www.bluecares.com for a list of participating hospitals.

Making Reservations for Popular Restaurants, Events, and Sights

If you want to be certain that you'll get tickets for special events or performances (the opera, a symphony concert, seasonal festivals), a reservation at a special restaurant, or admission to an extraordinary museum, think about booking these activities before you leave (or at least a few days ahead while on the road).

Top restaurants in Paris, London, and other major cities can have waiting lists up to two or three weeks long. Often, you can call the day before (or the day of) your planned dinner and get a reservation, but you may want to call further ahead to ensure a table at restaurants with hot, haute reputations.

Increase your chances of landing a table at a coveted eatery by reserving for lunch rather than the more popular dinner hour. Also, while traveling, you may want to reserve dinners at special restaurants a day or so ahead of time if missing a meal there would be a big disappointment.

If you want to make sure that you see a special musical or play in the West End, the Vienna Boys Choir, an opera at the ancient Roman amphitheater in Verona (or at any of Europe's opera houses), a symphony concert with a famous orchestra, or Shakespeare at the Globe, reserve your tickets several weeks before you leave. Call the box office direct, book at the theater's Web site (which allows you to peruse the schedule and pick your performance), or contact the local tourist office. Expect to pay a small service charge.

You can also contact a ticketing agency such as **Keith Prowse** (the U.K., France, Italy, Czech Republic, Austria, and Ireland; ☎ **800-669-8687**; www.keithprowse.com), **Edwards & Edwards/Global Tickets** (all of Europe; ☎ **800-223-6108**), or **Tickets.com** (the U.K., the Netherlands, Germany, Ireland, and Belgium).

If you don't have time before you leave, try to reserve tickets when you first arrive in town. To find out what's playing, pick up the local events magazine — such as *Time Out* in London or *Pariscope* in Paris — at a newsstand.

At several museums and sights across Europe (especially in Italy), you can call ahead and reserve an entry time. This feature can save you hours of standing in line at popular places such as Florence's Uffizi and Rome's Galleria Borghese (where reservations are mandatory and sell out weeks ahead of time).

Sights worth reserving ahead for are the Lipizzaner Horse Show in Vienna, the Galleria Borghese and Papal Audiences in Rome, the Uffizi Galleries and the Accademia (Michelangelo's *David*) in Florence, the Secret Itineraries tour of the Doge's Palace in Venice, Buckingham Palace and the Houses of Parliament summer tours in London, and the Military Tattoo at Edinburgh Castle in Scotland.

Even if a museum or sight does not offer advance booking, you may still be able to skip to the head of the line by buying a special attractions pass at the city's tourist office; the Paris Museum Pass, for example, allows you immediate entry at dozens of museums with no waiting.

Packing It Up

Here's a helpful packing suggestion: Take everything you think you need and lay it out on the bed. Now get rid of half. You'll have a better trip, and be more mobile, if you carry less.

So what are the bare essentials? Comfortable walking shoes, a camera, a versatile sweater and/or jacket, an all-purpose coat or windbreaker, a belt, toiletries, medications (pack these in your carry-on bag), and something to sleep in. Unless you attend a board meeting, a funeral, or one of the city's finest restaurants, you don't need a dress suit or a fancy dress. For everyday wear, you can rely on a pair of jeans or comfortable trousers and a sweater or pullover.

Put things that may leak, like shampoo and suntan lotion, in zippered plastic bags. Finally, put a distinctive identification tag on the outside so your bag is easy to spot on the luggage carousel.

Dressing as the locals do

Over the past couple of decades, a kind of universal, homogenous, brand-name fashion consciousness has erased many of the differences between younger Europeans and their American counterparts. If it's cool at home, it'll probably be considered cool in Europe. Older and more sophisticated Europeans, however, are still known for their savvy fashion sense. In Europe, even casual can be pretty chic.

Of course, comfort is essential, but you may feel more at ease if you look less like a tourist. Leave the silly garments at home (you know what they are) and pack a sensible, sporty outfit. If you're bringing only one pair of shoes, make sure they're comfortable and all-purpose enough so that you can wear them to restaurants and dressier spots. Nothing gives away the American traveler faster than running shoes worn for every occasion. In some classier restaurants, you may encounter a "smart casual" dress code, which means that no jeans or running shoes are allowed and that men must wear a jacket (sometimes a tie as well). Europe in general is becoming more casual about clothing, but dressing up for a special occasion or an evening out remains an important part of European life.

If your travel plans include visiting churches and cathedrals, keep in mind that some adhere to strict dress codes. St. Peter's Basilica in Rome, for example, turns people away who show too much skin. Plan ahead: Wear shorts or skirts that fall past the knee and shirts that cover your shoulders. During warmer seasons, layer a shirt over or under a sleeveless jumper, and in cooler temperatures, an oversize scarf can substitute for a wrap — a very chic look! Men, please leave behind the sleeveless T-shirts.

Sporting money belts

Many travelers like to tote their most important documents, such as plane tickets, rail passes, traveler's checks, credit cards, driver's license, and passport, in a money belt.

Money belts are flat pouches worn under clothing. You can choose from three kinds: one that dangles from your neck; one that fastens around your waist, over your shirttails but under your pants (larger and more safely concealed, but less comfortable); and one that sways by your pants leg, attached to your belt by a loop.

Don't take any keys except your house key and leave behind any unnecessary wallet items (department-store and gas-station credit cards, library cards, and so on).

Traveling without electronics

Electronics take up valuable luggage space, waste too much time, and blow hotel fuses. And you spend way too much time worrying about losing them or having them ripped off. In other words, leave them at home. Open your eyes and ears to Europe's sights and sounds! Take a small battery-operated alarm clock and maybe a small camera — and that's it.

If you're determined to lug around half of an electronics store, consider the following: American current runs on 110V and 60 cycles, and European current runs on 210V to 220V and 50 cycles. Don't expect to plug an American appliance into a European outlet without harming your appliance or blowing a fuse. You need a currency converter or transformer to decrease the voltage and increase the cycles.

You can find plug adapters and converters at most travel, luggage, electronics, and hardware stores.

Travel-size versions of popular items such as irons, hair dryers, shavers, and so on come with dual voltage, which means they have built-in converters (usually you must turn a switch to go back and forth). Most contemporary camcorders and laptop computers automatically sense the current and adapt accordingly — be sure to check the manuals, the bottom of the machine, or with the manufacturer to make sure you don't fry your appliance.

Mastering Communication

This section helps you figure out how to call another country — for example, in case you need to make advance reservations or book a hotel before you leave — and how to stay in touch while you're away from home.

Calling Europe from the United States

When calling Europe from the United States, you must first dial the **international access code (011)**, then the **country code,** and then (sometimes) the **city code** (usually dropping the initial 0, or in Spain's case, the initial 9). Country and city codes are listed in the "Fast Facts" section of each destination chapter in this book.

Only when you're calling a city from another area within the same country do you dial the initial 0 (or 9).

 Many countries (France, Italy, and Spain, among others) are now incorporating the separate city codes into the numbers themselves. In some cases, you still drop the initial 0; in others you do not. If all this seems confusing, don't worry: The rules for dialing each city are included in the destination chapters in this book.

Calling home from Europe

 No matter which calling method you choose, overseas phone rates are costly. But some money pits are avoidable. For example, *never* make a transatlantic call from your hotel room, unless you can spare lots of cash. Surcharges tacked onto your hotel bill can amount to a whopping 400 percent over what you pay if you make the call from a public pay phone. Most hotels even overcharge for local calls. Just ignore the phone in your hotel room; look for one in a nearby bar or cafe instead.

 Using a calling card is the simplest and most inexpensive way to call home from overseas. (Some credit cards even double as calling cards.) You just dial a local number — which is usually free, but keep in mind that some hotels will charge you for it — and then punch in the number you're calling plus the calling-card number (often your home phone number plus a four-digit PIN). The card comes with a wallet-size list of local access numbers in each country (these numbers are listed in the "Fast Facts" section of each destination chapter in this book). Before leaving home, set up a calling-card account with AT&T, MCI, or Sprint. If you're calling from a non-touch-tone country such as Italy, just wait for an American operator, who will put your call through, or for the automated system in which you speak your card's numbers out loud.

To make a collect call, dial a phone company's number and wait for the operator.

 Phone companies offer a range of calling-card programs. When you set up an account, tell the representative that you want the program and card most appropriate for making multiple calls from Europe to the United States.

Calling from the United States to Europe is often much cheaper than the other way around, so you may want to ask friends and family to call you at your hotel instead of you calling them. If you must dial direct from

Europe to the United States, first dial the international access code (often, but not always, 00), and then the country code for the United States (which is 1). After that 001, just punch in the area code and number as usual.

Using European pay phones

European and North American pay phones operate similarly. You'll find three types of phones in Europe: coin-operated, phone-card only (most common), and a hybrid of the two. Phone-card units are quickly replacing coin-operated phones all over the Continent.

Slide the phone card into the phone as you would an ATM card at a cash machine. You can buy prepaid cards in increments equivalent to as little as $2 or as much as $30, depending on the country. Single-country phone cards come in handy only if you plan on staying for a while or if you want to make direct long-distance calls. If you're visiting for only a few days and expect to make mainly local calls, just use pocket change or a smaller-increment prepaid card.

Calling cards (described in the preceding section) have made phoning North America from Europe cheap and easy from any pay phone, but some traditionalists still prefer heading to the post office or international phone office, where you make your call on a phone with a meter and then pay when you're done. This method is no cheaper than direct dialing from a pay phone, but at least you don't need to worry about remembering a bunch of numbers to get through.

Staying connected by cellphone

The three letters that define much of the world's **wireless capabilities** are GSM (Global System for Mobiles), a big, seamless network that makes for easy cross-border cellphone use throughout Europe and dozens of other countries worldwide. In the U.S., T-Mobile and AT&T Wireless use this quasi-universal system; in Canada, Fido and some Rogers customers are GSM; and all Europeans and most Australians use GSM.

If your cellphone is on a GSM system, and you have a world-capable multiband phone (Sony, Ericsson, Motorola, or Samsung all make models with this capability), you can make and receive calls across much of the globe. Just call your wireless operator and ask for international roaming to be activated on your account. Unfortunately, per-minute charges can be high, usually $1 to $1.50 in Western Europe.

That's why buying an "unlocked" world phone is important. Many cellphone operators sell "locked" phones that restrict you from using any removable computer memory phone chip (called a **SIM card**) other than the ones they supply. Having an unlocked phone allows you to install a cheap, prepaid SIM card (found at a local retailer) in your destination country. (Show your phone to the salesperson; not all phones work on all networks.) You'll get a local phone number and much, much lower calling rates. Getting an already locked phone unlocked can be a complicated process, but it can be done; just call your cellular operator and say you'll be going abroad for several months and want to use the phone with a local provider.

For many, **renting** a phone is a good idea. Although you can rent a phone from any number of overseas sites — including kiosks at airports — we suggest renting the phone before you leave home. That way you can give loved ones and business associates your new number, make sure the phone works, and take the phone wherever you go. This option is especially helpful for overseas trips through several countries, where local phone-rental agencies often bill in local currency and may not let you take the phone to another country.

Phone rental isn't cheap. You'll usually pay $40 to $50 per week, plus airtime fees of at least a dollar a minute. If you're traveling to Europe, though, local rental companies often offer free incoming calls within their home country, which can save you big bucks. The bottom line: Shop around.

Two good wireless rental companies are **InTouch USA** (☎ **800-872-7626**) and **RoadPost** (☎ **888-290-1606** or 905-272-5665; www.roadpost.com). You may find cheaper rates by renting through one of the big car-rental agencies, such as AutoEurope (www.autoeurope.com) or Avis (www.avis.com). Give them your itinerary, and they'll tell you what wireless products you need. InTouch will also, for free, advise you on whether your existing phone will work overseas; simply call ☎ **703-222-7161** between 9 a.m. and 4 p.m. EST, or go to http://intouchglobal.com/travel.htm.

Accessing the Internet in Europe

Travelers in Europe have any number of ways to check their e-mail and access the Internet while on the road. Of course, using your own laptop — or even a personal digital assistant (PDA) or electronic organizer with a modem — gives you the most flexibility. But even if you don't have a computer, you can still access your e-mail and even your office computer from cybercafes.

Nowadays, finding a city that *doesn't* have a few cybercafes is difficult. Although no definitive directory for cybercafes exists, two places to start looking are www.cybercaptive.com and www.cybercafe.com.

Aside from formal cybercafes, most **youth hostels** nowadays have at least one computer you can use to access the Internet, and most **public libraries** across the world offer Internet access free or for a small charge. Inexpensive hotels often have an Internet terminal in the lobby that you can use for free or pretty cheaply, but avoid **business centers** in the pricier hotels or in international chain properties, unless you're willing to pay exorbitant rates.

Most major airports now have **Internet kiosks** scattered throughout their gate areas. These kiosks, which you'll also see in tourist information offices, give you basic Web access for a per-minute fee that's usually higher than cybercafe prices. The kiosks' clunkiness and high price mean they should be avoided whenever possible.

To retrieve your e-mail, ask your **Internet Service Provider (ISP)** if it has a Web-based interface tied to your existing e-mail account. If your ISP doesn't have such an interface, you can use the free **mail2web** service (www.mail2web.com) to view and reply to your home e-mail. For more flexibility, you may want to open a free, Web-based e-mail account with **Yahoo! Mail** (http://mail.yahoo.com) or Microsoft's **Hotmail** (www.hotmail.com). Your home ISP may be able to forward your e-mail to the Web-based account automatically.

If you need to access files on your office computer, look into a service called **GoToMyPC** (www.gotomypc.com). The service provides a Web-based interface for you to access and manipulate a distant PC from anywhere — even a cybercafe — provided your "target" PC is turned on and has an always-on connection to the Internet (such as with a cable modem or DSL). The service offers top-quality security, but if you're worried about hackers, use your own laptop rather than a cybercafe computer to access the GoToMyPC system.

If you're bringing your own computer, which is frankly a hassle on a pleasure trip, **Wi-Fi** hot spots in hotels, cafes, and retailers provide high-speed connection without cable wires, networking hardware, or a phone line. You can get Wi-Fi connection one of several ways. Many laptops sold today have built-in Wi-Fi capability (an 802.11b wireless Ethernet connection). Mac owners have their own networking technology, Apple AirPort. For those with older computers, an 802.11b/**Wi-Fi card** can be plugged into your laptop.

You sign up for wireless access service much as you do cellphone service, through a plan offered by one of several commercial companies that have made wireless service available in airports, hotel lobbies, and coffee shops, primarily in the U.S. (followed by the U.K. and Japan). **Boingo** (www.boingo.com) and **Wayport** (www.wayport.com) have set up networks in airports and high-class hotel lobbies. iPass providers also give you access to a few hundred wireless hotel-lobby setups. Best of all, you don't need to be staying at the Four Seasons to use the hotel's network; just set yourself up on a nice couch in the lobby. The companies' pricing policies can be byzantine, with a variety of monthly, per-connection, and per-minute plans, but in general you pay around $30 a month for limited access — and as more and more companies jump on the wireless bandwagon, prices are likely to get even more competitive.

There are also places that provide **free wireless networks** in cities around the world. To locate these free hot spots, go to http://wiki.personal telco.net/WirelessCommunities.

If Wi-Fi is not available in your destination, most business-class hotels throughout the world offer dataports for laptop modems, and many hotels in Europe now offer free high-speed Internet access using an Ethernet network cable. You can bring your own cables (another hassle), but most hotels rent them for around $10. Call your hotel in advance to find out your options.

In addition, major ISPs have **local access numbers** around the world, allowing you to go online by simply placing a local call. Check your ISP's Web site or call its toll-free number and ask how you can use your current account away from home, and how much it'll cost. If you're traveling outside the reach of your ISP, the **iPass** network has dial-up numbers in most of the world's countries. You'll have to sign up with an iPass provider, who will then tell you how to set up your computer for each of your destinations. For a list of iPass providers, go to www.ipass.com and click on Individual Purchase. One solid provider is **i2roam** (☎ **866-811-6209** or 920-235-0475; www.i2roam.com).

Wherever you go, bring a **connection kit** of the right power and phone adapters, a spare phone cord, and a spare Ethernet network cable — or find out if your hotel supplies them to guests. European phone-jack converters and line testers are available from some travel and electronics stores and from catalogs such as Magellan's (www.magellans.com) or TravelSmith (www.travelsmith.com). Many European phone lines use the pulse system rather than touch-tone, so you may need to configure your dial-up software settings to cope.

Keeping Up with Airline Security Measures

With the federalization of airport security, security procedures at U.S. airports have generally become more stable and consistent. Generally, you'll be fine if you arrive at the airport at least **two hours** before an international flight.

Obviously, bring your **passport.** Be prepared to show it several times — to airline employees asking security questions, to the clerks checking you in, to the Transportation Security Administration (TSA) officials at the security checkpoint, and, on Europe-bound flights, to the gate attendants before you board the aircraft.

Many travelers have grown accustomed to paperless E-tickets, curbside luggage check-in, timesaving kiosks, and even checking in for flights online. But when you're flying internationally, you're still required to wait in line for check-in, answer security questions, show your passport, and then proceed to the security checkpoint with your boarding pass and photo ID.

Security checkpoint lines are getting shorter, but some doozies remain. If you have trouble standing for long periods of time, tell an airline employee; the airline will provide a wheelchair. Speed up security by **not**

wearing metal objects such as big belt buckles or oversized jewelry. If you have metallic body parts, a note from your doctor can prevent a long chat with the security screeners. Keep in mind that only **ticketed passengers** are allowed past security, except for folks escorting passengers or children with disabilities.

Federalization has standardized **what you can carry through security** and **what you can't.** The general rule is that sharp objects and bottled water are out, and nail clippers are okay. Any liquids or gels must be in a small container (3.4 ounces or less) and placed in a see-through quart-size plastic bag, which is put separately through the scanner. (After you've passed through security, you can buy bottled water and bring it on the plane.) Food and beverages you bring with you to the airport (rather than those purchased beyond the initial security screening checkpoints) must be passed through the X-ray machine. Travelers are generally allowed **one carry-on bag, plus one personal item** such as a purse, briefcase, or laptop bag. Carry-on hoarders can stuff all sorts of things into a laptop bag; as long as it has a laptop in it, it's still considered a personal item. The TSA has issued a list of restricted items; check its Web site (www.tsa.gov) for details.

Airport screeners may decide that your checked luggage needs to be searched by hand. Although the TSA recommends that you do not lock your checked luggage (because, if they search it, they have to break the locks), you can now purchase **TSA-approved locks** (also called Travel Sentry–certified and marked with a red diamond logo), which agents are able to unlock with a special key and secret combination. Check www.tsa.gov for a list of approved locks and the retailers who sell them. For more information on the locks, visit www.travelsentry.org.

Bringing Your Goodies Back Home

You *can* take your European goodies home with you, but restrictions exist for how much you can bring back for *free.* If you go over a certain amount, Customs officials impose taxes.

The personal exemption rule (how much you can bring back into the United States without paying a duty on it) is $800 worth of goods per person. On the first $1,000 worth of goods over $800, you pay a flat 3 percent duty. Beyond that, it works on an item-by-item basis. There are a few restrictions on amount: 1 liter of alcohol (you must be 21 or over), 200 cigarettes, and 100 cigars. Antiques more than 100 years old and works of fine art are exempt from the $800 limit, as is anything you mail home.

 You can mail yourself $200 worth of goods duty-free once a day; mark the package "For Personal Use." You can also mail gifts to other people without paying duty as long as the recipient doesn't receive more than $100 worth of gifts in a single day. Label each gift package "Unsolicited Gift." Any package must state on the exterior a description of the contents and their values. You can't mail alcohol, perfume (it contains alcohol), or tobacco products worth more than $5.

Items bought at a duty-free shop before returning to the United States still count toward your U.S. Customs limit. The "duty" that you're avoiding in these shops is the local tax on the item (such as state sales tax in the United States), not any import duty that may be levied by the U.S. Customs office.

If you need more information or would like to see a list of specific items you can't bring into the United States, check out the **U.S. Customs and Border Protection** Web site (www.cbp.gov).

The following list outlines a few items for residents of Canada, Australia, and New Zealand.

✔ Canada allows its residents of legal age a C$750 exemption, and you're allowed to bring back duty-free 200 cigarettes, 2.2 pounds of tobacco, 40 imperial ounces of liquor, and 50 cigars. In addition, you're allowed to mail gifts to Canada from abroad at the rate of C$60 a day, provided they're unsolicited and don't contain alcohol or tobacco (write on the package "Unsolicited gift, under $60 value"). *Note:* The C$750 exemption can be used only once a year and only after an absence of seven days. For a clear summary of Canadian rules, write for the booklet *I Declare,* issued by the **Canada Border Services Agency,** 2265 St. Laurent Blvd., Ottawa, ON K1G 4KE (☎ **800-461-9999** or 204-983-3500; www.cbsa-asfc.gc.ca).

✔ The duty-free allowance in Australia is A$900 or, for those 17 and under, A$450. Citizens 18 and older can bring in 250 cigarettes or 250 grams of loose tobacco and 2.25 liters of alcohol. A helpful brochure available from Australian consulates or Customs offices is *Know Before You Go.* For more information, call the **Australian Customs Service** at ☎ **1300-363-263,** or log on to www.customs.gov.au.

✔ The duty-free allowance for New Zealand is NZ$700. Citizens 18 and over can bring in 200 cigarettes or 50 cigars or 250 grams of tobacco (or a mixture of all three if their combined weight does not exceed 250 grams), plus 4.5 liters of wine and beer or 1.125 liters of liquor. New Zealand currency does not carry import or export restrictions. Most questions are answered in a free pamphlet available at New Zealand consulates and Customs offices: *New Zealand Customs Guide for Travellers, Notice no. 4.* For more information, contact **New Zealand Customs Service,** 17–21 Whitmore St., Box 2218, Wellington (☎ **04-473-6099** or 0800-428-786; www.customs.govt.nz).

Part III
The British Isles

The 5th Wave   By Rich Tennant

"Let me ask you a question. Are you planning to kiss the Blarney Stone, or ask for its hand in marriage?"

In this part . . .

A visit to the British Isles makes for a memorable, adventurous stop on any European vacation. London, the capital of the U.K., is considered by many to be the most exciting city in Europe, filled with an inexhaustible array of charms and attractions. From London, it's easy to make fascinating day trips to other parts of England, including Bath, Oxford, and the perennially mysterious ancient stones of Stonehenge. Farther north, in scenic Scotland, you can explore Edinburgh, hike the heather-clad highlands, and go "Nessie" hunting on Loch Ness. To the west, charming Ireland beckons, offering cosmopolitan pleasures in Dublin and some of the most glorious scenery in the world.

Chapter 10

London and the Best of England

The wondrous city of London is home to Buckingham Palace and Big Ben, the Tower of London and the Crown Jewels, Westminster Abbey and St. Paul's Cathedral, Piccadilly Circus and the British Museum. That's just the beginning of what you can see and do in this huge, happening city on the Thames. Spend the evening at the latest West End play, attend an opera or symphony, dance until dawn at the hippest clubs, and have a pint in the same pubs where Charles Dickens hung out. And if that's not enough, you have the River Thames to cruise, the Tate Modern to peruse, and all the shopping you're up for. London also has some of the world's foremost museums, including exhaustive collections of historical artifacts, paintings, and antiquities, and a stunning array of parks and architectural treasures.

Anything less than three days in London is simply not enough time to appreciate all that's here; four or five days is more reasonable. With this chapter, no matter how many days you have, you can begin to plan your explorations of what many consider to be the most exciting city in Europe.

Getting There

Air travel is the most convenient option for getting to London, although if you're coming from the Continent you can always hop a ferry or take the super-fast Eurostar train from Paris or Brussels through the Channel Tunnel (*Chunnel* for short).

Arriving by air

Transatlantic flights usually land west of the city at **Heathrow Airport** (☎ 0870-000-0123; www.heathrowairport.com). From Heathrow, you can take a 15-minute ride on the Heathrow Express train (☎ 0845-600-1515; www.heathrowexpress.com), with departures every 15 minutes to London's Paddington Station. One-way standard-class fare is £15 ($30); you can buy tickets at the airport (machines and ticket windows) or, for a £3 ($6) extra charge, on the train. Another option is a leisurely 50-minute Underground ride on the Piccadilly Line, which runs through the center of town and may drop you off at a more convenient point closer to your hotel. One-way fare to Paddington Station is £4 ($8).

Some flights (especially from the Continent) and charter planes land at **Gatwick Airport** (☎ 0870-000-2468; www.gatwickairport.com), 48km (30 miles) south of London and a 30-minute ride (£17/$34 one-way) on the Gatwick Express to London's Victoria Station (☎ 0845-850-1530; www.gatwickexpress.com), or at **London Stansted Airport** (☎ 0870-000-0303; www.stanstedairport.com), 56km (35 miles) northeast of town and a 45-minute ride (£15/$30 one-way) to London's Liverpool Street Station on the Stansted Express (☎ 0845-850-0150; www.stansted express.com).

Some flights from Britain and northern Europe land at **London City Airport** (☎ 020-7646-0000; www.londoncityairport.com), 14km (9 miles) east of the center. The Docklands Light Railway takes you into central London (about 20 minutes). A one-way fare is £4 ($8). EasyJet and other no-frills/low-cost European airlines are making little **London Luton Airport** (☎ 01582-405-100; www.london-luton.co.uk), 48km (30 miles) northwest of the city, a busy hub for budget flights from other parts of Britain and the Continent. From Luton Airport, take the free shuttle bus (eight minutes) to Luton's rail station and connect to a train (30 minutes) to London's King's Cross Station or next-door neighbor St. Pancras Station; one-way fares are £11 to £17 ($22–$34).

Arriving by rail

Trains coming from Dover (where ferries from the Continent land) arrive at either **Victoria Station** or **Charing Cross Station,** both in the center of town (10½ hours total travel time from Paris via the ferry route).

The direct Eurostar trains (www.eurostar.com) that arrive from Paris and Brussels via the Channel Tunnel (a trip of three hours — two after you factor in the time change) pull into the newly refurbished **St. Pancras International Station** in the northern part of Central London. If you're coming from Edinburgh, you arrive at **King's Cross Station,** also in the northern part of the city.

England

Orienting Yourself in London

London is a huge, sprawling city with over 7.5 million residents. Urban expansion has been going on around London for centuries, and the 1,601 sq. km (618 sq. miles) of Greater London consist of many small towns and villages that have been incorporated over time. Officially, 33 boroughs divide London, but most of its residents still use traditional neighborhood names, which we do as well in this guide.

Most of Central London lies north of the Thames River and is more or less bounded by the Circle Line Tube route. Central London, where you'll find most of the must-see attractions, is divided into **The City** and the **West End.** Several performing arts venues and the megapopular Tate Modern sit on the **South Bank,** right on the Thames.

Introducing the neighborhoods

Located on what now is the eastern edge of London's center, **The City** is the ancient square mile where the Romans founded the original settlement of Londinium. This area is home to St. Paul's Cathedral, the Tower of London, world financial institutions, and Fleet Street, the one-time center of newspaper publishing.

The **West End** is much larger and harder to classify. This lively center of London's shopping, restaurant, nightlife, and museum scene includes many neighborhoods.

One old West End neighborhood, **Holborn,** lies alongside The City and is filled with the offices of lawyers and other professionals. North of this district, the British Museum and the University of London lend a literary, academic feel to **Bloomsbury.** West of Bloomsbury, **Fitzrovia** is an old writer's hangout with shops and pubs that fade into Soho to the south. Farther to the west, the area called **Marylebone** attracts visitors to Madame Tussaud's and the stamping grounds of the fictional Sherlock Holmes.

The areas below Bloomsbury get livelier. **Covent Garden** and **the Strand** comprise an upscale restaurant, entertainment, and shopping quarter. To the west, **Soho,** once a seedy red-light district, is cleaned up and contains numerous eateries and nightclubs, as well as London's Chinatown. To the south is **Piccadilly Circus/Leicester Square,** where you find the bulk of London's theaters; lots of crowded pubs, bars, and commercial clubs; the biggest movie houses; and Piccadilly Circus, which is a swirling square of traffic with a statue of Eros in its center and neon-faced superstores all around.

Southwest of Piccadilly Circus are the old, exclusive residential streets of **St. James's** (imagine an old gentlemen's club and expand it several blocks in each direction). Northwest of St. James's (and west of Soho) is fashionable **Mayfair,** which is full of pricey hotels and tony restaurants. **Westminster,** running along the western bank of the Thames's north–south stretch, is the heart and soul of political Britain, home to Parliament and Buckingham Palace, Queen Elizabeth II's London home. Westminster flows into Victoria to the south. Centered on Victoria train station, this neighborhood remains genteel and residential, but has lots of B&Bs and small hotels. Northwest of Victoria and west of Westminster is **Belgravia,** an old aristocratic zone full of stylish town houses that's just beyond the West End.

West of the West End, the neighborhoods are divided north–south by enormous **Hyde Park.** South of Hyde Park stretch the uniformly fashionable residential zones of **Knightsbridge, Kensington,** and **South Kensington,** which are also home to London's grandest shopping streets. (Harrods department store is in Knightsbridge.) South of Belgravia and South Kensington is the artists' and writers' quarter of **Chelsea,** which manages to keep hip with the changing times — Chelsea's King's Road is where miniskirts debuted in the 1960s and punk in the 1970s.

North of Hyde Park are the more middle-income residential neighborhoods of **Paddington, Bayswater,** and **Notting Hill,** popular among budget travelers for their abundance of bed-and-breakfasts (B&Bs) and inexpensive hotels. Nearby **Notting Hill Gate** has become a hip fashion and dining center in its own right.

On the other side of the Thames is **Southwark** (*Suh*-thuk) — where tourism has recently exploded, thanks to the opening of Shakespeare's Globe Theatre, the Tate Modern (connected to St. Paul's Cathedral and The City by the elegant pedestrian-only Millennium Bridge), and an assortment of lesser sights. It's also an arts and cultural center, with major performance venues such as Royal Festival Hall and the National Theatre.

On a first-time or quick visit, you probably won't venture too far beyond this huge area of central London. If you do, the most likely candidates are the revitalized **Docklands,** a major housing and business development of the 1980s, or the **East End,** part of the real, working class of London and home to many recent immigrants, but becoming trendier by the day.

If you're exploring London to any extent, one of your most useful purchases will be **"London A to Z,"** one of the world's greatest street-by-street maps. This publication is the only one that lists every tiny alley and dead-end lane of the maze that is London. You can buy one at any bookstore and most newsstands. (Z, by the way, is pronounced "zed.")

Finding information after you arrive

London's tourist office (see the "Fast Facts: London" section at the end of this chapter) will provide useful information, as will a copy of *Time Out: London,* sold at any newsstand.

The **London Information Centre** (☎ 020-7292-2333; www.london informationcentre.com), smack-dab in the middle of Leicester Square right next to the TKTS booth, offers a free London map and general information to visitors, including a hotel booking service. Like the square, the info center is open late — from 8 a.m. to midnight seven days a week.

Getting Around London

The city of London is too spread out for you to rely solely on your feet to get from here to there. Driving in the city is a nightmare, and taxis are pretty expensive. Fortunately, London has an extensive public transportation system. At any Tube station or tourist center, pick up a copy of the map/pamphlet "Tube & Bus," which outlines the major bus routes and includes a copy of the Tube map. For information on all London public-transport options (Tube, buses, light rail) call **Transport for London** at ☎ 020-7222-1234, or visit www.tfl.gov.uk.

You can hop aboard London's buses, the Tube, and light rail systems with the **Travelcard** (in this section we just discuss "off-peak" prices, which are valid after 9:30 a.m. Mon–Fri and any time weekends and public holidays). You buy tickets according to how many zones you'll need to ride through. Zone 1 covers all of Central London and all the major attractions you want to see on an average visit; zone 2 is the next concentric ring out, getting in most of the outlying attractions. Charts posted in Tube stations help you figure out in which zones you'll be traveling.

By Tube (subway)

The quickest and most popular way to get around town is by London's subway system, known locally as the Tube or the Underground. The Underground is a complex network of lines and interchanges that make getting anywhere in London easy. For travel time, count on an average of three minutes between Tube stops. You can pick up a free Tube map in any station, or see the inside back cover of this book.

You can buy tickets from machines (they take coins and £5, £10, and £20 notes) or manned booths in Tube stations. A single ticket in zones 1 to 6 costs £4 ($8) adults. Children 5 to 10 ride for free on the Tube when accompanied by an adult with a valid ticket, and 11- to 18-year-olds and students can get discounted tickets if they have an Oyster card (see the nearby box, "Travel fast and cheap by Oyster").

Paying a full-price one-way fare every time you use the Underground is prohibitively expensive. To save money, consider buying a **Travelcard** or the new **Oyster card,** about the size of a credit card and easy to use — you just touch it over an electronic reader pad when entering and leaving an Underground station or a bus. Not only will you save money with either option, but you'll enjoy the freedom of nipping around London without worrying about paying each time you step onto a bus or the Underground. A **Day Travelcard,** valid in zones 1 and 2, costs £5.50 ($11) adults and £3.40 ($6.80) children. Three-day Travelcards covering zones 1 and 2 cost £17 ($34) adults and £8.70 ($17) children.

Travel fast and cheap by Oyster

The new Oyster card entitles Londoners to all sorts of travel discounts, but London visitors can benefit, too. You can buy an Oyster (at any ticket window) and put up to £90 ($180) in credit on it. With the Oyster, you automatically get substantial discounts every time you travel. The cost of a trip on the Underground, for instance, drops from £4 ($8) to £1.50 ($3), and a bus fare from £2 ($4) to 90p ($1.80). What's more, the daily amount you spend is automatically capped, so no matter how much you travel, you spend less than you would with a Travelcard: For example, the Oyster cap for travel all day in zones 1 and 2 is £6.30 ($13), compared to the £6.80 ($14) you pay for a peak Day Travelcard valid for travel in these zones.

By bus

Although you can use the Tube and its many transfer stations to tunnel your way just about anywhere in London, we suggest you ride the bus a few times — but not during rush hour — because riding the bus gives you a much better feel for the city layout than when you travel underground.

Bus-stop signs with a red slashed circle on white are compulsory stops, so you just wait and the bus will stop for you; if the slashed circle is white on red, you're at a request stop, and you have to wave down the bus.

The bus system in London is changing — and, sadly, that includes replacing the famous double-decker buses with ones that are twice as long and bend in the middle — although the "heritage" double-deckers continue to operate on some routes in Central London. You may also encounter new energy-efficient hydro-powered buses. On older buses, you just board the bus and — if you don't have a Travelcard — pay the conductor cash. However, on newer, Pay Before You Board (PBYB) lines — distinguishable by the fact that the route numbers have a yellow background on bus-stop signs — you must either have a Travelcard or buy a ticket from a machine before you board (all bus lines that have become PBYB have ticket machines at each stop).

Either way, a regular ride costs £2 ($4) adults, free for children 16 and under (with valid ID). **One-day bus passes** are available for £3.50 ($7) adults; **weekly passes** are £13 ($26) adults.

By taxi

London's Tube and buses can get you around town nicely, but you can also opt for a ride in one of London's fabled and incredibly spacious black cabs. The drivers are highly trained and experienced, and also incredibly knowledgeable about London information. In fact, many people use these drivers as auxiliary city guides, asking them for information as they ride. Prices, however, are far from a bargain. Fares change depending on the time of day, speed, and distance traveled. Fares and any extra charges are displayed on the meter next to the driver. Hail a taxi on the street or find one at a taxi *rank* (stand) outside major rail stations, hotels, department stores, and museums. To call for a taxi (an extra £2/$4 charge), dial ☎ **020-7272-0272,** 020-7253-5000, or 020-7432-1432. Take note, though: The meter begins running as soon as the driver picks up the call. For more info, visit www.tfl.gov.uk/pco.

The basic taxi fare begins at £2.20 ($4.40) and rises in increments of 20p (40¢) every 160m (525 ft.) or 34.5 seconds. Tip your cabbie 10 percent to 15 percent of the total fare.

Minicabs are meterless taxis that operate out of offices rather than driving the streets for fares. Minicabs are more useful at night when the Tube stops running and fewer regular taxis are available. Make sure you get one that is licensed by the Public Carriage Office (indicated by a sticker in the window with the diamond-shaped LICENSED PRIVATE HIRE VEHICLE hologram). Negotiate the fare before you get into the minicab. You can find minicab stands in popular spots, such as Leicester Square, or call the numbers in the preceding paragraph. Women may prefer Lady Cabs, with only women drivers (☎ **020-7254-3501**).

By foot

London sprawls, and what appears to be a short jaunt may actually be an epic trek. There are, however, pleasant walks throughout the city. Try out the new Millennium Bridge between St. Paul's and the Tate Modern in Southwark, the colorful back streets of Soho, or the pedestrian-only riverside walk along the South Bank.

Staying in London

 Hotel rates in London come at premium prices, especially when compared to other large European cities. To avoid exorbitant room rates, your best bet is to find a B&B or small hotel offering low(er) rates. You may not sleep in luxury, but you'll be able to afford the rest of your trip. Many hotels offer **weekend breaks** or special seasonal discounts that can get you 20 percent to 50 percent off a room. Always check the hotel's Web site for special offers, and refer to Chapter 8 for more money-saving tips on finding the best hotel rate.

 The two best **hotel booking services** are run by the Visit London tourist board (☎ **08456-443-010** or 020-7932-2020; www.visitlondonoffers. com) and the private LondonTown (☎ **020-7437-4370;** www.london town.com). Both offer discounted rooms.

Britain sports two types of **bed-and-breakfasts** these days: the old pension-type inn — often worn about the edges, and pretty hit-or-miss, but costing from about £45 ($90) per person — and the upscale private-home type of B&Bs that burgeoned in the 1990s (at rates from £80/$160 on up per person, £95/$190 for double occupancy). The place to find the cream of the crop among the latter type is the **Bulldog Club** (☎ 0870-803-4414; www.bulldogclub.com), a reservation service that lists tasteful private-home accommodations throughout London and the U.K. Not quite as exclusive, but still representing upscale B&Bs and apartments, is **Uptown Reservations** (☎ 020-7937-2001; www.uptownres.co.uk). Solid midrange agencies include **London Homestead Services** (☎ 020-7286-5155; www.lhslondon.co.uk), **London Bed & Breakfast Agency** (☎ 020-7586-2768; www.londonbb.com), **London B and B** (☎ 800-872-2632 in the United States; www.londonbandb.com), and the **Independent Traveller** (☎ 01392-860-807; www.gowithit.co.uk).

You can also consider staying at a **self-catering hotel,** where *you* do the cooking in the kitchen in your hotel room. For short stays and for one or two people, self-catering hotels don't always beat the competition's price. But for families and travelers who can't afford or don't want to eat out every meal, self-catering hotels can be a budget-saver. For comfort and convenience, **Astons Apartments** in South Kensington is among the best (see the listing in the following section). If you're interested in finding other self-catering options in London, contact **Refresh Accommodation** (☎ 0845-680-0080; www.refreshaccommodation.com).

For general tips on booking and what to expect from European accommodations, see Chapter 7.

London's top hotels and B&Bs

Astons Apartments
$$ South Kensington

Astons offers value-packed accommodations in three carefully restored Victorian redbrick town houses. Each studio has a compact kitchenette (great for families on a budget), a small bathroom, and bright, functional furnishings. (Because you can cook on your in-room stove, the English call these accommodations "self-catering" units.) The more expensive designer studios feature larger bathrooms, more living space, and extra pizzazz in the décor. Four-person apartments are also available. If you like the idea of having your own cozy London apartment (with daily maid service, but no breakfast), you can't do better. Free cribs, baby tubs, and baby-bottle sterilization equipment are available.

See map p. 132. 39 Rosary Gardens (off Hereford Square). ☎ *800-525-2810 in the U.S. or 020-7590-6000. Fax: 020-7590-6060.* www.astons-apartments.com. *Tube: Gloucester Road. Rack rates: £99–£138 ($198–$276) double. Rates don't include 17.5 percent VAT. AE, MC, V.*

Accommodations, Dining, and Attractions in Central London

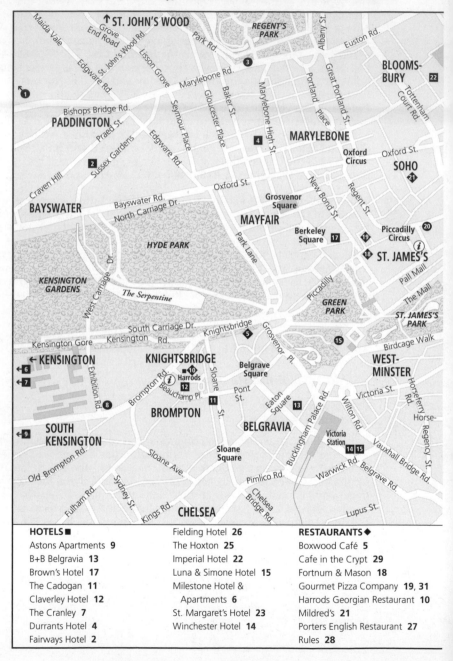

HOTELS ■

Astons Apartments **9**
B+B Belgravia **13**
Brown's Hotel **17**
The Cadogan **11**
Claverley Hotel **12**
The Cranley **7**
Durrants Hotel **4**
Fairways Hotel **2**

Fielding Hotel **26**
The Hoxton **25**
Imperial Hotel **22**
Luna & Simone Hotel **15**
Milestone Hotel &
 Apartments **6**
St. Margaret's Hotel **23**
Winchester Hotel **14**

RESTAURANTS ◆

Boxwood Café **5**
Cafe in the Crypt **29**
Fortnum & Mason **18**
Gourmet Pizza Company **19, 31**
Harrods Georgian Restaurant **10**
Mildred's **21**
Porters English Restaurant **27**
Rules **28**

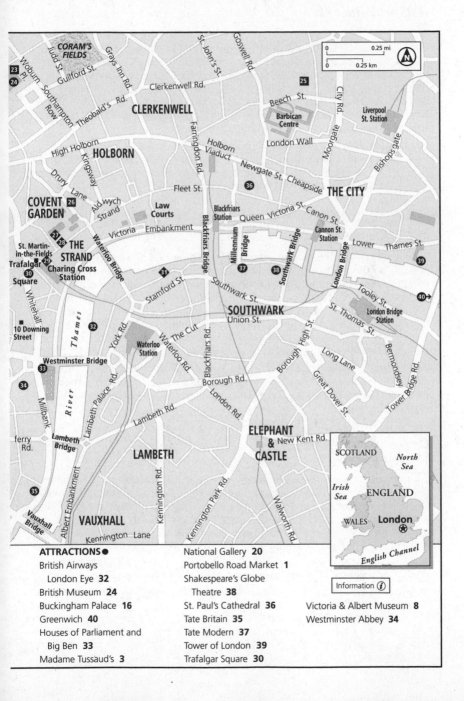

ATTRACTIONS●

British Airways
  London Eye **32**
British Museum **24**
Buckingham Palace **16**
Greenwich **40**
Houses of Parliament and
  Big Ben **33**
Madame Tussaud's **3**

National Gallery **20**
Portobello Road Market **1**
Shakespeare's Globe
  Theatre **38**
St. Paul's Cathedral **36**
Tate Britain **35**
Tate Modern **37**
Tower of London **39**
Trafalgar Square **30**

Victoria & Albert Museum **8**
Westminster Abbey **34**

Information ⓘ

B+B Belgravia
$$ Belgravia

Close to Victoria Station, this small, comfortable, and contemporary B&B favors simple, modern design over the old-fashioned chintzes and furniture of so many London B&Bs. Rooms have a spare, cool look and come with a tub or shower. The lobby is a nice little gathering spot where you can relax and get fresh tea and coffee 24/7. Breakfast is continental or English, cooked up right in front of your eyes in the open kitchen. Free wireless Internet access is available throughout.

See map p. 132. 64–66 Ebury St. ☎ *020-7259-8570. Fax: 020-7259-8591.* www.bb-belgravia.com. *Tube: Victoria (then a 10-minute walk south on Buckingham Palace Road, west on Eccleston Street, and south on Ebury Street). Rack rates: £107–£117 ($214–$234). English breakfast included. MC, V.*

The Cadogan
$$$$$ Chelsea

Memories of the Victorian era pervade this beautiful 65-room hotel, which is close to the exclusive Knightsbridge shops. The main floor includes a small, wood-paneled lobby and sumptuous drawing room (good for afternoon tea). The Cadogan (pronounced Ca-*dug*-en) is the hotel where Oscar Wilde was staying when he was arrested. (Room 118 is the Oscar Wilde Suite.) The large guest rooms, many overlooking Cadogan Place gardens, are quietly tasteful and splendidly comfortable, with large bathrooms. The sedate Edwardian restaurant is known for its excellent cuisine.

See map p. 132. 75 Sloane St. (near Sloane Square). ☎ *020-7235-7141. Fax: 020-7245-0994.* www.cadogan.com. *Tube: Knightsbridge or Sloane Square. Rack rates: £255–£355 ($510–$710) double. Continental breakfast £15 ($30); English breakfast £20 ($40). AE, DC, MC, V.*

Claverley Hotel
$$$ Knightsbridge

On a country-quiet cul-de-sac a few blocks from Harrods and the best of Knightsbridge shopping, this cozy place is one of London's best small hotels. Georgian-era accessories, 19th-century oil portraits, elegant antiques, and leather-covered sofas accent the public rooms. The 29 guest rooms are smart and cozy; marble bathrooms have tubs and power showers. The hotel offers an excellent English breakfast and great value for this tony area.

See map p. 132. 13–14 Beaufort Gardens (off Brompton Road). ☎ *800-747-0398 in the U.S. or 020-7589-8541. Fax: 020-7584-3410.* www.claverleyhotel.co.uk. *Tube: Knightsbridge. Rack rates: £149–£219 ($298–$438) double. Rates include English breakfast. AE, DC, MC, V.*

The Cranley
$$$ South Kensington

On a quiet street near South Kensington's museums, the Cranley occupies a quartet of restored 1875 town houses. Luxuriously appointed public rooms and 39 high-ceilinged, air-conditioned guest rooms — with original plasterwork, a blend of Victorian and contemporary furnishings, and up-to-the-minute in-room technology — make this property a standout. The bathrooms are large and nicely finished, with tubs and showers. Rates include tea with scones in the afternoon and aperitifs and canapés in the evening.

See map p. 132. 10–12 Bina Gardens (off Brompton Road). ☎ *800-448-8355 in the U.S. or 020-7373-0123. Fax: 020-7373-9497.* www.thecranley.com. *Tube: Gloucester Road. Rack rates: £120–£245 ($240–$490) double. Rates don't include 17.5 percent VAT. Continental breakfast £9.95 ($20). AE, DC, MC, V.*

Durrants Hotel
$$$ Marylebone

Opened in 1789 off Manchester Square, this 92-room hotel makes for an atmospheric London retreat. Durrants is quintessentially English, with pine- and mahogany-paneled public areas, a wonderful Georgian room that serves as a restaurant, and even an 18th-century letter-writing room. Most of the wood-paneled guest rooms are generously proportioned and nicely furnished, with decent-size bathrooms. Some rooms are large enough for families with children. The Wallace Collection, one of London's most sumptuous small museums, is right across the street.

See map p. 132. George Street (west of Oxford Street). ☎ *020-7935-8131. Fax: 020-7487-3510.* www.durrantshotel.co.uk. *Tube: Bond Street. Rack rates: £205 ($410) double. AE, MC, V.*

The Hoxton
$–$$ Shoreditch

This trendsetting "urban lodge" opened in 2007 and offers something quite unique for London: chic style at a cheap price. In fact, check their Web site because the Hoxton periodically holds incredible sales, and you may be able to nab a room for as little as £1 ($2)! The rooms are comfortable, well-designed, and refreshingly free of frou-frou. The beautifully tiled, shower-only bathrooms have every hotel in this price range beat by a mile. A simple bagged breakfast arrives at your room every morning, food and wine are sold in the lobby at supermarket prices, guests have access to high-speed computers (and free Wi-Fi throughout the hotel), and phone calls are incredibly cheap. In short, you'll find great value and no rip-offs. The trendy Shoreditch area is considered part of London's East End.

See map p. 132. 81 Great Eastern St. ☎ *020-7550-1000. Fax: 020-7550-1090.* www.hoxton hotels.com. *Tube: Old Street (then a 5-minute walk east on Old Street to Great Eastern). Rack rates: £59–£159 ($118–$318) double. Rates include continental breakfast. AE, MC, V.*

Luna & Simone Hotel
$ Westminster and Victoria

The outside of this big, stucco-fronted, family-run hotel gleams bright white, and each guest room has a tiled private bathroom with shower. The 36 rooms vary widely in size, but with their blue carpeting and cream-colored walls, they beat all the dowdy, badly designed hotels and B&Bs for miles around. The beechwood and marble-clad reception area is all new, too, as is the smart-looking breakfast room. The look throughout is refreshingly light, simple, and modern.

See map p. 132. 47–49 Belgrave Rd. (just west of Warwick Way). ☎ *020-7834-5897. Fax: 020-7828-2474.* www.lunasimonehotel.com. *Tube: Victoria. Rack rates: £70–£90 ($140–$180) double. Rates include English breakfast. MC, V.*

St. Margaret's Hotel
$$ Bloomsbury

This clean and comfortable old hotel is the best of a cluster of inexpensive accommodations that line a quiet street. The Marazzi family has offered kind, homey service for over 50 years. Rooms are carpeted and the furniture is worn but cared-for. Ask for a room in the rear of the hotel — those are the nicest. Though not all rooms have private bathroom, they do have sinks, TVs, and telephones. The breakfast is large and is included in the low rates. The British Museum is just around the corner — a huge plus. Stay more than one day, and the Marazzis will knock a couple of pounds off the nightly rate.

See map p. 132. 26 Bedford Place (near the Russell Square end of the street, 2 blocks west of the British Museum). ☎ *020-7636-4277. Fax: 020-7323-3066.* www.stmargaretshotel.co.uk. *Tube: Russell Square. Rack rates: £69 ($138) double without private bathroom; £95–£101 ($190–$202) double with private bathroom. Rates include breakfast. MC, V.*

Winchester Hotel
$ Westminster and Victoria

One of the best choices along Belgrave Road, this 18-room hotel is owned and managed by Jimmy McGoldrick, who goes out of his way to make his customers happy. Guests have been returning for 20 years; if you stay here, you'll understand why. Jimmy's staff maintains an extremely high level of service and cleanliness. The recently refurbished guest rooms are comfortable and well decorated. Each room has a small private bathroom with a good shower. Guests are served a big English breakfast in a lovely and inviting room. The sleek modernity that is displayed throughout is rare in small London hotels.

See map p. 132. 17 Belgrave Rd. ☎ *020-7828-2972. Fax: 020-7828-5191.* www.winchester-hotel.net. *Tube: Victoria. Rack rates: £85 ($170) double. Rates include English breakfast. No credit cards.*

London's runner-up accommodations

Fairways Hotel

$ **Paddington**   This large late-Georgian house from the 1820s exudes charming English ambience. *See map p. 132. 186 Sussex Gardens.* ☎ *020-7723-4871.* www.fairways-hotel.co.uk.

Fielding Hotel

$$ **Covent Garden**   This old-fashioned hotel has small, worn, but comfortable rooms and traditional charms. The hotel is located in one of the best parts of town, on a gas lamp–lit pedestrian street across from the Royal Opera House and near busy Covent Garden. *See map p. 132. 4 Broad Court, Bow Street.* ☎ *020-7836-8305.* www.thefieldinghotel.co.uk.

Imperial Hotel

$$ **Bloomsbury**   This large, full-service hotel isn't particularly glamorous, but it's well run and a terrific value right on Russell Square. *See map p. 132. Russell Square.* ☎ *020-7278-7871.* www.imperialhotels.co.uk.

Milestone Hotel & Apartments

$$$$$ **South Kensington**   You find superior service and a country house feeling in his small, stylish hotel wonderfully situated across from Kensington Gardens. *See map p. 132. 1 Kensington Ct.* ☎ *877-955-1515 in the U.S. or 020-7917-1000.* www.milestonehotel.com.

Dining in London

The British have long been mocked for the drab quality of their national cuisine (mushy peas, anyone?), and you can still find plenty of undistinguished food. But over the past two decades, London's top chefs have been paying lots of attention to the quality of old-fashioned dishes, adopting new culinary techniques, and using more international ingredients. This fusion of old-world tradition with new-world foodstuffs has led to the rise of **Modern British cuisine** and turned London into one of the culinary capitals of the world. Factor in London's variety of ethnic restaurants — locals go out for Indian the way Americans go out for Chinese — and you won't ever have to touch steak and kidney pie unless you want to.

If you're not interested in trying out the new culinary trends, Britain still has plenty of time-tested dishes for you to try. The **ploughman's lunch** is a hunk of bread, a chunk of cheese, butter, pickle (relish), and chutney. Two familiar meat pies are the **Cornish pasty** (beef, potatoes, onions, and carrots baked in a pastry shell) and **shepherd's pie** (lamb and onions under mashed potatoes; if beef is used, it's called cottage pie). The English are masters of roast beef, which is traditionally served with **Yorkshire pudding** (a popover-like concoction meant to soak up the juices).

You can also partake of oddly named British dishes such as **bangers and mash** (sausages and mashed potatoes), **bubble-and-squeak** (fried cabbage and potatoes), or **toad in the hole** (what Americans call pigs in a blanket). **Fish and chips** (fried fish with french fries) remains a popular staple.

Traditional **English breakfasts** — becoming rarer in these days of the continental croissant-and-coffee breakfast — include sausage, fried eggs, fried tomatoes, and toast with butter and jam. Even better is the tea ritual, detailed in the "More cool things to see and do" section, later in the chapter.

English cheeses are delicious and *puddings* (British for "desserts") tend to be very sweet. Of the former, blue-veined Stilton is the king and is best enjoyed with a glass of port wine. Regional delicacies pop up on the cheese board as well, one of the most famous being cheddar. If you prefer your meal to end with something sweet, try an English pudding. **Trifle** is sponge cake soaked with brandy, smothered in fruit or jam, and topped with custard. Light cream whipped with fresh fruit is called a **fool,** and a **treacle pudding** is a steamed trifle without the sherry and with syrup instead of fruit.

If you want to wash down your meal with a pint of bitter, make sure it's a proper English ale and not a wimpy import or lager. A few of the most widely available bitters are listed in the "More cool things to see and do" section, later in this chapter. More and more Brits drink wine, not beer, with their evening meal.

London is chockablock with restaurants, and **Soho** is the neighborhood with the densest concentration of (relatively) inexpensive eateries (Indian, Italian, Asian, and more). **Leicester Square/Piccadilly** is the easiest place to find a *Döner kebab* (a pita wrap with spiced lamb and a picante sauce) or other Middle Eastern street food. Some of the cheapest (but still excellent) Indian and Asian restaurants now cluster just south of the British Museum in the south end of **Bloomsbury** (around, not on, New Oxford Street).

Several of London's museums and sights have extremely good cafeterias or restaurants on the premises, so you don't have to leave the museums at lunchtime. You may want to plan on a meal in the **Tate Britain, Tate Modern, National Gallery, British Museum,** or **National Portrait Gallery.**

The most discriminating diners shop for their picnic delicacies in the gourmet food departments of **Fortnum & Mason,** 181 Piccadilly (see listing later in this section) or **Harrods,** 87–135 Brompton Rd. (see "More cool things to do," later in this chapter). **Marks and Spencer,** 458 Oxford St. (☎ 020-7935-7954), has a grocery department for less fancy staples. **Sainsbury's** is a fairly common supermarket chain where you can buy food to go (called *takeaway*).

Saving money on meals

Eating out in London can be mind-bogglingly pricey. So where do you go for lower-cost meals? Try pubs, cafes, sandwich bars, food halls in department stores, ready-made meals in supermarkets, pizza places, and ethnic restaurants — places where you're not paying for custom cooking and high-end personal service. If you opt for a pricier establishment, always find out whether the restaurant of your choice has a fixed-price menu. Many of London's top restaurants offer two- and three-course fixed-price meals that can slash an a la carte tab by one-third or more. Wine can cost you a bundle, so forgo that glass of chardonnay if you need to watch your budget. And try your splurge dining at lunch, when prices are often one-third of the cost at dinner and you get the same food. Note that in London and throughout England, tap water is not automatically brought to your table — you must specifically request it. Bottled mineral water (still or "fizzy") is more commonly drunk with meals than tap water.

The best **sandwich shops** in Central London are the **Pret à Manger** chain stores, which offer fresh, inventive, healthy sandwiches and fast counter service. You'll find them all over the city.

Boxwood Café
$$$$ Knightsbridge   MODERN BRITISH

This may be the most stylish kid-friendly restaurant in London, but grown-ups will find plenty of comforting delights on the menu, too. Created by chef-superstar Gordon Ramsay, Boxwood Café is chic without being fussy, and the same goes for the food, which emphasizes fresh and healthy dishes ranging from glazed pea and leek tart to fresh steamed fish, wine-braised veal, roast chicken salad, or steaks, plus simpler, more popular items for the kids.

See map p. 132. In the Berkeley Hotel, Wilton Place (on Brompton Road). ☎ *020-7235-1010. Tube: Knightsbridge. Reservations recommended. Main courses: £9–£25 ($18–$50); fixed-price lunch £25 ($50). AE, DISC, MC, V. Open: Daily noon to 3 p.m. (until 4 p.m. Sat–Sun) and 6–11 p.m.*

Cafe in the Crypt
$ Trafalgar Square   BRITISH

Eating in a crypt might not be everyone's idea of fun, but eating in this crypt — below St. Martin's-in-the-Fields Church on Trafalgar Square — is an inexpensive London dining experience that you won't forget. The food is basic but good, served cafeteria-style. Choose from a big salad bar, traditional main courses such as shepherd's pie, filled rolls, and delicious soups. One fixture is that most traditional of British desserts, bread-and-butter pudding (bread soaked in eggs and milk with currants or sultanas

---

Smoke-free dining and drinking

Gone are the days of smoke-filled London restaurants. An ordinance that went into effect throughout England in July 2007 prohibits smoking in restaurants and pubs. More and more restaurants are also prohibiting the use of cellphones in the dining room.

---

and then oven-baked). The cavernous, candlelit room, with its great stone pillars, is wonderfully atmospheric. The crypt is also a nice spot for a good, inexpensive afternoon tea.

See map p. 132. St. Martin-in-the-Fields, Duncannon Street (on Trafalgar Square). ☎ *020-7839-4342. Tube: Charing Cross. Reservations not accepted. Main courses: £6–£7.50 ($12–$15); fixed-price meal £5.25 ($11); afternoon tea £5 ($10). No credit cards. Open: Mon–Wed 10 a.m.–7:30 p.m.; Thurs–Sat 10 a.m.–10:15 p.m.*

Fortnum & Mason
$$$ St. James's   TRADITIONAL BRITISH

Fortnum & Mason, a posh, legendary London store that's a "purveyor to the Queen" and famous for its food section, has three restaurants. The mezzanine-level Patio is a good lunch spot, with a menu that offers an assortment of pricey sandwiches and main courses, including hot and cold pies (steak and kidney, curried fish and banana, chicken, and game) and Welsh rarebit (thick melted cheese poured over toast) prepared with Guinness stout. The lower-level Fountain offers breakfast and lunch, and the fourth-floor St. James's serves lunch and afternoon tea. The more well-heeled dine at St. James's, where the menu is traditionally British: For starters, try the kipper (smoked herring) mousse or potato and Stilton brûlée; main courses include pies and roast rib of Scottish beef. Although crowded with tourists, these three establishments remain pleasant places where you can get a good meal and a glimpse of the fading Empire. The Fountain and Patio are good places to dine with a family; ice-cream sundaes are a specialty.

See map p. 132. 181 Piccadilly. ☎ *020-7734-8040. Reservations accepted for St. James's only. Tube: Piccadilly Circus. Main courses: Lunch £11–£24 ($22–$48); fixed-price menu £20–£37 ($40–$74). AE, DC, MC, V. Open: St. James's and the Patio Tues–Sat 9:30 a.m.–5:30 p.m.; the Fountain Mon–Sat 8:30 a.m.–7:45 p.m.*

Gourmet Pizza Company
$ St. James's   PIZZA/PASTA

If you're in the West End or across the river in Southwark and want an economical lunch or dinner in a family-friendly environment, stop at one of these bright, pleasant spots. You can choose among 20 pizzas (pizza as in pie, not slice). Everything from a B.L.T. version to one with Cajun chicken and prawns is available; about half the choices are vegetarian, and some are vegan. The crusts are light and crispy, and the toppings are fresh and flavorful. Pasta dishes are also available. The new branch at Upper Ground, Gabriel's Wharf (☎ 020-7928-3188; Tube: London Bridge), is right on the river.

See map p. 132. 7–9 Swallow Walk (off Piccadilly), W1. ☎ 020-7734-5182. Reservations not accepted. Tube: Piccadilly Circus (then a five-minute walk west on Piccadilly and north on Swallow Street). Main courses: Pizzas £7–£10 (14–$20), pastas £8–£11 ($16–$22). AE, DC, MC, V. Open: Daily noon to 10:30 p.m. (until midnight at Gabriel's Wharf location).

Mildred's
$$ Soho VEGETARIAN

Considered by many to be London's best vegetarian restaurant, Mildred's is a busy, buzzy place. It isn't fancy, but that only seems to add to the hip ambience. There's always a pasta of the day and a variety of robustly flavored offerings such as organic lentil casserole with roasted pumpkin and squash, or sun-dried tomato, bean, and tarragon sausages. Try the sweet potato fries as a side, and don't forget dessert.

See map p. 132. 45 Lexington St., W1. ☎ 020-7494-1634. Reservations not accepted. Tube: Piccadilly Circus. Main courses: £7–£8.50 ($14–$17). No credit cards. Open: Mon–Sat noon to 11 p.m.

Porters English Restaurant
$$$ Covent Garden BRITISH

With so many pricey traditional restaurants in London, the Earl of Bradford took a gamble that the city had room for reasonably priced, well-prepared British cuisine. His instinct was correct, and Porters has become popular with people looking for the tastes they remember from old-fashioned family dinners. The meat pies and puddings are particularly good; try the unusually flavored lamb and apricot pie with mint and Lady Bradford's famous banana and ginger steamed pudding.

See map p. 132. 17 Henrietta St. (½ block off the Covent Garden square). ☎ 020-7836-6466. www.porters.uk.com. Reservations recommended. Tube: Covent Garden. Main courses: £11–£19 ($22–$38). AE, DC, MC, V. Open: Mon–Sat noon to 11:30 p.m.; Sun noon to 10:30 p.m.

Rules
$$$$$ Covent Garden BRITISH

In a clubby, 19th-century setting, Rules is the oldest restaurant in London, established in 1798. The restaurant serves up game from its own preserve and some of the most staunchly British food in town. You can't go wrong with the venison or wild fowl. Try the roast loin of Wiltshire rabbit, Irish sirloin steak with béarnaise sauce, or Gloucestershire pork chops with crackling and chutney — just make sure you cap the meal off with one of Rules's famous puddings. This truly is a special place, well worth a splurge.

See map p. 132. 35 Maiden Lane (1 block off the Strand). ☎ *020-7836-5314.* www.rules.co.uk. *Reservations recommended. Tube: Charing Cross or Covent Garden. Main courses: £16–£21 ($32–$42); fixed-price menu (Mon–Thurs 10 p.m.–11:30 p.m.) £19 ($38). AE, DC, MC, V. Open: Mon–Sat noon to 11:45 p.m.; Sun noon to 10:45 p.m.*

Exploring London

London is home to some of the world's greatest museums and nearly all of them are absolutely free. You can walk in and enjoy the antiquities of the British Museum, the Old Masters of the National Gallery, the contemporary greats in the Tate Modern, and the decorative arts in the Victoria & Albert Museum (known as the V&A). London's major churches — Westminster Abbey and St. Paul's Cathedral — *do* charge admission, and so does the Tower of London and Buckingham Palace.

London's top sights

British Airways London Eye
South Bank

As a piece of engineering, the 400-foot-high London Eye observation wheel is impressive. Each glass-sided elliptical module holds about 25 passengers, with enough space so that you can move about freely. Lasting about 30 minutes (equivalent to one rotation), the ride (or flight, as they call it) is remarkably smooth — even on windy days riders don't feel any nerve-twittering shakes. Providing that the weather is good, the wheel offers unrivaled views of London. It's a good idea to reserve your place (with a specific entry time) before you arrive; otherwise, you may have to wait an hour or more before you can get on the wheel.

See map p. 132. Bridge Road (beside Westminster Bridge). ☎ *0870-500-0600 (advance credit card booking; 50p/$1 booking fee added). Tube: Westminster. Admission: £13.50 ($27) adults, £11 ($22) seniors, £6.75 ($14) children 15 and under. Open: Daily 9:30 a.m. Last admission varies seasonally.*

British Museum
Bloomsbury

The British Museum ranks as the most visited attraction in London, with a splendid, wide-ranging collection of treasures from around the world. Permanent displays of antiquities from Egypt, Western Asia, Greece, and Rome are on view, as well as prehistoric and Romano-British, Medieval, Renaissance, Modern, and Oriental collections. Give yourself at least three unhurried hours in the museum. If you have only limited time, consider taking one of the 90-minute highlight tours offered daily at 10:30 a.m., 1 p.m., and 3 p.m.; the cost is £8 ($16). You can rent audio guides, which also cover museum highlights, for £3.50 ($7).

The most famous of the museum's countless treasures are the superb **Parthenon Sculptures** brought to England in 1801 by the seventh Lord

Elgin. These marble sculptures once adorned the Parthenon in Athens, and Greece desperately wants them returned. Other famous treasures include the **Egyptian Mummies;** the **Rosetta Stone,** which enabled archaeologists to decipher Egyptian hieroglyphics; and the **Sutton Hoo Treasure,** an Anglo-Saxon burial ship, believed to be the tomb of a seventh-century East Anglian king.

The museum's **Great Court,** inaccessible to the general public for 150 years, is now the museum's central axis, with a glass-and-steel roof designed by Lord Norman Foster. The circular building in the center, completed in 1857, once served as the museum's famous **Reading Room.** Completely restored, it now houses computer terminals where visitors can access images and information about the museum's vast collections.

See map p. 132. Great Russell Street (between Bloomsbury and Montgomery streets). ☎ *020-7323-8000. Tube: Russell Square. Admission: Free. Open: Sat–Wed 10 a.m.– 5:30 p.m.; Thurs–Fri 10 a.m.–8:30 p.m. Closed Jan 1, Good Friday, Dec 24–26.*

Buckingham Palace and the Changing of the Guard
St. James's Park and Green Park

Since 1837, when Victoria ascended the throne, all the majesty, scandal, intrigue, triumph, tragedy, power, wealth, and tradition associated with the British monarchy has been hidden behind the monumental facade of Buckingham Palace, the reigning monarch's London residence.

An impressive early-18th-century pile, the palace was rebuilt in 1825 and further modified in 1913. From August through September, when the royal family isn't in residence, you can buy a ticket to get a glimpse of the staterooms used by Elizabeth II and the other royals. You leave via the gardens, where the queen holds her famous garden parties each summer. Budget about two hours for your visit.

Throughout the year, you can visit the **Royal Mews,** one of the finest working stables in existence, where the magnificent Gold State Coach, used in every coronation since 1831, and other royal conveyances are housed (and horses stabled). The **Queen's Gallery,** which features changing exhibits of works from the Royal Collection, went through a refurbishment and reopened for the queen's golden jubilee in June 2002.

The famous **Changing of the Guard** takes place along Birdcage Walk and in front of Buckingham Palace at 11:30 a.m., daily from April through early June and on alternate days the rest of the year. You can check dates at www.royalcollection.org.uk.

You can purchase admission tickets to Buckingham Palace, and request a specific entry time, by calling ☎ **020-7766-7300.** All phone-charged tickets cost an additional £1.25 ($2.50). Also, you can purchase reduced-price tickets if you plan to visit more than one royal property.

See map p. 132. Buckingham Palace Road. Palace Visitor Office, Royal Mews, and Queen's Gallery ☎ *020-7839-1377 (9:30 a.m.–5:30 p.m.) or 020-7799-2331 (24-hour recorded info).* www.royalcollection.org.uk. *Tube: St. James's Park or Green Park. Admission (includes audio guide): Palace £16 ($32) adults, £14 ($28) seniors,*

£8.75 ($18) children 16 and under, £40 ($80) families (2 adults, 3 children 16 and under); Royal Mews £7.50 ($15) adults, £6.25 ($13) seniors, £4.80 ($9.60) children, £20 ($40) families; Queen's Gallery £8 ($16) adults, £7 ($14) seniors, £4 ($8) children, £20 ($40) families. Open: Palace July 31–Sept 29 (these dates fluctuate yearly by a day or two) daily 9:30 a.m.–6 p.m. (last admittance 3:45 p.m.); Royal Mews Mar 15–July and Oct Sat–Thurs 11 a.m.–4 p.m. (last admission 3:15 p.m.), Aug–Sept daily 10 a.m.–5 p.m. (last admission 4:15 p.m.); Queen's Gallery daily 10 a.m.–5:30 p.m. (last admittance 4:30 p.m.). Royal Mews and Queen's Gallery closed Dec 25–26. Visitors with disabilities must prebook for palace visits; Royal Mews and Queen's Gallery are wheelchair accessible.

Houses of Parliament and Big Ben
Westminster

The **Houses of Parliament,** situated along the Thames, house the landmark clock tower containing **Big Ben,** the biggest bell in the booming hourly chime that Londoners have been hearing for nearly 150 years. Designed by Sir Charles Barry and A. W. N. Pugin, the impressive Victorian buildings were completed in 1857. Covering approximately 3.2 hectares (8 acres), they occupy the site of an 11th-century palace of Edward the Confessor.

At one end (Old Palace Yard) you find the **Jewel House,** built in 1366 and once the treasury house of Edward III, who reigned from 1327 to 1377. The best overall view of the Houses of Parliament is from Westminster Bridge, but if you prefer, you can sit in the **Stranger's Gallery** to hear Parliamentary debate. The best way to see the Houses of Parliament, however, is to take a 75-minute **guided tour,** available Monday through Saturday from the end of July through most of September. The tours cost £12 ($24) for adults, £8 ($16) for seniors, £5 ($10) for children, and £30 ($60) for families; you can reserve by phone at ☎ 0870-906-3773, online at www.keithprowse.com, or by visiting the ticket office in Westminster Hall (at the Houses of Parliament). For the rest of the year, the procedure for getting a tour is much more difficult. If you're interested, you can find details on the Web at www.parliament.uk.

See map p. 132. Bridge Street and Parliament Square. ☎ 020-7219-4272. www. parliament.uk. Tube: Westminster (you can see the clock tower with Big Ben directly across Bridge Street when you exit the tube). Admission: Free. For tickets, join the line at St. Stephen's entrance. Open: Stranger's Gallery House of Commons Mon 2:30–10:30 p.m., Tues–Wed 11:30–7:30 p.m., Thurs 11:30 a.m.–6:30 p.m., most Fri 9:30 a.m.–3 p.m.; House of Lords Mon–Wed 2:30–10 p.m., Thurs 10 a.m.–7:30 p.m. Parliament isn't in session late July to mid-Oct or on weekends.

National Gallery
Trafalgar Square, St. James's

If you're passionate about great art, then you'll think that the National Gallery is paradise. This museum houses one of the world's most comprehensive collections of British and European paintings. All the major schools from the 13th to the 20th century are represented, but the Italians get the lion's share of wall space, with works by artists such as da Vinci, Botticelli, and Raphael. The French Impressionist and post-Impressionist works by Monet, Manet, Seurat, Cézanne, Degas, and van Gogh are splendid. And because you're on English soil, check out at least a few of Turner's stunning seascapes, Constable's landscapes, and Reynolds's society portraits. And you won't want to miss the Rembrandts. Budget at least two hours to enjoy the gallery. The second floor has a good restaurant for lunch, tea, or snacks.

See map p. 132. Trafalgar Square. ☎ *020-7747-2885.* www.nationalgallery. org.uk. *Tube: Charing Cross. Admission: Free. Open: Daily 10 a.m.–6 p.m. (Wed until 9 p.m.). Closed Jan 1 and Dec 24–26. The entire museum is wheelchair accessible.*

St. Paul's Cathedral
The City of London

After the Great Fire of 1666 destroyed the city's old cathedral, the great architect Christopher Wren was called upon to design St. Paul's, a huge and harmonious Renaissance-leaning-toward-baroque building. During World War II, Nazi bombing raids wiped out the surrounding area but spared the cathedral, so Wren's masterpiece, capped by the most famous dome in London, rises majestically above a crowded sea of undistinguished office buildings. Grinling Gibbons carved the exceptionally beautiful choir stalls, the only impressive artwork inside.

Christopher Wren is buried in the **crypt;** his companions in the crypt include Britain's famed national heroes: the Duke of Wellington, who defeated Napoleon at Waterloo, and Admiral Lord Nelson, who took down the French at Trafalgar during the same war. But many people want to see St. Paul's simply because Lady Diana Spencer wed Prince Charles here in what was billed as "the fairy-tale wedding of the century."

You can climb up to the **Whispering Gallery** for a bit of acoustical fun or gasp your way up to the very top for a breathtaking view of London. You can see the entire cathedral in an hour or less. St. Paul's is now linked to the Tate Modern on the South Bank by the pedestrian-only **Millennium Bridge,** designed by Lord Norman Foster.

See map p. 132. St. Paul's Churchyard, Ludgate Hill. ☎ *020-7246-8348.* www.st pauls.co.uk. *Tube: St. Paul's. Admission: £10 ($20) adults, £9 ($18) seniors, £3.50 ($7) children, £24 ($48) families. Guided tours: £3 ($6) adults, £2.50 ($5) seniors, £1 ($2) children 9 and under. Audio guides: £3.50 ($7) adults, £3 ($6) seniors and students. Open: Mon–Sat 8:30 a.m.–4 p.m.; no sightseeing on Sun (services only). Guided tours: Mon–Sat 11 a.m., 11:30 a.m., 1:30 p.m., 2 p.m. Audio guides: Available 8:30 a.m.–3 p.m. The cathedral is wheelchair accessible by the service entrance near the South Transept; ring the bell for assistance.*

Tate Britain
Pimlico

The Tate Gallery took this name to distinguish it from its new counterpart, Tate Modern (see the next listing). Tate Britain retains the older (pre–20th century) collections of exclusively British art, plus works by major British stars, such as David Hockney, and experimental works by Brits and foreigners living in Britain. Among the masterpieces on display in a host of newly refurbished galleries are dreamy works by the British pre-Raphaelites, the celestial visions of William Blake, bawdy satirical works by William Hogarth, genteel portraits by Sir Joshua Reynolds, pastoral landscapes by John Constable, and the shimmering seascapes of J. M. W. Turner. The collection is hung thematically rather than chronologically. Plan on spending at least two hours here. The gallery has a fine restaurant and a cafe on the lower level.

See map p. 132. Millbank, Pimlico. ☎ 020-7887-8000. www.tate.org.uk/britain. Tube: Pimlico. Bus: 77A for a more scenic route (it runs south along The Strand and Whitehall to the museum entrance on Millbank). Admission: Free. Audio guides: £3 ($6). Open: Daily 10 a.m.–5:50 p.m. Most of the galleries are wheelchair accessible, but call first for details on entry.

Tate Modern
South Bank

The former Bankside Power Station is the setting for the fabulous Tate Modern, which opened in May 2000. Considered one of the top modern-art museums in the world, it houses the Tate's collection of international 20th-century art, displaying major works by some of the most influential artists of this century: Pablo Picasso, Henri Matisse, Salvador Dalí, Marcel Duchamp, Henry Moore, and Frances Bacon among them. A gallery for the 21st-century collection exhibits contemporary art. Fans of contemporary art and architecture shouldn't miss this new star on the London art scene. Plan on spending at least two hours.

See map p. 132. 25 Sumner St. (on the South Bank just off the Millennium Bridge). ☎ 020-7887-8000. www.tate.org.uk/modern. Tube: Southwark or Blackfriars. Admission: Free; varying admission fees for special exhibits. Open: Sun–Thurs 10 a.m.–6 p.m.; Fri–Sat 10 a.m.–10 p.m. Tours: Free tours hourly 11 a.m.–3 p.m. Closed Jan 1 and Dec 24–26.

Tower of London
The City of London

Come early to beat the long lines at London's best medieval attraction, a site of intrigue, murder, and executions galore. The hour-long tours, guided by Beefeater guards, are highly entertaining and informative. Count on at least another full hour to explore on your own and to investigate the Crown Jewels, the Armory, and such. The Beefeaters take you past the Bloody Tower, where Sir Walter Raleigh awaited execution for 13 years and where King Edward IV's two young sons were murdered. You walk through the 900-year-old White Tower, still housing an armory of swords and plate mail, as well as a gruesome collection of torture instruments, and into Tower Green, where Thomas Moore, Lady Jane Grey, and two of Henry VIII's wives (Anne Boleyn and Catherine Howard) were beheaded.

All the gore should be enough trade-off for the kids when you have to wait in line to be whisked past the Crown Jewels on a moving walkway. Be sure to drool over the world's largest cut diamond, the 530-carat Star of Africa (set in the Sovereign's Sceptre), and to gape at Queen Victoria's Imperial State Crown (still worn on occasion), studded with over 3,000 jewels. Say hello to the resident ravens, who are rather pampered because legend holds that the Tower will stand as long as they remain; in 2006, they were put indoors so that they wouldn't contract avian flu.

See map p. 132. Tower Hill. ☎ 0870-756-6060. www.hrp.org.uk. *Tube: Tower Hill. Admission: £16 ($32) adults, £13 ($26) seniors and students, £9 ($18) children 5–15. Open: Mar–Oct Tues–Sat 9 a.m.–6 p.m., Sun–Mon 10 a.m.–6 p.m.; Nov–Feb Tues–Sat 9 a.m.–5 p.m., Sun–Mon 10 a.m.–5 p.m. Last admission half-hour before closing. Beefeater tours: Mon–Sat every half-hour starting at 9:30 a.m. and continuing until 2:30 p.m. (3:30 p.m. in summer); Sun tours begin at 10 a.m.*

Trafalgar Square
St. James's

After a major urban redesign scheme, Trafalgar Square reopened in 2003 with one side attached to the steps of the National Gallery, making access easier than it's ever been. Besides being a major tourist attraction, Trafalgar Square is the site of many large gatherings, including political demonstrations, Christmas revels, and New Year's Eve festivities. The square honors military hero Admiral Lord Nelson (1758–1805), who lost his life at the Battle of Trafalgar, fighting French and Spanish forces. **Nelson's Column,** with fountains and four bronze lions at its base, rises some 44m (145 ft.) above the square. At the top, a 4m-high (14-ft.) statue of Nelson (who was 5'4" tall in real life) looks commandingly toward **Admiralty Arch,** passed through by state and royal processions between Buckingham Palace and St. Paul's Cathedral. You don't really need more than a few minutes to take in the square. **St. Martin-in-the-Fields (☎ 020-7930-0089),** the famous neoclassical church at the northeast corner of Trafalgar Square, was designed by James Gibbs, a disciple of Christopher Wren, and completed in 1726.

See map p. 132. Bounded on the north by Trafalgar, on the west by Cockspur Street, and on the east by Whitehall. Tube: Charing Cross (an exit from the Underground station leads to the square).

Victoria & Albert Museum
South Kensington

The Victoria & Albert (known as the V&A) is the national museum of art and design. In the 145 galleries, filled with fine and decorative arts from around the world, you find superbly decorated period rooms, a fashion collection spanning 400 years of European designs, Raphael's designs for tapestries in the Sistine Chapel, the Silver Galleries, and the largest assemblages of Renaissance sculpture outside Italy and of Indian art outside India. The Canon Photography Gallery shows work by celebrated photographers. In

November 2001, the museum opened its spectacular new British Galleries. Allow at least two hours to cover just the basics.

See map p. 132. Cromwell Road. ☎ *020-7942-2000.* www.vam.ac.uk. *Tube: South Kensington (the museum is across from the Underground station). Admission: Free. Open: Daily 10 a.m.–5:45 p.m. (until 10 p.m. Fri). Closed Dec 24–26. The museum is wheelchair accessible (only about 5 percent of the exhibits include steps).*

Westminster Abbey
Westminster

The Gothic and grand Westminster Abbey is one of London's most important historic sites. The present abbey dates mostly from the 13th and 14th centuries, but a church has been on this site for more than a thousand years. Since 1066, when William the Conqueror became the first English monarch to be crowned here, every successive British sovereign except for two (Edward V and Edward VIII) has sat on the **Coronation Chair** to receive the crown and scepter. In the **Royal Chapels,** you can see the **chapel of Henry VII,** with its delicate fan vaulting, and the **tomb of Queen Elizabeth I,** who was buried in the same vault as her Catholic half-sister, Mary I, and not far from her rival Mary Queen of Scots. In **Poets' Corner,** some of England's greatest writers (including Chaucer, Dickens, and Thomas Hardy) are interred or memorialized. Other points of interest include the College Garden, cloisters, chapter house, and the Undercroft Museum, which contains the Pyx Chamber, with its display of church plate — the silver owned by the church. In September 1997, the abbey served as the site of Princess Diana's funeral; in 2002, the funeral service for the Queen Mother was held there. The abbey is within walking distance of the Houses of Parliament.

See map p. 132. Broad Sanctuary (near the Houses of Parliament). ☎ *020-7222-7110.* www.westminster-abbey.org. *Tube: Westminster. Bus: The 77A going south along The Strand, Whitehall, and Millbank stops near the Houses of Parliament, near the Abbey. Admission: £10 ($20) adults; £7 ($14) seniors, students, children 11–16; £24 ($48) families (2 adults, 2 children). Guided tours: Led by an Abbey Verger £5 ($10); call for times. Audio guides: £4 ($8). Open: Cathedral Mon–Fri 9:30 a.m.–3:45 p.m., Sat 9 a.m.–1:45 p.m. (closed Sun except for services); College Garden Apr–Sept 10 a.m.– 6 p.m., Oct–Mar 10 a.m.–4 p.m. There's ramped wheelchair access through the Cloisters; ring the bell for assistance.*

More cool things to see and do

✔ **Strolling Portobello Road Market:** Antiques collectors, bargain hunters, tourists, and deals on everything from kumquats to Wedgwood are what you find at London's most popular street market. The outdoor fruit and veggie market runs all week (except Sun), but on Saturday, starting at 5:30 a.m., the market balloons into an enormous flea and antiques mart. About 90 antiques shops line the roads around this section of London; so even during the week, you can browse their dusty treasures (serious shoppers pick up the Sat Antiques Market guide). To get to the market, take the Tube to Notting Hill Gate.

✔ **Embarking on a London pub crawl:** The drinker's version of a traditional London evening out starts around 5:30 p.m. at a favorite pub and continues from one pub to the next throughout the evening. Among the most historic and atmospheric ale houses are the historic **Ye Olde Cheshire Cheese** at Wine Office Court, off 145 Fleet St. (☎ 020-7353-6170), where Dr. Johnson once held court; Dryden's old haunt the **Lamb and Flag,** 33 Rose St. (☎ 020-7497-9504), known as "Bucket of Blood" from its rowdier days; the Art Nouveau **Black Friar,** 174 Queen Victoria St. (☎ 020-7236-5474); and **Anchor Inn,** 34 Park St. (☎ 0870-990-6402), where the present pub dates from 1757 — but a pub has been at this location for 800 years, with Dickens and Shakespeare as past patrons. Make sure you order some true English bitters, hand-pumped and served at room temperature. Try Wadworth, Tetley's, Flowers, and the London-brewed Young's and Fuller's. Most pubs are open Monday through Saturday from 11 a.m. to 11 p.m. and on Sunday from noon to 10:30 p.m. Pub opening hours were extended in 2005, so some of them now stay open until midnight and later.

✔ **Making a shopping pilgrimage to Harrods:** Posh, somewhat stuffy, and a bit snobbish (they may turn you away if you look too scruffy), **Harrods,** 87–135 Brompton Rd. (☎ 020-7730-1234; www.harrods. com), is the only store in the world that offers you any item you can possibly want and backs up its word. With 1.2 million square feet and 300 departments, the store carries just about everything. Its fabulous food halls are still the highlight of a visit — 500 varieties of cheese, anyone?

✔ **Raising your pinkies at a proper afternoon tea:** Tea (and, increasingly, coffee) is drunk around the clock, but "tea time" is between 3 and 5:30 p.m. That's when you can sit down and order a steaming pot of tea accompanied by a tiered platter of delicious finger sandwiches, slices of cake, and scones with jam and clotted cream. A full tea can run anywhere from £10 to £40 ($20–$80). One of London's classiest (and most expensive) afternoon teas is at **Brown's Hotel,** 29–34 Albemarle St. (☎ 020-7493-6020; www.brownshotel.com; Tube: Green Park). Less pricey — but just as good — are the teas at two of London's legendary department stores: the inimitable **Harrods Georgian Restaurant,** on the fourth floor, at 87–135 Brompton Rd. (☎ 020-7730-1234; www.harrods.com; Tube: Knightsbridge), and **Fortnum & Mason's** St. James's Restaurant, 181 Piccadilly (☎ 020-7734-8040; www.fortnumandmason.co.uk; Tube: Piccadilly Circus or Green Park).

✔ **Seeing a Shakespeare play at the Globe Theatre:** Shakespeare was once part owner and main playwright for a theater called the Globe, right on the Thames at Bankside. Shakespeare's Globe Theatre is a recently built replica of the O-shaped building, with an open center and projecting stage — the sort of space for which Shakespeare's plays were written. Performances are late April through early October; tickets for seats run £15 to £33 ($30–$66).

For only £5 ($10), you can stand in the open space right in front of the stage (tiring, and not so fun if it rains). Call ☎ 020-7401-9919 for the box office. Even if you don't stop for a show, make some time during the day to come for a tour (☎ 020-7902-1400; www.shakespeares-globe.org).

✔ **Club hopping:** The city that gave the world punk, new wave, techno, and electronica still has one of the world's most trend-setting clublands. The nature of the art means that any place we mention in this book will be considered out before the guide is, so do yourself a favor and pick up the _Time Out London_ magazine to find out what's hottest each week. A few perennial favorites (sure to be full of tourists) include the **Ministry of Sound,** 103 Gaunt St., SE1 (☎ 020-7378-6528; www.ministryofsound.com); the **Equinox,** Leicester Square, W2 (☎ 020-7437-1446); **Carwash,** 256 Old St., EC1 (☎ 0870-246-1966); and **Venom Club/The Zoo Bar,** 13–17 Bear St., WC2 (☎ 020-7839-4188).

✔ **Joining the thespians — an evening at the theater:** London rivals New York for the biggest, most diverse theater scene. The West End has dozens of playhouses, but you find many other venues as well. The _Time Out London_ and _What's On_ magazines list (and review) the week's offerings, as does the online Official London Theatre Guide (www.officiallondontheatre.co.uk). For tickets, your best bet is to go directly to the theater's box office, where you won't have to pay an additional booking fee; you can also buy them, and pay a booking fee, from **Keith Prowse** (☎ 800-223-6108 in the U.S., 0870-842-2248 in the U.K.; www.keithprowse.com), which has a desk in the main tourist office on Regent Street. Theater tickets can cost anywhere from £15 to £70 ($30–$140). If you want to try to get last-minute tickets at a discount, the _only_ official spot is Leicester Square's half-price TKTS ticket booth (www.officiallondontheatre.co.uk/tkts), open Monday through Saturday 10 a.m. to 7 p.m., Sunday noon to 3 p.m. The tickets there are usually half-price (plus a £2.50/$5 fee) and are sold on the day of the performance only. The most popular productions are usually not offered at TKTS.

✔ **Waxing historic at Madame Tussaud's:** Famous **Madame Tussaud's,** Marylebone Road (☎ 0870-400-3000; www.madame-tussauds.co.uk), is something between a still-life amusement ride and a serious gallery of historical likenesses. Madame herself took death masks from the likes of Marie Antoinette and other French royals beheaded in the Revolution; Ben Franklin (while very much alive) personally sat for her to mold a portrait. Some of the historical dioramas are interesting — although whether they're £20 ($40) worth of interesting is seriously up for debate. (Tickets for children are £16/$32; the prices for all tickets fall considerably if you enter after 5 p.m.). Besides the obligatory celebs and superstores on display, there's also a gore-fest Chamber of Horrors and a Spirit of London theme ride. The museum is open Monday through Friday from 9:30 a.m. to 5:30 p.m., Saturday and Sunday from 9 a.m. to 6 p.m.

🖝 **Setting your watch — a day in Greenwich:** London may set its watches by Big Ben, but Ben looks to the **Old Royal Observatory** at Greenwich for the time of day. This attractive Thames port and riverside village keeps Greenwich (mean) time, by which the entire world sets its clocks. At the observatory, you can straddle the prime meridian (0° longitude mark) and have one foot in each hemisphere. Then visit the **National Maritime Museum** and immerse yourself in the history of the British Navy. After that, head to the adjacent **Queen's House,** designed by Inigo Jones, completed in 1635, and later used as a model for the White House; today it's an art gallery. All three attractions are free and open daily from 10 a.m. to 5 p.m. (☎ **0870-780-4552** or 020-8312-6565; www.nmm.ac.uk). Unfortunately, that most famous of clipper ships, the *Cutty Sark,* suffered major fire damage in 2007 and is closed for a complete refit that will take years. **The Greenwich Tourist Information Centre,** Pepys Houses, Cutty Sark Gardens (☎ **0870-608-2000;** www.greenwich.gov.uk), can give you more information on all the historic attractions in Greenwich. You have several options for getting to Greenwich: You can take the Jubilee Tube line to North Greenwich (then bus no. 188 to the maritime heritage site); the train from Charing Cross Station; the Docklands Light Railway from the Tower Hill Tube stop; or the no. 188 bus from Russell Square. Our favorite mode of transport to this destination is by boat: Catch a ferry from Westminster Pier.

Guided tours

You can get an excellent overview of the city's layout, and see many of the architectural sights at a snappy pace, from the top of a double-decker bus on the **Original London Sightseeing Tour** (☎ **020-8877-1722;** www.theoriginaltour.com). You'll find boarding points for this hop-on/hop-off bus at 90 different stops throughout the city, including all the major attractions. At £19 ($38) for adults and £12 ($24) for kids, the Original Tour is the best overall, spinning a 90-minute loop of the top sights with five minutes (15 in winter) between buses. Tickets are good all day — if you buy tickets after 2 p.m., they're good the next day as well. With this tour you get a free boat ride on the Thames and some walking tours as well.

Of the many walking tour outfits in this city, by far the biggest and best is **London Walks** (☎ **020-7624-3978;** www.walks.com). For fun, education, and entertainment at a really low price ($6/$12 adults, free for children 14 and under with a parent), a London Walk is one of the best investments you can make in London. Two-hour themed walks with an expert guide take you through historic neighborhoods, on pub crawls, or for walks in the footsteps of Shakespeare, Churchill, Christopher Wren, or Jack the Ripper.

Suggested itineraries

In case you're the type who'd rather organize your own tours, this section offers some tips for building your own London itineraries.

If you have one day

To see London in a day takes full-throttle sightseeing. Reserve ahead for the 9:30 a.m. Beefeater tour at the **Tower of London.** After perusing the Crown Jewels there, take off for the **British Museum** (grab lunch along the way) to ogle the Rosetta Stone, Egyptian mummies, and Parthenon sculptures. Be at **Westminster Abbey** by 3 p.m. to pay homage to the British monarchs, English poets, and other notables entombed therein; then make your way over to have a look at **Buckingham Palace** and **Trafalgar Square.** Have an early pre-theater dinner at **Rules** and then spend the evening doing whatever floats your boat: attending a play or a concert, indulging in a pub crawl, or just enjoying the street scene and nighttime crowds milling around Piccadilly Circus and Leicester Square.

If you have two days

Begin **Day 1** at **Buckingham Palace,** where, if you time it right, you can watch the Changing of the Guard. Afterward, head for the **British Museum** to marvel at the spoils of the old empire. Move along to the stellar collection of Renaissance paintings in the **National Gallery,** stopping early on for a sandwich in the excellent cafeteria, and visiting **Trafalgar Square** afterward. Lunch tides you over until you get to fabled **Harrods** department store, where you can take a break from the window-shopping to indulge in an afternoon tea in the **Georgian Restaurant.** Spend the late afternoon however you like, but make sure you get tickets ahead of time for a play or show (whether it's Shakespeare at the Globe or a West End musical), and book ahead at **Rules** for a post-theater dinner (in fact, try to reserve a week or so beforehand).

Start off **Day 2** at the **Tower of London** on one of the excellent Beefeater tours. Spend the late morning climbing the dome of Christopher Wren's masterpiece, **St. Paul's Cathedral.** After a late lunch, be at the meeting place for the **London Walks** tour that intrigues you the most (several leave from near St. Paul's). Try to get to **Westminster Abbey** early enough to pop into the Royal Chapels before they close. Duck out and head over to have a look at the neighboring **Houses of Parliament** and the clock tower with **Big Ben.** The **British Airways London Eye** is right across the river and, on a clear day, offers a stupendous view of London. If it's a Friday or Saturday, you still have time afterward to hit the **Tate Modern,** which doesn't close until 10 p.m.

If you have three days

Spend the morning of **Day 1** in the **British Museum,** which catalogs human achievement across the world and throughout the ages. During lunch, call the **Globe Theatre** to find out whether a play is on for the next day at 2 p.m. (if so, book tickets). Try to finish lunch by 2 p.m. and then head to the nearest stop on the map for the **Original London Sightseeing Tours** and take the 90-minute bus loop past the major sights of London, which will include **Buckingham Palace** and **Trafalgar Square.** After you're good and oriented, plunge right into the Old Masters of the **National Gallery.** Have a traditional British dinner at **Rules** or **Porters English**

Restaurant and try to get to bed early; you need to wake up early the next morning.

Day 2 is the day for the London of the Middle Ages and Renaissance. Be at the **Tower of London** by 9:30 a.m. to get in on the first guided tour of this medieval bastion and its Crown Jewels. Afterward, visit **St. Paul's Cathedral** and grab some lunch. Then head across the Thames River on the Millennium Bridge to visit the **Tate Modern.** Afterward, stroll Bankside walkway along the Thames to tour Shakespeare's **Globe Theatre** and, if possible, experience one of the Bard's plays in the open-air setting the way he intended (plays start at 2 p.m.). The tour itself only takes an hour; a play takes two to four hours.

If you see a play, plan on a quick dinner; if you just do the tour, you have the late afternoon to spend as you like — perhaps squeeze in a visit to **Tate Britain** to marvel at the best of British art, or take a ride on the **British Airways London Eye.** Either way, finish dinner by 6:30 or 7 p.m. so that you can join whichever historic pub walk **London Walks** is running that evening (they start at 7 or 7:30 p.m.; the brochure tells you where to meet). After your introduction to British ales and pub life, call it a night.

Yesterday was medieval, but for **Day 3** you're going to stiffen your upper lip with some Victorian-era British traditions. Start out at 9 a.m. by paying your respects to centuries of British heroes, poets, and kings buried at **Westminster Abbey.** Drop by the **Victoria & Albert Museum** for miles of the best in decorative arts and sculpture. Have a snack (not lunch) on your way to the world's grandest and most venerable department store, **Harrods.** After a bit of browsing inside, stop by the fourth floor's **Georgian Restaurant** at 3 p.m. sharp for a proper British afternoon tea. Linger and enjoy your teatime.

Head over to **Big Ben** and the **Houses of Parliament** around 5:30 p.m. and, if government is in session (Oct–July), get in line to go inside and watch Parliament at work, vilifying one another in a colorfully entertaining way that makes the U.S. Congress seem like a morgue. Or, if you go gaga over musicals (or are itching to see a cutting-edge London play), go see a show. Either way, because you'll eat late, make sure you've reserved a restaurant that specializes in late, after-theater meals (**Rules** is a good choice).

Traveling beyond London

You can find enough in London to keep you busy for weeks, but a day trip into the English countryside is a magnificent way to spread your wings and enlarge your horizons. Our top choices are Bath, with its ancient Roman baths and stately 18th-century mansions; Salisbury, with its imposing Gothic cathedral and Stonehenge nearby; and Oxford, one of the world's greatest college towns.

The fastest and easiest way to reach these destinations is by train. **National Express** (☎ 08705-808-080; www.nationalexpress.com) offers guided bus trips, but the buses take much longer than the train.

Bath: Ancient Rome in Georgian clothing

When Queen Anne relaxed at the natural hot springs here in 1702, she made the village of Bath fashionable, but she wasn't exactly blazing new territory. The Romans built the first town here in A.D. 75, a small village centered on the same hot springs. The water was considered to be sacred and healing, so the Romans built a temple over the springs and dedicated it to Sulis Minerva — a deity that combined the Latin goddess of knowledge, Minerva, with Sulis, the local Celtic water goddess. In the 18th century, when the Georgians were laying out what would become Britain's most unified cityscape — with the help of architects John Wood, Sr., and John Wood, Jr. — they unearthed the ancient temple, Britain's best-preserved Roman ruins.

Bath, today, is a genteel foray into the Georgian world, with its memories of fashionable balls, gambling, gossip, and of course, "taking the waters." Highlights of a visit here include touring the excavated Roman temple and admiring the honey-colored stone architecture that drew, in its heyday, the likes of Dickens, Thackeray, and Jane Austen, the writer most associated with Bath. With its parks, squares, and curving crescents, Bath is a city of such architectural distinction that UNESCO has designated it as a World Heritage City. Although doable as a day trip from London, Bath's charms really come out after the day-trippers leave; savvy travelers plan to stay the night and next morning.

Getting there

Trains to Bath leave from London's Paddington Station every half-hour; the trip takes about 90 minutes. For train fares and schedules, call **National Rail** at ☎ 08457-484950 or go to www.nationalrail.co.uk. Once you're there, pick up maps and information at the **Tourist Information Centre** (☎ 01225-477-761; www.visitbath.co.uk), located on the square next to Bath Abbey in the center of town.

Free, two-hour **Mayor's Guides walking tours** leave from outside the Pump Room Sunday through Friday at 10:30 a.m. and 2 p.m., and Saturday at 10:30 a.m. From May through September, additional walks are offered at 7 p.m. on Tuesday, Friday, and Saturday.

Seeing the sights

Start your tour at the city's main square. A spin through the **Roman Baths Museum** (☎ 01225-477-785; www.romanbaths.co.uk) with your digital audio guide in hand gives you an overview of the hot springs from their Celto-Roman inception (the head of Minerva is a highlight) to the 17th/18th-century spa built over the hot springs. You can drink a cup of the famous waters (taste: *blech!*) upstairs in the elegant **Pump Room** (☎ 01225-477-785). This cafe/restaurant offers one of England's classic afternoon tea services, but you can also get a good lunch here, all to the musical accompaniment of a live trio or solo pianist. Lunch and tea are served daily. The museum is open November through February daily from 9:30 a.m. to 4:30 p.m., March through June and September through October daily from 9 a.m. to 5 p.m., and July and August from 9 a.m. to 10 p.m. Admission is £11 ($22) adults, £9 ($18) seniors, £6.80 ($14) children, and £30 ($60) families.

After seeing the museum and Pump Room, head out to the square to examine **Bath Abbey** (☎ 01225-422-462), a 16th-century church renowned for the fantastic, scalloped fan vaulting of its ceilings. The Abbey is open Monday through Saturday from 9 a.m. to 4:30 p.m. (until 6 p.m. Apr–Oct), Sunday from 1 to 2:30 p.m. and 4:30 to 5:30 p.m. Admission is £2.50 ($5).

The Jane Austen Centre, 40 Gay St. (☎ 01225-443-000; www.jane austen.co.uk), located in a Georgian town house on an elegant street where Austen once lived, is something to visit if you're a Jane Austen buff. Exhibits and a video convey a sense of what life was like in Bath during the Regency period, and how the city influenced Austen's writing. The center is open daily from 9:45 a.m. to 5:30 p.m. (July–Aug Thurs–Sat until 8:30 p.m.; Nov–Feb daily until 4:30 p.m.). Admission is £6.50 ($13) adults, £4.95 ($9.90) seniors and students, £3.50 ($7) children, £18 ($36) families. The **Regency Tea Rooms** on the second floor are a nice spot for afternoon tea (£6.95/$14).

Bath in and of itself is a major attraction, so plan to stroll as much as you can. Be sure to visit the architectural triumphs of **The Circus** and the **Royal Crescent,** both up on the north end of town. The latter has a highly recommended museum, **No. 1 Royal Crescent** (☎ 01225-428-126), a gorgeously restored 18th-century house with period furnishings. It's open mid-February through mid-October Tuesdays through Sundays from 10:30 a.m. to 5 p.m., and mid-October through November from 10:30 a.m. to 4 p.m.; admission is £5 ($10) adults, £4 ($8) seniors, and £12 ($24) families.

Where to stay

If you can swing the £185-and-up ($370) per-double price tag, *the* place to stay in Bath is bang in the middle of one of the city's architectural triumphs at the **Royal Crescent Hotel,** 16 Royal Crescent (☎ 888-295-4710 in the U.S., 0800-980-0987 or 01225-823-333 in the U.K.; Fax: 01225-339-401; www.royalcrescent.co.uk). If you stay here, you get to experience a contemporary version of Georgian splendor, with a private boat and hot-air balloon at your disposal (for a hefty additional sum). Otherwise, the elegant **Victorian One Three Nine,** Leighton House, 139 Wells Rd. (☎ 01225-314-769; Fax: 01225-443-079; www.139bath.co.uk), is a small, stylish, boutique B&B that's much more affordable. Rack rates are £65 to £150 ($130–$300) double.

Where to dine

A popular eatery in Bath's city center is **No. 5 Bistro,** 5 Argyle St.
(☎ 01225-444-499). The chef at this pleasant restaurant produces
mouthwatering daily specials such as steak, Provençal fish soup, char-
grilled loin of lamb, and vegetarian dishes. Main courses are £14 to £17
($28–$34).

Salisbury and Stonehenge: Inspired spires and outstanding standing stones

Many visitors hurrying out to see the famous stone circle known as
Stonehenge are surprised to find one of Europe's greatest Gothic cathedrals just 14km (9 miles) away. Salisbury, gateway to South Wiltshire and
its prehistoric remains, is a medieval market town that's a deserved
attraction in its own right. Although you can see the cathedral and
Stonehenge as a day trip from London, you have to rush to do it.

Getting there

Hourly trains travel from London's Waterloo Station to Salisbury
(pronounced *Sauls*-bur-ee) daily. From here, **Wilts and Dorset buses**
(☎ 01722-336-855; www.wdbus.co.uk) depart about every two hours
(starting at 10:25 a.m.) for the 40-minute trip out to Stonehenge, 14km
(9 miles) north of the city at the junction of the A303 and A344/A360.

Salisbury's **Tourist Information Centre** (☎ 01722-334-956; www.visit
salisbury.com) is on Fish Row.

Seeing the sights

Salisbury Cathedral, The Close (☎ 01722-555-120), the town's one
must-see attraction, dates from the 13th century and is the best example
of the Perpendicular Gothic style of architecture in all of England. The
123-m (404-ft.) spire is the tallest in the country and dominates the countryside. Step into the cathedral's exceptionally beautiful octagonal chapter house to see one of the four surviving original copies of the Magna
Carta, and then stroll through the serene cloisters. The suggested dona-
tion for admission is £5 ($10) for adults, £4.25 ($8.50) for seniors and students, £3 ($6) for children, and £12 ($24) for families. The cathedral is
open daily from 7:15 a.m. to 6:15 p.m. (until 7:15 p.m. June–Aug).

After exploring the cathedral, take some time to wander around the
Cathedral Close, the historic precinct housing the cathedral and sur-
rounded by old stone walls and the River Avon. Some of Salisbury's
finest houses are in the large Close, which includes some 75 buildings.
You can tour one of the best of the remaining houses: **Mompesson
House** (☎ 01722-335-659; www.nationaltrust.org.uk), built in 1701.
The house evokes the Queen Anne period so richly that period dramas
are often filmed here. (You may recognize the house from director Ang
Lee's 1995 *Sense and Sensibility*.) The house is open mid-March through

Still standing: the stones of Stonehenge

Stonehenge (☎ 01980-624-715; www.english-heritage.org), one of the world's most renowned prehistoric sites and one of England's most popular attractions, is a stone circle of megalithic pillars and lintels built on the flat Salisbury Plain some 3,500 to 5,000 years ago. As you walk around the site, and listen to the history of Stonehenge on the free audio guide, the majesty and mystery of these ancient stones will not be lost on you.

Stonehenge was almost certainly a shrine and/or ceremonial gathering place of some kind. A popular theory is that the site was an astronomical observatory because it's aligned to the summer solstice and can accurately predict eclipses based on the placement of the stones. Recent archaeological evidence has uncovered another ceremonial avenue nearby, leading experts to speculate that Stonehenge was also an important burial place. But in an age when experts think they know everything, Stonehenge still keeps its tantalizing secrets to itself. Admission is £6.30 ($13) adults, £4.70 ($9.40) seniors and students, and £3.20 ($6.40) children. Stonehenge is open daily from March 16 through May and September through October 15 from 9:30 a.m. to 6 p.m., June through August from 9 a.m. to 7 p.m., and October 16 to March 15 from 9:30 a.m. to 4 p.m.

October Saturday through Wednesday from 11 a.m. to 5 p.m.; admission for adults is £4.50 ($9). If you have time, walk through the nearby Water Meadows, where you can enjoy a view of the cathedral and surrounding landscape made famous by the painter John Constable in the early 19th century.

Where to stay

A double with breakfast at the comfortable **Mercure White Hart Hotel** (☎ 01722-327-416; www.mercure.uk.com), opposite Salisbury Cathedral, goes for £90 to £160 ($180–$320). More atmospheric is the **Red Lion Hotel** (☎ 01722-323-334; www.the-redlion.co.uk), an ancient coaching inn (now owned by Best Western) where the doubles with breakfast start at £134 ($268) and an open fire warms the pub.

Where to dine

For good homemade food in the center of Salisbury (overlooking the marketplace), go to **Harper's Restaurant,** 7–9 Ox Row, Market Square (☎ 01722-333-118). On the menu at this old-fashioned restaurant you'll find uncomplicated main courses such as lemon sole, burritos, deep-fried calamari, and Wiltshire sausages. Main courses run from £7.50 to £14 ($15–$28). **One Minster Street,** 1 Minster St. (☎ 01722-322-024), is the trendy new name for a wonderfully atmospheric chophouse and pub that dates to 1320 and that everyone still calls the Haunch of Venison. The menu at the third-floor restaurant combines contemporary international cuisine and traditional favorites; mains go for £7.50 to £15 ($15–$30). Do check out the ancient pub rooms, even if you don't dine here.

Oxford: The original college town

Oxford University, one of the world's oldest, greatest, and most revered universities, dominates the town of Oxford, about 87km (54 miles) north-west of London. Its skyline pierced by ancient tawny towers and spires, Oxford has been a center of learning for seven centuries (the Saxons founded the city in the 10th century). Roger Bacon, Sir Walter Raleigh, John Donne, Sir Christopher Wren, Dr. Samuel Johnson, Edward Gibbon, William Penn, John Wesley, Lewis Carroll, T. E. Lawrence, W. H. Auden, and Margaret Thatcher are just a few of the distinguished alumni who've taken degrees here. Even Bill Clinton studied at Oxford.

Although academically oriented, Oxford is far from dull. Its long sweep of a main street (High Street, known as "The High") buzzes with a cosmo-politan mix of locals, students, black-gowned dons, and foreign visitors. You can tour some of the beautiful historic colleges, each sequestered away within its own quadrangle (or quad) built around an interior court-yard; stroll along the lovely Cherwell River; and visit the Ashmolean Museum.

Getting there and taking a tour

Oxford is a comfortable day trip from London. Trains depart hourly from London's Paddington Station, take just over an hour, and cost £16 ($32) for a round-trip "cheap day return" ticket.

The **Oxford Information Centre,** 15–16 Broad St. (☎ **01865-726-871;** www.visitoxford.org), conducts two-hour **walking tours** of the town and its major colleges (but not New College or Christ Church). Tours leave daily at 11 a.m. and 2 p.m., with additional walks on Saturday at 10:30 a.m. and 1 p.m.; the cost is £6.50 ($13) adults, £3 ($6) children 5 to 15.

City Sightseeing (☎ **01708-864-340;** www.citysightseeing.co.uk) offers a one-hour **bus tour** (£9.50/$19) with hop-on/hop-off service. Buses depart daily from the train station starting at 9:30 a.m. and run every 15 to 20 minutes until 5 or 6 p.m., depending on the season.

Seeing the sights

Oxford University (☎ **01865-270-000;** www.ox.ac.uk) doesn't have just one, but 45 widely dispersed colleges serving some 16,000 students. Instead of trying to see them all (impossible in a day), focus on seeing a handful of the better-known ones. Faced with an overabundance of tourists, the colleges have restricted visiting to certain hours and to groups of six or fewer; in some areas, you aren't allowed in at all. Before heading off, check with the tourist office to find out when and what colleges you can visit, or take their excellent walking tour.

A good way to start your tour is with a bird's-eye view of the colleges from the top of **Carfax Tower** (☎ **01865-792-653**) in the center of the city. The tower is all that remains from St. Martin's Church, where William Shakespeare stood as godfather for a fellow playwright. The tower is open November through March daily from 10:30 a.m. to 3:30 p.m., and April through October from 10 a.m. to 5 p.m. Admission is £2 ($4) adults, £1 ($2) children 5 to 15.

The Oxford Story, 6 Broad St. (☎ 01865-790-055), packages Oxford's complexities into a concise and entertaining exhibit-cum-ride that takes you through 800 years of the city's history, reviewing some of the architectural and historical features that you may otherwise miss. It also fills you in on the backgrounds of the colleges and those people who've passed through their portals. Admission costs £7.25 ($15) for adults. The exhibit is open July and August daily from 9:30 a.m. to 5 p.m., and September through June daily from 10 a.m. to 4:30 p.m. (from 11 a.m. on Sun).

We recommend visits to the following three colleges:

- ✔ **Christ Church College** (☎ 01865-276-150), facing St. Aldate's Street, was begun by Cardinal Wolsey in 1525. Christ Church has the largest quadrangle of any college in Oxford and a chapel with 15th-century pillars and impressive fan vaulting. **Tom Tower** houses Great Tom, the 18,000-pound bell that rings nightly at 9:05 p.m., signaling the closing of the college gates. The college and chapel are open Monday through Saturday from 9 a.m. to 5 p.m., Sunday from 1 to 5:30 p.m. Admission is £4.90 ($9.80).

- ✔ **Magdalen** (pronounced *Maud*-lin) **College,** on High Street (☎ 01865-276-000), founded in 1458, boasts the oldest botanical garden in England and the most extensive grounds of any Oxford college; you even find a deer park. The 15th-century bell tower, one of the town's most famous landmarks, is reflected in the waters of the Cherwell River. You can cross a small footbridge and stroll through the water meadows along the path known as Addison's Walk. October through June, the college is open daily from 1 p.m. to dusk; July and August, it's open daily noon to 6 p.m. Admission is £3 ($6).

- ✔ **Merton College** (☎ 01865-276-310), dating from 1264, stands near Merton Street, the only medieval cobbled street left in Oxford. The college is noted for its 14th-century library, said to be the oldest college library in England (admission is £1/$2). On display is an *astrolabe* (an astronomical instrument used for measuring the altitude of the sun and stars) thought to have belonged to Chaucer. The library and college are open Monday through Friday 2 to 4 p.m., and Saturday and Sunday 10 a.m. to 4 p.m.; both close for a week at Easter and at Christmas.

East of Carfax is the famed **Bodleian Library,** Broad Street (☎ 01865-277-000), the world's oldest library, established in 1450. The **Radcliffe Camera,** the domed building just south of the Bodleian, is the library's reading room, dating from 1737. You can visit parts of the library on a one-hour guided tour (daily at 10:30 a.m., 11:30 a.m., 2 p.m., and 3 p.m.; £6/$12); call or stop in at the Bodleian bookstore for details.

If you only visit one museum in town, make it the **Ashmolean Museum** (☎ 01865-278-000; www.ashmolean.org), founded in 1683 and one of Britain's best. The impressive painting collection features works by Bellini, Raphael, Michelangelo, Rembrandt, and Picasso. The museum is open Tuesday through Saturday from 10 a.m. to 5 p.m. and Sunday from 2 to 5 p.m.; admission is free.

Where to stay

You can hole up for the night at the **Mercure Eastgate Townhouse**, 23 Merton St., The High (☎ 0118-971-4700; www.mercure.uk.com), originally a 17th-century coaching inn. The hotel is near the river, close to most of the colleges, with modern doubles going for £99 to £119 ($198–$238) with breakfast.

Where to dine

Browns, 5–11 Woodstock Rd. (☎ 01865-319-655), a large, casual, upbeat brasserie, is one of the best places to eat in Oxford. It serves hearty food, including a good traditional cream tea, and has a large convivial bar and a very pleasant outdoor terrace. Main courses run from £7 to £16 ($14–$32). If you don't want to spend a lot for lunch, stop in at **Mortons**, 22 Broad St. (☎ 01865-200-860). They make delicious sandwiches on fresh baguettes and serve a daily soup; open daily 8:30 a.m. to 5 p.m.

Fast Facts: London

American Express

You can find Amex foreign exchanges in terminals 3 and 4 at Heathrow (☎ 020-8759-6845) and in London at 78 Brompton Rd., Knightsbridge SW3 (☎ 020-7761-7905).

Area Code

The country code for the United Kingdom is **44**. The city code for most of Greater London is **020**. Many businesses instead use the new, non-geographical code of **0870**. When dialing either from abroad, drop the initial 0. To call London from the United States, dial **011-44-20**, and then the local number. See also "Telephone," later in this section.

Currency

Britain has so far opted out of adopting the euro. The basic unit of currency is the pound sterling (£), divided into 100 pence (p). There are 1p, 2p, 10p, 20p, 50p, £1, and £2 coins; banknotes are issued in £5, £10, £20, and £50.

The rate of exchange used to calculate the dollar values given in this chapter is $1 = 50p (or £1 = $2). Amounts over $10 have been rounded to the nearest dollar.

Doctors and Dentists

Most hotels have physicians on call. Medical Express, 117A Harley St., W1 (☎ 020-7499-1991; Tube: Oxford Circus), is a private clinic with walk-in medical service (no appointment necessary) Monday through Friday 9 a.m. to 6 p.m., and Saturday 10 a.m. to 2 p.m. Dental Emergency Care Service, Guy's Hospital, St. Thomas Street, SE8 (☎ 020-7188-7188; Tube: London Bridge), is open Monday through Friday 8:45 a.m. to 3:30 p.m. for walk-in patients.

Embassy

The U.S. Embassy and Consulate is at 24 Grosvenor Sq., W1 (☎ 020-7499-9000; www.usembassy.org.uk). For passport and visa information, visit the Special Consular Services Monday through Friday 8:30 to 11:30 a.m. and 2 to 5 p.m.

Emergency

Dial ☎ **999** to call the police, report a fire, or call for an ambulance.

Hospitals

See "Doctors and Dentists," earlier in this section.

Information

The main Tourist Information Centre, Britain & London Visitor Centre, 1 Lower Regent St., Piccadilly Circus, SW1 (Tube: Piccadilly Circus), provides tourist information to walk-in visitors Monday 9:30 a.m. to 6:30 p.m., Tuesday through Friday 9 a.m. to 6:30 p.m., and Saturday and Sunday 10 a.m. to 4 p.m. Another Tourist Information Centre is located in the Arrivals Hall of the Waterloo Terminal (Open: Daily 8:30 a.m.–10 p.m.). For general London information, call ☎ 0870-156-6366.

The London Information Centre in Leicester Square is open late seven days a week. See "Finding information after you arrive," earlier in this chapter.

Online you can get information at the national Visit Britain site (www.visit britain.org) and Visit London's site (www.visitlondon.com).

Internet Access and Cybercafes

The easyInternetCafe shops (www.easy internetcafe.com), located all over London and open daily from 8 or 9 a.m. to 11 p.m. or midnight, offer hundreds of terminals and charge the lowest rates in town — £1 ($2) per hour. Branches include 456–459

The Strand, just off Trafalgar Square, across from Charing Cross Station (Tube: Charing Cross); 9–13 Wilton Rd., opposite Victoria Station (Tube: Victoria); 9–16 Tottenham Court Rd. (Tube: Tottenham Court Road or Goodge); and 43 Regent St., in the Burger King on Picadilly Circus (Tube: Picadilly Circus).

Maps

The London A to Z (the *Z* is pronounced "zed") is a widely available street atlas that maps every teensy alleyway, mews, close, and street in all of London. Makes a great souvenir, too.

Newspapers and Magazines

The best way to find out what's going on around town, from shows to restaurants to events, is to buy a copy of the *Time Out London* magazine, published every Tuesday and available at newsstands. You can also get listings from *Time Out London*'s competitor, *What's On,* as well as from the *Evening Standard.*

Pharmacies

Boots (www.boots.com) is the largest chain of London *chemists* (drugstores). You find them located all over London. They're generally open Monday through Saturday from 9 a.m. to 10 p.m. and Sunday from noon to 5 p.m.

Police

In an emergency, dial ☎ **999** from any phone; no money is needed.

Post Office

The most central post office is the Trafalgar Square branch at 24–28 William IV St. (☎ 020-7930-9580), open Monday through Saturday from 8:30 a.m. to 5:30 p.m. Other post offices and *sub-post offices* (window newsagent stores) are open Monday through Friday 9 a.m. to 5:30 p.m. and

Saturday 9 a.m. to 12:30 p.m. Look for red POST OFFICE signs outside.

Safety

Security in the London Underground was dramatically increased following the 2005 terrorist attacks. In general, London is a safe city. As in any large metropolis, use common sense and normal caution when you're in a crowded public area or walking alone at night. The area around Euston Station has more purse snatchings than anywhere else in London.

Taxes

In England, a 17.5 percent value-added tax (VAT) is figured into the price of most items. Foreign visitors can reclaim a percentage of the VAT on major purchases of consumer goods (see Chapter 4 for more about this).

Taxis

See the "Getting Around London" section, earlier in this chapter.

Telephone

London has three kinds of pay phones — one that accepts only coins; the Cardphone, which takes only phone cards; and one that accepts both phone cards and credit cards. The minimum charge for a local call is 20p (40¢) for 55 seconds. Stick to small coins at coin-operated phones because they don't make change. Phone cards are sold at newsstands and post offices in amounts varying from £3 ($6) to £20 ($40). Credit card pay phones accept the usual credit cards — Visa, MasterCard, American Express — but the minimum charge is 50p ($1); insert the card and dial 144. For directory assistance, dial 192 for the United Kingdom or 153 for international; for operator-assisted calls, dial 100 for the United Kingdom or 155 for international.

To call the United States direct from London, dial 001 followed by the area code and phone number. To charge a call to your calling card or make a collect call home, dial AT&T (☎ 0800-890-011 or 0500-890-011), MCI (☎ 0800-279-5088), or Sprint (☎ 0800-890-877 or 0500-890-877). See also "Area Code," earlier in this section.

Transit Info

For 24-hour information on London's Underground, buses, and ferries, call Transport for London (☎ 020-7222-1234; www.tfl.gov.uk).

Chapter 11

Edinburgh and the Best of Scotland

In This Chapter

▶ Getting to Edinburgh
▶ Checking out the neighborhoods
▶ Discovering the best places to sleep and eat
▶ Exploring the city's highlights
▶ Heading into the Highlands or wandering west to Glasgow

*E*dinburgh is an attractive city full of distinguished architecture and devoted to the fine arts. Called the "Athens of the North," partly because of its renowned university and intellectual life (Sir Walter Scott and Robert Burns lived here, and Robert Louis Stevenson is a native son) and partly because some neoclassical ruins top one of its hills, Edinburgh's history lends it an air of old-fashioned romance. But don't be fooled. The city is also a modern, international business destination and enjoys some of the most happening nightlife in Britain. Edinburgh (*ed*-in-bur-ah) is a cultural capital of Europe and hosts a performing arts blowout every August called the Edinburgh International Festival (see "More cool things to see and do," later in this chapter). It also serves as a gateway to the fabled, heather-clad Highlands. It's possible to tour Edinburgh in a day, but it really deserves two or three.

 The Scots are a proud people with a long, turbulent history. Although Scotland is incorporated into the United Kingdom, the Scots are fiercely independent and increasingly autonomous. Use the word *Scotch* only to describe the whisky, the broth, or the prevailing northern mist. Calling a person Scotch is considered an insult. Refer to the locals here as *Scots* or *Scottish*.

Getting There

Scotland borders England to the north, so if you're coming to Edinburgh from London, the best choices are a quick one-hour flight or a scenic five-hour train ride that lets you off right in the middle of town.

Arriving by air

Edinburgh Airport (☎ **0870-040-0007**; www.edinburghairport.com) is just 10km (6 miles) west of town and handles flights from all over Great Britain and major cities on the Continent (including Amsterdam, Brussels, Frankfurt, Paris, Madrid, and Zurich). The airport is small and quite manageable. The information desk is located in the arrivals hall. To get into the city, you can take the **Airlink 100** bus (☎ **0131-555-6363**; www.flybybus.com), which leaves every ten minutes or so (every 30 minutes at night when the bus follows a slightly different route) for the 25-minute trip to downtown's Waverley Station. One-way fare is £3 ($6); round-trip is £5 ($10). You can buy tickets at the airport Airlink desk or onboard the bus. A 20-minute taxi ride from the airport to Edinburgh runs about £18 ($36). The taxi *rank* (stand) is to the left outside the arrivals hall.

Arriving by train or bus

Fast trains link London with Edinburgh's **Waverley Station,** at the east end of Princes Street. All trains depart from London **King's Cross Station,** except for the overnight train, which departs from London **Euston.** The journey takes 4½ hours during the day; overnight trains take 7¼ hours and have couchettes. *Coaches* (the term for buses here) from London cost less, but they take eight hours and arrive at a bus depot on St. Andrew Square.

Orienting Yourself in Edinburgh

Edinburgh is a port town of sorts; its outskirts rest on the **Firth of Forth,** an inlet of the North Sea. The center of town is an ancient volcanic outcrop crowned by **Edinburgh Castle.** Due east of the castle is Waverley Station. **Princes Street Gardens** stretches between the two and effectively divides the city into the Old Town to the south and the gridlike New Town to the north.

Introducing the neighborhoods

Hotels and shops fill **New Town,** developed in the 18th century. The major east–west streets of New Town are **Princes Street,** bordering the gardens named after it, and **George Street,** which runs parallel to Princes Street 2 blocks north.

The **Royal Mile,** the main thoroughfare of the **Old Town,** spills off the castle's mount and runs downhill to the east. It's a single road, but the Royal Mile carries several names: Lawnmarket, High Street, and Canongate. Farther to the south is the **University District,** one of the hot spots for Edinburgh's famed nightlife.

Finding information after you arrive

Edinburgh's tourist office (see the "Fast Facts: Edinburgh" section at the end of this chapter) is an excellent resource.

Scotland

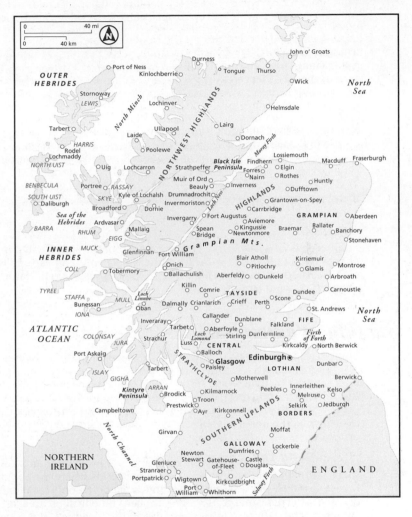

Getting Around Edinburgh

Because historic Edinburgh is not a big area, you can walk most of it easily. But if you plan to travel across town to catch a show or see a sight, consider hopping a bus or hailing a cab.

By bus

City buses (☎ **0131-555-6363;** www.lothianbuses.co.uk) are cheap and offer quick access to the residential districts that surround the city center (where you find the more inexpensive hotels and B&Bs). On Edinburgh buses, you pay a £1 ($2) flat fare (60p/$1.20 children 5–15) for any distance traveled; drop *exact change* in the slot. Night buses cost £2 ($4).

The **Dayticket** costs £2.50 ($5) for adults and £2 ($4) for children for a full day of unlimited rides. Purchase tickets from the driver as you board, but be sure to have the correct change.

By taxi

You can reach Edinburgh's tourist sights easily on foot, but a taxi may be useful if you're traveling longer distances or carrying luggage. Hail a cab or find one at a taxi rank at Hanover Street, Waverley Station, or Haymarket Station. To call a taxi, dial ☎ **0131-229-2468** or 0131-228-1211. Taxi fares start at £1.50 ($3) or £2.50 ($5) at night, and go up in 25p (50¢) increments every 45 seconds or 445 meters (¼ mile).

By foot

Edinburgh is an easily walked city, and most of the sights listed in this chapter won't take you too far from the city's center. An especially pleasant walk is down the Royal Mile (see "Exploring Edinburgh," later in this chapter).

Staying in Edinburgh

Edinburgh hotels are not cheap, and they all charge three different rates: off-season, high season, and festival season (the annual Edinburgh International Festival — see "More cool things to see and do," later in this chapter). If you don't book well in advance for festival time, you probably won't find a room, at least not anywhere near the city center. Even if you do book in advance, staying near the city center during the festival costs more than double the off-season price.

Luckily, Edinburgh has many pleasant suburbs no more than 20 minutes by bus from the center of town — neighborhoods where the rooms cost less year-round and where you can find some of the only available space during the festival. Inexpensive guesthouses fill one such area, around Dalkeith Road between Holyrood Park and the Meadows, just a ten-minute bus ride south of the Old Town.

The tourist office has a booklet listing local B&Bs and guesthouses, and the staff can help you find room in one or space in a regular hotel for a small fee.

For general tips on booking and what to expect from European accommodations, see Chapter 7.

Edinburgh's top hotels and B&Bs

Balmoral Hotel
$$$$$ New Town

Edinburgh's oldest luxury hotel is a 1902 city landmark with a clock tower, where kilted doormen welcome you to a slightly contrived Scottish experience. The Rocco Forte chain recently refurbished the hotel, and the large rooms are now outfitted in a Victorian-meets-contemporary-comfort style, discreetly cushy and with full amenities. The Michelin-starred Number One restaurant is refined and highly recommended for international cuisine, as is the modern brasserie-style Hadrian's. You can take afternoon tea in the Palm Court after a workout in the gym, a trip to the spa or sauna, or a dip in the indoor pool. The rack rates are exorbitant, so be certain to check the hotel's Web site for special offers and packages.

See map p. 168. 1 Princes St. (at the east end of the street, practically on top of the train station). ☎ *800-225-5843 in the U.S. or 0131-556-2414. Fax: 0131-557-3747.* www.thebalmoralhotel.com. *Bus: 3, 3A, 4, 8, 15, 26, 30, 31, 33, or 44 (but if you're arriving by train, you're already there). Rack rates: £345–£510 ($690–$1,020) double. Full Scottish breakfast £19 ($38); continental breakfast £14 ($28). AE, DC, MC, V.*

Bank Hotel
$$–$$$ Old Town

This unusual hotel is located right in the heart of Old Town and offers better value than all of its competitors along the Royal Mile. Built in 1923 as a branch of the Royal Bank of Scotland, it now offers a handful of individually decorated theme rooms (each named for a famous Scotsman) above Logie Baird's Bar, a lively ground-floor bar and restaurant. You'll find delightful touches throughout, and the bathrooms are as nice and comfortable as the rooms.

See map p. 168. Royal Mile at 1–3 S. Bridge St. ☎ *0131-622-6800. Fax: 0131-622-6822.* www.festival-inns.co.uk. *Bus: 4, 15, 31, or 100. Rack rates: £85–£125 ($170–$250) double. Rates include breakfast. AE, DC, MC, V.*

The Bonham
$$$–$$$$ New Town

Style is pumped up to a very high level at this New Town hotel occupying three Victorian town houses. The high-ceilinged, large-windowed guest rooms feature the best of contemporary furnishings against a bold palette of colors. Beds are huge and bathrooms as fine as you'll find. The hotel is very techno-friendly and every room has its own communication and entertainment center. The Restaurant at the Bonham offers fine dining.

See map p. 168. 35 Drumsheugh Gardens. ☎ *0131-226-6050. Fax: 0131-226-6080.* www.thebonham.com. *Bus: 41 or 42. Rack rates: £110–£250 ($220–$500) double. Rates include full Scottish breakfast. AE, MC, V.*

Accommodations, Dining, and Attractions in Edinburgh

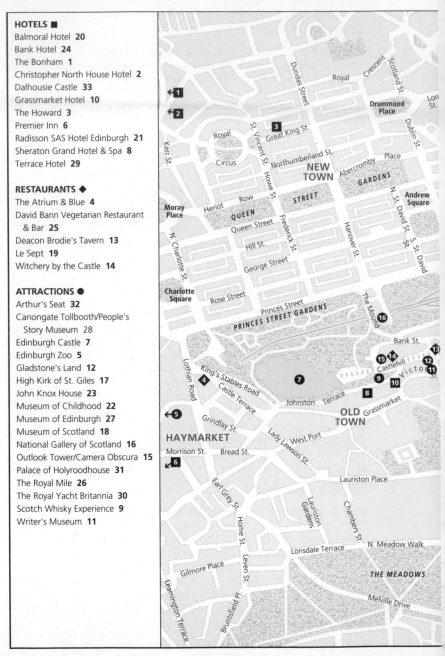

HOTELS ■

Balmoral Hotel **20**
Bank Hotel **24**
The Bonham **1**
Christopher North House Hotel **2**
Dalhousie Castle **33**
Grassmarket Hotel **10**
The Howard **3**
Premier Inn **6**
Radisson SAS Hotel Edinburgh **21**
Sheraton Grand Hotel & Spa **8**
Terrace Hotel **29**

RESTAURANTS ◆

The Atrium & Blue **4**
David Bann Vegetarian Restaurant
  & Bar **25**
Deacon Brodie's Tavern **13**
Le Sept **19**
Witchery by the Castle **14**

ATTRACTIONS ●

Arthur's Seat **32**
Canongate Tollbooth/People's
  Story Museum **28**
Edinburgh Castle **7**
Edinburgh Zoo **5**
Gladstone's Land **12**
High Kirk of St. Giles **17**
John Knox House **23**
Museum of Childhood **22**
Museum of Edinburgh **27**
Museum of Scotland **18**
National Gallery of Scotland **16**
Outlook Tower/Camera Obscura **15**
Palace of Holyroodhouse **31**
The Royal Mile **26**
The Royal Yacht Britannia **30**
Scotch Whisky Experience **9**
Writer's Museum **11**

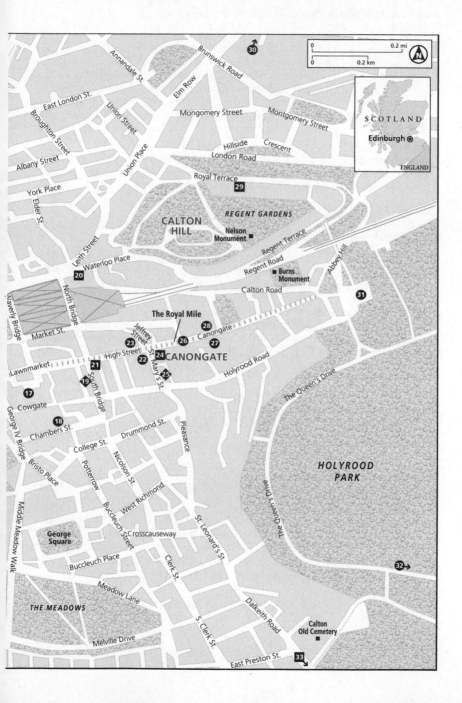

0.2 mi
0.2 km

SCOTLAND

Edinburgh ⊛

ENGLAND

Brunswick Road
30

Annandale St.
Elm Row
East London St.
Union Street
Mongomery Street
Montgomery Street
Broughton Street
Union Place
Hillside
Crescent
Albany Street
London Road
York Place
Royal Terrace
29
Elder St.
Leith Street

REGENT GARDENS

**CALTON
HILL**
Nelson
Monument ■

Regent Terrace

Abbey Hill

Waterloo Place
Regent Road
20
Burns
Monument

Calton Road
31

North Bridge
Waverley Bridge
The Royal Mile
28 Canongate
Jeffrey
Street
23 **26** **27**
Market St.
St. Mary's St.
High Street **22** **24** CANONGATE
21
Lawnmarket
19
Holyrood Road
South Bridge
25
17
Cowgate
George IV Bridge
18
Chambers St.
Drummond St.
Pleasance
Bristo Place
College St.
Potterrow
Nicolson St.
West Richmond
The Queen's Drive

**HOLYROOD
PARK**

Middle Meadow Walk
Buccleuch Street
Crosscauseway
**George
Square**
Clerk St.
St. Leonard's St.
Buccleuch Place
32➜
Meadow Lane
THE MEADOWS
S. Clerk St.
Dalkeith Road
Calton
Old Cemetery ■
Melville Drive
East Preston St.
33

Christopher North House Hotel
$$–$$$$ New Town

Christopher North, a famous and colorful figure in 19th-century Edinburgh, lived in this neoclassical town house from 1826 to 1854. The dramatic staircase and glass-roofed foyer ceiling are original, and the red-flocked hallway wallpaper re-creates a Victorian splendor, but the room furnishings are modern and the décor full of dramatic accents. Some of the rooms are rather small; suites are large and comfortably luxurious. Bathrooms throughout are ample and well equipped. Bacchus, the hotel's intimate restaurant, is one of Edinburgh's best-kept secrets.

See map p. 168. 6 Gloucester Place. ☎ 0131-225-2720. Fax: 0131-220-4706. www. christophernorth.co.uk. Bus: 19 or 80 to North West Circus Place. Rack rates: £98–£198 ($196–$296) double. Rates include full breakfast. AE, DC, MC, V.

Dalhousie Castle
$$$–$$$$$ Bonnyrigg

Staying right in charming Edinburgh is convenient, but you can travel just outside the town to find a 15th-century castle that offers all the medieval romance that you expect to find in Scotland. Henry IV, Sir Walter Scott, and Queen Victoria all resided at Dalhousie Castle, before it was renovated to provide luxurious, modern comforts. The castle's sylvan setting beside a flowing stream appeals to romantic and to outdoorsy types alike. The hotel organizes salmon and trout fishing, shooting, and horseback riding expeditions. Try the Dungeon Restaurant for a unique dining experience. The novelty of staying in a castle is usually a big hit with kids. Children 11 and under stay free in parent's room.

See map p. 168. Bonnyrigg (13km/8 miles southeast of Edinburgh). ☎ 01875-820-153. Fax: 01875-821-936. www.dalhousiecastle.co.uk. By car: Take the A7 13km (8 miles) southeast of Edinburgh toward Carlisle and turn right onto B704; the castle is just outside the village of Bonnyrigg. Rack rates: £135–£330 ($270–$660) double. Rates include full Scottish breakfast. AE, DC, MC, V.

The Howard
$$$$–$$$$$ New Town

Classic elegance, impeccable service, and gorgeous furnishings combine to make this one of Edinburgh's finest small deluxe hotels. Occupying three Georgian terrace houses, the Howard is refined but relaxed about it. The spacious guest rooms are impeccable, the bathrooms fabulous (some have free-standing "roll-top" Georgian-style bathtubs). Your dedicated butler is on call 24/7.

See map p. 168. 34 Great King St. ☎ 0131-550-3500. Fax: 0131-557-6515. Bus: 13, 23, 27, or C5. www.thehoward.com. Rack rates: £165–£295 ($330–$590) double. Rates include full breakfast. AE, DC, MC, V.

Sheraton Grand Hotel & Spa
$$$$$ **New Town**

A short walk from Princes Street, this upscale hotel has one of Europe's greatest spas attached to it. The spacious, traditionally furnished guest rooms are extremely comfortable and have nice bathrooms; the castle-view rooms on the top floors are the best. Very fine dining is available in the Grill Room; traditional afternoon tea is served in the graciously appointed hotel bar, called The Exchange. What really makes this hotel stand out, however, is the new and superlatively equipped spa, which contains a state-of-the-art gym, gorgeous indoor and outdoor pools, steam room and sauna, and a complete array of spa treatments. Children 12 and under stay free in parent's room.

See map p. 168. 1 Festival Sq. ☎ 800-325-3535 in the U.S. and Canada or 0131-229-9131. Fax: 0131-228-4510. Bus: 4, 15, or 44. www.starwoodhotels.com/sheraton. *Rates: £220–£260 ($385–$455) double. AE, DC, MC, V.*

Edinburgh's runner-up accommodations

Grassmarket Hotel
$ **Old Town** This centrally located budget hotel beneath the castle has reasonably priced rooms, which range from adequate to extra large, and bathrooms with showers. Nothing glamorous, but the location is great. Be aware that Grassmarket can be busy and noisy on weekend nights. *See map p. 168. 94 Grassmarket. ☎ 0131-220-2299.*

Radisson SAS Hotel Edinburgh
$$$–$$$$ **Old Town** The almost castlelike Radisson — formerly a Crowne Plaza — looks centuries older than its 15 years, due to Edinburgh's strict zoning rules for the Royal Mile. The hotel has smallish, amenity-filled rooms and a stellar location, plus a health club, pool, and restaurant (appetizing international cuisine in a dull subterranean environment). *See map p. 168. 80 High St. (on the Royal Mile just east of South Bridge). ☎ 888-201-1718 in the U.S., or 0131-557-9797.* www.radisson.com.

Terrace Hotel
$ **New Town** Terrace Hotel offers a bit of elegance — and 4m (14-ft.) ceilings — at a reasonable price in a historic Georgian home. *See map p. 168. 37 Royal Terrace (on the north side of Calton Hill near Regent Gardens). ☎ 0131-556-3423.* www.terracehotel.co.uk.

Premier Inn
$ **Old Town** Premier Inn is part of a massive hotel chain: zippo atmosphere, but some 278 clean, motel-like rooms at dirt-cheap rates (plus a full Scottish breakfast for under £5/$10). *See map p. 168. 1 Morrison Link (a ten-minute walk west of Edinburgh Castle). ☎ 0870-238-3319.* www.premierinn.com.

Dining in Edinburgh

Edinburgh boasts the finest restaurants in Scotland. You'll find an array of top restaurants serving Scottish, French, Modern European, and ethnic cuisines. The Scottish–French culinary connection dates back to the time of Mary Queen of Scots, though it's been much refined over the centuries. More and more restaurants are catering to vegetarians, too. Some of the dishes Edinburgh is known for include fresh salmon and seafood, game from Scottish fields, and Aberdeen Angus steaks. What's the rage at lunch? *Stuffed jacket potatoes* (baked potatoes with a variety of stuffings) are popular, but you can also get good sandwiches at coffee bars on the Royal Mile and in other locations around central Edinburgh.

At a Scottish high tea, you can sample freshly baked scones alongside some of the best fresh jams (especially raspberry), heather honeys, and marmalades in Europe. Also excellent are Scottish cheeses — look in particular for cheddars; the creamy, oatmeal-coated Caboc; and cottage cheeses.

The Atrium

$$$$ New Town   MODERN SCOTTISH/INTERNATIONAL

This stylish, award-winning restaurant next to the Traverse Theatre has been one of the top dining spots in Edinburgh since 1993. The menu draws inspiration from Scotland and all over the world. The offerings change daily but may include roast pumpkin soup; wild mushroom, truffle, and artichoke risotto; pan-fried halibut; or filet of Aberdeen Angus beef. Rosemary crème brûlée with mascarpone sorbet is one delectable dessert worth trying. Upstairs, the Atrium's sister restaurant, **Blue** (☎ **131-221-1222;** www.blue scotland.co.uk), offers lighter fare and lower prices.

See map p. 168. 10 Cambridge St. (off Lothian Road, beneath Saltire Court). ☎ **0131-228-8882.** www.atriumrestaurant.co.uk. *Reservations highly recommended. Bus: 2, 10, 11, 15, 15A, 16, 17, or 24. Main courses: Lunch £20–£24 ($40–$48); dinner £12–£20 ($24–$40); fixed-price dinner menu £27 ($54). AE, DC, MC, V. Open: Mon–Fri noon to 2 p.m.; Mon–Sat 6–10 p.m. Closed Christmas week.*

Have you had your haggis today?

Scotland's national "dish" is the infamous *haggis,* a fat, cantaloupe-size sausage traditionally made from sheep lungs, liver, and hearts mixed with spices, suet, oatmeal, and onions (there are newer vegetarian versions, too). Haggis smells horrible, but if you're looking for an authentic taste of Scotland, try it — if only once. **Charles MacSween and Son,** Dryden Road (☎ **0131-440-2555**), is the city's most time-honored purveyor.

David Bann Vegetarian Restaurant & Bar
$ New Town VEGETARIAN

All the current trends in vegetarian cooking are wonderfully summarized in this hip vegetarian restaurant around the corner from the new Scottish Parliament building. With its stylish décor and smooth jazzy background, it's a place where you want to linger. The chef creates vegetarian dishes inspired and influenced by the foods of India, China, and the Mediterranean. This is a good spot to come for a meatless Sunday brunch.

See map p. 168. 56–58 St. Mary's St. ☎ 0131-556-5888. Bus: 30 or 35. Reservations recommended for weekend dinner. Main courses: £8.50–£12 ($17–$24); snacks £3–£8 ($6–$16). AE, DC, MC, V. Open: Daily 11 a.m.–10 p.m.

Deacon Brodie's Tavern
$$ Old Town SCOTTISH/PUB GRUB

This tavern, established in 1806, is a favorite among the locals and tourists who are drawn to the old pub atmosphere, the good food, and the unusual story of its namesake, whose life inspired R. L. Stevenson to write *The Strange Case of Dr. Jekyll and Mr. Hyde.* A respectable city councilor and inventor by day, Brodie was a thief and murderer by night. In 1788, his dark side caught up with him, and after a trial, he was hanged on a gibbet he helped to perfect. Morbid history aside, the tavern serves decent pub food on the ground floor, but head upstairs to the wood-lined restaurant, where you may want a second helping of the beef steak pie (a variant on shepherd's pie).

See map p. 168. 435 Lawnmarket (the western spur of the Royal Mile, near St. Giles's Church). ☎ 0131-225-6531. Reservations recommended. Bus: 23, 27, 28, or 41. Main courses: £8–£16 ($16–$32). Open: Daily 10 a.m. to midnight (until 1 a.m. Fri–Sat).

Le Sept
$$ New Town FRENCH/SCOTTISH

This wonderful little restaurant has the look of a simple French bistro and offers a small but satisfying array of traditional French and Scottish dishes (plus a vegetarian choice). You can try rack of lamb, Scottish beef, or one of the daily fish dishes, such as grilled salmon. The crepes, both savory and dessert, are worth trying, too.

See map p. 168. 5 Hunter Sq. ☎ 0131-225-5428. Reservations recommended for dinner. Main courses: £10–£16 ($20–$32); fixed-price menu £16 ($32). AE, DC, MC, V. Open: Mon–Thurs noon to 2:15 p.m. and 6–10 p.m.; Fri–Sat noon–10 p.m.

Witchery by the Castle
$$$$$ Old Town SCOTTISH

This pretty and popular place with a subterranean dining room and dining by candlelight bills itself as the oldest restaurant in town and is said to be haunted by one of the many victims burned as a witch on nearby Castlehill between 1470 and 1722. The chef uses creative flair to create unfussy Scottish food, such as filet of Aberdeen Angus beef, pheasant, grilled halibut, and — most delectable and expensive of all — a platter of Scottish seafood and crustaceans with oysters, langoustines, clams, mussels, crab, smoked salmon, and lobster. For dessert, sample the passion fruit and mascarpone trifle or the warmed bitter chocolate torte. Some 550 wines and 40 malt whiskies are available.

See map p. 168. Castlehill (at the west end of the Mile, very near the Castle). ☎ *0131-225-5613.* www.thewitchery.com. *Reservations recommended. Bus: 23, 27, 28, 41, or 42. Main courses: £15–£50 ($30–$100); 2-course light lunches and pre-theater dinners £13 ($26). AE, DC, MC, V. Open: Daily noon to 4 p.m. and 5:30–11:30 p.m.*

Exploring Edinburgh

With the exception of the National Gallery, you'll find most of Edinburgh's most popular sights concentrated in Old Town, the rocky outcropping that overlooks the rest of the city.

Edinburgh's top sights

Edinburgh Castle
Old Town

No place in Scotland is filled with as much history, legend, and lore as Edinburgh Castle. Its early history is vague, but it's known that in the 11th century, Malcolm III (Canmore) and his Saxon queen, later venerated as St. Margaret, founded a castle on this spot. The oldest structure in Edinburgh is **St. Margaret's Chapel,** a small stone structure on the castle grounds dating from the 12th century.

The somber and sparsely furnished **State Apartments** include Queen Mary's Bedroom, where Mary Queen of Scots gave birth to James VI of Scotland (later James I of England). Scottish Parliaments used to convene in the **Great Hall.** For most visitors, the highlight is the **Crown Chamber,** housing the Honours of Scotland (Scottish Crown Jewels), used at the coronation of James VI, along with the scepter and sword of the state of Scotland. The storerooms known as the **French Prisons** were used to incarcerate captured French soldiers during the Napoleonic wars. Many of them made wall carvings still visible today.

See map p. 168. Castlehill. ☎ *0131-225-9846.* www.historic-scotland.gov.uk. *Bus: 23, 27, 28, 41, or 42. Admission: £11 ($22) adults, £9 ($18) seniors, £5.50 ($11) children. Open: Apr–Sept daily 9:30 a.m.–6 p.m.; Oct–Mar daily 9:30 a.m.–5 p.m. Last admission 45 minutes before close.*

Museum of Scotland
Old Town

Scotland's premier museum, built of pale Scottish sandstone, opened in 1998 to house the nation's greatest national treasures. There are many beautiful objects on display here, but the museum in some ways overwhelms the collections. Highlights include wonderful examples of ancient jewelry displayed in modern sculptures by Sir Eduardo Paolozzi; the Trappan treasure horde of silver objects found buried in East Lothian; the 12th-century Lewis chessmen; and, gruesomely, the "Maiden," an early guillotine. The roof terrace has great views of the city.

Chambers Street. ☎ *0131-247-4422.* www.nms.ac.uk. *Bus: 23, 27, 28, 41, 42. Admission: Free. Open: Mon–Sat 10 a.m.–5 p.m. (until 8 p.m. Tues); Sun noon to 5 p.m.*

National Gallery of Scotland
Princes Street Gardens

This honey-colored neoclassical temple houses one of the best midsize art museums in Europe, hung with a well-chosen selection of Old Masters and Impressionist masterpieces. Spend a morning (or at least half of one) here in the company of Rembrandt, Rubens, Andrea del Sarto, Raphael, Titian, Velázquez, El Greco, Monet, Degas, Gainsborough, and van Gogh. You may find yourself pleasantly surprised by the many works of largely unknown Scottish artists.

See map p. 168. 2 The Mound (in the center of Princes Street Gardens, behind the train station). ☎ *0131-624-6200 or 0131-332-2266.* www.nationalgalleries. org. *Bus: 23, 27, 28, 41, 42, or 45. Admission: Free. Open: Daily 10 a.m.–5 p.m. (until 7 p.m. Thurs).*

Palace of Holyroodhouse
Old Town

The royal palace of Scotland was originally the guesthouse of a 12th-century abbey (now in ruins). Of James V's 16th-century palace, only the north tower — rich with memories of his daughter, the political pawn Mary Queen of Scots — remains. You can see a plaque where Mary's court secretary Riccio was murdered by her dissolute husband and his cronies, and some of the queen's needlework is on display. Most of the palace was built in the late 17th century. Although Prince Charles held his roving court here at one time, the palace was only recently restored after years of neglect; it opened in November 2002. A quick visit takes about 45 minutes. Admission is by timed entry and includes an audio guide. You must book ahead of your visit.

Behind Holyroodhouse begins **Holyrood Park,** Edinburgh's largest. With rocky crags, a loch, sweeping meadows, and the ruins of a chapel, it's a wee bit of the Scottish countryside in the city, and a great place for a picnic. From the park, you can climb up a treeless, heather-covered crag, called **Arthur's Seat,** for breathtaking panoramas of the city and the Firth of Forth.

See map p. 168. Canongate (east end of the Royal Mile). ☎ *0131-556-5100 for required reservations.* www.royalcollection.org.uk. *Bus: 35 or 64. Admission: £9.80 ($20) adults, £8.80 ($18) seniors, £5.80 ($12) children under 17. Open: Mid-Mar to Oct daily 9:30 a.m.–6 p.m.; Nov to mid-Mar daily 9:30 a.m.–4:30 p.m. Last admission 45 minutes before close. Closed for parts of May, June, and July (see Web site for exact dates), and Dec 25–26.*

The Royal Mile
Old Town

Walking down the Royal Mile — the main drag of the Old Town that changes names from Lawnmarket to High Street to Canongate — takes you from Edinburgh Castle on the west end, downhill to the Palace of Holyroodhouse on the east. The various small museums of the Royal Mile tend to be open Monday through Saturday from 10 a.m. to 6 p.m. (a few stay open until 7:30 p.m. in summer and are open Sun from noon to 5 p.m.).

Some museums along the Royal Mile are free, but the ones listed below charge admission ranging from £1 to £8.95 ($2–$18). Simply strolling the Royal Mile from one end to the other takes 20 to 30 minutes. Add in another 20 to 30 minutes for each stop you want to make along the way.

Begin your mile tour at the **Scotch Whisky Experience,** 354 Castlehill (☎ 0131-220-0441; www.whisky-heritage.co.uk), where you find out all that you could possibly want to know about the making of single malts. The tour is expensive and somewhat cheesy, but you get to down a dram (or a soft drink) as part of your tour.

Across the street, housed in Outlook Tower, is **Camera Obscura and World of Illusions** (☎ 0131-226-3709; www.camera-obscura.co.uk). From the top of the tower, the live image of Edinburgh that you see projected by the camera obscura onto a white surface has been famous for over 150 years. The exhibits are updated to include modern advances in optics, such as laser holography.

At 477B Lawnmarket, **Gladstone's Land** (☎ 0131-226-5856; www.nts.org.uk) is a restored 17th-century home (open mid-Mar to Oct only). A nearby alley leads to Lady Stair's House, home to the **Writer's Museum** (☎ 0131-529-4901; www.cac.org.uk), which celebrates the lives and works of Scotland's three great scribes: Burns, Scott, and Stevenson.

Briefly a cathedral in the past, the **High Kirk of St. Giles** (☎ 0131-225-9442; www.stgiles.net) has changed so much over the ages that today the main draw is the Thistle Chapel, built onto the church's corner in 1911. The fiery John Knox, leader of the Scottish Reformation and perpetual antagonist to Mary Queen of Scots, served as the church's minister from 1559 to 1572.

Supposedly Knox lived a few doors down at 43–45 High St., although no actual historical evidence supports this theory. The **John Knox House** (☎ 0131-556-9579) is the only 16th-century building with projecting upper floors still existing on the Royal Mile.

Across the street at no. 42 is the **Museum of Childhood** (☎ 0131-529-4142; www.cac.org.uk), a museum full of toys from Victorian to recent times. Patrick Murray founded the museum even though he was a confirmed bachelor who insisted he was opening a museum of social science, not a romper room for kids — whom he reportedly detested.

As the Royal Mile becomes Canongate, you pass at no. 142 the **Museum of Edinburgh** (☎ 0131-529-4143; www.cac.org.uk). It resides in a restored

16th-century house filled with period rooms and collections detailing Edinburgh's past. Across the street is the clock-faced 1591 **Canongate Tollbooth,** a one-time council room, law court, and prison, now housing the **People's Story Museum** (☎ 0131-529-4057; www.cac.org.uk), an exhibit on working life in Edinburgh from the 18th century to today.

The Royal Yacht Britannia
Leith

Used by Queen Elizabeth II and the royal family from 1952 until it was decommissioned in 1997, this luxurious 124m (412-ft.) yacht is berthed in Leith (3km/2 miles from Edinburgh's center) and open to the public. You reach the famous vessel by going through a shopping mall to a visitor center, where you collect a portable audio guide keyed to the major state-rooms and working areas on all five decks. You can walk the decks where Prince Charles and Princess Diana strolled on their honeymoon, visit the drawing room and the little-changed Royal Apartments, and explore the engine room, the galleys, and the captain's cabin. An air of the 1950s still permeates the yacht. Give yourself at least an hour. It's fascinating.

Ocean Terminal, Leith. ☎ *0131-555-5566.* www.royalyachtbritannia.co.uk. *Bus: 11, 22, 34, 35, 36, or 49. Admission: £9.75 ($20) adults, £7.75 ($16) seniors, £5.75 ($12) children 5–15, £28 ($56) families (2 adults, 3 children). Open: Apr–Oct daily 9:30 a.m.–4:30 p.m.; Nov–Mar daily 10 a.m.–3:30 p.m.*

More cool things to see and do

- ✔ **Donning a kilt:** Thinking of sizing yourself for a kilt? The Highlander's dress used to be a 5m-long (16-ft.) plaid scarf wrapped around and around to make a skirt, with the excess thrown across the chest and up over the shoulder. After an 18th-century ban on the wearing of such traditional clan tartans, kilts became a fierce symbol of Scottish pride, and an industry was born. Today, a handmade kilt with all its accessories can run you well upwards of £500 ($1,000), but even if a tartan scarf or tie is more your stripe, the **Tartan Gift Shop,** 54 High St. (☎ 0131-558-3187), can help you identify your clan (or one close enough) and match you to one of its traditional tartans.

- ✔ **Visiting a few old Edinburgh haunts:** The most entertaining walks around the city are led after dark by the "dead" guides working for **Witchery Tours** (☎ 0131-225-6745; www.witcherytours.com). Each guide wears a costume representing an officially deceased Edinburgher whose ghost haunts this city. Your spirit guide leads you on a sometimes spooky, often goofy, and occasionally educational 90-minute tiptoe around the city's key historical and legendary spots. Called "Ghosts and Gore" and "Murder and Mayhem," the tours cost £7.50 ($15) for adults, £5 ($10) for children, and must be reserved in advance.

- ✔ **Witnessing the penguin parade at the zoo:** From April to September, at 2 p.m. daily, the **Edinburgh Zoo,** 134 Corstorphine Rd. (☎ 0131-334-9171; www.edinburghzoo.org.uk; Bus: 12, 26, or

31), herds the largest penguin colony in Europe out of its enclosure to run a few laps around a grassy park. Don't miss the gorillas, either (or the great view that stretches to the Firth of Forth).

✔ **Sampling the city's pubs and nightlife:** Edinburgh is an unsung nightlife capital, with a lively performing arts and theater scene year-round. More nighttime fun can be had at dance clubs, such as the always-trendy **Buster Browns,** 25 Market St. (☎ 0131-226-4224), and the **Bongo Club,** 37 Holyrood Rd. (☎ #0131-558-7604). The city is saturated with pubs and bars, especially in the Old Town around Grassmarket (**Black Bull,** no. 12; ☎ 0131-225-6636), Candlemaker Row (**Greyfriars Bobby's Bar,** no. 34; ☎ 0131-225-8328), and other university-area streets. In New Town, the slightly run-down Rose Street has a good row of pubs (try **Kenilworth,** no. 152; ☎ 0131-226-1773). Toss back a pint of bitter or set up your own tasting marathon of wee drams of single-malt Scotch whisky — the night is yours.

For a more archetypal Scottish evening, you can either go with the hokey or the traditional. A bagpipe-playing, kilt-swirling Scottish Folk Evening is staged at big hotels such as the Carlton Highland or King James. A less forced *ceilidh* (*kay*-lee — a folk-music jam session) happens nightly at the Tron Tavern, on South Bridge, or at any of the musical pubs listed in the *Gig* (available at newsstands and in pubs).

✔ **Attending the famous Edinburgh festivals:** Every August, Scotland's capital celebrates two to three weeks of theater, opera, arts, dance, music, poetry, prose, and even traditional culture (the bagpiping Military Tattoo parade uses the floodlit castle as a backdrop) during the **Edinburgh International Festival,** headquarters at The Hub on the Royal Mile on Castlehill (☎ 0131-473-2000 or 0131-473-2001; www.eif.co.uk).

The festival has also spawned multiple minifestivals, including celebrations that center on jazz, film, television, and books, and the famous **Fringe Festival,** headquartered at 180 High St. (☎ 0131-226-0026; www.edfringe.com), also held in August and offering hundreds of new plays and theater acts in every conceivable space around the city.

Guided tours

Lothian Buses (☎ 0131-555-6363; www.lothianbuses.co.uk) runs a fleet of double-deckers around the major Edinburgh sights; a full-day ticket for the Edinburgh Tour lets you hop on and off at any of two dozen stops. You can get tickets (valid for 24 hours) for the tour bus — £9 ($18) adults, £8 ($16) seniors and students, £3 ($6) children — at the starting point, Waverley Station. The same prices apply for the **City Sightseeing Tour** (☎ 0131-220-0770; www.guidefriday.com), which covers much the same ground, year-round, on a 60-minute tour. You can hop on at Waverley Bridge, Lothian Road, Royal Mile, Grassmarket, or Princes Street.

But perhaps the best way to see Edinburgh with a guide is to join one of the walking tours described in the "More cool things to see and do" section, earlier in this chapter.

Suggested itineraries

If you're the type who'd rather organize your own tours, this section offers some tips for building your own Edinburgh itineraries.

If you have one day

Start your early morning admiring Old Masters and Scottish Impressionists in the **National Gallery of Scotland.** Cross The Mound and climb Lawnmarket/Castlehill to glowering **Edinburgh Castle.** Tour the bits you like, and then start making your way down the **Royal Mile,** popping into the sights and shops that catch your fancy and stopping for a late Scottish lunch at Witchery by the Castle or, if your purse strings are tighter, Deacon Brodie's Tavern. Finish up with the Royal Mile in time to meet the **Witchery Tours** guide for 90 minutes of "Ghosts & Gore." Spend the evening hopping from pub to pub, with a pause to dine at Le Sept.

If you have two days

Begin Day 1 exploring Edinburgh's single greatest sight: **Edinburgh Castle.** After you have your fill of medieval battlements and royal history, head to the **National Gallery of Scotland** for a spell of art appreciation or to the **Museum of Scotland.** In the afternoon, hop in a cab or take a bus to Leith to visit the **Royal Yacht Britannia.** Dine at **Witchery by the Castle** or the **Atrium.**

Take Day 2 to enjoy the bustle, shopping, atmosphere, and some of the modest attractions found along the **Royal Mile.** Start from the top end at **Edinburgh Castle** and work your way down to the 16th-century royal **Palace of Holyroodhouse** anchoring the other end. In **Holyrood Park,** behind the palace, you can clamber up **Arthur's Seat** for the sunset. Finish off the day with a pub-crawl through the Old City and the University district.

If you have three days

Spend the first two days as discussed in the previous section and take Day 3 to get out of town, either to track down the Loch Ness Monster or get funky in Glasgow. (Both excursions are described in the next section.)

Traveling beyond Edinburgh

If you have a day or so to spare, consider heading out of town. We recommend either traveling north to enjoy the spectacular scenery of the Highlands (and perhaps catch a glimpse of that fabled sea monster) or going west to Glasgow, currently being reinvented as a splendid museum and shopping town.

On Nessie's trail: Inverness and Loch Ness

Many first-time visitors to the Highlands view Inverness — ancient seat of the Pictish kings who once ruled northern Scotland — merely as a steppingstone. Their real quest is for a glimpse of that elusive monster said to inhabit the deep waters of Loch Ness, a long finger of water stretching southwest from Inverness. The largest volume of water in Scotland, the loch is deeper than it looks — it's only 1.6km (1 mile) wide and 39km (24 miles) long, but at its deepest, it plunges 210 to 240m (700–800 ft.).

In truth, the Highlands hold more beautiful and rewarding spots, but no one can deny the draw of Loch Ness and its creature. Visiting the loch in a single day from Edinburgh is tough, but it can be done. Take the early train to Inverness, tour the loch in the late morning and early afternoon, and then bus back to Inverness to spend an afternoon seeing a few sights before boarding a late train back to Edinburgh or the overnight train to London.

Getting there

Seven trains daily connect Edinburgh and Inverness, and the trip is 3½ hours long. From Inverness, buses run hourly down the loch to Drumnadrochit (a 30-minute trip). To find the bus station, turn right as you exit the train station and then right again on Strothers Lane.

The **Inverness Tourist Office** (☎ 01463-234-353; Fax: 01463-710-609; www.visithighlands.com), at Castle Wynd off Bridge Street, can help you with the basics of Nessie-stalking and other loch activities ranging from lake cruises to monster-seeking trips in a sonar-equipped boat for around £10 to £25 ($20–$50).

If you just want a quick spin to Nessie's lair, **Highland Experience,** 2 Stoneycroft Rd., South Queensferry in Edinburgh (☎ 0131-331-1889; www.highlandexperience.com), offers a full-day Loch Ness Tour by bus that includes an hour-long lake cruise, a lunch stop at Spean Bridge, a stop at Glencoe, and a drive through the scenic countryside where Rob Roy, William "Braveheart" Wallace, and other cinematic icons of Scottish history made their names. The tour leaves daily from Waterloo Place in Edinburgh at 8 a.m. and costs £33 ($66) for adults and £31 ($62) for seniors 61 and older and children 15 and younger.

In Inverness, **Jacobite Coaches and Cruises,** Tomnahurich Bridge on Glenurquhart Road (☎ 01463-233-999; www.jacobitecruises.co.uk; take a taxi or bus no. 3, 3A, 4, or 4A from Church Road, 1 block straight ahead from the train station), runs half- and full-day tours of the loch. You can tour by boat (£9.50/$19 adults, £9/$18 seniors, £7/$14 children for 1-hour cruise) or take the coach-and-cruise (£21/$42 adults, £19/$38 seniors, £15/$30 children), which takes you by bus to Drumnadrochit, gives you a cruise on the loch, and brings you back. Jacobite runs tours year-round.

In Drumnadrochit, **Loch Ness Cruises,** behind the Original Loch Ness Visitor Centre (☎ 01456-450-395; www.lochness-centre.com), runs hourly Nessie-hunting cruises on the loch for £10 ($20) adults, £6 ($12) children, Easter to New Year's, weather permitting.

Seeing the sights

Despite being one of the oldest towns in Scotland, **Inverness** has been extensively rebuilt over the past century and a half and consequently looks rather modern. The castle looks old and impressive, but it was built between 1834 and 1847.

A short distance to the east of Inverness, on Auld Castlehill of the Craig Phadrig, is the most ancient area in town. This rise was the original site of the city castle, one of several Scottish sites that lay claim to the dubious distinction of being the place where Macbeth murdered King Duncan in 1040. Next to the castle sits the free **Inverness Museum and Art Gallery** (☎ 01463-237-114; www.invernessmuseum.com), which gives you the lowdown on the life, history, and culture of the Highlands.

Across the river are the Victorian **St. Andrew's Cathedral** (☎ 01463-225-553; www.invernesscathedral.co.uk) on Ardoss Street (check out the Russian icons inside) and the excellent **Balnain House,** 40 Huntly St. (☎ 0463-715-615), whose exhibition of Highland music displays include instruments (bagpipes, fiddles, harps) you can play and a great CD and gift shop. They also sponsor fantastic jam sessions Thursday nights year-round. Farther west lies **Tomnahurich,** or the "hill of the fairies," with a cemetery and panoramic views.

If you're driving around the lake, you have to make a choice: the main A82 along the north shore, passing such monster haunts as Drumnadrochit and Urquhart castle, or the more scenic southern shore route of natural attractions — pretty woodlands and the Foyers waterfalls. On a quick trip, the A82 offers more memorable scenery.

About halfway (23km/14 miles) down the A82 from Inverness is the hamlet of **Dumnadrochit,** unofficial headquarters of Nessie lore. You find two museums here devoted to Nessie. The **Loch Ness Exhibition Centre,** in a massive stone building (☎ 01456-450-573; www.lochness.com), is a surprisingly sophisticated look at the history of the loch (geological as well as mythological) and its famously elusive resident. The show takes a strict scientific view of the whole business of Nessie-hunting, really doing more to dispel and discredit the legends and sightings than to fan the flames of speculation. Admission is £5.95 ($12) adults, £4.50 ($9) seniors, £3.50 ($7) children, and £17 ($33) families.

The older and simpler **Original Loch Ness Monster Exhibition** (☎ 01456-450-342; www.lochness-centre.com), is more of a believers' haunt, running down the legend of the monster with a hackneyed old film, a lot

Nessie, the monster of the loch

The legend started in the sixth century after St. Colomba sent a monk swimming across the loch and a giant creature attacked him. After a harsh scolding from the saint, the monster withdrew. The legend, however, lives on.

Is Nessie the Loch Ness Monster that surfaced from the dark waters in the 16th century, slithering to shore, knocking down trees, and crushing three men with her tail? Or is she *Nessitera rhombopteryx,* a vestigial survivor from the age of the dinosaurs? Her basic description sounds like that of a plesiosaur — then again, it also kind of matches some species of sea snake.

No one knows for sure, but one definite fact is that the monster sightings increased in number after 1933, when the A82 road was built by blasting lakeshore rock. Shortly thereafter, innkeepers Mr. and Mrs. Spicer thought they saw something break the surface of the waters one night. The incident was reported on a slow news day in the local paper, and the rumor spread like wildfire.

In the end, the monster may be no more than the collective effect of faked photographs, water-surface mirages brought on by too much whisky, a few unexplained lake phenomena, and a string of lochside villages whose economies are based on spinning tall tales to visitors. Sonar soundings and a host of keen-eyed watchers have not yet managed to prove, or disprove, Nessie's existence, and that is more than enough reason for 200,000 visitors annually to come, cameras and binoculars in hand, to search for the monster of Loch Ness.

of "What is it?" photographs, accounts of Nessie sightings (along with other mythological creatures throughout the world, such as unicorns and Bigfoot), and a big ol' gift shop.

Almost 3km (2 miles) farther down the road (a half-hour walk), the ruins of **Urquhart Castle** (☎ 01456-450-551; www.historic-scotland.gov.uk) sit on a piece of land jutting into the lake. This castle holds the record for the most Nessie sightings. The 1509 ramparts encompass what was once one of the largest fortresses in Scotland, blown up in 1692 to prevent it from falling into Jacobite hands. When not packed with summer tourists, the grassy ruins can be quite romantic, and the tower keep offers fine loch views. The castle is open daily year-round from 9:30 a.m. to 6 p.m. (Oct–Mar until 5 p.m.). Admission is ₤6.50 ($13) adults, ₤5 ($10) seniors, and ₤3.25 ($6.50) children.

Where to stay and dine

One of the nicest places to stay in Inverness is the **Glen Mhor Hotel** (☎ 01463-234-308; Fax: 01463-713-170; www.glen-mhor.com), on the River Ness, with great views and excellent Scottish cuisine in its restaurants. Small doubles go for ₤65 to ₤115 ($130–$230). Steaks, seafood, and pizza can be had at the modern, laid-back Irish music pub **Johnny Foxes**

(☎ 01463-236-577; www.johnnyfoxes.co.uk), on Bank Street at Bridge Street. If you want to stay immersed in monster tales, shack up in Drumnadrochit at the **Polmaily House Hotel** (☎ 01456-450-343; Fax: 01456-450-813; www.polmaily.co.uk) for £65 ($130) per person, including breakfast.

Glasgow: A Victorian industrial city discovers culture

Glasgow was an Industrial Revolution powerhouse, the "second city of the British Empire," from the 19th to the early 20th century. With its wealth came a Victorian building boom, the architecture of which is only beginning to be appreciated.

A civic and mental makeover in the 1980s turned Glasgow from a depressed slum into a real contender for Edinburgh's title of cultural and tourist center of Scotland. With friendlier people and more exclusive shopping than the capital, and a remarkable array of art museums, Glasgow has made a new name for itself. Spend at least one night to drink in its renewed splendors.

Getting there and around

Half-hourly trains arrive in 50 minutes from Edinburgh; the eight daily trains (four on Sun) from London take almost six hours to arrive in Glasgow. Throughout the day, **CityLink** (www.citylink.co.uk) runs buses from Edinburgh to Glasgow. Glasgow's helpful **tourist office** (☎ 0141-204-4400; www.seeglasgow.com) is at 11 George Sq.

The old section of Glasgow centers around the cathedral and train station. The shopping zone of **Merchant's City** is west of High Street. Glasgow grew westward, so the finest Victorian area of the city is the grid of streets known as the **West End.** All these areas are north of the River Clyde. The city has a good bus system and an underground (subway) that swoops from the southwest in an arc back to the northwest. The £1.90 ($3.80) Discovery Ticket allows you one day's unlimited travel on Glasgow's underground after 9:30 a.m. Monday through Saturday (Sat tickets include Sun for free); it's the cheapest way to get around.

Seeing the sights

As far as sightseeing goes, Glasgow offers art, art, and more art. Luckily, admission to almost all of Glasgow's attractions is free. You'll find additional information about many of the museums listed in this section at www.glasgowmuseums.com. Make sure you fit in at least the **Kelvingrove Art Gallery and Museum,** on Argyle Street in the West End (☎ 0141-287-2699), which is strong on Italian and Dutch Old Masters, such as Botticelli, Bellini, and Rembrandt, as well as the moderns — Monet, Picasso, van Gogh, Degas, Matisse, Whistler, and Ben Johnson. A whole horde of Scottish artists is represented, too, with works dating from the 17th century to the present. Take your time perusing the collections of sculpture, ethnological artifacts, arms and armor, natural history, decorative arts, and relics of Scotland's Bronze Age. After a major refurbishment, the museum reopened in 2006.

The other great gallery of Glasgow is the **Burrell Collection** (☎ 0141-287-2550), about 6km (4 miles) southwest of the city center in Pollok Country Park. The huge assortment of art and artifacts was once a private collection. The collection is global and spans from the Neolithic era to the modern day, with special attention to ancient Rome and Greece, as well as paintings by Cézanne, Delacroix, and Cranach the Elder. Also in the park is the 18th-century mansion **Pollok House** (☎ 0141-616-6410), with a fine series of Spanish paintings by El Greco, Goya, Velázquez, and others.

The **Hunterian Art Gallery,** University Avenue (☎ 0141-330-5431; www.hunterian.gla.ac.uk), controls the estate of the great artist James McNeill Whistler (born American, but proud to be of Scottish blood). The gallery is housed in a painstaking reconstruction of Charles Rennie Mackintosh's home, an architectural treasure designed and built by the Art Nouveau innovator, the original of which was demolished in the 1960s.

Across the street from the Hunterian Art Gallery is the **Hunterian Museum** (☎ 0141-330-4221; www.hunterian.gla.ac.uk), which has a unique archaeological collection, ranging from dinosaur fossils to Roman and Viking artifacts — enough relics to give the kids a break from all those paintings. You can also see an exhibit on the travels of Captain Cook.

The kids — and certainly history buffs — may also get a kick out of the **People's Palace and Winter Gardens** (☎ 0141-554-0223) on Glasgow Green (Britain's first public park). Beyond a lush greenhouse filled with palms and a tearoom, the museum contains an assortment of artifacts from the Middle Ages and pertaining to Mary Queen of Scots, but the main collections focus on the life of an average Glaswegian in Victorian times.

Where to stay

The huge **Quality Hotel Central,** 99 Gordon St. (☎ 0141-221-9680; Fax: 0141-226-3948; www.qualityhotelglasgow.co.uk), near the central station, provides a tatty turn-of-the-last-century charm for £64 to £125 ($128–$250) per double; the tourist office can also help you book a room.

Where to dine

Revitalized Glasgow has plenty of refined international eateries these days, and the best of the lot has to be oddball **Rogano,** 11 Exchange Place, Buchanan Street (☎ 0141-248-4055; www.roganoglasgow.com) serving pricey traditional seafood in an atmosphere intended to re-create the Deco styling of the *Queen Mary;* you can also dine in the less-expensive bar or cafe.

Fast Facts: Edinburgh

American Express

Edinburgh's branch, 69 George St. (☎ 0131-718-2501), is open Monday through Friday from 9 a.m. to 5:30 p.m. and Saturday from 9 a.m. to 4 p.m.

Area Code

The country code for the United Kingdom is **44**. Edinburgh's city code is **0131**. If you're calling Edinburgh from outside the United Kingdom, drop the 0. In other words, to call Edinburgh from the United States, dial 011-44-131 and the number. To call the United States direct from Edinburgh, dial 001 followed by the area code and phone number.

Currency

As a member of the United Kingdom, Scotland is one of several European countries that have chosen not to adopt the euro.

The basic unit of currency is the pound sterling (£), divided into 100 pence (p). There are 1p, 2p, 10p, 20p, 50p, £1, and £2 coins; bank notes are issued in £5, £10, £20, and £50. Scottish banks can print their own money, so you may find three completely different designs for each note, in addition to regular British pounds. All different currency designs are valid.

The rate of exchange used to calculate the dollar values given in this chapter is $1 = 50p (or £1 = $2). Amounts over $10 have been rounded to the nearest dollar.

Doctors and Dentists

Your best bet is to ask your hotel concierge to recommend a doctor or dentist.

Embassies and Consulates

The U.S. Consulate, 3 Regent Terrace (☎ 0131-556-8315; www.usembassy.

org.uk/scotland), is open Tuesday and Thursday from 9 a.m. to 1 p.m. for walk-ins. The after-hours emergency number for U.S. citizens is ☎ 0122-485-7097.

Emergency

For police assistance, fire, or ambulance, dial ☎ **999**.

Hospitals

Try the Royal Infirmary, 1 Lauriston Place (☎ **0131-536-1000**; www.nhslothian.scot.nhs.uk; Bus: 23, 27, 28, 37, or 45).

Information

The main Edinburgh and Scotland Tourist Information Centre, 3 Princes St. (☎ 0845-22-55-121; www.edinburgh.org; Bus: all city-center buses), is at the corner of Princes Street and Waverley Bridge, above the underground Waverley Market shopping center. The office is open Monday through Saturday 9 a.m. to 6 p.m. (until 8 p.m. in May–Sept) and Sunday 10 a.m. to 6 p.m. (until 7 p.m. May–June and Sept, until 8 p.m. July–Aug). You'll also find an info desk at the airport. Scotland's tourism board runs www.visitscotland.com, another useful resource.

For transit information, call the Lothian Region Transport Office (☎ 0131-554-4494). For train information, contact ScotRail (☎ 0191-269-0203; www.firstgroup.com/scotrail).

Internet Access and Cybercafes

You can check your e-mail or send messages at easyEverything, 58 Rose St., just behind Princes Street (www.easyeverything.com; Bus: all Princes Street buses), open seven days a week from 7:30 a.m. to 10:30 p.m. Rates are around £1 ($2) for an hour.

Maps

The tourist office sells maps of Edinburgh for a small fee, or you can visit any bookstore.

Newspapers and Magazines

The Scotsman, the *Daily Record,* and the *Sunday Mail* all list goings-on about town.

Pharmacies

Edinburgh has no 24-hour pharmacies, but a branch of the drugstore Boots the Chemist, 48 Shandwick Place (☎ 0131-225-6757), is open Monday through Saturday from 9 a.m. to 9 p.m. and Sunday from 10 a.m. to 5 p.m.

Police

For police assistance, dial ☎ 999.

Post Office

You find Edinburgh's main post offices at 7 Hope St., off Princes Street (☎ 0131-226 6823), and 40 Frederick St. (☎ 0131-226-6937). Hours are Monday through Friday from 9 a.m. to 5:30 p.m. and Saturday from 9 a.m. to 12:30 p.m.

Safety

Violent crime is rare in Edinburgh, so you should feel safe walking around the city day or night. But keep in mind that the city's drug problem has produced a few muggings.

Taxes

In Scotland, a 17.5 percent value-added tax (VAT) is figured into the price of most items. Foreign visitors can reclaim a percentage of the VAT on major purchases of consumer goods. See Chapter 4 for more on this, or visit www.hmce.gov.uk/public/vat refunds/vatrefunds.htm.

Taxis

See "Getting Around Edinburgh," earlier in this chapter.

Telephone

A local call in Edinburgh costs 20p (40¢) for the first three minutes. Pay phones accept either coins or phone cards, which are sold at post offices or the tourist board.

To charge a call to your calling card or make a collect call home, dial AT&T (☎ 0800-890-011 or 0500-890-011), MCI (☎ 0800-279-5088), or Sprint (☎ 0800-890-877 or 0500-890-877).

Transit Info

See "Getting Around Edinburgh," earlier in this chapter.

Chapter 12

Dublin and the Best of Ireland

Called the Emerald Isle with good reason, Ireland is a lush, green land with a deep history. Ancient ruins and medieval monasteries, structures once inhabited by Celts, Vikings, Normans, and the English, dot the countryside. Ireland is the renowned home to literary giants, Irish whiskey, and a rich musical tradition.

The city of Dublin has exquisite museums and a thriving nightlife. But even more appealing is the beautiful, rural landscape and charming small towns that await you. Give Dublin two or three days and then take off to the Irish countryside.

Getting There

You can fly to Dublin from London in just one hour, making that by far the most convenient way to get to town — especially in light of the plodding train-to-overnight-ferry-to-commuter-rail alternative. But the following sections include your many options.

Arriving by air

Dublin International Airport (☎ 01-814-1111; www.dublin-airport. com) lies about 13km (8 miles) or 30 minutes north of the city. Inside the arrivals hall are multiple ATMs and a cellphone rental shop. The **Tourist Information Centre** (☎ 01-605-7700) can help with hotel reservations and assist you in planning your itinerary. It's open daily 8 a.m. to 8 p.m.

Aircoach (☎ 01-844-7118; www.aircoach.ie) runs to and from Dublin's City Centre every 15 minutes between 5 a.m. and midnight, and every hour between midnight and 5 a.m. The one-way fare is €7 ($11); round-trip is €12 ($19). You can buy a ticket onboard. Dublin Bus's **Airlink** service (routes 747 and 748; ☎ 01-873-4222; www.dublinbus.ie) also runs between the airport and City Centre. The 747 stops at O'Connell Street or the Central Bus Station; the 748 stops at the same bus station and at Heuston Rail Station. One-way fare is €6 ($9.60) adults, €3 ($4.80) children. The buses run from about 5:45 a.m. to about 10:50 p.m. depending on the day of the week.

Taxis line up outside the terminal for a quick, easy trip into town; fares average €17 to €27 ($27–$43).

Finally, several car-rental options are available at the airport. If you're staying in Dublin, however, we don't recommend renting a car.

Arriving by land

CIÉ (www.cie.ie) is a great place to find out about bus and train service across Ireland.

Most trains (from the west, south, and southwest) arrive at **Heuston Station** (☎ 01-703-2132), on the west end of town. Those from the north pull into the more centrally located **Connolly Station** (☎ 01-703-2358). **Buses** arrive at the **Busaras Central Bus Station** (☎ 01-836-6111) on Store Street near Connolly Station. For information, contact **Irish Rail** (☎ 1-850-366-222; www.irishrail.ie). For bus information, contact **Bus Éireann** ☎ 01-836-6111; www.buseireann.ie).

Arriving by sea

For information on getting to Ireland by ferry, check out www.irishferries.com, www.stenaline.com, or www.poirishsea.com.

If you arrive in Dún Laoghaire by ferry, you can take DART into town (trains run from about 6 a.m. to roughly midnight). If your ferry arrives at dawn, take bus no. 46A; it runs from the ferry docks to Parnell Square West from 6:25 a.m. to 10:30 p.m.

Orienting Yourself in Dublin

The city of Dublin is sprawling, but many of its sights are concentrated in the city center near the Liffery River. Most sights lie on the south side of the River Liffey, though several interesting sights exist on the north side around **Parnell Square.**

Introducing the neighborhoods

North of the Liffey, the main thoroughfare is called **O'Connell Street.** On the north side, O'Connell Street leads up to Parnell Square. O'Connell Street crosses a bridge of the same name to the south side, where it

Ireland

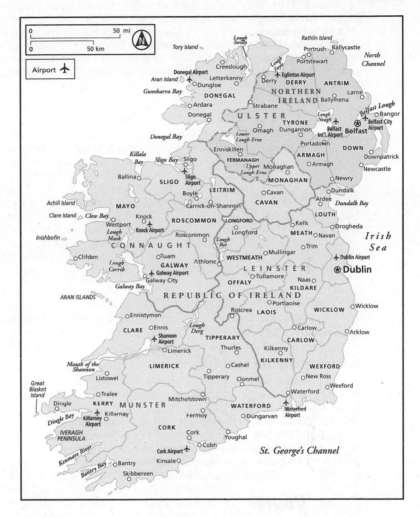

becomes a large traffic circle in front of the grand campus of **Trinity College.** The street then narrows again into the pedestrian **Grafton Street.** Grafton Street continues south to spill into **St. Stephen's Green,** which is something between a square and a gorgeous city park. Off the northeast corner of this square is a complex of huge buildings that house the government and various national museums and libraries. To the east of St. Stephen's Green lie several elegant Georgian Squares, including **Merrion Square** and **Fitzwilliam Square.** Farther to the southeast is the fashionable embassy and hotel-filled neighborhood of **Ballsbridge.**

Back at that traffic circle in front of Trinity College, College Green leads due west past the impressive Bank of Ireland building and becomes **Dame Street. Temple Bar,** Dublin's always fun pub-, club-, and restaurant-filled district lies between Dame Street and the Liffey. (Temple Bar is connected to the north side of the Liffey by the picturesque span of the **Ha'penny Bridge.**) Dame Street changes names regularly as it moves west, passing Dublin Castle before reaching **Christ Church Cathedral** on the edge of the city center.

Finding information after you arrive

Dublin Tourism (☎ 01-605-7700; www.visitdublin.com) operates two tourism centers throughout the city plus one in nearby Dún Laoghaire. In addition to the desk at the airport (see "Getting There," earlier in this chapter), you can find information at the main office in the former **Church of St. Andrew** on Suffolk Street (Open: July–Aug Mon–Sat 9 a.m.–7 p.m. and Sun 10:30 a.m.–5:30 p.m.; June and Sept Mon–Sat 9 a.m.–7 p.m. and Sun 10:30 a.m.–3 p.m.; Oct–May Mon–Sat 9 a.m.–5:30 p.m. and Sun 10:30 a.m.–3 p.m.); in **Dún Laoghaire Harbour** (Open: Mon–Sat 10 a.m.–1 p.m. and 2–6 p.m.); and at **14 Upper O'Connell St.** (Open: Mon–Sat 9 a.m.–5 p.m.)You can also get good information from **Tourism Ireland** (☎ 800-223-6470 in the U.S.; www.discoverireland.com/us).

Getting around Dublin by foot

The heart of Dublin is small, and with so many garden squares to stroll, it's eminently walkable.

Getting around Dublin by bus

Dublin's green double-decker buses (☎ 01-873-4222; www.dublinbus.ie) can transport you all over the city and suburbs. To take a bus, hop on, say where you want to get off, and pay the driver (you must have exact change, and bills are not accepted). Your fare is calculated by the distance traveled and runs from about €0.95 to €2.50 ($1.50–$4), except late at night when the rate is a flat €5 ($8) fare. A **Rambler Ticket** is valid for one, three, five, or seven days of unlimited travel on the bus system, and costs €6 ($9.60), €12 ($19), €19 ($30), and €23 ($37), respectively. For a ticket that combines travel on the bus and DART systems, see the following section. You can purchase Rambler Tickets online or at the bus depot at 59 Upper O'Connell St.

Getting around Dublin by DART (light rail)

The speedy Dublin Area Rapid Transit **(DART)** electric train (☎ 01-703-3504; www.dart.ie) is really for commuters, with only five stops you may need to know: three in the city center (Connolly, Tara Street, and Pearse), the Lansdowne Road station in Ballsbridge, and the Dún Laoghaire station at the ferry docks. It's usually not worth it to take DART within the city center because the stops are within such close walking distance to one another. DART tickets cost about €1.50 to about €5 ($2.40–$8). A **one-day pass** is €7.60 ($12) for DART only and €9.30 ($15) if you want to ride the buses as well. A **three-day pass** is €16 ($26), or €18 ($29) including bus travel.

Getting around Dublin by car

There is absolutely no need to drive in the walkers' paradise of Dublin City, and it will usually prove to be a nuisance because parking is scarce, especially around tourist attractions. If you do decide to drive in Dublin, remember to avoid parking in bus lanes or along curbs with double yellow lines — these are easy ways to get your tires clamped by parking officials. To park on the streets in Dublin, buy a parking disc at one of the black vending machines along the street and display it in the window of your car.

Getting around Dublin by Luas (tram)

Luas (☎ 1-800-300-604; www.luas.ie) is Dublin's sleek, shiny tram system. You probably won't need it if you're spending time in the center of the city, which is easily walkable. However, check out the map if you're traveling outside of the city center. It's also useful for moving between Connolly and Heuston stations. One-way fares run between €1.50 ($2.40) and €2.20 ($3.50), depending on your destination.

Getting around Dublin by taxi

Do not try to hail a taxi as it whizzes by you on the street. Instead, line up at one of the city's many *ranks* (stands), where taxis wait for their fares. You'll find ranks outside all the major hotels and transportation centers as well as on the busier streets, such as Upper O'Connell Street, College Green, and the north side of St. Stephen's Green.

You can also call a taxi. Try **A to B Cabs** (☎ 01-677-2222), **Castle Cabs** (☎ 01-831-9000), or **City Cabs** (☎ 01-873-1122). The starting fare for the first kilometer (⅔ mile) is €3.80 ($6.10) by day and €4.10 ($6.55) at night. For the next 14km (8⅔ miles), the fare is €0.95 ($1.50) per kilometer by day, €1.25 ($2) by night, rising to a maximum of €1.65 ($2.65) per kilometer. It costs an extra €2 ($3.20) if you order a cab by phone.

Staying in Dublin

You can find a lot of breathtaking, expensive hotels in central Dublin, but you can also find some great values if you look hard enough. A great alternative is to seek out one of the number of hotels housed in historic Victorian and Georgian buildings, or something funky — such as the Temple Bar neighborhood's **Oliver St. John Gogarty** (☎ 01-671-1822; www.gogartys.ie) — listed as a pub under "More cool things to see and do," later in this chapter — which has converted its upper floors

Accommodations, Dining, and Attractions in Dublin

Map legend:

- † Church
- ⓘ Information
- ✉ Post Office

Scale: 0 – 0.2 mi / 0 – 0.2 km

Map labels: North Circular Rd., Aughrim Street, Prussia St., Oxmantown Road, Manor Street, Kirwan, Grangegorman Upper, St. Brendan's Hospital, St. Lawrence Hospital, Dublin Zoo, Hospital, Collins, Brunswick Street North, North King Street, PHOENIX PARK, Infirmary Road, Arbour Hill, Blackhall Place, Queen Street, Smithfield St., Irish Whiskey Corner, Main Road, Montpelier Hill, Barracks, Bow St., Conyngham Road, Parkgate Street, King's Bridge, Benburb Street, Victoria's Bridge, Ellis Quay, Arran Quay, River Liffey, Wolfe Tone Quay, Heuston Station, Victoria Quay, Queen's Bridge, Island Street, Usher's Quay, St. John's Road, West Hospital, Steven's Lane, Guinness Brewery, Bonham St., Bridgefoot Street, Whitworth Bridge, Military Road, Irish Museum of Modern Art, St. Patrick's Hospital, Cook, Kilmainham Lane, St. James's Street, Thomas Street West, 31, Rainsford St., Cornmarket, THE LIBERTIES, Old Kilmainham, Basin Street Upper, Robert St., Bellevue, Bond St., Earl St. S., Pimlico, Meath Street, St. Patrick's Hospital, Marrowbone Lane, St. Kevin's Hospital, Grand Canal Bank, Cork Street, Ardee Street, Belfast, South Circular Road, Dublin, IRELAND, Dolphin's Barn Street, Brown Street, Hospital, O'Donovan Road

HOTELS ■
- ABC Guesthouse **1**
- Avalon House **26**
- Blooms **17**
- The Clarence **16**
- Grafton Guesthouse **23**
- Hotel Isaacs **5**
- Jurys Inn Christchurch **13**
- Kilronan House **30**
- The Morrison **8**
- Number 31 **29**
- Stauntons on the Green **28**
- Temple Bar Hotel **18**

RESTAURANTS ◆
- Beshoff **7**
- Elephant & Castle **19**
- The Mermaid Café **15**
- Queen of Tarts **10**
- The Tea Room **16**
- Winding Stair **9**

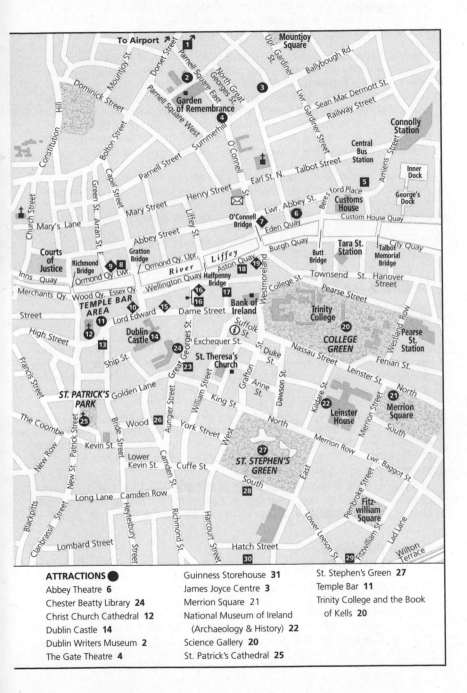

ATTRACTIONS ●

Abbey Theatre **6**
Chester Beatty Library **24**
Christ Church Cathedral **12**
Dublin Castle **14**
Dublin Writers Museum **2**
The Gate Theatre **4**

Guinness Storehouse **31**
James Joyce Centre **3**
Merrion Square **21**
National Museum of Ireland
  (Archaeology & History) **22**
Science Gallery **20**
St. Patrick's Cathedral **25**

St. Stephen's Green **27**
Temple Bar **11**
Trinity College and the Book
  of Kells **20**

into a hotel/hostel (€78–€86/$125–$138 for a twin room or €25–€40/ $40–$64 per person in the dorms) and a set of self-catering apartments (€140–€200/$224–$320).

Many areas outside Dublin's city center have bed-and-breakfasts (B&Bs), which generally offer inexpensive lodging in a friendly, small-inn atmosphere. **Dublin Tourism** (☎ 01-605-7777; www.visitdublin.com) can help you find a B&B room for a €5 ($8) fee; the agency books rooms in traditional hotels as well (see "Finding information after you arrive," earlier in this chapter). The embassy-filled residential area of **Ballsbridge,** a short DART ride from downtown, is one of the nicest (and safest) neighborhoods to stay in if you want to stay outside of the city center.

Note that Dublin hotels often quote their prices *per person,* not per room. The prices listed in this chapter are per room double occupancy, but wherever you stay, double-check the hotel's pricing policy so that you won't be in for any surprises when you check out.

For general tips on booking and what to expect from European accommodations, see Chapter 7.

Dublin's top hotels

The Clarence
$$$$ **Temple Bar, Dublin 2**

This high-class hotel has a lot to offer, including a terrific location at the doorstep of the lively Temple Bar area, an elegant modern look, and superior service. It's even touched by fame: The hotel is partly owned by Bono and The Edge of the Irish rock band U2. You may not want to leave your enormous bed, where you can bliss out to CDs on the room's stereo. Décor is simple and chic, with vivid colors gracing each room. The classy Octagon Bar, the wonderful Tea Room restaurant (reviewed in the "Dining in Dublin" section later in this chapter), and the full-service Therapy Spa are downstairs. The Clarence is among the city's top hotels — not as supertrendy as the Morrison, but just plain classy.

See map p. 192. 6–8 Wellington Quay. ☎ *01-407-0800. Fax: 01-407-0820.* www.the clarence.ie. *DART: Tara Street Station. Bus: 26, 66, 66A, 66B, 66D, 67, 67A. Rack rates: €370–€760 ($592–$1,216) double. Full Irish breakfast €28 ($45). AE, DC, MC, V.*

Grafton Guesthouse
$$ **Old City, Dublin 2**

This guesthouse is an incredible value, offering bright, cute, decent-size rooms at ridiculously low prices (by Dublin standards). Rooms are decorated with kitschy touches, such as wallpaper with bright flowers and mod lamps, and free WiFi is available for those who can't live without their Internet. The kicker is that this place is in a central location, on hip Great Georges Street, right near Grafton Street and Trinity College. Service is a little rushed but still friendly. Vegetarians should appreciate the vegetarian version of the traditional Irish breakfast, complete with nonmeat sausages. *See map p. 192. 26–27 S. Great Georges St.* ☎ *01-679-2041. Fax: 01-677-9715.* www. graftonguesthouse.com. *DART: Tara Street Station. Bus: 16A. Rack rates: €115–€145 ($184–$232) double. Rates include full breakfast. MC, V.*

Jurys Inn Christchurch
$$ Old City (near Temple Bar), Dublin 8

You can't beat Jurys for value if you're traveling as a family: This hotel group is one of the few in Ireland that doesn't charge extra if more than two people share a room. The rooms here are large and modern, with the standard hotel décor of floral fabrics. There's a lively pub downstairs, and the hotel offers baby-sitting services. The hotel is centrally situated at the top of Dame Street, right near Christ Church Cathedral and Dublin Castle (ask for a room with a view of the cathedral).

See map p. 192. Christ Church Place. ☎ *01-454-0000. Fax: 01-454-0012.* www.jurys inns.com. *DART: Tara Street Station. Bus: 49, 50, 51B, 54A, 56A, 65, 77, 77A, 78A. Rack rates: €112–€215 ($179–$344) for up to 3 adults or 2 adults and 2 children. Full Irish breakfast €12 ($19). AE, DC, MC, V.*

Kilronan House
$$$ St. Stephen's Green, Dublin 2

This small family-run hotel, with only 15 rooms, is one of the best places to stay if this is your first visit to Dublin. Terry Masterson, the hotel's friendly proprietor, makes a point to sit down with each guest to help plan an itinerary and to field questions about the city. Located on a quiet street within a ten-minute walk of St. Stephen's Green, the Georgian town house features many original details, such as beautiful ceiling molding, large bay windows, Waterford chandeliers, and hardwood floors in the public areas. The spacious rooms are modern, brightly painted, and filled with natural light — ask for one with a skylight. An excellent full Irish breakfast is served in the elegant dining room.

See map p. 192. 70 Adelaide Rd. ☎ *01-475-5266. Fax: 01-478-2841.* www.dublinn. com/kilronan.htm. *DART: Pearse St. Bus: 14, 15A, 15B, 44, 44N, 48A, 48N. Rack rates: €110–€170 ($176–$272) double. Rates include full breakfast. AE, MC, V.*

Number 31
$$$ St. Stephen's Green, Dublin 2

You know how guidebooks always say that certain hotels are "an oasis in a busy city"? Well, Number 31 really is. Designed by Sam Stephenson, one of Ireland's most famous modern architects, this guesthouse is tucked away behind a vined wall on a peaceful little lane about a ten-minute walk from St. Stephen's Green. The style inside is a marriage of modern design and country chic. The spacious rooms have intentionally weathered white wood country furniture and cozy quilts, plus little modern surprises such as a burnished gray mirrored wall and a sunken bathtub created with turquoise mosaic tiles. Sitting in the glass-walled conservatory; munching on homemade granola and delightful hot breakfast dishes; and chatting with Deirdre and Noel Comer, your warm hosts, you may want to move in permanently. Be sure to say hi to Homer, the resident Golden Labrador.

See map p. 192. 31 Lower Leeson Close, Lower Leeson St. ☎ *01-676-5011. Fax: 01-676-2929.* www.number31.ie. *Bus: 70X, 92. Rack rates:* €150–€320 ($240–$512) *double. Rates include full Irish breakfast. AE, DC, MC, V.*

Stauntons on the Green
$$$ St. Stephen's Green

Although less than 20 years old, this hotel on Dublin's central square has a historic feel — thanks in large part to the fact that it occupies a series of three 18th-century Georgian town houses. The windows are tall, ceilings high, and furnishings traditional, with fireplaces blazing in the public rooms. You see green every way you look; the back rooms open onto Iveagh Gardens.

See map p. 192. 83 St. Stephen's Green (on the south side of the Green). ☎ *01-478-2300. Fax: 01-478-2263.* www.stauntonsonthegreen.ie. *DART: Pearse Station. Bus: 11, 11A, 41X, 46A, 46B, 46C, 46D, 46E, 46X, 58X, 70X, 118, 127. Rack rates:* €149–€208 ($238–$333) *double. Rates include full Irish breakfast. AE, DC, MC, V.*

Temple Bar Hotel
$$$ Temple Bar, Dublin 2

This hotel has everything: a terrific location in the heart of Temple Bar, a welcoming and helpful staff, an airy Art Deco lobby, and a nice restaurant serving light fare under the glow of skylights. In fact, the only drawback to the hotel is the small size of the bedrooms, which feature mahogany furniture, deep green and burgundy colors, and firm double beds. Ask for a room away from the street if you're a light sleeper.

See map p. 192. Fleet Street. ☎ *01-612-9200. Fax: 01-677-3088.* www.temple barhotel.com. *DART: Tara Street Station. Bus: 7B, 7D, 11, 14A, 16, 16A, 46, 46A, 46B, 46C, 46D, 51N, 58X, 67N, 69N, 116, 121, 122, 150, 746. Rack rates:* €110–€145 ($176–$232) *double. Rates include full Irish breakfast. AE, DC, MC, V.*

Dublin's runner-up accommodations

ABC Guesthouse

$ North Dublin, Dublin 9 This guesthouse, located north of the city center, gets rave reviews for its kind and helpful hosts and its great value. *57 Drumcondra Rd. Upper.* ☎ *01-836-7417.* www.abchousedublin.com.

Avalon House

$ Old City, Dublin 2 This funky hostel, which plays host to a mix of travelers ranging from teens to young families to older groups of friends, is legendary among backpackers for its friendliness, clean rooms, and sense of community. You can chill out in the self-catering kitchen or in the airy Avalon Café, which offers hot drinks and pastries and often hosts free live entertainment. *See map p. 192. 55 Aungier St.* ☎ *or 01-475-0001.* www. avalon-house.ie.

Blooms

$$ **Temple Bar** Blooms is a large, modern hotel wedged strategically between Trinity College and Temple Bar. Many guests party the night away at Club M (www.clubm.ie), the hotel's sister nightclub. *See map p. 192. Anglesea Street, off Dame Street.* ☎ *01-671-5622.* www.blooms.ie.

Hotel Isaacs

$$-$$$ **O'Connell Street Area, Dublin 1** This moderately priced hotel is right across the street from the Bus Éireann station, close to Dublin's main shopping area and a mere five-minute walk from the city center. The building is a restored wine warehouse, and much of the original brickwork is still visible, giving it a lot of character. Rooms are modern and tastefully furnished. Il Vignardo, an Italian restaurant, is downstairs. *See map p. 192. Store Street.* ☎ *01-813-4700.* www.isaacs.ie.

The Morrison

$$$$ **North of the Liffey** This top-notch hotel, in league with the Clarence, is a utopia for those who love modern, minimalist style. The elegant, uncluttered bedrooms are decorated in cream, black, and cocoa, and are filled with amenities, including a state-of-the-art sound system. The service is pampering and flawless. Though the Morrison is located on the less-happening north side of the Liffey, it's within easy walking distance of Temple Bar, Dublin Castle, and many other top attractions. *See map p. 192. Lower Ormond Quay.* ☎ *01-887-2400.* www.morrisonhotel.ie.

Dining in Dublin

If you think of shepherd's pie, Irish stew, and mashed potatoes when you think of Irish cuisine, you're right. But that's only half the story: In the past few decades, Ireland has seen huge changes on the food scene. A stroll down a row of restaurants is like paging through a book about the world's cuisines. Especially in larger towns and cities, you can find everything from Italian restaurants that would make *The Sopranos* proud, to Indian restaurants serving fiery curries, to minimalist temples to sushi.

Along with these ethnic eateries is a bevy of restaurants creating innovative dishes that showcase the best of Ireland's sparkling fresh produce and incorporating international influences. Typical dishes? How about fresh Irish salmon served with wasabi-infused mashed potatoes or local free-range beef with a Thai curry sauce?

If you're in the market for traditional Irish dishes, your best bet is a pub, where you find hearty offerings such as Irish stew, thick vegetable soups, and ploughman's lunches (cheese, pickles, and bread). Pub grub hasn't escaped the influences of the last few decades. The dishes are better than ever, many chefs use as much local produce as possible, and international influences are found in many dishes. (Who knew that chili jam would go so well with Gubbeen, a West Cork cheese?) And you'd better sit down for this next bit: Many traditional pubs now squeeze salads and other healthy options onto the menu.

If you want something quick and inexpensive, try a pub or head for one of the loads of small cafes and lunch counters that offer soups and sandwiches. Even more plentiful are *chippers* and *take-aways,* fast-food places where you can get, among other things, traditional fish and chips.

You can't discuss Irish cuisine without mentioning beer. The Irish say that drinking Guinness from a can or bottle rather than enjoying a fresh pint drawn straight from the tap is like eating canned peaches rather than a ripened peach fresh off the tree. Guinness's lager is called *Harp,* and don't miss out on the Guinness rival from Cork, the dark *Murphy's.* Kilkenny's *Smithwicks* is the best when it comes to ales. For a break from the brew, quality hard cider is also on tap.

The Irish invented whiskey: The legend pins it on a sixth-century monk. Old Bushmills (established in 1608) is the oldest distillery in the world. The *e* isn't the only difference between Irish whiskey and Scotch or English *whisky;* the unique Irish distillation process gives the stuff a cleaner, less smoky flavor. Other brands to sample include John Jameson, Powers, Paddy's, Tullamore Dew, Murphy, and Dunphy. The Irish drink their whiskey *neat* — straight out of the bottle at room temperature. A few decades ago, they started dumping Irish whiskey into coffee, mixing in sugar, topping it off with whipped cream, and serving it to arrivals at the Shannon airport (hence, Irish coffee). This concoction may be touristy, but it's very, very tasty.

 If you have your heart set on eating at a posh restaurant in one of the larger cities during the summer or on a weekend (or on a summer weekend!), make reservations. For the poshest of the posh restaurants, it's a good idea to make reservations no matter what time of year it is.

 Dublin's restaurants often add a service charge of 10 percent to 17 percent to your bill, so when you're calculating a tip, double-check the bill to see if it's already been done.

Beshoff
$ Trinity Area, Dublin 2   FISH AND CHIPS

The fish here, and there's quite a variety (cod is the classic), is as fresh as can be, its juices sealed in by a fried golden-brown crust; the *chips* (fries) are cut fresh each day and are thick and deliciously dense. If you like salt and vinegar to begin with, you'll love how they complement fish and chips, so ask for them. Beshoff has seating, so you can pick up your food downstairs and then climb the stairs to find a table overlooking busy

Westmoreland Street. However, these meals tend to taste best when eaten on a park bench along the River Liffey.

See map p. 192. 6 Upper O'Connell St. ☎ *01-872-4400. DART: Tara Street Station. Bus: 10, 10A, 32X, 46A, 116, 145. Main courses: €6.90–€9 ($11–$14). No credit cards. Open: Mon–Sat 9 a.m.–10 p.m.; Sun 11 a.m.–9 p.m.*

Elephant & Castle
$$ Temple Bar, Dublin 2   AMERICAN

Locals and visitors alike pile into this immensely popular, buzzing joint in the heart of Temple Bar, which serves exceptional burgers, salads, omelets, and other American diner fare. Burger-slingers around the world should cross their fingers that Elephant & Castle doesn't open a branch in their town, because these juicy, flavorful burgers are excellent. This warm, relaxed restaurant, with its wood booths and funky paintings and photos, is the perfect place to watch the crowds of people who parade down Temple Bar.

See map p. 192. 18 Temple Bar St. ☎ *01-679-3121. DART: Tara Street Station. Bus: 7B, 7D, 11, 14A, 16, 16A, 46, 46A, 46B, 46C, 46D, 51N, 58X, 67N, 69N, 116, 121, 122, 150, 746. Main courses: €12–€23 ($19–$37). AE, DC, MC, V. Open: Mon–Fri 8 a.m.–11:30 p.m.; Sat and Sun 10:30 a.m.–11:30 p.m.*

The Mermaid Café
$$–$$$$ Dublin 2   NEW IRISH

This popular Dublin restaurant serves innovative dishes made with some of the freshest, most flavorful ingredients around. The menu changes seasonally, offering the likes of Irish Angus rib-eye steak with sage-and-mustard mashed potatoes and garlicky beans; yellowfin tuna with plum tomatoes, capers, mint, and wasabi mayonnaise; and a salad of asparagus and quail eggs with shaved Parmesan and greens. The crowd is always buzzing and chic; businesspeople descend on the restaurant at lunch, while dinner sees more couples and small groups. The surroundings are cozy and modern, featuring contemporary art, white wood walls, high-backed pine chairs, and solid pine tables. Save room for the unbelievable desserts, including pecan pie served with maple ice cream.

See map p. 192. 70 Dame St. ☎ *01-670-8236. Reservations recommended. DART: Tara Street Station. Bus: 39B, 49X, 50X, 65X, 77X. Main courses: €20–€33 ($32–$53). MC, V. Open: Mon–Sat 12:30–2:30 p.m. and 6–11 p.m.; Sun noon to 3:30 p.m. and 6–9 p.m.*

The Tea Room
$$$–$$$$ Temple Bar, Dublin 2   NEW IRISH

This is *the* place in Dublin to try out New Irish cuisine, which uses Ireland's bounty of fresh ingredients in imaginative dishes. Expect intriguing options such as the roast rack of Wicklow lamb marinated in Indian spices and pre-served lemon, served with a mixture of natural lamb juices and curry oil. Housed in the fabulous Clarence Hotel (reviewed earlier in this chapter), the Tea Room has an airy feel, with soaring ceilings, large windows, and blond wood.

See map p. 192. In the Clarence Hotel, 6–8 Wellington Quay. ☎ 01-407-0813. Reservations required. DART: Tara Street Station. Bus: 7B, 7D, 11, 14A, 16, 16A, 46, 46A, 46B, 46C, 46D, 51N, 58X, 67N, 69N, 116, 121, 122, 150, 746. Main courses: 3-course fixed-price dinner €55 ($88); 2-course fixed-price lunch €26 ($42). AE, DC, MC, V. Open: Mon–Fri 7 a.m.–11 a.m., 12:30–2:30 p.m., and 7–10:30 p.m.; Sat 7:30 a.m.– 11:30 a.m. and 7–10:30 p.m.; Sun 7:30 a.m.–11:30 a.m., 12:30–2:30 p.m., and 7–9:30 p.m.

Queen of Tarts
$ Dublin 2   BAKERY/CAFE

If you lived near this bakery and cafe, you might weigh about 900 pounds, and that would be tragic, because then you might not be able to fit through the door to sample more of their incredible desserts. Savory lunch tarts (such as a goat cheese, tomato, olive, and pesto combo), salads, sandwiches, and toothsome homemade soups attended by a thick slice of brown bread are served in a cheerful, casual yellow room. But the excellent lunch fare is just the opening act for the glorious desserts, including a tangy blackberry-and-apple crumble offset by sweet cream.

See map p. 192. 4 Corkhill (part of Dame Street across from Dublin Castle). ☎ 01-670-7499. DART: Tara Street Station. Bus: 49, 56A, 77, 77A, 123. Main courses: €2.50–€8.95 ($4–$14). No credit cards. Open: Mon–Tues 7:30 a.m.–7 p.m.; Wed–Sat 9 a.m.–8 p.m.; Sun 9:30 a.m.–8 p.m. Hours vary seasonally.

Winding Stair
$$$ Dublin 2   New Irish

The Winding Stair is the best new restaurant in Dublin, giving you the best of both worlds: traditional Irish ingredients presented with impeccable modern cooking skills. The chefs are obsessed with finding the top sources for their local ingredients, from the Irish Aberdeen beef (which is accompanied by sticky onions, garlic butter, and homemade French fries) to the fromage heaven that greets you on the Irish Cheese Board. And don't miss the desserts, especially the unbelievable sticky pear and ginger cake. The setting is casual and airy, with views over the River Liffey through ceiling-high windows. You may find yourself elbow-to-elbow with your fellow patrons, but with the good spirits, laughter, and transcendent food, you should hardly mind.

See map p. 192. 40 Ormond Quay (near the Ha'penny Bridge). ☎ 01-872-7320. DART: Tara Street Station. Bus: 68, 69, 69X. Main courses: €20–€25 ($32–$40). AE, MC, V. Open: Mon–Sat 12:30–3:30 p.m. and 6–10:30 p.m.; Sun 12:30–3:30 p.m. and 6–9:30 p.m.

Exploring Dublin

With the exception of the Dublin Writers Museum, the top sights in town are concentrated south of the River Liffey.

If you're planning on doing a lot of sightseeing, you'll definitely want to check out the **Dublin Pass** (☎ 01-605-7700; www.dublinpass.ie), a card that allows you expedited and "free" entry to more than 30 of Dublin's sights (the pass, of course, is not free), discounts on some of Dublin's best shops and restaurants, and a ride from the airport on Aircoach. All the major attractions listed in the upcoming "Dublin's top sights" section are covered by the pass except the Book of Kells. The pass, which you can buy at any of Dublin's tourism centers, is available for one, two, three, or six days. The **one-day pass** costs €31 ($50) adults, €17 ($27) children; the **two-day pass** costs €49 ($78) adults, €29 ($46) children; the **three-day pass** costs €59 ($94) adults and €34 ($54) children; and the **six-day pass** costs €89 ($142) adults and €44 ($70) children.

Dublin's top sights

Chester Beatty Library
Dublin 2

The Chester Beatty Library is one of those gems that often gets overlooked in favor of the flashier attractions of Dublin. But this extensive collection of books, artwork, manuscripts, and religious objects from around the world is worth at least a couple of hours of precious vacation time. On the first floor, you find an exhibit called Arts of the Book, an awe-inspiring and diverse collection of ancient books, from Egyptian Books of the Dead to medieval illuminated manuscripts. Narrated videos of craftspeople at work are found throughout the gallery, illuminating crafts such as bookbinding, papermaking, and printmaking. The second floor is dedicated to books and objects from many of the world's religious traditions. A beautifully created audiovisual explores religious practices and belief systems around the world. The treasures on this floor are numerous, including a Hindu cosmological painting from 18th-century Nepal; a standing Tibetan Buddha; and some of the earliest New Testament and Gospel texts, including the Gospel of St. John, written on Greek papyrus, circa A.D. 150 to 200. If you're hungry, the Silk Road Café offers terrific Mediterranean food.

See map p. 192. Dublin Castle. ☎ *01-407-0750.* www.cbl.ie. *Bus: 13, 16, 19, 123. Free admission. Open: Mon–Fri 10 a.m.–5 p.m.; Sat 11 a.m.–5 p.m.; Sun 1–5 p.m. Closed Mon Oct–Apr.*

Christ Church Cathedral
Dublin 8

Christ Church Cathedral, an Anglican/Episcopal church, has existed in various forms in this spot for almost a thousand years. The Vikings built a simple wood church at this location in 1038. In the 1180s, the original foundation was expanded into a cruciform, and the Romanesque cathedral was built in stone. The church you see today is the result of restoration and rebuilding on the 1180s building during the 1870s. The cathedral provides an informative self-guided tour brochure when you enter. Don't let all the soaring architecture above you make you forget to look down at the beautiful tile floor. On your way to the Peace Chapel of Saint Laud, check out the mummified rat and cat found in a pipe of the organ in the late 1860s. Your ticket also covers admission to the crypt, which houses the cathedral's Treasury. Visitors are welcome at services; just call ahead for times. Allow 45 minutes for your visit.

See map p. 192. Christic Church Place. ☎ *01-677-8099. DART: Tara Street Station. Bus: 49, 50, 65, 77. Admission: €6 ($9.60) adults, €4 ($6.40) seniors and students, free for children accompanied by a parent. Open: June–Aug daily 9 a.m.–6 p.m. (last admission at 5:30 p.m.); Sept–May daily 9:45 a.m.–5 p.m. Limited access during services.*

Dublin Castle
Dublin 2

This is not your typical storybook castle. It was built in the 13th century, but many additions were made over the following 800 years. Today, the castle looks like an encyclopedia of European architectural styles, from the 13th-century Norman Record Tower to the Church of the Holy Trinity, designed in 1814 in Gothic style. The castle now hosts official state functions, such as the president's inauguration, and the clock tower is home to the excellent Chester Beatty Library (reviewed earlier in this section). Forty-five-minute guided tours take you through many of the impressively furnished State Apartments, including the Drawing Room, which features a breathtaking Waterford crystal chandelier; the Throne Room, which holds what is believed to be an original seat of William of Orange; and Patrick's Hall, which boasts the banners of the knights of Saint Patrick and historical ceiling paintings. Don't miss the Church of the Holy Trinity, with its beautiful carved-oak panels and stained-glass windows.

See map p. 192. Cork Hill, off Dame Street. ☎ *01-645-8813. Bus: 49, 56A, 77, 77A, 123. Admission: €4.50 ($7.20) adults, €3.50 ($5.60) seniors and students, €2 ($3.20) children 11 and under. Guided tours are obligatory. Open: Mon–Fri 10 a.m.–4:45 p.m.; Sat–Sun 2–4:45 p.m.*

Dublin Writers Museum
North of the River Liffey

Ireland has produced a multitude of great writers — the short list includes Jonathan Swift, Oscar Wilde, James Joyce, Thomas Mann, Roddy Doyle, and Nobel Prize winners George Bernard Shaw, W. B. Yeats, and Samuel Beckett. This 18th-century house commemorates Ireland's famed scribes with first editions, letters, memorabilia, portraits, busts, and photos. Exhaustive and interesting text on the walls relates the biographies of the writers and explains Ireland's literary movements. The 30-minute audio tour gives brief descriptions of the writers and includes snippets of text read by actors and music appropriate to the display that you're looking at. (Don't be cowed by the listening device — it takes everyone a few minutes to master it.) Only true literary types need apply.

See map p. 192. 18 Parnell Square N. ☎ *01-872-2077.* www.writersmuseum.com. *DART: Connolly Station. Bus: 1, 2, 14, 14A, 16, 16A, 19, 19A, 33X, 39X, 41X, 48A, 58X, 70B, 70X. Admission: €7.25 ($12) adults, €6.10 ($9.75) seniors and students, €4.55 ($7.30) children 3–11, €21 ($34) families. Open: Mon–Sat 10 a.m.–5 p.m. (until 6 p.m. June–Aug); Sun and holidays 11 a.m.–5 p.m.*

Guinness Storehouse
Dublin 8

Though the actual Guinness Brewery is closed to the public, the Guinness Storehouse fills you in on everything you've ever wanted to know about "black gold." This temple to Guinness is housed in a 1904 building that was used for the fermentation process (when yeast is added to beer). The core of the building is a recently created seven-level, pint-shaped structure that could hold approximately 14.3 million pints of Guinness. The Storehouse explores every facet of Ireland's favorite beverage, from the ingredients that go into each batch to the company's advertising campaigns to the role of Guinness in Irish culture. Though the whole attraction evokes a sense of unabashed propaganda, the exhibits are beautifully done in a cool, modern design. With a lot to see, you'll definitely want to make time for the ingredients exhibit, which features a veritable beach of barley and a waterfall of Irish water; the intriguing exhibit about Guinness and Irish pubs around the world (did you know that the first Irish pub in Abu Dhabi opened in 1995?); and the fascinating display of Guinness advertisements through the years. Also don't miss the opportunity to pull your own pint of Guinness. The top-floor Gravity Bar is (literally) the Storehouse's crowning glory, offering 360-degree views of Dublin through floor-to-ceiling glass walls, and dispensing a free pint of black stuff to every visitor over the age of 18. Allow about two hours for your visit.

See map p. 192. St. James's Gate. ☎ *01-408-4800.* www.guinness-storehouse. com. *Bus: 51B, 51C, 78A, or 123. Admission: €14 ($22) adults, €10 ($16) seniors and students 18 and over, €8 ($13) students 17 and under, €5 ($8) children 6–12, free for children 5 and under. Price includes pint of stout or a soda. Open: Daily 8:30 a.m.– 5 p.m. (until 7 p.m. July–Aug).*

St. Patrick's Cathedral
Dublin 8

St. Patrick's Cathedral, the national cathedral of the Church of Ireland, derives its name from the belief that, in the fifth century, Saint Patrick baptized converts to Christianity in a well that once existed on this land. Though there have been churches on this spot since the fifth century, the glorious church that stands today was built in the early 13th century, with restorations to the west tower in 1370 and the addition of a spire in 1749. Volunteers provide an informative map pamphlet that guides you through the church, explaining the highlights of the interior. Be sure to visit the moving memorial of author and social critic Jonathan Swift. Beautiful matins (Sept–June Mon–Fri 9:40 a.m.) and evensongs (Mon–Fri 5:45 p.m. and Sun 3:15 p.m.) are sung here. Allow 45 minutes for a visit.

See map p. 192. Patrick's Close. ☎ *01-475-4817.* www.stpatrickscathedral. ie. *DART: Tara Street Station. Bus: 49, 49A, 49X, 54A, 54N. Admission: €5.50 ($8.80) adults, €4.20 ($6.70) seniors and students; services free. Open: Mar–Oct Mon–Sat 9 a.m.–6 p.m. and Sun 9–11 a.m., 12:45–3 p.m., and 4:15–6 p.m.; Nov–Feb Mon–Fri 9 a.m.–6 p.m., Sat 9 a.m.–5 p.m., and Sun 10 a.m.–11 a.m. and 12:45–3 p.m.*

Trinity College and the Book of Kells
Dublin 2

Trinity College, founded in 1592 by Elizabeth I, looks like the ideal of an impressive, refined, old-world college, with Georgian stone buildings and perfectly manicured green lawns. The campus sits in the middle of the busy city, but within its gates, everything is composed and quiet. As you wander the cobbled paths around Trinity, you can imagine the days when former students Oscar Wilde, Samuel Beckett, Jonathan Swift, and Bram Stoker (a great athlete at Trinity) pounded the same pavement on their way to class.

The jewel in Trinity College's crown is the **Book of Kells,** along with its attending exhibit, housed in the Old Library. This manuscript of the four gospels of the Bible was painstakingly crafted by monks around A.D. 800. The gospels are written in ornate Latin script, and the book is filled with stunning, vivid illustrations, including intricate Celtic knots and fantastical animals. The engaging exhibit that leads to the Book of Kells (and three other ancient Irish religious texts) explains the historical context in which the books were created and reveals the techniques used in their creation. You get to see only one page of the Book of Kells on each visit (they turn a page each day). Be sure to check out the upstairs Long Room after you go through the exhibit. Allow 2½ hours for your visit.

If you're a longtime science lover, check out the new Science Gallery (see description later in the next section) while you're on the Trinity Campus.

See map p. 192. Main entrance on College Street at the eastern end of Dame Street. Walk 2 blocks south of the River Liffey from O'Connell Street Bridge; entrance is on your left. Walk through the front entrance arch, and follow signs to the Old Library and Treasury. ☎ *01-896-1000 for Trinity College information or 01-896-1661 for Book of Kells information.* www.tcd.ie/Library. *DART: Tara Street Station. Bus: 10, 10A, 11, 11B, 13, 13A, 39B. Admission: College grounds free; Old Library and Book of Kells €8 ($13) adults, €7 ($11) students, free for children 11 and under. Open: May–Sept Mon–Sat 9:30 a.m.–5 p.m., Sun 9:30 a.m.–4:30 p.m.; Oct–Apr Mon–Sat 9:30 a.m.–5 p.m., Sun noon to 4:30 p.m. Closed for 10 days during Christmas holiday.*

More cool things to see and do

✔ **Spending an evening in the pubs and clubs of Temple Bar:** The eclectic, hopping **Temple Bar** area is a favorite with many visitors. This area, a few streets along the Liffey, is packed with pubs, shops, bars, cafes, galleries, theaters, and outdoor markets. The neighborhood has its own tourist office at 27 Eustace St. (☎ 01-677-2397; www.visit-templebar.com). In summer, ask at the tourist office about "Diversions Temple Bar," an arts and culture program that includes movie screenings, dance performances, and Irish music and storytelling sessions. Events are free of charge, but tickets (available at the Temple Bar tourist office) are required.

Strolling about is the best way to visit Temple Bar. Proper pub-hopping here includes **Flannery's,** 48 Temple Bar (☎ 01-478-2238); **Farringtons,** East Essex Street (☎ 01-671-5135); and **Oliver St. John Gogarty,** 58–59 Fleet St. (☎ 01-671-1822), and its catty-cornered neighbor **Auld Dubliner,** Temple Bar and Anglesea streets (☎ 01-677-0527). **Lillie's Bordello,** Adam Court off Grafton Street (☎ 01-679-9204), is still one of the hottest Dublin clubs after ten years, with a lipstick-red interior and the members-only (you can pay to be a member) "Library" room. **Renards,** 35–37 S. Frederick St. (☎ 01-677-5876), pulls in celebrities and locals alike, with three floors of bars, dancing, and frequent live jazz. **Ri-Rá,** 1 Exchequer St. (☎ 01-671-1220), fills up every night with dancers getting down to funk, jazz, and other grooves. No need to pub-hop just in Temple Bar, though. Make sure you also hit Dublin's oldest and greatest pub, the **Brazen Head,** west of Temple Bar at 20 Lower Bridge St. (☎ 01-679-5186), as well as the Victorian **Doheny and Nesbitt,** 5 Lower Baggot St. (☎ 01-676-2945), the literary **Davy Byrnes,** 21 Duke St. (☎ 01-677-5217), and two musical bars, **The Cobblestone,** 77 North King St. (☎ 01-872-1799), and **O'Donoghues,** 15 Merrion Row (☎ 01-676-2087). Officially, Dublin's pubs are generally open from 10:30 a.m. to 11:30 p.m. (until 12:30 a.m. Fri–Sat). Some pubs are licensed to stay open later on weekends.

✔ **Tapping your feet on a musical pub crawl: The Musical Pub Crawl** (☎ 01-475-3313; www.discoverdublin.ie) is a fabulous experience for anyone even remotely interested in Irish music. Two excellent musicians guide you from pub to pub, regaling you with Irish tunes and songs; cracking many a joke; and filling you in on the instruments used in Irish music, the history of the music, and the various types of tunes and songs. The nightly tour begins in the upstairs room at **Oliver St. John Gogarty's pub** at the corner of Fleet and Anglesea streets in Temple Bar. Show up at 7:30 p.m. nightly April through October, Thursday, Friday, and Saturday nights in February, March, and November.

✔ **Researching your Irish roots:** Forty million Americans have some Irish in them. Hundreds of Americans come to Ireland every year to seek out their ancestors here, and the Irish are much obliged to help (sometimes for a modest fee). First, the freebie services. The **National Library** (☎ 01-603-0200; www.nli.ie) and the **National Archives** (☎ 01-407-2300, or for Northern Ireland, ☎ 020-8876-3444; www.nationalarchives.ie, or for Northern Ireland, www.national archives.gov.uk) are great places to start your search. The **Office of the Registrar General** in County Roscommon (☎ 01-663-2900; www.groireland.ie) retains all the records on births, deaths, and marriages in the Republic of Ireland. The Web sites of commercial (for-a-fee) ancestor-research firms **Irish Genealogy** (www.irish genealogy.ie) and **Irish Roots** (www.irishroots.net) both have good links lists to lots of local resources.

✔ **Discovering literary and theatrical Dublin:** If the Dublin Writers Museum (see "Dublin's top sights" earlier in this chapter) isn't enough, immerse yourself in literary Dublin by checking out the definitive **James Joyce Centre,** 35 N. Great George's St. (☎ 01-878-8547; www.jamesjoyce.ie), and the **Abbey Theatre,** 26 Lower Abbey St. (☎ 01-878-7222; www.abbeytheatre.ie).

One of the most fun ways to visit the Dublin of books is to take the **Literary Pub Crawl** (☎ 01-670-5602; www.dublinpubcrawl.com), a popular guided walking tour that meets at the Duke Pub at 9 Duke St. (Apr–Oct Mon–Sat 7:30 p.m., Sun noon and 7:30 p.m.; Nov–Mar Thurs–Sat 7:30 p.m., Sun noon and 7:30 p.m.). Or try the **James Joyce Dublin Walking Tour** (☎ 01-878-8547; www.jamesjoyce.ie), offered through the Joyce Centre.

Another great experience is seeing a play at the **Abbey Theatre,** 26 Lower Abbey St. (☎ 01-878-7222; www.abbeytheatre.ie), founded by W. B. Yeats and Lady Gregory in 1904 (plays are performed Mon–Sat at 8 p.m.), or the more avant-garde **Gate Theatre** (☎ 01-874-4045; www.gate-theatre.ie).

✔ **Immerse yourself in the history of Dublin:** On the Original History Tour, nicknamed the "Seminar on the Street," Trinity history students and graduates give a relatively in-depth account of Irish history as they guide you to some of the city's most famous sites, including Trinity, the Old Parliament House, Dublin Castle, City Hall, Christ Church, and Temple Bar. This tour is likely to thrill history buffs and anyone interested in the details of Irish history, and may bore anyone looking for short anecdotes. Tours cost €12 ($19) and are given daily May through September at 11 a.m. and 3 p.m., April and October daily at 11 a.m., and November through March Friday, Saturday, and Sunday at 11 a.m. Contact Historical Walking Tours (☎ 01-688-9412; www.historicalinsights.ie) or just show up at the front gates of Trinity College a bit before the tour begins.

✔ **Exploring an artsy Science Gallery:** Trinity College's new **Science Gallery,** Trinity College at Pearse Street (☎ 01-896-4091), hosts hands-on exhibits that blur the lines between art and science. A recent exhibit about light featured offerings ranging from a life-size playable Pong game projected on an old building across the street to an interactive artistic rendition of the Northern Lights.

Shopping

This is the country that invented duty-free, so you'd be remiss not to purchase a few items of local craft and tradition, from tweeds and tin whistles to Waterford crystal, woolen sweaters, and whiskey. Dublin has several "anything and everything Irish" stores, which are like department store–size gift shops that cater exclusively to travelers. Several have high quality control and are great if you're on a tight time schedule (all but one of the following are on Nassau Street, across from the south flank of Trinity College). Head for **House of Ireland,** 37–38 Nassau St. (☎ 01-671-1111; www.houseofireland.com), or the nearby **Kilkenny Shop,** 5–6 Nassau St. (☎ 01-677-7066). You don't have to go all the way to the Aran Islands to pick up thick Irish woolen sweaters. **Blarney Woollen Mills,** 21–23 Nassau St. (☎ 01-451-6111), has everything from traditional sweaters to kilts, shawls, and scarves. For trendy Irish styles, you can't beat **Avoca,** 11–13 Suffolk St. (☎ 01-677-4215).

Guided tours

For a general feel of the city, **Dublin Bus** (☎ 01-873-4222; www.dublin bus.ie) operates a very good, 75-minute hop-on/hop-off **Dublin City Tour** that connects 23 major points of interest, including museums, art galleries, churches and cathedrals, libraries, and historic sites. The tour departs from the Dublin Bus office at Cathal Brugha Street, but you can pick it up at any of the 23 stops. Fares are €15 ($24) adults, €6 ($9.60) children 13 and under, and €13 ($21) seniors and students; the ticket is valid for 24 hours. The bus operates daily from 9:30 a.m. to 6:30 p.m.

Suggested itineraries

If you're the type who'd rather organize your own tours, this section offers some tips for building your own Dublin itineraries.

If you have one day

If you just have **one day** and really want to pack the sightseeing in, take the **Dublin Bus** "Hop-On Hop-Off" tour so that you can see as many attractions as possible in the most efficient way.

Take in **Trinity College** and the **Book of Kells** first, and then wander around the excellent shopping areas of Grafton Street and Nassau Street. Grab lunch and picnic in **Merrion Square.** In the afternoon, visit the nearby **National Museum.**

Treat yourself to a delicious dinner at the **Winding Stair** before meeting up with the **Musical Pub Crawl.**

If you have two days

If you have **two days,** follow the itinerary for Day 1. On the morning of the second day, take the **Historical Walking Tour.** Then head over to the **Chester Beatty Library** to gaze at the gorgeous books and art housed within.

Eat lunch at a pub, and then head out to see **St. Patrick's Cathedral** and the **Guinness Storehouse.** Drop into the **Queen of Tarts,** 4 Corkhill, across from Dublin Castle (☎ 01-670-7499), for an afternoon treat on your way back to Temple Bar.

Stroll Temple Bar, and splurge for dinner at **Tea Room** before joining up with the **Jameson's Literary Pub Crawl.**

If you have three days

Spend **Day 1** and **Day 2** as described in the preceding section, and take **Day 3** to tour the prehistoric **mound tombs,** north of Dublin, or the **Wicklow Mountains** and **Glendalough,** to the south (both covered in the following section).

Traveling the Irish Countryside

Lovely as Dublin is, you should really see a bit of Ireland's famed countryside. Scenic drives abound, and the excursions in this section take you past ruined churches and impressive mansions, along rocky shorelines, and through rolling, verdant landscapes dotted with sheep. The best way to explore the countryside is by car.

North of Dublin to passage tombs and ruined medieval abbeys

Prehistoric sites and ruined abbeys draw visitors to the area around the Boyne River Valley, north of Dublin. If you plan a tightly packed day, you can easily visit all the sights below on a long day trip.

Getting there

The most convenient base for the region is the town of Drogheda, which has regular rail and bus links with Dublin. The **tourist office** here is located on Mayoralty Street (☎ **041-983-7070;** www.drogheda.ie). The prettiest area in the region is Carlingford, which is about 45km (28 miles) north of the Boyne Valley attractions.

Mary Gibbons Tours (☎ **01-283-9973;** www.newgrangetours.com) offers an excellent bus tour of Meath from Dublin.

Seeing the sights

Top honors for sightseeing go to **Newgrange** and **Knowth,** Ireland's most famous and most accessible passage tombs. Newgrange is an 11m-high (36-ft.) burial chamber made of stones — some weighing up to 16 tons. It's a watertight engineering triumph built well over 5,000 years ago, before Stonehenge or the Egyptian pyramids were even contemplated. You can take part in a guided visit down the 18m (60-ft.) passage to the center of the tomb. There, you'll be greeted with a beautiful surprise. Knowth is a tomb of similar size to Newgrange, used from the Stone Age through the 1400s. Tours do not begin at Newgrange but at the **Brú Na Bóinne Visitor Centre,** south of the river Boyne on the L21, 3km (2 miles) west of Donore (☎ **041-988-0300;** www.heritageireland.ie), and some distance from Newgrange itself.

The center is open daily year-round, but hours vary: March, April, and October, it's open daily from 9:30 a.m. to 5:30 p.m.; May and the last two weeks of September, it's open daily from 9 a.m. to 6:30 p.m.; June through mid-September, it's open daily from 9 a.m. to 7 p.m.; and November through February, it's open daily from 9:30 a.m. to 5 p.m. The last tour is offered 90 minutes before closing; the last admission to the visitor center is 45 minutes before closing. The center restricts the number of people visiting the site, so expect to spend about an hour viewing the center before your 45-minute tour of Newgrange. Admission to the center and Newgrange is €5.80 ($9.30) adults, €4.50 ($7.20) seniors, €1.60 ($2.55) children and students, and €11 ($18) families. The addition of Knowth to your tour will cost about €2 ($3.20) more.

Located 10km (6 miles) northwest of Drogheda are the remains of the monastery **Monasterboice,** now represented mainly by its quiet, monumental cemetery. Here you can see plenty of Celtic high crosses, including the best preserved in Ireland, **Muiredeach's High Cross,** a 5m-tall (17-ft.) example from A.D. 922 (look at the beautifully preserved "Taking of Christ" panel just above the base). Nearby are the ruins of **Mellifont Abbey** (☎ 041-982-6103), a 12th-century religious community. Monasterboice is open daily during daylight hours and is free. Mellifont Abbey is open May through September daily 10 a.m. to 6 p.m. Admission is €2.10 adults ($3.35), €1.30 ($2.10) seniors, and €1.10 ($1.75) children and students.

Where to stay and dine
You can stay in Drogheda at the **Ballymascanlon House Hotel** (☎ 042-935-8200; www.ballymascanlon.com). If you opt to stay in charming Carlingford, up north a ways, you won't want to miss the welcome at **Shalom House,** on Ghan Road (☎ 042-937-3151; www.jackiewoods.com), and the baked goods at **Georgina's Bakehouse and Tea Rooms,** on Castle Hill (☎ 042-937-3346).

South of Dublin: Mansions and monasteries in County Wicklow
Just an easy 15-minute drive south of downtown Dublin gets you to the gardens of County Wicklow. The sights south of Dublin can easily be visited on a day trip.

Getting there
Dublin's tourist office has information on County Wicklow; otherwise, you'd have to drive all the way through the region to Wicklow Town and the area **tourism office** (☎ 0404-20-173; www.wicklow.ie) on Fitzwilliam Square. You can see the best of this area by car, but if you're not renting a car, you can catch a ride with **Bus Eireann** (☎ 01-836-6111; www.buseirann.ie), which takes busloads of travelers from Dublin to the major sights year-round. If you don't have a car and you want to see Glendalough, make a reservation for the fun, daylong **Wild Wicklow Tour** (☎ 01-280-1899; www.wildwicklow.ie).

Seeing the sights
A few miles south of Dublin on the N11, just past the town of Enniskerry, you'll find **Powerscourt Gardens** (☎ 01-204-6000; www.powerscourt.ie). These gardens are the finest in Wicklow County, which is saying a lot, because the county is known for its abundance of exceptionally beautiful gardens. First laid out from 1745 to 1767, the gardens were redesigned in Victorian style from 1843 to 1875. The gardens have many different facets, among them a wooded glen graced with a stone round tower that was

modeled on Lord Powerscourt's dining-room pepper pot, a magical moss-covered grotto, a formal Italianate area with a circular pond and fountain presided over by sculptures of winged horses, and a walled garden where blazing roses cling to the stone. About 6km (4 miles) on is the 120m (400-ft.) **Powerscourt Waterfall,** the tallest in Ireland. The gardens are open year-round from 9:30 a.m. to 5:30 p.m. during the summer and 9:30 a.m. to dusk in the winter.

The old Military Road (R115) slices through the wildest heights of the **Wicklow Mountains.** This eerie peatscape, covered with heather and reddish scrub, looks as if it belongs somewhere on Mars, with only the Sally Gap pass and Glenmacnass waterfalls breaking up the moody boglands.

At Laragh, detour west to visit one of the most magical of Ireland's ruined monastic sites, **Glendalough** (☎ 0404-45-325), which is filled with high crosses, round towers, pretty lakes, and medieval stone buildings. During the summer, the tour buses can be frequent. Glendalough is open daily mid-March to mid-October from 9:30 a.m. to 6 p.m. The rest of the year, it's open from 9:30 a.m. to 5 p.m.

Driving rings around County Kerry

To partake in Irish culture at its best, check out County Kerry. Irish traditions flourish here, from music and storytelling to good pub *craic* (a Gaelic word that, roughly translated, means "a great vibe"). In addition, you can find several of the country's few remaining Gaelic-speaking pockets here. The 177km (110-mile) **Ring of Kerry,** a scenic route circling the Iveragh Peninsula, is Ireland's most famous — and most tour bus–engulfed — drive.

Because this area is heavy with tour buses, most visitors take the Ring counterclockwise from Killarney, which makes the heavy traffic easier to manage. The only thing less fun than driving on the left side of a twisty, narrow two-lane road along a cliff and sharing it with a constant stream of giant buses much too wide for their lane is doing the same thing with all those buses *coming directly at you.*

You can visit the Ring in a long day, but give the whole area two or three days in order to take some trips off the beaten path on the Iveragh Peninsula and to spend time on the less-visited **Dingle Peninsula.**

Getting there

Frequent daily train and bus service arrives from Ireland's big cities into Killarney, the region's main town and tourist center. Killarney also houses the region's main **tourist office** (☎ 064-31-633; www.killarneyonline. com) in the Town Hall off Main Street.

County Kerry

Seeing the sights

Driving the Ring in County Kerry, a stretch of route N70 with plenty of signage, is by far the most popular activity in this region. The winding route provides thrilling, dramatic views of the sea and the high inland mountains, and passes through a succession of charming villages, each with its own unique points of interest. Highlights include the **Kerry Bog Village Museum** at Glenbeigh (thatched cottages re-created for tourists), **Cahirciveen** (the main town), **Staigue Fort** (a well-preserved, Iron Age, drystone fortress), the town of **Sneem** (cottages in festive colors), and the charming, picturesque town of **Kenmare,** where you'll enjoy fine hotels, restaurants, shopping, and pubs.

About halfway around the Ring, you can detour onto **Valentia Island,** connected to the mainland by a bridge and home to the **Skellig Experience Centre** (☎ **066-947-6306**), where exhibits introduce you to the endangered natural habitats and medieval monastery of the dramatic Skellig Islands off the coast. The center offers weather-dependent cruises around the islands.

Though the Ring of Kerry is justifiably popular, the less frequented circular drive around the **Dingle Peninsula,** one inlet to the north of the Inveragh, is even more scenic. Dingle's **tourist office** (☎ **066-915-1188**) is on the Quay in Dingle Town, the main town. Dingle is also home to Fungie, the resident dolphin of Dingle Bay. To arrange a swim with Fungie (he's not in captivity, so there's no guarantee that he'll show up), call ☎ **066-915-1967.**

Another gem in Kerry is **Killarney National Park** (☎ **064-35-960**), a beautiful area full of lakes, waterfalls, castles, woodlands, bogs, and the manor house, gardens, and romantically ruined abbey of **Muckross.**

Where to stay and dine

You may feel as though you're staying in a friend's house at **Blackstones House** (☎ **066-976-0164;** www.glencar-blackstones.com), a cozy farmhouse B&B located off the Ring of Kerry in the mountains, next to a rushing river. **Packies,** Henry Street, Kenmare (☎ **053-41-508**), a hip, cheerful restaurant, serves up delectable dishes that range from traditional Irish to modern, internationally influenced fare.

Fast Facts: Dublin

American Express

Dial ☎ 1-850-882-028 to report lost or stolen traveler's checks or cards.

Area Code

Ireland's country code is **353**. Dublin's city code is **01**. If you're calling from outside Ireland, drop the initial 0. To call Dublin from the United States, dial 011-353-1, followed by the number.

Currency

In January 2002, Ireland's national currency changed from the Irish punt to the euro (€). The euro is divided into 100 cents, and there are coins of .01, .02, .05, .10, .20, .50, 1, and 2. Paper-note denominations are 5, 10, 20, 50, 100, 200, and 500 euros. Rates of exchange used to calculate the dollar value given in this chapter are €1 = $1.60. Amounts over $10 have been rounded to the nearest dollar.

Doctors and Dentists

In an emergency, ask your hotel to call a doctor for you, or go to the hospital (see "Hospitals," later in this section). Otherwise, call the Eastern Health Board Headquarters, Dr. Steeven's Hospital, Dublin (☎ 01-679-0700), which can also arrange a doctor visit.

Embassies and Consulates

The U.S. Embassy (☎ 01-668-8777; Fax: 01-668-9946) is at 42 Elgin Rd.

Emergency

Dial ☎ 999 for police, fire, or an ambulance.

Hospitals

The two best hospitals for emergency care in Dublin are St. Vincent's Hospital, Elm Park, Dublin 4 (☎ 01-221-4000), on the south side of the city; and Beaumont

Hospital, Beaumont Road, Dublin 9 (☎ 01-809-3000), on the north side.

Information

The main Dublin Tourism office is in St. Andrew's Church (☎ 01-605-7700; www.visitdublin.com), at Suffolk Street, a block west of Grafton Street. In addition to information about Dublin, they can provide you with information about the rest of the country and Northern Ireland. For specifics on this and other offices, see "Finding information after you arrive," near the beginning of this chapter.

The Temple Bar district has its own tourist office at 27 Eustace St. (☎ 01-677-2397; www.visit-templebar.com).

The Dublin Bus number is ☎ 01-873-4222, and the Web site is www.dublinbus.ie. The number for Dublin Area Rapid Transit (DART) is ☎ 01-703-3504; its Web site is www.dart.ie. For Bus Eireann (coaches throughout Ireland), call ☎ 01-836-6111 or visit www.buseireann.ie.

Internet Access and Cybercafes

Central Cyber Cafe, 6 Grafton St. (☎ 01-677-8298; www.centralcafe.ie), is in the heart of town. Its sister location is Global Internet Cafe at 8 Lower O'Connell St. (☎ 01-878-0295; www.centralcafe.ie).

Maps

Good maps are available at the Dublin Tourism Centre, Suffolk Street, and online through the Tourism Centre's Web site at www.visitdublin.com/travel/maps.

Newspapers and Magazines

The *Irish Times* (www.ireland.com) publishes a daily arts and entertainment guide. The best events listings are found in *In Dublin* (www.indublin.ie) and *Event*

Guide (www.eventguide.ie), and at www.hotpress.com. *Where: Dublin* is geared to travelers and features restaurant, shopping, and entertainment information.

Pharmacies

Hamilton, Long & Co., 5 O'Connell St., Dublin 1 (☎ 01-874-8456), is a central pharmacy with extended hours.

Police

Dial ☎ 999 in an emergency to get the Garda (police). Dublin's Tourist Victim Support Service (☎ 01-478-5295) is located in the Garda headquarters on Harcourt Square.

Post Office

Dublin's main post office is on O'Connell Street (☎ 01-705-7000) and is open Monday through Saturday from 8 a.m. to 8 p.m.

Safety

Late-night crime is not uncommon, so don't walk back to your hotel alone after pub closing time (11:30 p.m. most nights); get a taxi. Be especially careful around O'Connell Street and its side streets after the pubs close.

Taxes

In Ireland, a value-added tax (VAT) of about 21 percent is figured into the price of most items. International visitors can reclaim this VAT on major purchases of consumer goods (see Chapter 4).

Taxis

See "Orienting Yourself in Dublin," earlier in this chapter.

Telephone

Although some pay phones accept both euro coins (in denominations of €0.10, €0.20, €0.50, €1, and €2) and phone cards, most only accept phone cards, which you can buy at supermarkets, convenience stores, and post offices. The minimum charge is €0.50 (80¢).

To call the United States from Ireland directly, dial 001 followed by the area code and phone number. To charge a call to your calling card or to make a collect call home, dial AT&T (☎ 1-800-550-000), MCI (☎ 1-800-551-001), or Sprint (☎ 1-800-552-001).

Transit Info

See "Orienting Yourself in Dublin," earlier in this chapter.

Part IV
Central Europe

In this part . . .

Welcome to Central Europe, the home of some of the most romantic cities in the world. There's dreamy Prague, the "new" showcase city of Eastern Europe, and chic, sophisticated Paris — where fine food, high fashion, and great art are part and parcel of everyday life. In atmospheric Amsterdam, you can cruise the 17th-century canals, discover museums crammed with Rembrandts and van Goghs, have a peek at the infamous Red-Light District, and visit the house where Anne Frank and her family hid from the Nazis. In Munich, you can explore a city that revels in all the oompah-band cheeriness of Bavaria and offers all the refinements of a great cultural center. Fascinating Vienna, a city renowned for its musical heritage, offers a roster of fabulous cultural enjoyments. In the Bernese Oberland of Switzerland, you can scale the Alps on thrilling gondola rides, visit ice palaces carved into glaciers, and marvel at the soaring mountaintop vistas.

Chapter 13

Paris and Environs

● ●

In This Chapter

▶ Getting to Paris

▶ Checking out the neighborhoods

▶ Discovering the best places to sleep and eat

▶ Exploring the highlights of the City of Light

▶ Side-tripping to Versailles and Chartres

● ●

All clichés are based in truth and those about Paris are no different: Paris is the City of Light. It's a moveable feast. It's the world capital of romance, birthplace of bohemians and Impressionists, muse to Hemingway and Gertrude Stein (who coined the term *Lost Generation*), and the high temple of haute cuisine. You can (and probably will) grow faint from so much great art at the Louvre, cruise the Seine past one of the world's most famous cathedrals, and gaze at the prison where Marie Antoinette spent her last days. You can sip a *pastis* in a neighborhood cafe, dine stupendously in a tiny bistro, or steal kisses while taking in the view from the Pont des Arts footbridge.

Romanticizing this city is easy — just as it's easy to belittle it. Even Parisians seem to be losing a little heart. No doubt friends have regaled you with their best rude-French stories, and you've heard that the museums are crowded, the traffic is horrendous, the pollution vile, the Champs-Elysées has become a commercialized strip mall, and everything is too expensive.

Don't let these obstacles keep you from having a good time. Prepare yourself for residents' wariness of visitors, and you'll be pleasantly surprised when they show you how warm they can be. To beat the museum crowds, go early. To avoid traffic, take the Métro (subway), one of the most reliable and convenient transportation systems around. Or ride one of the many bikes for rent around the city in Mayor Bertrand Delanoë's continuing quest to cut down on pollution and make Paris greener.

Sure, fast-food joints have mushroomed and movie multiplexes now dominate the Champs-Elysées, but you can find elegant, authentic Paris elsewhere, even a block away from the tourist crowds. And although you can spend all your cash in Paris, there is no city with more great values on everything from meals and hotels to shopping and museums. You have to be willing to search those bargains out, and this chapter helps you find some of them.

Finally, although those positives and negatives exist, they are by no means the sum of the city. Paris strikes a lively balance between the vibrant, modern metropolis of the 21st century (where residents can talk on cell-phones in subway cars) and the majestic, historic city of Napoleon. It's a city of hip nightclubs, cutting-edge cuisine, and the highest fashion, as well as one of venerable museums, legendary cafes, and sweeping 18th- and 19th-century grandeur. This balance keeps Paris intriguing and addic-tive, and visitors and faithful admirers return year after year.

Getting There

Getting to the center of Paris is easy whether you're arriving by plane or train. Getting around the city is a breeze, too, thanks to the efficient Métro subway system.

Arriving by air

Most international flights land at **Charles de Gaulle Airport** (☎ 01-48-62-22-80; www.adp.fr), also known as Roissy, 23km (14 miles) northeast of the city. Most of the big-name transatlantic airlines arrive at terminals 1 and 3; Air France and its affiliates, intra-European carriers, and airlines serving the rest of the world arrive at Terminal 2. Several ATMs are located in the arrivals halls of the terminals.

If you aren't overloaded with baggage and/or small children, the RER B (commuter train) line runs into the center of Paris for 8.20€ ($13) adults, 5.80€ ($9.30) children. The train is easy, cheap, and convenient, and you can ride to and from the airport from 5 a.m. to midnight daily. Free shuttle buses connect terminals CDG 1 and CDG 2 to the RER ticket counter and train station. (Look for illustrated signs showing a bus, or get directions from English-speaking personnel at the information desks located on every arrivals-level floor.)

Buy the **RER** ticket at the RER ticket counter and hang onto it in case of ticket inspection. (You can be fined if you can't produce your ticket for an inspector.) In any case, you need your ticket later to get off the RER system and into the Métro (where you must buy a subway ticket to enter). Individual tickets cost 1.50€ ($2.40), but if you plan on staying a few days, a *carnet* (pack of ten) costs only 11€ ($18). A ticket counter and ticket machines are at each Métro entrance.

Depending where your hotel is located, you exit the subway either on the Right Bank or the Left Bank. From the airport station, trains depart about every 15 minutes for the half-hour trip into town and stop on the **Right Bank** at Gare du Nord and Châtelet–Les Halles, and on the **Left Bank** at St-Michel, Luxembourg, Port-Royal, and Denfert-Rochereau, before heading south out of the city.

France

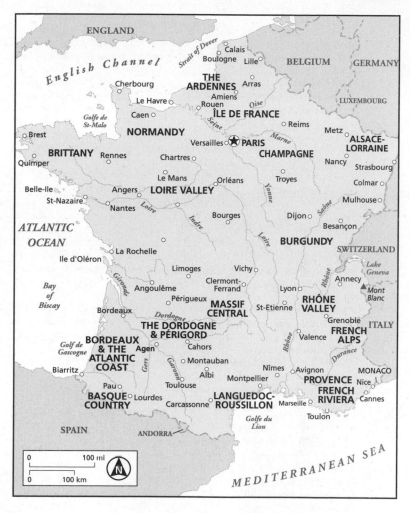

ENGLAND

English Channel

Strait of Dover

Calais
Boulogne   Lille
BELGIUM   GERMANY

Cherbourg   **THE**   Arras
ARDENNES
Amiens
Le Havre   Rouen   Oise   LUXEMBOURG
Golfe de   Caen   **ÎLE DE FRANCE**
St-Malo
Brest   **NORMANDY**   Reims   Metz
Versailles ★ **PARIS**   Marne   **ALSACE-**
BRITTANY   Rennes   **CHAMPAGNE**   **LORRAINE**
Quimper   Chartres   Nancy
Strasbourg
Le Mans   Orléans   Troyes   Colmar
Belle-Ile   Angers   **LOIRE VALLEY**   Yonne   Mulhouse
St-Nazaire   Nantes   Loire
Bourges   Dijon   Saône
ATLANTIC   Besançon
OCEAN   Indre   Loire   **BURGUNDY**
Ile d'Oléron   La Rochelle   SWITZERLAND
Lake
Limoges   Vichy   Geneva
Bay   Clermont-   Annecy
of   Angoulême   Ferrand   Lyon   Rhône   Mont
Biscay   Périgueux   **MASSIF**   St-Etienne   **RHÔNE**   Blanc
Bordeaux   **CENTRAL**   **VALLEY**
Dordogne   Grenoble   ITALY
THE DORDOGNE   Valence   **FRENCH**
& PÉRIGORD   Rhône   **ALPS**
Golf de   **BORDEAUX**   Agen   Cahors   Durance
Gascogne   **& THE**
Biarritz   **ATLANTIC**   Montauban   Nîmes   Avignon   MONACO
COAST   Gers   Garonne   Albi   Montpellier   **PROVENCE**   Nice
Pau   Toulouse   **FRENCH**
BASQUE Lourdes   **LANGUEDOC-**   **RIVIERA**   Cannes
COUNTRY   Carcassonne **ROUSSILLON**   Marseille
Golfe du   Toulon
SPAIN   ANDORRA   Lion

0   100 mi
0   100 km

MEDITERRANEAN SEA

Métro stations such as Châtelet–Les Halles have numerous stairways and long corridors; you'll want to avoid taking the RER if you have a lot of baggage.

If you aren't in a hurry to get into Paris proper, another cheap way to get to town is by the bus service run by Air France. Les Cars Air France will drop you off near such central Paris locations as the Arc de Triomphe, Gare Montparnasse, Gare de Lyon, and Invalides. Buy your ticket directly from the driver for 14€ ($22) from Charles de Gaulle, 10€ ($16) from Orly (a 15 percent discount is given to groups of four or more). It takes about an hour, sometimes more, from Charles de Gaulle, about

45 minutes from Orly, depending on traffic. Look for signs on the arrivals level for the gates where the bus is located, or go to www.airfrance.com before your trip.

Another option is taking a taxi, but it's not cheap: Around 50€ ($80) from 7 a.m. to 8 p.m. and about 15 percent more at other times.

Some charter flights, as well as many national flights, land 14km (8½ miles) south of town at **Orly Airport** (☎ 01-49-75-15-15; www.adp.fr). French domestic flights land at Orly Ouest, and intra-European and inter-continental flights land at Orly Sud. Shuttle buses connect these terminals, and other shuttles connect them to Charles de Gaulle every 30 minutes or so. ATMs and information desks are located in the arrivals hall of both terminals. A taxi from Orly to central Paris costs around 40€ ($64) and takes anywhere from 25 minutes to an hour. You can also take one of two commuter trains. If you're staying on the Left Bank, take the **RER C line** by catching a free shuttle bus from Exit G, Platform 1, at Orly Sud, or Exit G on the arrivals level at Orly Ouest, to the **Rungis** station, where RER C trains leave every 15 minutes for **Gare d'Austerlitz** (near the Jardin des Plantes, in the 13th *arrondissement* (municipal district); see "Orienting Yourself in Paris," below, for details about Paris's arrondissements). A one-way fare is 6€ ($9.60). The trip into the city takes 40 minutes, making various stops along the Seine on the **Left Bank.**

If you're staying on the **Right Bank,** you can take the **Orlyval/RER B line** to **Antony** Métro station. You connect at the **Antony** RER station, where you board the RER B train to Paris. Hold onto the ticket because you'll need it to get into the Métro/RER system. A trip to the Châtelet station on the Right Bank takes about 50 minutes and costs 9.30€ ($15).

Arriving by rail

Paris has many rail stations, but most international trains arrive at one of four places. The **Gare du Nord** serves northern Germany, Belgium, the Netherlands, Denmark, and London. It's the destination for both the **Eurostar** direct train that uses the **Channel Tunnel** (or Chunnel) — a dozen trains daily for a three-hour trip, four hours with the time change — as well as trains arriving on the last leg of the old-fashioned and highly not recommended route: London to Dover by train; Dover to Calais by ferry; and Calais to Paris by train (10½ long hours for the trip). Trains from the southwest (the Loire Valley, Pyrénées, Spain) arrive at the **Gare d'Austerlitz.** Those from the south and southeast (the Riviera, Lyon, Italy, Geneva) pull in at the **Gare de Lyon.** Trains coming from Alsace and eastern France, Luxembourg, southern Germany, and Zurich arrive at the **Gare de l'Est.** The **Gare Montparnasse** serves as the point for all trains from western and southwestern France, including Bordeaux and Chartres. All train stations connect to Métro stations with the same name. All Paris train stations are located within the first 15 arrondissements, and are easily accessible.

Orienting Yourself in Paris

The Seine River divides Paris between the *Rive Droite* (Right Bank) to the north and the *Rive Gauche* (Left Bank) to the south. The city of Paris's origins date back thousands of years to the **Ile de la Cité,** an island in the Seine that is still the center of the city and home to **Cathédrale de Notre-Dame.**

The city is divided into 20 numbered *arrondissements* (municipal districts). The layout of these districts follows a distinct snail-like pattern. The first (abbreviated 1er for *premiere*) arrondissement is the dead center of Paris, comprising an area around Notre-Dame and the Louvre. From there, the rest of the districts spiral outward, clockwise, in ascending order. The lower the arrondissement number, the more central the location. The last two digits of the postal code denote the actual arrondissement, so an address listed as Paris 75003 is in the third arrondissement, and 75016 is in the 16th.

Introducing the neighborhoods

Traditionally people consider the Right Bank to be more upscale, with Paris's main boulevards such as avenue Montaigne and rue du Faubourg-St-Honoré, and museums such as the **Louvre.** The old bohemian half of Paris is on the Left Bank, with the **Latin Quarter** around the university.

Among the major arrondissements (for visitors) on the Right Bank is the 3e. Called **Le Marais,** this bustling neighborhood manages to remain genuinely Parisian amid the swirl of tourism in the city center, but sadly, super-chic boutiques are chasing out Paris institutions such as Jo Goldenberg, the venerable Jewish deli. The 4e includes most of **Ile de la Cité** and its posh neighbor, **Ile St-Louis;** the **Beaubourg pedestrian zone;** and the **Centre Pompidou** modern-art complex.

The 1er includes the **Louvre** neighborhood and the tip of **Ile de la Cité.** The 8e — a natural extension westward of the 1er — is Paris's most upscale area, consisting of ritzy hotels, fashion boutiques, fine restaurants, and upscale town houses. The 8th arrondissement centers on the grandest boulevard in a city famous for them: the **Champs-Elysées.** The sidewalks of this historic shopping promenade were recently cleaned up and widened. Now no more than a string of international chain stores and movie theaters, the Champs-Elysées has become merely a shadow of its former elegant self. For expensive boutique shopping, walk directly north of the Champs to **Rue Faubourg St-Honoré,** where you'll find Pierre Cardin, Chanel, Yves St. Laurent, and Christian Lacroix, among others.

From **Place de la Concorde** — an oval plaza at the western end of the **Louvre** complex, where French royalty met the business end of a guillotine during the Revolution — the Champs-Elysées beelines east–west to the **Arc de Triomphe.** The Arc is one of the world's greatest triumphal

Paris Neighborhoods

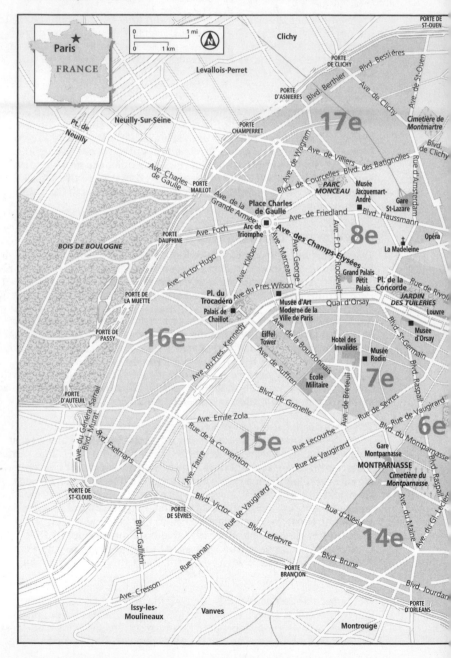

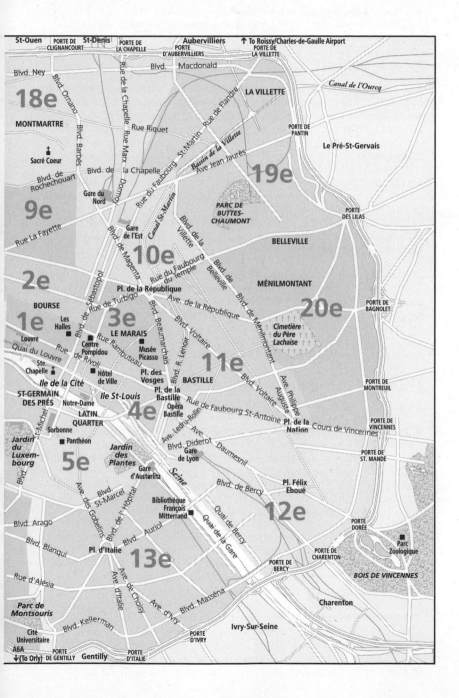

arches, a monument to France's unknown soldier and to the gods of car-insurance premiums (surrounding the Arc is a five-lane traffic circle where, it seems, anything goes). From the top of the Arc running in a straight line, you can see its counterpart, the 110m-high (361-ft.) Grande Arche de la Défense, in neighboring St-Denis.

Still echoing with the ghosts of Picasso's Paris, in the northerly reaches of the Right Bank lies **Montmartre,** topped by the fairy-tale gleaming white basilica of **Sacré-Coeur,** and trampled by tourists. The neighborhood is so distinct and (despite the numerous visitors) charming that it gets its own write-up under "More cool things to see and do," later in this chapter.

Left Bank arrondissements include the 5e, the famous old **Latin Quarter,** named for the language spoken by students attending the Sorbonne who gave it its once-colorful atmosphere. These days, the quarter is another sad Parisian shadow of former glory, its bohemia replaced by gyro stands, souvenir shops, and hordes of tourists wondering why the Latin Quarter was ever famous.

The adjacent 6e retains some of its counterculture charm. The students of **Paris's Fine Arts School** help liven up things here, especially in the now highly fashionable but still somewhat artsy **St-Germain-des-Prés** neighborhood of cafes, brasseries, and restaurants. Tucked into a wide arc of the Seine, the 7e intrudes a bit on the **St-Germain** neighborhood, but its major features are the **Musée d'Orsay,** the new **Musée du Quai Branly,** the **Tour Eiffel** (Eiffel Tower), and the **Musée Rodin.**

Finding information after you arrive

The city's **tourist information office,** L'Office du Tourisme et des Congrès de Paris (www.parisinfo.com), maintains two full-service welcome centers. Both offer basic information about attractions in the city, help with last-minute hotel reservations, make booking for day trips, and sell transportation and museum passes — but for a small fee. The first, in Gare du Nord (Métro: Gare du Nord), beneath the glass roof, is open daily from 8 a.m. to 6 p.m. The second, the Opéra-Grands Magasins Welcome Center, 11 rue Scribe (Métro: Opéra or Chaussée d'Antin), is open Monday through Saturday from 9 a.m. to 6:30 p.m.

Several auxiliary offices, or welcome centers, are scattered throughout the city. The office in Gare de Lyon (Métro: Gare de Lyon) is open Monday through Saturday from 8 a.m. to 6 p.m. The welcome center in Gare du Nord is open daily from 8 a.m. to 6 p.m. There are two offices in Montmartre: one at 21 place du Tertre (Métro: Abbesses), open daily from 10 a.m. to 7 p.m., and the other on the median strip facing 72 bd. Rochechouart (Métro: Anvers), open daily from 10 a.m. to 6 p.m. The welcome center in the Louvre (Métro: Palais Royal or Musée du Louvre) is open daily from 10 a.m. to 6 p.m., while the nearby Pyramides office, 25 rue des Pyramides (Métro: Pyramides), is open June through October daily from 9 a.m. to 7 p.m., and November through May daily from 10 a.m. to

6 p.m. Paris's convention center, Paris Expo (Métro: Porte de Versailles), has an information desk open 11 a.m. to 7 p.m. during trade fairs.

Getting Around Paris

Paris has an extensive public-transportation system that makes it easy for you to get around without having to rent a car. Transport tickets are good on the Métro, bus, and RER lines. Individual tickets cost 1.50€ ($2.40), but a *carnet* (pack of ten) costs only 11€ ($18).

Two types of cards offer unlimited travel on all forms of public transportation: the "tourists'" Paris Visite and the locals' *Carte Orange Hebdomadaire* (Weekly Card Orange). You won't find mention of the less-expensive Carte Orange on the English-language version of www.ratp. fr, but that doesn't mean you can't get the same savings a Parisian can; you just have to ask for it.

The **Carte Orange** costs 16€ ($26) for zones 1 and 2 and 22€ ($35) for zones 1, 2, and 3. You'll need to provide a passport-size photo (or snap one at photo booths in major train and Métro stations). Make sure you get the *hebdomadaire* (weekly) and not the *mensuel* (monthly). The card is valid Monday through Sunday and on sale Monday through Wednesday of the same week, and Thursday through Sunday for the following week.

Avoid buying the card on Wednesday, the last day it's on sale for the week in which it's valid, because you won't get your money's worth.

Buy the **Paris Visite** (the regular pass covers zones 1–3, which include all of central Paris and many of its suburbs) if you're in Paris for only a day or two. At 8.50€ ($14) for one day or 14€ ($22) for two days (children 4–11 pay half-price; children 3 and under ride free), you'll still beat the price of the Carte Orange. However, the three-day 19€ ($30) and the five-day 28€ ($45) Visites are a waste of money.

More comprehensive Visite passes covering zones 1 through 6 (all the 'burbs, including Disneyland Paris) cost almost, or more than, twice as much, depending on the duration of your pass.

Don't pay for passes that carry you beyond zone 3; most of the interesting monuments lie within zones 1 and 2.

By Métro (subway) and RER

The Paris **Métro** (☎ 32-46 within France, for information in English at 0.34€/55¢ per minute; www.ratp.fr) is one of the best subways in Europe, a clean, efficient, and well-interconnected system. Using a Métro map (there's one on the inside front cover of this book), find which numbered line you want to take and the name of the last station in the direction you want to go. In the Métro tunnels, follow signs for that line and that last station to get on the train going the right way.

You may have to transfer to another line to get to your destination (although usually not more than once per trip). When transferring, follow the signs labeled CORRESPONDENCE to the next line. Don't follow a SORTIE sign, unless you want to exit. You can make unlimited transfers on one ticket as long as you don't exit the system — although you may often find yourself walking long distances in the tunnels that connect some transfer stations.

Most of the lines are numbered, but some are assigned letters. The lettered lines (A, B, C, and D) are technically not the Métro but are part of the overlapping RER network. This high-speed commuter light-rail system services only major stops within the city and extends much farther out into the suburbs. The RER uses the same tickets as the Métro (except when you're traveling way out into the 'burbs, for which you have to buy a separate ticket), and you can transfer freely between the two systems.

The wait for arriving RER trains can be longer than the wait for a regular subway train, so consider this before using the RER within the city.

Some RER lines are particularly useful; the C line, for instance, follows the left bank of the Seine closely (no Métro line does this) and also heads out to Versailles. Both ends of all RER lines split off like the frayed ends of a rope as they leave the city, so make sure the train you board is heading out to the numbered fork you want (for example, the C line has eight different end destinations, C1 through C8). Maps on the platforms show you the routes of each fork, and TV displays tell you when the next half-dozen trains will be arriving and which number each one is.

By bus

Some people automatically discount the bus system in Paris because the congested traffic conditions make the ride generally less efficient than the Métro system (and, if you take it during rush hour, quite crowded). However, if you're tired of wandering around underground tunnels, the bus system provides a dual service: transportation and a very cheap sightseeing tour of Paris. Almost every bus line makes a trip along the Right Bank of the Seine, giving passengers a glimpse of Ile St. Louis, Notre-Dame, and often the fortified walls of the Louvre. The bus you're on may also pass any number of the beautiful avenues, fountains, or sculptures that make Paris a beautiful city. Although the bus is not always as quick as the Métro and can get caught in rush-hour traffic, it stops in places that the Métro cannot and provides a refreshing and sunny alternative. Buses use the same tickets as the Métro, but a single ticket is only good for two *sections* to reach your destination, which can make bus trips expensive. If you're traveling through three or more sections, you need to punch two tickets.

You can find separate maps for each bus route posted at bus stops, and each map has a blue-and-red bar running along the bottom. You can also find maps and information online at www.ratp.fr. The stops that appear directly above the blue section of this bar are within that stop's two-section limit. For stops appearing above the red section(s) of the bar, you need to use two tickets. When the number of a bus route is written in black on a white circle, it means that the bus stops there daily; when it's written in white on a black circle, it means the bus doesn't stop there on Sundays or holidays.

By taxi

Because cabs in Paris are scarce, picking up one at a stand may be easier than hailing one in the street. Be careful to check the meter when you board to be sure you're not also paying the previous passenger's fare, and if your taxi lacks a meter, make sure to settle the cost of the trip before setting out. Calling a cab to pick you up is more expensive because the meter starts running when the cab receives the call, but if you need to do it, call **Alpha Taxis** (☎ **01-53-60-63-50**).

The initial fare for up to three passengers is 2.20€ ($3.50) and, between 10 a.m. and 5 p.m., rises 0.86€ ($1.40) for each kilometer. Between 5 p.m. and 10 a.m., the standing charge remains the same, but the per-kilometer charge rises to 1.12€ ($1.80). An additional fee of 1€ ($1.60) is imposed for luggage weighing more than 5kg (11 lbs.) or for an extra bag. A fourth passenger incurs a 2.85€ ($4.55) charge.

By foot

Paris is a wonderful city for walking. Tourist attractions are spread throughout the city, but many areas — along the Seine, in the cemeteries, across the Pont Neuf — make for lovely strolls. Don't expect to take the Métro to the Eiffel Tower and then duck back underground quickly; you'll want to savor the scene.

On Sundays and public holidays, many Paris streets are closed to traffic and open to pedestrians. The *Paris Respire* initiative includes the Seine expressway on the Left Bank, between the Eiffel Tower and the Musée d'Orsay; the expressway on the Right Bank, between Place de la Concorde and Pont Charles de Gaulle; and the streets just south of Jardin de Luxembourg. Also included are two areas beyond Paris's ring road: the Boie de Boulogne and Boie de Vincennes. These areas are terrific venues for running, inline skating, or just ambling.

Staying in Paris

Paris has more than 2,200 hotels — chains, deluxe palace-like accommodations, hotels that cater to business travelers, budget hotels, and mom-and-pop establishments — so you're sure to find a bed. The general assumption, still holding true (but tenuously) these days, is that the Right Bank has more upscale hotels, while the bohemian Left Bank boasts more inexpensive options. On your first visit, you may want to stay pretty close to the center of town, but don't fret if the only room

Accommodations, Dining, and Attractions in Paris

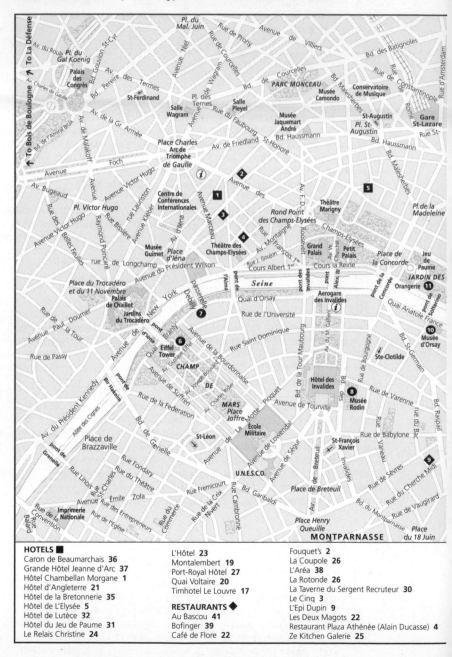

HOTELS ■
Caron de Beaumarchais **36**
Grande Hôtel Jeanne d'Arc **37**
Hôtel Chambellan Morgane **1**
Hôtel d'Angleterre **21**
Hôtel de la Bretonnerie **35**
Hôtel de L'Elysée **5**
Hôtel de Lutèce **32**
Hôtel du Jeu de Paume **31**
Le Relais Christine **24**

L'Hôtel **23**
Montalembert **19**
Port-Royal Hôtel **27**
Quai Voltaire **20**
Timhotel Le Louvre **17**

RESTAURANTS ◆
Au Bascou **41**
Bofinger **39**
Café de Flore **22**

Fouquet's **2**
La Coupole **26**
L'Aréa **38**
La Rotonde **26**
La Taverne du Sergent Recruteur **30**
Le Cinq **3**
L'Epi Dupin **9**
Les Deux Magots **22**
Restaurant Plaza Athénée (Alain Ducasse) **4**
Ze Kitchen Galerie **25**

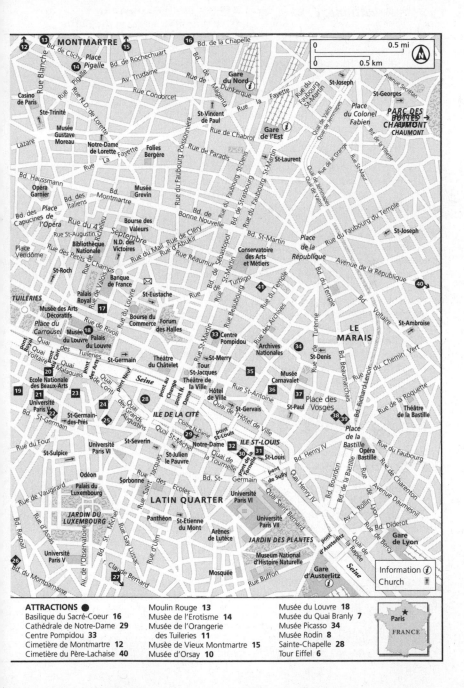

0 0.5 mi
0 0.5 km

MONTMARTRE
Place Pigalle
Bd. de Clichy
Bd. de Rochechuart
Bd. de la Chapelle
Rue Blanche
Rue Pigalle
Av. Trudaine
Rue de
Magenta
Gare du Nord
Dunkerque
St-Joseph
Avenue Secretan
St-Georges
Casino de Paris
Rue N.D. de Lorette
Rue Condorcet
Rue la Fayette
Place du Colonel Fabien
PARC DES BUTTES CHAUMONT
CHAUMONT
Ste-Trinité
St-Vincent de Paul
Rue du Faubourg St-Martin
Quai de Valmy
Musée Gustave Moreau
Notre-Dame de Lorette
Rue La Fayette
Folies Bergère
Rue de Chabrol
Gare de l'Est
St-Laurent
Quai de Jemmapes
Quai de Valmy
Lazare
Rue de Paradis
Rue du Faubourg St-Denis
Rue du Faubourg St-Martin
Rue de la Grange
Rue St-Maur
Bd. de la Villette
Bd. Haussmann
Opéra Garnier
Bd. des Italiens
Bd. Montmartre
Musée Grevin
Bd. de Bonne Nouvelle
Bd. de Strasbourg
Bd. St-Martin
Rue du Faubourg du Temple
St-Joseph
Place Vendôme
Bd. des Capucines
Place de l'Opéra
Rue du 4 Septembre
Rue Richelieu
Bourse des Valeurs
N.D. des Victoires
Rue du Mail
Rue de Cléry
Rue d'Abukir
Rue Réaumur
Bd. de Sebastopol
Rue St-Martin
Conservatoire des Arts et Métiers
Place de la République
Avenue de la République
Rue St-Augustin
Bibliothèque Nationale
Rue des Petits Champs
Place Vendôme
St-Roch
Banque de France
Palais Royal
Rue de Valois
Rue du Louvre
St-Eustache
Rue de Turbigo
Rue Beaubourg
Rue du Temple
Bd. du Temple
Bd. Voltaire
TUILERIES
Musée des Arts Décoratifs
Place du Carrousel
Musée du Louvre
Palais du Louvre
Rue de Rivoli
Bourse du Commerce
Forum des Halles
Centre Pompidou
Archives Nationales
St-Denis
Bd. de Turenne
LE MARAIS
St-Ambroise
Quai du Louvre
St-Germain
Théâtre du Châtelet
St-Merry
Tour St-Jacques
Musée Carnavalet
Bd. Beaumarchais
Bd. Richard-Lenoir
Rue du Chemin Vert
Rue de la Roquette
Théâtre de la Bastille
Quai Voltaire
Quai Malaquais
Pont des Arts
Pont Neuf
Seine
Pont au Change
Pont N. Dame
Théâtre de la Ville
Hôtel de Ville
Rue St-Antoine
St-Paul
Place des Vosges
Ecole Nationale des Beaux-Arts
Université Paris V
Rue St-Germain
St-Germain-des-Prés
Quai des Grands Augustins
ILE DE LA CITÉ
Quai de l'Hôtel de Ville
St-Gervais
Place de la Bastille
Opéra Bastille
Rue du Faubourg
Rue de Charenton
Avenue Daumesnil
Rue du Four
St-Sulpice
Université Paris VI
St-Severin
Quai St-Michel
Cloître N.Dame
Notre-Dame
ILE ST-LOUIS
St-Louis
Bd. Henry IV
Bd. Bourdon
Bd. de la Bastille
Odéon
Sorbonne
St-Julien le Pauvre
Quai de la Tournelle
Quai de Béthune
Pont de Sully
Quai Henry IV
Rue de Lyon
Bd. Diderot
Palais du Luxembourg
Rue des Ecoles
Bd. St-Germain
Université Paris VI
Quai Saint Bernard
Gare de Lyon
JARDIN DU LUXEMBOURG
LATIN QUARTER
Panthéon
St-Etienne du Mont
Arènes de Lutèce
Université Paris VII
JARDIN DES PLANTES
Pont d'Austerlitz
Gare de Bercy
Université Paris V
Mosquée
Museum National d'Histoire Naturelle
Rue Buffon
Gare d'Austerlitz
Seine
Bd. du Montparnasse
r. Claude Bernard

Information (i)
Church

ATTRACTIONS ●

Basilique du Sacré-Coeur **16**	Moulin Rouge **13**	Musée du Louvre **18**
Cathédrale de Notre-Dame **29**	Musée de l'Erotisme **14**	Musée du Quai Branly **7**
Centre Pompidou **33**	Musée de l'Orangerie	Musée Picasso **34**
Cimetière de Montmartre **12**	des Tuileries **11**	Musée Rodin **8**
Cimetière du Père-Lachaise **40**	Musée de Vieux Montmartre **15**	Sainte-Chapelle **28**
	Musée d'Orsay **10**	Tour Eiffel **6**

you can find is out in *les boondocks*. Getting to the **Louvre** by Métro from the 16e only takes a few minutes longer than it does from the **Latin Quarter.** Besides, most repeat visitors find themselves drawn away from the tourist center in favor of a more authentic Parisian neighborhood. For a price, you can find that authenticity as close by as the **Marais** or **St-Germain-des-Prés.**

In addition to the November-to-February low season, July and August are also slow in Paris, and you can bargain for good rates. Multiple trade fairs during May, June, September, and October tend to book up the city's four-star and luxury hotels.

The tourist offices (see "Finding information after you arrive," earlier in this chapter) will book a room for you, and they also broker last-minute rooms that upper-class hotels have a hard time moving, so you may luck into a deep discount on a posh pad.

Paris offers additional options for lodging — renting an apartment, for example. Nothing beats living in Paris as a Parisian. In your own **apartment,** you can cook with fresh produce from the local markets, taste fine wines that would be too expensive in a restaurant, and entertain new friends. Although the daily rate can be higher than a budget hotel, the room will be larger, you can save money on meals, and in the end, you may end up paying the same rate you would for room and board at a hotel — or less. Companies offering attractive apartments at reasonable prices are **Apartment Living in Paris** (www.apartment-living.com), which is run by French real estate brokers, and **Lodgis.com** (www.lodgis.com). **Paris Vacation Rentals** (www.rentals-paris.com) is an agency that deals in short-term rentals of upscale apartments at very good prices.

Paris's top hotels

Grande Hôtel Jeanne d'Arc
$ The Marais (4e)

Located right in the heart of the charming Marais district off the pretty Place Ste-Catherine, this hotel is often booked up to two months ahead of time by regulars. Rooms are small to decent-sized with large windows, card-key access, and large bathrooms, but storage space is a bit cramped. Other room features include direct-dial telephones, cable TV, and bedside tables. Some rooms don't have a view, so if this is important to you, make sure to request a view when you reserve. The hotel can be a little noisy, but you're near the Musée Picasso, place des Vosges, and the Bastille; the fabulous Au Bistro de la Place is just one of the charming restaurants in the square next door.

See map p. 228. 3 rue de Jarente (between rue de Sévigné and rue de Turenne, off rue St-Antoine). ☎ *01-48-87-62-11. Fax: 01-48-87-37-31. Métro: St-Paul, Bastille. Rack rates: 78€–116€ ($125–$186) double. Breakfast 6€ ($9.60). MC, V.*

Hôtel d'Angleterre
$$$ St-Germain-des-Prés (6e)

The high-beamed ceilings of this 18th-century Breton-style inn offer a slice of U.S. history: When this was the British Embassy in 1783, the papers recognizing American independence were prepared here. Some rooms have exposed stone walls and four-poster canopy beds, and all boast period furnishings, carved-wood closet doors, and silk wall hangings. The "apartments," with two bedrooms, are ideal for families. The homey common lounge has a piano, and in summer you can breakfast in a small lush courtyard. Check the Web site for specials.

See map p. 228. 44 rue Jacob (off rue Bonaparte). ☎ *01-42-60-34-72. Fax: 01-42-60-16-93.* www.hotel-dangleterre.com. *Métro: St-Germain-des-Prés. Rack rates: 200€–320€ ($320–$512) double. Rates include in-room breakfast. AE, DC, MC, V.*

Hôtel de la Bretonnerie
$$ The Marais (4e)

This cozy hotel in the heart of the Marais boasts classic French style in each of its rooms with unique décor, from Empire divans or Louis XIII chairs to Napoleon III tables. The nicest are the *chambres de charme,* some with canopy beds, some country-style with heavy beams and floral-print walls. *Classique* rooms are smaller but still have nice touches, such as the occasional four-poster bed. The snug duplexes are defined by beamed ceilings and huge curtained windows. The vaulted stone breakfast room with a pastel fresco adds a nice touch.

See map p. 228. 22 rue St-Croix-de-la-Bretonnerie (between rue des Archives and rue Vieille-du-Temple). ☎ *01-48-87-77-63. Fax: 01-42-77-26-78.* www.hotel bretonnerie.com. *Métro: Hôtel de Ville. Rack rates: 160€–185€ ($256–$296) double. Breakfast 9.50€ ($15). MC, V.*

Hôtel de L'Elysée
$$$ Champs-Elysées (8e)

Wallpaper of stamped 18th-century etchings, built-in closets, half-headboards, stuccoed ceilings, and a cozy sitting room with a fireplace just off the lobby give this hotel close to the Champs-Elysées a homey feel. The wonderful but small mansard suite no. 60 features wood beams overhead and skylights set into the low, sloping ceilings, which provide peek-a-boo vistas of Parisian rooftops and a perfectly framed view of the Eiffel Tower. All fifth- and sixth-floor rooms enjoy at least rooftop views, the former from small balconies. *Note:* You must climb an additional 15 steps to the top-floor rooms after the elevator lets you off — a consideration for those with a lot of luggage.

See map p. 228. 12 rue des Saussaies. ☎ *01-42-65-29-25. Fax: 01-42-65-64-28.* www.france-hotel-guide.com/h75008efsh.htm. *Métro: Champs-Elysées-Clemenceau or Miromesnil. Rack rates: 150€–275€ ($240–$440) double. Breakfast 12€ ($19). AE, DC, MC, V.*

Hôtel de Lutèce
$$$ Ile St-Louis (4e)

The Lutèce is located on a street lined with restaurants and shops, just a five-minute stroll from Notre-Dame, and occupies a converted 17th-century house accented with rustic details such as wood-beam ceilings and terra-cotta floors. It has comfy rooms that are large for such a central (and chic) location, even if a few bathtubs could use curtains (many Europeans would scoff at such a luxury). **Des Deux-Iles** (☎ 01-43-26-13-35), a sibling hotel, is a few doors down at no. 59; between the two of them, there's a pretty good chance you can get a room.

See map p. 228. 65 rue St-Louis-en-l'Ile (on the main drag of the island). ☎ 01-43-26-23-52. Fax: 01-43-29-60-25. www.paris-hotel-lutece.com. *Métro: Pont-Marie. Rack rates: 189€ ($302) double. Breakfast 11€ ($18). AE, V.*

Hôtel du Jeu de Paume
$$$$ Ile St-Louis (4e)

This is one of Paris's more unusual hotels, an impressive, airy, three-story, ancient wood skeleton inside a former *jeu de paume* (a precursor to tennis) court. Scoop, a friendly Golden Retriever welcomes you to an interior that seamlessly weaves modern and ancient, incorporating public lounges, indoor and outdoor breakfast terraces, and a glass elevator. Most accommodations are on the snug to medium size, but the simplicity of the stylishly modern décor under hewn beams keeps rooms from feeling cramped. The three standard duplexes with spiral stairs are roomier, but if you're staying five days or longer and want true bliss, check into one of the hotel's two apartments. The three-bedroom apartment is a duplex, with two bedrooms and a living room below and a bedroom above, two bathrooms, and a private terrace overlooking the small stone garden rimmed with flowers, where guests — it can accommodate five people — can breakfast in nice weather.

See map p. 228. 54 rue St-Louis-en-L'Ile. ☎ 01-43-26-14-18. Fax: 01-40-46-02-76. www.jeudepaumehotel.com. *Métro: Pont-Marie. Rack rates: 275€–435€ ($440–$696) double; 545€ ($872) 3-person suite; 600€–900€ ($960–$1,440) apartment. Breakfast 18€ ($29). AE, DC, MC, V.*

Le Relais Christine
$$$$$ St-Germain-des-Pres (6e)

Passing through the cobbled courtyard to enter this early 17th-century building, you feel less like you're checking into a hotel and more like a baron or baroness arriving at your own country manor house, with a cordial staff to match. Many of the largish rooms are done in a contemporary relaxed style, with such added touches as antique desks or chairs; the grandest has a Louis XIII décor. Most suites are duplexes, with sitting areas downstairs, marble bathrooms sporting double sinks, and a lofted bedchamber. The basement breakfast room, formerly a kitchen with a massive fireplace for show, is installed under the low rough vaulting of a 13th-century abbey founded by Saint Louis himself. A tranquil garden filled with flowers makes this hotel a true haven from the yuppie bustle in the neighborhood outside.

See map p. 228. 3 rue Christine (off rue Dauphine, between bd. St-Germain and the Pont Neuf). ☎ *01-40-51-60-80. Fax: 01-40-51-60-81.* www.relais-christine.com. *Métro: Odéon or St-Michel. Rack rates: 370€–460€ ($592–$736) double. Breakfast 25€–32€ ($40–$51). AE, DC, MC, V.*

Port-Royal Hôtel

$ **Latin Quarter (5e)**

Although this hotel, owned by the same family since its creation in 1930, is on the far edge of the Latin Quarter, the Métro stop down the block keeps you only minutes from the city's center. Its incredible rates come with surprisingly nice and clean rooms. You have to pay a nominal fee for showers (unless you have a bathroom en suite), but they're modern and don't run out of hot water. In short, it's a decent and completely unshabby hotel at hostel prices.

See map p. 228. 8 bd. Port-Royal (near av. des Gobelins). ☎ *01-43-31-70-06. Fax: 01-43-31-33-67.* www.hotelportroyal.fr. *Métro: Gobelins. Rack rates: 79€–89€ ($126–$142) double with bathroom; 53€ ($85) double without bathroom. Breakfast 5.50€ ($8.80). No credit cards.*

Paris's runner-up accommodations

Caron de Beaumarchais

$$ **The Marais (4e)** Caron de Beaumarchais is a boutique hotel at budget rates, with an antiques-laden salon in place of a reception area and rooms outfitted like those of an 18th-century Marais town house — wood ceilings and a touch of gold around the carved filigree of curving chair backs and mirror frames. Rooms in the front are largest. *See map p. 228. 12 rue Vieille-du-Temple (off rue de Rivoli).* ☎ *01-42-72-34-12.* www.carondebeaumarchais. com.

Hôtel Chambellan Morgane

$$$ **Trocadéro (16e)** This small yet elegant hotel is comfortable and has standard contemporary furniture and trim. Located in a quiet bourgeois neighborhood, its location gives close and easy access to the Arc de Triomphe, the Champs-Elysées, and the Eiffel Tower. *See map p. 228. 6 rue Keppler (in between av. Marceau and av. d'Iéna, south of the Arc de Triomphe).* ☎ *01-47-20-35-72.* www.hotel-paris-morgane.com.

L'Hôtel

$$$$ **St-Germain-des-Prés (6e)** This hotel is no longer the flophouse where Oscar Wilde died in 1900. In fact, in 2007, *Harper's Bazaar* voted it the best urban hotel in the world. It's a funky velvet-and-marble monument, with 20 smallish, carefully decorated rooms and furnishings ranging from Louis XV and Empire styles to Art Nouveau. Customer service can be a bit

frosty. *See map p. 228. 13 rue des Beaux-Arts (between rue Bonaparte and rue de Seine, 1 block from the Quai Malaquais).* ☎ **01-44-41-99-00.** www.l-hotel.com.

Montalembert

$$$$$ St-Germain-des-Prés (7e) Montalembert is one of Paris's top hotels, with a unique meld of contemporary design, Art Deco fashion, and French tradition (and amenities such as in-room VCRs, fax machines, and modem lines). Deluxe bedrooms are Louis-Phillipe style, with heavily lacquered chestnut and gold Art Deco furnishings; junior suites are located on upper floors and offer superb views of Paris, some of them from beneath mansard roofs. Check the Web site for "long-stay" specials for three or more nights. *See map p. 228. 3 rue de Montalembert (off rue de Bac, behind the church of St Thomas d'Aquin).* ☎ **01-45-49-68-68.** www.montalembert.com.

Quai Voltaire

$$ St-Germain-des-Prés (7e) The Quai Voltaire has clean and simple midsize rooms. The dreamy Parisian view that overlooks the Seine to the Louvre across the way comes with a price: traffic noise from the *quai* that even the double-glazed windows don't quite drown out. *See map p. 228. 19 quai Voltaire.* ☎ **01-42-61-50-91.** www.quaivoltaire.fr.

Timhotel Le Louvre

$$ Louvre (1er) Two blocks from the Louvre, this was once a writers' and artists' crash pad, but has been relentlessly renovated into cookie-cutter blandness by a chain selling itself to the business set. Good value, but service can be frosty. *See map p. 228. 4 rue Croix-des-Petits-Champs (off rue St-Honoré, 2 blocks east of the Palais Royal).* ☎ **01-42-60-34-86.** www.timhotel.com.

Dining in Paris

Yes, Paris—and the rest of the country—is a feast. Traditional haute cuisine — a delicate balance of flavors, sauces, and ingredients blended with a studied technique — includes such classics as *blanquette de veau* (veal in an eggy cream sauce), *pot-au-feu* (an excellent stew of fatty beef and vegetables), *coq au vin* (chicken braised in red wine with onions and mushrooms), *bouillabaisse* (seafood soup), and that hearty staple *boeuf bourguignon* (beef stew with red wine).

But when people started thinking healthy a few decades back, buttery, creamy, saucy French cuisine quickly found itself on the outs. So the French invented *nouvelle cuisine,* which gave chefs an excuse to concoct new dishes — still French, mind you, but less fattening because they use fewer heavy creams and less butter and serve smaller portions.

When the nouvelle trend lost steam (in part because of its miniscule portions), people began spinning off more healthful and/or more creative cooking styles. Add to these styles the mix of French regional restaurants and the many ethnic dining rooms, and you'll never want for variety.

A French economic crisis in the 1990s forced many restaurants to lower their prices, and some top chefs found opportunity in the downturn by opening up *baby bistros,* small, relaxed eateries with menus designed by the biggest names in the business and prices up to 75 percent below what you'd pay in these chefs' flagship restaurants. Wildly popular, most baby bistros are still going strong a decade later.

Your waiter or the restaurant's wine steward should be able to pair your meal with an appropriate vintage wine. Or better yet, check out *Wine For Dummies,* 4th Edition, by Ed McCarthy and Mary Ewing-Mulligan (Wiley Publishing, Inc.). Ordering wine by the bottle can jack up the cost of your meal in no time, so be careful. Table wine by the liter carafe or *demi* (half a liter) is always cheaper. The top reds are produced in Bordeaux, Burgundy, Beaujolais, and the Loire and Rhone valleys. Great whites hail from Alsace, the Loire, Burgundy (if you can afford it, Meursault is simply a wonder), and Bordeaux. And don't forget that sparkling white wine from the vineyards east of Paris called Champagne.

Some people may be intimidated by the idea of sitting down to what many consider the most refined food on the planet. Don't sweat it. The only people with a need to impress anyone are the chef and kitchen staff. Have your waiter suggest some dishes, and then just sit back and enjoy the flavors.

If you're looking for a meal in a hurry, try Paris's greatest street food, crepes, sold at sidewalk stands and from store windows. They're best when cooked fresh on the spot for you, but in touristy areas, crepe stands often make up stacks in advance and merely reheat them on the griddle when you approach.

You can visit a supermarket or gourmet store for your picnic supplies, but shopping at the little local food stores and street markets is more fun. Pick up a baguette at the *boulangerie* (bakery), cured meats and the like at a *charcuterie,* and other groceries at an *épicerie.* Top it all off with some fruit, pastries from a *pâtisserie,* a bottle of wine, and you're set.

Au Bascou
$$ Le Marais (3e)   BASQUE

In a simple and softly lit rustic interior, some of the best Basque dishes in Paris can be found here. (The Basque region is the corner of southwestern France, resting along the Spanish border, and is known for its distinct dialect and the excellent culinary skills of its citizens.) Consider starting with a *pipérade basquaise* (a light terrine of eggs, tomatoes, and spices) before moving on to roast wild duck or rabbit in a red-wine sauce. A bottle of Irouléguy, a smooth red Basque wine, makes a nice accompaniment to meals. The service, though friendly, at times can leave a lot to be desired. You may want to save this place for a night when you don't want to linger over dinner.

See map p. 228. 38 rue Réaumur (between rue du Temple and rue de Turbigo). ☎ *01-42-72-69-25. Reservations recommended. Métro: Arts et Métiers. Main courses: 18€ ($29). AE, MC, V. Open: Mon–Fri noon to 2 p.m. and 8–10:30 p.m.*

Bofinger
$ Bastille (4e) ALSATIAN

Parisians like to joke that the clientele at this famous restaurant near the Bastille is made up of tourists and elderly locals. But Bofinger, which first opened in 1864, continues to pack them in, with waiters in long white aprons delivering hearty cuisine, much of it based on the Franco-Germanic cooking of the Alsace region — lots of *choucroute* (sauerkraut, usually served with sausages or other cuts of pork). The downstairs dining room is ornately decorated with Art Nouveau flourishes and a glass-domed ceiling. Upstairs is cozier with wood paneling. It's owned by the Flo brasserie chain, which means that you'll see similar menus in the chain's other restaurants, which include Julien and Brasserie Flo. Service can be whirlwind. Brasseries are good for off-hours dining, tending to stay open until 1 a.m.

See map p. 228. 5–7 rue de la Bastille (just off place de la Bastille). ☎ *01-42-72-87-82. www.bofingerparis.com. Reservations recommended. Métro: Bastille. Fixed-price menus: Lunch Mon–Fri 24€ ($38); dinner daily and lunch Sat–Sun 32€ ($51) with half-bottle of wine. AE, DC, MC, V. Open: Mon–Fri noon to 3 p.m. and 6:30 p.m.– 1 a.m.; Sat–Sun noon to 1 a.m.*

L'Aréa
$$ Marais/Bastille (4e) MIDDLE EASTERN/BRAZILIAN

Trendy artist types, musicians, and locals have been packing the house for Brazilian–Middle Eastern food at this inexpensive happening joint near place Bastille since the early 1990s. Owner Edward Chuaka was born in Brazil to Lebanese parents, and his menu not only shows it but attracts a big crowd of regulars. Choose from starters such as *Filezinho à Carioca* (ground beef marinated in red wine) or a *Mezzé* plate of hummus, tabbouleh, and other assorted Lebanese salads; and from main courses such as *Moqueca de Peixe* (filet of dorado served in a sauce of coconut milk, tomato, peppers, and palm over rice) and *Grillades Libanaises* (skewers of Lebanese sausage, beef, lamb, and chicken served with tabbouleh and potatoes). Go early to get a seat; the place gets full later in the evening, with people waiting at the bar and spilling into the quiet rue des Tournelles.

See map p. 228. 10 rue des Tournelles. ☎ *01-42-72-96-50. Métro: Bastille. Main courses: 13€–19€ ($21–$30); fixed-price lunch menu 15€ ($24); fixed-price dinner menu 28€ ($45). AE, MC, V. Open: Tues–Fri noon to 3 p.m.; Sat 4 p.m.–2 a.m.; Sun noon to 4 p.m. and 6 p.m. to midnight.*

La Taverne du Sergent Recruteur
$$ Ile St-Louis (4e) FRENCH

Supposedly, unscrupulous army sergeants would get potential young recruits drunk in this 17th-century eatery, and the saps would wake up in the barracks the next day as conscripts. These days the only danger is overeating, because the fixed-price menu is a great value. Appetizers include unlimited baskets of crudités (vegetables) or sausages, and wine glasses are bottomless. The menu includes a selection of basic main dishes, such as duck confit and leg of lamb, and a choice of cheeses and dessert after the meal. Kids tend to like the simple fare.

See map p. 228. 41 rue St-Louis-en-l'Isle (on the main drag of the Ile St-Louis, just off rue des Deux Ponts). ☎ *01-43-54-75-42.* www.lesergentrecruteur.com. *Reservations recommended. Métro: Pont-Marie. Fixed-price menu: 41€ ($66) with wine. AE, MC, V. Open: Mon–Sat 7 p.m.–2 a.m.; Sun noon to 2 a.m.*

Le Cinq
$$$$ Champs-Elysées (8e)   HAUTE CUISINE

Chef Phillippe Legendre has earned two Michelin stars for this restaurant in the Four Seasons Georges V, where every element is in place, from the gray-and-gold dining room with its high ceilings and overstuffed chairs to the Limoges porcelain and Riedel stemware created for the restaurant. The sumptuous and inventive cuisine is served by the perfect wait staff. Diners may start with an eggplant risotto, with a carpaccio of *cèpes* (mushrooms) from Sologne, served with black truffles, and then continue with milk-fed Pyrenées lamb roasted in sesame and mint cream. For dessert, a Manjari chocolate soufflé flavored with orange or the chef's choice of assorted chocolate desserts may be on the menu. The wine list here is magnificent; if he has time, chief sommelier Thierry Hamon may even give you a tour of the cellar.

See map p. 228. 31 av. George V (in the Four Seasons George V Hotel). ☎ *01-49-52-71-54. Métro: George V. Reservations required. Main courses: 80€–260€ ($128–$416); light tasting menu 135€ ($216); gourmet tasting menu (without beverage) 210€ ($336). AE, MC, V. Open: Daily noon to 2:30 p.m. and 6:30–11 p.m.*

L'Epi Dupin
$ St-Germain-des-Prés (7e)   FRENCH

L'Epi Dupin is still perhaps the best of the baby bistros (see the introduction to this section) and a good value as well. Chef François Pasteau pairs fine modern bistro cuisine with an antique French setting of hewn beams and stone walls (though tables are quite close together). The food, which Pasteau buys fresh daily at the Rungis green market, runs to traditional rural French, with lighter, modern alternatives such as salmon carpaccio or endive tatin with goat cheese. Service, though friendly, can be seriously rushed as staff scramble to accommodate three seatings a night.

See map p. 228. 11 rue de Dupin (between rue de Sèvres and rue du Cherche Midi). ☎ *01-42-22-64-56. Reservations strongly recommended. Métro: Sèvres Babylone. Fixed-price menus: 25€ ($40) lunch, 35€ ($56) dinner. AE, MC, V. Open: Mon 7:30–10:30 p.m.; Tues–Fri noon to 2:30 p.m. and 7:30–10:30 p.m. Closed 3 weeks in Aug.*

Restaurant Plaza Athénée (Alain Ducasse)

$$$$$ Champs-Elysées (8e)   FRENCH (MODERN/TRADITIONAL)

This multistarred Michelin chef divides his time between his restaurants in Paris, New York, and Monaco. His "modern and authentic" dishes reflect the room created by celebrated designer Patrick Jouin (the chandeliers have 10,000 crystal pendants) and contain produce from every corner of France — rare local vegetables, fish from the coasts, and dishes incorporating turnips, celery, turbot, cuttlefish, and Bresse fowl. Specialties may include duck foie gras from the Landes region served with frozen black tea, or thick, oozing slabs of pork grilled to a crisp.

See map p. 228. In the Hotel Plaza Athénée, 25 av. Montaigne. ☎ *01-53-67-65-00.* www.alain-ducasse.com. *Métro: FDR or Alma-Marceau. Reservations required. Main courses: 85€–175€ ($136–$280); fixed-price menus 240€–360€ ($384–$576). AE, DC, MC, V. Open: Mon–Wed 7:45–10:15 p.m.; Thurs–Fri 12:45–2:15 p.m. and 7:45–10:15 p.m. Closed mid-July to mid-Aug.*

Ze Kitchen Galerie

$$ St-Germain-des-Prés (6e)   MODERN BISTRO

William Ledeuil opened this hip and sophisticated place in 2002 near the trendy Les Bookinistes, where he previously worked as chef. It is indeed an art gallery and kitchen: the walls of the spacious and spare dining room feature as their only decoration artwork that changes every three months. The innovative, Asian-inspired menu, created from a tiny windowed kitchen at the far side of the room, changes every five weeks. The menu is broken down into categories of soups, pastas, and grilled (*à la plancha*) items. Starters may include a soup of snail and *conchiglie* pasta, flavored with a horseradish-parsley emulsion, or duck ravioli with Thai herbs. Mains may be grilled milk-fed lamb served with a spicy teriyaki and orange condiment, or grilled sea scallops with lemongrass and kumquat confit and a coriander-flavored potato croquette. Because portions are small, you'll more than likely have room for dessert, which may include tasty ginger-orange cake served with a blood-orange sorbet.

See map p. 228. 4 rue des Grands Augustins. ☎ *01-44-32-00-32.* www.zekitchen galerie.fr. *Métro: St-Michel. Reservations recommended. Main courses: 22€–30€ ($35–$51). AE, DC, MC, V. Open: Mon–Fri noon to 2:30 p.m. and 7–11 p.m.; Sat 7–11 p.m.*

Exploring Paris

By far Paris's best buy is the **Paris Museum Pass,** formerly known as the Carte Musées et Monuments (www.parismuseumpass.fr). This card lets you into most Parisian sights free (the only notable exceptions are the **Eiffel and Montparnasse towers** and the **Marmottan** museum). It's offered in three versions: a two-consecutive-day pass (30€/$48), a four-consecutive-day pass (45€/$72), and a six-consecutive-day pass (60€/$96). The biggest benefit is that you don't have to wait in line at most museums and monuments! You just saunter up to a separate window, and they wave you through. You can buy the pass at any branch of the tourist office, at most museums and monuments, and at any Fnac store (a French chain store selling electronics and music), one of which is conveniently located at 74 Champs-Elysées.

Paris's top sights

Cathédrale de Notre-Dame (Notre-Dame Cathedral)
Ile de la Cité (4e)

"Our Lady of Paris" is the heart and soul of the city. The Gothic church constructed between the 12th and 14th centuries dominates the Seine and the Ile de la Cité, as well as the history of Paris. Notre-Dame is a study in Gothic beauty and gargoyles, at once solid, with squat, square facade towers, and graceful, with flying buttresses around the sides. It's been remodeled, embellished, ransacked, and restored so often that it's a wonder it still has any architectural integrity at all (during the Revolution, it was even stripped of its religion and rechristened the Temple of Reason).

A circular bronze plaque in the cathedral marks Kilomètre Zéro, from which all distances in France have been measured since 1768. And in many ways, Notre-Dame is the center of France. Crusaders prayed here before leaving for the holy wars. Napoleon crowned himself emperor here, and then crowned his wife Josephine empress. When Paris was liberated during World War II, General de Gaulle rushed to this cathedral to give thanks.

Visiting Notre-Dame takes a good hour to 90 minutes out of your day. The highlight for kids will undoubtedly be climbing the 387 narrow and winding steps to the top of one of the towers for a fabulously Quasimodo view of the gargoyles and of Paris (set aside at least 45 minutes for this, more during high tourist season — and note that the entrance to the towers is outside the cathedral on the left side of the facade on rue du Cloître-Notre Dame). However, if you plan to visit the tower, go early in the morning. Lines stretch down the square in front of the cathedral during the summer. If you do find yourself caught in a line, you have a chance to admire the Bible stories played out in intricate stone relief around the three great portals on the facade. Much of the facade was (poorly) restored once in the 18th century and then again (as well as could be done) in the 19th. If you're keen to see some medieval originals, the upper tier of the central portal is ancient, and much of the sculpture on the right-hand portal has also survived from 1165 to 1175.

The main draw, however, is the three enormous rose windows, especially the 69-foot diameter north window (left transept), which has retained almost all its original 13th-century stained glass. Save Notre-Dame for a sunny day to see the best light effects.

One last thing you shouldn't forget to do is to walk around the building. Those famous flying buttresses at the very back, holding up the apse with 50-foot spans of stone strength, are particularly impressive. Around the south side and the back are gardens in which to rest and enjoy the structure, as well as a small playground. Cross the Seine to admire the entire effect from the quay on the Left Bank. Free guided tours in English are on offer Wednesday, Thursday, and Saturday (donations are appreciated).

At the opposite end of the square (about 60m/200 ft.) from the cathedral's front door, a flight of steps leads down to the **Archaeological Crypt** (☎ 01-55-42-50-10), a 260-foot gallery extending under Notre-Dame's square. This excavation includes the jumbled foundations, streets, and walls of a series of Parises, including the medieval and Roman cities. You can even see a house from Lutèce — the town built by the Celtic Parisii tribe that flourished on the Ile de la Cité over 2,000 years ago. The crypt is open Tuesday through Sunday from 10 a.m. to 6 p.m.; admission is 3.30€ ($5.30) adults, 1.60€ ($2.55) students 14 to 26, free for children 13 and under.

See map p. 228. 6 place du Parvis de Notre-Dame, on Ile de la Cité. ☎ 01-42-34-56-10. www.notredamedeparis.fr. *Métro: Cité. Admission: Cathedral free; towers 7.50€ ($12) adults, 4.80€ ($7.70) students 18–25, free for children 17 and under. Exact change required for admission to towers. Open: Cathedral daily 8 a.m.–6:45 p.m. (until 7:15 p.m. Sat–Sun); treasury Mon–Fri 9:30 a.m.–6 p.m., Sat 9:30 a.m.–6:30 p.m., Sun 1:30–6:30 p.m.; towers Jan–Mar and Oct–Dec daily 10 a.m.–5:30 p.m., Apr–Sept daily 10 a.m.–6:30 p.m., and June–Aug daily 10 a.m.–6:30 p.m. (until 11 p.m. Sat–Sun); crypt daily 10 a.m.–6 p.m. Free museum tours in English Wed, Thurs, and Sat 2:30 p.m.; visits start inside at the great organ.*

Centre Pompidou
The Marais (4e)

Brightly colored escalators, elevators, air-conditioning, and tubular passages resembling a giant gerbil habitat run along this building's facade, but the inside is a wonderfully spacious haven in which to view, touch, or listen to modern art and artists. The Pompidou is Paris's homage to 20th-century creativity. Aside from the gallery of modern art, see exhibits on industrial design, music research, photography, and the history of film. Even if you don't want to spend an hour or two with the exhibits inside, come by to shake your head at the wildly colorful and controversial transparent inside-out architecture — which was outrageously avant-garde in the 1970s, but by 1998 had deteriorated so badly they had to shut it down for 18 months of repairs — and to watch the street performers on the sloping square out front.

See map p. 228. Place Georges Pompidou. ☎ 01-44-78-12-33. www.centre pompidou.fr. *Métro: Rambuteau. Admission: 10€ ($16) adults (12€/$19 early May to mid-Aug), 8€ ($13) students 18–25 (9€/$14 early May to mid-Aug), free for children 17 and under. Open: Wed–Mon 11 a.m.–9 p.m. Last admission 8 p.m.*

Musée de l'Orangerie des Tuileries
Jardin des Tuileries (1er)

Since spring 2006, visitors have been delighting in the newly renovated Musée de l'Orangerie, which underwent repairs for close to a decade. The highlight of the Orangerie is its two oval rooms wrapped nearly 360 degrees with Monet's *Nymphéas,* the waterlily series he painted especially for the Orangerie, and these rooms were the primary focus of the renovations. The immense and awe-inspiring murals simply pop from their spotless cream-white walls, lit brightly enough to accentuate all the beautifully emotional colors. But don't make the waterlily paintings your sole reason to visit. Since 1984, the museum has also housed the remarkable John Walter and Paul Guillaume art collection, comprising works by Cézanne, Renoir, Rousseau, Matisse, Modigliani, Dérain, Picasso, and Soutine, among other artists.

See map p. 228. Jardin des Tuileries, 1er. ☎ *01-44-77-80-07. Métro: Concorde. Admission: 7.50€ ($12) adults, 5.50€ ($8.80) students 25 and under; free for all first Sun of month. Open: Wed–Mon 12:30–7 p.m. (until 9 p.m. Fri). Closed May 1 and Dec 25.*

Musée d'Orsay
St-Germain-des-Prés (7e)

In 1986, this brilliantly renovated train station opened to the public, giving the world one of its greatest museums of 19th-century art with an unsurpassed collection of Impressionist masterpieces. Many of the works are so widely reproduced that you may wander through with an eerie feeling of déjà vu. Degas's ballet dancers and *l'Absinthe;* Monet's women in a poppy field, his *Rouen Cathedral* painted under five different lighting conditions, and his giant *Blue Waterlilies;* van Gogh's *Restaurant de la Siréne,* self-portraits, peasants napping against a haystack, and *Bedroom at Arles; Whistler's Mother;* and Manet's groundbreaking *Picnic on the Grass* and *Olympia,* which together helped throw off the shackles of artistic conservatism and gave Impressionism room to take root.

Give yourself three hours, including a lunch break in the museum's gorgeous, turn-of-the-20th-century Musée d'Orsay restaurant on the middle level, or the Café des Hauteurs with a great view of the Seine through the enormous clock window. Check the Web site for combined admission with the Musée Rodin.

See map p. 228. 1 rue Bellechasse or 62 rue de Lille. ☎ *01-40-49-48-14.* www.musee orsay.fr. *Métro: Solférino. RER: Musée-d'Orsay. Admission: 8€ ($13) adults 26 and over, 5.50€ ($8.80) adults 18–25 and for everyone after 4:15 p.m. (except Thurs); free for children 17 and under and for everyone first Sun of month. Open: Tues–Wed and Fri–Sun 9:30 a.m.–6 p.m.; Thurs 9:30 a.m.–9:45 p.m. Last admission 30 minutes before close.*

Musée du Louvre (Louvre Museum)
Louvre (1er)

The magnificent Louvre palace evolved during several centuries, first opening as a museum in 1793, and it would take you a month of visits to see the more than 35,000 treasures it houses. But a visit to the Louvre doesn't have to be overwhelming. The museum is organized in three wings — Sully, Denon, and Richelieu — over four floors, exhibiting art and antiquities from

Oriental, Islamic, Egyptian, Greek, Etruscan, Roman, European, and North and South American civilizations, and sculpture, objets d'art, paintings, prints, drawings, and the moats and dungeon of the medieval Louvre fortress.

When you're in a hurry, but you want to do the Louvre on your own, do a quick, "best of the Louvre" tour on either Wednesday or Friday when the museum is open until 9:45 p.m. Start with Leonardo da Vinci's *Mona Lisa* (Denon wing, first floor); on the same floor nearby are two of the Louvre's most famous French paintings, Géricault's *The Raft of Medusa* and Delacroix's *Liberty Guiding the People*. Next, visit the *Winged Victory* and Michelangelo's *Slaves* (both Denon wing, ground floor) before seeing the *Venus de Milo* (Sully wing, ground floor). After that, let your own interests guide you.

You can take three steps that will help your Louvre experience be an enjoy-able one. First, **buy your tickets in advance.** If you're in the United States or Canada, you can purchase tickets online from www.ticketweb.com (don't be put off by the "Paris, CA" location denoted on the Web site; this is the Louvre in Paris, France) and have them delivered to your home before departure. Others can use www.fnac.com or www.ticketnet.com. (All online ticket outlets charge a service fee.) If you happen to be strolling on the Champs-Elysées before you visit the Louvre, you can visit the Fnac location at 74 Champs-Elysées and buy your ticket in person there. Second, **grab a free map of the Louvre** at the information desk under the pyramid, get a free guide, and look for the brochure for visitors in a hurry. The Virgin bookstore in the Carrousel du Louvre sells many comprehensive guides and maps in English, as well as the guidebook, *The Louvre, First Visit.* And third, **take a guided tour.** You can try a 90-minute tour by a museum guide (☎ 01-43-20-53-17) that covers the most popular works and gives you a quick orientation to the museum's layout. Times and prices vary. Ask at the information desk inside the Louvre beneath the pyramid. Also, before you leave for your trip, access the museum's terrific comprehensive Web site, www.louvre.fr. A self-guided tour of the masterpieces of the Louvre is already mapped out for you.

I. M. Pei's glass pyramid is the main entrance to the museum; pregnant women, visitors with children in strollers, and those with disabilities have priority. Avoid this entrance and its long lines by using the **99 rue de Rivoli/Carrousel du Louvre** entrance; take the Métro to the Palais Royal-Musée du Louvre stop, which deposits passengers into the Carrousel; or take the stairs at the **Porte des Lions** near the Arc du Triomphe du Carrousel (the arch resembling a smaller Arc de Triomphe). Those who already have tickets or have the Paris Museum Pass can use the special entrance to the Louvre at the **passage Richelieu,** between rue de Rivoli and the courtyard.

Tickets are valid all day, so you can enter and exit the museum as many times as you prefer. Admission is reduced after 6 p.m. on Monday and Wednesday, and free the first Sunday of each month.

See map p. 228. ☎ 01-40-20-53-17 for the information desk, or 08-92-68-46-94 to order tickets. www.louvre.fr. *Métro: Palais-Royal-Musée du Louvre. Admission: 9€ ($14), 6€ ($9.60) after 6 p.m. Wed and Fri, free for children 17 and under; free for everyone (but crowded) first Sun of month. Open: Wed–Mon 9 a.m.–6 p.m. (until 10 p.m. Wed and Fri). The entrance, or entresol, with its information desks, medieval Louvre exhibit, cafes, post office, and shops, stays open daily until 9:45 p.m.*

Musée du Quai Branly
St-Germain-des-Prés (7e)

This is the newest art museum in Paris, just a block from the Eiffel Tower, opening in June 2006 to much fanfare. Designed by Jean Nouvel, who also designed the Fondation Cartier and the Institut du Monde Arabe, there is plenty of glass to let in light. Housed in four spectacular buildings, with a garden walled off from the quai Branly, the art, sculpture, and cultural materials of a vast range of non-Western civilizations are separated into sections that represent the traditional cultures of Africa, East and Southeast Asia, Oceania, Australia, the Americas, and New Zealand. The pieces come from the now-defunct Musée des Arts Africains et Océaniens, the Louvre, and the Musée de l'Homme. Temporary exhibits are shown in boxes all along the 180m (600-ft.) exhibition hall. Tribal masks of different cultures are among the most impressive. Allow two hours for a full visit; also take a stroll in the carefully manicured garden, or refresh yourself in the small cafeteria across from the main building. There are numerous entrances to the museum grounds from the area near the Eiffel Tower, but the main entrance is on quai Branly.

See map p. 228. 27 or 37 quai Branly and 206 or 218 rue de l'Université, 7e. ☎ 01-56-61-70-00. Métro: Alma-Marceau, cross le pont d'Alma, turn right, and follow along the Seine until you come across a large glass-paneled wall, which among other things, will say MUSÉE DU QUAI BRANLY. *RER: Pont d'Alma. Admission: 13€ ($21) adults, 9.50€ ($15) seniors and students 18–26, free for children 17 and under. Open: Tues–Sun 11 a.m.–7 p.m. (until 9 p.m. Thurs–Fri). Ticket counters close 45 minutes before the museum.*

Musée Picasso (Picasso Museum)
The Marais (3e)

This museum, in a historic *hôtel particulier,* or mansion, in the Marais, was created in 1973 by Picasso's heirs, who donated his personal art collection to the state in lieu of paying $50 million worth of outrageous inheritance taxes. You can pay a visit to the Musée Picasso on each trip to Paris and see something different each time because the works are rotated in this space, which isn't, unfortunately, large enough to house everything. The spectacular collection includes more than 200 paintings, nearly 160 sculptures, 88 ceramics, and more than 3,000 prints and drawings. Every phase of Picasso's prolific 75-year career is represented. A visit here is well worth the trip; make sure to walk around the neighborhood afterward to shop the trendy boutiques and fill up on falafel from one of the numerous stands on and around rue des Rosiers.

See map p. 228. 5 rue de Thorigny (in the Hôtel Salé). ☎ *01-42-71-25-21.* www. musee-picasso.fr. *Métro: Chemin-Vert, St-Paul, or Filles du Calvaire. Admission: 6.50€ ($10) adults 26 and over, 4.50€ ($7.20) ages 18–25, free for children 17 and under. Admission during special exhibitions may be slightly higher. Open: Apr–Sept Wed–Mon 9:30 a.m.–6 p.m.; Oct–Mar Wed–Mon 9:30 a.m.–5:30 p.m.*

Musée Rodin (Rodin Museum)
Les Invalides (7e)

After the critics stopped assailing Rodin's art, they realized that he had been the greatest sculptor since Michelangelo, and the studio where Rodin worked from 1908 until his death in 1917 was opened as a museum to house some of the artist's greatest works. Among the museum's 2,000 rose bushes in its gardens you can see *The Thinker, The Gate of Hell, The Burghers of Calais,* and *Balzac.* Inside are many famed sculptures — *The Kiss, The Three Shades, The Hand of God, Iris* — along with some of Rodin's drawings and works by his friends and contemporaries, such as his lover Camille Claudel. You can view all the works in 45 minutes. Or, if you don't want to go inside, pay the 1€ ($1.60) admission to visit just the gardens. Check the Web site for combined admission with Musée d'Orsay.

See map p. 228. 77 rue de Varenne (in the Hôtel Biron). ☎ *01-44-18-61-10.* www. musee-rodin.fr. *Métro: Varenne or St François Xavier. Admission: 6€ ($9.60) adults 26 and over, 4€ ($6.40) adults 18–25, free for children 17 and under. Open: Apr–Sept Tues–Sun 9:30 a.m.–5:45 p.m., Oct–Mar Tues–Sun 9:30 a.m.–4:45 p.m. Last admission 30 minutes before close.*

Sainte-Chapelle
Ile de la Cité (4e)

Save Sainte-Chapelle for the early afternoon of a sunny day, because the effect of its 15 perfect stained-glass windows soaring 50 feet high to a star-studded vaulted ceiling is purely kaleidoscopic. Each of the 1,134 stained-glass scenes depicts a biblical story. Louis IX had this Gothic chapel, which is actually two chapels, constructed one on top of the other; built between 1246 and 1248, it housed the Crown of Thorns he purchased for an exorbitant sum. Some evenings the upper chapel becomes a venue for classical music concerts, and the effects of the chandelier lights dancing off the windows is magical.

See map p. 228. 4 bd. du Palais (in the Palais de Justice on the Ile de la Cité). ☎ *01-53-40-60-97.* http://sainte-chapelle.monuments-nationaux. fr/en. *Métro: Cité, Châtelet–Les-Halles, or St-Michel. RER: St-Michel. Admission: 7.50€ ($12) adults 26 and over, 4.80€ ($7.70) adults 18–25, free for children 17 and under. Open: Mar–Oct daily 9:30 a.m.–6 p.m.; Nov–Feb daily 9 a.m.–5 p.m.*

Tour Eiffel (Eiffel Tower)
Les Invalides (7e)

Did you know that the Eiffel Tower's usefulness as a transmitter of telegraph — and later, radio and TV — signals saved it from demolition?

Designed as a temporary exhibit for the Paris Exhibition of 1899, Gustave Alexandre Eiffel's tower rises 317m (1,056 ft.) above the banks of the Seine, and Eiffel managed to rivet together all 7,000 tons of it (with 2.5 million rivets) in less than two years.

Critics of the day assailed its aesthetics, but no one could deny the feat of engineering. The tower remained the tallest man-made structure in the world until the Chrysler Building stole the title in 1930, and its engineering advances paved the way for the soaring skyscraper architecture of the 20th century. The restaurants and bars on the first level are pricey but not bad. The view from the second level is an intimate bird's-eye view of Paris; from the fourth level, you can see the entire city spread out below and, on a good day, as far out as 68km (42 miles). Visibility is usually best near sunset; pausing for vistas at all levels takes about 90 minutes.

Some advice: Six million people visit the Eiffel Tower each year. To avoid loonnnggg lines, go early in the morning or in the off-season. If this isn't possible, allow at least three hours for your visit: one hour to line up for tickets and another two just to access the elevators on levels one and two. If you must eat at the tower, food is available at the Altitude 95 restaurant on the first floor, which is simply gorgeous but overpriced for the quality of its meals, and there are a first-floor snack bar and second-floor cafeteria, also not the best of values. The best food at the Eiffel Tower is also its most expensive: The Michelin-starred Jules Verne, one of Paris's most celebrated restaurants, is on the Eiffel Tower's second level.

See map p. 228. Champs-de-Mars. ☎ *01-44-11-23-23.* www.tour-eiffel.fr. *Métro: Trocadéro, Ecole-Militaire, Bir-Hakeim. RER: Champ-de-Mars–Tour Eiffel. Admission: First level by elevator 4.80€ ($7.70) adults, 2.50€ ($4) children 11 and under; second level by elevator 7.80€ ($12) adults, 4.30€ ($6.90) children 11 and under; to second level 4€ ($6.40) adults, 3.10€ ($4.95) children 3–11. Open: Mid-June to early Sept daily 9 a.m.–12:45 a.m., early Sept to mid-June daily 9:30 a.m.–11:45 p.m.*

More cool things to see and do

✓ **Squandering the day away in a cafe:** Many European cultures have a third place, between home and work, where citizens play out their lives. In Paris, it's the cafe, a sort of public extension of the living room; after all, they don't have nearly as much space as North Americans with our vast fruited plains and purple mountain majesties. In the cafe, you can sit all day reading the paper over a single cup of coffee or order a light meal or a glass of regional wine. Ensconce yourself indoors or stand at the bar (this is cheaper!), but most people choose to sit outside — in a glassed-in porch in winter or on the sidewalk in summer — because one of the cafe's biggest attractions is the people-watching — and all without the harsh scent of cigarettes. A law that banned smoking in most public places was passed in February 2007; cafes and restaurants had 11 more months to get with the program. Many cafes now have outside dining year-round (with the help of heat lamps), where diners can comfortably eat and smoke without feeling much cold.

Here are some classic cafes: **Les Deux Magots,** 6 place St-Germain-des-Prés (☎ 01-45-48-55-25; www.lesdeuxmagots.fr), established in 1914, was the haunt of Picasso, Hemingway, and Sartre, who wrote a whole trilogy holed up at a table in its neighboring **Café de Flore,** 172 bd. St-Germain-des-Pres (☎ 01-45-48-55-26; www.cafe-de-flore.com), a Left Bank cafe frequented by Camus and Picasso and featured in Gore Vidal novels. The Champs-Elysées may no longer be Paris's hot spot, but **Fouquet's** at no. 99 (☎ 01-40-69-60-50) is an institution with good past reviews by such legends as Chaplin, Churchill, FDR, and Jacqueline Kennedy Onassis. Henry Miller had his morning porridge at **La Coupole,** 102 bd. du Montparnasse (☎ 01-43-20-14-20), a brasserie that also hosted the likes of Josephine Baker, John Dos Passos, Salvador Dalí, and F. Scott Fitzgerald. Finally, you can make a pilgrimage to the Art Nouveau interiors of **La Rotonde,** 105 bd. du Montparnasse (☎ 01-43-26-48-26), risen like a phoenix from the ashes of its namesake that once stood here. In *The Sun Also Rises,* Hemingway writes of the original, "No matter what cafe in Montparnasse you ask a taxi driver to bring you to . . . they always take you to the Rotonde."

✔ **Paying homage to the cultural giants at Cimetière du Père-Lachaise (Père-Lachaise Cemetery):** Though it's well off the beaten path, visiting this small city of the dearly departed is well worth the trip. Chopin, Gertrude Stein, Delacroix, Proust, Rossini, Oscar Wilde, Georges Bizet, Ingres, Isadora Duncan, Pissaro, Molière, Edith Piaf, Modigliani, and The Doors' Jim Morrison — you couldn't imagine most of these people getting together in life, but they fit well together in death. Pick up the map of the graves and spend a morning under the trees of this vast and romantic cemetery of rolling hills and historic tombs. To get there, take the Métro to Père-Lachaise.

✔ **Strolling through Montmartre, the original bohemian 'hood:** Although inundated by tourists these days, Montmartre, an old artists' neighborhood crowning a hill at Paris's northern edge (the 18e), still has an intriguing village flavor. The Abbesses Métro stop is in Montmartre itself, but get off one stop early at Pigalle.

Here you're on the northwest edge of Paris's red-light district, centered on the sex shop–lined boulevard de Clichy, which features such hangers-on as the **Moulin Rouge** at no. 87 (☎ 01-53-09-82-82; www.moulinrouge.com), which has been packing in audiences since 1889 with its bare-breasted can-can, and the surprisingly quasi-tasteful **Musèe de l'Erotisme** (Museum of the Erotic) at no. 72 (☎ 01-42-58-28-73), which is open from 10 a.m. to 2 a.m.; admission is 8€ ($13).

Work your way uphill to the **Basilique du Sacré-Coeur** (☎ 01-53-41-89-00; www.sacre-coeur-montmartre.com), the domed white neo-Byzantine basilica built from 1876 to 1919 that towers over the city. Climb the dome for a vista that, on clear days, extends 56km (35 miles).

Some of Montmartre's quirkiest sights include a pair of windmills, visible from rue Lepic and rue Girardon, and Paris's only vineyard, on rue des Saules. Next-door to the latter, at rue St-Vincent 12, is the **Musèe de Vieux Montmartre** (Museum of Old Montmartre; ☎ 01-49-25-89-37), dedicated to the neighborhood in a house that was at times occupied by van Gogh, Renoir, and Utrillo.

Pay your respects to the writers Stendhal and Dumas, the composers Offenbach and Berlioz, and the painter Degas at their graves in the **Cimetière de Montmartre** on avenue Rachel. Finish the evening at 22 rue des Saules in **Au Lapin Agile** (☎ 01-46-06-85-87; www.au-lapin-agile.com) — called Café des Assassins in Picasso and Utrillo's day. The cover, including first drink, is a steep 24€ ($38) adults, 17€ ($27) for students with a valid school ID.

✔ **Window-shopping with the best of them:** Paris is a world shopping capital. On boulevard Haussmann rise Paris's two flagships of shopping, the department stores **Au Printemps** (no. 64) and **Galeries Lafayette** (no. 40). Au Printemps is a bit more modern and American-styled, and Galeries Lafayette is more old-world French, but both are very upscale and carry the ready-to-wear collections of all the major French designers and labels. Or try the Left Bank's only department store, the exquisite **Le Bon Marché**, which carries international designers and wonderful cosmetics and has one of Paris's best grocery stores, Le Grand Épicerie, next door.

If you prefer to shop designer boutiques, the best concentrations of stores are in the adjoining 1er and 8e. No single street offers more shops than the long rue du Faubourg St-Honoré/rue St-Honoré and its tributaries. Even if you can't afford the prices, having a look is fun. Big fashion houses, such as **Hermès** (no. 24), hawk ties and scarves, **Au Nain Blue** (no. 406) has one of the fanciest toy emporiums in the world, and the prices at **La Maison du Chocolat** (no. 225) are as rich as the confections.

Some of the best food shopping is concentrated on place de la Madeleine, 8e, home to **Fauchon** (at no. 26), Paris's homage to the finest edibles money can buy (although it faces serious competition from neighbor **Hediard**, no. 21). Jewels glitter on place **Vendôme,** 1er, at **Cartier** (no. 23), **Chaumet** (no. 12), and **Van Cleef & Arpels** (no. 22). Stink like the best of them with discounts on French perfumes at **Parfumerie de la Madeleine,** 9 place de la Madeleine, 8e.

✔ **Having a flea market fling:** If the prices at **Cartier, Hermès,** and the like set your head to spinning, you may have more luck at the **Marché aux Puces de St-Ouen/Clignancourt,** the city's most famous flea market (closed Sun). It's a group of several markets comprising almost 3,000 stalls, along avenue de la Porte de Clignancourt and rue des Rosiers. Ignore the stalls that begin popping up at the Porte de Clignancourt underpass and selling cheap junk, and turn left onto rue des Rosiers. Be alert for pickpockets. At press time, ATMs were few, so make sure to carry enough money in a safe place.

Usually, Monday is the best day to get a bargain, because the crowds are fewer and vendors are anxious for the dough. Keep in mind, though, that you can get a better price if you speak French and show that you're serious about and respectful of the merchandise.

Hours vary with the weather and the crowds, but stalls are usually up and running between 7:30 a.m. and 6 p.m. Take the Métro to Porte de Clignancourt; from there, turn left and cross boulevard Ney, and then walk north on avenue de la Porte de Clignancourt.

✔ **Cruising the Seine:** Is there anything more romantic than slipping down the current of one of the world's great rivers past famous cathedrals, museums, palaces — and the prison where Marie Antoinette spent her last days? Well, perhaps killing the canned PA sightseeing commentary and getting rid of all the other camera-clicking tourists would help the romantic mood, but if it's mood you're after, you can always take a more refined, though wildly expensive, dinner cruise.

The classic *Bateaux-Mouches* float down the Seine is offered by several companies, the biggest being **Bateaux Parisiens** (☎ 01-46-99-43-13; www.bateauxparisiens.com), which departs from quai Montebello or from pont d'Iena at the foot of the Eiffel Tower, and **Les Vedettes du Pont-Neuf** (☎ 01-46-33-98-38; www.vedettes dupontneuf.com), which leaves from Pont Neuf on the Ile de la Cité. Vessels depart every half-hour (less often in winter). Regular one-hour trips with multilingual commentary cost 10€ ($16) adults, 5€ ($8) children 3 to 12, free for children 2 and under. Departure intervals and fares are the same for both companies listed here.

After dark, the boats sweep both banks with megapowered floodlights — illuminating everything very well, but sort of spoiling the romance. These tend to be touristy, too, as are the more refined luncheon or dinner cruises, which are more expensive — 52€ to 72€ ($83–$115) for lunch and 95€ to 150€ ($152–$240) for jacket-and-tie dinner cruises — and the food is only so-so. The setting, however, can't be beat.

A cheaper, and less-contrived, alternative to the daytime tour is the **Batobus** (☎ 08-25-01-01 [0.15€/25¢ per minute for the call]; www.batobus.com), a water taxi with no piped-in commentary that stops every 25 minutes at eight major points of interest: the **Eiffel Tower,** the **Musée d'Orsay, St-Germain-des-Prés, Notre-Dame,** the **Jardin des Plantes, Hôtel de Ville, Louvre,** and the **Champs-Elysées.** A day ticket costs 12€ ($19) adults, 6€ ($9.60) children 15 and under. Batobus runs mid-March through May and September through the beginning of November every 25 to 30 minutes from 10 a.m. to 7 p.m. (until 9:30 p.m. June–Aug); from November through January 8 and from February 3 through mid-March, Batobus runs every half-hour from 10:30 a.m. to 4:30 p.m.

✔ **Paying a visit to le Mickey:** Contrary to popular belief, more visitors head to **Disneyland Paris** (☎ 407-934-7639 in the U.S., 01-60-30-60-53 in Paris; www.disneylandparis.com) than to the Louvre. The theme park, a slightly Europeanized version of California's Disneyland, with both familiar and new versions of rides and those contrived cultural areas, has been a fantastic success and inundated with guests since its opening day. The early financial troubles that occurred when more people than expected stayed in Paris rather than in the Disney hotels have been reversed.

To get there, take the A line RER from such central Paris RER/Métro stops as Châtelet–Les-Halles, Nation, or Gare de Lyon to Marne-la-Vallée/Chessy, within walking distance of the park. The RER station is in zone 5 of the public-transport system, so the cheapest way there (and back again) is to buy a single-day Mobilis pass good through zone 5, which costs 13€ ($21). Admission to the park from April through November is 57€ ($91) adults, 49€ ($78) children 3 to 11, free for children 2 and under. The hours of Disneyland Paris vary with the weather and season, so call before setting out. In general, however, the park is open daily from 9 a.m. to 8 p.m. It sometimes opens an hour later in mid-May, mid-June, and September and October.

Guided tours

The top tour-bus company in town is Grayline's **Cityrama** (☎ 01-44-55-60-00; www.cityrama.com), which has a 1½-hour, top-sights tour daily at 10 a.m., 11:30 a.m. and 2:30 p.m.; the cost is 20€ ($32) adults, 10€ ($16) children 4 to 11, free for children 3 and under. Cityrama also offers various full-day tours of Paris from 78€ to 100€ ($125–$160), and three- and four-hour historic- and major-sights tours starting at 48€ ($77). The four-hour "Seinorama" tour (daily at 2:15 p.m.) includes a drive up the **Champs-Elysées,** a one-hour cruise on the Seine, and a stroll to the second floor of the **Eiffel Tower.** It costs 48€ ($77) adults, 24€ ($38) children 11 and under.

Cityrama also offers a variety of Paris by Night tours with bus trips around the illuminated city and perhaps a dinner and Seine Cruise starting from 27€ ($43); more deluxe packages include a show at the **Moulin Rouge** or **Paradis Latin** or dinner in the **Eiffel Tower** (prices start at 98€/$157). Cityrama offers free pickup from some hotels, or you can meet at its office at 2 rue des Pyramides (Métro: Pyramides), between rue St-Honoré and rue de Rivoli (across from the **Louvre**).

L'Open Tour (www.ratp.fr) offers three hop-on/hop-off routes for 29€ ($46) for a one-day pass or 32€ ($51) for a two-day ticket. Use your Paris Visite card to get the one-day ticket for 22€ ($35).

Paris Walks (☎ 01-48-09-21-40; www.paris-walks.com) is a popular English-language outfit offering fascinating two-hour guided walks with such themes as Paris during the Revolution, Hemingway's Paris, the

Marais, the Village of Montmartre, Chocolate Tour, the Latin Quarter, and the Two Islands. Call for tours being offered during your visit and for where and when to meet — usually at a Métro station entrance at 10:30 a.m., and again at 2:30 p.m. Tours cost 10€ ($16) adults, 8€ ($13) students 24 and under, and 5€ ($8) children. They also offer weekend jaunts to places such as **Fontainebleau** or **Monet's Gardens** at Giverny or **Normandy landing beaches** by car.

Or try **Paris à Pied** (☎ 800-594-9535 in the U.S.; www.parisapied.com), which is geared toward first-time visitors to Paris. The three-hour tours are especially good: The Heart of Old Paris, the Latin Quarter, Montmartre, and the Marais. Tours cost $59 (guides prefer to be paid in dollars) and are made up of no more than six people.

Take a fun bike tour with **Fat Tire Bike Tours,** 24 rue Edgar Faure, 15e (☎ 01-56-58-10-54; www.fattirebiketoursparis.com). Friendly American guides take you on day or night bike tours of the city, with much irreverent though knowledgeable commentary. The tours last three to four hours. Day tours are April through October at 11 a.m. and 3 p.m., and November through March at 11 a.m. (closed Dec 25). Night tours, which are beautiful (especially the ride past the Grand Pyramid through the courtyard at the Louvre), take place April through October nightly at 7 p.m.; March nightly at 6 p.m.; and November and February 15 to February 28 on Saturday, Sunday, Tuesday, and Thursday at 6 p.m. Reservations are optional for day tours but required for night. The day tour costs 24€ ($38) adults, 22€ ($35) students; the night tour runs 28€ ($45) adults, 26€ ($42) students. You can combine both tours for 44€ ($70) adults, 48€ ($77) students. Look for the yellow meeting-point sign in front of the Pilier Sud (South Pillar) of the Eiffel Tower (PILIER SUD is spelled out above the ticket booth) for the bike tour. Bike rental is also available at 2.50€ ($4) per hour, 15€ ($24) for 24 hours. Cash, check, or credit card deposit of 250€ ($400) per bike is required.

In 2007, Mayor Bertrand Delanoë launched the Vélib bicycle rental program, bringing 10,000 bikes into the city, placing them in specially built bike racks in high-pedestrian destinations, and charging a nominal fee for their rental (1€/$1.60 for the first hour). The program was so successful, especially after 1 a.m. when the Métro closes, that 10,000 more bikes were ordered and more bike racks constructed.

Suggested itineraries

If you'd rather organize your own tour and you have a limited amount of time to sample the sights of Paris, try these recommendations for hitting the highlights.

If you have one day

Paris in a day? Better start out as early as possible and wear your most comfortable shoes: Be at **Cathédrale de Notre-Dame** when it opens at 8 a.m. Spend an hour poking around inside and climbing its tower (entrance to the towers is outside on the left side on rue du Cloître-Notre Dame) before hustling across the river to visit the **Musée du Louvre** at a dead trot. You only have time for the top stuff here; pay your respects to *Mona Lisa* and the *Venus de Milo* and have lunch in the cafeteria. Cross the Seine again to pop into the **Musée d'Orsay** and spend two hours or so admiring its horde of Impressionists and other French greats. As the sun sets over your full day in Paris, head to the **Eiffel Tower** to toast the City of Light from its heights. Descend and treat yourself to a first-class dinner to celebrate your day in one of the world capitals of cuisine.

If you have two days

Plunge right in on the morning of **Day 1** with the **Musée du Louvre.** Lunch in the food hall, and by midafternoon, trot over to the **Eiffel Tower** before sunset to get your requisite picture and drink in the panorama of Paris. Have a classy dinner in a fine Parisian restaurant, or dine intimately at a tiny bistro.

Be at **Cathédrale de Notre-Dame** early (8 a.m.) on **Day 2** to beat the crowds, and then clamber up the cathedral towers after they open to examine the famed gargoyles up close. Notre-Dame affords a much more intimate view across Paris than the Eiffel Tower does. When you get back to ground level, cross the square in front of the cathedral and descend into the **Archaeological Crypt** to puzzle out Paris's earliest origins.

Continue to the far end of the square for the jewel-box chapel of **Sainte-Chapelle,** hidden amid the government buildings. Grab some lunch on your way to the **Musée Picasso.** Don't stay too long with the works of this 20th-century master (leave by no later than 2:30 p.m.) because one of Paris's biggies lies ahead: the Impressionist treasure-trove of the **Musée d'Orsay.** Stay there as long as possible before heading off to dinner.

If you have three days

Spend **Day 1** and **Day 2** as described in the preceding section. **Day 3** is day-trip time. Catch the RER out to **Versailles** to spend a day exploring the palace to end all palaces, where a string of kings Louis held court in the powdered-wig exuberance of the 17th century. Take at least one guided tour, and save time to wander the acres of gardens.

Return to Paris by late afternoon so you can take the Métro out to the original bohemian quarter of **Montmartre** to watch the sun set from the steps of **Sacré-Coeur.** Wander the streets, peek at windmills and vineyards, or people-watch and write postcards at a classic Parisian cafe where you can rustle up some dinner.

Traveling beyond Paris

The day trips from Paris are as impressive as the in-town attractions. Among the many nearby destinations are two that exhibit the France of old in royal and religious splendor — the palaces at **Versailles** and the marvelous cathedral at **Chartres.**

Versailles: Palace of the Sun King

Versailles, with its extravagant 17th-century palace and gardens, is Paris's best and easiest day trip. Versailles takes up at least a day and in summer is packed by 10 a.m. Go seriously early (the grounds open at 9 a.m.) or wait to go late — after 3:30 p.m. you pay a reduced fare, and the tour buses have cleared out. In summer especially, this strategy gives you plenty of time to tour the emptying palace and, because the grounds are open until sunset, the extensive gardens as well. In fact, you may want to visit late afternoon on a day when Versailles hosts one of its evening concerts; for a schedule go to www.chateauversailles.fr and look for Palace of Versailles shows.

Getting there

You can zip out to Versailles from Paris in half an hour on the RER C line (you want the C5 heading to Versailles–Rive Gauche station). Versailles is in zone 4 of the public-transport system, so the Mobilis one-day pass will run you 9.30€ ($15) — covering not just there and back but also your Métro ride to Rive Gauche. Keep in mind that it's free if you have a Eurail pass. From the train station to the palace is a 15-minute stroll, or you can take a shuttle bus.

Seeing the sights

What started in 1624 as a hunting lodge for Louis XIII was turned by Louis XIV into a palace of truly monumental proportions and appointments over his 72-year reign (1643–1715). The Sun King made himself into an absolute monarch, the likes of which hadn't been seen since the Caesars, and he created a palace, which is more like a small city that he believed to be befitting of his stature.

You can wander the **State Apartments, Hall of Mirrors** (where the Treaty of Versailles ending World War I was signed), and **Royal Chapel** on your own (or with an audio tour), but taking one of the guided tours is much more informative and gets you into many parts of the palace not open to the casual visitor. These tours are popular and fill up fast, so your first order of business should be to head to the tour reservations office and sign up for one. You may have to wait an hour or more, so book an even later tour and use the intervening time to explore the magnificent gardens.

Le Nôtre (who designed Greenwich Park in London and the Vatican Gardens in Rome) laid out the hundreds of acres of palace grounds in the most exacting 17th-century standards of decorative gardening. The highlights are the ⅔-mile-long **Grand Canal,** once plied by a small warship and Venetian gondolas; the **Grand Trianon,** a sort of palace away from home for when the king wanted a break from the main château; and the **Petit Trianon,** a jewel of a mansion done in fine neoclassical style.

Nearby is Marie Antoinette's fairy-tale **Hameau,** or hamlet, created so Her Majesty could enjoy a cleaned-up version of peasant life. Here the queen fished, milked the occasional cow, and watched hired peasants lightly toil at the everyday tasks she imagined they did in the country — she even had a little "house in the faux country" built here, sort of a thatched mansion.

Versailles has complicated hours and admissions. The **château** (☎ 01-30-84-76-18) is open Tuesday through Sunday from 9 a.m. to 6:30 p.m. (until 5:30 p.m. Nov–Mar). Your best bet is to buy the one-day all-access pass, which allows entry to the palace, Grand and Petit Trianons, gardens, and estate of Marie Antoinette, as well as audio-guide tours of the palace and gardens for 20€ ($32) weekdays and 25€ ($40) weekends March through October (16€/$26 weekends Nov–Feb). The **park** and **gardens** are open year-round, from 8 a.m. in summer and 9 a.m. in winter until sunset. Admission to the park and gardens is free. Admission is free for all venues for children under 18.

On Sundays in May through October, there is a weekly fountain water show, called *Les Grandes Eaux Musicales,* which is accompanied by classical music and costs 8€ ($13) for adults and 6€ ($9.60) for students, children 17 and under, and people with disabilities. Also in summer, special nighttime displays of fireworks and illuminated fountains take place, usually on Sundays for 19€ ($30) and 15€ ($24). For more information on the summer spectacles, visit www.chateauversailles-spectacles.fr.

You can buy your tickets online at www.chateauversailles.fr; e-ticket holders can use a special express line and skip the long wait for tickets. You can also buy a Forfait Loisirs Chateau de Versailles pass at any French national rail station (Gare Montparnasse, Gare du Nord, Gare de l'Est, and so on). The pass provides round-trip transportation by RER and Métro to Versailles, "queue-skipping" entry to the chateau and the Grand and Petit Trianons and other attractions, as well as entry to evening musical spectacles *(Les Grands Eaux Musicales).* It costs 22€ ($35) on weekdays, and 26€ ($42) on weekends April through November. Look for TRANSILIEN signs or ask personnel at the information booths in the train stations to direct you to the correct ticketing agent.

Five to nine **guided visits** are offered (a few are in French only, and the tour of the garden's groves runs only in summer). Standard tours of the château book early; go directly to the information booth in the South Minister's wing of the palace upon your arrival to book a space. If you're interested in a more in-depth and themed tour, call ☎ 01-30-83-77-89 or visit www.chateauversailles.fr to see what's scheduled. Tours vary in price.

Chartres Cathedral: A Gothic masterpiece

The French sculptor Rodin dubbed this building "The Acropolis of France." Upon laying eyes on this greatest of High Gothic cathedrals, Napoleon declared, "Chartres is no place for an atheist." Perhaps the would-be emperor had been moved by the ethereal world of colored light that fills the cathedral (still the fourth-largest church in the world) on a sunny day, streaming through an awe-inspiring 2,500 sq. m (27,000 sq. ft.) of 12th- and 13th-century stained glass, turning the church walls into quasi-mystical portals to heaven. Budget three-quarters of a day for Chartres, returning to Paris for dinner.

Getting there

You can see all this for around a 26€ ($46) round-trip train ticket from Paris's Gare Montparnasse, less than an hour's ride away. The tourism office (☎ 02-37-18-26-26) is right on the place de la Cathédral.

Seeing the sights

The first **cathedral** (☎ 02-37-21-75-02; www.diocese-chartres.com) was built in the fourth century atop a Roman temple. Many historians hold that the site was religious even before the Romans invaded Gaul (Celtic France), and there's evidence that Druids worshipped in a sacred grove here centuries before Christ.

You can spend hours just scrutinizing the charismatic 12th-century sculptures adorning the main **Royal Portal,** and their 13th-century cousins around to the north and south sides of the church as well. The Royal Portal is part of the west facade, which, along with the base of the south tower, is the only part of the Romanesque church to survive an 1194 fire.

The cathedral was quickly rebuilt in the 13th century, and the rest remains an inspiring tribute to High Gothic architecture. Tear your eyes from the stained glass inside for at least long enough to admire the 16th- to 18th-century choir screen, whose niches are filled with statuettes playing out the Life of the Virgin.

You can take an excellent guided group tour in English for 10€ ($16) Monday through Saturday at noon or 2:45 p.m. (as long as there is no religious service, including funerals) with Malcolm Miller, who has been doing this for more than 40 years and has even written a book on the cathedral. No need to reserve; just meet inside the cathedral at the gift shop. Miller also gives private tours for groups up to 15 at 10€ to 15€ per person. ($16–$24) Call ☎ 02-37-28-15-58, or e-mail millerchartres@aol.com for more information. The cathedral is open daily from 8:30 a.m. to 7:30 p.m.

Climb the tower for gargoyle close-ups Monday through Saturday from 7:30 a.m. to noon and from 2 to 7 p.m., and also on Sunday from 8:30 a.m. to noon and from 2 to 7 p.m.; admission is 6.20€ ($9.90) adults 26 and over, 4.20€ ($6.70) adults 18 to 25, free for children 17 and under. Note that the stone stairs are steep and winding and the climb isn't for everyone. Make time to explore the cobbled medieval streets in the *Vieux Quartier* (Old Town) and visit the 16th- to 19th-century paintings in the **Musée des Beaux-Arts de Chartres,** 29 Cloître Notre-Dame (☎ 02-37-90-45-80).

Where to stay and dine

If you decide to make a night of it, rest your weary head for 98€ to 124€ ($157–$198) per double at the **Hôtel Châtelet,** 6–8 Jehan-de-Beauce (☎ **02-37-21-78-00;** Fax: 02-37-36-23-01; www.hotelchatelet.com), within walking distance of the cathedral. Many of the antique-styled rooms have panoramic views of the cathedral. When hunger strikes, head to 5 rue au Lait for modern French cuisine at **La Vieille Maison,** a celebrated restaurant in a 14th-century building, complete with Louis XIV furnishings (☎ **02-37-34-10-67**).

Fast Facts: Paris

American Express

The full-service office at 11 rue Scribe (☎ 01-47-14-50-00) is open Monday through Friday from 9 a.m. to 6:30 p.m. (until 7:30 p.m. May–Sept). The bank is also open Saturday from 9 a.m. to 5:30 p.m., but the mail-pickup window is closed.

Area Code

France's country code is 33. Calling anywhere within the country's borders requires dialing a ten-digit phone number (it already includes the city code) even if you're calling another number from within Paris. To call Paris from the United States, dial 011-33, and then drop the initial 0 of the French number and dial just the remaining nine digits. Some calls beginning with 08, usually to information lines, cost money.

Currency

The French franc gave way to the euro (€) in 2002. The euro is divided into 100 cents, and there are coins of .01, .02, .05, .10, .20, .50, 1, and 2. Paper-note denominations are 5, 10, 20, 50, 100, 200, and 500 euros. The exchange rate used in this chapter is 1€ = $1.60. Amounts over $10 have been rounded to the nearest dollar.

Doctors and Dentists

SOS Médecins (☎ 01-47-07-77-77) recommends physicians. SOS Dentaire (☎ 01-43-37-51-00 or 01-42-61-12-00) will locate a

dentist for you. The U.S. Embassy also provides a list of doctors.

Embassies and Consulates

The embassy of the United States, 2 av. Gabriel, 8e (☎ 01-43-12-22-22; france. usembassy.gov; Métro: Concorde), is open Monday through Friday from 9 a.m. to 6 p.m. Passports are issued at its consulate at 2 rue St-Florentin, 1er (☎ 01-43-12-22-22; Métro: Concorde), Monday through Friday from 9 a.m. to noon. The consulate is open Monday through Friday from 9 a.m. to 12:30 p.m. and 1 to 3 p.m.; it's closed on all French and U.S. holidays.

Emergency

Dial ☎ 17 for the police *(gendarmerie).* To report a fire or if you need an ambulance, call ☎ 18 *(Sapeurs-Pompiers)* or ☎ 15 for SAMU *(Service d'Aide Medicale d'Urgence),* a private ambulance company.

Hospitals

Both the American Hospital of Paris, 63 bd. Victor-Hugo in Neuilly-sur-Seine (☎ 01-46-41-25-25), and the Hertford British Hospital, 3 rue Barbes in Levallois-Perret (☎ 01-46-39-22-22; Métro: Anatole France), are staffed by English-speaking physicians.

Information

The city's tourist information office, L'Office du Tourisme et des Congrès de Paris (www.parisinfo.com), maintains two full-service welcome centers. Both offer basic information about attractions in the city, help with last-minute hotel reservations, make booking for day trips, and sell transportation and museum passes — but for a small fee. The first, in Gare du Nord (Métro: Gare du Nord), beneath the glass roof, is open daily from 8 a.m. to 6 p.m. The second, the Opéra-Grands Magasins Welcome Center, 11 rue Scribe (Métro: Opéra or Chaussée d'Antin), is open Monday through Saturday from 9 a.m. to 6:30 p.m.

Several auxiliary offices, or welcome centers, are scattered throughout the city. The office in Gare de Lyon (Métro: Gare de Lyon) is open Monday through Saturday from 8 a.m. to 6 p.m. The welcome center in Gare du Nord is open daily from 8 a.m. to 6 p.m. There are two offices in Montmartre — one at 21 place du Tertre (Métro: Abbesses), open daily from 10 a.m. to 7 p.m., and the other on the median strip facing 72 bd. Rochechouart (Métro: Anvers), open daily from 10 a.m. to 6 p.m. The welcome center in the Louvre (Métro: Palais Royal or Musée du Louvre) is open daily from 10 a.m. to 6 p.m., while the nearby Pyramides office, 25 rue des Pyramides (Métro: Pyramides), is open June through October daily from 9 a.m. to 7 p.m., and November through May daily from 10 a.m. to 6 p.m. Paris's convention center, Paris Expo (Métro: Porte de Versailles), has an information desk open 11 a.m. to 7 p.m. during trade fairs.

To reserve tickets for shows, exhibitions, or theme parks, visit www.ticketnet.fr or call ☎ 08-92-392-100 (0.34€/55¢).

Internet Access and Cybercafes

There is no single chain of Internet cafes in Paris, so the best way to find one is to wander around the streets in the Latin Quarter, home to the Sorbonne and other colleges, which is the best thing to do while in Paris anyway. Rates start at around 1.50€ ($2.40) for the first ten minutes. Most hotels now have wireless Internet (Wi-Fi) or free or low-cost computer access in the salon or lobby area.

Maps

The tourist office map is not bad at all, and even the Métro maps give you a pretty good idea of where you're going in terms of big monuments in Paris. But, if you want to be absolutely sure of where you are in the maze of streets near Place St. Michel or the Marais, buy a Paris Pratique, a thin, dark-blue street atlas with big and clear pages that many Parisians rely on to find their way. You can find them at any French bookstore after you arrive, or at Monoprix, the Target-like all-in-one stores you find all over Paris. Also popular, though its maps are much smaller, is the red-covered Plan de Paris.

Newspapers and Magazines

Paris has a terrific events/nightlife/sightseeing weekly called *Pariscope* (www.pariscope.fr), sold at every newsstand for 0.40€ (65¢). A competitor is *L'Officiel des Spectacles,* costing a mere 0.35€ (55¢). You may also want to pick up the free English-language *Paris Voice* (http://parisvoice.com), which is widely available at hotels and English-speaking venues.

Pharmacies

All pharmacies sport green neon crosses, and one in each neighborhood remains open all night. Check any pharmacy door for a list of those open at night, or try the 24-hour Pharmacie Les Champs, 84 av. des Champs-Elysées, 8e (☎ 01-45-62-02-41; Métro: George-V), in the Galerie des Champs-Elysées shopping center. A Left Bank option is Pharmacie des Arts, 106 bd. du Montparnasse, 14e (☎ 01-43-35-44-88; Métro: Vavin), which is open until midnight

Monday through Saturday; on Sunday, it closes at 9 p.m.

Police

Dial ☎ **17** for the police.

Post Office

The most convenient post office (www.laposte.fr) is at the Louvre, 52 rue du Louvre (☎ 01-40-28-20-00), open 24 hours. All other Paris post offices are open Monday through Friday from 8 a.m. to 7 p.m., Saturday from 9 a.m. to noon.

Safety

Paris is a relatively safe city with little violent crime, but there is plenty of petty theft. Around popular tourist sites, on the Métro, and in the station corridors lurk pickpockets — often children — who aren't afraid to gang up on you, distract you by holding or waving an item near your face, and then make off with your wallet. It only takes seconds, so hold onto your wallet or purse and yell at or push away your attackers — don't hold back just because they're children. Look out for thieves around the Eiffel Tower, the Louvre, Notre-Dame, Montmartre, and other popular tourist sites.

Taxes

In France, a 19.6 percent value-added tax (VAT) is figured into the price of most items. Foreign visitors can reclaim a percentage of the VAT on major purchases of consumer goods (see Chapter 4).

Taxis

See "Getting Around Paris," earlier in this chapter.

Telephone

Public phone booths in Paris seem to be going the way of the dinosaur since the advent of cellphones. You may find a coin-operated phone in a cafe or restaurant, but most public phone booths are equipped to take *cartes à puces* (European credit cards or other cards with a microchip that are inserted directly into the phone) or *cartes à code,* which have a code you dial before dialing a number. If you don't have a cell-phone with you, the *cartes à code* will be the most convenient because you can use the card on the phone in your hotel. *Cartes à code* start at 7.50€ ($12) for about an hour's worth of phone access. You can buy them at any *tabac.* For directory assistance, dial ☎ 12. To make international calls, dial ☎ 00 to access international lines.

To charge your call to a calling card or call collect, dial AT&T at ☎ 0-800-99-0011; MCI at ☎ 0-800-99-0019; or Sprint at ☎ 0-800-99-0087. To call the United States direct from Paris, dial 00 (wait for the dial tone), and then dial 1 followed by the area code and number.

Transit Info

See "Getting Around Paris," earlier in this chapter, or call ☎ 32-46 (0.34€/55¢ per minute) for information in English, or consult www.ratp.fr.

Chapter 14

Amsterdam and Environs

. . . .

In This Chapter

▶ Getting to Amsterdam
▶ Checking out the neighborhoods
▶ Discovering the best places to sleep and eat
▶ Exploring the city's highlights
▶ Side-tripping to Haarlem and the tulip-filled bulb belt
▶ Searching out windmills and Europe's largest sculpture garden

. . . .

Few cities have such an eclectic mix of sights as Amsterdam, from the basest of pleasures to the most somber reflections on human cruelty, taking in sublime art along the way. Spanning from the Renaissance to the modern period, the Dutch presence and strength in the fine arts is an obvious tourist draw — how could it be otherwise, with Rembrandt, Frans Hals, Jan Vermeer, Vincent van Gogh, and Piet Mondrian among the names on its roster? Visitors also come to shop for diamonds, to drink Dutch beers such as Heineken and Amstel in *brown cafes* (so-called because the best of them are stained brown from years of smoke), or to see the tulip fields and the windmills.

A tradition of encouraging high art and tolerance while discouraging prudish morality laws has endowed Amsterdam with some of its greatest attractions. The cityscape is one of the most beautiful anywhere, with its 300-year-old town houses lining well-planned and scrupulously mani-cured canals. Dutch leniency toward drugs and prostitution has grown into a huge tourism industry, luring students and other hip, mellow types to the city's "smoking coffeehouses," and visitors of all stripes who giggle and gawk at the legal brothels in the (in)famous Red-Light District.

To really appreciate Amsterdam, you should plan on spending at least three days here.

Getting There

Thanks to Amsterdam's continuing popularity with visitors who are eager to sample its free-for-all lifestyle, getting to Amsterdam by air or rail couldn't be easier.

Holland (The Netherlands)

Arriving by air

Amsterdam's ultramodern, single-terminal **Schiphol Airport** (☎ **0900-0141** from inside Holland or 31-20-794-0800 from outside; www.schiphol.nl), 13km (8 miles) southwest of the center city, is served by international airlines from across the Atlantic and around Europe and the world.

The Holland Tourist Information desk in Arrivals Hall 2 is open daily from 7 a.m. to 10 p.m. There you can get help making last-minute accommodations reservations. You can also buy train tickets for Amsterdam

Centraal Station. Also in the arrivals hall is a communications point for Internet and e-mail and a bunch of ATMs.

Regular trains provide a connection from Schiphol Airport to Centraal Station in about 20 minutes for 3.80€ ($6.10). Or ask your hotel if it has its own shuttle bus or is on the route served by the Connexxion Schiphol Hotel Shuttle that can whisk you straight to many hotels and close to others — for 12€ ($19). If convenience is your priority, the easiest way to transport yourself and your luggage from the airport to your hotel is to wait in line for a taxi, for a steep 40€ ($64).

Arriving by rail

Trains from Brussels, Paris, Berlin, and other points around Europe arrive in Amsterdam at **Centraal Station,** built in the 19th century on an artificial island in the IJ channel that separates the center city from the northern district. Stationsplein, the square in front of the station, has a VVV Amsterdam tourist office (a second office is inside the station) and a tram and bus terminal. You can take a tram to your hotel, or pick up a taxi from the taxi stand outside the station.

Load up on transit information and maps, and purchase transit cards at the **GVB Tickets & Info** office (see "Getting Around Amsterdam," later in this chapter), right next to the VVV office outside the station.

Orienting Yourself in Amsterdam

Infiltrated by canals, Amsterdam is like Venice. On a map, it looks like half of a spider web, with the canals as the threads radiating out from the center in tight, concentric arcs. Here, you'll find it easier to think in terms of the canals and six major squares as opposed to addresses, compass directions, and streets.

Introducing the neighborhoods

Try to remember a few street names, starting with Damrak. Think of Damrak as the backbone of the **Centrum** (Center), a neighborhood made up of a few straight canals and a tangle of medieval streets. Damrak runs from Centraal Station at its north end straight down to the **Dam,** the square in the heart of the city where the first dam was built across the Amstel River (hence the city's original name Amstelledamme, later to become Amsterdam).

Out the other end of the Dam, Damrak changes to **Rokin,** which curves down to the square and busy transportation hub of Muntplein. East of Muntplein, on the Center's southeast corner, is **Waterlooplein,** home to one of the city's premier performance venues and a flea market.

Next is the **Grachtengordel** (Canal Belt), wrapped around the Centrum in a big arc. This zone is a series of three concentric canals — Herengracht, Keizersgracht, and Prinsengracht — laid out with 17th-century regularity. The earlier Singel canal can be considered the inner edge of this belt, and the Singelgracht canal forms an outer boundary to the neighborhood. To the south lies **Museumplein,** where you find the city's three greatest art museums (one is currently partially closed for refurbishment and another has moved its collection out while refurbishment proceeds — in both cases until 2009), the finest shopping, and some of the best small hotels.

The **Jordaan,** a grid of small streets between Prinsengracht and Singelgracht, at the northwestern end of the Canal Belt, is a blue-collar neighborhood that has grown fashionable but hasn't been destroyed by gentrification; it has a roster of good restaurants. On the other side of the Canal Belt southwest of Muntplein is **Leidseplein,** the bustling, throbbing center of Amsterdam's liveliest quarter of restaurants (few of them A-list), nightclubs, and theaters. Nearby is **Pieter Cornelisz Hooftstraat,** known locally as "the P. C. Hooft," Amsterdam's most fashionable shopping street, and so small as to give some idea of the position fashion holds in the city's list of priorities.

The watery arc of Singel/Amstel River/Oude Schans canal surrounds the oldest part of the Center and runs from Centraal Station south to Muntplein, with the Dam in the middle. This area is where you find the **Rosse Buurt** (Red-Light District).

The most upscale residential district (of interest to upwardly mobile Amsterdammers but not so much to visitors) is **Amsterdam-Zuid** (South). **Amsterdam-Oost** (East), east of the Center, is a fairly pleasant, residential working-class and immigrant neighborhood, with attractions such as Artis Zoo and the Tropical Museum. Across the IJ waterway from Centraal Station lies **Amsterdam-Noord** (North), a district that has been a dull "dormitory" suburb up until now, though there are signs that this is beginning to change for the better.

Finding information after you arrive

In the Netherlands, tourist offices are indicated by the letters VVV — for *Vereniging voor Vreemdelingenverkeer,* if you must know — usually in a blue-and-white triangle sign. Amsterdam's main VVV office is just outside Centraal Station at Stationsplein 10. There's also an office in the station itself at Platform 2b, and a branch in the heart of town, in a kiosk facing Stadhouderskade 1. Call for tourist info at ☎ **0900-400-4040** from inside Holland, which costs 0.40€ (65¢) per minute, and 31-20-551-2525 from outside (at the usual rate for an international call), or use the Web site www.amsterdamtourist.nl. An information desk covering all the Netherlands is at the airport (see "Arriving by air," earlier in this chapter).

Getting Around Amsterdam

The best way to see Amsterdam is to travel on foot, by tram, or on a bicycle. Amsterdam's efficient trams (streetcars), buses, and Metro (subway) trains make getting around the city exceedingly simple. Public transportation begins around 6am and the regular service ends around midnight. After that, there are infrequent night buses.

By 2009, all public transportation in the Netherlands should be using an electronic stored-value card called the **OV-chipkaart** in place of the old tickets. There are three main types of OV-chipkaart: *personal cards* that can be used only by their pictured owner; *anonymous cards* that can be used by anyone; and *throwaway cards*. The personal and anonymous cards, both valid for five years, cost 7.50€ ($12) and can be loaded and reloaded with up to 30€ ($48). Throwaway cards, which are likely to be the card of choice for short-term visitors, cost 2.50€ ($4) for one ride and 4.80€ ($7.70) for two rides. Reduced-rate cards are available for seniors and children. Electronic readers on Metro and train-station platforms and onboard trams and buses deduct the correct fare; just hold your card up against the reader at both the start and the end of the ride.

Keep in mind that inspectors, sometimes undercover, may demand to see your card at any time. If you haven't paid, you'll be fined 37€ ($59) on the spot, plus the fare.

Maps showing the city's transit network are posted at most tram/bus shelters and all Metro stations. A free transit map is available from VVV tourist offices and from the **GVB Amsterdam Tickets & Info** office (☎ **0900-9292;** www.gvb.nl) on Stationsplein, in front of Centraal Station. You can buy transit cards from this office, from sales points and automats at Metro and train stations, and from some bus and tram drivers and conductors.

By tram, bus, and subway

Ten of Amsterdam's 16 tram lines begin and end at Centraal Station (and one more passes through). The Dam, Muntplein, Leidseplein, and Museumplein are the other main tram connection points. This is also true for buses.

The doors on trams and buses don't open automatically; you have to press the DEUR OPEN button. On some lines you board at the back of the tram and deal with the conductor, not the driver; on others you have to get a card ahead of time. If all else fails, keep in mind that Amsterdam is a city made for walking.

The city's four Metro (subway) lines — 50, 51, 53, and 54 — don't serve most areas you'll likely want to visit. But from Centraal Station you can use Metro trains to reach both Nieuwmarkt and Waterlooplein in the central zone.

By foot

The ring of canals making up the center city are not only easy to get around on foot, they also make for some of the most lovely walking in all of Europe — but watch out for bicycles! Amsterdammers really tear down those bike lanes, and tourists unused to this system are constantly getting knocked over. Just pretend the bike lane is the same as a street filled with cars, and look both ways before you cross. The museums and parks of Museumplein are quite a hike from Damrak; you'll probably want to take a tram (or, more scenically, a canal boat) to get there.

By bike

So you'd rather see Amsterdam as an Amsterdammer would? Why not rent a pedal-bike and tool around the canals? See "More cool things to see and do," later in this chapter for information.

By car

Don't drive in Amsterdam, for several reasons: The city is a jumble of one-way streets, narrow bridges, and trams and cyclists darting every which way. Tough measures are in place to make driving as difficult as possible. No-parking zones are rigorously enforced and the limited parking spaces are expensive. And if all that's not bad enough, car break-ins are common. Outside the city, driving is a different story and you may want to rent a car to tour.

By taxi

Taxis are easy to find at the stands in front of most major hotels and at Leidseplein, Rembrandtplein, and Centraal Station. To call for a taxi, dial ☎ 020-777-7777. Initially, the charge (which includes service) is 3.10€ ($4.95) and then 1.90€ ($3.05) per kilometer (⅗ mile).

Staying in Amsterdam

Many of those picturesquely tall, gabled houses lining canals and historic streets have been converted into hotels, but be forewarned: Dutch staircases give new meaning to the word *steep*. The older the building, the more difficult it is for a hotel to get permission to install an elevator (and the more costly it is to do it), so if stairs present a problem for you, be sure to ask before booking.

A room with a canal view costs more, but it's often worth it for the atmosphere; plus, these rooms are often better outfitted and sometimes larger than the rooms without views.

All the places that we suggest are located in pleasant, safe neighborhoods. For July and August, you want to make hotel reservations well in

Accommodations, Dining, and Attractions in Central Amsterdam

HOTELS ■
Acro Hotel **13**
Ambassade Hotel **10**
Amstel Botel **20**
Amsterdam American **11**
Avenue Hotel **17**
Bilderberg Hotel Jan Luyken **14**
The Bridge Hotel **28**
Owl Hotel **12**
Rembrandt Centrum **6**
RHO Hotel **25**
Toren **5**

RESTAURANTS ◆
Bordewijk **1**
De Prins **3**
D'Vijff Vlieghen **7**
Fifteen **22**
Kantjil & de Tijger **9**
Pancake Bakery **2**

ATTRACTIONS ●
Amsterdams Historisch
   Museum **8**
Anne Frankhuis **4**
Erotic Museum **24**
Hash Marihuana &
   Hemp Museum **26**
Joods Historisch Museum **27**
Ons' Lieve Heer op Solder **19**
Red-Light District **23**
Rijksmuseum **16**
Sexmuseum Amsterdam **18**
Stedelijk Museum CS **21**
Tropenmuseum **29**
Van Gogh Museum **15**

✝ Church
ⓘ Information
✉ Post office
— Railway

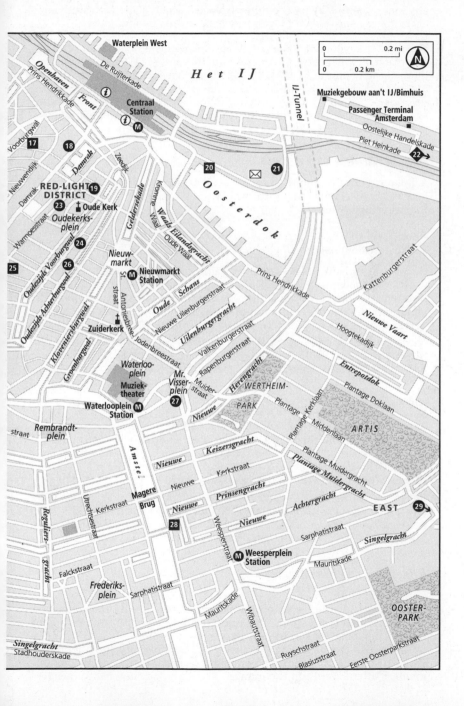

advance — especially for the budget places, which fill up with students eager to test Amsterdam's legendary lenient drug policy.

 The Amsterdam tourist office (see "Fast Facts: Amsterdam," at the end of this chapter) will reserve a room for you for a 15€ ($24) fee if you contact them ahead of time at ☎ **0900-400-4040** or, from outside the Netherlands, 31-20-551-2525 (Fax: 020-201-8850; www.amsterdamreservations.nl; reservations@atcb.nl). There is no fee if you book online. The office will also reserve a last-minute room for you on the spot at one of their offices in the city for a 4€ ($6.40) fee, plus a refundable room deposit.

Amsterdam's top hotels

A 5 percent city tax applies to rooms at all Amsterdam hotels. Some hotels include this tax in the room rate; others add it to the rate. Be sure to check this when reserving.

Acro Hotel
$ Near Museumplein

One of Amsterdam's not-so-secret bargains, the Acro has bright, clean, and well-kept small rooms close to the city's major museums and P. C. Hooftstraat's shops. With a shower in every room, a full Dutch breakfast included in the rates, and the hopping Leidseplein restaurant quarter just across the canal, what more could you ask for?

See map p. 264. Jan Luijkenstraat 44 (near the corner with Honthorststraat). ☎ 020-662-0526. Fax: 020-675-0811. www.acro-hotel.nl. *Tram: 2 or 5 to Hobbemastraat. Rack rates: 75€–150€ ($120–$240) double. Rates include breakfast. AE, DC, MC, V.*

Avenue Hotel
$$$ Center

The Avenue has all the bland, standardized charm of any international chain. But for solid, reliable comfort (if smallish rooms), American-style amenities at a great price, and a safe location near the rail station, you can do no better. The full Dutch breakfast adds local color.

See map p. 264. Nieuwezijds Voorburgwal 33 (one street east of Spuistraat, just a few minutes' walk from Centraal Station). ☎ 020-530-9530. Fax: 020-530-9599. www.embhotels.nl/avenue. *Tram: 1, 2, 5, 13, or 17 to Nieuwezijds Kolk. Rack rates: 112€–190€ ($179–$304) double. Rates include breakfast. AE, DC, MC, V.*

Bilderberg Hotel Jan Luyken
$$$ Near Museumplein

Nestled in a trio of 19th-century buildings between the city's top museums and P. C. Hooftstraat's shops, this boutique hotel, boasting refined amenities and personalized service, is a good splurge option. You get the best of both worlds here: an intimate inn with comfortably furnished bedrooms (though some are smaller than you might reasonably expect) and complimentary afternoon tea in the lounge — and a pricey hotel with business services, modern bathrooms, and several bars, patios, and dining spaces for relaxing.

See map p. 264. Jan Luijkenstraat 58 (between Honthorststraat and Van de Veldestraat). ☎ *020-573-0730. Fax: 020-676-3841.* www.bilderberg.nl. *Tram: 2 or 5 to Hobbemastraat. Rack rates: 129€–159€ ($206–$254) double. Rates include breakfast. AE, DC, MC, V.*

Rembrandt Centrum
$$ Canal Belt

In the center of canal land, the Rembrandt Centrum has many canal-side rooms. Whether you stay in the main 18th-century house or one of the small 16th-century homes lining the Singel out back, you have a good chance of getting a canal view. The rooms are more modern than their settings: They have a full complement of amenities, almost all are of a generous size, and the odd wood beam or fireplace is a reminder of the building's history.

See map p. 264. Herengracht 255 (below Raadhuisstraat). ☎ *020-622-1727. Fax: 020-625-0630.* www.rembrandtcentrum.com. *Tram: 1, 2, 5, 13, 14, or 17 to the Dam. Rack rates: 125€–205€ ($200–$328) double. Rates include breakfast. AE, DC, MC, V.*

RHO Hotel
$$ Center

This hotel in a former gold-company building is one of the most conveniently located in Amsterdam — on a quiet side street off the Dam. The Art Nouveau lobby hints at the hotel's origins as an early-20th-century theater. Unfortunately, the rooms are thoroughly modern and functional. The hotel provides all the amenities and is an excellent price for this level of comfort.

See map p. 264. Nes 5–23 (just off the southeast corner of the Dam). ☎ *020-620-7371. Fax: 020-620-7826.* www.rhohotel.com. *Tram: 1, 2, 4, 5, 9, 13, 14, 16, 24, or 25 to the Dam. Rack rates: 100€–170€ ($160–$272) double. Rates include breakfast. AE, MC, V.*

Toren
$$$$ Canal Belt

With its antique elegance in two side-by-side buildings dating from 1617 on a posh stretch of canal, this family-run boutique hotel, completely restyled in 2008 by local interior design guru Wim van de Oudeweetering, is justifiably considered one of Amsterdam's "hidden treasures." The style varies from room to room, going from understated elegance, via plush Italianate, to something that comes perilously close to resembling a classy 19th-century bordello — but with a whirlpool bathtub.

See map p. 264. Keizersgracht 164 (near Raadhuisstraat, close to the Westerkerk and Anne Frank House). ☎ *020-622-6352. Fax: 020-626-9705.* www.toren.nl. *Tram: 13, 14, or 17 to Westermarkt. Rates: 130€–250€ ($208–$400) double. Breakfast 12€ ($19). AE, DC, MC, V.*

Amsterdam's runner-up accommodations

Ambassade Hotel

$$$$ **Canal Belt** This hotel fills out ten 17th-century canal houses with fashionable charm at relatively affordable prices. Almost all rooms look through floor-to-ceiling windows over the canal. *See map p. 264. Herengracht 341.* ☎ *020-555-0222.* www.ambassade-hotel.nl.

Amstel Botel

$ **Center** Amstel Botel is nothing if not unique: a huge houseboat with 176 cabins. The botel is moored on the Amsterdam harbor (the best cabins feature water views), very near the temporary home of the Stedelijk Museum. Kids enjoy the novelty of staying on a boat. *See map p. 264. Oosterdokskade 2–4, just east of Centraal Station.* ☎ *020-626-4247.* www.amstel botel.com.

Amsterdam American

$$$$ **Leidseplein** An Art Nouveau gem dating from 1900 (and restored in 2008), the American faces the city's liveliest square, and has rooms that are modern yet refined and a stylish feel emanating from its famed Art Deco Café Americain. *See map p. 264. Leidsekade 97.* ☎ *020-556-3000.* www.amsterdam american.com.

The Bridge Hotel

$$ **On Amstel River** This place has huge rooms and modern amenities overlooking the "Skinny Bridge" over the Amstel River. *See map p. 264. Amstel 107–111, near Magere Brug.* ☎ *020-623-7068.* www.thebridgehotel.nl.

Owl Hotel

$$ **Near the Museumplein** The Owl is a neat little hotel on the Vondel-park, just a few short blocks from Museumplein. *See map p. 264. Roemer Visscherstraat 1, off Eerste Constantijn Huygensstraat.* ☎ *020-618-9484.* www.owl-hotel.nl.

Dining in Amsterdam

As the capital of a trading nation and former imperial power in the Caribbean and Far East, Amsterdam has a good selection of restaurants serving all sorts of cuisines, from Dutch to Indonesian. Traditional Dutch cuisine tends to be hearty and rather uninventive, but it's still good and filling (and it has been joined by a more inventive, fusion local style).

Traditional specialties include *Hutspot* (beef rib stew) and *pannekoeken*, massive pancakes that can be eaten topped with sugar or fruit as a dessert or with meats and cheeses as a main course. Consider a Dutch beer such as Heineken, Grolsch, or Amstel (all light *pils* brews), or a Belgian white or dark beer to complement your main dish.

If you're looking for something more exotic, the dish to try is the Indonesian feast called *rijsttafel*. This "rice table" smorgasbord consists of 17 to 30 tiny dishes, offering you a taste of some of the best food the former Dutch colony has to offer — Amsterdam is famous for its excellent Indonesian restaurants.

Small sandwiches called *broodjes* are the traditional snack of Amsterdam. They're available everywhere, but the best are at the specialty *broodjeswinkel* **Eetsalon Van Dobben,** at Korte Reguliersdwarsstraat 5–9, off Rembrandtplein (☎ 020-624-4200; www.vandobben.com), or **Broodje van Kootje,** at Leidseplein 20 (☎ 020-623-2036). You can buy ultrafresh picnic supplies at the market on Albert Cuypstraat, at the health-foody Boerenmarkt Farmers' Market at Noordermarkt, or in Albert Heijn supermarkets (there's one at the corner of Leidsestraat and Koningsplein).

Bordewijk
$$$$ Jordaan   FRENCH

Against a starkly modern setting, the food is richly textured and tastefully French, with modern accents and Italian and Asian twists. The food is accompanied by attentive, but not overbearing, service. The constantly changing menu may include rib roast in a Bordelaise sauce or red mullet with wild spinach. An outdoor terrace on the square makes dining alfresco even more attractive.

See map p. 264. Noordermarkt 7 (at the north end of Prinsengracht). ☎ *020-624-3899.* www.bordewijk.nl. *Reservations required. Tram: 1, 2, 5, 13, or 17 to Martelaarsgracht; Stop/Go minibus to Noordermarkt. Main courses: 20€–29€ ($32–$46); fixed-price menu 39€–54€ ($62–$86). AE, MC, V. Open: Tues–Sun 6:30–10:30 p.m.*

De Prins
$$ Canal Belt   DUTCH/FRENCH

One of the best deals in the city, this tiny neighborhood place is so popular for its inexpensive brown cafe–style food that tables fill up fast. In a 17th-century canal-side house, Dutch and French dishes are expertly prepared at remarkably low prices. This is one of your best bets for an opportunity to mix with the locals. It's also open late — the kitchen closes at 10 p.m., but the cafe stays open until 1 a.m.

See map p. 264. Prinsengracht 124 (near the Anne Frank House). ☎ *020-624-9382.* www.deprins.nl. *Reservations not accepted. Tram: 13, 14, or 17 to Westermarkt. Main courses: 10€–16€ ($16–$26); plate of the day 14€ ($22); specials 11€–15€ ($18–$24). AE, DC, MC, V. Open: Daily 10 a.m.–1 a.m.*

D'Vijff Vlieghen
$$$ Canal Belt   DUTCH

An Amsterdam institution, "The Five Fliers" resides in a string of five 17th-century canal-front buildings. The place offers a variety of historical décors and an excellent cuisine prepared by a chef determined to prove that traditional recipes can be exquisite. Try the wild boar with stuffed apples or smoked turkey filet with cranberry. If gin is your drink of choice, check out the list of Dutch gins with more than 40 selections. You can often sit outdoors here in summer.

See map p. 264. Spuistraat 294–302 (below Raadhuisstraat). ☎ *020-530-4060.* www. thefiveflies.com. *Reservations recommended on weekends. Tram: 1, 2, or 5 to Spui. Main courses: 20€–28€ ($32–$45), seasonal menus 33€–39€ ($53–$62). AE, DC, MC, V. Open: Daily from 5:30 p.m.*

Fifteen
$$$–$$$$ Waterfront   CONTINENTAL/ITALIAN

London celebrity chef Jamie Oliver's hot spot has both a full-menu restaurant and an adjoining trattoria serving less-elaborate (and less-expensive) fare. Drop-dead-gorgeous staff, clientele, and food, with dishes like a salad of the day with figs, prosciutto, Gorgonzola, and toasted almonds on field greens; seafood risotto; linguini with horse mushrooms and thyme; or pan-fried calf's liver with balsamic figs and pancetta.

See map p. 264. Pakhuis Amsterdam, Jollemanhof 9. ☎ *0900-343-8336.* www. fifteen.nl. *Reservations required for restaurant. Tram: 10 or 26 to Rietlandpark. Restaurant fixed-price menu 46€ ($74); trattoria main courses 23€–29€ ($37–$46). AE, DC, MC, V. Open: Restaurant daily noon to 3 p.m. and 6 p.m.–1 a.m.; trattoria Mon–Sat noon to 3 p.m. and 5:30 p.m.–1 a.m.*

Kantjil & de Tijger
$$$ Canal Belt   JAVANESE/INDONESIAN

Modernist and popular, the "Antelope & the Tiger" emphasizes cool over traditional color, but it succeeds at being deliciously hot on the plate. It features a great *rijsttafel* for two, a tasty *nasi goreng Kantjil* (fried rice with pork kebabs and stewed beef), and other specialties such as shrimp in coconut dressing. The multilayered cinnamon cake is worth saving room for.

See map p. 264. Spuistraat 291–293 (beside Spui). ☎ *020-620-0994.* www.kantjil. nl. *Tram: 1, 2, or 5 to Spui. Main courses: 13€–16€ ($21–$26); rijsttafel for 2 people 43€–55€ ($69–$88). AE, DC, MC, V. Open: Daily 4:30–11 p.m.*

Pancake Bakery
$ Canal Belt   DUTCH/PANCAKES

The name says it all: This canal-side joint does one thing only — *pannekoeken* — and it does it great. One of these disks topped with Cajun chicken or curried turkey and pineapple may be your dinner. For dessert, fruit compotes, syrups, and ice cream are typical pancake stuffings. Its décor is simple and slightly rustic, but in summer join the crowds (and the syrup-seeking bees) at the long tables outside with a canal view.

See map p. 264. Prinsengracht 191 (1 block from the Anne Frank House). ☎ *020-625-1333.* www.pancake.nl. *Tram: 13, 14, or 17 to Westermarkt. Main courses: 4.75€–11€ ($7.60–$18). AE, MC, V. Open: Daily noon to 9:30 p.m.*

Exploring Amsterdam

 The **I amsterdam card** gets you into most Amsterdam museums, including all listed here except the Anne Frank House, plus a free canal cruise and free rides on public transportation. It costs 33€ ($53) for 24 hours, 43€ ($69) for 48 hours, or 53€ ($85) for 72 hours, and you can buy the card at any tourist office. If you're under 26, you can buy a **Cultureel Jongeren Pas** (CJP — Cultural Youth Passport), entitling you to discounts at 1,500 places (museums, movie theaters, concerts, record stores, and so on) across the Netherlands. The pass costs 15€ ($24) and is good for a year; for more info, go to www.cjp.nl.

Amsterdam's top sights

Amsterdams Historisch Museum (Amsterdam Historical Museum)
Center

Housed in a 17th-century orphanage building, and with exhibits that cover 700 years of city history, this fascinating museum gives you a better understanding of everything you see as you explore Amsterdam. Gallery by gallery, century by century, you learn how a fishing village became a major world trading center. The main focus is on the city's 17th-century Golden Age, a period when Amsterdam was the richest city in the world, and some of the most interesting exhibits are of the trades that made it rich. You can also view many famous paintings by Dutch masters. Next to the museum is the **Schuttersgalerij** (Civic Guard Gallery), a narrow chamber bedecked with 17th-century group portraits of city militiamen; the open hours for this gallery are the same as for the museum, and admission is free.

See map p. 264. Kalverstraat 92, Nieuwezijds Voorburgwal 357, and Sint-Luciënsteeg 27 (next to the Begijnhof). ☎ *020-523-1822.* www.ahm.nl. *Tram: 1, 2, 4, 5, 9, 14, 16, 24, or 25 to Spui. Admission: 7€ ($11) adults, 5.25€ ($8.40) seniors, 3.50€ ($5.60) children 6–18. Open: Mon–Fri 10 a.m.–5 p.m.; Sat–Sun and holidays 11 a.m.–5 p.m. Closed Jan 1, Apr 30, Dec 25.*

Anne Frankhuis (Anne Frank House)

Canal Belt

As 13-year-old Anne Frank began her diary in July 1942, she dealt with the usual problems of adolescence, including feelings about her family and the boy next door. She also included the defining fact of her life: She was Jewish and had just moved into a hidden apartment with seven other people, comprising two families and a family friend, as the Nazis occupied Amsterdam. Anne lived here for two years, with only a crack in the window and some pictures of movie stars on the wall to remind her of the outside world.

The Franks and their companions were betrayed eventually, and they all were deported to concentration camps. Anne went first to Auschwitz, and then was moved to Bergen-Belsen when the Nazis retreated. She died of typhus just weeks before the camp was liberated. Of the eight people who lived in the attic, only her father, Otto, survived. His model of the rooms as they looked in those years of concealment and Anne's photos on the walls are all that adorn the small apartment hidden behind a swinging bookcase. A photograph downstairs details the Holocaust in Amsterdam, and the bookshop carries copies of Anne's remarkable diary in dozens of languages. Half a million people come to pay their respects here every year, so expect crowds and arrive early, or, in summer, late.

See map p. 264. Prinsengracht 267 (just above Westermarkt). ☎ *020-556-7105.* www. annefrank.org. *Tram: 13, 14, or 17 to Westermarkt. Admission: 7.50€ ($12) adults, 3.50€ ($5.60) children 10–17. Open: Mid-Mar to June and 1st 2 weeks Sept Sun–Fri 9 a.m.–9 p.m., Sat 9 a.m.–10 p.m.; July–Aug daily 9 a.m.–10 p.m.; mid-Sept to mid-Mar daily 9 a.m.–7 p.m.; Jan 1 noon to 7 p.m.; May 4 9 a.m.–7 p.m.; Dec 21 and 31 9 a.m.– 5 p.m.; Dec 25 noon to 5 p.m. Closed Yom Kippur (usually in late Sept or early Oct).*

Joods Historisch Museum (Jewish Historical Museum)
Waterlooplein

To dig deeper into the history of Amsterdam's Jewish population, visit this vast museum in what was the heart of the Jewish district. It chronicles the 400 years of Jewish history and culture in the city. Ever a tolerant country, the Netherlands welcomed hundreds of mainly Sephardic Jews fleeing persecution in Spain and Portugal in the 15th and 16th centuries. Although at first restricted to certain trades such as diamond-cutting, by 1796, Jews in Amsterdam were granted full civil rights (unheard of in that era in Europe), a position they enjoyed until the Nazi occupation.

Across the street at Mr. Visserplein 3, the **Portuguese Synagogue,** built in 1665, is the only still-functioning temple to survive from that period.

See map p. 264. Jonas Daniël Meijerplein 2–4 (off Waterlooplein). ☎ *020-626-9945.* www.jhm.nl. *Tram: 9 or 14 to Waterlooplein. Admission: 7.50€ ($12) adults, 4.50€ ($7.20) seniors and students, 3€ ($4.80) children 13–17. Open: Daily 11 a.m.–5 p.m. (to 9 p.m. Thurs); Jan 1 noon to 5 p.m. Closed Rosh Hashanah (2 days, usually in Sept), Yom Kippur (usually in late Sept or early Oct).*

Ons' Lieve Heer op Solder (Our Lord in the Attic)
Center

In the heart of the Red-Light District, this tiny, well-preserved baroque church spreads across the connected third floors of three 17th-century homes. Today Amsterdam is famed for its tolerance, but in the 16th and 17th centuries, the practice of any religion except for the official Calvinist Dutch Reformed Church was forbidden. To worship, Jews, Mennonites, Lutherans (for a time), and, in this instance, Catholics, had to go underground — or aboveground, as the case may be — and hold services in secret. One of the houses below the church has been restored for visitors — it's the oldest house in Amsterdam open to the public.

See map p. 264. Oudezijds Voorburgwal 40 (3 blocks from Centraal Station, on the far side of Damrak). ☎ *020-624-6604.* www.opsolder.nl. *Tram: 1, 2, 4, 5, 9, 13, 14, 16,*

17, 24, 25, or 26 to Centraal Station. Admission: 7€ ($11) adults, 5€ ($8) students, 1€ ($1.60) children 5–18. Open: Mon–Sat 10 a.m.–5 p.m.; Sun 1–5 p.m. Closed Jan 1, Apr 30.

Rosse Buurt (Red-Light District)

Dutch pragmatism and tolerance has led to the establishment of the best-known, safest, and cleanest prostitution zone of any Western city. The Rosse Buurt's sheer openness has made the district one of Amsterdam's major sightseeing attractions. Amsterdam never presumed to have the capability to stop the world's oldest profession, so it decided to regulate prostitution and confine the licensed brothels to the old city streets surrounding the Oude Kerk (Old Church).

These houses of ill repute display their wares behind plate-glass windows. The storefronts of some of the prettiest 17th-century homes in Amsterdam are occupied by women half-naked or wrapped in leather watching TV, darning socks, reading books, and otherwise occupying themselves until a customer comes along. At such time, they either close the blinds or abandon the window for the privacy of an inner room. Prostitutes pay their taxes, and the state ensures that they have regular medical checkups and health coverage.

The district is mostly frequented by five types of people. Three are harmless: lots of giggling and gawking tourists, darty-eyed career guys in suits, and the age-old sailors. Two other types can be scary and tragic: unlicensed prostitutes strung out on heroin and trolling the streets, and packs of shifty, seedy men who look as though all they do is indulge in drugs and brothels.

Come prepared to be provoked or saddened by the sight of scantily clad women behind glass, who manage to look bored and provocative at the same time — and be even more careful and aware than usual. Don't take any pictures — they don't want their faces recorded, so you could find your digital camera being pitched into one of the canals. You'll be pretty safe here during the day, but by night either steer clear entirely or stick only to the main streets if you're alone (this is doubly good advice if you're female) — and leave your valuables at the hotel.

Surprisingly, for all of the flesh trade's dominance, the district is still inhabited by its share of "real" people who take their kids to school, walk their dogs, shop at local stores, and eat out in a plethora of international restaurants. In recent years, the city government has cut the number of red-light rooms by a third and is moving to shut down some of the live sex shows. Boutiques and other small businesses are being encouraged to move in, with the general aim of "raising the tone" of the neighborhood — and curtailing its links to organized crime and human trafficking.

See map p. 264. The Red-Light District fills the streets around the northern half of the canals Oudezijds Achterburgwal and Oudezijds Voorburgwal. Tram: 4, 9, 14, 16, 24, or 25 to the Dam, and then duck behind the NH Grand Hotel Krasnapolsky.

Rijksmuseum
Museumplein

Although it doesn't get as much publicity as the Louvre or the Uffizi, Amsterdam's Rijksmuseum is one of the top museums in Europe. Not surprisingly, it houses the largest collection of Dutch masters in the world. Rembrandt is the star of the show, with a couple of self-portraits, the gruesome *Anatomy Lesson,* the racy *The Jewish Bride,* and his masterpiece, *The Night Watch,* which is the defining work for the Golden Age of Dutch painting.

But note that most of the Rijksmuseum is closed through 2010 for massive renovations. In the meantime, a "mini-Rijksmuseum" remains open in the Philips Wing, comprising some 400 masterpieces, while other elements of the collections have been split up among temporary exhibits all over the Netherlands (including ten masterpieces, by the likes of Jan Steen and Rembrandt, at the Rijksmuseum's Schiphol Airport annex) or lent out to traveling shows.

Frans Hals is well represented, with *The Merry Drinker* being one of his best portraits. You find party scenes courtesy of Jan Steen, Pieter de Hooch's intimate interiors, still lifes by Hans Bollongier, and four Vermeer paintings, including the famed *Woman Reading a Letter* and *The Kitchen Maid.*

See map p. 264. Philips Wing, Jan Luijkenstraat 1 (at Museumplein). ☎ *020-674-7000.* www.rijksmuseum.nl. *Tram: 2 or 5 to Hobbemastraat. Admission: 10€ ($16) adults, free for children 18 and under. Open: Daily 9 a.m.–6 p.m. (until 8:30 p.m. Fri). Closed Jan 1.*

Stedelijk Museum CS
Near Centraal Station

For modern art from Impressionism to the present, spend a morning at the Stedelijk. The permanent collections and regularly staged exhibits highlight many movements and styles of the past century. Of particular interest are Gerrit Rietveld's *Red Blue Chair* and paintings by Mondrian — two major forces in the Dutch abstract De Stijl movement, which prefaced the Bauhaus and modernist schools. You also find a large collection by the Russian Kazimir Malevich, who experimented with supersaturated color in a style he called *Suprematism.* Picasso, Chagall, Cézanne, Monet, Calder, Oldenburg, Warhol, Jasper Johns, and Man Ray are featured artists. The Stedelijk is currently being housed in a modern business high-rise on the east end of the same island as Centraal Station, but its real home — closed for major renovations until sometime in 2009 (or even later) — is a 1895 northern neo-Renaissance structure at Museumplein.

See map p. 264. Oosterdokskade 5 (just east of Centraal Station). ☎ *020-573-2911.* www.stedelijkmuseum.nl. *Tram: 1, 2, 4, 5, 9, 13, 14, 16, 17, 24, 25, or 26 to Centraal Station. Admission: 9€ ($14) adults; 4.50€ ($7.20) seniors, students, and children 7–16. Open: Daily 10 a.m.–6 p.m. Closed Jan 1.*

Van Gogh Museum
Near Museumplein

The most famous modern artist of the Netherlands died an underappreciated, tormented genius who sold only one painting in his lifetime — to his brother. Bouts of depression landed him in an asylum at one point and at another led him to hack off his own ear after an argument with the painter Gauguin. Yet even while the artistic establishment was virtually ignoring him, van Gogh managed to carry the freedom of Impressionism to new heights, and he created an intensely expressive style all his own.

This monument to the artist offers a chronological progression of his works, including 200 paintings and 500 drawings, alongside letters and personal effects (some of which are featured in the paintings on display). A few of his more famous canvases here include *The Potato Eaters, Sunflowers, The Bedroom at Arles, Gauguin's Chair, Self Portrait with a Straw Hat,* and *The Garden of Daubigny.* At the end of the exhibit hangs the powerful *Crows over the Cornfield,* one of the last paintings van Gogh completed in 1890 prior to committing suicide at the age of 37.

See map p. 264. Paulus Potterstraat 7 (at Museumplein). ☎ *020-570-5200.* www.van goghmuseum.nl. *Tram: 2, 3, 5, or 12 to Van Baerlestraat. Admission: 13€ ($20) adults, 2.50€ ($4) children 13–17. Open: Daily 10 a.m.–6 p.m. (until 10 p.m. Fri). Closed Jan 1.*

More cool things to see and do

☑ **Cruising the canals:** Amsterdam has 165 canals spanned by more than 1,280 bridges, so your trip won't be complete until you take a canal cruise on a glass-roofed boat with multilingual commentary (recorded or live). This is the best way to get a feel for the city and see its gabled houses, humpback bridges, busy harbor, and some unforgettable sights. These sights include the unlikely **Cat Boat,** a temporary home for dozens of furry felines who are *supposed* to detest being anywhere near water. Most canal-boat tours depart from Damrak or near the Rijksmuseum or Muntplein and last an hour. Tours run every 15 to 30 minutes in summer (9 a.m.–9:30 p.m.), every 45 minutes in winter (10 a.m.–4 p.m.), and cost around 9€ ($14) for adults, and 6€ ($9.60) for children 4 to 12.

Similar tours are operated by nearly a dozen other companies, though two of the biggest are **Holland International** (☎ 020-625-3035) and **Rederij Lovers** (☎ 020-530-1090). Romantics should try one of the two-hour night cruises with wine and cheese, cocktails, tapas, or some other option, or a two- or three-hour dinner cruise. The snack-type cruises cost around 30€ ($48); dinner cruises around 75€ ($120). Reservations are required.

☑ **Tramping to the sex museums:** These places are as squeaky clean as their subject matter allows and are full of giggling tourists. Of the two, the **Sexmuseum Amsterdam,** Damrak 18 (☎ 020-622-8376), has more of a carnival-like atmosphere, with a section of antique porn photographs that border on being of historical interest and a room of everything you either do or don't want to know about deviant sexual practices. Admission is 3€ ($4.80); the museum is open daily from 10 a.m. to 11:30 p.m. The **Erotisch** (Erotic) **Museum,** Oudezijds Achterburgwal 54 (☎ 020-624-7303), is more clinical and adds some mock-ups of an S&M "playroom" and a re-created alley from the Red-Light District in the good old days. Admission is 5€ ($8); the museum is open daily from noon to midnight.

✔ **Drinking beer in a brown cafe, gin in a *proeflokaal:*** When the Dutch want to go to the proverbial place where everybody knows their name, they head to the neighborhood *bruine kroeg* (brown cafe — so-called because they're stained from decades of smoke). This is the best place to try Dutch beer, where glasses drawn extra frothy from the tap are beheaded by a knife-wielding bartender. You can find hundreds of these cafes throughout the city, but here are a few of the best: **Café Chris,** Bloemstraat 42 (☎ 020-624-5942), has been around since 1642 and plays opera music on Sunday nights; **Gollem,** Raamsteeg 4 (☎ 020-626-6645), has over 200 beers to offer; **Hoppe,** Spui 18–20 (☎ 020-420-4420), is an always-crowded classic from 1670; touristy **Reijnders** has some great people-watching on the Leidseplein at no. 6 (☎ 020-623-4419); and **De Vergulde Gaper,** Prinsengracht 30 (☎ 020-624-8975), is another good place for people-watching, with terrace tables and an atmospheric interior.

After you've become familiar with the local beer, try the hard liquor the Dutch made famous. Visit a gin-tasting house, or a *proeflokaal,* which looks like a brown cafe but is usually owned by the distillery itself. It's customary to take the first sip no-hands, slurping it from the brim-filled shot glass as you lean over it. Try **Brouwerij 't IJ,** Funenkade 7 (☎ 020-320-1786 or 020-622-8325), in a now-defunct windmill near the harbor (good beers from its own brewery, too); minuscule **Café 't Doktertje,** Rozenboomsteeg 4 near Spui (☎ 020-626-4427), which has lots of antiques and tasty fruit brandies; or the 1679 **Wijnand Fockink,** Pijlsteeg 31 (☎ 020-639-2695), where they've already heard all the English jokes about their name. They also display a series of liqueur bottles painted with portraits of all the city's mayors since 1591.

✔ **Hanging out with hemp:** It really wouldn't be Amsterdam without its fascination with intoxicating weeds (see the nearby sidebar, "Lighting up"). In the Red-Light District, the **Hash Marihuana & Hemp Museum,** Oudezijds Achterburgwal 148 (☎ 020-623-5961; www.hashmuseum.com; Tram: 4, 9, 14, 16, 24, or 25 to the Dam), will teach you everything you ever wanted to know, and much you maybe didn't, about hash, marijuana, and related products. The museum does not promote drug use but aims to make you better informed. In a cannabis garden on the premises, plants at various stages of development fill the air with a heady, resinous fragrance. Some exhibits shed light on cannabis's medicinal use and on hemp's past and present uses as a natural fiber. Among several artworks is David Teniers the Younger's painting, *Hemp-Smoking*

Peasants in a Smoke House (1660). Admission is 5.70€ ($9.10) adults, free for children 12 and under (when accompanied by an adult). The museum is open daily from 10 a.m. to 10 p.m. (closed Jan 1, Apr 30, Dec 25).

✔ **Spending an afternoon in the tropics:** In East Amsterdam, the **Tropenmuseum,** Linnaeusstraat 2, at Mauritskade (☎ 020-568-8200; www.kit.nl/tropenmuseum; Tram: 7, 9, 10, or 14 to Mauritskade), investigates the indigenous cultures of the country's former colonies in India, Indonesia, and the Caribbean. The best exhibits are set up as typical villages you can wander through. They're so realistic that you almost wonder where all the inhabitants went. This place may be a good bet when the kids' (or your own) interest in Dutch Old Masters starts flagging and you need a change of pace. Admission is 7.50€ ($12) adults, 6€ ($9.60) seniors and students, and 4€ ($6.40) ages 6 to 17. The museum is open daily from 10 a.m. to 5 p.m. (to 3 p.m. Dec 5, 24, and 31; closed Jan 1, Apr 30, May 5, Dec 25).

✔ **Cycling around Amsterdam on two wheels:** The Dutch are avid bicyclists: The country is home to 15 million people . . . and 12 million bikes. The streets are divided into lanes for cars, lanes for pedestrians, and lanes for bikes (each even has its own stoplights). Renting a bike is one of the best ways to explore Amsterdam away from the tram routes and major sights (quiet Sun are best). The only hills are the humps of the bridges over scenic canals. For rentals, try **MacBike,** Stationsplein (☎ 020-620-0985), at Centraal Station. Prices start at 9.50€ ($15) per day and 31€ ($50) per week.

Guided tours

For a quick overview of town, take a bus tour from **Keytours Holland,** Paulus Potterstraat 8 (☎ 020-305-5333), or **Best of Holland,** Damrak 34

Lighting up

We officially can't condone this, but we also can't write about Amsterdam without mentioning the special class of "coffeehouses" in town, where the drug of choice isn't caffeine. Under pressure from the European Union, the Netherlands is cracking down on drugs, but the country is still lenient with marijuana. Contrary to popular belief, weed *is* illegal here, but police unofficially tolerate possession of a small amount — less than 5 grams — for personal use. These venerable establishments are allowed to sell small amounts of grass and hash — they even have marijuana menus! They can also sell joints (rolled with tobacco) and various hash products, coffee, tea, and juice, but no food. The most famous smoking coffee shop is **Bulldog,** the main branch of which is at Leidseplein 17 (☎ 020-625-6278) in — get this — a former police station, but almost any other one will have more of a typically Amsterdam, ahem, atmosphere.

(☎ 020-420-4000). A typical one-hour city tour costs around 16€ ($26); a two-hour tour, around 20€ ($32).

Mike's Bike Tours (☎ 020-622-7970; www.mikesbiketoursamsterdam. com) offers half-day tours around the canals in town, and a ride outside the city to see windmills and a cheese farm and clog factory (touristy, but fun). The cost is 22€ ($35) adults, 19€ ($30) students, and 15€ ($24) kids 11 and under; there's a discount of 5€ ($8) if you bring your own bike. Meet daily at 12:30 p.m. (except May 16–Aug 31, when there are two tours, at 11:30 a.m. and 4 p.m.) near the reflecting pool behind the Rijksmuseum (Tram: 2, 3, or 5). December through February, you have to book in advance (minimum three people).

And don't forget about touring Amsterdam from the canals' point of view; see "More cool things to see and do," earlier in this chapter. Amsterdam's most innovative tour has to be the **Canal Bus** (☎ 020-622-2181; www. canal.nl), a trio of color-coded boats that stop near most of the city's museums and attractions, including all those mentioned in this chapter. The full-day fare — valid until noon the next day — is 18€ ($29) adults, 12€ ($19) ages 12 and under, and includes discounts on admissions for some museums. The boats leave every half-hour from Centraal Station.

Suggested itineraries

If you're pressed for time and prefer to organize your own tour, this section offers tips for building your own Amsterdam itinerary.

If you have one day

Start off the day early with a canal cruise at 9 a.m. Get to the **Rijksmuseum "The Masterpieces"** when it opens and spend about an hour enjoying the Rembrandts and Vermeers. Then pop down the block for another hour in the company of Holland's towering master modernist at the **Van Gogh Museum.** Head to the **Pancake Bakery** for a quick canal-side lunch, and then stroll up the street to pay your respects at the **Anne Frankhuis.**

Because Amsterdam attracts all types, we leave the late afternoon up to you: Explore the town by bike, titillate at one of the sex museums, stroll the canals, or make the rounds of the brown cafes (or the other kind of cafe). In the early evening, take the requisite shocked spin through the Red-Light District — before sunset if possible (that is, before the seedy night elements come out, but while the ladies are putting their best, er, feet forward for the businessmen who stop by on their way home). Cap the day off with an Indonesian feast at **Kantjil & de Tijger.**

If you have two days

Start off **Day 1** with the ol' canal cruise — the best intro to the charming side of Amsterdam that money can buy. Head to the masterpieces in the **Rijksmuseum** next and spend two hours or so perusing the Old Masters.

After lunch, pay homage to The Earless One at the nearby **Van Gogh Museum.** Head back up to the Centraal Station neighborhood to check out the modern art **Stedelijk Museum CS** before wandering back down to Damrak to spend the early evening visiting the **Red-Light District.** Settle in for a thoroughly Dutch dinner at **Restaurant d'Vijff Vlieghen.**

Begin **Day 2** indulging in a favorite Dutch pastime: Rent a bike and tool around on your own, or take one of Mike's excellent guided bike tours. Lunch at the **Pancake Bakery** before seeing the **Anne Frankhuis,** and then head across to the old part of town to see the Oude Kerk and the church **Ons' Lieve Heer op Solder** (Our Lord in the Attic), hidden inside a canal-side mansion. Spend the early evening hopping between brown and gin cafes, and then poke around the Leidseplein district for a funky little Indonesian restaurant (**Bojo,** at Lange Leidsedwarsstraat 51, is a decent budget bet) for dinner.

If you have three days

Spend **Day 1** and **Day 2** as outlined in the preceding section, and take **Day 3** to visit the re-created folk village of **Zaanse Schans** in the morning and **Haarlem** in the afternoon, or — especially if you're in town for the spring flower season — Haarlem in the morning, followed by a drive, bike ride, or train trip through the flower-bedecked **Bollenstreek.** Find out more about these sights in the next section.

Traveling beyond Amsterdam

Several interesting destinations are an easy day trip from Amsterdam — among them the tulip region near Haarlem, the traditional museum-village of Zaanse Schans, and the Vincent van Gogh paintings galore at the Kröller-Müller Museum in the Hoge Veluwe National Park.

Discovering the other Haarlem

Haarlem makes perhaps the most pleasant day trip from Amsterdam, offering a much more laid-back and less hectic version of a tidy Dutch city. Haarlem boasts a great museum, too.

Getting there

Every half-hour or so, a train makes the 20-minute jaunt to Haarlem from Amsterdam. The local **VVV tourist office** (☎ **0900-616-1600** or 31-23-616-1600 from outside Holland; www.vvvzk.nl) is just outside the station at Stationsplein 1.

Seeing the sights

The town's pretty central square, Grote Markt, is anchored by the late-Gothic church Sint-Bavokerk, better known as the **Grote Kerk.** Inside are artist Frans Hals's tombstone and a cannonball that embedded in the wall during the Spanish siege of 1572 to 1573. The church also houses one of the world's great organs, a 68-stop, 5,068-pipe beauty built by Christian Müller from 1735 to 1738 — Handel, Liszt, and a ten-year-old Mozart all came to play it. From about mid-May to late October, you can enjoy free, hour-long organ recitals; these are generally Tuesdays at 8:15 p.m. and Thursdays at 3 p.m., with occasional specials on other days. On the church's south side, 17th-century shops and houses nestle together like barnacles. These were built so that they could be rented for additional income to help with the church's upkeep.

Haarlem's biggest attraction is the **Frans Hals Museum,** Groot Heiligeland 62 (☎ 023-511-5775; www.franshalsmuseum.nl), set up in the home for retired gentlemen where the painter spent his last days in 1666. Frans Hals's works make up the bulk of the collections, but many Dutch painters from the 16th century to the present are represented as well. The works are all displayed in 17th-century-style rooms that often bear a striking resemblance to the settings in the works themselves. Admission is 7.50€ ($12) adults 25 and over, 3.75€ ($6) ages 19 to 24. It's open Tuesday through Saturday from 11 a.m. to 5 p.m. and Sunday from noon to 5 p.m. (closed Jan 1, Dec 25).

Where to stay and dine

Hotel Carillon (☎ 023-531-0591; www.hotelcarillon.com) has clean 80€ ($128) doubles in the heart of town at Grote Markt 27. Close by, the tiny restaurant **Dijkers,** Warmoestraat 5–7 (☎ 023-551-1564), serves hearty lunches such as Thai green curry and lighter fare such as club and toasted sandwiches.

Stopping to admire the tulips

Believe it or not, tulips aren't even Dutch! They came to the Netherlands from Turkey in the 1590s. By 1620, tulips gained popularity and growers couldn't keep up with the demand. By the year 1636, rare tulip bulbs were being sold for their weight in gold. Bulbs have come down in price since then, but the Netherlands is still one of the world's largest producers of flowers.

The **Bollenstreek** is Amsterdam's bulb belt, home of the tulip. It's located between Haarlem and Leiden and stretches across a 19-mile strip of land. These lowlands along the North Sea are fields of gladioli, hyacinths, lilies, narcissuses, daffodils, crocuses, irises, dahlias, and the mighty tulip for miles as far as the eye can see. January is when the earliest blooms burst into color, and the floral show doesn't slow down until the end of May. Mid-April, though, is the Time of the Tulip.

Getting there

Haarlem is just a quick 20-minute ride by train from Amsterdam. Buses run between Haarlem and Leiden to service the region.

Seeing the sights

If you're here between around March 20 and May 20, rush to the **Keukenhof Gardens** in Lisse (☎ 0252-465-555; www.keukenhof.nl), to see its 8 million-plus bulbs in full bloom over 32 hectares (80 acres). These are perhaps the top floral gardens on Earth. Open daily from 8 a.m. to 7:30 p.m., there are cafeterias on-site so you don't have to miss any of the surrounding chromatic spectacle. Admission is a steep 14€ ($22) adults, 13€ ($21) seniors, 6€ ($9.60) children ages 4 to 11. Take bus no. 54 from Leiden.

One of the bulb-field region's chief attractions is just 10km (6 miles) south of Amsterdam at the **Bloemenveiling** (Flower Auction) in Aalsmeer (☎ 0297-393-939; www.flora.nl). Nineteen million cut flowers daily (and two million other plants) are auctioned at a speedy pace. As you watch from the visitors' gallery, giant dials tick down rapidly from 100 to 1 — as the numbers count down, the price drops — and the first bidder to buzz in on that lot stops the clock at that price and gets the bouquet. Because only one bid gets the goods, it's like a huge game of chicken. The auction runs Monday through Friday from 7 to 11 a.m. (try to show up before 9 a.m. for the best action). Admission is 5€ ($8) adults, 3€ ($4.80) children ages 6 to 11. Bus no. 172 heads to Aalsmeer from outside Amsterdam's Centraal Station.

Tilting at windmills

Luckily, when the Dutch paved the way for progress, they also set aside space for preservation. As industrialization of the countryside north of Amsterdam started during the first half of the 20th century, people realized that a way of life and mode of architecture was rapidly disappearing. In the late 1950s, dozens of local farms, houses, and windmills dating from that ever-popular 17th century were broken down, carted off, and reassembled into a kind of archetypal "traditional" village called **Zaanse Schans,** where the Dutch 17th century lives on.

Getting there

Zaanse Schans is about 16km (10 miles) northwest of Amsterdam, just above the town of Zaandam, to which there are numerous daily trains from Amsterdam (a 12-minute ride). Bus no. 91 departs about hourly from outside central Station to Zaanse Schans, a 30-minute ride. The **tourist office** (☎ 075-616-8218; www.zaanseschans.nl) is in the ultramodern Zaans Museum, at Schansend 7.

Seeing the sights

Although Zaanse Schans is a little bit of a tourist trap, it's not just a sightseeing attraction — people actually live in most of the cottages and houses, doing their daily tasks in as much an early 18th-century way as possible. The grocery stores and the like are truly from a different era, and a few of the buildings are museums for the public, including the four working windmills. Three of the town's windmills are open to visitors for

2.50€ ($4) each for adults, and 1.50€ ($2.40) children ages 6 to 12, but they keep widely varying hours — roughly 9 or 10 a.m. to 4 or 5 p.m., with shorter hours November through March (go to www.zaansemolen. nl for details). The little **Molenmuseum** (Windmill Museum) in the village is open Tuesday through Friday 11 a.m. to 5 p.m., Saturday and Sunday 1 to 5 p.m. Admission is 3.50€ ($5.60) adults, 3€ ($4.80) seniors, free for children 17 and under. Short cruises on the Zaan River are also popular.

If you'd like to see some more impressive windmills, head 106km (66 miles) south of Amsterdam to the **Kinderdijk** region below Rotterdam (☎ 078-691-5179; www.kinderdijk.org). Nineteen functioning, old-fashioned windmills built from 1722 to 1761 dot the landscape like sailboats, turning their 13m-long (42-ft.) sails slowly in the wind on Saturdays from 1:30 to 5:30 p.m. in July and August. For the rest of the year, they just sit there looking picturesque. The visitor's mill is open to the public April through September, daily from 9:30 a.m. to 5:30 p.m. Take the train from Amsterdam's Centraal Station to Rotterdam, and then the metro to Zuidplein, and then bus no. 154.

Biking to the Kröller-Müller Museum

One of the Netherlands's top modern-art museums and Europe's largest sculpture garden is the **Kröller-Müller Museum,** set in the middle of the **Hoge Veluwe,** a 5,500-hectare (13,750-acre) national park of heath, woods, and sand dunes. This is a great Dutch excursion and can easily be done as a day trip from Amsterdam.

Getting there

Trains scheduled twice hourly run from Amsterdam to Arnhem in 65 minutes. From Arnhem's station, hop on bus no. 12, which stops in the park both at the museum and at the visitor center/cafeteria (☎ 0318-591-627), where you can pick up maps of the park.

Before taking that bus in Arnhem, do some advance reconnoitering by popping into the city's **VVV tourist office** (☎ 0900-112-2344; www.vvv arnhem.nl) at Stationsplein 45 outside the station to pick up park info and maps.

Seeing the sights

Biking is the primary form of transportation in the **Hoge Veluwe National Park** (☎ 0900-464-3835; www.hogeveluwe.nl); grab a free white bike by any entrance or at the visitor center — just drop it off before you leave. As you bike through the calm, lush greenery of the park, you may catch glimpses of red deer, foxes, wild boar, or badgers. Under the visitor center lies the **Museonder,** a series of displays and tunnels dedicated to underground ecology, open daily 10 a.m. to 5 p.m. (until 6 p.m. Apr–Oct). The park itself is open daily November through March 9 a.m. to 6 p.m., April 8 a.m. to 8 p.m., May and August 8 a.m. to 9 p.m., June and July 8 a.m. to 10 p.m., September 9 a.m. to 8 p.m., and

October 9 a.m. to 7 p.m. Admission to the park is 7€ ($11) adults, 3.50€ ($5.60) children ages 6 to 12.

The **Kröller-Müller Museum** (☎ 0318-591-241; www.kmm.nl), within the park, displays paintings from radically different artists and eras, all side-by-side like wallpaper. The museum displays a rotating selection of its 278 (!) works by van Gogh. Other featured artists include Picasso, Mondrian, Seurat, Monet, and Braque.

 The 11-hectare (27-acre) **sculpture garden** behind the museum features work by Rodin, Oldenburg, Henry Moore, Barbara Hepworth, Mark di Suvero, and Lipchitz. Jean Dubuffet's enormous *Jardin d'Emaille* is an interactive artscape of the sculptor's patented white with black lines, raised above ground level, so you have to climb a set of stairs. This enables you to wander around on the art (which should make it interesting for kids). The museum is open Tuesday through Sunday from 10 a.m. to 5 p.m.; the sculpture garden closes a half-hour earlier. Admission to the museum is another 7€ ($11) adults, 3.50€ ($5.60) children ages 6 to 12, on top of the park fee.

Fast Facts: Amsterdam

American Express

There is no longer an American Express office in Amsterdam.

Area Code

The country code for the Netherlands is **31.** Amsterdam's city code is **020,** but drop the initial 0 if you're calling from outside the Netherlands. To call Amsterdam from the United States, dial 011-31-20, and then the number.

Currency

The currency of the Netherlands is the euro (€), divided into 100 euro cents. There are coins of 1, 2, 5, 10, 20, and 50 cents, and 1 and 2 euros. (Holland does not use the 1-cent and 2-cent coins, but rounds prices up or down to the nearest 5 cents.) Paper-note denominations are 5, 10, 20, 50, 100, 200, and 500 euros. The exchange rate used in this chapter is 1€ = $1.60. Amounts over $10 have been rounded to the nearest dollar.

Doctors and Dentists

For 24-hour doctor and dentist referrals, contact the Central Doctors Service (☎ 020-592-3434). For 24-hour first-aid service, see "Hospitals," later in this section.

Embassies and Consulates

Embassies are in The Hague (Den Haag). The U.S. Consulate in Amsterdam is at Museumplein 19 (☎ 020-575-5309; http://netherlands.usembassy.gov; Tram: 2, 5, 12, or 16), open for visits Monday through Friday from 8:30 to 11:30 a.m.

Emergency

For police assistance, an ambulance, or the fire department, call ☎ **112.**

Hospitals

Onze Lieve Vrouwe Gasthuis is close to the center city, at Oosterpark 9 (☎ 020-599-9111; www.olvg.nl; Tram: 3, 7, or 10). You can reach the giant Academisch Medisch

Centrum at Meibergdreef 9 (☎ 020-566-9111; www.amc.uva.nl) from the center of Amsterdam on the Metro train to Holendrecht station in suburban Amsterdam Zuidoost. Also see "Doctors," earlier in this section.

Information

Amsterdam's main VVV tourist office is just outside Centraal Station at Stationsplein 10. You also find an office in the station itself, and an agency branch at the Canal Company kiosk on Stadhouderskade, at Leidseplein. Call for tourist info on ☎ 0900-400-4040, or go to the Web site www.amsterdamtourist.nl. You can find an information desk covering all the Netherlands in Schiphol Plaza at the airport.

Internet Access and Cybercafes

Many hotels offer Internet access. The Mad Processor, Kinkerstraat 11–13 (☎ 020-612-1818; www.madprocessor.com), is open daily from noon to 1 or 2 a.m.; access is 2€ ($3.20) per hour.

Maps

Though the tourist office hands out a decent enough freebie map, it pays to pick up a more detailed one from any newsstand or bookstore.

Newspapers and Magazines

The tourist office publishes a 1.95€ ($3.10) monthly magazine called *Amsterdam Day by Day* (in English) covering events and exhibitions alongside the usual attractions, museums, shopping, and restaurant info.

Pharmacies

An *apotheek* is a pharmacy that fills prescriptions; a *drogerji* sells toiletries. The most central apotheek is called Dam Apotheek, Damstraat 2 (☎ 020-624-4331). For a list of the local pharmacies whose

turn it is to stay open at night or on weekends, check the door of any *apotheek;* a sign will direct you to the nearest late-night pharmacy.

Police

Call ☎ 112 for the police.

Post Office

The main TNT post office, Singel 250 (☎ 076-527-2727), is open Monday through Friday from 7:30 a.m. to 6:30 p.m., and Saturday from 9 a.m. to noon.

Safety

Although violent crime is rare, the Dutch tolerance of drugs invites drug-related crime. Protect yourself against pickpockets in all tourist areas, on public transportation, and around Damrak, the Dam, and the Red-Light District. The Red-Light District becomes less than savory after dark, particularly as the evening wears on and tourists have returned to their hotels. Avoid this area at night; we recommend that you don't wander the district alone or call attention to yourself. If you simply must walk through this area late at night, at least make sure you're in a group of people.

Taxes

In Amsterdam, a value-added tax (BTW) is figured into the price of most items. As a visitor from outside the European Union, you can reclaim 13.75 percent of the BTW on consumer goods, as long as you spend at least 50€ ($80) in a single participating store in a single day (see Chapter 4).

Taxis

See "Getting Around Amsterdam," earlier in this chapter.

Telephone

Almost all pay phones in the Netherlands accept only phone cards, which are sold at newsstands, post offices, tobacconists, and train stations — confusingly, different types of cards are required for the orange-and-gray phones in train stations than for the green phones everywhere else. While talking, watch the digital reading: It tracks your decreasing deposit, so you know when your card is out. For directory assistance, call ☎ 0900-8008.

To charge a call to your calling card, dial AT&T (☎ 0800-022-9111), MCI (☎ 0800-023-5103), or Sprint (☎ 0800-022-9119). To call the United States from the Netherlands direct, dial 00-1 followed by the area code and number.

Transit Info

Amsterdam's public transportation system is operated by GVB Amsterdam (☎ 0900-9292; www.gvb.nl). You can visit the GVB Tickets & Info office on Stationsplein, in front of Centraal Station.

Chapter 15

Munich and Bavaria

● ●

In This Chapter

▶ Getting to Munich

▶ Checking out Munich's neighborhoods

▶ Discovering the best places to sleep and eat

▶ Exploring the city's highlights

▶ Heading into Bavaria with stops at Neuschwanstein and Dachau

● ●

Munich (München, pronounced *Mewn*-shin, in German), the capital of Bavaria, is a town that likes to celebrate. **Oktoberfest,** which yearly draws some seven million revelers, starts in September and lasts for 16 days. From January through February, the city goes into party mode again and celebrates **Fasching** (Carnival), a whirl of colorful parades, masked balls, and revelry. Throughout the year, people gather in the giant beer halls and beer gardens to quaff liters of beer, listen to the oompah bands, and have a good time.

Oom-pah-pah aside, Munich is also a rich, elegant, sophisticated city, with an unparalleled array of artistic and cultural treasures. World-class museums, palaces, concert halls, and theaters are part and parcel of life in the Bavarian capital. If you believe the polls, Munich is the Germans' first choice as a desirable place to live. Many Germans — especially the 1.5 million people who live in Munich — think of the city as Germany's secret capital. Munich offers so much to visitors that we recommend you give yourself at least three days here.

Getting There

With one of the most modern airports in the world and one of the largest train stations in Europe, Munich's status as a major travel hub means that you'll have no trouble finding your way there.

Arriving by air

The ultramodern **Flughafen München** (Munich Airport; ☎ **089-97-500;** www.munich-airport.com) is 29km (18 miles) northeast of Munich. At the information desks on levels 3 and 4 of the main concourse, you can make hotel reservations for Munich and the surrounding area. The desks

Germany

are open daily from 6 a.m. to 11 p.m. A 24-hour Internet point is in the airport's center area, and ATMs are located throughout the airport.

Near Terminal 1 or Terminal 2 you can catch the S8 S-Bahn (light-rail train), which leaves the Flughafen (airport) stop every ten minutes for the 45-minute trip to Munich (8.80€/$14). The **Lufthansa Airport Bus** (☎ **089-323-040**) runs between the airport (the stop is in front of the Central Area) and Munich's main train station; the trip takes about 40 minutes and costs 10€ ($16).

Arriving by train

Trains to Munich arrive at the **Hauptbahnhof,** on Bahnhofplatz near the city center. It's one of Europe's largest train stations, with a hotel, restaurants, shopping, and banking facilities. A train information office, on the mezzanine level, is open daily from 7 a.m. to 8 p.m. Connected to the rail station are the city's extensive **S-Bahn** light-rail system and the **U-Bahn** subway system.

For help or tickets, skip the lines and head to the private **EurAide** agency (www.euraide.de), a travel agency staffed by English-speakers and geared toward helping rail-pass holders by selling tickets and supplements and helping you plan rail journeys from Munich (Room 3 next to Track 11). The office is open June through October 3 daily from 7:45 a.m. to noon and 1 to 6 p.m.; in winter, hours vary.

Orienting Yourself in Munich

Munich's major sights are not confined to its **Altstadt,** or old center, as in many European cities. Cultural attractions are spread across town.

Introducing the neighborhoods

The **Altstadt** is an oval-shaped pedestrian-only district on the west bank of the Isar River. Munich's **Hauptbahnhof** (main train station) lies just west of the Altstadt. **Marienplatz,** the Altstadt's most important square, is where you find several important churches, the **Residenz** (former royal palace), the **National Theater,** and the **Viktualienmarkt,** a wonderfully lively outdoor market. Between Marienplatz and the National Theater is the **Platzl** quarter, famed for its nightlife, restaurants, and the landmark **Hofbräuhaus,** the most famous beer hall in the world.

Odeonsplatz, to the north of Marienplatz, is Munich's most beautiful square. Running west from Odeonsplatz is Briennerstrasse, a wide shopping avenue that leads to **Königsplatz** (King's Square). Flanking this large square, in an area known as the **Museum Quarter,** are three neoclassical buildings constructed by Ludwig I and housing Munich's antiquities collections. Another triad of world-famous art museums — the **Alte Pinakothek** (Old Masters Gallery), the **Neue Pinakothek** (New Masters Gallery), and the **Pinakothek Moderne Kunst** (Gallery of Modern Art) — also lie in the Museum Quarter, just northeast of Königsplatz.

Ludwigstrasse connects the Altstadt with **Schwabing,** a former artists' quarter located north of the Altstadt and known for its cafes, restaurants, and nightlife. **Olympiapark,** site of the 1972 Olympics, is northwest of Schwabing. The sprawling park known as the **Englischer Garten** is located east of Schwabing. **Theresienwiese,** site of the annual Oktoberfest, and **Schloss Nymphenburg** (Nymphenburg Palace), one of Germany's most beautiful palaces, are both located west of the Altstadt.

Finding information after you arrive

The main tourist office, **Fremdenverkehrsamt** (☎ 089-2339-6500; www.muenchen.de), is at the Hauptbahnhof at the south exit opening onto Bayerstrasse. Open Monday through Saturday from 9 a.m. to 6:30 p.m. and Sunday from 10 a.m. to 6 p.m., it offers a free map of Munich and a **hotel booking service** (☎ 089-2339-6555). You can also get tourist information in the town center on Marienplatz inside the Rathaus Monday through Friday from 10 a.m. to 8 p.m. and Saturday from 10 a.m. to 4 p.m.

Getting around Munich

Munich is a large city and the best way to explore is by walking and using the excellent public transportation system. Subways **(U-Bahn)**, trams **(Strassenbahn)**, buses, and light-rail lines **(S-Bahn)** make getting anywhere in the city easy. In the Altstadt, you can walk to all the attractions — in fact you have to, because the Altstadt is a car-free zone. For information, call the public transportation authority, **MVV**, at ☎ 089-210-330, or visit them on the Web at www.mvv-muenchen.de.

Buses, trams, S-Bahns, and U-Bahns all use the same **tickets,** which you buy at machines marked FAHRKARTEN in S-Bahn/U-Bahn stations; the machines display instructions in English. You can also buy tickets in the tram or from a bus driver. Tickets must be **validated** in the machines found on platforms and in buses and trams: Stick your ticket into the machine, which stamps it with the date and time. A validated ticket is good for two hours. You can transfer as often as you like to any public transportation as long as you travel in the same direction.

Munich has four concentric fare zones. Most, if not all, of your sightseeing will take place in Zone 1, which includes the city center. A **single ticket** *(Einzelfahrkarte)* in Zone 1 costs 2.20€ ($3.50). (If you have a Eurail pass, you can use it on the S-Bahn.) A **day ticket** *(Tageskarte)* for unlimited trips within the inner zone costs 5€ ($8); a three-day ticket costs 13€ ($21).

By U-Bahn and S-Bahn (subway and light rail)

The **S-Bahn** is a state-run commuter train line that covers a wider area than the U-Bahn and is often aboveground; the **U-Bahn** runs mostly underground as a city subway. In the center of Munich, they're both subways, providing visitors with an overlapping, interchangeable set of networks. The major central U-Bahn/S-Bahn hubs are Hauptbahnhof, Karlsplatz, Marienplatz, Sendlingertor, and Odeonsplatz. The most useful of the U-Bahn lines (**U3** and **U6**) run north–south through the city center and stop at Sendlingertor, Marienplatz, and Odeonsplatz before going to Schwabing.

By tram and bus

Trams and buses are great for getting to a few areas within the Altstadt and for traveling out into greater Munich, but they're less effective at getting you where you want to go in the center of town. Tram no. 19 runs along Maximilianstrasse and the northern part of the Altstadt before heading to Hauptbahnhof. Tram no. 18 trundles from Hauptbahnhof through Sendlinger Top and Isartor right to the Deutsches Museum.

By taxi

With Munich's efficient public transportation system, you don't need to take taxis — and at their steep prices, you probably won't want to. The initial charge is 2.70€ ($4.30) and then 1.60€ ($2.55) for each kilometer up to 5, 1.40€ ($2.25) per kilometer for kilometers 5 through 10, and 1.25€ ($2) for each kilometer over 10. You're charged an extra 0.50€ (80¢) per bag for luggage. You can hail a cab on the street if the rooftop light is illuminated, or you call a taxi to pick you up by dialing ☎ 089-21-610, 089-19-410, or 089-450-540, but you'll pay 1€ ($1.60) more for the convenience.

Staying in Munich

Munich has a healthy supply of hotel rooms that serve a large tourist population, as well as a commercial and industrial trade. Unfortunately, year-round demand keeps prices high.

Rates in Munich rise when a trade fair is in town, during the summer tourist season, and during Oktoberfest. You'll want to book a room well in advance for the city's big keg party, or you'll pay high prices or end up a long way from the center — or both.

If you arrive in town without a hotel, the tourist office can land a room for you. Call them at ☎ 089-2339-6555, or see "Finding information after you arrive," earlier in this chapter, for locations.

Munich's top hotels

Bayerischer Hof
$$$$ Altstadt

This full-service luxury hotel dates from 1841 and has individually deco-rated rooms with large bathrooms, plus a health club with a pool and sauna. Rooms range from medium-size to extremely spacious, each with plush duvets; many beds are four-posters. Décor ranges from Bavarian provincial to British country-house chintz. The large bathrooms have tub/shower combos, private phones, and state-of-the-art luxuries.

See map p. 292. Promenadeplatz 2–6. ☎ *800-223-6800 in the U.S. or 089-21-200. Fax: 089-212-0906.* www.bayerischerhof.de. *Tram: 19. Rack rates: 245€–410€ ($392–$656) double. Champagne breakfast buffet 23€ ($37). AE, DC, MC, V.*

Hotel Am Markt
$ Altstadt

You may have to hunt to find this budget favorite near Munich's outdoor market. The owner keeps the place spotless, welcoming all sorts of visitors from families to students to stars of stage and opera. Rooms are sparse but functional, small but comfortable. This is one place that doesn't raise prices for Oktoberfest.

See map p. 292. Heiliggeistrasse 6 (a tiny alley between the Tal and the Viktualien-markt). ☎ 089-225-014. Fax: 089-224-017. www.hotelinmunich.de. *U-Bahn or S-Bahn: Marienplatz, and then walk under the arches of the Altes Rathaus, and the hotel is down the first right turn off the Tal. Rack rates: 69€–73€ ($110–$117) double without bathroom; 90€–99€ ($144–$158) double with bathroom. Rates include breakfast. MC, V.*

Hotel An der Oper
$$$ Altstadt

This five-story hotel, dating from 1969, is wonderfully situated for sight-seeing and shopping in the Altstadt. The décor is basic modern without being particularly distinguished. The 68 rooms are on the small side but have double-glazed windows and small sitting areas. The bathrooms are small, too, and come with showers.

See map p. 292. Falkenturmstrasse 10 (just off Maximilianstrasse, near Marienplatz). ☎ 089-290-0270. Fax: 089-2900-2729. www.hotelanderoper.com. *Tram: 19. Rates: 180€–270€ ($288–$432) double. Rates include breakfast. AE, MC, V.*

Hotel Opera
$$$$ Altstadt

A turn-of-the-20th-century Italianate building with a courtyard and garden houses this small, elegant, boutique hotel. The 25 distinctively decorated rooms have country antiques or a cool, modern look. Some of the rooms have small balconies. Rooms in the rear on the third and fourth floors are quieter but also smaller than those facing the street. The bathrooms have a tub and shower. The hotel is a short walk from chic Maximilianstrasse and several major attractions.

See map p. 292. St.-Anna-Strasse 10. ☎ 089-210-4940. Fax: 089-2104-0977. www.hotel-opera.de. *U-Bahn: Lehel. Rates: 190€–275€ ($304–$440) double. Rates include breakfast. AE, MC, V.*

Hotel Vier Jahreszeiten Kempinski München
$$$$$ Altstadt

This grand old hotel, built in 1858 for Maximilian II to accommodate the overflow of guests from his nearby Residenz, is worth the splurge if you appreciate discreet service, constantly renovated rooms, a rooftop pool, a bevy of fine restaurants, boutique shops, posh accommodations, and the

Accommodations, Dining, and Attractions in Munich

HOTELS ■
Advokat Hotel **34**
Bayerischer Hof **13**
Eden Hotel Wolff **10**
Gästehaus Englischer
  Garten **14**
Hotel Am Markt **32**
Hotel An der Oper **25**
Hotel Jedermann **8**
Hotel Opera **22**
Hotel Vier
  Jahreszeiten Kempinski
  München **23**
Platzl Hotel **33**

RESTAURANTS
Alois Dallmayr **20**
Augustinerkeller **9**
Boettner **24**
Donisl **27**
Halali **18**
Hirschgarten **3**
Hofbräuhaus am Platzl **29**
Nürnberger Bratwurst
  Glöckl am Dom **26**

ATTRACTIONS
Alte Pinakothek **12**
Altes Rathaus and
  Spielzeugmuseum **30**
Bayerisches
  Nationalmuseum **17**
Chinesischer Turm **15**
Cuvilliés Theater **19**
Deutsches Museum **35**
Englischer Garten **16**
Marienplatz **31**
Neue Pinakothek **11**
Neues Rathaus and
  Glockenspiel **28**
Residenz Palace **21**
Schloss Nymphenburg **1**

**SCHLOSS
NYMPHENBURG INSET**
Amalienburg **4**
Badenburg Pavilion **5**
Magdalenenklause **7**
Marstallmuseum **2**
Pagodenburg **6**

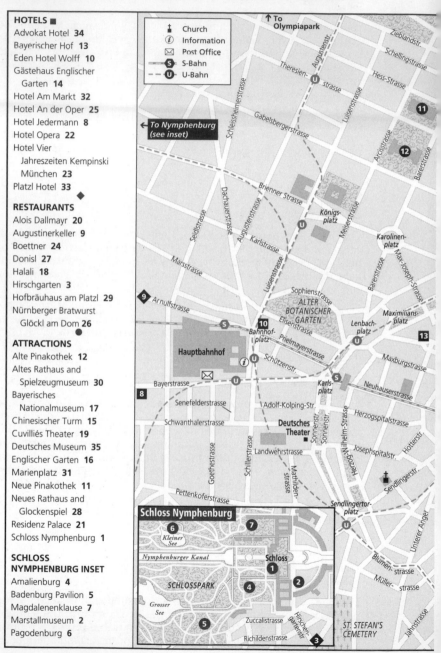

✝ Church
ⓘ Information
✉ Post Office
Ⓢ S-Bahn
Ⓤ U-Bahn

↑ To Olympiapark

← To Nymphenburg (see inset)

Zieblandstr.
Schellingstrasse
Theresien-strasse
Hess-Strasse
Schleissheimerstrasse
Gabelsbergerstrasse
Luisenstrasse
Arcisstrasse
Barerstrasse
Brienner Strasse
Dachauerstrasse
Augustenstrasse
Königs-platz
Meiserstrasse
Karolinen-platz
Seidlstrasse
Karlstrasse
Max-Joseph-Strasse
Marsstrasse
Luisenstrasse
Sophienstrasse
ALTER BOTANISCHER GARTEN
Elisenstrasse
Maximilians-platz
Lenbach-platz
Arnulfstrasse
Bahnhof-platz
Prielmayerstrasse
Hauptbahnhof
Schützenstr.
Maxburgstrasse
Bayerstrasse
Karls-platz
Neuhauserstrasse
Senefelderstrasse
Adolf-Kolping-Str.
Herzogspitalstrasse
Schwanthalerstrasse
Deutsches Theater
Sonnenstr.
Sonnenstr.
Josephspitalstr.
Hotterstr.
Goethestrasse
Schillerstrasse
Landwehrstrasse
Herzog-Wilhelm-Strasse
Pettenkoferstrasse
Mathilden-strasse
Sendlingerstr.
Sendlingertor-platz

Schloss Nymphenburg
Kleiner See
Nymphenburger Kanal
Schloss
SCHLOSSPARK
Grosser See
Zuccalistrasse
Richildenstrasse
Hirschgartenstr.
ST. STEFAN'S CEMETERY
Unterer Anger
Blumen-strasse
Müller-strasse
Jahnstrasse

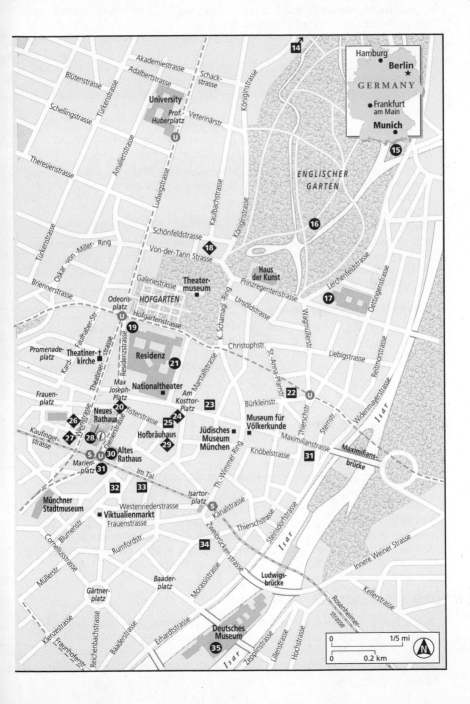

proximity of shopping, theater, and galleries. The least expensive rooms are in the uninteresting 1972 wing; if you're splurging anyway, go for the modern rooms in the original building. Check the Web site for special offers.

See map p. 292. Maximilianstrasse 17 (3 blocks from the Residenz and hard to miss). ☎ *800-426-3135* or *089-21-250. Fax: 089-2125-2000.* www.kempinski-vier jahreszeiten.de. *Tram: 19. Rates: 240€–490€ ($384–$784) double. AE, DC, MC, V.*

Munich's runner-up accommodations

Advokat Hotel

$$$ **Altstadt** This minimalist contemporary hotel sits comfortably between Isartorplatz and the river. *See map p. 292. Baaderstrasse 1.* ☎ *089-216-310.* www.hotel-advokat.de.

Eden Hotel Wolff

$$$ **Near train station** This large hotel across from the train station has been redone with a pleasantly modern look. Most of the 211 rooms are fairly large, and all are decorated in a comfortable, unobtrusive style. *See map p. 292. Arnulfstrasse 4.* ☎ *089-551-150.* www.ehw.de.

Gästehaus Englischer Garten

$$ **Schwabing** This 25-room guesthouse near the Englischer Garten is quiet, charming, and an excellent value. The rooms are small to medium in size and decorated with a homey mixture of antiques, old-fashioned beds, and Oriental rugs. *See map p. 292. Liebergesellstrasse 8.* ☎ *089-383-9410.* www.hotelenglischergarten.de.

Hotel Jedermann

$-$$ **Near train station** *Jedermann* means "everyman," and that translates here into affordable, family-friendly prices (as well as cribs and cots, adjoining rooms, and breakfast). This pleasant, family-run hotel offers a central location and 55 comfortable rooms, most with shower-only bathrooms. *See map p. 292. Bayerstrasse 95.* ☎ *089-543-240.* www.hotel-jedermann.de.

Platzl Hotel

$$-$$$$ **Altstadt** If you're looking for a gulp of old-fashioned Bavarian ambience, this "medieval" hotel, across from the Hofbräuhaus — Munich's famous beer hall — is one of the best choices in Munich. *See map p. 292. Sparkassenstrasse 10.* ☎ *089-237-030.* www.platzl.de.

Dining in Munich

Munich is a city that loves to eat, and eat big. Homemade dumplings are a specialty, as are all kinds of sausages and *Leberkäse,* a large loaf of sausage eaten with freshly baked pretzels and mustard. *Schweinbraten,* another Bavarian specialty, is a braised loin of pork served with potato dumplings and rich brown gravy. Filling the city are all kinds of fine restaurants, small cafes and bistros, and beer halls that serve food. Inexpensive sausages, soups, and snacks are sold from outdoor stalls all around the Viktualienmarkt, too.

Wurstel (sausages) come in many shapes, sizes, and stuffings. Look for *Bratwurst* (finger-sized seasoned pork), *Frankfurter* (the forerunner of hot dogs), *Blütwurst* (blood sausage), *Leberwurst* (liver), and, Munich's specialty, *Weisswurst* (veal, calf brains, and spleen, spiced to mild deliciousness and boiled). The proper way to eat *Weisswurst* is to cut it in half, dip the cut end in mustard, and suck the filling out of the casing in one fell slurp.

Another word you may see on menus is *Knödel,* which means "dumpling." *Knödel* may be made of *Semmel* (bread), *Leber* (liver), or *Kartoffel* (potato). You can usually get these specialties in a beer hall tavern, where people sit communally at big tables. The outdoor *Biergarten* is a wonderful Munich tradition. For more on this, see "More cool things to see and do," later in this chapter. If you want a refreshing nonalcoholic drink, served everywhere, ask for *Apfelsaftschorle,* apple juice mixed with sparkling water.

 Now about that beer. Munich is one of the world's beer capitals, and if you're a beer drinker, you'll definitely want to try light beer (*light* refers to the color, not the calories). You can get light beer in a giant liter-size mug called *ein Mass.* At Oktoberfest tents, if you order *ein Bier,* you usually get a half-liter; if you want the giant one, you need to order it by name.

Munich beer types include: *Weissbier* (made with wheat); *Pils* (ale); *Dunklesbier, Bock,* or *Dopplebock* (all dark beers); and the beer-and-lemonade spritzer called *Radlermass.* All beers are made under the strictest quality guidelines and almost never contain preservatives. *Helles* means light-colored beer; *dunkles* is dark beer.

Alois Dallmayr
$$–$$$$ Altstadt DELICATESSEN/CONTINENTAL

In business for almost 300 years, Alois Dallmayr is the most famous delicatessen in Germany, and one of the most elegant. Downstairs you can buy fine food products; upstairs in the dining rooms you can order a tempting array of dishes, including herring, sausages, smoked fish, and soups. A crowd always fills the restaurant at lunchtime. The informal cafe is much less expensive than the dressier restaurant.

See map p. 292. Dienerstrasse 14–15. ☎ *089-213-5100.* www.dallmayr.de. *Reservations recommended. U-Bahn or S-Bahn: Marienplatz. Main courses: Cafe 8.50€–19€ ($14–$30); restaurant 35€–44€ ($56–$70); fixed-price menu 59€–118€ ($94–$189). AE, DC, MC, V. Open: Cafe Mon–Sat 9:30 a.m.–7 p.m.; restaurant Tues–Sat noon to 2 p.m. and 7–10 p.m.*

Boettner
$$$$$ Near the Residenz   INTERNATIONAL

Boettner, with its famous wood-paneled interior and inspired international cuisine, remains one of the most popular restaurants in town. The food here has a lighter but still rich touch, mixing seafood and truffles into the general Franco-Bavarian mélange of ingredients. Fresh asparagus, available in the spring, is a noteworthy entree. It'll be difficult, but try to save room for dessert; your taste buds will thank you.

See map p. 292. Pfisterstrasse 9 (off Platzl square just north of the Hofbräuhaus). ☎ *089-221-210. Reservations strongly recommended. U-Bahn or S-Bahn: Marienplatz. Main courses: 25€–50€ ($40–$80). AE, DC, MC, V. Open: Mon–Sat 11:30 a.m.–3 p.m. and 6–10 p.m.*

Donisl
$$ On Marienplatz   BAVARIAN/INTERNATIONAL

Munich's oldest beer hall has summer tables outside and skylit, pine-paneled galleries inside. The Bavarian cuisine menu features the traditional *Weisswurst* (spicy pork sausage), but the restaurant also serves specials that draw from many culinary traditions (when the chef offers duck, dive for it). An accordion player makes the atmosphere feel that much more Bavarian.

See map p. 292. Weinstrasse 1 (just above Marienplatz). ☎ *089-220-184.* www. bayerischer-donisl.de. *Reservations recommended. U-Bahn or S-Bahn: Marienplatz. Main courses: 8€–17€ ($13–$27). AE, DC, MC, V. Open: Daily 9 a.m. to midnight.*

Halali
$$$ North of the Residenz   FINE BAVARIAN

Refined, but still traditionally Bavarian, Halali features a candlelit dining room decorated with stag's horns to add authenticity to the overall hunting motif. The restaurant serves popular Bavarian dishes — *Blütwurst* (blood sausage), venison, and other game — but with delicate flavors and attractive presentations. Red wine, not beer, is the beverage of choice in this upscale eatery.

See map p. 292. Schönfeldstrasse 22 (3 long blocks north of Odeonsplatz). ☎ *089-285-909. Reservations required. U-Bahn: Odeonsplatz. Main courses: 15€–27€ ($24–$43); fixed-price menu 25€–50€ ($40–$80). AE, MC, V. Open: Mon–Fri noon to 3 p.m.; Mon–Sat 6 p.m. to midnight.*

Hofbräuhaus am Platzl
$–$$ Altstadt   GERMAN

A boisterous atmosphere prevails in Munich's huge and world-famous beer hall. In the tap room on the ground floor, you sit on benches at wooden tables as a brass band plays; a big courtyard occupies this level, too. Upstairs are a number of smaller, quieter dining rooms. The beer is

Hofbrau, which is served by the "mass," equal to about a quart. The food is heavy and hearty, with a menu that includes several sausages, *Schweinsbraten* (roasted pork), *Spanferkel* (roast suckling pig), and stuffed cabbage rolls. Everything on the menu is translated into English.

See map p. 292. Am Platzl 9. ☎ *089-290-1360. U-Bahn or S-Bahn: Marienplatz. Main courses: 5€–12€ ($8–$19). No credit cards. Open: Daily 9 a.m. to midnight.*

Nürnberger Bratwurst Glöckl am Dom
$$ Near Marienplatz   BAVARIAN

This place is our choice for best traditional Munich beer-hall grub. You can't get any more Bavarian than rustic dark-wood tables and carved chairs and tin plates full of wurstel. Since 1893, this place has served up the finger-size sausage specialty of nearby Nürnburg. A platter of assorted wursts, a pretzel, and a tankard of Augustiner Bollbier or Tucher Weissbier make the perfect meal.

See map p. 292. Frauenplatz 9 (off the back end of the cathedral). ☎ *089-291-9450.* www.bratwurst-gloeckl.de. *Reservations recommended. U-Bahn or S-Bahn: Marienplatz. Main courses: 6€–13€ ($9.60–$21). No credit cards. Open: Daily 9:30 a.m. to midnight.*

Exploring Munich

If you're planning to visit two or three of Munich's famous art museums, you'll save money with a two-day **combined ticket,** available Monday through Saturday for 9€ ($14) adults, 6€ ($9.60) seniors and students. The ticket gets you into both the **Alte** and **Neue Pinakothek,** as well as the **Pinakothek der Moderne** of 20th-century art, Barerstrasse 40 (☎ 089-2380-5360; www.pinakothek.de/pinakothek-der-moderne), which otherwise charges 9.50€ ($15) admission. On Sundays, admission to several of Munich's top museums is reduced to 1€ ($1.60).

Munich's top sights

Alte Pinakothek (Old Masters Gallery)

Pinakothek means "painting gallery," and the nearly 800 paintings on display in this enormous building represent the greatest European artists of the 14th through the 18th centuries. You'll find paintings by Italian Renaissance artists Giotto, Filippo Lippi, Botticelli, Leonardo da Vinci *(Madonna and Child),* Raphael *(Holy Family),* Titian *(Christ with the Crown of Thorns* is one of his most mature works), and Tintoretto. The Dutch and Germans are well represented here, with Albrecht Dürer's *Self Portrait* (from around 1500) acting as the centerpiece of the collection. Many artists before Dürer painted themselves into the background or crowds in large works as a kind of signature, but Dürer was the first to make himself, the artist, the star of the show. Prior to this portrait, full frontal portraiture had been used only to portray Christ.

The museum is so immense that you could easily spend several days exploring. To make the most of your time, pick up a museum guide at the information desk, decide which paintings you particularly want to see, and then spend at least two to three hours. A free audio tour in English is available in the lobby, and free tours highlighting various parts of the vast collection take place on Monday at 3 p.m. and Wednesday at 6:30 p.m.

See map p. 292. Barer Strasse 27 (off Theresienstrasse). ☎ *089-2380-5216.* www. pinakothek.de/alte-pinakothek. *Tram: 27 to Pinakothek. Admission: Mon–Sat 5.50€ ($8.80) adults, 4€ ($6.40) seniors and students, free for children 14 and under; Sun 1€ ($1.60). Open: Tues–Sun 10 a.m.–6 p.m. (until 8 p.m. Tues).*

Bayerisches Nationalmuseum (Bavarian National Museum)

This museum contains three vast floors of sculpture, painting, folk art, ceramics, furniture, and textiles, as well as clocks and scientific instruments. The objects on view are among Bavaria's greatest historic and artistic treasures. A major highlight is the **Riemenschneider Room,** which contains works in wood by the great sculptor Tilman Riemenschneider (1460–1531). The museum also contains a famous collection of Christmas Nativity cribs from Bavaria, Tyrol, and southern Italy. Give yourself at least an hour just to cover the highlights.

See map p. 292. Prinzregentenstrasse 3 (off the southeast corner of the Englischer Garten). ☎ *089-211-2401.* www.bayerisches-nationalmuseum.de. *U-Bahn: U4 or U5 to Lehel. Tram: 20. Bus: 53. Admission: Tues–Sat 5€ ($8) adults, 4€ ($6.40) seniors and students; Sun 1€ ($1.60). Open: Tues–Sun 10 a.m.–5 p.m. (until 8 p.m. Thurs).*

Deutsches Museum (German Museum of Science and Technology)

Located on the Museumsinsel, an island in the Isar River, this is the largest science and technology museum in the world and one of the most popular attractions in Germany. Its huge collection of scientific and technological treasures includes the first electric locomotive (1879); the first electric generator, called a *dynamo* (1866); the first automobile (1886); the first diesel engine (1897); and the laboratory bench at which the atom was first split (1938). This hands-on, kid-friendly museum has interactive exhibits and an English-speaking staff to answer questions and demonstrate glass blowing, papermaking, and how steam engines, pumps, and historical musical instruments work.

The **Automobile** department in the basement is noteworthy, with a collection of luxury Daimler, Opel, and Bugatti vehicles. On display in the **Aeronautics** section is a biplane flown by the Wright brothers in 1908, the first airliner (1919), and an assortment of military aircraft. Spending half a day here is easy.

The Deutsches Museum is one of the few museums in Munich that is open on Monday.

See map p. 292. Museuminsel 1 (on an island in the Isar river). ☎ *089-21-791.* www.deutsches-museum.de. *U-Bahn: U1 or U2 to Fraunhoferstrasse. S-Bahn:*

Isartorplatz. Tram: 18. Admission: 8.50€ ($14) adults, 3€ ($4.80) children 6 and older, free for children 5 and under, 17€ ($27) families. Open: Daily 9 a.m.–5 p.m.

Marienplatz

This large pedestrian-only square (see map p. 292) in the heart of the Altstadt is also the old heart of Munich. Chances are, you'll return here again and again, because many of the city's attractions are clustered in the vicinity. On the north side of Marienplatz is the **Neues Rathaus** (New City Hall), built in 19th-century neo-Gothic style and famous for its **Glockenspiel,** the mechanical clock that performs a miniature tournament several times a day (daily at 11 a.m., noon, and 5 p.m. Mar–Oct). You can take an elevator to the top of the Rathaus's tower for a good view of the city center (open Apr–Oct daily 10 a.m.–7 p.m., Nov–Mar Mon–Fri 10 a.m.–5 p.m.); admission is 4.50€ ($7.20) adults, 0.75€ ($1.20) children 6 to 18. To the right of the Neues Rathaus stands the **Altes Rathaus** (Old City Hall), with its plain, 15th-century Gothic tower. Inside is the **Spielzeugmuseum** (☎ 089-294-001), a historical toy collection (open daily 10 a.m.–5:30 p.m.); admission is 2.50€ ($4) adults, 0.50€ (80¢) children.

See map p. 292. In the center of the Altstadt. U-Bahn or S-Bahn: Marienplatz.

Neue Pinakothek (New Art Museum)

Housed in a postmodern building cross from the Altes Pinakothek, the Neue Pinakothek showcases 19th-century German and European art, starting right around 1800. Artists whose works are on view include Thomas Gainsborough, Joshua Reynolds, William Turner, Francesco Goya, Caspar David Friedrich, Vincent van Gogh, and Paul Gauguin, among many others. A tour of the highlights takes a couple of hours; an audio tour in English is free with your admission.

See map p. 292. Barer Strasse 29 (off Theresienstrasse). ☎ 089-2380-5195. www. pinakothek.de/neue-pinakothek. Tram: 27 to Pinakothek (the museum entrance is across the street). Admission: 5.50€ ($8.80) adults, 4€ ($6.40) seniors and students, 1€ ($1.60) Sun. Open: Wed–Mon 10 a.m.–6 p.m. (until 8 p.m. Wed).

Residenz Palace

This magnificent building was the official residence of the Wittelsbach family, the rulers of Bavaria, from 1385 to 1918. Added to and rebuilt over the centuries, the palace is a compendium of various architectural styles, including German and Florentine Renaissance, and Palladian. Artisans painstakingly restored the Rezidenz, which was almost totally destroyed in World War II. The must-sees are the **Residenz Museum,** with arts and furnishings displayed in some 130 rooms; the **Schatzkammer** (Treasury), with three centuries' worth of accumulated treasures, including the Bavarian crown jewels; and the **Altes Residenztheater,** a stunning rococo theater. You enter both the Residenz Museum and the Schatzkammer from Max-Joseph-Platz on the south side of the palace. On the north side of the palace is the Italianate **Hofgarten** (Court Garden), laid out between 1613 and 1617.

The Residenz is so big that they open separate sets of rooms in the morning (10 a.m.–2:30 p.m. for Circular Tour I) and the afternoon (12:30–4 p.m. for Circular Tour II).

Around the corner is the beautiful **Cuvilliés Theater,** named after its architect, a former court jester who became one of southern Germany's most important architects. Enjoy concerts and opera here in summer; Mozart's *Idomeneo* premiered here in 1781. It's also called the **Residenztheater.**

See map p. 292. Max Joseph Platz 3. ☎ 089-290-671. www.schloesser.bayern. de. *Tram: 19 to Nationaltheater (the palace is on the same square as the theater). U-Bahn: Odeonsplatz (the palace is southeast across the square). Admission: Combined ticket for Residenz Museum and Schatzkammer 9€ ($14) adults, 8€ ($13) students and children; Residenztheater 3€ ($4.80) adults, 2€ ($3.20) students and children. Open: Apr–Oct 15 daily 9 a.m.–6 p.m.; Oct 16–Mar daily 10 a.m.–4 p.m.*

Schloss Nymphenburg

Schloss Nymphenburg, the Wittelsbach family's summer residence, is one of the most sophisticated and beautiful palaces in Europe. Begun in 1664, the palace took more than 150 years to complete. In the first of its four pavilions you come to the **Great Hall,** decorated in a vibrant splash of rococo colors and stuccowork. In the south pavilion, you find Ludwig I's famous **Gallery of Beauties** with paintings by J. Stieler (1827–1850). The beauties include Lola Montez, the raven-haired dancer whose affair with Ludwig caused a scandal.

To the south of the palace buildings, in the rectangular block of low structures that once housed the court stables, is the **Marstallmuseum,** where you find a dazzling collection of ornate, gilded coaches and sleighs, including those used by Ludwig II. The **Porzellansammlung** (Porcelain Collection; entrance across from the Marstallmuseum) contains superb pieces of 18th-century porcelain.

A canal runs through the 500-acre **Schlosspark,** stretching all the way to the far end of the formal, French-style gardens. In the English-style park, full of quiet meadows and forested paths, you find the **Badenburg Pavilion,** with an 18th-century swimming pool; the **Pagodenburg,** decorated in the Chinese style that was all the rage in the 18th century; and the **Magdalenenklause** (Hermitage), meant to be a retreat for prayer and solitude. Prettiest of all the buildings in the park is **Amalienburg,** built in 1734 as a hunting lodge for Electress Amalia; the interior salons are a riot of flamboyant colors, swirling stuccowork, and wall paintings. From central Munich, you can easily reach the palace by tram in about 20 minutes. You need at least half a day to explore the buildings and grounds.

A factory on the grounds of Schloss Nymphenburg still produces the famous Nymphenburg porcelain. **Porzellan-Manufaktur-Nymphenburg,** Nördliches Schlossrondell 8 (☎ 089-179-1970), has a sales room and exhibition center open Monday through Friday from 8:30 a.m. to 5 p.m.

See map p. 292. Schloss Nymphenburg 1 (8km/5 miles northwest of the city center). Tram: 12, 16, or 17 to Romanplatz, and then walk 10 minutes west to the palace

About Oktoberfest

For about three weeks starting in mid-September, tens of thousands of people converge on Munich to partake of the legendary Oktoberfest (www.muenchen.de). What is it, exactly? Well, sort of a giant keg party with oompah bands, food, and drunken revelry that's not always pretty to watch. Some 5 million liters of beer are reputedly quaffed during Oktoberfest, which started in 1810 as a celebration for Prince Ludwig's marriage to Princess Therese. Most of the action centers on the Theresienwiese park fairgrounds, southwest of Hauptbahnhof, but the whole city has a distinct party air (just follow the smell of the beer). You must reserve a hotel room months in advance.

entrance. ☎ *089-179-080.* www.schloesser.bayern.de. *Admission: Palace grounds free; all attractions 10€ ($16) adults, 8€ ($13) seniors, free for children 6 and under. Open: Apr 1–Oct 15 daily 9 a.m.–6 p.m.; Oct 16–Mar 31 daily 10 a.m.–4 p.m. Badenburg and Magdalenenklause closed Oct 16–Mar 31.*

More cool things to see and do

✔ **Eating lunch at a Biergarten:** Bring your own food, and order mugs of beer. Biergartens are generally open from 10 a.m. to 10 p.m. or midnight. They usually offer simple sandwiches, and pretzels and other snacks are always available. Try these Biergartens: the **Biergarten Chinesischer Turm** (☎ 089-383-8730), in the heart of the Englischer Garten Park beneath a Chinese pagoda; the **Augustinerkeller,** Arnulfstrasse 52 (☎ 089-594-393; www.augustinerkeller.de), several long blocks past Hauptbahnhof; and the **Hirschgarten** (☎ 089-172-591; www.hirschgarten.de), in Nymphenburg Park, the world's largest beer garden, with room for 8,000 guzzlers.

✔ **Spending an afternoon in the Englischer Garten:** Munich's famous city park is one of the largest (373 hectares/922 acres) and most beautiful city parks in Europe. Established in 1789, the Englischer Garten is also the oldest public park in the world. You can wander for hours along the tree-shaded walks, streams, and lake, and admire the view of Munich's Altstadt from the round, hilltop temple called the Monopteros, constructed in the 19th century. The banks of the Eisbach, the stream that runs through the park, are popular nude-sunbathing spots. A giant beer garden occupies the plaza near the **Chinesischer Turm** (Chinese Tower).

Guided tours

Gray Line Tours (☎ 089-5490-7560; www.grayline.com) offers two standard orientation bus tours. If your time is limited, the Express Tour is a straightforward affair — just hop on in front of Hauptbahnhof and buy your 13€ ($21) ticket onboard. The hour-long tour is delivered in eight languages; departures are every 20 minutes daily until 5 p.m. (until 4 p.m. Nov–Mar).

The longer 2½-hour, 18€ ($29) Grand Circle tour offers the same hop-on/hop-off privileges but goes farther afield to Schloss Nymphenburg and the Olympic Area, where you can climb its 292.6m (960-ft.) Olympic Tower. Gray Line also runs half- and full-day guided tours to the castle of Neuschwanstein.

Munich Walk Tours (☎ 0171-274-0204; www.munichwalktours.de), con- ducted in English, are a great way to acquaint yourself with Munich's his- tory and architecture. The company offers several options; the meeting point for all walks is the Neue Rathaus, directly under the Glockenspiel on Marienplatz. No need to reserve; you pay the guide (identifiable by a yellow sign). The 2¼-hour City Walk Tour starts daily at 10:45 a.m., with an additional walk at 2:45 p.m. daily from May through mid-October and Friday and Saturday year-round. The cost for each tour is 10€ ($16).

Perhaps the most enjoyable way to see town is with the English-speaking ex-pats at **Mike's Bike Tours** (☎ 089-2554-3988 or 0172-852-0660; www. mikesbiketours.com). Mike's offers four-hour, 24€ ($38; price includes bike) spins around the sights of central Munich (including 45 minutes in a beer garden). The daily tours leave at 12:30 p.m. in March through mid-April and September through November 10; from mid-April through August, they depart daily at 11:30 a.m. and 4 p.m. All tours meet 15 min- utes before setting off, under the tower of the Altes Rathaus on Marienplatz.

Suggested itineraries

If you're the type who likes to strike out on your own, this section offers tips for building your own Munich itinerary.

If you have one day

Start the day off with a tour of the **Residenz Palace,** the most impressive downtown palace in Europe. Visit the Old Masters paintings in the **Alte Pinakothek** before heading down to **Marienplatz** around noon to take in the clock-tower show and enjoy a late lunch in a beer hall or (if it's summer) the Biergarten in the middle of the Viktualienmarkt.

Enjoy the displays in the **Bayerisches Nationalmuseum** after lunch, and then set off for what everyone really comes to Munich for: drinking enor- mous tankards of beer. Have dinner downstairs in **Nürnberger Bratwurst Glöckl am Dom** — or just nibble on wurstel as you crawl from beer hall to beer hall.

If you have two days

Spend Day 1 as described in the preceding section. On the morning of Day 2, head out to **Schloss Nymphenburg** for more royal splendor. In the late afternoon, stroll the **Englischer Garten** (look for the modern art galleries that ring its southern edge), or investigate the scientific wonders of the **Deutsches Museum.**

If you have three days

Spend Days 1 and 2 as described in the previous sections. On the morning of Day 3, head out of town, either to the somber concentration-camp museum at **Dachau** or, if you get an early start, to see Mad King Ludwig's fantastical **Neuschwanstein** castle. Depending on what time you get back into town, wind down with one last stein of beer at one of the Biergartens mentioned earlier in this chapter.

Traveling beyond Munich

The Bavarian Alps is a region of spectacular scenery; any trip from Munich into the surrounding countryside is bound to be unforgettable. In addition to the excursions mentioned here, Munich is just two to three hours away from **Innsbruck** by train. Innsbruck is covered as an excursion from Vienna, Austria, in Chapter 16.

Neuschwanstein: Mad King Ludwig's fairy-tale castle

Ever wonder where Walt Disney got the idea for Cinderella Castle at his theme parks? He drew direct inspiration — and even consulted some original blueprints — from Bavaria's storybook castle, Neuschwanstein.

King Ludwig II — in many ways the epitome of a 19th-century German Romantic — built or renovated many a castle for himself. But the only project that would completely satisfy his restless, reckless nature was to create a castle that looked like something from a story by the Brothers Grimm.

Neuschwanstein was the result and is still a stunning, dreamlike sight, perched halfway up a forested mountain near a waterfall. The structure features slender towers, ramparts, and pointy turrets done in pale gray. Sadly, the castle was never quite finished, and the king got to live in his half-completed fantasy for only 170 days before his mysterious death. (Some say he committed suicide; others say that he was murdered.)

Getting there and buying tickets

From Munich, you can visit Neuschwanstein in a day, but you may find it more relaxing to stay overnight in the nearby town of Füssen and trek to Neuschwanstein from there. As Bavaria's biggest tourist draw, Neuschwanstein is packed by 9 a.m., and the crowd doesn't thin out until 4 p.m. or so. (In summer, you may have to wait a couple of hours just to take the 35-minute tour.) You can't avoid the crowds, but you can take a late train into Füssen the night before in order to arrive at Neuschwanstein with the first tourist wave.

This trip is most easily made by car, but you can also use **public transportation** from Munich. Take one of the nearly hourly trains to Füssen (a two-hour trip), from which hourly buses make the ten-minute trip to the castle parking lot. A much easier way to get there is by the 10½-hour Linderhof/Neuschwanstein **bus tour** offered by Gray Line Tours (☎ 089-5490-7560; www.grayline.com), which leaves Munich daily April through October at 8:30 a.m. and costs 49€ ($78) plus admission to the castles (Linderhof is another of Ludwig's castles).

When driving into this castle complex (Neuschwanstein and the adjacent castle of Hohenschwangau are usually referred to on road signs as *Königsschlösser,* or "Royal Palaces"), you have your choice of **parking lots** in Schwangau, that little tourist center by the lake. Park in Lot D for the quickest (but steepest) walk up to Neuschwanstein (20–30 minutes). Go farther down the road to the big lot on the right if you want to take the longer (but less steep) paved road up (30–45 minutes). It's a fairly strenuous hike either way.

A **ticket office** (☎ 0836-930-830) near the parking lot of the castles sells tickets for both Hohenschwangau and Neuschwanstein. You can see the castles only on guided tours, which last about 35 minutes each. Tours in English are available throughout the day. A **combined "Kings Ticket"** lets you visit both castles for 17€ ($27) adults, 15€ ($24) seniors and students. Individual tickets are 9€ ($14) adults, 8€ ($13) seniors and students, free children 17 and under. You can order tickets online at www.ticket-center-hohenschwangau.de. Neuschwanstein is open April through September daily 9 a.m. to 6 p.m., October through March daily 10 a.m. to 4 p.m.; Hohenschwangau closes a half-hour earlier.

For the easiest route from the ticket office up to Neuschwanstein's entrance, take the **shuttle bus** that leaves from near Hotel Lisl, overshoots the castle, and stops at Marienbrücke, a bridge across the gorge above Neuschwanstein (2€/$3.20 uphill, 1€/$1.60 downhill, or 3€/$4.80 round-trip). This lets you walk (steeply) back downhill in ten minutes to the castle and gives you a great view of the castle with Alpsee Lake in the background. **Horse-drawn carriages** leave from the Müller Hotel (5€/$8 uphill, 2.50€/$4 downhill).

Seeing the sights

The tour of **Neuschwanstein** (www.neuschwanstein.de) shows you some of the castle's most theatrical details, including the king's bedroom — almost every inch covered in intricately carved wood — his neo-Byzantine-Romanesque Throne Room, and the huge Singers Hall, covered with paintings that refer to the work of composer Richard Wagner.

Ludwig was enthralled by Wagner's music; he supposedly convulsed and writhed in such bliss to the strains of the composer's operas that his aides feared he was having an epileptic fit. Ludwig bailed Wagner out of debt and poured money into whatever project the composer desired.

This was the sort of thing that earned Ludwig II the moniker "Mad King Ludwig," but the monarch probably wasn't certifiable. Although beloved by his subjects as a genial and well-meaning ruler, Ludwig's withdrawal into his fantasies caused him to lose touch with his court and the political machinations in Munich. In 1886, he was deposed in absentia, and a few days later his body was found drowned, under suspicious circumstances, in a few feet of water at the edge of a lake.

At the bottom of Neuschwanstein's hill is the tiny village/parking lot of Schwangau, which serves as a lunch stop for tour-bus crowds. Across the road and up a short hill is **Hohenschwangau** (☎ **08362-930-830;** www.hohenschwangau.de), a sandy-colored castle restored in neo-Gothic style by Ludwig's father (Maximilian II). By comparison to Neuschwanstein, it's almost ordinary, but tours (usually in German, unless enough English speakers show up) can prove interesting. Ludwig made his home in Hohenschwangau for 17 years.

The Nazi concentration camp at Dachau

In 1933, in a little town outside Munich called Dachau, SS leader Heinrich Himmler set up Nazi Germany's first concentration camp. Between 1933 and 1945, 206,000 prisoners were officially registered here, and countless thousands more were interned without record. Spending an hour or two at Dachau is a sobering experience, to say the least — here you confront the darkest side of Germany's history.

Getting there

To get to Dachau from Munich, take a 20-minute ride on the S2 **S-Bahn train** from Marienplatz. From Dachau station, bus no. 724 or 726 takes you to the camp. For information on the town, visit www.dachau.info; for information on the concentration-camp memorial site, call ☎ **08131-669-970** or visit www.kz-gedenkstaette-dachau.de. **Gray Line Tours** (☎ **089-5490-7560;** www.grayline.com) in Munich leaves from the Bahnhofplatz at Herties Department Store for a 4½-hour tour of Dachau (25€/$40) from mid-May through mid-October on Saturdays at 1:30 p.m.

Seeing the sights

The taunting Nazi slogan *Arbeit Macht Frei* (Work Brings Freedom) is inscribed on the gate where you enter. Allied troops razed the 32 prisoners' barracks to the ground when they liberated the camp in 1945, but two have been reconstructed to illustrate the squalid living conditions. Each barrack was built to house 208 people; by 1936, they accommodated up to 1,600 each.

In 2002, parts of the Dachau Concentration Camp Memorial were redesigned to focus on the fate of the prisoners and to integrate the still-existing historic buildings into the reworked permanent exhibition. Visitors now follow the route of the prisoners, enter rooms in which citizens were stripped of all their belongings and rights, and where, after disinfecting, they were given a striped prison uniform. Inscribed boards show the rooms' original conditions and functions. Captions are in German and English.

The former kitchen is now a museum with photographs documenting the rise of the Nazis and the persecution of Jews, communists, Gypsies, homosexuals, and others. You can watch a short documentary film (the English version usually shows at 11:30 a.m. and 3:30 p.m.).

The ovens of the crematorium and a gas chamber disguised as showers are at the back of the camp. No prisoners were gassed at Dachau (though more than 3,000 Dachau inmates were sent to an Austrian camp to be gassed); this room was used for beatings and cruel interrogations. Although Dachau, unlike other camps such as Auschwitz in Poland, was primarily for political prisoners and not expressly a death camp, more than 32,000 people died here, and thousands more were executed. The camp is scattered with Jewish, Catholic, and Protestant memorials.

The camp is open Tuesday through Sunday from 9 a.m. to 5 p.m.; admission is free; 2½-hour guided tours (3€/$4.80) are conducted in English at 12:30 p.m. (also at 11 a.m. Sat–Sun in summer).

Fast Facts: Munich

American Express

American Express has an office at Promenadeplatz 6 (☎ 089-2280-1465) open Monday through Friday from 9 a.m. to 6 p.m. and Saturday from 9:30 a.m. to 12:30 p.m.

Area Code

Germany's country code is **49**. The city code for Munich is **089**. If you're calling Munich from outside Germany, drop the city code's initial 0. In other words, to call Munich from the United States, dial 011-49-89 and the number.

Currency

The Deutsche Mark gave way to the euro in 2002. The euro is divided into 100 cents, with .01, .02, .05, .10, .20, .50, 1€, and 2€ coins. Paper-note denominations are 5, 10, 20, 50, 100, 200, and 500 euros. The exchange rate used in this chapter is 1€ = $1.60. Amounts over $10 have been rounded to the nearest dollar.

Doctors and Dentists

The American, British, and Canadian consulates keep a list of recommended English-speaking physicians. For emergency doctor service, call ☎ 089-551-771 or 01805-191-212. For an English-speaking dentist, try the Gemeinschaftspraxis (Partnership Practice for Dentistry), Rosenkavalierplatz 18 (☎ 089-928-7840).

Embassies and Consulates

The U.S. Consulate, Königstrasse 5 (☎ 089-28-880; www.usembassy.de), is open Monday through Friday from 1 to 4 p.m. A Consulate General Office for the United Kingdom is located at Bürkleinstrasse 10, 80538 (☎ 089-21-10-90). Canada maintains a consulate at Tal 29, 80331 (☎ 089-2-19-95-70). The Australian government does not maintain an office in Munich, but if you need assistance, contact their consulate in Berlin at Wallstrasse 76-79 10179 (☎ 030-8-80-08-80). New Zealand's embassy is also in Berlin, Friedrichstrasse 60 (☎ 030-20-62-10).

Emergency

For an ambulance, call ☎ 112. For emergency doctor service, phone ☎ 089-551-771 or 01805-191-212. Call the police at ☎ 110. Report a fire at ☎ 112.

Hospitals

Munich's main hospitals are the Red Cross Hospital in Neuhausen (Ärztliche Bereitschaftspraxis im Rotkreuz Krankenhaus), Nymphenburger Strasse 163 (☎ 089-1278-9790), and the Schwabing Hospital (Ärztliche Bereitschaftspraxis im Krankenhaus Schwabing), Kölner Platz 1 (☎ 089-3304-0302).

Information

For specifics on Munich's tourist information offices, see "Finding information after you arrive," near the beginning of this chapter.

Internet Access and Cybercafes

You can send e-mails or check your messages at the Times Square Online Bistro, Bayerstrasse 10A (☎ 089-550-8800), open daily from 7 a.m. to 1 a.m. There's an easyInternet cafe (☎ 089-260-0230) with more than 450 terminals across from the main train station at Bahnhofplatz 1. It's open daily from 6 a.m. to 1.a.m.

Maps

The center of Munich is pretty small, so the map the tourist office gives out should serve you just fine.

Newspapers and Magazines

The tourist office hands out a monthly events calendar called *Monatsprogramm*. You may also want to pick up the ex-pat magazine *Munich Found* (www.munichfound.de) — full of events, news, and articles of interest to foreigners in Munich — on newsstands.

Pharmacies

Apotheke (pharmacies) in Munich rotate the duty of staying open nights and weekends. For the location of the nearest 24-hour pharmacy, check the sign in the window of any pharmacy. The International Ludwigs-Apotheke, Neuhauser Strasse 11 (☎ 089-1894-0300), is open Monday through Friday from 9 a.m. to 8 p.m. and Saturday from 9 a.m. to 4 p.m.

Police

Call the police at ☎ 110.

Post Office

A large post office is at Bahnhofplatz 1 (☎ 089-599-0870; www.deutschepost.de), across from the train station, and is open Monday through Friday from 7 a.m. to 8 p.m., Saturday from 9 a.m. to 4 p.m., and Sunday from 9 a.m. to 3 p.m.

Safety

You probably don't have to worry about violent crime, but you should be alert to possible pickpockets or purse-snatchers in popular areas such as the Marienplatz and around the Hauptbahnhof, especially at night.

Taxes

In Germany, a 16 percent value-added tax (VAT) is figured into the price of most items. Foreign visitors can reclaim a percentage of the VAT on purchases of 25€ ($40) or more in a single store (see Chapter 4).

Taxis

See "Getting Around Munich," earlier in this chapter.

Telephone

Pay phones in Munich take phone cards, which are available in various denominations from newsstands. To charge your call to a calling card, you can call AT&T (☎ 0800-225-5288), MCI (☎ 0800-888-8000), or Sprint (☎ 0800-888-0013). To call the United States direct, dial 001 followed by the area code and phone number.

Transit Info

For public transportation information, visit www.mvv-muenchen.de. For train info, visit www.bahn.de. For more, see "Getting Around Munich," earlier in this chapter.

Chapter 16

Vienna and the Best of Austria

. . . .

. . . .

More than any other European city, Vienna maintains a link with the past. In attitude, architecture, and interior décor, Vienna still reverberates with the stately elegance of the Hapsburg Dynasty, which ruled the Austro-Hungarian Empire in the 18th and 19th centuries. The city on the Danube is pure refinement: Its imperial palaces and art museums delight, its rococo churches and ornate beer taverns excite, and its nostalgic cafes and awe-inspiring concert halls thrill.

Vienna lays claim to one of Europe's richest and most varied musical heritages. The birthplace of the waltz, it's home to the likes of Mozart, Haydn, Beethoven, Schubert, the Strauss family, Brahms, Mahler, and the Vienna Boys' Choir. Plan for at least two or three days in Vienna — or slightly longer to take in all the sights and give yourself time just to walk, sample delectable pastries, and people-watch in a fantastic capital that stands at the crossroads of Europe.

Getting to Vienna

Vienna lies a brief five-hour train ride from both Munich and Prague, making the city a convenient destination to reach by air or rail. Once here, you'll find that most attractions are concentrated in a small part of the city center.

Arriving by air

Wien Schwechat airport (☎ 01-70-070; www.viennaairport.com) is 19km (12 miles) southeast of the city. If you're traveling with your own

Austria

laptop, you'll be able to take advantage of several wireless hot spots throughout the airport. The information desk is located in the arrivals hall, where there are also two ATMs.

The **City Airport Train** (☎ **01-25-250;** www.cityairporttrain.com) connects the terminal with Wien Mitte train station in just 16 minutes for 8€ ($13). Buses (☎ **01-930-000**) cost 6€ ($9.60), leave every 20 minutes, and stop in the center at Südtiroler Platz (20 minutes), Südbahnhof (25 minutes), and Westbahnhof (35 minutes). The S7 S-Bahn service is the cheapest (3€/$4.80) but also the slowest (35 minutes or more). It leaves every 30 minutes for stops at Wien Mitte and Wien Nord.

Arriving by rail

By train, you arrive in Vienna at **Westbahnhof** from northern Europe or **Südbahnhof** from southern Europe (central Europe arrivals are split between the two). Trains from Prague and Berlin occasionally arrive at the northerly **Franz-Josef Bahnhof,** and if you're coming from Prague or the airport, you may disembark at **Wien Mitte/Landstrasse** on the eastern edge of the city.

 The **U-Bahn** (subway) and tram system runs between these stations and the center of town — except Südbahnhof, from which you can catch the D tram to the center. (Look for the tram in a terminal on the station's east side, not right out in front near the other tram stop.)

Orienting Yourself in Vienna

Vienna's inner city is the oldest part of town and home to the most spectacular sights and almost all the hotels and restaurants recommended in this chapter.

 When you're trying to figure out a **Viennese address,** remember that the building number comes *after* the street name. A number before the name, especially a Roman numeral, indicates the *bezirk* (city district) in which the address resides. (The inner city is "I bezirk.")

Introducing the neighborhoods

The **Ringstrasse,** or Ring Road, encircles the inner city with an elegant, tree-lined thoroughfare. This boulevard follows the outline of the medieval city walls of yesteryear. The road is studded with many of Vienna's most prized gems: churches, palaces, and museums. Although the Ring is a continuous stretch of road, its name changes often. Just remember this: Any road whose name ends in *-ring* (such as Opern Ring or Kärntner Ring) is part of this avenue.

Forming the northeast border of the old city is the **Danube Canal** (the actual famed river, which isn't really blue, is farther northeast). The northward-running shopping boulevard **Kärntnerstrasse** begins where Kärntner Ring becomes Opern Ring at the Staatsoper opera house. This avenue bisects the inner city to **Stephansplatz,** the epicenter of town and home of St. Stephan's Cathedral.

The only place you're likely to venture outside of Vienna's Ring is the refined neighborhood of **Karlsplatz** (just southeast of the Staatsoper), with its namesake church, history museum, and major U-Bahn (subway) junction. You may also head west of the Ring a bit to the **Naschmarkt,** a fresh produce market, and maybe a touch farther beyond that to **Mariahilferstrasse,** the wide shopping street that runs from the Opern Ring to **Westbahnhof** train station.

Finding information after you arrive

Vienna's tourist office is an excellent resource. You'll find it behind the Staatsoper, at Kärntnerstrasse 38 (☎ **01-24-555;** www.wien.info). Hours are daily from 9 a.m. to 7 p.m.

Getting Around Vienna

You use the same ticket for all Viennese public transportation. Tickets are available at *Tabak-Trafiks* (tobacco/newsstands), automated machines at major stops and U-Bahn stations, and on trams (though they cost 0.50€/80¢ more onboard). A single (one-ride) ticket costs 1.70€ ($2.70), which is also the price of two rides for a child. Kids five and under ride free. A one-day pass for 5.70€ ($9.10) and a three-day pass for 14€ ($22) are also available.

A potential cost-saving option, if you're going to be doing lots of sightseeing, is the 19€ ($30), 72-hour **Vienna Card** (see the introduction to "Exploring Vienna," later in this chapter, for details).

By U-Bahn (subway)

Although inner-city Vienna is ideal for hoofing it, you need public transportation for some of the longer hauls. To get where you want to go as quickly as possible, the **U-Bahn** (subway) is your best bet. The U3 heads from Westbahnhof station through the center of town, stops at Stephansplatz, and then proceeds on to Wien Mitte/Landstrasse station. The U1 cuts north to south through the center of town, stopping at Karlsplatz, Stephansplatz, Swedenplatz (near the Danube Canal), and Praterstern/Wien Nord (at the Prater city park). The U2 curves around the Ring's west side to Karlsplatz, where it ends, and the U4 continues circling around the Ring's eastern half before heading north to the Friedensbrücke stop (the closest to Franz-Josef Bahnhof).

By tram or bus

For a more scenic way to get about town, try the tram. Lines include 18 (Südbahnhof to Westbahnhof), D (hedging around much of the Ring before veering off to Südbahnhof), and 1 and 2 (circling along the Ring — 1 goes clockwise, 2 goes counterclockwise).

You can also take buses that crisscross the center of town (1A, 2A, and 3A) or head out to the 'burbs.

By taxi

Although you can see most of the major sites in Vienna on foot, you may prefer the comforts of a taxi for trips from the airport or train station to your hotel. Be aware that taxis won't cruise the streets of Vienna looking for you. Instead, you need to hire taxis at stands located throughout the city, or call ☎ **31-300,** 60-160, 81-400, or 40-100 (a 2.50€/$4 charge is added onto your fare when you call a cab).

The basic fare for one passenger is 2.50€ ($4), plus 1.09€ ($1.75) per kilometer for the first 4km, and then .90€ ($1.45) for each kilometer after that. You pay a 1€ ($1.60) surcharge for luggage and a 0.10€ (15¢) surcharge between 11 p.m. and 6 a.m. and on Sundays and holidays (and the per-kilometer rate goes up to 1.31€/$2.10). Each additional passenger costs 1€ ($1.60) more. Rides to the airport (☎ 676-380-5797) also cost extra, or you can get a taxi for a flat rate, around 35€ to 45€ ($56–$72).

Staying in Vienna

If you're on a shoestring budget, you can find a concentration of cheap, plain hotels around Westbahnhof, a short tram ride from the center of town. This area is usually safe at night, except as you near Karlsplatz, a pretty plaza that junkies claim after dark. Vienna's popularity booms in late spring and late summer, and rooms can get scarce, so reserve ahead.

The **tourist office** (see "Finding information after you arrive," earlier in this chapter) can help you find lodging in a hotel or private home.

Vienna's top hotels

Hotel Astoria
$$$$ Near the Staatsoper

Recapturing the twilight days of the Austro-Hungarian Empire, this classic hotel has a frayed but cared-for elegance. Its location is prime for shopping and visiting the opera house and the cathedral. Avoid the dark and cramped interior rooms, and try your luck at getting one of the front rooms (outside, Kärntnerstrasse is pedestrian-only, so you won't be disturbed much at night). Although hard to snag, the large, light-filled "superior" corner rooms, featuring lovely marble fireplaces, stucco wall decorations, and 19th-century furnishings, are definitely worth asking about (however, as the staff laments, "we have only so many corners"). Check the hotel's Web site for the cheapest rates and special packages; lower rates are available for stays of two nights or more.

See map p. 314. Kärntnerstrasse 32–34 (entrance actually on side road Führichgasse, 4 blocks north of Kärntner Ring). ☎ *01-51-577. Fax: 01-515-77582.* www.austria-trend.at/asw. *U-Bahn: Stephansplatz. Rack rates: 160€–300€ ($256–$480) double. Rates include breakfast. AE, DC, MC, V.*

Hotel Kärntnerhof
$$ North of Stephansdom

Take just a few minutes' walk north of the cathedral to find this comfortable hotel, modest but not spare, with pricing right for most budgets. The near-modern accommodations are a bit worn and frayed at the edges (an overhaul of some of the older bathrooms would be welcome), but the facilities are sparkling clean. If you're traveling with a group or family, ask about the three roomier apartments, each of which has two bedrooms joined by a short hall.

See map p. 314. Grashofgasse 4 (near the corner of Kollnerhof and Fleischmarkt). ☎ *01-512-1923. Fax: 01-513-222-833.* www.karntnerhof.com. *U-Bahn: Stephansplatz. Rack rates: 105€–162€ ($168–$259) double. Rates include breakfast. AE, DC, MC, V.*

Accommodations, Dining, and Attractions in Vienna

HOTELS ■
Hotel am Stephansplatz **24**
Hotel Astoria **18**
Hotel Austria **32**
Hotel Kärntnerhof **30**
Hotel Mercure Secession Wien **4**
Hotel Neuer Markt **20**
Hotel Post **33**
Hotel Royal **26**
Hotel Wandl **23**
Pension Altstadt Vienna **2**
Pension Nossek **22**
Pension Pertschy **21**

◆

RESTAURANTS
Augustinerkeller **19**
Café Demel **15**
Café Landtmann **17**
Drei Husaren **27**
Figlmüller **29**
Griechenbeisl **31**
Kardos **35**
Österreicher im MAK
 Gasthof & Bar **34**
Ristorante Firenze Enoteca **28**

●

ATTRACTIONS
Akademie der Bildenden
 Künste-Gemaldegalerie **5**
Burgkapelle **11**
Grinzing **1**
Hofburg Palace **10**
Kaiserappartments **13**
Kunsthistoriches Museum **7**
Museum für Völkerkunde **8**
MuseumsQuartier **6**
Neue Burg **9**
Prater **36**
Schatzkammer **12**
Schloss Schönbrunn **3**
Spanische Reitschule **14**
Staatsoper **16**
Stephansdom **25**

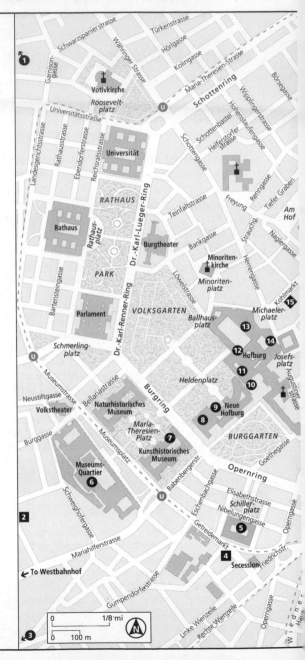

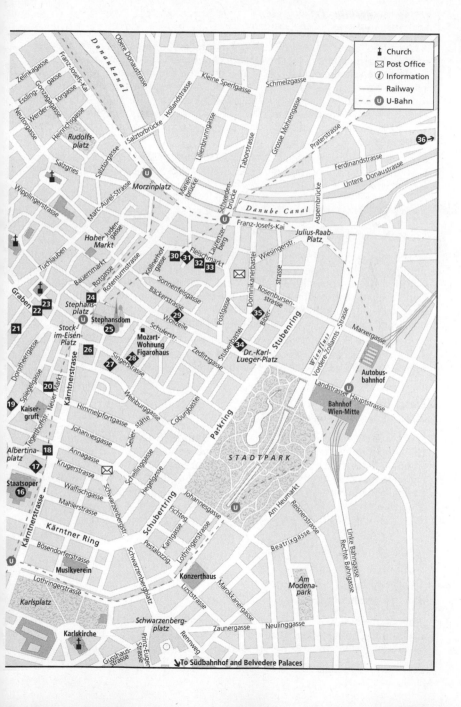

Legend:
- Church
- Post Office
- Information
- Railway
- U-Bahn

Hotel Mercure Secession Wien
$$ Just southeast of the Ringstrasse

A favorite of entertainers, this modern hotel is redone with contemporary modular furnishings every few years. Art lovers appreciate the location behind the Academy of Fine Arts and near the Kunsthistoriches Museum. The Mercure's comfortable apartments, which feature small kitchenettes (a nearby produce market can help you take care of the details), are suitable for families and groups. The main street is noisy, so light sleepers should request a room in the rear. Only a few rooms have air-conditioning, so be sure to ask for it.

See map p. 314. Getreidemarkt 5. ☎ *01-588-380. Fax: 01-5883-8212.* www.mercure. com. *U-Bahn: Karlsplatz. Rack rates: 99€–180€ ($158–$288) double. Breakfast 14€ ($22). AE, DC, MC, V.*

Hotel Royal
$$$$ Near Stephansdom

At the intersection of two prestigious streets on a corner of the cathedral square, this hotel offers good value at a great location. Don't miss the piano in the antiques-filled lobby — it was once owned by Wagner. You don't stay at the Royal for history, however; this place was built in 1960. For the best accommodations, choose one of the corner rooms, which have spacious foyers and balconies overlooking the Stephansdom.

See map p. 314. Singerstrasse 3 (at the corner with Kärntnerstrasse). ☎ *01-515-680. Fax: 01-513-9698.* www.kremslehnerhotels.at. *U-Bahn: Stephansplatz. Rack rates: 150€–255€ ($240–$408) double. Rates include breakfast. AE, DC, MC, V.*

Hotel Wandl
$$$$ Near Stephansdom

Halfway between the cathedral and the Hofburg, this inn has been run by the same family for generations. Pleasant, good-size rooms feature functional furniture. Only one doesn't have a private bathroom, which means that you can save big-time if you choose that one, and you don't even have to share the bathroom down the hall — it's yours alone. Be sure to ask for a room with a view of St. Stephan's steeple.

See map p. 314. Petersplatz 9. ☎ *01-534-550. Fax: 01-534-5577.* www.hotel-wandl. com. *U-Bahn: Stephansplatz. Rack rates: 158€–205€ ($253–$328) double. Rates include breakfast. AE, DC, MC, V.*

Pension Altstadt Vienna
$$$ Near Kärntnerstrasse

This is an undiscovered gem for those who like their hotels small and charming. The premises were converted from a century-old private home in the mid-1990s by noted connoisseur of modern art, Otto Wiesenthal. The comfortable, cozy rooms are reminiscent of a stately English home.

See map p. 314. Kirchengasse 41. ☎ *01-522-6666. Fax: 01-523-4901.* www.altstadt. at. *U-Bahn: Volkstheater. Rack rates: 139€–189€ ($222–$302) double. Rates include breakfast. AE, DC, MC, V.*

Pension Pertschy
$$ Near Stephansdom

One of Vienna's most atmospheric hotels — and a bargain to boot — Pension Pertschy sits smack-dab in the middle of town. This family-owned and -operated hotel is situated in a gorgeous baroque building (dating back to 1723). Rooms are decorated in old-fashioned Biedermeier style and include lovely chandeliers (a few even have 200-year-old ceramic heaters). Take advantage of one of the hotel's larger, homelike rooms, which have sofas or easy chairs.

See map p. 314. Habsburgergasse 5 (just off the Graben). ☎ *01-534-490. Fax: 01-534-4949.* www.pertschy.com. *U-Bahn: Stephansplatz. Rack rates: 105€–167€ ($168–$267) double. Rates include breakfast. DC, MC, V.*

Vienna's runner-up accommodations

Hotel am Stephansplatz

$$$$$ Near Stephansdom   This hotel may be mostly modern (although some rooms have rococo stylings), but its location, right on the cathedral square, is the most central in Vienna. *See map p. 314. Stephansplatz 9.* ☎ *01-534-050.* www.hotelamstephansplatz.at.

Hotel Austria

$ North of Stephansdom   Hotel Austria lies, in all its functional glory, just a few blocks north of the cathedral, in a quiet residential neighborhood just a few minutes' stroll from the tourist sights. The cheapest rooms don't have private bathrooms. *See map p. 314. Am Fleischmarkt 20.* ☎ *01-51-523.* www.hotelaustria-wien.at.

Hotel Neuer Markt

$$ Near Kärntnerstrasse   Hotel Neuer Markt occupies a baroque building on a fountain-blessed square, in the perfect location, halfway between the cathedral and the opera house. *See map p. 314. Seilergasse 9.* ☎ *01-512-2316.* www.hotelpension.at/neuermarkt.

Hotel Post

$ North of Stephansdom   Hotel Post is another ancient hotel that once hosted the likes of Mozart and Haydn; today, below the comfy, modern bedrooms, a cafe/wine bar still pipes in their music. Rooms without a bathroom are the true bargain. *See map p. 314. Fleischmarkt 24.* ☎ *01-515-830.* www. hotel-post-wien.at.

Pension Nossek

$ Near Stephansdom Pension Nossek was once home to Mozart and has been a simple, sensible inn on the main shopping drag near the royal palace since 1909. *See map p. 314. Graben 17.* ☎ *01-5337-0410.* www.pension-nossek.at.

Dining in Vienna

Viennese cooking is varied and palate-pleasing — with German, Swiss, and Italian influences, as well as more eastern-tinged Turkish, Hungarian, and Balkan flavors. Far and away, Vienna is most famous for being the birth-place of *Wiener schnitzel,* a simple, flat cutlet of pork or veal, breaded and fried (traditionally in lard), which is then tucked into a roll as a sandwich or served on a plate that can barely contain it.

Tafelspitz is another delicious (and dyed-in-the-wool) Viennese dinner-time meal. This boiled beef dish, served with applesauce topped with horseradish shavings, has been popular for centuries — in fact, Emperor Franz Joseph was noted for eating it daily. From Hungary (the other half of the Austro-Hungarian Empire), the Viennese pantry has several spicy influences; look for paprika popping up in a variety of dishes, especially in the flavorful pork or beef stew called *goulash.*

The Ottoman Turks besieged Vienna frequently throughout the 16th and 17th centuries and in the process introduced the city to a beverage that would eventually become one of Vienna's passions — *kaffee* (coffee). (For a preview of the best Viennese cafes, head to the section "More cool things to see and do," later in this chapter.) And of course, mouth-watering pastries are a necessity with any cup of kaffee. Vienna's world-renowned baked goods include *strudel,* which comes with numerous tempting fillings (*apfelstrudel* with apple is still the reigning pastry king). Other irresistible choices include *gugelhupf* (cream-filled horns) and *rehrucken* (chocolate cake encrusted with almonds).

Ready to overload on chocolate? Set your sights on sampling some *Sachertorte,* the original chocolate lover's delight (made unique by a touch of apricot jam). The **Hotel Sacher,** Philharmonikerstrasse 4 (☎ 01-514-560; www.sacher.com), was the birthplace of this tempting creation in 1832, but found itself engaged in a long legal battle with **Café Demel,** Kohlmarkt 14 (☎ 01-535-17170; www.demel.at), during the 1960s over the right to call its dessert delight the "Original Sachertorte." Although the Hotel Sacher won, your taste buds will be hard-pressed to tell the difference, so sample the sweets at both.

Top Austrian beers include lighter fare such as Gold Fassl, Kaiser, and Weizengold (a wheat beer). Or, if you prefer richer brews, try Gösser Spezial and Eggenberger Urbock (the latter dates back to the 17th century and is one of the world's most powerful beers).

When it comes to enjoying the best of Austria's wines, you'll find that whites dominate. Although the pinnacle white is the fruity Grüner Veltiner, the country's dry Rieslings are also celebrated, along with several fine chardonnays and Pinot Blancs. Also, keep your palate open to sample some Eiswein, a special Austrian dessert wine made from grapes that are allowed to ripen on the vine until after the first frost hits. This unusual growing process freezes water in the grapes and concentrates the fruit's alcohol level and taste. And don't forget about schnapps, delightfully flavored liqueurs distilled from various fruits.

Augustinerkeller
$$ Near the Staatsoper AUSTRIAN

Serving simple but tasty meals such as schnitzel, spit-roasted chicken, and tafelspitz since 1954, this restaurant in a vaulted brick cellar under the Hofburg Palace features long communal tables and a good selection of Viennese beer and wine. Touristy elements — including wandering accordion players in the evenings — tend to drive away the locals, but coming here is a fun dining experience, with ample, palette-pleasing food.

See map p. 314. Augustinerstrasse 1 (a little way off Albertinaplatz, across from Augustinia church). ☎ *01-533-1026. Reservations not necessary. U-Bahn: Stephansplatz. Main courses: 11€–23€ ($17–$37); buffet 28€ ($45). AE, DC, MC, V. Open: Daily 10 a.m. to midnight.*

Drei Husaren
$$$$$ Near Stephansdom VIENNESE/INTERNATIONAL

Decorated with Gobelin tapestries and antiques, this fine establishment has been regarded as Vienna's top eatery since World War I. You can sample both traditional and more inventive Viennese cuisine, including an hors d'oeuvres table filled to the brim with more than 35 goodies, *kalbsbrücken Metternich* (the chef's specialty veal dish), and cheese-filled crepes served with a chocolate topping.

See map p. 314. Weihburggasse 4 (off Kärtnerstrasse, 2 blocks south of Stephansplatz). ☎ *01-512-1092.* www.drei-husaren.at. *Reservations required. U-Bahn: Stephansplatz. Main courses: 29€–39€ ($46–$62); 6-course tasting menu 83€ ($133); fixed-price lunch 34€–44€ ($54–$70). AE, DC, MC, V. Open: Daily noon to 3 p.m. and 6 p.m.–1 a.m. Closed mid-July to mid-Aug.*

Figlmüller
$$$ Near Stephansdom VIENNESE

This perennially popular Viennese *beisel* (tavern) is home to *Wiener schnitzel* so colossal it overflows the plate. The dining room (dating back more than 500 years) has an aged glow from thousands of delighted diners who've settled down to generous helpings of salads, sausages, tafelspitz, and goblets of exceptional wine.

See map p. 314. Wollzelle 5 (go 1 block north on Rotenturmstrasse from Stephansplatz and turn right; the restaurant is up an alley half a block down on the left). ☎ *01-512-6177.* www.figlmueller.at. *Reservations recommended. U-Bahn: Stephansplatz. Main courses: 7.50€–15€ ($12–$24). MC, V. Open: Daily 11 a.m.–10:30 p.m. Closed Aug.*

Griechenbeisl
$$$ North of Stephansdom   AUSTRIAN

Beethoven and Mark Twain (among other fans) certainly can't be wrong. This 550-year-old restaurant with its iron chandeliers and low vaulted ceilings has been a favorite for centuries. Taste buds thrill to hearty dishes such as venison steak, Hungarian goulash, and an excellently prepared tafelspitz. Plus, the accordion and zither music gets the feet tapping.

See map p. 314. Fleischmarkt 11 (from Swedenplatz, take Laurenzerberg away from the Canalto Fleischmarkt and turn right). ☎ *01-533-1977 or 01-963-1030.* www.griechenbeisl.at. *Reservations required. Tram: N or Z. Main courses: 13€–20€ ($21–$32). AE, DC, MC, V. Open: Daily 11 a.m.–1 a.m. Closed Dec 24.*

Kardos
$$ East of Stephansdom   HUNGARIAN/BALKAN

Huge portions and elements of Vienna's eastern heritage await you at Kardos. From its Gypsy-rustic accents and deep wooden booths to its exotic fare that includes such tasty treats as rolls stuffed with spiced pork, Balkan fish soup, and grilled meats, Kardos highlights the days when Austria's influence extended far and wide. Get the ball rolling with the Hungarian apricot aperitif *barack.*

See map p. 314. Dominikanerbastei 8 (take Wollzeile several long blocks east of Stephansdom and turn left up Stuben Bastei, which becomes Dominikaner Bastei). ☎ *01-512-6949.* www.restaurantkardos.com. *Reservations recommended. U-Bahn: Schwedenplatz. Main courses: 9€–21€ ($14–$34). AE, MC, V. Open: Mon–Sat 11:30 a.m.–2:30 p.m. and 6–11:30 p.m. Closed Aug.*

Österreicher im MAK Gasthof & Bar
$$ Near Bahnhof Wien-Mitte   VIENNESE

This deeply respected culinary destination occupies a pair of rooms on the street level of the Museum der Angewanten Kunst (MAK). One is an enormous and echoing room capped with one of the most elaborate coffered and frescoed ceilings in town; the other is a smaller, postmodern, glass-sided room with a ceiling that rolls back during clement weather for a view of the sky. There's also a garden terrace. Since 2006, the culinary inspiration behind all this is Helmut Österreicher, a chef who has helped to redefine the tenets of modern Viennese cuisine — a lighter reinterpretation of what dining with the Habsburgs really meant. The menu is divided into two categories, one featuring "classical" and the other "modern" Viennese cuisine.

See map p. 314. In the Museum der Angewanten Kunst (MAK), Stubenring 5.
☎ *01-714-0121. Reservations recommended. U-Bahn: Stubentor. Main courses:*
13€–22€ ($21–$35). AE, DC, MC, V. Open: Daily 11:30 a.m.–11:30 p.m.

Ristorante Firenze Enoteca
$$$$ **Near Stephansdom   TUSCAN/ITALIAN**

If you're experiencing schnitzel overdose, head over to the premier Italian
eatery in Vienna. The delightful décor, with reproduced frescoes, recalls
the Renaissance, while the cuisine highlights central Italian staples such
as spaghetti with seafood, penne with salmon, and succulent veal cutlets.
Take a break from beer and get yourself a bottle of smooth Chianti.

*See map p. 314. In the Hotel Royal, Singerstrasse 3 (1 short block south of
Stephansplatz, Singerstrasse branches off to the left/east; the restaurant is 2 blocks
down).* ☎ *01-513-4374. Reservations recommended. U-Bahn: Stephansplatz. Main
courses: 14€–30€ ($22–$48). AE, DC, MC, V. Open: Daily noon to 3 p.m. and 6 p.m. to
midnight.*

Exploring Vienna

If you're going to be in town for few days, pick up the **Vienna Card,**
which gives you three days of unlimited public transportation plus discounts at 30 city sights and museums (as well as on a load of restaurants, shops, bars, nightlife venues, tours, and other attractions). The
card costs 19€ ($30) and is available at the tourist office, hotel desks,
or U-Bahn stations.

Because several museums fall under the purview of the Kunsthistoriches
Museum, you can get several combination tickets. The 23€ ($37) Bronze-
ticket covers the main Kunsthistoriches Museum and the Schatzkammer
and Neue Burg at the Hofburg (all reviewed in this section). The 26€ ($42)
Silberticket takes in those plus the Austrian Theater Museum. The 28€ ($45)
Goldticket covers all that, plus the Lipizzaner Museum and Wagenburg.

Vienna's top sights

Akademie der Bildenden Künste-Gemaldegalerie (Academy of Fine Arts)
If time permits, try to make at least a quick stop at this small but choice
gallery with a fine painting collection that covers the 14th to 17th centuries. The collection features a 1504 *Last Judgment* by Hieronymus Bosch
(a major influence on the Surrealists), a *Self-Portrait* by Van Dyck, and
works by Rubens, Guardi, Rembrandt, and Cranach the Elder.

See map p. 314. Schillerplatz 3 (just south of the Staatsoper). ☎ *01-5881-6225.* www.
akademiegalerie.at. *U-Bahn: Karlsplatz. Admission: 7€ ($11) adults, 4€ ($6.40)
seniors and students. Open: Tues–Sun 10 a.m.–6 p.m.*

Hofburg Palace

A wonder of connective architecture, the palace of Hofburg (actually the Hapsburgs' winter home) is a jumbled complex that was added on to from 1279 to 1913. It spreads out over several blocks and features numerous entrances, but the main entrance on Michaelerplatz ushers you into the majestic courtyard that leads to the Imperial Apartments, or **Kaiserappartments** (☎ 01-533-7570; www.hofburg-wien.at). Here you'll also find the Imperial Silver and Porcelain Collection containing 18th- and 19th-century Hapsburg table settings, and the Sissi Museum dedicated to the beloved 19th-century empress Elisabeth.

The **Schatzkammer** (Imperial Treasury) is another choice attraction at the Hofburg (☎ 01-533-7931; www.khm.at). Head left from the In der Burg courtyard and enter through the Swiss Court. The treasury, Europe's greatest, houses a collection of historic gems and jewelry likely to impress even the most jaded of tourists.

The **Neue Burg** (New Castle) is yet another section of the palatial estate worth visiting (☎ 01-525-240; www.khm.at). Constructed in the early 20th century, the building's elegantly curving exterior houses several collections. Collections include (in descending order of interest): historical musical instruments (many used by famous composers; try the audio tour even though it's in German — it features wonderful snippets of period music); arms and armor; and classical statues (mainly from the Greco-Turkish site of Ephesus). An entrance next door (closer to the Ringstrasse) leads to the **Museum für Völkerkunde** (Museum of Ethnology), featuring the only intact Aztec feather headdresses in the world (☎ 01-525-240; www.ethno-museum.ac.at). At press time, this museum was closed for renovation.

See map p. 314. The palace takes up many square city blocks, but the main entrance is on Michaelerplatz. Each section has its own phone number and Web site, which are listed in the preceding description. U-Bahn: Herrengasse or Stephansplatz (walk down Graben, and then left onto Kohlmarkt). Tram: 1, 2, D, or J. Admission: Kaiserappartments 10€ ($16) adults, 7€ ($11) students 25 and under, 5€ ($8) children 6–15 (free for children 5 and under); Neue Burg (including the Museum für Völkerkunde) 10€ ($15) adults, 6€ ($8.70) children; Schatzkammer 10€ ($16) adults, 6€ ($9.60) seniors, children, and students (free for children 5 and under). Open: Kaiserappartments daily 9 a.m.–5 p.m.; Neue Burg and Schatzkammer (including the Museum für Völkerkunde) Wed–Mon 10 a.m.–6 p.m.

Kunsthistoriches Museum (Museum of Fine Arts)

An amazingly diverse art collection awaits you in this 100-room museum. Start with ancient Egyptian and Greco-Roman art, work your way through the Renaissance, and then move on to the Flemish, Dutch, and German masters such as Memling, Van Dyck, Rembrandt, and especially Breughel the Elder (the majority of his known works are here).

Masterpieces include Dürer's *Blue Madonna*, Vermeer's *The Artist's Studio*, and works by Italian masters Titian, Raphael, Veronese, Caravaggio, and Giorgione. Top ancient works consist of a Roman onyx cameo of the

Gemma Augustea, and a roly-poly blue hippopotamus from 2000 B.C. Egypt (which also serves as the museum's mascot). Also check out Archimboldo's idiosyncratic and allegorical still lifes–cum-portraits, in which the artist cobbles together everyday objects to look like a face from afar. Craggy, wooden-faced *Winter* is really Francis I of France, and flame-haired *Fire* may be Emperor Maximillian II himself.

See map p. 314. Maria Theresien Platz (across the Burgring from the Neue Burg). ☎ *01-525-240.* www.khm.at. *U-Bahn: Mariahilferstrasse. Tram: 52, 58, D, or J. Admission: 10€ ($16) adults, 7.50€ ($12) seniors and students, free for children 5 and under. Guided tours in English at 11 a.m. and 3 p.m. 2€ ($3.20). Open: Daily 10 a.m.– 6 p.m. (until 9 p.m. Thurs).*

MuseumsQuartier

Installed in former Hapsburg stables, MuseumsQuartier is one of the largest cultural complexes in the world. It's like combining the Guggenheim Museum in New York with that city's Museum of Modern Art. Toss in the Brooklyn Academy of Music, a children's museum, an architecture and design center, lots of theaters and art galleries, along with video workshops — and much more — and you've got it. There's even a tobacco museum.

Our favorite attraction here is the **Leopold Museum** (☎ 01-525-700; www. leopoldmuseum.org) with its brilliant collection of Austrian art. We'd visit it for no other reason than it contains the world's largest treasure-trove of the works of Egon Schiele (1890–1918), ranked by some critics right up there with van Gogh and Modigliani. Schiele died at the age of 27, but Leopold has more than 2,500 drawings and watercolors along with 330 oil canvases. There's so much more, including works by Gustav Klimt.

Of almost equal importance is the **Kunsthalle Wien** (☎ 01-521-8933; www. kunsthallewien.at), a showcase for both classic modern art and contemporary cutting-edge paintings. Every artist from Picasso to Andy Warhol is represented here — yes, even Ms. Yoko Ono, not the world's greatest painter, although she married well. From Expressionism to cubism to abstraction, the art is magnificently spread across five floors.

A final attraction, **Museum of Modern Art Ludwig Foundation** (MUMOK; ☎ 01-525-000; www.mumok.at) presents one of the most outstanding collections of modern art in central Europe, even American pop. The museum features five exhibition levels (two of which are underground). From cubism to surrealism, major art movements are grouped together. The fabled names of the 20th century, including Jasper Johns and Roy Lichtenstein, are on ample display.

See map p. 314. Museumsplatz 1. ☎ *01-523-5881 for MQ Point, the complex's information center.* www.mqw.at. *U-Bahn: MuseumsQuartier. Admission: Leopold Museum 10€ ($16) adults, 7€ ($11) seniors, 5.50€ ($8.80) students and children 8–18, free for children 7 and under; Kunsthalle Wien 11€ ($17) adults, 8.50€ ($14) seniors, students, and children; MUMOK 10€ ($16) adults, 8€ ($13) seniors, 6.50€ ($10) students 19 and over, 4€ ($6.40) students 14–18, 2€ ($3.20) children 6–13. Open: MQ Point daily 10 a.m.–7 p.m.; Leopold Museum Wed–Mon 10 a.m.–6 p.m. (until 9 p.m.*

Thurs); Kunsthalle Wien Thurs–Tues 10 a.m.–7 p.m. (until 10 p.m. Thurs); MUMOK Tues–Sun 10 a.m.–6 p.m. (until 9 p.m. Thurs).

Schloss Schönbrunn (Schönbrunn Palace)

You have to travel about 4 miles from Vienna's center to experience this palace — but it's definitely worth the effort. Schloss Schönbrunn was the baroque playground of Empress Maria Theresa and served as the Hapsburgs' summer palace after its completion in the mid-18th century. Only 40 of the sprawling palace's 1,441 rooms are open to visitors.

Two different self-guided tours lead the way through state apartments that brim with gorgeous chandeliers and old-world detail. The basic Imperial Tour guides you through 22 rooms; the Grand Tour includes 40 rooms, including 18th-century interiors from the time of Maria Theresa. (Be sure to call ahead for tour costs and times; summertime tours leave as frequently as every 30 minutes.)

Your visit is not compete without a jaunt through the extravagant rococo gardens, complete with faux "Roman ruins" and a baroque coffeehouse that overlooks the gardens (a fantastic photo op). If imperial coaches are your thing, don't miss the Wagenburg carriage museum.

See map p. 314. Schönbrunner Schlossstrasse. ☎ *01-8111-30.* www.schoenbrunn.at. *U-Bahn: U4. Admission: Imperial Tour 9.50€ ($15) adults, 7.90€ ($13) students, 5.90€ ($9.50) children 14 and under; Grand Tour 13€ ($21) adults, 9.90€ ($16) students, 7.90€ ($13) children 14 and under; gardens 2.90€ ($4.70) adults, 2.40€ ($3.90) seniors and students, 1.70€ ($2.70) children 6–15. Open: Palace Apr–June and Sept–Oct daily 8:30 a.m.–5 p.m., July–Aug daily 8:30 a.m.–6 p.m., and Nov–Mar daily 8:30 a.m.–4:30 p.m.; gardens daily 9 a.m. to sunset.*

Staatsoper (State Opera House)

One of the world's greatest opera meccas, the regal Staatsoper has a marvelous musical heritage dating all the way back to its 1869 opening with a performance of Mozart's *Don Giovanni.* Mahler and Strauss — among other classical musical titans — have served as its musical directors. Take a short 40-minute tour during the day or, even better, catch a thrilling performance in the evening (see "More cool things to see and do," later in this chapter).

See map p. 314. Opern Ring 2. ☎ *01-514-44-2606.* www.staatsoper.at. *U-Bahn: Oper or Karlsplatz. Tram: 1, 2, D, J, 62, or 65. Admission: Tours 5€ ($8) adults, 4€ ($6.40) seniors, 2€ ($3.20) students and children 14 and under. Open: The ever-changing schedule of tours (1–3 English-language tours offered daily, usually between 1 and 3 p.m.) is posted at an entrance on the right (east) side.*

Stephansdom (St. Stephan's Cathedral)

The heart of Vienna lies in this visual and cultural landmark from the 12th to 14th centuries. (Mozart's 1791 pauper funeral was held here.) Visit the fanciful tombs, an impressive 15th-century carved wooden altar, and a crypt filled with urns containing the entrails of the Hapsburgs. See the quintessential Viennese vista, with its colorful pattern of mosaiclike tiling, from atop the 450-foot, 343-stepped *Steffl* (south tower). The unfinished north tower (named for its *Pummerin* bell) offers a less impressive view, but you can catch a glimpse of the Danube.

See map p. 314. Stephansplatz 1. ☎ 01-51-552-3667. www.stephansdom.at. *U-Bahn: Stephansplatz. Admission: Church free; north tower 4€ ($6.40) adults, 1.50€ ($2.40) children 15 and under; south tower 3€ ($4.80) adults, 1€ ($1.60) children 14 and under; church tours 4€ ($6.40) adults, 1.50€ ($2.40) children 14 and under; evening tours, including tour of the roof, 10€ ($16) adults, 5€ ($8) children 14 and under. Open: Church daily 6 a.m.–10 p.m., except during services; north tower Nov–Mar daily 8:30 a.m.–5 p.m., Apr–Oct daily 8:30 a.m.–5:30 p.m. (to 6 p.m. July–Aug); south tower daily 9 a.m.–5:30 p.m.; church tours in English Apr–Oct daily 3:45 p.m.*

More cool things to see and do

✔ **Spending a night at the opera:** Vienna's Staatsoper is a truly world-class theatrical venue, and you don't want to miss experiencing a performance, even if you don't consider yourself an opera aficionado. The season runs September through June, and you can get tickets at a variety of prices (5€–254€/$8–$406) at the box office one month in advance (☎ 01-514-442-606), the day after the season opens (☎ 01-514-44-2421), or on the Web (www.staatsoper.at).

You can save money and try your luck by purchasing last-minute tickets the day of a performance, or you can show up at least three hours before the performance to get in line for standing-room-only space — it costs only 2€ ($3.20), or 3.50€ ($5.60) for the Parterre. Bring a scarf and tie it around the railing at your standing spot — that's all you need to do to save your place. Then wander through the glittery rooms and circulate among the black-tie crowd until the performance begins.

When the summer heat chases the company out of the State Opera House, get your opera fix at **open-air concerts** — from Mozart and the Vienna Boys' Choir to Lenny Kravitz and David Bowie — at Schloss Schönbrunn. The Schloss itself also stages musical concerts year-round; call for info (☎ 01-8111-3239; www.imagevienna.com).

✔ **Drinking java, eating strudel, and people-watching at a Kaffeehaus:** Legend has it that Vienna's first coffeehouse was established in 1683 — and certainly, they've been a vibrant part of Viennese culture ever since. One of the grandest places, the chandeliered **Café Landtmann,** Dr. Karl Lueger Ring 4 (☎ 01-241-000; www.landtmann.at), was once a fave of Freud's.

The granddaddy of all Viennese cafes is **Café Demel** (☎ 01-535-17170; www.demel.at), which moved to Kohlmarkt 14 in 1888 and hasn't changed its ornate décor since. You can enjoy your *kaffee* in a variety of ways, the most popular being *schwarzer* (black), *melange* (mixed with hot milk), or *mit schlagobers* (topped with whipped cream).

✔ **Seeing the Vienna Boys' Choir:** Dating all the way back to 1498, this Viennese institution has been the training ground for many talented musicians, including Joseph Haydn and Franz Schubert. Catch a sonorous Sunday or holiday Mass (Jan–June and mid-Sept to Christmas) at 9:15 a.m. in the **Hofburg's Burgkapelle,** with accompanying members of the Staatsoper chorus and orchestra. You can pick up tickets at the box office the preceding Friday from 5 to 6 p.m. Get in line early — this is one of the few times you find people shelling out 5€ to 29€ ($8–$46) to go to church. The boys also warble at a weekly afternoon concert somewhere in town (the venue and times vary), and in summer often put on evening concerts at the Schloss Schönbrunn (for info on that last one, visit www.theviennaboyschoir.com). Contact them at ☎ 01-216-3942 or go to www.wsk.at to see their upcoming concert schedule (these kids travel *a lot*).

✔ **Riding the Riesenrad in the Prater:** Courtesy of Johann Strauss, Sr., in 1820, this former imperial hunting ground on the Danube Canal is the birthplace of the waltz. Aside from the lovely grounds, visit the Prater Park to experience its year-round amusement park/fair that's bursting with restaurants, food stands, and a beer garden. Also, take a spin on the Riesenrad — at 67m (220 ft.) and 100 years, one of the world's oldest (and slowest) operating Ferris wheels (www.wienerriesenrad.com), open daily from 10 a.m. until at least 8 p.m. (to 10 p.m. Mar, Apr, and Oct; until midnight May–Sept). Admission is 8€ ($13) adults, 3.20€ ($5.10) children 3 to 14, 20€ ($32) families (two adults, two kids).

✔ **Watching the horse ballet at the Spanische Reitschule (Spanish Riding School):** You don't have to attend a show to see the world-famous Lipizzaner horses strut their stuff. The Hofburg's school teaches complicated baroque horse choreography, based on 16th-century battle maneuvers. The horses and riders practice regularly (Feb–June 19, Aug 30–Oct 16, and Dec 2–29 Tues–Sat 10 a.m.–1 p.m.). You can purchase training session tickets from your travel agent or at the door for 15€ ($24) adults, 12€ ($19) seniors, 8€ ($13) children. Get them in advance at the visitor center on Michaelerplatz 1, or at the door at Josefsplatz, Gate 2.

However, if only the full, 80-minute show will do (Mar–June and Sept to mid-Dec most Sun 11 a.m.; plus Sat 11 a.m. Apr–May; and Fri 6 p.m. May and Sept), reserve a ticket as far in advance as possible by visiting www.spanische-reitschule.com. Tickets run 35€ to 160€ ($56–$256) for seats, 20€ to 28€ ($32–$45) for standing room. (Children 2 and under not admitted, but children 3–6 attend free with adults.) Hour-long dressage training sessions to classical music sometimes take place during the show season Fridays at 10 a.m., and you can observe for 25€ ($40), though tickets are limited and tend to sell out quickly.

✔ **Taking a *heuriger* crawl in Grinzing:** *Heuriger* is the name of both Viennese new wines and the country taverns that serve them. Most *heuriger* are centered around the fringes of the famous Vienna Woods, just a 15-minute tram ride northwest of the city center. The tradition's capital is Grinzing, home to about 20 taverns (take tram no. 38 from the underground station at Schottentor, a stop on the U2 U-Bahn, and tram nos. 1, 2, and D).

Because of the rising popularity of *heuriger* crawling, the village works hard to maintain its medieval look. Stroll down Cobenzigasse and sample the wine at *heuriger* along the way while you enjoy the sounds of accordion and zither music.

Guided tours

You find plenty of **city orientation tours,** but why pay $20 when a tram ticket and a good map gets you the same thing minus the stilted commentary? Buy an all-day ticket, step onto the **no. 1 or 2 tram,** and ride it all the way around the Ring, hopping on and off at sights where you want to spend time. The whole ride only takes half an hour if you don't get off. After you're oriented, you can abandon the tram to visit the sights off the Ring, such as the Hofburg Palace and Stephansdom. The tourist office has a brochure called **Walks in Vienna** that can fill you in on other, more organized guided tours.

Suggested itineraries

If you're the type who'd rather organize your own tours, this section offers some tips for building your own Vienna itineraries.

If you have one day

Be at the **Hofburg Palace** and in the **Kaiserappartments** at 9:15 a.m. to admire the excesses of the Hapsburgs, and in the **Schatzkammer** around 10 a.m. for its impressive medieval crown jewels and other royal artifacts.

Exit the Hofburg by the main Michaelerplatz entrance and start strolling up Kohlmarkt, pausing to indulge in a coffee and snack or early lunch amid the 19th-century elegance of **Cafe Demel.** Turn right on the Graben to arrive at **Stephansdom.** Tour the cathedral, climb its south tower for a city panorama, and then start waltzing your way down the main pedestrian drag, Kärntnerstrasse. Settle into the ground-floor cafe of the **Hotel Sacher** for a sinfully delicious Sachertorte.

Continue to the end of Kärntnerstrasse where it hits the Ring. Admire the **Staatsoper** exterior and, unless you'll be getting standing-room-only tickets (for which you'll return here shortly), stop into the box office to pick up discounted day-of-performance tickets for tonight's opera. Then hop tram no. 1, 2, or D heading west/clockwise (left) around the Ring, go one stop, and get off at Burgring for the **Kunsthistorisches Museum** and an hour and a half to two hours of exquisite paintings and ancient statues.

If you got tickets to the opera, get right back on tram no. 1 or 2 and ride it clockwise halfway around the Ring road, past the greatest glories of Viennese architecture. Get off at Schwedenplatz and transfer to the U1; go two stops north, getting off at Praterstern. Enjoy the city park–cum–carnival of Prater by taking a late-afternoon spin on the **Reisenrad** (Ferris wheel) and tossing back a few tall cold ones in the **Biergarten** before returning to the **Staatsoper** half an hour before the performance begins. You can also stop for dinner along the way, or just have some schnitzel in the Prater. If you have plenty of time to make it to the opera at your leisure, get off the U1 at Schwedenplatz again and simply get back on tram no. 1 or 2 to continue all the way around the Ring to the opera house. If you dallied too long in the Prater, stay on the U1 all the way to Karlsplatz, 2 blocks south of the Staatsoper. If you're still hungry after the proverbial fat lady sings, stop at nearby **Augustinerkeller,** which stays open until midnight.

Fans of standing-room-only tickets need to plan their evening like so: Depending on the hour when you get out of the museum, you either have time (half an hour) to ride tram no. 1 or 2 clockwise almost all the way around the Ring Road (getting off back at the Staatsoper), or you can just mosey the 2 long blocks back (counterclockwise) to the opera house. You need to pick up a snack to eat while waiting in line at the opera house — be there by 5 p.m. for the best spots. Have dinner late at **Augustinerkeller,** after the performance is over.

If you have two days

Spend **Day 1** as outlined in the preceding section. That's a pretty packed day, so take **Day 2** to relax at Vienna's suburban sights. Head out in the morning to **Schloss Schönbrunn** for even more imperial excess than you saw at the Hofburg. After marveling at Hapsburgian opulence and taking a spin through the gardens, return downtown on the U4, transferring at Karlsplatz to the U2 toward Schotten Ring. Get off at the Schottentor stop and hop tram no. 38 out to Grinzing for an afternoon of *heuriger* (country tavern) crawling, snacking, and drinking your way through Vienna's specialty foods and white wines. If you're in town during the season (and booked tickets long before you left on this trip), get back to town by 6:30 p.m. so you can take in the 7 p.m. show of the Lipizzaner horses at the famed **Spanische Reitschule.**

If you have three days

Days 1 and 2 in the preceding sections give you all the best Vienna has to offer. Take **Day 3** for a big day trip out to the lovely Austrian village of **Innsbruck.** For information about Innsbruck, see the next section.

Traveling beyond Vienna: Innsbruck

Although Innsbruck is technically in Austria, traveling there from Munich, Germany (see Chapter 15), is much faster and more convenient.

This section provides directions from both Munich and Vienna, and it's a perfect excursion to do en route from one to the other.

Innsbruck, famous for hosting the Winter Olympics as well as the imperial family of the Austro-Hungarian Empire, is a sleepy little gem of a town, bordered by the stupendous Alps and a milky white river. The village is a good starting point for hiking, skiing, and scenic driving.

Getting there

Ten daily trains arrive at Hauptbahnhof from Vienna (five hours away), passing through Salzburg (two hours away); 14 trains arrive from Munich daily (one-and-a-half to two hours away).

The **tourist office** is at Burggraben 3, a road that rings the Altstadt at the end of Maria Theresien Strasse (☎ 0512-598-500; Fax: 0512-598-50107; www.innsbruck-tourism.at). It's open Monday through Friday 8 a.m. to 6 p.m., Saturday 8 a.m. to noon.

If you'll be doing heavy-duty sightseeing, purchase the **Innsbruck Card** to get free access to all city sights and free public transportation. The tourist office sells cards for 25€ ($40) for one day, 30€ ($48) for two days, or 35€ ($56) for three days. Children get a 50 percent discount.

Seeing the sights

Walking the Maria Theresien Strasse, you pass through a triumphal arch and reach the rustic, souvenir shop–lined **Herzog Friedrich Strasse**. The **Stadtturm** tower (☎ 512-58-7113) is at the end of the street, offering panoramic views of the surrounding Alps. The tower is open June through September daily from 10 a.m. to 8 p.m., October through May daily from 10 a.m. to 5 p.m. Admission is 3€ ($4.80) adults, 2.50€ ($4) seniors and students, or 1.50€ ($2.40) children 14 and under.

The street ends in a wide spot, which the **Goldenes Dachl** (☎ 0512-581-111) overlooks. The structure is basically an overblown imperial balcony erected and gilded for Emperor Maximilian I in the 16th century as a box seat for the festivities on the square below. Admiring it from below is enough, although its Maximilian-oriented museum is open October through April Tuesday through Sunday from 10 a.m. to 12:30 p.m. and 2 to 5 p.m., May through September daily from 10 a.m. to 6 p.m. Admission is 4€ ($6.40) adults, 2€ ($3.20) children, 8€ ($13) families.

Turn right on Universitätsstrasse, and then left on Rennweg for a half-hour tour of the exuberant, curving baroque stylings of Maria Theresa's **Hofburg Palace** (☎ 0512-587-186), open daily from 9 a.m. to 5 p.m. Admission is 5.50€ ($8.80) adults, 4€ ($6.40) seniors, 3.65€ ($5.85) students, 1.10€ ($1.75) children 14 and under. Next-door is the equally rococo **Dom** (cathedral). Across from the Hofburg at no. 2 Universitätsstrasse is the **Hofkirche** (☎ 0512-584-302; www.hofkirche.at), containing a massive, statue-ridden monument to Maximilian I. It's open

Monday through Saturday from 9 a.m. to 5 p.m. (to 5:30 p.m. July–Aug), Sunday 1 to 5 p.m. Admission is 4€ ($6.40) adults, 2€ ($3.20) students, 1.50€ ($2.40) children 14 and under. Its neighbor is the **Tiroler Volkskunst-Museum** (☎ 0512-5948-9510; www.tiroler-volkskunst museum.at), a folk museum celebrating everyday life in the history of the Tyrol district. The museum is open daily from 9 a.m. to 5 p.m. (to 5:30 p.m. July–Aug), but it's closed noon to 1 p.m. on Sunday. Admission is 4€ ($6.40) adults, 3.50€ ($5.60) students, 2€ ($3.20) children 14 and under. The 8€ ($13) "Combi card" covers adult admission to both the Hofkirche and the museum.

Outside the Alstadt is the **Alpenzoo**, Weiherburggasse 37 (☎ 0512-292-323; www.alpenzoo.at), which clings to the alpine cliffs and features regional wildlife. The zoo is open daily 9 a.m. to 6 p.m. (until 5 p.m. in winter). Admission is 7€ ($11) adults, 5€ ($8) students, 3.50€ ($5.60) children 6 to 15, 2€ ($3.20) children 4 to 5. From the center, cross the Inn River, turn right, and follow the signs a long way; you can also take bus no. N, D, E, or 4 from the Altes Landhaus on Maria-Theresien Strasse.

The zoo sits at the base of the **Hungerburg plateau** (☎ 0512-586-158), which offers panoramic city views. In summer, the Hungerburgbahn cog railway ascends from the corner of Rennweg and Kettenbrücke at 15-minute intervals daily from 9 a.m. to 8 p.m., and then runs at 30-minute intervals until 10:30 p.m. The rest of the year, the railway operates at hourly intervals daily from 8:30 a.m. to dusk (5–6 p.m.). Round-trip fares on the cog railway cost 5.60€ ($8.95) adults and 2.80€ ($4.50) children.

Where to stay and dine

Please your palate at the inexpensive **Restaurant Ottoburg**, Herzog Friedrich Strasse 1 (☎ 0512-584-338), an Austrian tradition since 1745. The **Hotel Goldene Krone**, Maria Theresien Strasse 46 (☎ 0512-586-160; Fax: 0512-580-1896; www.goldene-krone.at), features modern comforts and baroque touches, in a lovely house just outside the Altstadt. Doubles run 76€ to 106€ ($122–$170) and include breakfast.

Fast Facts: Vienna

American Express

Vienna's American Express office is located at Kärntnerstrasse 21–23 (☎ 01-515-1100). Hours are Monday through Friday from 9 a.m. to 5:30 p.m., Saturday 9 a.m. to noon.

Area Code

Austria's country code is **43**; Vienna's city code is **01**. Drop the 0 if calling from outside Austria. To call Vienna from the United States, dial ☎ 011-43-1 followed by the phone number; to call Vienna from another Austrian city, dial 01 and then the number.

Currency

For its currency, Austria is part of the euro system. The same euros you used in Germany, France, or Italy are valid in Austria. The euro is divided into 100 cents, and there are coins of 0.01, 0.02, 0.05, 0.10,

0.20, 0.50, 1€, and 2€. Paper-note denominations are 5, 10, 20, 50, 100, 200, and 500 euros. The exchange rate used in this chapter is 1€ = $1.60. Amounts over $10 have been rounded to the nearest dollar.

Doctors and Dentists

For a list of English-speaking doctors, call the Vienna Medical Association at ☎ 01-1771 (or, during the nighttime in an emergency, ☎ 40-144). Dr. Wolfgang Molnar at the Ambulatorium Augarten (☎ 01-330-3468; www.ambulatorium.com) is the panel physician for the U.S. Embassy — and you can always contact the consulate for a list of English-speaking physicians, though virtually every doctor or dentist in Vienna and throughout Austria is English-speaking. For dental emergencies, call Dr. Lydia Hofmann, Breitenfurterstrasse 360–368 (☎ 01-333-6796).

Embassies and Consulates

The U.S. Embassy's consulate (☎ 01-31-339; www.usembassy.at) is located at Gartenbaupromenade 2–4, A-1010 Vienna. It handles lost passports, tourist emergencies, and other matters, and is open Monday through Friday from 8:30 a.m. to noon (and after-hours for emergency service through 5 p.m.).

Emergency

Dial ☎ 144 for an ambulance; call the police at ☎ 133; or report a fire by calling ☎ 122.

Hospitals

For emergency medical care, go to the Neue Allgemeine Krankenhaus at Währinger Gürtel 18–20 (☎ 01-4040-001501); take tram no. 5 or 33 to the entrance at Spitalgasse 23. (At night, bus nos. N6 and N64 stop at the main entrance.)

Information

The helpful Vienna Tourist Board office is behind the Staatsoper, at Kärntnerstrasse 38 (☎ 01-24-555; Fax: 01-2455-5666; www.wien.info). Hours are daily 9 a.m. to 7 p.m.

Internet Access and Cybercafes

Mediencafe im Amadeus, Kärntnerstrasse 19, on the fifth floor of Steffl (☎ 01-5131-45017), offers free Web surfing Monday through Friday 9:30 a.m. to 7 p.m., Saturday 9:30 a.m. to 5:30 p.m.

Located at Rathausplatz 4 (☎ 01-405-2626), Cafe Einstein is a cool cafe with a historic-looking pub and lots of atmosphere. Hours are Monday through Friday from 7 a.m. to 2 a.m., Saturday 9 a.m. to 2 a.m., Sunday 9 a.m. to midnight.

Cafe Stein, Wahringerstrasse 6–8 (☎ 01-319-7241; www.cafe-stein.com), is open daily 10 a.m. to 11 p.m.

Maps

The tourist office hands out a decent city map, and because the center is rather small, it's easy to navigate with it.

Newspapers and Magazines

The tourist office (see "Information," earlier in this section) has a series of informative pamphlets on a variety of Viennese tourist activities, as well as free copies of the events rag *Wien Monatsprogramm*.

Pharmacies

Vienna's pharmacies are generally open Monday through Friday from 8 a.m. to noon and 2 to 6 p.m., Saturday 8 a.m. to noon. Look for signs outside each pharmacy that list which drugstores are open during the off-hours.

Police

Call the police at ☎ 133.

Post Office

The main post office is at Fleischmarkt 19 (☎ 01-5138-3500; www.post.at); it's open Monday through Friday 8 a.m. to 5 p.m.

Safety

Vienna has its share of purse-snatchers and pickpockets, so be especially cautious in crowded, touristy areas, especially Kärntnerstrasse between Stephansplatz and Karlsplatz. You should also be careful when taking out your wallet or opening your purse in public areas; many pitiable children who beg for money are accompanied by adult thieves who snatch wallets and run. The only central area that can become somewhat scary after dark is Karlsplatz, which is frequented by heroin addicts.

Taxes

In Austria, a value-added tax (VAT) is figured into the price of most items. Luxury items such as jewelry are taxed 34 percent, while clothing and souvenirs are taxed 20 percent. As a foreign visitor, you can reclaim a percentage of the VAT if you spend more than 75€ ($120) in a single shop (see Chapter 4).

Taxis

See "Getting Around Vienna," earlier in this chapter.

Telephone

All public phones take coins. Some phones take prepaid phone cards called *Wertkarte*, which you can purchase from post offices, newsstands, and tobacconists.

To charge a call to your calling card or credit card, insert a nominal fee into the pay phone and dial ☎ 0-800-200-247 for AT&T, ☎ 0-800-999-762 for MCI, or ☎ 0-800-200-236 for Sprint. To call the United States direct from Austria, dial 001 and then the area code and phone number. For an international operator, dial 09. For Austrian directory assistance, dial ☎ 11811; for international directory assistance, call ☎ 11813.

Transit Info

See "Getting Around Vienna," earlier in this chapter. For transportation information, call ☎ 01-790-9100 or go to www.wiener linien.at.

Chapter 17

Bern and the Swiss Alps

● ●

In This Chapter

▶ Finding your way to Bern and the Swiss Alps

▶ Exploring the neighborhoods of Bern

▶ Discovering Bern's best hotels, restaurants, and attractions

▶ Finding the best of Switzerland's other great cultural capitals: Zurich and Basel

▶ Heading into the alpine countryside and the Bernese Oberland

● ●

*T*he Swiss capital of Bern is a fine place to visit and — unlike Switzerland's larger cities — still has an almost medieval, Swiss-village feel. But the real attractions of this country are those mighty, snow-covered Alps. In this chapter, we cover Bern fully, hit the cultural highlights of Basel and Zurich, and then head south into the Bernese Oberland, a region that encompasses the legendary 4,092m (13,642-ft.) peak of the Jungfrau, Queen of the Alps.

Getting There

Bern has direct rail connections to the surrounding countries. This includes service via a high-speed rail line from France, making the train a quick and scenic option. The city itself is compact enough that after you're here, navigation is a breeze.

Arriving by air

The tiny **Bern-Belp Airport** (☎ **031-960-2111;** www.alpar.ch), about 9.7km (6 miles) south of the city, receives flights from several major European cities. A shuttle bus runs from the airport to the city's train station, where you can find the tourist office. The 20-minute trip costs 14F ($14). A taxi from the airport to the city costs about 60F ($60). Most European and transatlantic passengers fly into **Zurich's Kloten Airport** (www.zurich-airport.com), from which one to two trains per hour make the 90-minute trip direct to Bern. The cost for a one-way ticket is 82F ($82).

Arriving by rail

Bern's **Hauptbahnhof train station** (☎ **031-328-1212;** www.sbb.ch) is at the west end of the **Altstadt** (Old Town). Ticketing, track access, and lockers are in the basement. Luggage storage and train and tourist info are on the ground floor. For national rail information, visit www.sbb.ch, call ☎ **0900-300-300** (1.19F/$1.19 per minute), or use the computers in the **SBB train info office** (across from the tourist office) to look up and print out your itinerary.

If you leave the train station from the exit nearest the tourist office, you'll be facing south; turn left to head into the **Altstadt,** or Old Town.

Orienting Yourself in Bern

The **Aare River** is Bern's defining geological feature. It makes a sharp, U-shaped bend around the Altstadt, with the **Hauptbahnhof** (train station) at the open (western) end of the U. From here, you can follow the **Spitalgasse** east into the heart of the Altstadt. The street's name soon changes to **Marktgasse,** the main road of the Old Town.

Introducing the neighborhoods

Bern's medieval section, the **Altstadt,** is small and easily navigable on foot. Tucked into a sharp, U-shaped bend of the Aare River, the Altstadt is made up of five long, arcaded streets (whose names change at every block), two large squares (**Bärenplatz Waisenhausplatz/Bundesplatz** and **Kornhausplatz/Casinoplatz**), and a dozen cross streets. Lots of shop-lined passageways, not shown on most maps, cut to buildings from one main drag to another. Just south of the Altstadt, across the Aare, are several museums and the embassy district (take the Kirchenfeldbrücke Bridge to get here).

Finding information after you arrive

The **Bern Tourist Office** (☎ **031-328-1212;** Fax: 031-328-1277; www.berninfo.com) is in the **Hauptbahnhof.** It's open June through September daily from 9 a.m. to 8:30 p.m.; October through May, it's open Monday through Saturday 9 a.m. to 6:30 p.m. and Sunday 10 a.m. to 5 p.m. A smaller info station is inside the building at the Bear Pits (offering a free 20-minute multimedia show called *Bern Past and Present*); it's open June through September daily 9 a.m. to 6 p.m., October and March through May daily 10 a.m. to 4 p.m., and November through February Friday through Sunday 11 a.m. to 4 p.m.

Getting Around Bern

You can buy two types of public-transit tickets (accepted for both buses and trams): the 2F ($2) version, which is good to travel up to six stops

Switzerland

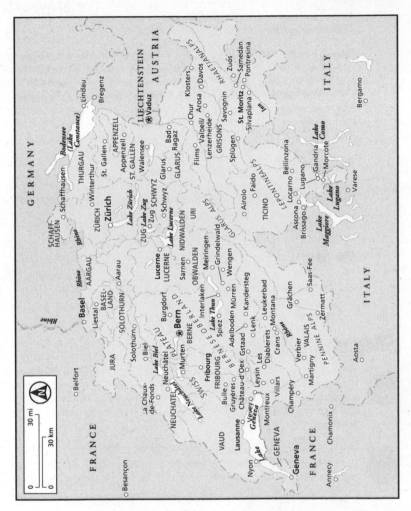

and valid for 45 minutes, and the 3.60F ($3.60) version for longer rides over six stops and for up to 90 minutes. You won't need more than six stops to get to any of the hotels, restaurants, or attractions in this chapter, so always get the cheaper ticket. Buy your ticket from the machine at each stop. You can purchase a daily ticket for 12F ($12), but you'd have to make five or more trips a day (unlikely) to save any money.

By tram and bus

Bern's **bus and tram system** (☎ 031-321-8844; www.berninfo.com) is extensive, but the Altstadt is small enough to cover on foot. However, if you're visiting the **Bear Pits,** you may want to take bus no. 12 on the way back uphill toward the city center and station. Most buses and trams begin and end their routes around the **Hauptbahnhof,** and many on **Bubenbergplatz** just to the station's south.

"Moonliner" night buses (www.moonliner.ch) run Thursday through Saturday three or four times between midnight and 4 a.m. (Thurs usually just at 12:30 a.m.), and cost 5F ($5). The most useful is the M3, which runs from the train station to the Altstadt, across the river past the Bear Pits, and returns via the casino. Several others are designed specifically to get partiers from outlying clubs and dance clubs back to the central train station.

By taxi

If you're only sightseeing in Altstadt, you can see it all on foot. If, however, you want to take a taxi to your hotel, you can catch a cab at the train station, Casinoplatz, or Waisenhausplatz; or you can call ☎ 031-371-1111, 031-331-3313, 031-311-1818, or 031-301-5353.

By foot

The compact historic center of Bern is only a few blocks wide — and a joy to wander. Most of the sights listed here won't take you too far from that walkable center.

Staying in Bern

 Bern is small for a national capital, and conventions and international meetings overbook it regularly. For this reason, this section features some of the town's larger hotels to try to maximize your chances of finding a room. No matter when you plan to visit, make reservations far in advance.

 The folks at the Bern tourist office (☎ 031-328-1212; Fax: 031-328-1277; www.berninfo.com) will book you a room for free, or you can use the big hotel board and free phone just outside the tourist office (at the top of the escalators down to the train tracks).

Bern's top hotels

Allegro Bern
$$$$ Altenberg

This is the hippest, savviest, and most sophisticated hotel in town, with a flair for elegance. Guests appreciate the panoramic view of the medieval town center of Bern and the Swiss Alps. That's reason enough to check in — that and the fact that this is the best-rated hotel in town for comfort and a sense of grace. Set just across the river from the town's historic core,

Accommodations, Dining, and Attractions in Bern

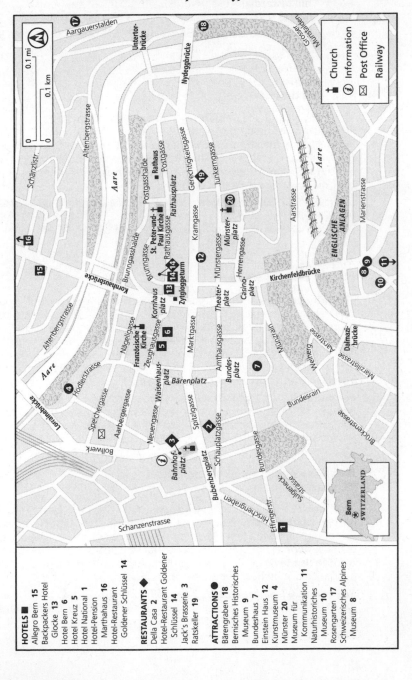

Legend:
- ✝ Church
- ⓘ Information
- ⊠ Post Office
- — Railway

HOTELS ■
Allegro Bern **15**
Backpackers Hotel Glocke **13**
Hotel Bern **6**
Hotel Kreuz **5**
Hotel National **1**
Hotel-Pension Marthahaus **16**
Hotel-Restaurant Goldener Schlüssel **14**

RESTAURANTS ◆
Della Casa **2**
Hotel-Restaurant Goldener Schlüssel **14**
Jack's Brasserie **3**
Ratskeller **19**

ATTRACTIONS ●
Bärengraben **18**
Bernisches Historisches Museum **9**
Bundeshaus **7**
Einstein Haus **12**
Kunstmuseum **4**
Münster **20**
Museum für Kommunikation **11**
Naturhistoriches Museum **10**
Rosengarten **17**
Schweizerisches Alpines Museum **8**

the hotel runs as efficiently as a Swiss clock. You'll find grand comfort everywhere, especially in the midsize to spacious bedrooms.

See map p. 337. Kornhausstrasse 3. ☎ *031-339-55-00. Fax 031-339-55-10.* www.allegro-hotel.ch. *Bus: 20. Rack rates: 209F–370F ($209–$370) double. Breakfast 18F ($18) per person. AE, DC, MC, V.*

Hotel Bern
$$$$ Altstadt

This massive hotel is popular with diplomats and business travelers who are drawn to its modern rooms and large selection of in-house restaurants. Rooms facing the streets are bigger and brighter than those opening onto the small inner courtyard. The cheaper rates apply during weekends and holidays. Children under 16 stay free in their parents' room (or at a 20 percent discount in a separate one).

See map p. 337. Zeughausgasse 9 (just off Kornhausplatz). ☎ *031-329-2222. Fax: 031-329-2299.* www.hotelbern.ch. *Bus/Tram: 3, 5, 9, 10, 12, or 30. Rack rates: 240F–310F ($240–$310) double. Rates include breakfast. AE, DC, MC, V.*

Hotel National
$$ Near Hauptbahnhof

The prices are low at this imposing 1908 castle-in-the-city, but it's a bit lifeless. The elevator doesn't make it up to the fifth floor, where the bathrooms and furnishings are newer and the modern double-glazed windows more efficient at blocking traffic noise from the boulevard below. Accommodations are larger than most in Bern, with patterned rugs atop the carpet and a hodgepodge of faux antique and modular furnishings. The hotel incorporates the popular South American–themed Shakira bar.

See map p. 337. Hirschengraben 24 (just south of the train station). ☎ *031-381-1988. Fax: 031-381-6878.* www.nationalbern.ch. *Bus: 9, 10, or 16. Rack rates: 120F ($120) double without bathroom; 140F–160F ($140–$160) double with bathroom. Rates include breakfast. AE, DC, MC, V.*

Hotel-Restaurant Goldener Schlüssel
$$ Altstadt

Jost Troxler runs his hotel and restaurant with care (see the "Dining in Bern" section, later in this chapter, for a review of the latter), and keeps the prices low for an inn just "99 steps" from the clock tower. The modular furnishings are beginning to show wear but remain sturdy. Rooms on the back overlook a medieval Bern sweep of rooftops and are the quietest (except for the charming hourly chimes of the nearby bell tower).

See map p. 337. Rathausgasse 72 (just off Kornhausplatz). ☎ *031-311-0216. Fax: 031-311-5688.* www.goldener-schluessel.ch. *Bus/Tram: 3, 5, 9, 10, 12, or 30. Rack rates: 168F–195F ($168–$195) double. Rates include breakfast. MC, V.*

Bern's runner-up accommodations

Backpackers Hotel Glocke

$ **Altstadt** For the cheapest night, this former hotel, right on the main square in town (a bit noisy, but located perfectly), improved dramatically when it was taken over and turned into a hostel, with a shared kitchen and cheap laundry facilities. There are even private rooms available for 140F ($140) per double, if you don't want a bed in a dorm at 31F ($31) per person. *See map p. 337. Rathausgasse 75.* ☎ *031-311-3771.* www.bernbackpackers.com.

Hotel Kreuz

$$$ **Altstadt** The Hotel Kreuz is another large business-oriented hotel with many amenities, like its neighbor the Hotel Bern. Many rooms hide foldaway beds for families. *See map p. 337. Zeughausgasse 39–41.* ☎ *031-329-9595.* www.hotelkreuz-bern.ch.

Hotel-Pension Marthahaus

$$ **North of the Altstadt** The Marthahaus is Bern's only pension, with inexpensive rates and rooms a bit larger than those of the central hotels — plus the lady who runs it is a sweetheart. Rooms with private bathrooms (32F/$32) also come with TVs and phones and have slightly nicer furnishings. *See map p. 337. Wyttenbachstrasse 22a (north of the Aare River).* ☎ *031-332-4135.* www.marthahaus.ch.

Dining in Bern

Switzerland has taken culinary influences from the surrounding countries of Germany, France, and Italy, giving Swiss cooking a very international flavor. Cheese is a holey Swiss ingredient. There are about 100 varieties besides the sour, hole-riddled Emmentaler we generically refer to as "Swiss cheese." Emmentaler and Gruyère, along with white wine, garlic, and lemon, often get thrown together in a melting crock and carried to your table — fondue, one of the country's specialties.

Another national specialty is *raclette,* created when half a wheel of cheese is held over an open fire. As the exposed surface begins to melt, the wheel is rushed over to you, and a melted layer is scraped off on your plate. The dish is eaten with hunks of brown bread.

To go with your cheese, the Swiss offer the omnipresent and delicious *rösti* (a sort of hash brown), lake fish, or sausages. Another typical Bernese dish is the *Bernerplatte,* a plate of sauerkraut or beans, piled with sausages, ham, pigs' feet, bacon, or pork chops.

An excellent way to wash all this down is with one of Switzerland's fine white or light red wines or a handcrafted local beer. Swiss chocolates are some of the world's finest (Nestlé is a Swiss company). Although some locals eat chocolate at breakfast, many Americans find that a bit too rich so early in the morning.

Cheap cafes and restaurants line Bern's two main squares, **Bärenplatz** and **Kornhausplatz**. Lining the arcaded streets of the city are kiosks selling *donner kebab* (pita stuffed with spicy lamb and a hot sauce), various Asian nibblers, pizzas, pretzel sandwiches, and *Gschnätzltes* (a Bern specialty of fried veal, beef, or pork; order yours *sur chabis,* with sauerkraut).

For a variety of quick-bite options, head to the indoor marketplace **Markthalle,** Bundesplatz 11, which features lots of small food booths hawking prepared specialty foods to take away or to enjoy at a small table. The hours are Monday through Friday 8 a.m. to 7 p.m. (until 9 p.m. Thurs), and Saturday 8 a.m. to 4 p.m. The supermarkets **Migros** (Marktgasse 46/ Zeughausgasse 31) and **Coop** (in the Ryfflihof department store on Neuengasse) sell fresh picnic ingredients, and both have inexpensive cafeterias where meals generally cost less than 20F ($20). They're both open Monday 9 a.m. to 6:30 p.m.; Tuesday, Wednesday, and Friday 8 a.m. to 6:30 p.m.; Thursday 8 a.m. to 9 p.m.; and Saturday 7 a.m. to 4 p.m.

Della Casa
$$$ Altstadt   SWISS

This creaky local legend, housed in a building from the 1500s, has been around for more than a century. The low-ceilinged, wood-paneled rooms are cozy and inviting; the service is friendly and furious. The staff weaves expertly among the large, crowded tables to bring the abundant portions of ravioli and *lamm-médaillons* (tender lamb medallions in a rich sauce) with Swiss efficiency. If you feel like loosening your wallet straps (and your belt), splurge on the local specialty *Bernerplatte,* an enormous platter of grilled meats served over beans and kraut — it'll cost 45F ($45) but will probably tide you over for two meals. Most regulars prefer the jovial tavern atmosphere on the ground floor to the fancier, more sedate dining room upstairs.

See map p. 337. Schauplatzgasse 16. ☎ *031-311-2142.* www.della-casa.ch. *Reservations recommended. Bus/Tram: 9, 10, 12, or 16. Main courses: Lunch 22F–26F ($22–$26); dinner 24F–40F ($24–$40). AE, DC, MC, V. Open: Apr–Sept Mon–Fri 9:30 a.m.–11:30 p.m., Sat 9:30 a.m.–3 p.m.; Oct–Mar Mon–Sat 9:30 a.m.–11:30 p.m.*

Hotel-Restaurant Goldener Schlüssel
$$ Altstadt   SWISS

You can tuck into hearty Swiss peasant cooking such as *Bauern Bratwurst erlebnis* (a 200g/7-oz. sausage under an onion sauce with *rösti*), or one of several vegetarian dishes of Indian or Mexican inspiration in this converted stone-and-wood 16th-century stable. Wash it all down with a half-liter bottle of a local Bern brew, *Mutzenbügler.*

See map p. 337. Rathausgasse 72 (just off Kornhausplatz). ☎ *031-311-0216. Reservations recommended. Bus/Tram: 9, 10, or 12. Main courses: 18F–35F ($18–$35). Open: Sun–Thurs 7 a.m.–11:30 p.m.; Fri–Sat 7 a.m.–12:30 a.m.*

More Bern museums

Bern's only truly great museum is the **Kunstmuseum**, although the **Bernisches Historisches Museum** is also worth a visit. (You find listings for both of these museums under "Bern's top sights," earlier in this chapter.)

The best of the rest is the **Schweizerisches Alpines Museum (Swiss Alpine Museum)**, Helvetiaplatz 4 (☎ 031-350-0440; www.alpinesmuseum.ch), explaining all you ever wanted to know about the Alps via maps, do-it-yourself slide shows, and a whole collection of scale relief models of alpine regions, some dating from 1800. Admission is 10F ($10) adults, 7F ($7) seniors and students, and 3F ($3) children 6 to 16; hours are Monday 2 to 5 p.m. and Tuesday through Sunday 10 a.m. to 5 p.m. (closed from noon to 2 p.m. mid-Oct to May).

Others that may pique your interest are the **Naturhistoriches Museum (Natural History Museum)**, Bernastrasse 15 (☎ 031-350-7111; www.nmbe.unibe.ch), not the best of its kind, but you can pay your respects to Barry (1800–1814), the most famous of the old rescue Saint Bernards (he saved more than 40 people before retiring to Bern at age 12), and the **Museum für Kommunikation (Museum of Communication)**, Helvetiastrasse 16 (☎ 031-357-5555; www.mfk.ch), covering everything from stamps to cellphones. The admission for the Museum of Communication is 9F ($9) for all comers; the Natural History Museum charges 7F ($7) adults and 5F ($5) students. Both keep hours roughly Tuesday through Sunday 10 a.m. to 5 p.m.; the Natural History Museum opens at 9 a.m. weekdays and is also open Mon 2–5 p.m.

Jack's Brasserie (Stadt Restaurant)
$$$$$ **Altstadt FRENCH/CONTINENTAL**

Nostalgically outfitted in a style that evokes a Lyonnais bistro, Jack's bustles in a way that's chic, convivial, and matter-of-fact, all at the same time. The best dishes on the menu include the kind of *wiener schnitzels* that hang over the sides of the plate, a succulent sea bass, veal head vinaigrette for real regional flavor, tender pepper steaks, and smaller platters piled high with salads, risottos, and pastas.

See map p. 337. In the Hotel Schweizerhof, Bahnhofplatz 11. ☎ 031-326-8080. www.schweizerhof-bern.ch. *Tram: 3, 9, or 12. Reservations recommended. Main courses: 25F–65F ($25–$65); fixed-price menu 85F ($85). AE, DC, MC, V. Open: Mon–Fri 6:30 a.m.–11:30 p.m.; Sat–Sun 8 a.m.–11:30 p.m.*

Ratskeller
$$$$ **Altstadt SWISS**

This starched-tablecloth restaurant is a bit pricey (the laid-back brick-vaulted *keller* [cellar] underneath is cheaper), but for professional service and excellent meat dishes, this is one of the best splurge deals in town for a quiet, understated dinner. The *Oberlander rösti* (cheesy *rösti* layered with bacon and topped by a fried egg) is a house specialty.

See map p. 337. Gerechtigkeitsgasse 81. ☎ 031-311-1771. Reservations recommended. Bus: 12. Main courses: 20F–54F ($20–$54); fixed-price lunch 18F–22F ($18–$22). AE, DC, MC, V. Open: Daily 11:30 a.m.–2 p.m. and 6–11 p.m. (cellar open only at lunch).

Exploring Bern

Bern's historic center is scenic and walkable, with low-key sights such as a dozen statue-topped fountains dating back to the 1500s and the **Zytgloggeturm (Clock Tower),** on Kramgasse at the corner with Bärenplatz, which for more than 460 years has treated Bern to a mechanical puppet show four minutes before every hour. May through October, there's a 45-minute tour of the clock's inner workings daily at 11:30 a.m. (July–Aug also at 4:30 p.m.); admission is 10F ($10) adults, 5F ($5) children.

The **BernCard** is good for unlimited travel on the local trams and buses, 25 percent discounts on city and clock-tower tours, and free entry to most city sights and museums. It costs 20F ($20) for one day, 31F ($31) for two days, or 38F ($38) for three days, and is sold at the tourist offices and major museums.

Bern's top sights

Bernisches Historisches Museum (Bern Historical Museum)
South of the Altstadt

Switzerland's second-largest historical museum is housed in a fanciful faux-medieval castle from 1894 and contains a rich collection of artifacts. Here you find a bit of everything, from Burgundian suits of armor, furnishings and decorative arts, and Flemish tapestries to the original 15th-century carvings from the cathedral's *Last Judgment* portal and dioramas of everyday life in Bern over the past three centuries. The Oriental collection (mostly Islamic), is rendered all the more fascinating by its post-industrial display cases.

See map p. 337. Helvetiaplatz 5. ☎ 031-350-7711. www.bhm.ch. *Tram: 3 or 5. Admission: 13F ($13) adults, 8F ($8) seniors and students, 4F ($4) children 6–16. Open: Tues–Sun 10 a.m.–5 p.m.*

Einstein Haus (Einstein House)
Altstadt

A young German dreamer named Albert Einstein was working in the Bern patent office in 1905 when he came up with $E = mc^2$. While living in this house, he devised his famous Special Theory of Relativity, which revolutionized 20th-century science. The modest museum consists mainly of photos and photocopied letters, most translated into English.

See map p. 337. Kramgasse 49. ☎ 031-312-0091. www.einstein-bern.ch. *Bus: 12. Admission: 6F ($6) adults, 4.50F ($4.50) students and children, free for children 5* *and under. Open: Mar–Sept daily 10 a.m.–5 p.m.; Oct–Dec 16 Tues–Fri 10 a.m.–5 p.m., Sat 10 a.m.–4 p.m. Closed Dec 17–Feb.*

Kunstmuseum (Fine Arts Museum)
Altstadt

This museum preserves the world's largest collection of paintings and drawings by Bern native Paul Klee, offering a unique insight into this early-20th-century master's skill with color and expression. Although the galleries also have a smattering of pieces by the likes of Fra Angelico, Duccio, and Delacroix, the museum's particular strength is late-19th- and early-20th-century art: a few works each by the best Impressionists and Surrealists, along with paintings by Kandinsky, Modigliani, Matisse, Picasso, Léger, Pollock, and Rothko.

See map p. 337. Hodlerstrasse 12. ☎ *031-328-0944.* www.kunstmuseumbern.ch. *Bus: 20 or 21 (or 5-minute walk from train station). Admission: 7F ($7) adults, 5F ($5) students; special exhibitions 18F ($18). Open: Tues–Sun 10 a.m.–5 p.m. (until 9 p.m. Tues).*

Münster (Cathedral)
Altstadt

On Münsterplatz, with its 16th-century Moses fountain, is Bern's Gothic cathedral from 1421, with enormous stained-glass windows and an elaborate *Last Judgment* carved over the main door (most of it is reproduction; the originals are in the Bernisches Historisches Museum). The biggest draw of the cathedral is its 90m (300-ft.) belfry, the highest in Switzerland, which offers a panoramic view across Bern and its river, with the Alps in the distance.

See map p. 337. Münsterplatz. ☎ *031-312-0462. Bus: 12. Admission: Cathedral free; belfry 3F ($3) adults, 1F ($1) children 7–16. Open: Easter Sun–Oct Tues–Sat 10 a.m.–5 p.m. and Sun 11:30 a.m.–5 p.m.; Nov to the day before Easter Tues–Fri 10 a.m. to noon and 2–4 p.m., Sat 10 a.m. to noon and 2–5 p.m., and Sun 11:30 a.m.–2 p.m. The belfry closes 30 minutes before the church.*

More cool things to see and do

- ✔ **Floating down the Aare:** Unlike most capital cities, Bern has a river so unpolluted that the locals actually swim in it regularly. In warm weather, join the Bernese for a short hike up the river and then a leisurely float down the Aare to a free public beach just below the Altstadt. (Make sure you get out at the beach, because a dam/waterfall is the river's next stop.)

- ✔ **Feeding the bears:** Bern's unique sight is the **Bärengraben** (Bear Pits), just on the other side of Nydeggbrücke Bridge from the Altstadt. Here you find up to 12 well-fed live examples of Bern's civic symbol roaming around. The city has had bear pits since at least 1441 — formerly on the square still named Bärenplatz, here since 1875. The bears are out daily 9 a.m. to 4 p.m. (until 5:30 p.m. in summer); the keeper sells 3F ($3) baggies of fruit to feed them —

these hairy fellows ham it up to get you to drop them a piece of apple or carrot. *Remember:* They're strict vegetarians. To the Bear Pits' left, a long path leads up the hillside to a ridge planted with Bern's fragrant **Rosengarten** (Rose Garden), with killer views over medieval Bern.

✔ **Observing how a federal government can operate on just $5 per citizen per year:** Switzerland began as a confederation of three forest *cantons* (states) in 1291. Today's 23 cantons retain a remarkable degree of autonomy and governmental powers, making this one of the West's least centralized democracies. The federal chambers meet only four times a year for three-week sessions to debate legislative issues and foreign treaties. If you'd like a glimpse into such a lean federal machine, you can tour the 1902 **Bundeshaus** (Parliament), Bundesplatz (☎ **031-322-8522;** www.bundeshaus.ch), the dome of which was modeled loosely on that of Florence's cathedral. Free tours are given Monday through Saturday at 9 a.m., 10 a.m., 11 a.m., 2 p.m., 3 p.m., and 4 p.m. (except when Parliament is in session, at which time you can observe from the galleries).

✔ **Shopping 'til you drop (chocolates, watches, and Swiss army knives):** Bern has almost 4 miles of virtually continuous shopping arcade running down its three parallel main streets, with even more shops crowding the alleys and corridors connecting them.

Switzerland is home to **Nestlé, Lindt,** and those triangular **Toblerone** chocolates. You can get these famous factory-made chockies at **Merkur,** Spitalgasse 2 (☎ **031-322-3080;** www.merkur.ch). If you want handmade sweets from a traditional confectioner, head to **Confiserie Abegglen,** Spitalgasse 36 (☎ **031-311-2111;** www.confiserie-abegglen.ch), or **Confiserie Tschirren,** Kramgasse 73 (☎ **031-812-2122;** www.swiss-chocolate.ch) and in the Markthalle at Bubenbergplatz 9.

If you're in the market for a fine watch, the shop with the most reasonable prices is **Columna,** Spitalgasse 4 (☎ **031-311-0975**). If you're using this guide mainly to save enough to afford that 4,200F ($4,200) Rolex (that's the cheapest model), put on your best and head to the burnished wood shrine of **Bucherer,** Marktgasse 38 (☎ **031-328-9090;** www.bucherer.ch).

You can find knives, watches, cuckoo clocks, and a little bit of everything Swiss (or imagined to be Swiss) at general souvenir shops such as **Swiss Plaza,** Kramgasse 75 (☎ **031-311-5616**), or **Boutique Regina,** Gerechtigkeitgasse 75 (☎ **031-311-5616**).

Guided tours

The **Bern Tourist Office,** in the Hauptbahnhof (☎ **031-328-1212;** Fax: 031-328-1277; www.berninfo.com), sponsors a **two-hour bus tour** of the center and major sights with a multilingual guide. The tour costs 40F ($40) adults and 15F ($15) children 16 and under; it runs daily at 11 a.m. (Nov 2–Apr, Sat only).

A **90-minute walking tour** of the Altstadt costs 18F ($18) adults, 9F ($9) children 16 and under; it leaves at 11 a.m. daily from June through September (plus daily in Apr at 2:30 p.m.). June through September, you can also see the city from below via a 90-minute raft tour daily (55F/$55 adults, 30F/$30 children 16 and under); this is a genuine rubber-raft deal, not a cruise-type river boat, meaning you help paddle and need to bring a swimsuit. You have to contact the tourist office to see when these are running — they require a minimum of four people to sign up before it's a go — but they tend to float around 5 p.m.

Suggested itineraries

If you're the type who'd rather organize your own tours, this section offers some tips for building your own Bern-centered itineraries.

If you have one day

You can do the best of Bern easily in a day. First thing, head to the **Kunstmuseum** to commune with the works of Paul Klee and other old and modern masters. At 11 a.m., take a tour of **Bundeshaus.** Then just head up to **Marktgasse** and start strolling downhill toward the far end of the **Altstadt,** taking in the ambience of the city, with its soft gray stone buildings with their coats of arms and red-tiled roofs and the cobbled streets with their statue-topped fountains. Pop into the **Einstein Haus** before having lunch at **Klötzlikeller.**

After lunch, mosey across the river to visit the bears at the **Bärengraben** and climb up to the **Rosengarten** for a beautiful vista across Bern. Head back into the Altstadt and detour left up Junkerngasse to visit the **Münster** after the cathedral reopens at 2 p.m., and climb its tower for another great cityscape. If you have time left, cross the river to the south to check out the **Bernisches Historisches Museum** before it closes at 5 p.m. End with a traditional Swiss dinner at **Della Casa.**

If you have two days

Spend **Day 1** as the one-day itinerary, but save the **Bernisches Historisches Museum** for the morning of **Day 2.** On **Day 2,** after the historical museum and before lunch, check out the **Schweizerisches Alpines Museum,** plus any of the others that catch your fancy. After lunch, head up to Bern's mini-mountain, the **Gurtenkulm,** or spend the afternoon shopping downtown. If you have only two days for all Switzerland, forget all that and spend **Day 2** in the Alps (see "Visiting the Bernese Oberland," later in this chapter).

If you have three days

You've covered all of Bern's major sites (see the preceding sections), so on **Day 3,** get up early and splurge 240F ($240) on a round trip to the **Jungfraujoch,** Europe's highest train station, slung 3,400m (11,333 ft.) up between two of the mightiest Alps (see "Visiting the Bernese Oberland," later in this chapter).

Traveling beyond Bern

The two excursions in this section take you to nearby urban destinations — Zurich, the banking capital of Europe, and Basel, a college town with an amazing repository of art. For trips into the countryside, see "Visiting the Bernese Oberland," later in this chapter.

Zurich: Swiss counterculture meets high finance

Switzerland's largest city and banking capital, Zurich is the prettiest of the country's big cities. Its oldest quarter is spread over the steep banks on either side of the swan-filled **Limmat River,** which flows out of the Zürichsee (Lake Zurich).

Zurich has always been a hotbed of radicalism and liberal thought. The Swiss Protestant Reformation started here in the 16th century, and the 20th century has drawn the likes of Carl Jung, Lenin (who spent World War I here, planning his revolution), Thomas Mann, and James Joyce, who worked on *Ulysses* in Zurich and returned a month before his death in 1941. Joyce's grave in **Friedhof Fluntern cemetery** (take tram no. 2) is near those of Nobelist Elias Canetti and *Heidi* author Joanna Spyri.

Your best bet is to spend a relaxing 48 hours in Zurich, but you can get a surprisingly good feel for the city in just a day.

Getting there

Zurich is well connected with Europe's major cities and is only 75 to 120 minutes from Bern by train. Trains arrive at **Hauptbahnhof** (the main train station) on the riverbank at the north end of town. The tourist office (☎ **01-215-4000;** Fax: 01-215-4044; www.zuerich.com) is at the train station, Bahnhofplatz 15.

From the station, the tree-shaded shopping street of **Bahnhofstrasse** runs south, paralleling the **Limmat** a few blocks away, all the way to the shores of the **Zürichsee.** Running off to the left of this street is a series of medieval alleys that lead down to the river. Several bridges cross the river to the wide **Limmatquai Street.** Narrow side streets lined with shops lead to the other half of the old city.

You need to hop a **tram** or **bus** (www.zvv.ch) for some of the outlying sights and hotels, even though you can get to most of central Zurich on foot. The cost is 6F ($6) for rides up to one hour, and 7.80F ($7.80) for a **Tageskarte,** a 24-hour ticket.

The **ZürichCARD** (www.vbz.ch) costs 33F ($33) for 24 hours, 34F ($34) for 72 hours, and covers all public transport and free admission to 43 museums (plus a free "welcome drink" at two dozen local restaurants).

Seeing the sights

The 13th-century **St. Peter's Church** at St. Petershofstaat 6 has the largest clock face in Europe — 9m (29 ft.) across with a 4m (12-ft.) minute hand. Nearby is one of Zurich's top sights, the Gothic **Fraumünster** church, with five 1970 stained-glass windows by artist Marc Chagall.

From here, cross the Münsterbrücke over the Limmat River to reach Zurich's cathedral, the twin-towered **Grossmünster.** Founded on a site said to have been chosen by Charlemagne's horse (he bowed his head on the spot where a trio of third-century martyrs were buried), its construction ran from 1090 to the 14th century. Swiss artist Alberto Giacometti designed the stained glass in 1933. Climb the tower (3F/$3) from March 15 to October 31 for a great city view.

A long walk up Kirchgasse from the church and a left on Seiler Granben/ Zeltweg takes you to Heimplatz and the **Kunsthaus** (☎ 01-253-8484; www.kunsthaus.ch), Zurich's fine-arts museum. The main collection starts with the Impressionists of the late 19th century and runs to contemporary times, featuring works by Monet, Degas, Cézanne, Chagall, Rodin, Picasso, Mondrian, Marini, and especially the Swiss-born Giacometti. Admission is 12F to 18F ($12–$18) for adults, 8F to 16F ($8–$16) for students (free for children 15 and under) — more when one of the frequent special exhibits is on — and it's closed Monday (you can also take tram no. 3 here). Wednesdays, admission is free to all.

 Zurich's cheapest sight is the park lining the mouth of the Zürichsee. You can stroll the west bank of the lake up and down the **General Guisan quai** (at the end of Bahnhofstrasse), which leads to an arboretum. Also at the base of Bahnhofstrasse are the piers from which dozens of steamers embark for tours of the lake. A full-length tour of the lake costs 23F ($23) in second class and 38F ($38) in first class. A shorter boat ride on the northern third of the lake costs 7.80F ($7.80). For more information, contact the **Zürichsee Schiffahrtsgesellschaft** (☎ 01-487-1333; www.zsg.ch).

Where to stay and dine

Zur Oepfelchammer, Rindermarkt 12, just off the Limmat (☎ 01-251-2336), serves up reasonably priced Swiss and French cuisine in a friendly, atmospheric setting. Although pricey at 550F to 850F ($550–$850) double, the romantic **Hotel zum Storchen,** Am Weinplatz 2 (☎ 01-227-2727; Fax: 01-227-2700; www.storchen.ch), is the best bet in town — a 640-year-old inn right on the river in the center of Zurich's Altstadt. The tourist office can help you find someplace cheaper or other rooms if you can't find a room here.

Basel: Three, three, three countries in one!

The Swiss answer to Four Corners, USA, is Basel, a university city that features a pylon on the **Rhine River** where you can walk in a circle and move from Switzerland into Germany, then France, and back into Switzerland (the spot's called **Dreiländereck**). Basel's number of museums (27) makes it an art capital of Switzerland, and the city claims Hans Holbein the Younger (along with thinker Friedrich Nietzsche) among its famous past residents. Non–art lovers needn't bother visiting, but give the city at least a day or two if you're a fan of modern and contemporary art.

Getting there

Half-hourly trains make the 60- to 75-minute trip from **Bern** and arrive at **SBB Hauptbahnhof.** A small branch of the tourist office can be found in the train station, but the main office (☎ **061-268-6868;** Fax: 061-268-6870; www.baseltourismus.ch) is on the Rhine at Schifflände 5, just past the Mittlere Bridge (take tram no. 1). Basel's compact, historic center lies mainly on the south bank of the Rhine River.

Seeing the sights

Although the elaborately carved face of the impressive 14th-century **Münster** (cathedral) is the pride of Basel, this city is really about museums. Top honors go to the eclectic collections of the **Kunstmuseum** (Fine Arts Museum), St. Alban Graben 16 (☎ **061-206-6262;** www.kunst musumbasel.ch). This museum has everything from Holbein the Younger and Konrad Witz to van Gogh, Picasso, Klee, Chagall, Rodin, and Alexander Calder.

Next door is the **Museum für Gegenwartskunst** (Museum for Contemporary Art; ☎ **061-206-6262;** www.kunstmuseumbasel.ch), with art ranging from the 1960s to the present day by the likes of Bruce Nauman, Joseph Beuys, and Donald Judd. Admission (covering both museums) is 18F ($18). Nearby you can also find the **Kunsthalle,** Steinenberg 7 (☎ **061-206-9900;** www.kunsthallebasel.ch), whose changing installations by contemporary artists are advertised on banners throughout town. Admission is 10F ($10). Most Basel museums are closed on Monday.

The city also has the **Basler Zoologischer Garten,** Binningerstrasse 40 (☎ **061-295-3535;** www.zoobasel.ch), a world-renowned zoo just a seven-minute stroll from the train station, with 600 species represented. Open daily May through August 8 a.m. to 6:30 p.m., March through April and September through October 8 a.m. to 6 p.m., and November through February 8 a.m. to 5:30 p.m.; admission is 16F ($16) adults, 14F ($14) seniors, 12F ($12) students 17 to 25, and 6F ($6) children 6 to 16.

Where to stay and dine

The restaurant **Gasthof zum Goldenen Sternen,** St. Alban-rheinweg 70, at the Rhine's edge (☎ **061-272-1666;** www.sternen-basel.ch), has served up a good, inexpensive medley of French-accented Swiss and Continental dishes since 1421. Art aficionados with shallow pockets will want to stay just across the river from the main part of town at the **Hotel Krafft am Rhein,** Rheingasse 12 (☎ **061-690-9130;** Fax: 061-690-9131; www.hotel krafft.ch), overlooking the Rhine. The setting is 19th century, and the rooms are modern and comfy. Rates are 250F to 310F ($250–$310) double.

Visiting the Bernese Oberland

The triple peaks of the **Eiger** (3,908m/13,025 ft.), **Mönch** (4,035m/13,450 ft.), and **Jungfrau** (4,093m/13,642 ft.) dominate the Jungfrau region. A trip to the area can be a thrilling, scenic ride on trains that hug (or punch through) cliffsides and ski-lift gondolas that dangle high above mountain glaciers.

The gateway to the Bernese Oberland is **Interlaken,** a bustling resort town in the foothills of the Alps that is flanked by a pair of lakes and is just a one-hour train ride from Bern. Interlaken itself doesn't have too much to hold your interest, but it makes an optimal base for forays into the Bernese Oberland.

The Alps are scattered with tiny villages and quaint resort towns. One of the most visitor-friendly of these is **Mürren,** where we recommend a few restaurants and hotels. The region calls for at least three or four days, but on the tightest of schedules you can take an overnight train to Interlaken, switch for a train up to **Jungfraujoch** to spend the day, and make it back to Interlaken by evening for another overnight train out — but that's pushing it.

Getting there

Two trains per hour run between Bern and Interlaken (a 50- to 60-minute ride), some requiring a change in Spiez. Get off at Interlaken's **Westbahnhof station** for the main part of town, or disembark at **Ostbahnhof station** to transfer to trains into the Jungfrau region.

Finding information after you arrive

For information on the Bernese Oberland and the Alps, the **Tourist Office of Interlaken** (☎ **033-826-5300;** Fax: 033-826-5375; www.interlaken.ch) is the unofficial central information bureau, with maps and advice on getting around the region. It's a seven-minute walk from Westbahnhof train station, in the Hotel Metropole at Höheweg 37. The tourist office is open May through October Monday through Friday 8 a.m. to noon and 1:30 to 6 p.m., Saturday 8 a.m. to 2 p.m. (open through the midday break in May, June, and Oct); July through September, hours are Monday through Friday 8 a.m. to 6:30 p.m., Saturday 8 a.m. to 5 p.m., and Sunday 10 a.m. to noon and 5 to 7 p.m. You find **Mürren's Tourist Office** in the Sportzentrum (☎ **033-856-8686;** Fax: 033-856-8696; www.muerren.ch).

General info on the Bernese Oberland is available at www.berner oberland.ch. Timetables for the major trains and cable cars are supplied in English at www.jungfraubahn.ch.

Learning the lay of the land

Interlaken lies on the brief stretch of the Aare River (the same river that runs to Bern) that connects two lakes, **Lake Thun** and **Lake Brienz** — hence the city's name, which means "between the lakes." Its busiest tourist area stretches between the two train stations along the Aare. The road that connects the stations is **Bahnhof Strasse,** which becomes the parklike **Höheweg.**

Now about the **Alps:** The Bernese Oberland is large, but the information in this chapter concentrates on the western half — it's the most popular and the easiest to reach from Interlaken. Imagine you're standing in Interlaken and looking south toward the Alps. Low mountains lie directly in front of you. Behind them, to the east, is a trio of enormous peaks called **Eiger, Mönch,** and, the most famous, **Jungfrau.**

Farther off to the west (right) is the slightly more modest peak of the **Schilthorn.** Running south from Interlaken between the Jungfrau and Schilthorn is a wide valley called the **Lauterbrunnen;** this is where the area's main train line leads to various alpine destinations. (Halfway up the valley in the town of Lauterbrunnen is a station where you may transfer trains frequently.)

Scattered throughout the upper reaches of this valley are many small resorts and alpine towns, such as **Mürren** (at the base of the **Schilthorn**) and **Wengen** (halfway to the **Jungfrau**). Between Interlaken and Lauterbrunnen town, a valley that branches off to the east from Lauterbrunnen Valley interrupts the Alpine foothills. Train tracks lead to here to the village of **Grindelwald.**

Getting around the Bernese Oberland

Unfortunately, the various scenic and private rail lines — not to mention funiculars, ski lifts, and cable cars — that connect the peaks and towns are ridiculously expensive. Rail passes, such as Swissrail or Eurail, only get you a 25 percent discount at most. Always ask about discounts for children, seniors, students, and so on. For each of the sights in this chapter, we give directions and some idea of the frequency of trains and connections.

Traveling around the Bernese Oberland means plenty of train changes, but this usually turns out to be kind of fun (if pricey). The wait between connections is most often five to ten minutes. Because trains tend to run hourly, it's fairly easy to hop off at any station, go see whatever town you're in, and pick up the transfer an hour or two later.

 The tourist office in Interlaken has Bernese Oberland transportation maps (get one if you plan to explore) and schedules of the whole system. The staff is usually very good at helping you work out an itinerary. A summer **Bernese Oberland Regional Pass** (www.regiopass-berner oberland.ch) gets you seven days of travel (three days for free, four days at 50 percent off) for 267F ($267), or 15 days (five days free, ten days at 50 percent off) for 322F ($322), but again the pass gets you only a discount on the **Jungfraujoch and Schilthorn rides.**

The Bernese Oberland

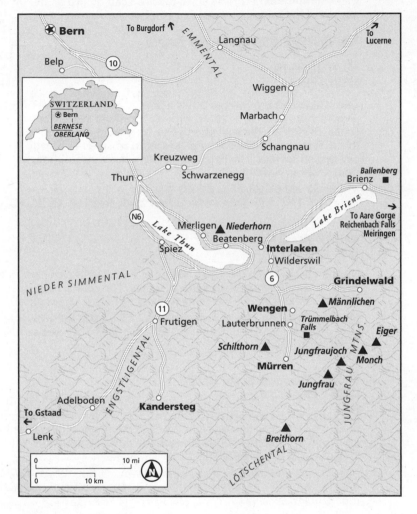

 TIP

Staying in the Bernese Oberland

At Interlaken and Bernese Oberland resorts, you receive a "guest card" from your hotel for significant discounts on everything from the **Jungfrau train** to adventure outfitters. If your hotel doesn't give you one, be sure to ask for it.

Interlaken certainly doesn't lack hotels, but it also doesn't lack visitors to fill them. If you're having trouble finding a room, check out the hotel billboards at each train station, or visit the tourist office (at the Hotel Metropole), which can book you a room for free. The tourist offices of

Mürren and other Bernese Oberland towns can help you find rooms as well, but these burgs are so small that you can do just as well by following one of the many hotel signs as you exit the station.

The Bernese Oberland's top hotels

Hotel Alpenruh
$$$$ Mürren

One of Mürren's top choices is this alpine-cozy but fully accessorized hotel next to the cable-car station, with an excellent restaurant and private sauna. Best of all, the staff gives you a free voucher for a morning ride up to the Schilthorn where you can breakfast in style — already a 48F ($48) per-person savings. The hotel stays open year-round, although the restaurant closes in November.

Mürren. ☎ *033-856-8800. Fax: 033-856-8888.* www.alpenruh-muerren.ch. *Rack rates: 190F–270F ($190–$270) double. Rates include breakfast. AE, DC, MC, V.*

Hotel Weisses Kreuz
$$$ Interlaken

On the classiest drag in town, which is basically a city park, this year-round hotel has functionally spartan rooms. The comfort is good, the price is right, and the people-watching from its terrace is unparalleled.

Höheweg (at the corner with Jungfraustrasse). ☎ *033-822-5951. Fax: 033-823-3555.* www.weisseskreuz.ch. *Rack rates: 190F–290F ($190–$290) double. Rates include breakfast. AE, DC, MC, V.*

Victoria-Jungfrau Grand Hotel
$$$$$ Interlaken

If you can swing the price tag, you can join a long list of dignitaries and royalty by checking into this massive 1865 landmark of over-the-top alpine architecture. Antiques fill the rooms, the most expensive of which overlook the park of Höheweg and the Alps beyond.

Höheweg 41 (several blocks from Interlaken West station). ☎ *033-828-2828. Fax: 033-828-2880.* www.victoria-jungfrau.ch. *Rack rates: 680F–760F ($680–$760) double. Breakfast 40F ($40). AE, DC, MC, V.*

The Bernese Oberland's runner-up accommodations

Alpina Hotel
$$ **Mürren** The Alpina offers lower prices than the Alpenruh and panoramic clifftop vistas across the Lauterbrunnen Valley. ☎ *033-855-1361.* www.muerren.ch/alpina.

Chalet-Hotel Oberland
$$$ **Interlaken** The Chalet-Hotel Oberland is another modernish hotel offering somewhat nicer, newer, and roomier accommodations at similar

prices to the Splendid (no views, though). *Postgasse 1 (just off Interlaken's main drag).* ☎ *033-827-8787.* www.chalet-oberland.ch.

Splendid

$$$ **Interlaken** The Splendid is a nondescript modern hotel with comfy rooms, all the amenities, glimpses of the mountains, and a popular corner pub featuring Internet access. Rooms without a bathroom, of course, are cheaper. *Höheweg 33 (in the center of Interlaken).* ☎ *033-822-7612.* www.splendid.ch.

Dining in the Bernese Oberland

Most hotels in Bernese Oberland resort towns either require or offer some meals in their own restaurants — and, in fact, there aren't enough non-hotel restaurants to go around. But don't despair. The hotel food is usually quite good. However, if possible, try not to sign up for full board; that way, at least one meal a day you can try the food at *other* hotel dining rooms in town.

For a primer on Swiss foods, see "Dining in Bern," earlier in this chapter.

In Interlaken, you can fill your daypack for picnics and hikes at Migros supermarket, just to the right of the Westbahnhof, or at the huge co-op supermarket center across from the Ostbahnhof. You also find a co-op market in Mürren.

Hirschen
$$$ **Matten SWISS**

There has been a Gasthaus Hirschen here since 1666, an oasis of old-fashioned flavors and alpine hospitality in touristy Interlaken. The low wood-paneled ceilings and overdressed tables strike an odd balance somewhere between rustic and fussy, but you'll be glad the fussiness spreads to their exacting standards in the kitchen — this is by far the best Swiss dining in town. Try the *Hirschen Platte* for two, a platter of grilled meats with *rösti* and a salad.

Hauptstrasse 11 (in Matten, the southerly neighborhood of Interlaken). ☎ *033-822-1545.* www.hirschen-interlaken.ch. *Reservations recommended. Main courses: 12F–42F ($12–$42). AE, DC, MC, V. Open: Wed–Fri 4–11 p.m.; Sat–Sun 9 a.m.–11:30 p.m.*

Restaurant im Gruebi
$$$ **Mürren SWISS**

This restaurant excels in both mountain views (from its outdoor terrace or the glassed-in hexagonal dining room) and local cuisine, from herb-flavored rack of lamb for two to fondue bourguignon.

In the Hotel Jungfrau (follow signs from the station). ☎ *033-856-6464.* www.hotel jungfrau.ch. *Reservations recommended. Main courses: 15F–40F ($15–$40); 4-course fixed-price menu 38F ($38). AE, DC, MC, V. Open: Daily 7:30 a.m.–9:15 p.m. Closed mid-Apr to mid-June and mid-Oct to mid-Dec.*

Restaurant Piz Gloria
$$$ Schilthorn SWISS

To cap off an idyllic trip to the Swiss Alps, dine in Europe's most stratospheric restaurant — it slowly rotates atop a 2,941m (9,804-ft.) mountain. If you can tear your eyes away from the view for a moment, sample the hearty Hungarian goulash or sirloin steak. This place is also a good place to have a high-altitude breakfast if you catch the first cable car up.

Atop Schilthorn Mountain, above Mürren. ☎ *033-855-2141. Reservations suggested, but not required. For directions, see "A bit of Bond history atop the Schilthorn," later in this chapter. Main courses: 18F–35F ($18–$35). AE, DC, MC, V. Open: Summer daily 7:25 a.m.–6 p.m.; winter daily 7:55 a.m.–5 p.m. Closed Nov 6–Dec 1, 1 week in Apr, and during blizzards.*

Exploring the Bernese Oberland

Prepare for the unique climate of the skyscraping Alps before you get on that train to the top of the world. A warm sunny day in Interlaken may still be sunny atop the Jungfrau, but the wind can bring temperatures deep into negative territory, so bring a heavy jacket. The sun reflects strongly off all that snow, and UV rays are more concentrated, so be sure to wear sunglasses and sunscreen. The highest peaks poke into a very thin atmosphere (about 30 percent less oxygen than at sea level), so overexerting yourself into dizziness and hyperventilation is easy.

Check the weather conditions and forecasts before you set off into the mountains. An overcast day can make an excursion to the panoramic terraces of Jungfrau or Schilthorn a moot point, and avalanche warnings may crimp your skiing or hiking plans. Displayed on TVs at train stations, tourist offices, and hotel rooms are the live Webcam video feeds of the **Jungfraujoch,** the **Schilthorn,** and the **Männlichen** peaks — which are also live-linked at www.swisspanorama.com. In addition, the Web site for Interlaken (www.interlakentourism.ch) links to several local weather-forecasting sites — most in German, but pretty easy to figure out. Real-time forecasts are also available by phone at ☎ 162.

The queen peak at Jungfraujoch

The most spectacular and rewarding excursion in the region is to **Jungfraujoch,** where at 3,400m (11,333 ft.) — the highest rail station in Europe — your breath quickens from the stupendous views and the extremely thin air. An elevator takes you up from the station to the even higher **Sphinx Terrace** viewpoint to look out over Europe's longest glacier, the 25km (16-mile) **Great Aletsch,** whose melt-off eventually makes its way to the Mediterranean.

The view goes on seemingly forever — on a clear day, you can even see as far as Germany's **Black Forest.** One of the popular attractions is the **Eispalast (Ice Palace),** a warren of tunnels carved into a living glacier and filled with whimsical ice sculptures, including a family of penguins and a sumo wrestler. You can eat at a mediocre restaurant (25F/$25 fondue) or a cafeteria up top if you didn't pack a lunch.

Trains run half-hourly from **Interlaken's Ostbahnhof** (two-and-a-half hours; 172F/$172). You change once in **Lauterbrunnen** (☎ 033-828-7038), pause in **Wengen,** and change again in **Kleine Scheidegg** (☎ 033-828-7623) before making the final run to **Jungfraujoch station** (☎ 033-828-7901). This popular route has run since 1894, so the transfers are smooth.

Four of the last six miles of track are in tunnels, but the train pauses a few times to let you peer out to windows in the rock at the glaciated surroundings. On your way back down, you can change trains at **Kleine Scheidegg** to detour west to **Grindelwald.** For more information, contact the Jungfraubahnen directly at ☎ 033-828-7233 or on the Web at www.jungfraubahn.ch.

A bit of Bond history atop the Schilthorn

A favorite excursion is to take a ride from **Mürren** — home to a fabulous **Sportzentrum** sports complex, with an indoor pool, outdoor skating rink, squash, tennis, curling facilities, and more — up the dizzying cable car to the 2,941m (9,804-ft.) peak of the **Schilthorn.** The trip takes you across the Lauterbrunnen Valley with views of the **Big Three peaks,** so you get a great panorama of the Alps' poster children. The summit shares its scenic terrace with the **Restaurant Piz Gloria** (see "Dining in the Bernese Oberland," earlier in this chapter).

When the financiers building Europe's most spectacularly sighted restaurant atop the Schilthorn went over budget, James Bond came to the rescue. A film company used the half-finished structure to play the role of "Piz Gloria," headquarters of evil SPECTRE leader Telly Savalas in *On Her Majesty's Secret Service.* George Lazenby (filling in for 007 between Sean Connery and Roger Moore), fought bad guys while hanging from the cable-car lines (and on skis, and in a bobsled . . .). After shooting wrapped, the film company helped pay for the restaurant's completion and, because the movie provided such great advance publicity, the restaurant decided to take its stage name.

Trains run every half-hour to **Mürren** from **Interlaken's Ostbahnhof,** with a change at Lauterbrunnen (60 minutes; 16F/$16). When the funicular-train line from Lauterbrunnen to Mürren is snowed in, take the hourly Postbus (15 minutes; 4F/$4) to Stechelberg and the half-hourly **Schilthornbahn cable car** (☎ 033-826-0007; www.schilthorn.ch) up to Gimmelwald (first stop) and then on to Mürren (10 minutes; 15F/$15). Half-hourly cable cars from Mürren get you to the top of the **Schilthorn** in 20 minutes (96F/$96 round-trip total from Stechelberg — 66F/$66 round-trip from Mürren — with a 25 percent discount if you take the "early-bird" run before 7:30 a.m.; discounts for various rail- and ski-pass holders). If you're up for a workout, you can hike up in a rather demanding, but exhilarating, five hours (a 1,309m/4,363-ft. climb).

Mürren's **Tourist Office** is in the Sportzentrum (☎ 033-856-8686; Fax: 033-856-8696; www.muerren.ch).

Skiing and other outdoorsy stuff

If you came to Switzerland hoping to log a few miles of **Alpine skiing,** you can't do better than **Wengen,** a resort under the looming **Jungfrau trio** and near the **Lauterbrunnen Valley** with some 23 lifts (from cable car to T-bar) and access to most of the region's major ski areas (Wengen, Männlichen, and Kleine Scheidegg). There are half-hourly trains here from **Interlaken's Ostbahnhof,** with a change in Lauterbrunnen (45–55 minutes; 13F/$13). Those arriving by car have to leave their wheels in the garage down in Lauterbrunnen (☎ 033-855-3244) and take the train up to car-free Wengen.

The tourist office (☎ 033-855-1414; Fax: 033-855-3060; www.wengen-muerren.ch) can help you make sense of the multitude of trails, some 20 lifts (both cable car and chair), and more than 7 miles of cross-country terrain. They can also point you toward rental outfitters and the local branch of the famous **Swiss Ski School** (☎ 033-855-2022; www.skiwengen.ch). Less intrepid sports enthusiasts can skate or curl in town.

When there isn't much snow, Wengen sports more than 310 miles of hiking trails (most open in summer only, but 31 miles open in winter, too). One of the most popular is a fairly flat jaunt along the wide ridge of the Männlichen massif, from the top of the Männlichen cable-car station (☎ 033-854-8080) to Kleine Scheidegg (90 minutes; descending gradually about 167m/555 ft.). A bit more of a workout, but wonderfully scenic, is the steady uphill walk from **Wengen** to **Kleine Scheidegg,** with a panorama of the **Jungfrau** group (two-and-a-half to three hours; 778m/2,594-ft. climb).

Even more spectacular hikes are available in **Lauterbrunnen Valley** (Lauterbrunnen town is 15 minutes by train or 90 minutes by foot below Wengen). From Lauterbrunnen, take the hourly postal bus or walk, in 45 minutes, to **Trümmelbach Falls** (☎ 033-855-3232; www.truemmelbach.ch), actually ten stair-stepped waterfalls in one, created by glacial melt-off from the surrounding mountains, thundering down the deep crevice of a gorge at 20,000 liters per second. April through November, you can ride an elevator up the inside of the cliff to stroll behind the cascades daily 9 a.m. to 5 p.m. (July–Aug 8:30 a.m.–6:30 p.m.); bring a raincoat. Admission is 11F ($11) adults and 4F ($4) children 6 to 16. Also near Lauterbrunnen, **Staubbach Falls** is a 300m (1,000-ft.) ribbon of water plunging straight down the valley's cliffside at the edge of Lauterbrunnen town.

Hikes in the hills from Grindelwald

Cars can reach **Grindelwald,** so this resorty village in the eastern alpine foothills gets more crowded than its less-accessible neighbors. However, the village is also one of the best bases for hiking. Half-hourly trains from **Interlaken's Ostbahnhof** take 36 minutes and cost 9.80F ($9.80). Be sure you're on the right car; the train splits in half at Lauterbrunnen

The **Tourist Office** (☎ **033-854-1212;** Fax: 033-854-1210; `www.grindelwald.travel/de/welcome.cfm`) has trail maps covering everything from easy scenic rambles to rock climbing up the sheer eastern face of **Mount Eiger.** Or **Grindelwald Sports** (☎ **033-854-1280;** `www.grindelwaldsports.ch`) can organize guided hikes of all degrees of difficulty, from glacier-climbing lessons to an easy, three-hour guided romp along the foot of Mount Eiger.

An hour's hike up to **Milchbach** brings you to the base of the **Obere Gletscher** glacier, whose milky white runoff gives the spot its name. If you continue 45 minutes up the side of the glacier, you're treated to the **Blue Ice Grotte.** Glacial ice turns a deep, resonant blue as you get down into it, and you can take a spin inside a slowly creeping glacier here for 6F ($6) mid-May through October daily 9 a.m. to 6 p.m. A postal bus can run you back down to town in 15 minutes.

Fast Facts: Bern

Area Code

Switzerland's country code is **41.** Bern's city code is **031.** If you're calling Bern (or any other Swiss destination) from beyond Switzerland's borders, drop the city code's initial 0. To call Bern from the United States, dial ☎ 011-41-31 followed by the phone number.

Currency

Switzerland has so far opted out of adopting the euro. The basic unit of currency is the Swiss franc (we abbreviate it F, though sometimes you'll see it as CHF), which is composed of 100 centimes. At press time, the Swiss Franc and the U.S. dollar were trading at par (i.e., 1F = US$1). Although this specific ratio can and probably will change by the time you get to Switzerland, we advise that you use the conversions within this chapter only as a rough guideline for a situation that most experts define as economically volatile.

Doctors and Dentists

For a list of doctors and dentists, visit the U.S. consulate (see the following listing) or call the national English-speaking tourist hot line at ☎ 157-5014 (2.13F/$2.13 per minute).

Embassies and Consulates

The U.S. Embassy, Jubiläumsstrasse 93 (☎ 031-357-7011; `http://bern.usembassy.gov`; Bus: 19), is open Monday through Friday from 9 a.m. to 12:30 p.m. and 1:30 to 5:30 p.m.

Emergency

Dial ☎ **117** for the police; ☎ **144** for an ambulance; ☎ **118** to report a fire; and ☎ **140** (not a free call) for car breakdown.

Hospitals

For emergency care, go to the 650-year-old Insel Hospital, Freiburgstrasse (☎ 031-632-2111; `www.insel.ch`).

Information

The Bern Tourist Office (☎ 031-328-1212) is in the Hauptbahnhof (train station). For specifics on it, and on other offices, see "Finding information after you arrive," near the beginning of this chapter.

Internet Access and Cybercafes

The traveler's best bet in Bern is the BZ Café, Zeughausstrasse 14 (☎ 031-327-1188). Run by *Berner Zeitung,* the local daily paper, the cafe lets you use the half-dozen computers with lightning ISDN access for free. (Yes, it's popular, but they even have some Sega game systems for you to play while you wait.)

Maps

The map handed out for free by the tourist office is more than adequate for ambling about the tiny town center.

Newspapers and Magazines

Aside from the local daily *Berner Zeitung* (German only), there's no particular magazine or newspaper for visitors in the city, but the tourist office has scads of pamphlets and announcements on current events, shows, concerts, and the like.

Pharmacies

Central-Apotheke Volz & Co., Zeitglockenlaub 2 (☎ 031-311-1094; www.central-apotheke-volz.ch), staffs English-speaking attendants. Located near the Clock Tower, it's open Monday 9 a.m. to 6:30 p.m., Tuesday through Friday 7:45 a.m. to 6:30 p.m., and Saturday 7:45 a.m. to 4 p.m.

Police

Dial ☎ 117 for the police.

Post Office

Bern's main post office (☎ 031-311-1094; www.post.ch) is at Schanzenpost 1 (behind the train station), open Monday through Friday 7 a.m. to 9 p.m., Saturday 8 a.m. to 4 a.m., and Sunday 4 to 9 p.m. There are several branches throughout the Altstadt.

Safety

With the exception of the park that surrounds Parliament, where heroin addicts roam after dark, you should feel comfortable on the streets of central Bern, day or night. But take the same precautions you'd take in any city to protect yourself against crime.

Taxes

Switzerland's value-added tax (VAT) on consumer goods is 7.6 percent. Foreigners who spend more than 400F ($400) at one store can reclaim it by requesting the necessary forms at the store.

Taxis

See "Getting Around Bern," earlier in this chapter.

Telephone

A local call in Bern costs 0.80F (80¢). Switzerland's phone system is highly advanced — most booths contain digital, multilingual phone books — and few phones accept coins anymore. You can use your major credit cards in most pay phones, or buy a *Taxcard* (prepaid phone card) in denominations of 5F ($5), 10F ($10), and 20F ($20) from the train station or any newsstand, gas station, or post office. For direct dialing internationally, you may want the Value Card versions for 20F ($20) or 50F ($50). Dial ☎ 111 (not free) for directory assistance.

To charge your call to a calling card (or make an operator-assisted call), dial the appropriate number: AT&T (☎ 0-800-890-011), MCI (☎ 0-800-890-222), or Sprint (☎ 0800-899-777). To call direct from Bern abroad, dial 00 followed by the country code (1 for the United States), the area code, and the number.

Transit Info

See "Getting Around Bern," earlier in this chapter.

Chapter 18

Prague and Environs

● ●

In This Chapter

▶ Getting to Prague

▶ Checking out the neighborhoods

▶ Discovering the best hotels, restaurants, and attractions

▶ Exploring beyond Prague

● ●

*P*rague emerged from behind the Iron Curtain in 1989 to shine once again as a world-class city. Cobbled streets weave past baroque palaces, lively beer halls, glowering castles, and light-infused cathedrals. In summer, some of the best street musicians in Europe play on elegant bridges spanning the swan-filled river.

When the Communist Bloc disintegrated with the Soviet Union's breakup, a group of Czech activist writers and artists, led by Václav Havel, encouraged Czechoslovakia to make a peaceful transition from communism to democracy. The movement, which many called the "Velvet Revolution," also peaceably redrew the ancient dividing line between the Czech and Slovak republics. Prague became the hot new destination, a "Paris of the '90s" for Gen-Xers imitating Hemingway's expat routine. But because of rapid expansion, the city's magic was doused by skyrocketing prices and tainted by the influx of Western culture. But Prague has finally revived itself.

In summer, backpackers and bus-tour groups flock to the city — if you're looking for a romantic setting, pick another season. And you may hear more English than Czech spoken on the streets of the Old Town. In the fall and winter, the crowds are gone, and Prague is all yours. Look for the magic, and spend several days of your trip here to fully capture the city's dreamy flavor. The skyline is dotted with spires, steeples, and towers, and Prague becomes a fairy-tale place at sunrise and sunset.

With a little practice, you can pronounce tongue-twisting Czech words with ease. Vowels are usually short, but any accent makes them long. Consonants are pronounced more or less as in English, except slightly roll your *r*'s, and c sounds like *ts*, č sounds like *ch*, ch sounds like *k, j* sounds like *y,* ř sounds like *rsh,* š sounds like *sh,* w sounds like *v,* and z sounds like the slurred *zh* sound in *azure* or *pleasure.* Pronounce consonants followed by an apostrophe *(d, n, t)* as if there were a *y* following them. For example, *děkuji* (thank you) is pronounced dyeh-*koo*-ee; *chci* (I would like . . .) is spoken ktsee; and *náměstí* (square) is pronounced naah-mee-*stee.*

Getting There

To get to your hotel, you can pick up a bus or taxi at the airport; train stations are connected to the subway lines. Although subway stations abound in central Prague, the best way to explore the city is on foot.

Arriving by air

Prague's small **Ruzyne airport** (☎ 220-113-314; www.prg.aero), is 19km (12 miles) west of the city center. Inside the manageable arrivals hall is an information desk that doesn't hand out city maps but will tell you how to get downtown. Several ATMs are located throughout the hall.

From the airport, a half-hourly ČEDAZ (☎ 220-114-296; www.cedaz.cz) shuttle bus runs every 30 minutes to náměstí Republiky, for 120Kč ($7.45). City bus no. 100 is an express heading right from the airport to the Zličín Metro stop (west end of the B line) in 15 minutes; bus nos. 119 and 254 zip to the Dejvická stop (western terminus of the A Metro line) in 20 minutes. A ticket on any technically costs 18Kč ($1.10), but because you'll want to hop on the Metro after you get there, buy the transfer ticket, which costs 26Kč ($1.60) — annoyingly, you'll also have to buy a 13Kč (80¢) ticket for each piece of luggage.

A taxi from the airport downtown should cost around 650Kč ($40). You can line up for a taxi at the curb, but you're more likely to get a fair deal and a lower rate if you call one of the radio taxi companies listed under "By taxi," later in this chapter (though you'll have to wait ten minutes or more).

Arriving by rail

Trains arrive in Prague either at the **Hlavní Nádraží** (Main Station) on the east edge of Nové Město, or, from Berlin and other northerly points, at the smaller **Nádraží Holešovice** (Holešovice Station) across the river to the north of the city center.

Both train stations, especially the main one, which has recently undergone a massive reconstruction, are seedy and chaotic. Dozens of hoteliers practically assault you the instant you step off the train, trying to sell you a hotel room — very annoying. Just ignore them and push ahead. If you want a reputable accommodations agency, see the "Staying in Prague" section, later in this chapter.

The Czech Republic

Orienting Yourself in Prague

Central Prague is divided into four main neighborhoods that straddle both sides of the **Vltava River,** which flows through the city from the south and then curves off to the east. **Staré Město** (Old Town) is tucked into a bend of the river (on the east bank), hemmed in by the Vltava on the north and west and by the continuous arc of streets **Národní/ 28.Října/Na Příkopě/Revoluční** on the south and east.

Introducing the neighborhoods

Staré Město, which means Old Town, is Prague's center. You find meandering streets dating back to the Middle Ages and wide boulevards from more-recent centuries. Filled with restaurants, cafes, and gorgeous Gothic and baroque architecture, the area is a great place to spend most of your time. Within Staré Mĕvsto is **Josefov,** the famed old Jewish quarter. The focal point of the Old Town is **Staroměstské náměstí** (Old Town Square).

Surrounding the Old Town on all but the riverside is the **Nové Město** (New Town). Much less interesting than the Old Town or the Malá Strana district (described later in this section), New Town is comprised mostly of office and apartment buildings. Still, you may enjoy the National Theater here, and the hotels are generally less expensive than those in Old Town.

In the center of Nové Město is **Václavské náměstí** (Wenceslas Square), a 4-block-long divided boulevard sloping gradually up to the dramatic neo-Renaissance National Museum. The strip down the middle (for pedestrian traffic) is lined on both sides with sausage stands and neoclassical and Art Nouveau buildings. (This area has been called New Town since its 1348 founding; the fact that much of that medieval neighborhood was replaced in the 19th and 20th centuries by an even newer New Town is just a coincidence.)

You cross a statue-lined **Karlů most** (Charles Bridge) from the Old Town into the **Malá Strana,** the "Little Quarter" on the west bank of the Vltava River. Above the Malá Strana is the small **Hradčany,** the "Castle District," which houses **Pražský Hrad** (Prague Castle), the city's major sight. Over the centuries, many palaces (several now housing museums) and monasteries have gathered around this traditional seat of government.

Beyond Prague's four traditional neighborhoods, the city has sprawled outward in every direction. One outlying neighborhood that you may want to visit is on the eastern edge of New Town. **Vinohrady** was named after the vineyards (owned by the king) that once filled this upscale residential zone. If Prague has a modern trendy district, Vinohrady is it — clean, full of shops and restaurants, and just a short hop from the city center on the Metro line A.

Finding information after you arrive

Prague Information Service (PIS), at Staroměstské náměstí 1, at the Old Town Hall (☎ 12-444; www.pis.cz), is one of the information offices in town. PIS is open Monday through Friday 9 a.m. to 7 p.m., Saturday and Sunday 9 a.m. to 6 p.m. (Nov–Mar, it closes at 6 p.m. during the week and at 5 p.m. on Sat and Sun). You'll find other branches at Rytířská 31, in the main train station and (summer only) in the tower over the Malá Strana end of Charles Bridge.

Getting Around Prague

You can use the same tickets for all of Prague's public transportation. The 18Kč ($1.10) nepřestupní ("no change") version is good for 20 minutes or five metro stops, but you cannot change to another bus/tram (you can transfer within the Metro). With the 26Kč ($1.60) přestupní ("change") version, you can make unlimited bus, tram, or Metro transfers within the 75-minute time limit (90 minutes 8 p.m.–5 a.m. and on weekends). There are also one-day (100Kč/$6.20), three-day (300Kč/$19), and five-day (500Kč/$31) passes available.

You can buy tickets from machines at Metro stations, newsstands marked TABÁK or TRAFIKA, and DP ticket kiosks.

By Metro (subway)

Prague's Metro (subway) system does a good job of covering the town with only three lines: A, B, and C. Each line intersects the other two only once: A and B at Můstek (the north end of Václavské náměstí), A and C at Muzeum (the south end of Václavské náměstí), and B and C at Florenc (a regional bus station).

By tram and bus

The tram system, supplemented by buses, is a more complete network that effectively covers much of central Prague. In winter, the tram seats are heated. Beware of tram nos. 22 and 23: Many people call them the "pickpocket trams" because of the pickpockets who prey on riders. The lines pass by the National Theater and head through the Malá Strana up to Prague Castle. Staré Město has only a few public trams and buses following its boundary roads. Several lines skirt the riverbank (especially tram no. 17) to hit Staroměstské náměstí, which also has a Metro line A station.

By taxi

You probably don't want to use a taxi unless your hotel is a great distance from Prague's center. The taxi drivers are notorious for ripping off unsuspecting tourists. If you must take a taxi, call a radio cab. In a pinch, hail one on the street, but be careful — you may end up with an unlicensed mafia cab (*mafia* here means that you're likely to be taken for a ride — financially, that is).

Wherever you get the cab, keep an eye on the meter. The display window on the left shows your fare; the window on the right should read 1, 2, 3, or 4, indicating the rate you're being charged. (The higher the number, the higher the rate.) Unless you venture far out from the center of town, the window on the right shouldn't read anything but 1 (although the parking lot of the main railway station is zoned 2). The initial charge should be 40Kč ($2.50) and then 28Kč ($1.75) per kilometer. If the rate is increasing by more than that, question it.

Don't let a taxi driver cover the meter's displays or change the rate as he changes gears. Let the cabbie see you making a note of the taxi number and any other identifying info as you get into the cab, and sit in the front seat to keep an eye on the driver.

Your chances of getting an honest cabbie are better if you call a radio-cab company (most Praguers tell you *never* to hail a cab, especially ones waiting around tourist sights). Because a radio cab's trip is logged in an office, inflating the fare is more difficult for the driver. Companies with English-speaking dispatchers include **AAA Taxi** (☎ 14-014) and **ProfiTaxi** (☎ 844-700-800).

Staying in Prague

Prague is an expensive city, probably the most expensive in Eastern Europe. Prices soared in the years after the fall of the Iron Curtain but have since stabilized and, in some cases, gone down as competition has increased. The priciest rooms are in the most desirable neighborhoods: Staré Město and Malá Strana.

The Czech Republic is a member of the European Union (EU). Although the country has promised to eventually change to the EU's common currency, the euro, this won't happen for several years, until there is even more convergence in economic strength. In the meantime, things generally are more expensive as the gross domestic product (GDP) grows. Even though wider access to better-quality suppliers and the competition created by it led to lower prices on some goods, luxurious items and electronics are still more expensive than in Western Europe. On the other hand, food and services are cheaper and more affordable.

The rapid capitalist invasion has also led to some dubious business practices. Many hotels charge one price for Czechs and another for foreign tourists. It's annoying but unavoidable. Hotels won't give you a good exchange rate from koruna to dollars, so don't pay your bill in dollars or euros (though most business-oriented hotels still tie their rates to one of those two stable currencies).

Remember: As soon as you step off the train at the station, you're accosted by an army of hotel representatives trying to sell you a good deal on a room. These deals are almost always a scam. Either the hotels have an inconvenient location, don't look anything like the "creative" photos suggest, or charge hidden extra fees not included in the quoted rates. If you need help finding a room, go to a legitimate agency instead.

Plenty of these agencies can help you find a hotel room, a pension, or even a full apartment. The most reputable is **AVE Ltd.** (www.avtravel. cz), with desks at the PIS offices (for open hours see "Finding information after you arrive" earlier in this chapter) — in the **Old Town Hall** at Staroměstské náměstí 1 (☎ 224-223-613) — as well as in the arrival halls of the main rail station (☎ 224-223-226; open daily 6 a.m.–11 p.m.), the Nádraží Holešovice station (☎ 266-710-514; open daily 7 a.m.–8:30 p.m.), and the airport (☎ 220-114-650; open daily 7 a.m.–10 p.m., until 9 p.m. in winter).

Prague's top hotels

Betlem Club
$$ Staré Město

The Betlem Club is a pleasant enough hotel in a quiet corner of the Old Town across the street from the church where Jan Hus started his Protestant revolution. Most of the rooms are done in shades of brown, tan, gray, brass, and the odd orange splash, but they are immaculately kept. They're oddly shaped, but most are of a good size (except for some of the top-floor mansard rooms, which can be comically cramped).

See map p. 366. Betlémské náměstí 9. ☎ *222-221-575. Fax: 222-220-580.* www. betlemclub.cz. *Metro: Národní Třída. Rack rates: From 2,600Kč ($161) double. Rates include breakfast. AE, MC, V.*

Hotel Evropa
$ Nové Město

You may be impressed by the remarkable, statue-topped Art Nouveau facade (from around 1903–1905) and classy sidewalk cafe of Prague's prettiest hotel. Unfortunately, the rooms seem to belong to a different hotel entirely. They vary widely in size and décor. Most are merely adequate, and some verge on dingy, but many also have a bit of faded low-rent, turn-of-the-20th-century style hanging about. The rooms on the high-ceilinged first two floors make for quite an enjoyable stay.

See map p. 366. Václavské náměstí 25. ☎ *224-215-387. Fax: 224-224-544.* www. evropahotel.cz. *Metro: Můstek or Muzeum. Rack rates: 1,950Kč–2,600Kč ($121–$161) double without bathroom; 3,000Kč–3,800Kč ($186–$236) double with bathroom. Rates include breakfast. AE, MC, V.*

Hotel Kampa
$$$ Malá Strana

The Kampa is a Best Western affiliate inhabiting a 17th-century armory on a quiet side street across the river, about a five-minute walk from the Charles Bridge. The simple, whitewashed, somewhat large rooms are boringly institutional but comfy enough. Try to get one overlooking the river or nearby park. The restaurant is a trippy cellar joint outfitted in that faux-medieval crossed-swords-on-the-wall style.

See map p. 366. Všehrdova 16 (just off Újezd). ☎ *257-404-444. Fax: 257-404-333.* www.euroagentur.cz. *Metro: Malostranská. Rack rates: 140€–270€ ($224–$432) double (rates quoted only in euros). Rates include breakfast. AE, DC, MC, V.*

Hotel Paříž
$$$$ Staré Město

This whimsically fantastic Czech Art Nouveau behemoth was built in 1904 at the edge of the Old Town. It is, hands-down, *the* choice for luxury in town, with far more character than most Prague business hotels. The large rooms were overhauled in 1998 and fitted with a modern interpretation of Art Deco — soft sofas and chairs in a sitting corner and contemporary prints on the walls. The lobby is flanked by the Café de Paris and the Sarah Bernhardt, serving French and international delicacies, the ceilings feature Art Nouveau chandeliers, and the walls are wrapped with aqua and gold mosaics.

See map p. 366. U Obecního domu 1 (off Náměstí Republiky). ☎ *222-195-195. Fax: 224-195-907.* www.hotel-pariz.cz. *Metro: Náměstí Republiky. Rack rates: 155€– 275€ ($248–$440) double (rates quoted only in euros). AE, DC, MC, V.*

Accommodations, Dining, and Attractions in Prague

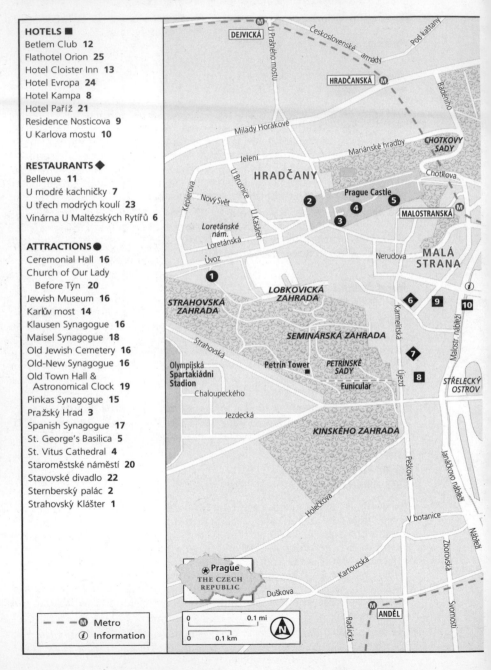

HOTELS ■
Betlem Club **12**
Flathotel Orion **25**
Hotel Cloister Inn **13**
Hotel Evropa **24**
Hotel Kampa **8**
Hotel Paříž **21**
Residence Nosticova **9**
U Karlova mostu **10**

RESTAURANTS ◆
Bellevue **11**
U modré kachničky **7**
U třech modrých koulí **23**
Vinárna U Maltézských Rytířů **6**

ATTRACTIONS ●
Ceremonial Hall **16**
Church of Our Lady
   Before Týn **20**
Jewish Museum **16**
Karlův most **14**
Klausen Synagogue **16**
Maisel Synagogue **18**
Old Jewish Cemetery **16**
Old-New Synagogue **16**
Old Town Hall &
   Astronomical Clock **19**
Pinkas Synagogue **15**
Pražský Hrad **3**
Spanish Synagogue **17**
St. George's Basilica **5**
St. Vitus Cathedral **4**
Staroměstské náměstí **20**
Stavovské divadlo **22**
Sternberský palác **2**
Strahovský Klášter **1**

DEJVICKÁ Ⓜ
Československé armády
Pod kaštany
U Pražského mostu
HRADČANSKÁ Ⓜ
Badeniho
Milady Horákové
Mariánské hradby
CHOTKOVY SADY
Jelení
HRADČANY
Chotkova
Keplerova
U Brusnice
Nový Svět
U kasáren
Loretánské nám.
Loretánská
Úvoz
Prague Castle
⓶
⓸
⓹
⓷
MALOSTRANSKÁ Ⓜ
Nerudova
MALÁ STRANA
Ⓘ
⓵
LOBKOVICKÁ ZAHRADA
STRAHOVSKÁ ZAHRADA
⓺ Ⓝ Ⓘ
Karmelitská
Maloštr. nábřeží
Strahovská
SEMINÁRSKÁ ZAHRADA
⓻
Olympijská Spartakiádní Stadion
Petřín Tower ■
PETŘÍNSKÉ SADY
Ⓝ
STŘELECKÝ OSTROV
Chaloupeckého
Funicular
Újezd
Jezdecká
KINSKÉHO ZAHRADA
Peškova
Janáčkovo nábřeží
Holečkova
V botanice
Nábřeží
Zborovská
⊛ Prague
THE CZECH REPUBLIC
Dušková
Kartouzská
Ⓜ ANDĚL
Radlická
Svornosti

─ ─ Ⓜ Metro
ⓘ Information

0   0.1 mi
0   0.1 km
N

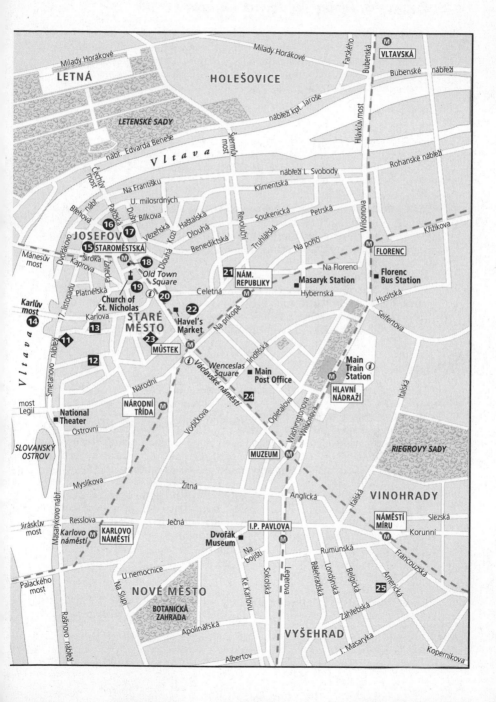

Prague's runner-up accommodations

Flathotel Orion

$ **Vyšehrad** This apartment hotel is Prague's best family value. All rooms are one- or two-bedroom flats, sleep up to six, and have well-equipped kitchens. Comfortable, but not imaginative. *See map p. 366.* *Americká 9.* ☎ *246-030-246.* www.hotel.cz/orion.

Hotel Cloister Inn

$$ **Staré Město** Stylish simplicity defines this moderate hotel right in the Old Town. The spacious rooms are fitted with modern furnishings and bright colors, and there's even free Internet, tea, and coffee in the lobby. *See map p. 366. Konviktská 14.* ☎ *224-211-020.* www.cloister-inn.cz.

Residence Nosticova

$$$$ **Malá Strana** This baroque palace tucked into Malá Strana's back streets retains its stone staircase and Imperial style. All ten units are sumptuously decorated suites, and all are worthy of a visiting dignitary. *See map p. 366. Nosticova 1.* ☎ *257-312-513.* www.nosticova.com.

U Karlova mostu

$$$ **Malá Strana** This former brewery on Na Kampě Island has been turned into a lovely inn, complete with beamed ceilings in many rooms. Your choices of view are a quiet cobbled square or the river and Charles Bridge. *See map p. 366. Na Kampě 15.* ☎ *257-531-430.* www.archibald.cz.

Dining in Prague

Traditional Czech cuisine is usually simple and hearty. Soups are meaty and frequently flavored with garlic. A favorite is *hovězí polévka s játrovými knedlíčky* (liver dumplings in beef stock). Praguers are fond of dumplings, called *knedlíky,* made of potatoes *(bramborové)* or bread *(houskové)* and sliced into discs. Dumplings are side dishes to such favorites as *svíčková na smetaně,* a beef pot roast sliced and served with a creamy and rich vegetable sauce and a sour cranberry chutney.

Also check out *pečená kachna,* roast duck with bacon dumplings and sauerkraut. Game dishes, such as *zvěřina* (venison), *zajíc* (hare), *bažant* (pheasant), and *husa* (goose), are usually roasted. Popular freshwater fish are *pstruh* (trout) and *kapr* (carp). Hungarian *guláš* (beef goulash) is a good, cheap standby for quick lunches. The best desserts are *ovocné knedlíky* (fruit dumplings), *vdolek* (jam tarts), and chocolate- or fruit-filled *palačinky* (crepes).

Czech *pivo* (beer) is a great brew. Light-colored beer is *světlé* (*svyet*-lay); dark beer is *černé* (*cher*-nay). This is the home of **Pilsner Urquell,** the country's famed lager (the brewery also makes a smooth, for-local-consumption-only beer, **Gambrinus**). If you're a beer-drinker, you may also want to try **Staropramen** (the most common Prague suds), and **Velkopopovický Kozel** (a wonderful dark beer).

By far, the most renowned Czech beer is **Budvar,** the original Budweiser — although it's nothing like the watery, mass-produced American beverage. (Budvar and Anheuser-Busch have been fighting for years over the name rights.)

 With the exception of some of the better restaurants and the tourist-trap places nearest the sights, meals in Prague can be very inexpensive. One of the trade-offs is remarkably poor service, a relic of the Communist era, when restaurant patrons received their meals only at the extreme convenience of the server. When service is haughty, ignore it and don't tip; when service is scarce, just chalk it up to economic growing pains. As investors start finer restaurants in Prague, their attention to service and food presentation should raise the bar for the rest of the industry.

 Watch out for these restaurant rip-offs:

✔ **Every item brought to your table may be charged to your bill, including bread, bowls of nuts, and so on.** Often, these small items turn out to be ridiculously expensive. Make sure that you know the price of everything before you eat it.

✔ **Examine your bill closely at the end of the meal to make sure it isn't padded with items that you didn't order.** Also, some restaurants doctor the amount written on a credit-card slip, so you may want to write the total, in words, somewhere on the slip.

For quick eats, tasty, tiny, open-faced sandwiches called *chlebíčky* are all the rage at **U Bakaláře** (Celetná 13). Sidewalk stands hawk *klobásy* (grilled sausages) and *párky* (boiled frankfurters) served with bread and *hořčice* (mustard).

Bellevue
$$$$$ Staré Město INTERNATIONAL

At Bellevue, one of the city's finest restaurants, you can enjoy your food surrounded by live music and, if you scam a window seat, a view of Prague Castle. The international menu varies from spinach tagliatelle in a salmon cream sauce to braised rabbit, always well prepared and presented. But the veggie dishes are less than thrilling. Sunday brunch features live jazz.

See map p. 366. Smetanovo nábřeží 18. ☎ *222-221-443.* www.vzatisigroup.cz. *Reservations highly recommended. Metro: Staroměstská. Main courses: 490Kč–890Kč ($30–$55). AE, DC, MC, V. Open: Mon–Sat noon to 3 p.m. and 5:30–11 p.m.; Sun 11 a.m.–3 p.m. and 5:30–11 p.m.*

U modré kachničky
$$$ Malá Strana CZECH/GAME

This very private and relaxing Art Nouveau–style space is renowned for its traditional Czech game dishes. The interior contains a series of small dining rooms with vaulted ceilings and playfully frescoed walls. Service is professional and friendly, and the refined cookery manages to rise above most "Bohemian cuisine" in town, while still remaining adamantly Czech — lots of duck and venison alongside salmon, trout, and rabbit (but you can get beef, pork, and chicken as well).

See map p. 366. Nebodviská 6 (a small street parallel to Karmelitská, south of the castle). ☎ *257-320-308.* www.umodrekachnicky.cz. *Reservations recommended. Tram: 12, 22, or 23. Main courses: 240Kč–685Kč ($15–$42). AE, MC, V. Open: Daily noon–4 p.m. and 6:30–11:30 p.m.*

U třech modrých koulí
$$ Staré Město REFINED CZECH

If you'd like to sample the best of fine Czech cuisine but don't quite have the scratch to pay for U modré (preceding listing) or the Vinárna (following listing), make reservations at "The Three Blue Balls," another of Prague's excellent, candlelit, cellar restaurants — but one without the airs (or high prices) of its culinary compatriots. The cooking, though, is top-notch, as it has been since 1816. The duck breast in cabernet is tender, and the beef medallions in a honey-wine sauce are absolutely delicious.

See map p. 366. Havelská 8 (just off Uhelnýtrh). ☎ *224-238-130.* www.trikoule.cz. *Reservations recommended. Metro: Můstek. Main courses: 155Kč–310Kč ($9.60–$19). AE, MC, V. Open: Daily noon to 4 p.m. and 5:30 p.m. to midnight.*

Vinárna U Maltézských Rytířů (Knights of Malta)
$$$ Malá Strana REFINED CZECH

This is one of Prague's most beloved eateries, a bastion of Czech food, good flavors, and warm welcomes. Seating is limited (especially in the atmospheric, candlelit basement), so reserve ahead to enjoy duck breast with cranberry sauce, a lamb cutlet, or pasta with fresh vegetables. The apple strudel with ice cream and eggnog is a must for dessert.

See map p. 366. Prokopská 10 (off Karmelitská). ☎ *257-530-075.* www.umaltezsky chrytiru.cz. *Reservations recommended. Metro: Malostranská. Main courses: 325Kč–600Kč ($20–$37). AE, MC, V. Open: Daily 1–11 p.m.*

Exploring Prague

Although Prague's classical music and the Czech Republic's unmatched beer are reasons to visit, the primary draw for many is simply walking along the winding cobblestone streets and enjoying the unique atmosphere. This section points out highlights to look for along the way.

Prague's top sights

Jewish Prague

Josefov

The **Jewish Museum** in Prague is the organization managing all the Jewish landmarks in Josefov, which forms the northwest quarter of Old Town. Jews lived in Prague before the 10th century, but by the 12th century, they were confined to a small part of town. At the time, this area was walled off. Ironically, even though 88,000 of the country's 118,000 Jews died during the Holocaust, Nazi occupiers spared this center of Jewish culture. Hitler planned to put all the scrolls, torahs, and other artifacts he collected while exterminating Jews across Europe on display in Prague, turning Josefov into a "museum to a vanished race."

Most of those seized items were returned in 1994 to the Diaspora from which they had been taken, but more than 39,000 local items (and more than 100,000 books) from Bohemia and Moravia stayed here in Prague as part of the Jewish Museum, its collections split among several synagogues. You can see Josefov's highlights in 45 minutes to an hour, but we recommend spending a morning here.

The area has become so insanely popular that it now operates a bit disconcertingly like a theme park: You go to a central ticketing office to pick up your multi-admission ticket, which has timed entries to each of the neighborhood's sights, in order.

Your first stop is right next to the ticketing office window at the **Klausen Synagogue** (on U Starého Hřbitova), now deconsecrated and containing the first half of a collection that illustrates the fascinating sociocultural history of the Czech Jews. The exhibits continue in the nearby **Ceremonial Hall,** the cemetery's former mortuary hall, highlighting the customs and traditions surrounding illness and death, including a fascinating series of small paintings depicting all the steps in funeral ceremonies (which, for some frustrating reason, are no longer hung all together in one room, nor are they presented in chronological order, rendering it a bit difficult to make sense of it all).

Next up, behind these buildings, is one of Prague's most evocative sights: the **Old Jewish Cemetery,** off U Starého Hřbitova, behind a high wall. This Jewish burial ground dates to the 15th century — when Jews couldn't bury their dead outside of the ghetto. Within this 1-block plot, they had to find final resting places for some 20,000 to 80,000 deceased (the exact number is unknown). Consequently, they stacked the bodies 12 deep in some places. The shady, overgrown, undulating ground is blanketed with some 12,000 time-worn tombstones lurching and tilting in varying degrees of disrepair. The air is melancholy yet serene. This is one sight in Jewish Prague that you don't want to miss. The somewhat elaborate sarcophagus is of the holy man Rabbi Loew, who died in 1609.

Josefov's most moving sight is next door, the **Pinkas Synagogue** on Široká, built in the flamboyant High Gothic style of the 16th century. From 1950 to 1958, Holocaust survivors painted on the inside walls the names of 77,297 Czech Jews who died under the Nazi regime. The Communist regime closed the synagogue and, claiming that dampness was leading to the deterioration of the walls, had the place replastered. As soon as communism ended and the synagogue was reopened, the Jews began the meticulous, four-year task of inscribing those names back on the walls. After Prague's disastrous summer 2002 floods filled this low-lying area with water and mud, they had to break out the paintbrushes yet again and start re-lettering all the names on the lower few feet of the walls. Upstairs are drawings (from a collection of 4,000) made by Jewish children while interned at the nearby Terezín Nazi camp (see "Traveling beyond Prague," later in this chapter). Of the 8,000 children who passed through there on the way to concentration camps, only 242 survived.

Two blocks over and down sits the next stop, the 16th-century **Maisel Synagogue,** on Maiselova, a renovated space that contains an exhibit of historical Jewish objects from the 10th to the 18th centuries. Part II of this collection (18th century to the present) resides several blocks to the east, up Široká, in the gorgeous neo-Renaissance/Iberian-styled 1868 **Spanish Synagogue,** on Dušní; it was reopened in late 1998 after a decades-long restoration of its lush, Moorish-inspired decorations.

There's one other sight in Jewish Prague that's still an active temple and, therefore, not part of the Jewish Museum group: the **Old-New Synagogue,** at červená 2, built in 1270 and the only Gothic temple of its kind remaining. The small interior is beautiful, with high ceilings crisscrossed with five-ribbed fan vaulting. (Gothic church vaulting uses four ribs, but because those ribs represent the cross, the Jews decided five would be a bit more appropriate.) Admission to this one is a ridiculous extra 200Kč ($12), paid at a shop across the street from the entrance.

See map p. 366. The ticket window is at U Starého Hřbitova 3a (right in the crook of an elbow-shaped street between Břehová and Pařížská). ☎ ***222-317-191.*** www.jewish museum.cz. *Metro: A to Staroměstská. Tram: 17, 18, 51, or 54. Bus: 135 or 207. Admission: 290Kč ($18) adults, 190Kč ($12) seniors and students. Open: Nov–Mar Sun–Fri 9 a.m.–4:30 p.m.; Apr–Oct Sun–Fri 9 a.m.–6 p.m.*

Karlův most (Charles Bridge)
Between Malá Strana and Staré Město

This may be the loveliest and liveliest bridge anywhere in Europe. The statue-lined Charles Bridge is bustling with people throughout the day and evening — tourists, musicians, street performers, caricature artists, and crafts peddlers. The 510m (1,700-ft.) span was constructed in the 14th century, but the majority of statues date from the early 18th century. (Actually, what you see on the bridge are copies; most of the originals have been moved inside for protection from the weather.)

Two of the earliest statues include the 1629 crucifix near the Old Town end (great effects during sunrise or sunset) and, halfway across, the haloed statue of St. John Nepomuk (1683), which honors the holy man tortured to death by King Wenceslas IV and then tossed off the bridge. A bronze plaque under the statue describes the event; rub the shiny, worn figure of the plummeting saint for good luck.

Climb the towers at either end for great bridge and city spire panoramas. Both are open daily from 10 a.m. to 6 p.m. (sometimes hours change Nov–Mar).

Prazský Hrad (Prague Castle)
Hradčany

Prague Castle, sternly overlooking Prague, is its own tiny city. Work began in the ninth century and seems never to stop, with constant renovations taking place. Massive fortifications enclose the castle, which spills over with churches, palaces, buildings, shops, and alleys that take a full day to explore properly. (You may be able to make a *quick* run-through in two to three hours.) This is Prague's only truly must-see sight. The massive cathedral is one of Europe's grandest Gothic churches.

Construction on **St. Vitus Cathedral,** the castle's centerpiece, began under Emperor Charles IV in 1344. After a long interruption, it was finished in the 19th and 20th centuries in a neo-Gothic style that tried to follow the original plans closely. The mosaic over the door dates from 1370. The light-filled interior of the cathedral contains the sumptuously decorated **Chapel of St. Wenceslas** (built in the 14th–16th centuries). The sarcophagi of Bohemian kings are stored in the crypt.

The **Royal Palace** was the home to kings for more than 700 years, beginning in the ninth century. The vaulted Vladislav Hall is still used for state occasions, such as the inauguration of the Czech president, but the Czechs don't celebrate like they used to. In the Middle Ages, knights on horseback entered through the Rider's Staircase for indoor jousting competitions.

St. George's Basilica was built in the tenth century and is the oldest Romanesque structure in Prague. Its adjacent **convent** houses a museum of Gothic and baroque Bohemian art (☎ 257-531-644; www.ngprague.cz), part of the National Gallery museums system and hence subject to a separate admission fee of 100Kč ($6.20) adults, 50Kč ($3.10) seniors and students; it's open Tuesday through Sunday from 9 a.m. to 5 p.m.

The row of tiny houses clinging to the inside base of the castle ramparts was known as **Golden Lane,** because they were once home to goldsmiths and shopkeepers; today the area houses souvenir stands and cafes. Franz Kafka worked, and perhaps lived, for a time at no. 22. Whether alchemists practiced their craft of trying to turn lead into gold on this "golden" lane is a point of debate. Some say yes, but others point to a similar lane off the left flank of St. Vitus Cathedral as "Alchemy Central."

See map p. 366. Main entrance at Hradčanské náměstí. ☎ *224-373-368.* www. hrad.cz. *Metro: A to Malostranská or Hradčanská. Tram: 22 or 23. Admission: Free for St. Vitus Cathedral and the grounds; 2-day combination ticket to main castle attractions (Royal Palace, St. George's Basilica, Powder Tower, Golden Lane, and Daliborka Tower) 350Kč ($22) adults, 175Kč ($11) students. Open: Information/ticket office daily 9 a.m.–4 p.m. (until 3 p.m. in winter); grounds daily 6 a.m. to midnight (until 11 p.m. in winter); individual buildings daily 9 a.m.–5 p.m. (until 4 p.m. in winter).*

Staroměstské náměstí (Old Town Square)
Staré Město

A massive memorial to the 15th-century religious reformer and martyr Jan Hus graces Prague's most gorgeous baroque square, Staroměstské. Beautiful buildings surround the square, which is perpetually crowded with street performers, tourists, and the general bustle of the city. Sit at an outdoor cafe table, and just watch it all for a while.

You can climb the tower in the **Old Town Hall** (☎ 724-508-584) for views across the rooftops, but its most popular feature is the **Astronomical Clock.** Rather than tell the hour, this 15th-century timepiece keeps track of moon phases, equinoxes, and various Christian holidays tied to them. On every hour from 8 a.m. to 8 p.m., the clock puts on a glockenspiel-style show of marching apostles and dancing embodiments of evil.

Here's a grisly tale for you: The architect of the clock, Master Hanus, did such a good job that the city council feared he might one day build a better one elsewhere. To ensure that their clock remained superior, they had him blinded. As the legend goes, Master Hanus, in despair and hoping for revenge, jumped into the clock's mechanism, crushing himself and throwing the works off-kilter for a century.

The **Church of Our Lady Before Týn** stands out with its twin multi-steepled towers. The structure is mainly Gothic, dating from 1380, and is the seat of Prague's Protestant congregation.

See map p. 366. Staroměstské náměstí. Metro: A to Staroměstská. Tram: 17, 18, 51, or 54. Bus: 135 or 207. Admission: Old Town Hall 60Kč ($3.70) adults, 40Kč ($2.50) seniors and students; plus another 30Kč ($1.85) adults, 20Kč ($1.25) seniors or students to climb the tower. Open: Old Town Hall Mar–Oct Mon 11 a.m.–6 p.m., Tues–Sun 9 a.m.–6 p.m.; Nov–Feb Mon 11 a.m.–5 p.m., Tues–Sun 9 a.m.–5 p.m.

Šternberský palác (National Gallery at Šternberk Palace)
Hradčany

Prague's main art gallery is housed in a gorgeous late-17th-century palace near the Castle. The collection spans the 15th to 20th centuries, including paintings by Rembrandt, Brueghel the Elder, Klee, and Munch. The finest piece is Dürer's huge *Feast of the Rosary,* painted in 1506.

See map p. 366. Hradčanské náměstí 15 (across from the main entrance to Prague Castle). ☎ 233-090-570. www.ngprague.cz. Metro: A to Malostranská or Hradčanská. Tram: 22 or 23. Admission: 130Kč ($8.05) adults, 80Kč ($4.95) students and children. Open: Tues–Sun 10 a.m.–6 p.m.

Strahovský Klášter (Strahov Monastery)
Malá Strana

Founded in 1140 by the Premonstratensian monks (an order that still lives here), this monastery was rebuilt in the Gothic style of the 13th century. It's renowned for its libraries, both the collections — more than 125,000 volumes, many of them priceless illuminated manuscripts — and for the long baroque hall that houses the philosophy and theology books. The ceiling fresco of the *Struggle of Mankind to Know Real Wisdom* is not to be missed. Also check out the baroque Church of Our Lady.

See map p. 366. Strahovské nádvoří 1. ☎ *233-107-711.* www.strahovskyk laster.cz. *Tram: 22 or 23. Admission: 80Kč ($4.95) adults, 50Kč ($3.10) students 26 and under. Open: Daily 9 a.m. to noon and 1–5 p.m.*

More cool things to see and do

✔ **Going concert-hopping:** Dozens of classical concerts are offered every evening throughout town — in churches and concert halls, in intimate private chambers and large public halls, under street arches, and in the squares. Many estimate that more musicians per capita live in the Czech Republic than anywhere else. The **Prague Information Service** (see "Finding information after you arrive," earlier in this chapter) sells tickets at all its offices via the agency **Ticketpro** (☎ 296-329-999; www.ticketpro.cz), or you can contact **Bohemia Ticket** at Na Příkopě 16 (☎ 224-215-031; www.bohemiaticket.cz).

In the city that gave the world the composers Smetana and Dvořák, and where Mozart wrote *Don Giovanni* and found greater acclaim than in his native Austria, you find a smorgasbord of offerings to choose from: an organ concert in the Týn Church, a chamber ensemble in a defunct monastery, or the Czech Philharmonic in the 19th-century **Dům umělců** (Rudolfinum), Alšovo nábřeží 12 (☎ 227-059-352; www.rudolfinum.cz).

The *Prague Post* lists most events around town, or you can just wander the Old Town, especially around Staroměstské Square, where you find the highest concentration of posters proclaiming the week's concerts and venues. If it's playing, attend Mozart's *Don Giovanni* in the venue where it premiered, the restored 1783 **Stavovské divadlo** (Estates' Theater), Ovocný trh 1 (☎ 224-902-322; www.nd.cz). This theater is the only baroque performance space preserved just as it appeared in Mozart's day.

✔ **Making friends in a beer hall:** "Wherever beer is brewed, all is well. Whenever beer is drunk, life is good." So goes the Czech proverb. Praguers love their *pivo* (beer) — they consume 320 pints per year per Czech — and they love their local *hospoda* (pub or beer hall). Beer halls serve as gathering places for almost everyone.

Refer to the "Dining in Prague" section, earlier in this chapter, for information about the different types of Czech beer. Also note this beer-hall etiquette:

- Share tables. Always ask *Je tu volno* (Is this spot taken)?

- Put a coaster in front of you if you want beer. Never wave down the waiter — he'll ignore you entirely.

- Nod at the waiter and hold up your fingers for how many beers you want. He'll leave a marked slip of paper at your table with the drinks.

The waiter visits you twice (at the most), so when he comes around again, order all the beer you'll want for the rest of your stay. Pay him when he drops off your drinks, or you may have to wait for hours.

Check out the famous beer hall, **U Fleků,** Křemencova 11 (☎ 224-934-019; www.ufleku.cz), a brewery from 1459 — rather touristy, but great brewskis, plus there's a cheesy-but-fun brass band in the courtyard garden. Or go to the 1466 **U Medvídků,** na Perštýně 7 (☎ 224-211-916; www.umedvidku.cz), for real Budvar on tap and good Czech pub grub. For a real, albeit famous, Praguer's bar, hit **U Zlatého tygra,** Husova 17 (☎ 222-221-111), a smoky haunt of writers and politicians.

✔ **Visiting a park along the river:** Letná Park (Letenské sady) is a wide, flat swath of trees and shrubs on the western bank of the Vltava River, north of Malá Strana. It has plenty of picnic spots, lots of paths winding through the trees and along the river, and even a beer garden in summer on the park's north side. Walk along the river tossing bread to, and making friends with, Prague's famed mute swans. Tram nos. 1, 8, 25, and 26 get you there.

✔ **Renting a paddle boat:** The Vltava is a beautiful river, filled with graceful swans and spanned by dramatic bridges. You may feel compelled to become a part of it — but don't. It's so polluted that swimming is out of the question. From March through September, you can rent paddle boats (80Kč/$4.95 per hour) and rowboats (60Kč/$3.70 per hour) from **Půjčovna** at the docks of Slovanský ostrov, an island 2 blocks south of the National Theater.

Next door, at **Rent-A-Boat "Slovanka,"** you can rent a rowboat with a lantern at the bow in the evenings (until 11 p.m.) and row around the river under the romantic moonlight and floodlit spires of the city. This boat costs you 80Kč ($4.95) per hour. Rent-A-Boat also stays open until October (Nov if the weather holds).

Guided tours

Plenty of outfits run **bus tours** of the city. Try these for the best reputation and prices:

✔ **Martin Tour** (☎ 224-212-473; www.martintour.cz) runs a variety of city tours (general, Jewish Prague, historical, river cruises) lasting from 75 minutes to three-and-a-half hours. Tours cost from 250Kč to 750Kč ($16–$47). You can hop on at Staroměstské náměstí, Náměstí Republiky, Melantrichova, or Na Příkopě.

✔ **Premiant City Tour** (☎ 606-600-123 or 224-946-922; www.premiant. cz) also runs city intro, historical/Jewish Prague, and river cruises lasting two to three-and-a-half hours. The cost is 250Kč to 850Kč ($16–$53). Hour-long bus tours cost 250Kč ($16). All tours leave from Na Příkopě 23.

If you're interested in a walking tour, try **Prague Airport Transfers** (☎ 222-554-211 or 777-777-237; www.prague-airport-transfers. co.uk). Tours meet under the Astronomical Clock on Staroměstské náměstí (look for the person with the ID badge holding a red umbrella). Most tours — Prague Castle and the Royal Route (daily 11 a.m.), Old Jewish Quarter (daily 10 a.m. and 2 p.m.), Undiscovered Prague (Mon, Wed, Fri, Sun 11 a.m.), Old Prague — 1,000 years of architecture (Tues, Thurs, Sat 11 a.m.), and the Ghost Walk (Tues, Thurs, Sat 6:30 p.m.) — last about 90 minutes to two hours each and cost 300Kč to 400Kč ($19–$25). The Superior Tour of Prague includes lunch, drinks, a boat cruise, a tram ride, and a Walks of Prague CD (daily 10 a.m.–4 p.m.) and costs 1,000Kč ($62).

Suggested itineraries

If you're the type who'd rather organize your own tours, read this section for tips on building your own Prague itineraries.

If you have one day

Spend a full morning exploring **Prazský Hrad** (Prague Castle) — the **Cathedral, the Royal Palace, St. George's Basilica,** and other sights nearby. Make your way down to the river, grab an eat-as-you-go lunch along the way, and cross the remarkable **Karlův most** (Charles Bridge) into the **Staré Město** (Old Town). Take your first left to walk up into **Josefov,** and spend the afternoon in the museums, synagogues, and cemetery of the Jewish quarter.

When evening falls, make your way to the lovely heart of Prague, the baroque building–lined square **Staroměstské nám,** where dozens of billboards, posters, and ticket hawkers allow you to browse for the best classical concert to suit your tastes. If you don't want to leave things to chance, stop by a Prague Information Service (PIS) office (see "Finding information after you arrive," earlier in this chapter) when you get to town and book tickets in the morning — the best concerts do sometimes sell out. If it's summer, you can pick up tickets when you're crossing the Charles Bridge around lunchtime — a PIS office/ticket booking center is in the base of the tower at the **Malá Strana** end of the bridge.

If you have two days

Spend all of **Day 1** in the **Malá Strana.** Start off at **Pražský Hrad,** but take a bit more time after seeing the big sights to enjoy some of the temporary exhibits that rotate through its galleries and halls. Pop into **Šternberský palác** (National Gallery at Šternberk Palace) afterward for a dip into Renaissance and baroque art. Then make your way down to **Malostranské nám,** exit it on **Karmelitská** street, and take the first left down **Prokopská,** which becomes **Nebovidská,** to have a Czech lunch at **U Modré Kachničky.**

After lunch, continue down Nebovidská to **Hellichova,** take a right, cross Karmelitská, and wind your way up through the **Seminářská Zahrada** (Seminary Gardens) to the library and frescoes inside the **Strahovský Klášter** (Strahov Monastery) at the western edge of the gardens. Hop on tram no. 22 and ride it all the way around to the back side of Prague Castle to **Malostranské náměstí** again, where you can get off and mosey on down to **Karlův most,** crossing back into the **Staré Město** to rustle up some dinner and a concert.

Start off **Day 2** in **Josefov,** exploring the sights, synagogues, and culture of Jewish Prague. If Prague's Jewish history intrigues you, leave early enough (by 1 p.m.) to get to Florenc station and grab a bus for the hour's ride outside town to the Nazi internment camp at **Terezín** (see "Traveling beyond Prague," later in this chapter). If you've had your fill at Josefov, spend your afternoon wandering the **Staré Město,** popping into its baroque churches, relaxing with the locals in Staroměstské náměstí, and browsing for the evening's concert. Dine at **U třech modrých koulí,** or just get some goulash at a pub.

If you have three days

Spend **Day 1** and **Day 2** as outlined in the preceding section, and on **Day 3** head out to imposing **Karlštejn Castle.** If you plan to visit **Terezín,** definitely do it on the afternoon of Day 2, because on Day 3, you want to be back in Prague early enough to engage in a rewarding wander around the **Staré Město** in the late afternoon. (Be sure to catch the sunset over the **Karlův most.**)

Traveling beyond Prague

Several fascinating destinations lie just a short bus or train ride from the city center. You can explore a 14th-century castle and a "model" Nazi internment camp that was designed to mask Hitler's true motives.

Medieval Karlštejn Castle

This highly picturesque, 14th-century castle perched scenically above the river is Prague's most popular day trip. (Tour companies love coming here, where more than 350,000 people visit annually.)

It takes only a few hours to get here, see the castle, and return to Prague, but you can stick around for lunch and enjoy Karlštejn's small-town setting. (But be aware that it's usually quite crowded.)

Getting there

You can get to the castle by train in about 45 minutes. The trains leave from Prague's Smíchov Station (take Metro line B to Smíchovské nádraží).

Martin Tour (☎ **224-212-473;** www.martintour.cz) does five-hour trips to Karlštejn Castle Tuesday through Sunday for 950Kč ($59), leaving at

Day Trips from Prague

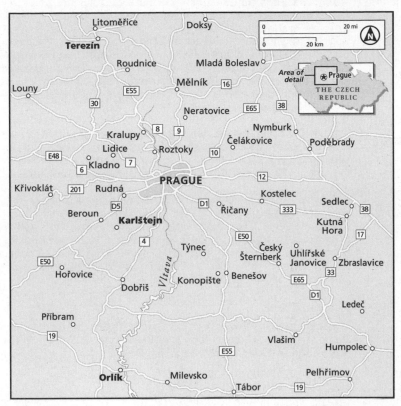

10 a.m. and including lunch; **Premiant City Tour** (☎ 606-600-123 or 224-241-072; www.premiant.cz) does it in four hours Tuesday through Sunday (at 9 a.m., including lunch) for 990Kč ($61). From April through September, you may want to ride instead with **Central European Adventures** (☎ 222-328-879; http://cea51.tripod.com), whose 680Kč ($42) price includes transportation from Prague (8:30 a.m. at the Astronomical Clock) to the castle, a guide, plus a 29km (18-mile) round-trip bike excursion to a nearby cave — but not castle admission. (All tours run Tues–Sun only.)

This is a one-trick town, so you won't find a tourism office; just hike up to the castle and the admissions office for information.

Seeing the castle

The walk uphill to **Karlštejn Castle** (☎ 311-681-370; www.hrad karlstejn.cz) from the train station is a rigorous mile, but the view from the castle across the fertile river valley makes the climb worth it.

(Unfortunately, no buses are available for those who can't manage the walk.) Charles IV built the fortress (between 1348 and 1357) to protect the crown jewels, which have been moved.

A 19th-century restoration stripped the place of later additions and rebuilt the castle in line with how folks from the Romantic era thought a medieval castle should look (close to the original, but a bit fanciful in places). You can get inside only by guided tour, which takes you through parts of the South Palace to see the Audience Hall and Imperial Bedroom — both impressive in an austere, medieval way.

The castle's most spectacular room, the famed Holy Rood Chapel with its ceiling of glass "stars," is only visible on the longer version of the tour — and because that is limited to 12 visitors per hour, it's worth calling ahead to reserve (☎ 274-008-154) and paying the 40Kč ($2.50) booking fee.

Admission for a 50-minute tour is 220Kč ($14) adults and 120Kč ($7.45) students; a 70-minute tour is 300Kč ($19) adults, 150Kč ($9.30) students. The castle is open Tuesday through Sunday, in May, June, and September from 9 a.m. to noon and 12:30 to 5 p.m.; July and August from 9 a.m. to noon and 12:30 to 6 p.m.; April and October from 9 a.m. to noon and 1 to 4 p.m.; and November, December and March from 9 a.m. to noon and 1 to 3 p.m. (closed Jan and Feb).

Where to dine

The main road leading up to the castle is littered with souvenir shops and restaurants. The best food is at **Restaurace Blanky z Valois,** a cozy place serving good Czech food with a French twist.

The Nazi camp at Terezín

Terezín was built as a city/fortress in the 19th century. The Nazi camp here served mainly as a transfer station in the despicable traffic of human cargo — sending Jews, homosexuals, Gypsies, and political dissidents on to other, more deadly destinations. At least half of the 140,000 people who passed through Terezín ended up in the death mills of Auschwitz and Treblinka.

Terezín's infamy is that it was the site of one of the most effective public-relations deceptions perpetrated by SS leader Heinrich Himmler. In 1944, the Nazis allowed three Red Cross workers to visit the camp to see whether the horrible rumors about SS methods were true. Instead, they found a self-governed modern ghetto with children studying at school, stores stocked with goods, internees apparently healthy — and none of the overcrowding that they had suspected. The Red Cross had no idea that all this was elaborately staged.

Getting there

Terezín is an hour's bus ride from Florenc station. You need a full morning to fully explore the camp. **Wittmann Tours,** Mánesova 8, Praha 2

(☎ **222-252-472;** www.wittmann-tours.com), has by far the best Terezín tour available; all guides are either survivors of the camp or experts on it. This seven-hour tour leaves Prague at 10 a.m. (May–Oct daily; Mar 15–Apr and Nov–Dec Tues, Thurs, Sat, and Sun), includes lunch, and costs 1,150Kč ($71) adults, 1,000Kč ($62) students. **Martin Tour** (☎ **224-212-473;** www.martintour.cz) tours Terezín in five hours and costs 1,100Kč ($68); **Premiant City Tour's** (☎ **606-600-123** or 224-241-072; www.premiant.cz) visit also lasts five hours and costs 1,150Kč ($71).

The **information office** (☎ **416-782-225;** www.pamatnik-terezin.cz) is on the town's main square, Náměstí čs, Armády 84.

Seeing the camp

The **Main Fortress** (Hlavní Pevnost) houses a **Ghetto Museum,** detailing life in this camp and the rise of Nazism. The museum is open daily from 9 a.m. to 6 p.m. (until 5:30 p.m. in winter). The prison barracks, execution grounds, and isolation cells are in the **Lesser Fortress,** a ten-minute walk away, open daily from 8 a.m. to 6 p.m. (until 4:30 p.m. in winter). In front is the **Jewish Cemetery,** where bodies exhumed from Nazi mass graves were properly reburied. The cemetery is open Sunday through Friday from 10 a.m. to 5 p.m. (until 4 p.m. in winter). The **Magdeburg Barracks** re-create a Ghetto dormitory. Here you see displays on Ghetto art and music. The barracks is open daily from 9 a.m. to 6 p.m. (until 5:30 p.m. in winter).

Admission to either the Ghetto Museum or the Lesser Fortress alone is 160Kč ($9.90) adults, 130Kč ($8.05) children. A combined ticket for all attractions costs 200Kč ($12) adults, 150Kč ($9.30) children.

Where to dine

As you may expect, Terezín doesn't offer many places to eat. However, in the main parking lot you can buy snacks and drinks at a small stand. Inside the Main Fortress, near the museum, is a decent, inexpensive restaurant with Czech fare.

Fast Facts: Prague

American Express

Prague has two American Express offices. The main one is at Václavské náměstí 56, Praha 1 (☎ 222-800-237), and is open daily from 9 a.m. to 7 p.m. There's another office at Staroměstské náměstí 5 (☎ 224-818-388), open daily from 9 a.m. to 7:30 p.m.

Area Code

The country code for the Czech Republic is **420.** Prague no longer has a separate city code. Instead, old numbers have had the former city code (2) grafted onto the front of them — if you see any number in outdated literature presented as "02-213 . . ." just drop the 0. In other words, to call Prague from the United States, dial 011-420 followed by the number.

Currency

The Czech unit of currency is called the koruna (Kc) and is divided into 100 hellers. Roughly, $1 equals 16Kc, or 10Kc equals 62¢. Czech coins include 50 hellers and 1, 2, 5, 10, 20, and 50 koruna. Bills come in denominations of 50, 100, 200, 500, 1,000, 2,000, and 5,000 koruna.

Doctors and Dentists

Unicare Medical Center, Na dlouhém lánu 11 (☎ 235-356-553, or 608-103-050 after hours; www.unicare.cz), has physicians in most specialties, as well as dentists; open Monday through Friday 8 a.m. to 8 p.m., Saturday 9 a.m. to 4 p.m. See also "Hospitals," later in this section.

Embassies and Consulates

The consulate services of the U.S. Embassy, Tržiste 15, Praha 1 (☎ 257-022-000; www.usembassy.cz), are open daily from 9 a.m. to noon. The Canadian Embassy, Muchova 6, Praha 6 (☎ 272-101-800), is open Monday to Friday from 8:30 a.m. to 12:30 p.m. and 1:30 to 4:30 p.m. The U.K. Embassy, Thunovská 14, Praha 1 (☎ 257-402-111), is open Monday to Friday from 8:30 a.m. to 12:30 p.m. and 1:30 to 5 p.m. You can visit the Australian Honorary Consul, Klimentská 10, Praha 1 (☎ 296-578-350) Monday to Friday from 9 a.m. to 1 p.m. and 2 to 5 p.m. The Irish Embassy is at Tržiste 13, Praha 1 (☎ 257-530-061), and is open Monday to Friday from 9 a.m. to 1 p.m. and 2 to 5 p.m. The New Zealand Honorary Consul is located at Dykova 19, Praha 10 (☎ 222-514-672), and visits here are by appointment.

Emergency

In a general emergency, dial ☎ 112. Dial ☎ 158 to call the police, or ☎ 150 to report a fire. For an ambulance, call ☎ 155.

Hospitals

In a medical emergency, head to Motol Hospital's 24-hour Center for Foreigners, V Úvalu 84 (☎ 224-433-681). If it's between 7:30 a.m. and 4:30 p.m., try the Foreigner's Medical Clinic at Na Homolce Hospital, Roentgenova 2, Praha 5 (☎ 257-272-174; www.homolka.cz).

Information

Prague Information Service (PIS), at Staromestské námestí 1 (☎ 12-444; www.pis.cz), is one of the information offices in town. For specifics on it, and on other offices, see "Finding information after you arrive," near the beginning of this chapter.

Internet Access and Cybercafes

Bohemia Bagel, Masná 2 (☎ 224-811-560; www.bohemiabagel.cz) has dozens of terminals open Monday through Friday 7 a.m. to midnight, Saturday and Sunday 8 a.m. to midnight — plus, great bagels. To surf for free (three computers; no time limit; long waits) or get your Wi-Fi on, head to the pubby restaurant Jáma, V jáme 7 (☎ 224-222-383; www.jamapub.cz).

Maps

The maps printed in some of the tourist-office handouts aren't bad, but you really should pick up a better one at a newsstand or bookstore.

Newspapers and Magazines

Newsstands carry an English-language weekly newspaper, *The Prague Post* (www.praguepost.com), packed with useful information and events calendars. You can also pick up *Culture in Prague,* a monthly bilingual events calendar.

Pharmacies

A Czech pharmacy is called a *lékárna.* Several pharmacies remain open 24 hours a day, including Palackého 5, Praha 1 (☎ 224-946-982), and Lékárna U Andela, Stefánikova 6, Praha 5 (☎ 257-320-918).

Police

Dial ☎ **158** to call the police.

Post Office

The main post office is at Jindřišská, just off Václavské náměstí (☎ 221-131-111; www.cpost.cz), open 24 hours.

Safety

Walking or taking the Metro or trams alone at night is safe, but always be on the lookout for pickpockets, especially on Charles Bridge, around parts of Old Town, and on public transportation. Václavské náměstí (Wenceslas Square) is a little seedy during the day and is traveled mainly by prostitutes at night.

Taxes

A 19 percent value-added tax (VAT) is built into the price of most goods and services. You can get a refund on the VAT as long as you spend more than 2,000Kc ($124) in a single shop (see Chapter 4).

Taxis

See "Getting Around Prague," earlier in this chapter.

Telephone

A local call in Prague costs at least 4Kc (25¢) for 104 seconds of local time or 35 seconds of long distance (longer after 7 p.m.). Pay phones accept either coins or phone cards, sold at post offices, tobacconists, or newsstands in denominations ranging from 150Kc to 500Kc ($9.30–$31). Coin-operated phones do not make change, so insert money as needed, but use smaller coins. Here's something to confuse you: A Czech dial tone sounds like a busy signal in the United States; the Czech busy signal sounds like a U.S. dial tone. For Czech directory assistance, call ☎ 1180; for international directory assistance, dial ☎ 1181. To dial direct internationally, press 052, the country code, and the number.

To charge a call to your calling card, dial AT&T (☎ 00-800-222-55288) or MCI (☎ 00-800-001-112; not accessible from cellphones). To call the United States direct from Prague, dial 001 followed by the area code and number.

Transit Info

Call ☎ 221-111-122 for train info, or go online to the Czech Railways site at www.cdrail.cz or see the timetable at www.vlak.cz. For intercity buses, call ☎ 900-149-144 or go to www.vlak-bus.cz. For the city transport system, call ☎ 296-191-817 or go to www.dpp.cz. For more, see "Getting Around Prague," earlier in this chapter.

Part V
Mediterranean Europe

The 5th Wave   By Rich Tennant

"Get your room key ready, Margaret!"

In this part . . .

Ah, bright and sunny Mediterranean Europe. You can enjoy winding coastal drives and long moonlit dinners, gemlike islands and afternoon siestas, and ripe olives and fine wine. The Mediterranean life runs at a slower pace and is more laid-back than that of Northern and Central Europe.

Here you can discover the ruins of ancient Greece and Rome. But a few dusty rocks and chipped columns do not make a Western civilization. We also guide you to the treasures — masterpieces by Michelangelo, Raphael, Donatello, da Vinci, Botticelli, and many, many others — that fill the museums and churches of Rome, Florence, and Venice.

From there, you head to Spain. Madrid boasts its own share of artistic treasures, but excursions to Toledo and Segovia give you a taste of the country's stunning landscape. Barcelona awaits with its distinctively whimsical architecture and vibrant, happening nightlife. And finally, it's off to the history surrounding Athens and the warm simplicity and sunshine of Santoríni in the Greek Islands.

Chapter 19

Rome and Southern Italy

• •

In This Chapter

▶ Getting to Rome
▶ Checking out the neighborhoods
▶ Discovering the best hotels, restaurants, and attractions
▶ Side-tripping to Naples, Herculaneum, and Pompeii

• •

The Eternal City's 2,000-year-old ruins — including major sights such as the Roman Forum, the Pantheon, and, of course, the Colosseum — hint at Rome's glorious past. But Rome didn't stop there: Medieval buildings are rare because they've been swept away by the blooming Renaissance, followed by the bursting baroque, which turned churches and *palazzi* into magnificent museums filled to the brim with the greatest art by the greatest artistic masters — Michelangelo, Raphael, Borromini, Bernini, Botticelli, and Caravaggio. Modern Rome hasn't sat on its laurels, and this bustling city is rich in cultural and artistic events, as well as simpler joys: a morning cappuccino, a deliciously hearty meal.

Rome is also the gate to southern Italy: the bay of Naples, beloved by ancient Romans, welcomes visitors with its riches. Thanks to high-speed trains, you can now visit **Naples, Pompeii,** or **Herculaneum** as a day trip from the capital.

As one saying goes, it would take a lifetime to see all of Rome, but you can get a good sampling of its wonderful flavors in three or four days. Because you won't see everything before you depart, be sure to toss a coin into the Trevi Fountain — legend has it that, if you do, you're destined to return someday.

Getting There

Rome is a perennially popular destination, with plenty of flights available on a wide variety of international airlines, and trains from all over Europe.

Arriving by air

Most international flights land at **Leonardo da Vinci International Airport,** also called **Fiumicino** (☎ **06-65951;** www.adr.it), 29km (18 miles) west of the city. The airport is compact, with three terminals connected by a long corridor, with departures on one level and arrivals below. There you'll find ATMs (one per terminal), as well as 24-hour currency-exchange machines, a *cambio* (change) office (open 8:30 a.m.–7:30 p.m.), a tourist info point, and a help desk for last-minute hotel reservations. Public transportation — including **taxis,** and car-rental shuttle buses — is outside along the sidewalk. The flat rate to hotels in the historic district is 40€ ($64) with a Rome-licensed taxi. (At press time, Fiumicino-licensed taxis were still charging 60€/$96, a quirk that the administration was working to resolve.) The ride will take between 40 minutes with no traffic, to well over an hour at rush hours.

Beware of Gypsy cabdrivers who approach you as you exit the arrival gate: They'll easily charge you double the regulated cab rates. Regulation taxis are white with a checkered line on the sides, have a meter and a city license inside, and wait at the regular stand.

The **train station** is on the second floor of a building attached to the terminal; follow the TRENI signs. You can buy tickets there from the ticket booth, the tobacconist store, and from vending machines for the **Leonardo Express,** a first-class-only express to the main rail station, Stazione Termini (30 minutes; 9.50€/$15). You can also take a local train every 20 minutes to the Tiburtina or Ostiense rail stations (final destination marked ORTE or FARA SABINA; 45 minutes; 5€/$8) from the same tracks. The local train fare is included in **transportation passes** (see "Getting Around Rome," later in this chapter).

Many charter and continental flights land at the smaller **Ciampino Airport** (☎ 06-7934-0297 or 06-794-941), 16km (10 miles) south of the city. **Taxis** are by far the easiest way to get to town from Ciampino. The flat rate to Rome's central hotels is 30€ ($48) for the 45-minute trip. You can also take a **shuttle bus: Terravision** (☎ 06-7949-4572; www.terravision.it) and **Schiaffini** (☎ 06-713-0531; www.schiaffini.com) run a shuttle service to Termini station for 8€ ($13).

Arriving by rail

Trenitalia, the national train service (☎ 892-021; www.trenitalia.it), offers cheap, reliable, and frequent service to Rome from every domestic and international destination. The majority of trains headed for Rome stop at **Termini,** the main station on Piazza dei Cinquecento (☎ 800-431784; www.romatermini.it). A few long-haul trains may stop only at the Tiburtina station northeast of the center; you'll find all kinds of public transportation at either station.

Finding information after you arrive

Rome has established about a dozen tourist info points near popular sights. See "Information" under "Fast Facts: Rome" at the end of this chapter for addresses.

Italy

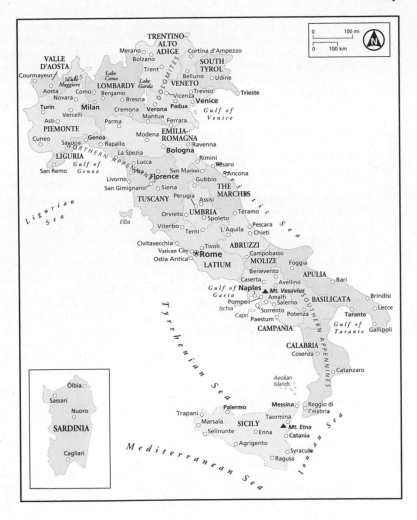

Getting Around Rome

Although there is much you can do on foot, Rome is quite vast — it's Italy's largest city — and finding your way even just within the historic district can be a tad complicated. Using a good map will help you figure out the lay of the land (see "Maps" under "Fast Facts: Rome" at the end of this chapter).

By taxi

Taxi rates are reasonable in Rome. The meter starts at 2.33€ ($3.75) and adds 0.78€ ($1.25) for every kilometer (⅝ mile) if you're moving at up to 20kmph (12 mph); for every 141m (462 ft.) if you're going faster; and for every 19.2 seconds if you're stuck in traffic. The night surcharge is 2.58€ ($4.15), and the Sundays and holiday one is 1.03€ ($1.65). Radio taxi calls have a surcharge of between 2€ and 6€ ($3.20–$9.60), depending on the distance from the call center. Taxi rides originating from Termini train station apply a surcharge of 2€ ($3.20). They're a great resource for getting to your hotel from the train station and traveling around at night, after the buses and Metro stop running.

Taxis in Italy don't cruise, so you usually can't hail a taxi on the street unless you happen to find one that's returning to a stand. If you need a taxi, call ☎ **06-88177,** 06-6645, 06-4994, or 06-5551 for radio taxi service, or walk to one of the many stations scattered around town at major squares and stations.

By subway, tram, and bus

You purchase a 1€ ($1.60) *biglietto* (ticket) to ride any public transportation within Rome. Tickets are good for 75 minutes, during which you may board the Metro system one time and transfer buses as frequently as you need — just stamp your ticket on the first bus and the final bus. You can also buy daily (4€/$6.40), three-day (11€/$18), or weekly (16€/$26) passes. Look for passes and tickets at *tabacchi* (tobacconist shops indicated by a brown-and-white T sign), Metro stations, newsstands, and machines near major bus stops. Keep your ticket with you as you travel in order to avoid paying a fine.

Because of Rome's rich ancient heritage, its Metro system is small and not especially developed (it seems that whenever the city attempts to add a new leg to the subway, it encounters ruins that archaeologists must examine). The Metro's two lines, the orange A line and the blue B line, intersect at Termini.

The Colosseum, Circus Maximus, and Cavour stops on the B line don't offer full elevator/lift service and aren't accessible for people with disabilities.

Thankfully, Rome has a much more developed bus and tram system; still they're very crowded at rush hour, and traffic jams are endemic. The lines you'll use the most are the diminutive **electric buses** that ride in the tiny, narrow streets of the historical district (**116** and **116T** from the Gianicolo hill to Villa Borghese; **117** from Piazza del Popolo to San Giovanni in Laterano; **118** from Piazzale Ostiense to Appia Antica; and **119** from Piazza del Popolo to Largo Argentina), as well as **23** (Prati to Aventino), **62** (Castel Sant'Angelo to Repubblica), **64** (Termini to Vatican), **87** (Prati to Colosseum), **492** (Tiburtina railroad station to Vatican Museums), and **910** (Termini to Villa Borghese). Rome also has a few tram lines; they aren't as spectacular as the cable cars in San Francisco, but they're fun to ride;

8 goes from Largo Argentina to Trastevere, and **3** passes by the Basilica di San Giovanni and the Colosseum. Most buses run daily from 5:30 a.m. to 12:30 a.m., but some stop at 8.30 p.m. After-hours, night lines marked with an N run hourly, leaving the ends of the line on the hour. For bus information, call ☎ **800-431784** or visit www.atac.roma.it.

Staying in Rome

Finding a hotel in Rome has become easier than ever: Many hotels have been recently refurbished, several new ones have opened, and hundreds of B&Bs have appeared. On the less bright side, prices have risen sharply in recent years. Off-season has shrunk to a few weeks in January, February, August, and November. The best way to get a deal is to plan in advance; see Chapter 7 for money-saving tips on booking your accommodations, and on what to expect from your hotel: globalization may be here as everywhere, but cultural differences remain alive and well.

If you arrive without a room reservation (something that's not advisable), you'll find a help desk for last-minute hotel reservations at the airport and one at Termini station.

Rome's top hotels

Albergo del Senato
$$$ Pantheon

This elegant hotel has an ideal location across from the Pantheon. Guest rooms are spacious — the suites are palatial — and beautifully furnished, with antiques and quality reproductions, marble-top tables, and hardwood floors. The marble bathrooms are huge (for Rome) and nicely appointed. The terrace has a spectacular view and is perfect for enjoying Rome's sunsets. It has been recently wired for Wi-Fi Internet connection.

See map p. 392. Piazza della Rotonda 73. ☎ *06-678-4343. Fax: 06-699-40297.* www.albergodelsenato.it. *Bus: 60, 175, or 492 to the Corso; 116 to Pantheon. Rack rates: 390€ ($624) double. AE, DC, MC, V.*

Hotel Aventino
$$ Aventino

We love this hotel located in our favorite area of Rome, convenient to most attractions and enjoying the gift of silence. It's housed in a charming villa surrounded by its own garden. Guest rooms are moderate in size but not cramped, and pleasantly decorated with ornate period furniture, elegant fabrics, and beautiful wooden floors. Bathrooms are not large, but they're modern and with functional showers.

See map p. 392. Via San Domenico 10. ☎ *06-570057. Fax: 06-578-3604.* www.aventino hotels.com. *Tram: 3 to Piazza Albania, and then take Via di Sant'Anselmo. Metro: Circo Massimo and Piramide. Rack rates: 270€ ($432) double. Rates include buffet breakfast. AE, DC, MC, V.*

Accommodations, Dining, and Attractions in Rome

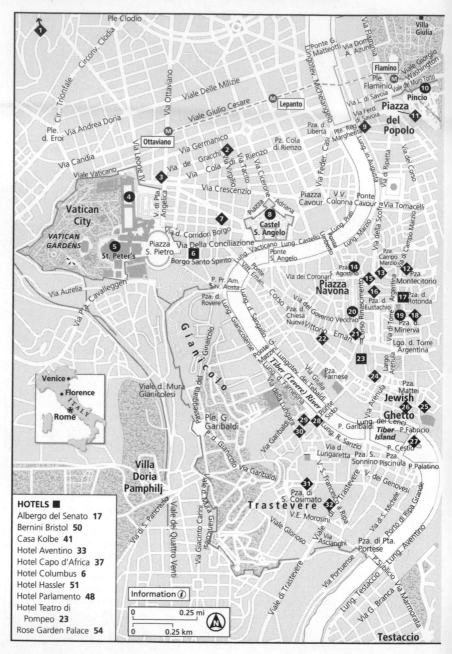

Ple Clodio

Villa Giulia

Via Flaminia

Viale Giorgio Washington

Ponte G. Matteotti

Via Domizio A. Azunio

Flamino

Ple. Flaminio

Viale del Muro Torto

Lungotev. Michelangelo

Via L. di Savoia

Pincio 10

Via Flaminio

Lepanto

Pza. d. Libertá

Via Ferd di Savoia

Piazza del Popolo 11

Ple. d. Eroi

Via Andrea Doria

Viale Delle Milizie

Via Ottaviano

Viale Giulio Cesare

Ottaviano

Via Germanico

Pze. Reg Margherita

Via di Ripetta

Via del Corso

Via Candia

Via de' Gracchi 2

Via Cola di Rienzo

Pz. Cola di Rienzo

Via di Augusta

Viale Vaticano

3

Via Cola

Via Tacito

Via Virgilio

Via Federt Cesi

Via Leone IV

Via Crescenzio

Via Cicerone

Piazza Cavour

V.V. Colonna

Ponte Cavour

Via Tomacelli

V. di Pta. Angelica

4

Piazza Adriana

7

Castel S. Angelo 8

Piazza della Scrofa

Via di Campo Marzio

Vatican City

VATICAN GARDENS

Via d. Corridori Borgo

Via Della Conciliazione

Lung. Vaticano

Ponte S. Angelo

Ponte Umberto

S. Agostino

Pza. Campo Marzio

12 Pza. Montecitorio

5

St. Peter's

Piazza S. Pietro

6

Borgo Santo Spirito

Lung.Castello

Via dei Coronari

Via Argentina

13

Via Aurelia

Via Pta Cavalleggeri

P. Pr. Am. Sav. Aosta

Pza. d. Rovere

Lung. d. Sangallo

Lung.Tor di Nona

14 15

Piazza Navona

Pza. d. S. Eustachio

16

17 Pza. d. Rotonda

G i a n i c o l o

Lung. Gianicolense

Corso Vittorio Eman.

Pza. d. Governo Vecchio

20

Corso Rinascimento

19 18

Pza. d. Minerva

Chiesa Nuova

21

Via di Torre Argentina

Lgo. d. Torre Argentina

22

23

Pza. Farnese

24

Tiber (Tevere) River

Venice

Florence

Rome

ITALY

Viale d. Mura Gianicolesi

Via Giulia

Lungotev. dei Tebaldi

Lung. d. Farnesina

Largo Arenula

Pza. Mattei

26 25

Jewish Ghetto

Ponte Sisto

Ple. G. Garibaldi

29 28

Tiber Island

P.Fabricio

27

Via di Pta. Pancrazio

Via Garibaldi

30

P. Cestio

Villa Doria Pamphilj

Viale d. Gianicolo Via Garibaldi

Via d. Lungaretta

Pza. S. Sonnino

Pza. Piscinula

P. Palatino

Via di S. Francesco a Ripa

V. dei Genovesi

31

Pza. di S. Cosimato

32

Via Porto di Ripa Grande

Trastevere

V.E. Morosini

Viale di Trastevere

Via di S. Michele

Viale Glorioso

Viale Trastevere

Viale Asciangh

Pza. di Pta. Portese

P.Subblicio

Lung. Aventino

Via di Porta Portese

Lung. Testaccio

Via G. Branca

Via Marmorata

Testaccio

Information (i)

0   0.25 mi
0   0.25 km

N

HOTELS ■

Albergo del Senato **17**
Bernini Bristol **50**
Casa Kolbe **41**
Hotel Aventino **33**
Hotel Capo d'Africa **37**
Hotel Columbus **6**
Hotel Hassler **51**
Hotel Parlamento **48**
Hotel Teatro di
  Pompeo **23**
Rose Garden Palace **54**

RESTAURANTS ◆
Alberto Ciarla **31**
Angelino ai Fori **43**
Bolognese **11**
Checco er Carettiere **29**
Da Benito e Gilberto **7**
Da Giggetto **25**
Er Faciolaro **18**
Fattoria la Parrina **15**
Forno Food e Café **13**
Gelateria alla Scala **30**
Gelateria Cecere **46**
Gelateria dei Gracchi **2**
Giolitti **12**
Grappolo d'Oro - Zampanò **22**
Il Barroccio **18**
Il Gelato **16**
Il Tempio del Buongustaio **3**
L'Antico Forno di
    Piazza Trevi **45**
La Pergola **1**
Osteria Ponte Sisto **28**
Pica **24**
Pizza Al Taglio **44**
Pizza a Taglio **9**
PizzaBuona **21**
Pizza Forum **38**
Pizza Rustica **26**
Pizzeria Ivo **32**
Sora Lella **27**

ATTRACTIONS ●
Borghese Gallery **56**
Caracalla Baths **34**
Castel Sant'Angelo **8**
Catacombs of
    Saint Callixtus **36**
Colosseum **39**
Keats–Shelley
    Memorial House **52**
Palatine Hill **40**
Palazzo Altemps **14**
Palazzo Massimo
    alle Terme **49**
Pantheon **19**
Pincio Gardens **10**
Roman Forum **42**
Santa Agnese in Agone **20**
St. Peter's Basilica **5**
Trevi Fountain **47**
Trinità dei Monti **53**
Vatican Museums and
    Sistine Chapel **4**
Via Appia Antica **35**
Villa Borghese **55**

Hotel Hassler
$$$$$ Piazza di Spagna

If money is no object, this luxury hotel is the place to be in Rome, with its fantastic location up the Spanish Steps and its sophisticated elegance. The basic double rooms are not as opulent and spacious as their deluxe doubles, which are basically junior suites, but you enjoy the same top amenities (including a state-of-the-art health center and free bicycles to take to nearby Villa Borghese). Furnishings are classic or modern, with extra-comfortable beds, carpeted floors, and luxury fabrics and linens. Bathrooms are wonderful, marble-clad retreats. We highly recommend the hotel's restaurant **Imàgo** with splendid views of Rome.

See map p. 392. Piazza Trinita dei Monti 6. ☎ *06-699340. Fax: 06-678-9991.* www. hotelhasslerroma.com. *Metro: Barberini, and then take Via Sistina downhill to your right and walk all the way to the end. Rack rates: 660€–935€ ($1,056–$1,496) double. Rates include buffet breakfast. AE, DC, MC, V.*

Hotel Teatro di Pompeo
$$ Campo de' Fiori

Located in the lively and historic neighborhood by Campo de' Fiori, this is a good, moderately priced choice with plenty of charm. The name of the hotel refers to the ancient Roman theater, dating from 55 B.C., that lies beneath the hotel — some of its structure can still be seen in the breakfast room. The rest of the building is much newer — that is, from the 15th century — as you see by the beamed ceilings in some of the rooms. The rooms are spacious for this ancient area of Rome, and the white plaster walls, hardwood floors, and simple furnishings give it an old-fashioned charm. The tiled bathrooms are small but with new fixtures. Three more rooms are in a nearby annex, on the third floor with no elevator.

See map p. 392. Largo del Pallaro 8. ☎ *06-6830-0170. Fax: 06-6880-5531.* www.hotel teatrodipompeo.it. *Bus: 64 to Sant'Andrea della Valle, and then walk east on Via dei Chiavari and turn right. Rack rates: 210€ ($336) double. Rates include buffet breakfast. AE, DC, MC, V.*

Rose Garden Palace
$$$$ Via Veneto

In the exclusive area around Via Veneto, this is a new hotel housed in a Liberty (Italian Art Nouveau) building from the beginning of the 20th century. The eponymous rose garden is a lovely inner garden, perfect for a private stroll. Charm isn't the only thing you'll find here, however; the amenities are top notch. The marble bathrooms have both showers and bathtubs; the rooms themselves are large; and the entire hotel is furnished with very sleek yet inviting modern décor. A new health club and even a swimming pool are on-site. Check their special Internet rates.

See map p. 392. Via Boncompagni 19. ☎ *06-421741. Fax: 06-481-5608.* www. rosegardenpalace.com. *Bus: 116 to Via Boncompagni, and then walk north 1 block. Rack rates: 385€–440€ ($616–$704) double. Rates include buffet breakfast. AE, DC, MC, V.*

Rome's runner-up accommodations

Bernini Bristol

$$$$ **Via Veneto** One of the best hotels in Rome, particularly for its great position — just at the foot of Via Veneto — it offers impeccable service at (relatively) moderate rates. Guest rooms are elegant, some in classical and others in modern luxury style; all have beautiful marble bathrooms. The best rooms open onto great views over Rome. From the splendid rooftop restaurant, the Olympus, you can enjoy a 360-degree view over Rome. *See map p. 392. Piazza Barberini 23.* ☎ *06-488931.* www.berninibristol.com.

Casa Kolbe

$ **Near the Forum** If you love archaeology and don't need too many amenities, this monastically quiet converted convent may be perfect. On the little-traveled side street hugging the west flank of the Palatine Hill, it offers roomy, basic, institutional rooms. *See map p. 392. Via S. Teodoro 44.* ☎ *06-679-4974.*

Hotel Capo d'Africa

$$$ **Colosseo** This elegant new hotel is located on an atmospheric street between the Colosseum and San Giovanni, close to most of the sights of ancient Rome. Known for its excellent service, it offers comfortable rooms furnished in a warm, modern-ethnic style. The marble bathrooms are good size and nicely outfitted. *See map p. 392. Via Capo d'Africa 54.* ☎ *06-772801.* www.hotelcapodafrica.com.

Hotel Columbus

$$$ **Near the Vatican** Michelangelo's patron, Pope Julius II, once owned this lovely 15th-century *palazzo* — located just blocks from the entrance to St. Peter's — and certainly the place feels like a Renaissance castle, complete with oil paintings and tapestries. Guest rooms are fairly simple yet comfortable. The good restaurant opens into the wonderful garden courtyard for good weather. *See map p. 392. Via della Conciliazione 33.* ☎ *06-686-5435.* www.hotelcolumbus.net.

Hotel Parlamento

$$ **Pantheon** Steps from Piazza di Spagna, Trevi Fountain, and the Pantheon, this hotel occupies the third and forth floors of a 15th-century building and offers good accommodations at excellent prices. Rooms are bright and spacious, with tiled floors; large beds; and comfortable bathrooms, some of them with tubs. Weather permitting, breakfast is served on the pleasant roof terrace. Air-conditioning is an extra charge of 12€ ($19) per day (to be booked at the time of your reservation). *See map p. 392. Via delle Convertite 5, off Piazza San Silvestro.* ☎ *06-6992-1000.* www.hotel parlamento.it.

Dining in Rome

Typically, a complete meal in Rome is a multicourse affair that could last for hours; in today's faster-paced world, however, this happens less frequently, especially at lunch. Rome offers a great choice, from down-to-earth trattorie and *osterie* preparing excellent traditional Roman fare to elegant restaurants that count among the best in the country. Restaurants crowd the historical center, with the highest concentration in the area around Campo de' Fiori, in Trastevere, and in the Navona/Pantheon and Trevi areas, in that order.

Traditional Roman cuisine is based on simple food, "poor people fare." It may be unsophisticated, but it's quite good. Among the *primi* (first courses), favorite Roman specialties include *pasta all'amatriciana* (a tomato-and-bacon sauce with pecorino cheese), and its tomatoless version called gricia; *pasta all'arrabbiata* (tomato sauce with bacon and lots of hot red pepper); *gnocchi* (potato dumplings in a tomato-based sauce — note that these are traditionally served on Thurs only); *cannelloni* (pasta tubes filled with meat or fish and baked); and ricotta and spinach ravioli. Among favorite *secondi* (main courses) are *abbacchio* (young lamb) — roasted with herbs or *scottadito* (small grilled cutlets) — and *saltimbocca alla romana* (veal or beef, stuffed with ham and sage and sautéed in a Marsala sauce). For the more adventurous, there is *trippa alla romana* (tripe Roman style). Desserts are few, mostly gelato (rich, creamy ice cream), creamy *zabaglione* (made with sugar, egg yolks, and Marsala wine), or *tiramisu* (layers of mascarpone cheese and espresso-soaked ladyfingers).

The best-known wines of Rome come from the nearby Castelli Romani, the hill towns to the east of the city. Worth trying are the white Frascati — very dry and treacherously refreshing — and the red Velletri.

Alberto Ciarla
$$$ Trastevere   ROMAN/SEAFOOD

This restaurant will satisfy both gourmets looking for creative dishes and those after traditional Roman cuisine. The chef claims to have invented the *crudo* ("raw" — as in raw fish) Italian style, and keeps researching new flavors: The ever-changing menu may list *millefoglie con mousse di dentice in salsa al vino bianco* (napoleon with local fish mousse in white-wine sauce) or his revisitation of the classic *zuppa di fagioli e frutti di mare* (bean and seafood stew). The tasting menus range from Roman tradition (50€/$80) to the chef's grand cuisine (84€/$134).

See map p. 392. Piazza San Cosimato 40. ☎ 06-581-8668. Reservations recommended. Tram: 8. Main courses: 18€–31€ ($29–$50). AE, DC, MC, V. Open: Mon–Sat 8:30 p.m.–12:30 a.m. Closed 10 days in Jan and 10 days in Aug.

Angelino ai Fori
$$ Colosseo   ROMAN/SEAFOOD/PIZZA

A local favorite, this is another stronghold of Roman cuisine, which may appear like a tourist trap because of its perfect location across from the Roman Forum but is actually an authentic traditional restaurant. Highly recommended are *bucatini all'amatriciana, saltimbocca alla romana* (sautéed veal with ham and sage), and — when on the menu — *pollo alla Romana* (chicken stewed with red and yellow peppers). It also serves nice fish dishes that vary with market offerings (check its display by the entrance door). The terrace is a great plus in the good season, but service may get slow.

See map p. 392. Largo Corrado Ricci 40. ☎ *06-679-1121. Reservations recommended. Metro: Colosseo. Main courses: 7€–18€ ($11–$29). AE, DC, MC, V. Open: Wed–Mon noon to 3:15 p.m. and 7–11 p.m. Closed Jan.*

Bolognese
$$$ Piazza del Popolo   BOLOGNESE

Elegant and hip, this restaurant serves well-prepared food at moderate prices in a nicely appointed dining room or, in good weather, on the outdoor terrace. Even Romans admit that Bologna has produced some good dishes, like the lasagna prepared so well here. The *tagliatelle alla Bolognese* (homemade pasta with tomato and meat sauce) and the *fritto di verdure e agnello* (tempura of vegetables and lamb tidbits) are mouthwatering. End with something from the unusually large selection of delicious desserts.

See map p. 392. Piazza del Popolo 1. ☎ *06-361-1426. Reservations required. Bus: 117 or 119. Main courses: 14€–29€ ($22–$46). AE, DC, MC, V. Open: Daily Tues–Sun 12:30–3 p.m. and 8:15 p.m. to midnight. Closed 3 weeks in Aug.*

Checco er Carettiere
$$ Trastevere   ROMAN

This traditional trattoria is still faithful to the old Italian-cuisine values of fresh ingredients and professional service. It even prepares the fish for you at your table. The *bombolotti all'amatriciana* is excellent, as are the *abbacchi scottadito* (grilled lamb chops) and the *coda alla vaccinara* (oxtail stew). Homemade desserts round out the menu nicely.

See map p. 392. Via Benedetta 10, near Piazza Trilussa. ☎ *06-580-0985. Reservations recommended. Bus: 23 or 115 to Piazza Trilussa. Main courses: 13€–18€ ($21–$29). AE, DC, MC, V. Open: Daily 12:30–3 p.m.; Mon–Sat 7:30–11:30 p.m. Closed for lunch Sun–Mon July–Aug.*

Da Benito e Gilberto
$$ San Pietro   SEAFOOD

Don't expect a written menu and a lot of time to make up your mind in this informal restaurant; you'll have to listen to the daily offerings and recommendations of your waiter, and then go for it. Don't worry; you won't regret it: The quality of the ingredients and the preparation of the food are out-

Lunch on the go in Rome

Pizza is a very good choice, both for a quick and inexpensive meal and to make children happy; they will love going to one of the ubiquitous pizza parlors (standing up only) for a quick bite. The best — and most convenient — are **Pizza**, Via del Leoncino 28 (☎ **06-686-7757**); **Pizza a Taglio**, Via della Frezza 40 (☎ **06-322-7116**); **Pizza**, Via della Penna 14 (☎ **06-723-4596**); **Pizza Rustica**, Via del Portico d'Ottavia (☎ **06-687-9262**) and Via dei Pastini 116 (☎ **06-678-2468**); **Il Tempio del Buongustaio**, Piazza del Risorgimento 50 (☎ **06-683-3709**); **Pizza Al Taglio**, Via Cavour 307 (☎ **06-678-4042**); and **PizzaBuona**, Corso Vittorio Emanuele II 165 (☎ **06-689-3229**). **Pizza Forum**, Via San Giovanni, in Laterano 34 (☎ **06-700-2515**) is a sit-down pizzeria with very fast service.

Another good — and cheap — alternative is to have a sandwich standing up at a bar counter. Of course, you can also sit down if you prefer, and pay the table service surcharge.

Finally, in fine weather, you can have great picnics in the Pincio Gardens, Villa Borghese, and the Gianicolo. For your supplies, try **Fattoria la Parrina**, Largo Toniolo 3, between Piazza Navona and the Pantheon (☎ **06-6830-0111**), which offers wonderful organic cheese, wine, and veggies; **L'Antico Forno di Piazza Trevi**, Via delle Muratte 8 (☎ **06-679-2866**), where you'll find superb focaccia and bread, as well as a variety of other items; and the bakery — both savory and sweet goods — **Forno Food e Café**, with several small shops around the Pantheon.

standing. The *pasta e fagioli con frutti di mare* (bean and seafood soup) is warm and satisfying; the *tagliolini alla pescatora* (homemade pasta with seafood), delicate; and the *fritto di paranza* (fried small fish), delicious. Also try the grilled daily catch.

See map p. 392. Via del Falco 19, at Borgo Pio. ☎ 06-686-7769. Reservations required several days in advance. Bus: 23 or 81 to Via S. Porcari. Main courses: 12€–18€ ($19–$29). AE, MC, V. Open: Tues–Sat 7:30–11:30 p.m. Closed Aug.

Da Giggetto
$$ Teatro Marcello   JEWISH ROMAN

For decades, this famous restaurant has been the destination of Romans who want to taste some of the specialties of Jewish Roman cuisine. Some Romans say Giggetto is a little past its prime, but it's still a good place to sample such specialties as *carciofi alla giudia* (crispy fried artichokes), as well as traditional Roman dishes such as *fettuccine all'amatriciana* and *saltimbocca alla romana*.

See map p. 392. Via del Portico d'Ottavia 21. ☎ 06-686-1105. Reservations recommended. Bus: 63 or 23, and then walk north behind the synagogue. Main courses: 12€–18€ ($19–$29). AE, DC, MC, V. Open: Tues–Sun 12:30–3 p.m.; Tues–Sat 7:30–11 p.m. Closed 2 weeks in Aug.

Er Faciolaro
$ Pantheon   ROMAN/PIZZA

Here we come, as generations of Romans have done before us and keep doing, for the sympathy of the service and the homemade food, which includes some of the hard-to-find classics of Roman cuisine. Favorite pasta dishes include the *trofie cacio e pepe* (fresh pasta with pecorino cheese and black pepper) and the *spaghetti alla gricia,* but many come for the *trippa alla romana* (tripe in a light tomato sauce) and the *coda alla vaccinara* (oxtail stew). They also serve beans (*fagioli,* hence the name) prepared in various manners, and excellent pizza. The restaurant across the street (**Il Barroccio;** Via dei Pastini 13; ☎ 06-678-3896) has the same owner and a similar menu.

See map p. 392. Via dei Pastini 123. ☎ *06-678-3896. Reservations recommended on weekends. Bus: 64 to Corso Vittorio Emanuele. Main courses: 8€–18€ ($13–$29). MC, V. Open: Tues–Sun 12:30–3 p.m.; daily 7:30 p.m.–1 a.m.*

Grappolo d'Oro–Zampanò
$ Campo de' Fiori   CREATIVE ITALIAN/PIZZA

This very successful restaurant serves well-rounded dishes, homemade bread, and good pizza (no pizza on Mon). The outdoor terrace is a pleasant plus. The seasonal menu may include *ravioli di parmigiano e scorza di limone con riduzione di basilico e pomodorini* (Parmesan and lemon zest ravioli with basil and cherry tomatoes reduction) or *carré d'agnello con spuma di sedano* (rack of lamb with celery mousse). Desserts are simple but tasty.

See map p. 392. Piazza della Cancelleria 80. ☎ *06-689-7080. Reservations recommended. Bus: 64 to Corso Vittorio Emanuele. Main courses: 8€–18€ ($13–$29). AE, DC, MC, V. Open: Sat–Sun 12:30–3 p.m.; daily 7:30–11 p.m. Closed Aug.*

La Pergola
$$$$ Monte Mario   CREATIVE ITALIAN

This is one of the best and most magical restaurants in Italy. The breathtaking panorama with Rome laid out at your feet, the elegance of the

---

Looking for a gelato break?

Why waste your time — and calories — with industrial ice cream when you can have handmade gelato? Here are a few of the best in Rome: **Giolitti,** Via Uffici del Vicario 40 (☎ 06-699-1243; Minibus: 116), is the oldest gelato parlor in Rome and is reliably excellent. **Il Gelato,** Piazza Sant'Eustachio 47, near the Pantheon (no phone) is one of the newest but a highly recommended addition. **Pica,** Via della Seggiola 12 (☎ 06-6880-3275; Tram: 8), near Campo de' Fiori, is another good address. Near Fontana di Trevi, head for **Gelateria Cecere,** Via del Lavatore 84 (☎ 06-679-2060; Bus: 116 or 492). In Trastevere, try **Gelateria alla Scala,** Via della Scala 5 (☎ 06-581-3174; Tram: 8); and, in Prati, **Gelateria dei Gracchi,** Via dei Gracchi 272 (☎ 06-321-6668; Metro: Lepanto).

furnishings, and the professional service — both kind and discreet — all add to Chef Heinz Beck's masterly handling of the best Italian ingredients, to make for a perfect experience. The *tortellini verdi con vongole e calamaretti* (green tortellini with clams and squid) and *triglia su ragout di carciofi* (red mullet served over a ragout of artichokes) are delectable. The tasting menu is a perfect way to sample several inventions at once (and highly recommended is a tasting menu of desserts). Finding your way up here by public transportation would be impressive but laborious; take a taxi.

See map p. 392. In the Rome Cavalieri Hilton, Via A. Cadlolo 101, up the Monte Mario hill. ☎ *06-3509-2152.* www.cavalieri-hilton.it. *Reservations necessary. Main courses: 36€–54€ ($58–$86). AE, DC, MC, V. Open: Tues–Sat 7:30–11 p.m. Closed Jan 1–23 and 2 weeks in Aug.*

Osteria Ponte Sisto
$ Trastevere ROMAN

Offering traditional Roman fare, this famous *osteria* has been a longstanding destination for locals and tourists alike. Try the delicious *risotto al gorgonzola* (Italian rice cooked with Gorgonzola cheese) or, if you dare, some truly Roman specialties such as *trippa alla romana* (tripe in a light tomato sauce) or oxtail stew.

See map p. 392. Via Ponte Sisto 80, off Piazza Trilussa. ☎ *06-588-3411. Reservations recommended. Bus: 23 or 115 to Piazza Trilussa. Main courses: 9€–16€ ($14–$26). AE, MC, V. Open: Thurs–Tues noon to 3 p.m. and 7–10:30 p.m. Closed Aug.*

Pizzeria Ivo
$ Trastevere PIZZA

One of Rome's most established *pizzerie,* Ivo is as popular with locals as it is with visitors. Luckily, the place is big! Here you can enjoy an entire range of appetizers — fried zucchini flowers, *bruschetta,* deep-fried and stuffed olives — as well as excellent pizza, crostini, and calzones. We love the seasonal pizza with *fiori di zucca* (zucchini flowers) and the *capricciosa* (prosciutto, carciofini, and olives).

See map p. 392. Via di San Francesco a Ripa 158. ☎ *06-581-7082. Reservations not necessary. Tram: 8 to Via di San Francesco a Ripa (on the right off Viale Trastevere). Main courses: 8€–12€ ($13–$19). DC, MC, V. Open: Wed–Mon 12:30–3:30 p.m. and 7:30–11 p.m.*

Sora Lella
$$ Trastevere ROMAN

This family-run restaurant — created by the sister of the famous Roman actor Aldo Fabrizi and run today by his son and grandsons — was already a Roman institution, but with the recent renovations in the dining room and on the menu, it has won new admirers. The gnocchi are superb, and complementing the solid traditional menu are many new dishes, such as the delicious *polpettine al vino* (small meatballs in a wine sauce). Tasting menus and a vegetarian menu are available, and the traditional Roman *contorni,* such as *cicoria* (dandelion greens) and *carciofi* (artichokes), are exceptional.

See map p. 392. Via di Ponte Quattro Capi 16, on Isola Tiberina, in the river between the center and Trastevere. ☎ 06-686-1601. Reservations recommended. Bus: 23, 63, or 115 to Isola Tiberina. Main courses: 14€–20€ ($22–$32). AE, DC, V. Open: Mon–Sat noon to 2 p.m. and 7–11 p.m. Closed Aug.

Exploring Rome

Advance reservations for the **Borghese Gallery** are mandatory (**Ticketeria; ☎ 06-32810** or 199-757510 within Italy; Fax: 06-3265-1329; www.ticketeria.it) and cost 2€ ($3.20); you can buy full-price tickets online for an extra service fee of 1€ ($1.60).

We highly recommend booking a guided tour for the **Vatican Museums** — if only to avoid the horrendous queues at the ticket booth — with their office (minimum 1 week and maximum 1 month in advance by fax only; see listing later in this chapter).

To beat the crowds at the **Colosseum,** buy your ticket at the Palatine Hill ticket booth, at the main Visitor Center of Via Parigi 5 (see "Fast Facts: Rome" at the end of this chapter), or, if you have access to a printer, online at **Pierreci** (**☎ 06-3996-7700;** www.pierreci.it; Mon–Sat 9 a.m.–1:30 p.m. and 2:30–5 p.m. local time), for a service fee of 1.50€ ($2.40), and then print the ticket yourself.

Rome's top attractions

Castel Sant'Angelo (Hadrian's Mausoleum)
San Pietro

This "castle" is a perfect example of recycling Roman style: It began as a mausoleum to hold the remains of Emperor Hadrian, was then transformed into a fortress, and is now a museum. Built in A.D. 123, it may have been incorporated into the city's defenses as early as 403 and was attacked by the Goths (one of the barbarian tribes who pillaged Rome in its decline) in 537. Later, the popes used it as a fortress and hideout, and for convenience they connected it to the Vatican palace by an elevated corridor — the *passetto* — which you can still see near Borgo Pio, stretching between St. Peter's and the castle. Castel Sant'Angelo houses a museum of arms and armor; you can also visit the elegant papal apartments from the Renaissance, as well as the horrible cells in which political prisoners were kept (among them sculptor Benvenuto Cellini). On Saturday, Sunday, and holidays, you can take an interesting guided tour in English on the prisons inside the castle for 3€ ($4.80); reserve in advance at the phone number below. Count about two hours for a full visit.

See map p. 392. Lungotevere Castello 50. ☎ 06-681-9111. www.castelsantangelo. com. Bus: 62 or 64 to Lungotevere Vaticano. Admission: 5€ ($8). Audio guides: 4€ ($6.40). Open: Tues–Sun 9 a.m.–7:30 p.m., Dec 31 9 a.m.–2 p.m. Ticket booth closes 1 hour earlier. Closed Jan 1 and Dec 25.

Catacombe di San Callisto (Catacombs of Saint Callixtus)
Park of Appia Antica

These are the best, most impressive catacombs in Rome, with 20km (12½ miles) of tunnels and galleries underground descending as low as 18m (60 ft.) under. (It's pretty cold down there during the summer, so bring a sweater.) Early Christians held mass, celebrated their rites, and buried their dead in underground hideouts; these catacombs were created inside abandoned quarries and were organized over four levels, with some of the original paintings and decorations still intact. The visit is led by a guide who gives an explanatory introduction and then takes you down, without further ado, for a 30-minute walk; lingering for questions and taking photos once underground is not allowed.

Via Appia Antica 110. ☎ *06-5130-1580.* www.catacombe.roma.it. *Bus/Metro: Metro A to San Giovanni stop, then bus no. 218 to Fosse Ardeatine stop. Admission: 5€ ($8). Open: Thurs–Tues 9 a.m. to noon and 2–5 p.m. Closed Jan 1, Feb, Easter, and Dec 25.*

Colosseum and Palatine Hill
Colosseo

The Colosseum, along with St. Peter's Basilica, is Rome's most recognizable monument. Begun under the Flavian Emperor Vespasian and finished in A.D. 80, it was named the Amphiteatrum Flavium. The nickname came from the colossal statue of Nero that was erected nearby in the second century A.D. The Colosseum could accommodate up to 73,000 spectators for entertainment that included fights between gladiators and battles with wild animals. In the labyrinth of chambers beneath the original wooden floor of the Colosseum, deadly weapons, vicious beasts, and gladiators were prepared for the mortal combats. (Contrary to popular belief, the routine feeding of Christians to lions is a legend.) The Colosseum was damaged by fires and earthquakes, and eventually abandoned; it was then used as a marble quarry for the monuments of Christian Rome until Pope Benedict XV consecrated it in the 18th century. Next to the Colosseum is the **Arch of Constantine,** built in A.D. 315 to commemorate the emperor's victory over the pagan Maxentius in A.D. 312. Pieces from other monuments were reused, so Constantine's monument includes carvings honoring Marcus Aurelius, Trajan, and Hadrian. The Colosseum now houses special exhibitions as well as performances.

Adjacent to the Colosseum is **Palatine Hill.** This is one of our preferred spots in Rome: Huge blocks of brick surrounded by trees and greenery testify mutely to what was once an enormous residential complex of patrician houses and imperial palaces, built with the grandiose ambitions of the emperors. This hill is also where Romulus drew the original square for the foundation of Rome and the first houses were built: Indeed, excavations in the area uncovered remains that date back to the eighth century B.C. **Casa di Livia** (Livia's House) is one of the best-preserved homes. Housed in what was the Palace of Caesar — later transformed into a convent — the **Palatine Museum** is where the most precious artwork recovered from the archaeological excavations of the Palatino is

Don't pass up these deals

If you're planning extensive sightseeing, **Roma Pass** may just be the ticket. The 20€ ($32) pass is valid for three days and grants you free admission to two attractions, discounts on all others, and public transportation (bus, subway, and trains) until midnight of the third day. You can buy the pass online (www.romapass.it), by phone (☎ 06-0608), or at all tourist information points and participating museums.

If you're planning an extensive visit to the sites of ancient Rome, the best deal is the seven-day **Roma Archeologia Card** for 20€ ($32) (22€/$35 if a special exhibit is on at the Colosseum), granting admission to the **Colosseum, Palatine Hill,** the **Roman Forum,** all the sites of the **National Roman Museum** (Palazzo Altemps, Palazzo Massimo, Terme di Diocleziano, and Crypta Balbi), **Caracalla Baths,** and the two paying sites of the **Park of the Via Appia Antica** (Mausoleum of Cecilia Metella and Villa of the Quintili). You can purchase the card at the Visitor Center of Via Parigi 5 and at all participating sites (except Via Appia). The least crowded are Crypta Balbi; Via delle Botteghe Oscure 31, off Largo Argentina; and Terme di Diocleziano, Viale E. de Nicola 78, off Piazza dell Repubblica, near Termini.

The **Villa Borghese Card** gives you free admission to one of the attractions of **Villa Borghese** (which include **Borghese Gallery,** the National Gallery of Modern Art, the zoo, and more; see "More cool things to see and do," later in this chapter), discounted admissions to all others, and 10 percent off purchases at the museums' bookshops, as well as at the bar-restaurant in the Casa del Cinema and in the zoo. The card is for sale for 10€ ($16) at all participating sites and tourist information points.

conserved, including frescoes and sculptures (admission is included in your ticket). Guided tours are available in English and Spanish daily at 11:30 a.m. for 4.50€ ($7.20); it's best to book in advance. Depending on your pace and whether you visit the museum, you should consider spending between one-and-a-half and two-and-a-half hours for your visit.

See map p. 392. Colosseum: Via dei Fori Imperiali. Palatine Hill: Via di San Gregorio 30, off Piazza del Colosseo. ☎ 06-3996-7700 for reservations. Metro: Colosseo. Minibus: 117. Admission: 9€ ($14) plus 2€ ($3.20) for exhibitions. Ticket includes Roman Forum. Audio guides: Colosseum 4.50€ ($7.20), Palatine Hill 4€ ($6.40). Open: Daily 9 a.m. to 1 hour before sunset. Ticket booth closes 1 hour earlier. Closed Jan 1, May 1, and Dec 25.

Galleria Borghese (Borghese Gallery)
Parioli

This unique art gallery was created in 1613 by Cardinal Scipione Borghese inside a splendid building surrounded by a grandiose park for the enjoyment of his special guests (**Villa Borghese,** see "More cool things to see and do," later in this chapter). A mentor for the arts, the cardinal put together the most stunning small collection on view in Italy with sculptures such as Canova's sensual reclining *Paulina Borghese as Venus Victrix*

(Paulina was Napoleon's sister) and the breathtaking *David* by Gian Lorenzo Bernini. The extensive painting collection contains many masterpieces: Caravaggio's haunting self-portrait as *Bacchus*, young Raphael's *Deposition*, and Tiziano's *Sacred and Profane Love*. Many other artists are also represented in this dazzling display of genius. *Note:* Reservations (for a 2-hour slot) are mandatory for admission.

Pick up your reserved ticket by showing your reservation code to the ticket booth at least 30 minutes before your allotted time slot, and be on time for admission, or you'll lose your reservation, miss your turn, and have to pay again for the next available time.

See map p. 392. Piazzale del Museo Borghese. ☎ *06-841-7645.* www.galleria borghese.it. *Reservations required at* ☎ *06-32810 or* www.ticketeria.it. *Bus: 52, 53, or 910 to Via Pinciana, behind the villa; 490 to Viale San Paolo del Brasile inside the park. Minibus: 116 to the Galleria Borghese. Metro: Line A to Spagna, and take the Villa Borghese exit and walk up Viale del Museo Borghese. Admission: 14€ ($22), if no special exhibit 11€ ($18). Admission price includes booking fee. Audio guides: 5€ ($8). Guided tours: 5€ ($8). Open: Ticket booth Tues–Sun 8:30 a.m.– 6:30 p.m. with admission at 9 a.m., 11 a.m., 1 p.m., 3 p.m., and 5 p.m. Closed Jan 1, May 1, and Dec 25.*

National Roman Museum
Piazza Navona and Piazza della Repubblica

Modern Rome's huge collection of ancient Roman artifacts has been spread throughout several locations. Set aside at least an hour to visit the 15th-century **Palazzo Altemps,** located behind Piazza Navona, which houses the **Ludovisi Collection,** one of the world's most famous former private art collections. The single most important piece is the **Trono Ludovisi,** a fifth-century-B.C. Greek masterpiece, finely carved to depict Aphrodite Urania rising from the waves on one side; a female figure offering incense on another; and a naked female playing a flute on yet another. The remarkable *Dying Gaul,* depicting a man apparently committing suicide with a sword, was commissioned by Julius Caesar and placed in his gardens to commemorate his victories in Gaul.

Schedule at least two hours to visit the museum of antiquity, **Palazzo Massimo alle Terme,** including — at the upper level — a magnificent collection of floor mosaics and frescoes. Entire rooms from the **Villa of Livia** on the Palatine Hill have been reconstructed here, and you can enjoy the frescoes as they were meant to be. *Note:* You can visit the fresco collection

Cover up

Bare shoulders, halter tops, tank tops, and shorts (or skirts) above the knee will lead to your being turned away at the entrance of churches and other Catholic sites — no kidding, and no matter your age and sex. Dress appropriately, or carry a large scarf to cover the offending parts.

by guided tour only — you can sign up when you enter, but it's best to make an advance reservation. On the lower floors, you'll find a huge sculpture collection with the striking satyr pouring wine, a Roman copy of the original by Greek sculptor Praxiteles; the *Daughter of Niobe,* from the Gardens of Sallust; and an *Apollo* copied from an original by Phidias, one of the greatest ancient Greek sculptors.

See map p. 392. Palazzo Altemps: Piazza Sant'Apollinare 46. Palazzo Massimo alle Terme: Largo di Villa Peretti 1 (Piazza dei Cinquecento). ☎ 06-3996-7700. Bus: For Palazzo Altemps, 116 to Via dei Coronari, and then walk away from Piazza Navona; for Palazzo Massimo alle Terme, 64 or 70. Metro: For Palazzo Massimo alle Terme, line A or B to Termini. Admission: 7€ ($11); 10€ ($16) if special exhibitions are on. Ticket is valid 3 days and includes Crypta Balbi and Diocletian Baths. Audio guides: 4€ ($6.40). Open: Tues–Sun 9 a.m.–7.45 p.m. Ticket office closes 1 hour earlier. Closed Jan 1 and Dec 25.

Pantheon
Navona/Pantheon

Rome's best-preserved monument of antiquity, the imposing Pantheon was built by the Emperor Hadrian in A.D. 125 as a temple for all the gods (from the ancient Greek *pan theon,* meaning "all gods"). It was eventually saved from destruction by being transformed into a Christian church in A.D. 609. Most of the marble floor is original, and the beautiful coffered dome, whose 5.4m (18-ft.) hole *(oculus)* lets in the light (and sometimes rain) of the Eternal City, is an architectural marvel which inspired Michelangelo when he was designing the dome of St. Peter's, though he made the basilica's dome 0.6m (2 ft.) smaller. Inside, you'll find the tombs of the painter Raphael and of two of the kings of Italy. Crowds always congregate in the square in front, **Piazza della Rotonda,** one of the nicest squares in Rome. A half-hour should be enough to take in the highlights of the monument, plus another hour to soak in the atmosphere from the terrace of one of the cafes.

See map p. 392. Piazza della Rotonda. ☎ 06-6830-0230. Minibus: 116. Admission: Free. Open: Mon–Sat 8:30 a.m.–7:30 p.m.; Sun 9 a.m.–6 p.m.; holidays 9 a.m.–1 p.m.

Piazza di Spagna and the Spanish Steps
Piazza di Spagna

The piazza and its famous steps are one of the favorite meeting places of Rome, and sometimes in the good season you can hardly see the floor because it's crowded with locals and visitors. The atmosphere is festive and convivial, though, and especially romantic in spring, when the steps are decorated with colorful azaleas. The front yard of the Spanish ambassador's residence in the 16th century, it was then far less hospitable, as the unwary could be press-ganged into the Spanish army. In more recent times, the piazza's most famous resident was English poet John Keats, who lived and died in the house to the right of the steps, now the **Keats–Shelley Memorial House** (☎ 06-678-4235; open Mon–Fri 9 a.m.–1 p.m. and 3–6 p.m., Sat 11 a.m.–2 p.m. and 3–6 p.m.); admission is 4€ ($6.40). The steps lead to the **Trinità dei Monti church,** whose towers loom above. At the foot of the steps, the boat-shaped fountain by Pietro Bernini, father of Gian Lorenzo, is one of the most famous in Rome.

See map p. 392. Via del Babuino and Via dei Condotti. Metro: Line A to Spagna. Minibus: 117 or 119 to Piazza di Spagna.

Piazza Navona
Navona/Pantheon

The most beautiful piazza in Rome is also one of the most popular hangouts, lined with cafes and crowded with craft artists and mimes. Built on the ruins of the **Stadium of Domitian** from the first century A.D., where chariot races were held (note the oval track form), it has kept its public role to these days. Between the 17th and 19th centuries, the bottom of the square was flooded for float parades in the summer, and now it's where the traditional Epiphany market — a colorful affair full of toys and sweets — is held during the three-week Christmas period. The piazza is dominated by the twin-towered facade of **Santa Agnese in Agone,** a baroque masterpiece by Borromini, and Bernini's **Fountain of the Four Rivers,** with massive figures representing the Nile, Danube, della Plata, and Ganges — the figure with the shrouded head is the Nile, because its source was unknown at the time. Built in 1651, it is crowned by an obelisk, a Roman copy from Domitian's time. Bernini also designed the figures of the **Fountain of the Moor** at the piazza's south end. (The tritons and other ornaments are 19th-century copies made to replace the originals, which were moved to the Villa Borghese lake garden.)

See map p. 392. Just off Corso Rinascimento. Bus: 70 or 116 to Piazza Navona.

Roman Forum
Colosseo

This was the heart of public life in Ancient Rome, with all the main administrative, religious, and commercial venues. The Forum lies in the valley between the Capitoline Hill, site of the great Temple of Jupiter, and the Palatine Hill, where the royal palace and the palaces of the noblest families were located. The Forum was built at the end of the seventh century B.C. in this once marshy area, and a huge drainage and sewer canal was dug under the forum: the **Cloaca Massima,** still in use. The main street of the forum was **Via Sacra,** the "sacred street," so called because it led to the main temples on the Capitoline Hill (today, Piazza del Campidoglio); you can still walk a stretch of it. Of the few standing buildings, the **Arch of Septimius Severus,** built in A.D. 203 to commemorate this emperor's victories, and nearby the **Curia,** an imposing square building where the Senate once met; many of the walls were heavily restored in 1937, but the marble-inlay floor inside is original from the third century A.D. Also well preserved is the **Temple of Antoninus and Faustina** (the Emperor Antoninus Pius, who succeeded Hadrian in A.D. 138), because it was turned into a church and given a baroque facade **(Chiesa di San Lorenzo in Miranda).** The other arch in the Forum is the **Arch of Titus** who reigned as emperor from A.D. 79 to 81. Nearby is the hulking form of the fourth-century **Basilica of Constantine and Maxentius,** a small corner of what were Rome's law courts. As Rome grew, the Forum became too small to accommodate the needs of the imperial capital, and it was gradually expanded by the various emperors; Via dei Fori Imperial was built on top of the **Imperial Fori,** but you can visit the impressive ruins (entrance at Trajan Market, Via 4 Novembre 94; ☎ **06-0608;** www.mercatiditraiano.it); admission is 6.50€ ($10).

 We recommend using an audio guide or signing up for a guided tour. The tour of the Forum in English is at 1 p.m. daily and lasts about an hour. Ask at the ticket booth or make a reservation.

See map p. 392. Largo della Salara Vecchia, off Via dei Fori Imperiali. ☎ *06-699841, or 06-3996-7700 for reservations.* http://archeoroma.beniculturali.it. *Metro: Colosseo. Minibus: 117. Admission: 11€ ($18), 9€ ($14) if no exhibition at the Colosseum. Ticket includes admission to Colosseum and Palatine Hill. Guided tours: 3.50€ ($5.60). Audio guides: 4€ ($6.40). Open: Daily 8:30 a.m. to 1 hour before sunset. Last admission 1 hour before closing. Closed Jan 1, May 1, and Dec 25.*

St. Peter's Basilica
San Pietro

In 324, Emperor Constantine commissioned a sanctuary to be built on the site of St. Peter's tomb. The first apostle was thought to have been buried here under a simple stone, and excavation and studies commissioned by the Vatican under the basilica have confirmed that thesis. The original basilica stood for about 1,000 years, but with its accrued importance and stability, the papacy decided it was time for renovations. Works begun in 1503 following designs by the architects Sangallo and Bramante. Then Michelangelo was appointed to finish the magnificent dome in 1547 but he died — in 1564 — before seeing its work completed, and his disciple Giacomo della Porta finished the job. The inside of the basilica is almost too huge to take in; walking from one end to the other is a workout, and the opulence will overpower you. On the right as you enter is Michelangelo's exquisite *Pietà,* created when the master was in his early 20s. (Because of an act of vandalism in the 1970s, the statue is kept behind reinforced glass.) Dominating the central nave is Bernini's 29m-tall (96-ft.) **baldaquin,** supported by richly decorated twisting columns. Completed in 1633, it was criticized for being excessive and because the bronze was supposedly taken from the Pantheon. The canopy stands over the papal altar, which in turn stands over the symbolic tomb of St. Peter. A **bronze statue of St. Peter** (probably by Arnolfo di Cambio, 13th century) marks the tomb; its right foot has been worn away by the millions of pilgrims kissing it in the traditional devotional gesture to salute the pope. By the apse, above an altar, is the **bronze throne** sculpted by Bernini to house the remains of what is, according to legend, the chair of St. Peter.

 To visit **Michelangelo's dome** and marvel at the astounding view, you have to climb some 491 steps. Make sure that you're ready and willing to climb, however, because after you've started up, you're not allowed to turn around and go back down. If you want to take the elevator as far as it goes, it'll save you 171 steps, and you'll pay an additional 1€/$1.60). On busy days, expect to wait in line to get a lift.

Beneath the basilica are grottoes, extending under the central nave of the church. You can visit them and wander among the tombs of popes. The excavations proceed farther down, to the paleo-Christian tombs and architectural fragments of the original basilica that have been found here, but you need to apply in writing at least three weeks beforehand to arrange for a visit. Plan on at least two hours to see the entire basilica.

See map p. 392. Piazza San Pietro, entrance through security checkpoint on the right-hand side under the colonnade. ☎ *06-6988-3712. Fax: 06-6988-5518. Bus: 40, 62, or 64. Metro: Ottaviano/San Pietro, and then walk along Viale Angelico to the Vatican. Admission: Basilica and grottoes free; dome 4€ ($6.40), 7€ ($11) with elevator; treasury 6€ ($9.60). Open: Oct–Mar basilica daily 7 a.m.–6 p.m., dome daily 8 a.m.– 4:45 p.m., treasury daily 9 a.m.–5:15 p.m., grottoes daily 7 a.m.–5 p.m.; Apr–Sept basilica Thurs–Tues 7 a.m.–7 p.m. and Wed noon to 7 p.m., dome Thurs–Tues 8 a.m.– 5:45 p.m. and Wed noon to 5:45 p.m.; treasury Thurs–Tues 9 a.m.–6:15 p.m. and Wed noon to 6:15 p.m., grottoes Thurs–Tues 7 a.m.–6 p.m. and Wed noon to 6 p.m.*

Trevi Fountain
Trevi

The imposing Trevi Fountain, fronting its own little piazza, existed for centuries in relative obscurity before it became one of the must-see sights of Rome, thanks to the film *Three Coins in the Fountain*. Crowded with thousands of tourists who have their picture taken as they throw a coin into it, you'll have to come late at night or early in the morning to have a tranquil moment to actually appreciate the artwork. The fountain was begun by Bernini and Pietro da Cortona, but there was a 100-year lapse in the work, and it wasn't completed until 1751 by Nicola Salvi. The central figure is Neptune, who guides a chariot pulled by plunging sea horses. *Tritons* (mythological sea dwellers) guide the horses, and the surrounding scene is one of wild nature and bare stone.

Of course, you have to toss a coin in the Trevi, something all kids love to do. To do it properly (Romans are superstitious), hold the coin in your right hand, turn your back to the fountain, and toss the coin over your left shoulder. According to tradition, the spirit of the fountain will then see to it that you return to Rome one day.

See map p. 392. Piazza di Trevi. Bus: 62. Minibus: 116 or 119. Take Via Poli to the fountain.

Vatican Museums and Sistine Chapel
San Pietro

This enormous complex of museums could swallow up your entire vacation, with its tons of Egyptian, Etruscan, Greek, Roman, paleo-Christian, and Renaissance art. Among the several museums, the **Gregorian Egyptian Museum** holds a fantastic collection of Egyptian artifacts; the **Gregorian Etruscan Museum,** a beautiful collection of Etruscan art and jewelry; the **Ethnological Missionary Museum,** a large collection of artifacts from every continent, including superb African, Asian, and Australian art; and the **Pinacoteca** (picture gallery) contains a splendid collection of medieval and Renaissance masterpieces, from Leonardo da Vinci's *St. Jerome* in Room 9, to Giotto's luminous *Stefaneschi Triptych* in Room 2, to Raphael's *Transfiguration* in Room 8.

Also part of the museums are the **Stanze di Raffaello** (Raphael's Rooms), the private apartments of Pope Julius II: four rooms completely frescoed by the artist, the largest depicting the life of the first Christian emperor, Constantine, including his triumph over Maxentius and his vision of the cross. Along the way, you'll come across the **Borgia Apartments,** designed for Pope Alexander VI (the infamous Borgia pope), and the **Chapel of Nicola V,** with floor-to-ceiling frescoes by Fra Angelico.

But, of course, it is the **Sistine Chapel,** Michelangelo's masterpiece, that is the crowning glory of the museums. Years after their restoration, conflict continues over whether too much paint was removed, flattening the figures. On the other hand, the brilliant color has been restored. The *Creation of Adam* and the temptation and fall of Adam and Eve are the most famous scenes. Michelangelo also painted a terrifying and powerful *Last Judgment* on the end wall.

Binoculars or even a hand mirror will help you appreciate the Sistine ceiling better; your neck tires long before you can take it all in. Just think how poor Michelangelo must have felt while painting it flat on his back atop a tower of scaffolding!

Visiting all the museums in one day is impossible: **Four color-coded itineraries** (A, B, C, or D), take you to the highlights of the museums: They range from one-and-a-half to five hours, and all end at the Sistine Chapel. Audio guides are essential.

If you booked the two-hour tour (Mar–Oct 10:30 a.m., noon, and 2 p.m.; Nov–Feb 10:30 a.m. only), which includes museums, Raphael's Rooms, and the Sistine Chapel, you'll need to take the fax confirmation you received to the Guided Tour desk 15 minutes before your scheduled tour time. (The line is to the right of the regular ticket-booth line at the main entrance of the museums.)

The museums are free the last Sunday of each month — and everyone knows it. Be prepared for huge mobs — or pay your way at another time.

See map p. 392. Viale Vaticano, to the northeast of St. Peter's Basilica. ☎ *06-6 988-3332. Reservations for guided tours* ☎ *06-6988-4676. Fax: 06-6988-5100.* visiteguidate.musei@scv.va. *Metro: Cipro. Bus: 19, 81, 492. Admission: 14€ ($22) adults, 8€ ($13) children 13 and under; free last Sun of each month. Audio guides: 6€ ($9.60). Guided tours: 30€ ($48). Open: Mon–Sat 8:30 a.m.–6 p.m.; last Sun of each month 8:30 a.m.–2 p.m. Last admission 2 hours before closing. Closed Jan 1, Jan 6, Feb 11, Mar 19, Easter, Easter Mon, May 1, Ascension Thurs (usually in May or June), Corpus Christi Day (usually in May or June), Aug 14 and 15 or Aug 15 and 16, Nov 1, Dec 8, Dec 25, and Dec 26.*

More cool things to see and do

After you've covered all of Rome's musts — and there are plenty — you'll have plenty more to choose from, including the following:

✔ Behind **Caracalla Baths,** Via delle Terme di Caracalla 52 (☎ **06-3996-7700;** http://archeoroma.beniculturali.it; open Mon 9 a.m.–2 p.m., Tues–Sun 9 a.m. to one hour before sunset; ticket booth closes one hour earlier; closed Jan 1, May 1, and Dec 25) starts the **Via Appia Antica.** Admission is 6€ ($9.60), and your ticket is valid for seven days and includes admission to Mausoleum of Cecilia Metella and Villa of the Quintili in the Appia Antica Park. Today a public park (☎ **06-513-0682;** www.parcoappiaantica.org; Bus: Archeobus, 118, 218, or 360) this is a section of the original ancient Roman road — the **Regina Viarum** (Queen of Roads) — which was built in 312 B.C. as the highway between Rome and Capua. It was on this road that St. Peter, in flight from Rome, had his vision of Jesus and turned back toward his martyrdom (the spot is marked by a small church, named *Domine Quo Vadis* after the words of Peter to Christ). The street is an archeological paradise, still paved with the original large, flat basalt stones, and lined with the remains of villas, tombs, and monuments against the background of the beautiful countryside. We highly recommend visiting the Catacombs of San Callisto (see earlier in this chapter) as well as the **Mausoleum of Cecilia Metella** (Via Appia Antica 161) and the impressive **Villa dei Quintili** (Via Appia Nuova 1092), a huge patrician villa. These last two attractions observe the same hours and admission as Caracalla Baths. The best way to visit this park's attractions is via the hop-on/hop-off **Archeobus** (see "Guided tours," later in this chapter) or by renting bicycles at the park visitor center, **Cartiera Latina** (Via Appia Antica 42), or at the **Bar Caffè dell'Appia Antica** (Via Appia Antica 175). Bikes rent for 3€ ($4.80) per hour or 10€ ($16) for the whole day.

✔ Surrounding the Borghese Gallery (see earlier in this chapter), you'll find **Villa Borghese,** one of Rome's most beautiful parks. Inside the park is a romantic small lake where you can rent rowboats, and **Piazza di Siena,** a picturesque oval track surrounded by tall pines, used for horse races and for Rome's international horse-jumping event, the **Concorso Ippico Internazionale di Roma,** in May. The park connects to the south to the famous **Pincio Gardens,** with their panoramic terrace overlooking **Piazza del Popolo** — another one of Rome's wonderful piazze — and offering one of the best views of the city, particularly striking at sunset. Children play areas and merry-go-rounds are available in both gardens, as are **bike rentals** (Via dell'Uccelliera, near the Borghese Gallery; Piazzale M.Cervantes, near the zoo; Viale J. W. Goethe, off Viale del Museo Borghese, leading to the Borghese Gallery; and Pincio Gardens). To the northwest of the park is Rome's zoo, called **Bioparco** (☎ **06-360-8211;** www.bioparco.it; Open: Oct–Mar daily 9:30 a.m.–5 p.m., Apr–Sep daily 9:30 a.m.–6 p.m., last admission one hour earlier); admission is

8.50€ ($14) adults, 6.50€ ($10) children 12 and under. Also north-west of Villa Borghese is the **National Gallery of Modern Art** (Viale delle Belle Arti 131; ☎ **06-3229-8221;** www.gnam.arti.beni culturali.it; Open: Tues–Sun 8:30 a.m.–7:30 p.m., last admission 40 minutes before closing); admission is 9€ ($14).

✔ With showrooms of all big names of high fashion, design, and antiques in the triangle formed by the streets between Piazza del Popolo, the Spanish Steps, and the Corso, Rome is a **shopping** para-dise: Via de' Condotti has **Gucci** (no. 68A), **Valentino** (no. 13), **Fragiacomo** (no. 35), **Ferragamo** (nos. 65, 73–74), **Bulgari** (no. 10), and **Battistoni** (no. 61A). The ever-popular **Benetton** has locations throughout Rome but also on Piazza di Spagna (nos. 67–69). Via Frattina is home to **Max Mara** (no. 28), **Brighenti** (no. 7–8), **Anatriello del Regalo** (no. 123), and **Fornari** (no. 133). In Via Borgognona, you'll find **Givenchy** (no. 21), **Fendi** (no. 36–40), and **Gianfranco Ferré** (no. 42B). Via del Babuino offers the relatively affordable "Emporio" of **Armani** (no. 140), **Oliver** (no. 61), **Olivi** (no. 136), **Alberto di Castro** (no. 71), and **Fava** (no. 180). A bit far-ther south, where Via Tritone hits the Corso at no. 189, is **La Rinascente,** Rome's biggest and finest upscale department store. The area on the other side of the Corso is full of nice little shops.

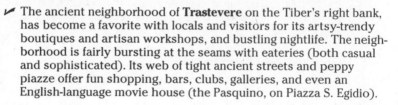

✔ The ancient neighborhood of **Trastevere** on the Tiber's right bank, has become a favorite with locals and visitors for its artsy-trendy boutiques and artisan workshops, and bustling nightlife. The neigh-borhood is fairly bursting at the seams with eateries (both casual and sophisticated). Its web of tight ancient streets and peppy piazze offer fun shopping, bars, clubs, galleries, and even an English-language movie house (the Pasquino, on Piazza S. Egidio).

Guided tours

The French writer Stendhal once wrote, "As soon as you enter Rome, get in a carriage and ask to be brought to the Coliseum [sic] or to St. Peter's. If you try to get there on foot, you will never arrive: Too many marvelous things will stop you along the way."

Taking a tour — by bus now — as you first arrive still is an excellent idea. The local transportation authority **Atac** offers three excellent hop-on/hop-off tours (☎ **06-4695-2252** daily 8 a.m.–8 p.m. for reservations and info; www.trambus.com/servizituristici.htm):

✔ **110 Open** red double-decker buses leave from Piazza dei Cinquecento (across from Termini railroad station) every ten min-utes between 8:40 a.m. and 7:40 p.m. for their 11-stop loop around Rome's major historic sights (16€/$26 adults, 7€/$11 children 6–12, free for children 5 and under).

✔ **Archeobus** green buses leave from the same stop every 40 minutes between 9 a.m. and 4 p.m. (10€/$16, 8€/$13 for those with Roma Pass; see the "Don't pass up these deals" sidebar, earlier in this chapter, for details about the Roma Pass) for a 15-stop itinerary of ancient Rome taking in the Appian Way Park.

✔ **Roma Cristiana** yellow double-decker buses leave from Via della Conciliazione, across from St. Peter's, for two different loops that take in all the major religious sites in Rome: the St. Peter's loop (every 25 minutes), and the St. Paul's Basilica loop (every 50 minutes) between 8:30 a.m. and 7:30 p.m. (15€/$24 for one day and one line, and 20€/$32 for two days/two lines); ten of its stops are actually also near major nonreligious attractions.

A wonderful way to experience Rome is sailing down the Tiber by taking a **boat tour** run by **Compagnia di Navigazione Ponte San Angelo,** Ponte Sant'Angelo, across from Castel Sant'Angelo (☎ **06-678-9361;** www. battellidiroma.it), offering day tours and evening cruises. Prices range from 12€ ($19) for the one-hour tour to 56€ ($90) for the candlelight dinner cruise.

Enjoy Rome, Via Varese 39, 3 small blocks north off Stazione Termini (☎ **06-445-1843;** www.enjoyrome.com; open Mon–Fri 8:30 a.m.–2 p.m. and 3:30–6:30 p.m., Sat 8:30 a.m.–2 p.m.) offers a variety of three-hour walking tours, including a night tour that takes you through the historical center, and a tour of Trastevere and the Jewish Ghetto. All tours cost 26€ ($42) adults and 20€ ($32) for those 25 and under, including some admissions.

Suggested itineraries

So much to see, so little time. The following three itineraries offer recommendations on how best to spend your time in Rome.

If you have one day

It's a tall order to try to see the Eternal City in what amounts to the blink of an eye. But if you don't have more than a day to spend here, we recommend the following: Head to Termini train station early in the morning and take the **110 Open stop-and-go bus tour.** Get off at the **Colosseum** for a visit, and then walk through the **Roman Forum.** You can then take your bus again and get off at the stop near **Piazza Navona** to visit this famous piazza. Then stroll to the nearby **Pantheon** and have lunch at **Grappolo d'Oro–Zampanò.** Enjoy some shopping in the area after lunch before getting back on your bus. Head to **St. Peter's Basilica,** where you'll get off to visit the church. After your visit, climb back on the bus and get off at the stop near the **Trevi Fountain** for a visit to the world's most famous fountain. Continue then toward **Piazza di Spagna and Spanish Steps,** enjoying a bit of shopping on your way. Have a special dinner at **La Pergola.**

If you have two days

On **Day 1,** you can begin as in the preceding section, spending more time visiting the archaeological area, including the **Palatine Hill.** In the afternoon, head for **Galleria Borghese,** where you made your advance reservations. After your visit, stroll down through the **Pincio Gardens** overlooking **Piazza del Popolo,** if possible at sunset. Have your *aperitivo* here at **La Casina Valadier.**

On **Day 2** follow Day 2 in the next section, but skip the visit inside **Castel Sant'Angelo** to squeeze in a pick at **Piazza Navona** and the **Pantheon** on your way to the **Spanish Steps.** After your visit at **Trevi Fountain,** have your last dinner in Rome at **La Pergola.**

If you have three days

Start on **Day 1** as in the "If you have one day" itinerary, and spend your morning imbibing in ancient Rome. After a nice lunch at **Angelino ai Fori,** get back on your bus and finish the tour (it's a loop) to scope out the rest of Rome; get off at the stop near **Piazza Navona** to visit this famous piazza, and stroll into the **Pantheon** for a visit. Have dinner at **Er Faciolaro** (see "Dining in Rome," earlier in this chapter).

On **Day 2,** get up early and head for the **Vatican Museums** to see the **Sistine Chapel,** and continue your visit with **St. Peter's Basilica.** You'll then be ready for a good lunch at **Da Benito e Gilberto.** In the afternoon, see **Castel Sant'Angelo** and cross the river Tiber over Ponte Sant'Angelo. You can then walk north along the river and turn right at Via del Clementino toward the **Spanish Steps** and **Piazza di Spagna.** Stroll to the **Trevi Fountain** after dinner.

On **Day 3,** take a boat tour in the morning, and then explore the funky medieval neighborhood of **Trastevere,** on the south side of the river Tiber, having lunch in one of the local restaurants. In the afternoon, head for **Galleria Borghese,** where you've made your advance reservation. After your visit, stroll down through the **Pincio Gardens** overlooking **Piazza del Popolo,** if possible at sunset. Have your *aperitivo* here at **La Casina Valadier,** and then head to **La Pergola** for your last dinner in Rome.

Traveling beyond Rome

If you can tear yourself away from Rome, consider catching a glimpse of the splendors of the south, and hop onto a high-speed train for Naples.

Naples: A splendid art city welcoming visitors once again

Thanks to high-speed trains, Naples is only a little over an hour away from Rome, making it possible to see its historic district — with its castles, medieval and baroque churches full to the brim with artworks, unique museums, and a most romantic waterfront promenade — or the famed archaeological area of Pompeii or Herculaneum as a day trip from the capital. If you can, though, take the time to explore this vivid, intense destination by spending a couple of nights.

Getting there

The small but well-run Capodichino airport (☎ 081-789-6259; www.gesac.it) — 7km (4 miles) from the city center and only 15 minutes away by public transportation — receives daily flights from Italian and European destinations, including connecting flights from the United States.

If you're coming as a day trip from Rome, book yourself on one of the new high-speed trains (☎ 892021; www.trenitalia.it), and in 87 minutes you'll be in Napoli's Stazione Centrale (☎ 081-554-3188) on Piazza Garibaldi, on the northeastern edge of the historic district; you can also take one of the frequent regular trains, taking two-and-a-half hours. Outside the station, you'll find taxis and public transportation.

You'll find a small tourist info point inside the rail station (☎ 081-268799; open Mon–Sat 9 a.m.–7 p.m.), and better ones in Via San Carlo 9, off Piazza del Plebiscito (☎ 081-402394), in Via Santa Lucia 107 (☎ 081-240-0914), and in Piazza del Gesù (☎ 081-551-2701), all open Monday through Saturday 9 a.m. to 1:30 p.m. and 2:30 to 7 p.m.

Seeing the sights

Before heading out to explore Naples, consider purchasing an **artecard** (☎ 800-600-601 in Italy, or 06-3996-7650; www.campaniartecard.it), the area's most comprehensive sightseeing pass. The pass grants unlimited public transportation and free admission to two attractions and a 50 percent discount to all other eligible locales out of an extensive list including all the region's major museums and archaeological areas. The Naples-only three-day version costs 13€ ($21), and the three-day all-sites version costs 25€ ($40); seven-day and youth versions are available. You can buy it at the Capodichino airport (a good idea if you're planning to use the Alibus bus, which is included), the *molo beverello* (harbor), the train station of Napoli Centrale, as well as major hotels, some news kiosks, and all participating attractions.

We recommend the **City Sightseeing** hop-on/hop-off bus tour (☎ 081-551-7279; www.napoli.city-sightseeing.it), which provides a great introduction to the city as well as convenient transportation between major attractions. Its three one-hour itineraries all start from Piazza Municipio/Parco Castello: **Line A** travels inland to Museo di Capodimonte (Apr daily 9:45 a.m.–4:30 p.m., May–Sept daily 9:45 a.m.–5:15 p.m.); **Line B** goes along the seaside to Posillipo (Apr–Sept daily 9:30 a.m.–5 p.m.); and **Line C** heads up the cliff to the Carthusian Monastery of San Martino on the Vomero (May–Sept daily 10 a.m.–4:45 p.m.). Check the schedule — it changes often. You can get tickets onboard for 22€ ($35) adults, 11€ ($18) children 6 to 15, and 66€ ($106) for families (up to two adults and three children). Tickets are valid for all lines for 24 hours. You get a 10 percent discount if you have the **artecard** (see the preceding paragraph). In the off season, you'll move best by **taxi.**

Then you can wander through the narrow streets of the Città Antica to the **Duomo,** Via Duomo 147 (☎ 081-449097 Duomo and 081-421609 museum; Metro: Piazza Cavour), Naples's cathedral decorated with artworks by great masters including Perugino and Domenichino, and its mosaic-covered fourth-century baptistery. Admission to the Duomo is free; admission to its accompanying museum is 10€ ($16), but it's eligible for a 25 percent discount with the artecard. The Duomo is open Monday through Saturday 8 a.m. to 12:30 p.m. and 4:30 to 7 p.m., and Sunday and holidays 8 a.m. to 1:30 p.m. and 5 to 7:30 p.m. The museum's hours are Tuesday through Saturday 9 a.m. to 6:30 p.m., and Sunday and holidays 9 a.m. to 7 p.m.

Lesser known to foreign visitors than the Uffizi, Naples's picture gallery, the **Museo di Capodimonte,** Via Miano 1 (☎ 081-749-9111; www.musis.it; Bus: 24 or R4 to Parco Capodimonte), holds a splendid collection with works by Mantegna, Raphael, Titian, Caravaggio, Botticelli, Masaccio, and Perugino, among others. You should not miss the royal apartments, full of priceless objects and artwork, as this was a hunting "lodge" for the Bourbon kings. Admission is 7.50€ ($12), and 6.50€ ($10) after 2 p.m. Audio guides rent for 4€ ($6.40). The museum is open Thursday through Tuesday 8:30 a.m. to 7:30 p.m. (ticket booth closes 1 hour earlier); it's closed January 1 and December 25.

If you're planning a visit to Pompeii and Herculaneum, make time to visit the **National Archaeological Museum,** Piazza Museo Nazionale 19 (☎ 081-440166; Metro: Museo or Piazza Cavour), the world's oldest antiquity museum and one of the richest. Here you'll find entire rooms from Pompeii, Herculaneum, and other nearby sites, reconstructed with the original frescoes, as well as a treasure-trove of mosaic floors, sculptures, and carved objects. Admission is 6.50€ ($10), and audio guides rent for 4€ ($6.40). The museum is open Wednesday through Monday 9 a.m. to 7:30 p.m. (ticket booth closes one hour earlier); it's closed January 1 and December 25.

Finish your day with an evening at **Teatro di San Carlo,** Via San Carlo 93 (☎ 081-400300; Fax: 081-400902; www.teatrosancarlo.it; Bus: R2 or R3 to Via San Carlo), the world's first opera house — and one of the most beautiful — a neoclassical jewel said to have better acoustics than Milan's famous La Scala (you can sign up for a guided tour at ☎ 081-553-4565; open Thurs–Mon 9 a.m.–5:30 p.m., other days by reservation only). Or stroll along the waterfront promenade of **Via Partenope,** graced by Naples's most famous landmark, **Castel dell'Ovo,** a picturesque fortress built on a small promontory projecting into the beautiful harbor.

Where to stay and dine

You'll be welcome like royalty at **Grand Hotel Vesuvio,** Via Partenope 45 (☎ 081-764-0044; Fax: 081-663527; www.vesuvio.it; Rack rates: 430€–440€/$688–$704 double, including buffet breakfast). Like one of the family is the more moderate but still elegant **Hotel Miramare,** Via Nazario Sauro 24 (☎ 081-764-7589; Fax: 081-764-0775; www.hotel miramare.com; Rack rates: 282€–357€/$451–$571 double, including buffet breakfast). Modern **Una Hotel Napoli,** Piazza Garibaldi 9

(☎ 081-563-6901; Fax: 081-563-6972; www.unahotels.it; Rack rates: 261€/$418 double, including buffet breakfast), is a stylish new hotel that is convenient to the train station.

For a taste of real Neapolitan pizza, head to **Brandi,** Salita Sant'Anna di Palazzo 1, off Via Chiaia (☎ 081-416928; open Tues–Sun 12:30–3:30 p.m. and 7:30 p.m. to midnight). For local seafood specialties, go to **La Cantinella,** Via Cuma 42, off Via Nazario Sauro (☎ 081-764-8684; open Mon–Sat 12:30–3:30 p.m. and 7:30 p.m. to midnight; closed one week in Jan and three weeks in Aug).

Herculaneum and Pompeii: The world's most famous ancient Roman archaeological areas

Buried beneath volcanic ash and pumice stone in Mount Vesuvius's A.D. 79 eruption, the ruins of Pompeii have been easier to excavate than those in Herculaneum, bringing to light almost the whole town. The huge site — four times larger than Herculaneum — is impressive. Because it was covered in hard volcanic mud — and the new town was built over it — only a small part of Herculaneum has been excavated, but this is highly interesting, having yielded rich and elaborated buildings, as well as woodwork that only partially burned.

Getting there

From Naples, board the **Circumvesuviana** railway (Corso Garibaldi; ☎ 800-053939; www.vesuviana.it; Metro: Garibaldi). For Pompeii, take the Sorrento line and get off at the **Pompei Scavi** stop (the Pompei stop on the other line is the modern town; don't take that). The station is near the entrance of the archaeological area. The 45-minute ride is 2.20€ ($3.50). For Herculaneum, take either the Poggiomarino or the Sorrento line, both of which stop at **Ercolano Scavi;** outside the station you'll find a shuttle bus to the site. The 20-minute ride costs 1.70€ ($2.70). Trains leave every half-hour on either line.

Seeing the sights

You'll need water, comfortable shoes, and a hat and sunscreen in summer to visit these large sights in comfort.

We recommend signing up for an official guided tour, particularly for Pompeii; you can do so at the entrance or in advance by phone or online (☎ 081-857-5347; www.pompeiisites.org), and at www.arethusa.net; a number of buildings — the most interesting — are accessible by guided tour only: **Casa del Menandro** (visits every 30 minutes Sat–Sun 2–4 p.m.); **Casa degli Amorini Dorati** and **Casa dell'Ara Massima** (each daily, every 30 minutes, 9 a.m.–6 p.m.); and **Suburban Baths,** a set of private thermal baths attached to a sumptuous villa set in a splendid, panoramic spot by the western town wall overlooking the sea (daily, every 30 minutes, 10 a.m.–1:30 p.m.). *Note:* At press time, the baths were closed for restoration.

Smaller then Pompeii — about a third smaller estimate the experts — **Herculaneum,** Corso Resina (☎ 081-857-5347; www.pompeiisites.org), was the glitzier seaside resort for VIPs during Roman times. It's estimated that, at the time of the eruption, Herculaneum was a town of about 5,000. Among the most interesting public buildings are the elegantly decorated **thermal baths** and the **Collegio degli Augustali,** lavishly decorated with marble floors and frescoes. This building had a custodian; he was found sleeping in his bed, which you can still see in his small room. The best example of private architecture is the **House of the Stags,** so named for the sculpture found inside — an elegant town house overlooking the sea built around uncovered atriums and terraces, and lavishly decorated. The **House of the Mosaic of Neptune** was a merchant's house, and you can see his shop lined with cabinets and merchandise still on the counter.

Pompeii was an important commercial town as well as a residential resort, and its urban fabric was a mix of elegant villas, shops, and more modest housing. The excavated **Archaeological Area,** Porta Marina, off Via Villa dei Misteri (☎ 081-857-5347; www.pompeiisites.org), is huge — about 44 hectares (109 acres) — representing about two-thirds of the original town; at the time of the eruption, Pompeii had about 35,000 inhabitants.

Organized around three poles — the **Forum,** the **theater district** by the **triangular forum,** and the games and sports area with the **Palestra** and the **Amphitheater** — this large town followed the classic Roman grid of almost perpendicular streets, both residential and commercial, lined with taverns and shops. Nearest to the entrance is the **Forum** — covering 5,388 square meters (58,000 sq. ft.) — surrounded by three important buildings: the **Basilica** (the meeting hall and the city's largest single structure), the **Macellum** (covered market), and the **Temple of Jupiter.** The theater district is farther along, with the beautiful **Teatro Grande** — a structure that could hold 5,000 — and the smaller **Odeion** — for only about 1,000. Nearby are the **Stabian Baths,** the finest thermal baths to have survived from antiquity. Still in good condition, they're richly decorated with marble, frescoes, and mosaics. At the other end of town are the **Amphitheater** — from 80 B.C., it's the oldest in the world — and the magnificent **Palestra,** the sports compound, with exercise areas and a swimming pool that must have been wonderful: huge and surrounded by trees, of which you can see the casts of the stumps. Among the best private homes, the most elegant is the **House of the Vettii,** belonging to two rich merchants, where you can admire a frescoed dining room in the coloring that has become famous as Pompeiian red. The largest is the **House of the Faun,** so called because of the bronze statue of a dancing faun that was found there; the house takes up a city block and has four dining rooms and two spacious inner gardens.

Admission to Herculaneum and Pompeii is 11€ ($18) each, and they're open daily November through March 8:30 a.m. to 5 p.m. and April through October 8:30 a.m. to 7:30 p.m. (last admission is 90 minutes earlier). Both sites are also included with the artecard (see "Seeing the sights" in the earlier section on Naples); alternatively, if you have time to visit both Herculaneum and Pompeii, you can get a cumulative ticket for 20€ ($32); it's valid for three days and gives you access to three other archaeological sites in the Vesuvian area — Oplontis, Stabiae, and Boscoreale.

Where to stay and dine

We like **Hotel Forum**, Via Roma 99 (☎ **081-850-1170;** Fax: 081-850-6132; www.hotelforum.it; rack rates: 120€–170/$192–$272 double, including buffet breakfast), with an excellent location not far from the excavations and modern, spacious guest rooms.

At **Il Principe,** Piazza Bartolo Longo, in the center of modern Pompei (☎ **081-850-5566;** open Tues–Sun 12:30–3 p.m. and Tues–Sat 8–11 p.m.), you'll have your chance to try — and, we hope, enjoy — some ancient Roman concoctions in an "authentic" Pompeian dining room or in the pleasant outdoors; it also serves well-prepared modern favorites.

Fast Facts: Rome

American Express

The office is at Piazza di Spagna 38 (☎ 06-67641; Metro: Line A to Spagna) and is open Monday through Friday 9 a.m. to 5:30 p.m. and Saturday 9 a.m. to 12:30 p.m. It's closed major local holidays.

Area Code

The local area code is **06** (see "Telephone," later in this section, for more on calling to and from Italy).

Currency

The euro replaced the lira back in 2002. The euro is divided into 100 cents, and there are coins of 0.01, 0.02, 0.05, 0.10, 0.20, 0.50, 1€, and 2€. Paper-note denominations are 5, 10, 20, 50, 100, 200, and 500 euros. The exchange rate used to calculate the dollar value given in this chapter is 1€ equals $1.60. Amounts over $10 are rounded to the nearest dollar.

Doctors and Dentists

Contact your embassy or consulate to get a list of English-speaking doctors or dentists.

Embassies and Consulates

All embassies maintain a 24-hour referral service for emergencies: United States (Via Vittorio Veneto 121; ☎ 06-46741), Canada (Via Salaria 243; ☎ 06-854441), Australia (Via Antonio Bosio 5; ☎ 06-852721), New Zealand (Via Zara 28; ☎ 06-441-7171), United Kingdom (Via XX Settembre 80; ☎ 06-4220-0001), and Ireland (Piazza Campitelli 3; ☎ 06-697-9121).

Emergencies

For an ambulance, call ☎ **118;** for the fire department, call ☎ **115;** for the police, call ☎ **113** or **112;** for any road emergencies, call ☎ **116.**

Hospitals

The major hospitals in the historic center are the Santo Spirito (Lungotevere in Sassia 1; ☎ 06-68351 or 06-6835-2241 for first aid), and the Fatebenefratelli on the Isola Tiberina (Piazza Fatebenefratelli 2; ☎ 06-68371 or 06-683-7299 for first aid).

Information

The tourist information hot line at ☎ 06-0608 will provide you with information in four languages, including English, from 9 a.m. to 7 p.m.

The main tourist office (Via Parigi 5; ☎ 06-488991; www.romaturismo.com; open Mon–Sat 9 a.m.–7 p.m.) maintains tourist info points at Termini rail station (☎ 06-4890-6300); Largo Goldoni/Via del Corso, at Via Condotti (☎ 06-6813-6061); Via Minghetti, off Via del Corso near Fontana di Trevi (☎ 06-678-2988); Via Nazionale, in front of the Palazzo delle Esposizioni (☎ 06-4782-4525); Via dei Fori Imperiali, near the Roman Forum (☎ 06-6992-4307); Piazza di Cinque Lune, off Piazza Navona (☎ 06-6880-9240); Lungotevere Castel Sant'Angelo (☎ 06-6880-9707); Piazza San Giovanni in Laterano (☎ 06-7720-3535); and Piazza Sonnino, in Trastevere (☎ 06-5833-3457).

The Holy See maintains its own tourist office. It is located in Piazza San Pietro (☎ 06-6988-4466; open Mon–Sat 8:30 a.m.–6 p.m.), under the colonnade to the left as you face the entrance to St. Peter's Basilica.

For cultural events, the best is the monthly *The Happening City,* distributed for free at the tourist information kiosks. For information on restaurants and nightlife, you can buy the magazines *Time Out Rome; Wanted in Rome,* an all-English publication; or *Roma C'è,* in Italian but with a section in English (it comes out on Thurs).

Internet Access

Most hotels in Rome offer free Internet access to their guests. In addition, Internet cafes are everywhere. One good chain is Internet Train (www.internettrain.it) with locations at Via delle Fornaci 22, near San Pietro (open Mon–Sat 6:30 a.m.–8:30 p.m. and Sun 6:30 a.m.–1 p.m.); Piazza

Sant'Andrea della Valle 3, near Piazza Navona (open Mon–Fri 10:30 a.m.–11 p.m. and Sat–Sun 10:30 a.m.–8 p.m.), and Via delle Fratte di Trastevere 44/b (open daily 10 a.m.–10 p.m.). Another is Yex, with a perfect location off Corso Vittorio Emanuele II, only steps from Piazza Navona (Piazza Sant'Andrea della Valle 1; open daily 10 a.m.–10 p.m.). Charges usually run around 5€ ($8) for one hour.

Maps

The free tourist-office map is quite good, but it doesn't have a *stradario* (street directory); you can buy one at any newsstand and many bookstores.

Pharmacies

Centrally located 24-hour pharmacies are at Termini station (☎ 06-488-0019), Piazza Risorgimento 44 (☎ 06-3973-8166), Via Arenula 73 (☎ 06-6880-3278), Corso Rinascimento 50 (☎ 06-6880-3985), and Piazza Barberini 49 (☎ 06-487-1195).

Police

Dial ☎ 113.

Post Office

The central post office is in Piazza San Silvestro 19, off Via del Tritone and Via del Corso. It's open Monday through Friday from 8:30 a.m. to 6:30 p.m. and Saturday from 8:30 a.m. to 1 p.m.

The Vatican also has a post office (under the colonnades to the right). You'll have to use Vatican stamps and post your mail in the Vatican mailboxes.

Restrooms

Public toilets are few and far apart: outside the Colosseum on the southeast side; halfway up the steps from Piazza del Popolo to the Pincio, on the left side. Facing St. Peter's, you can find toilets under the colonnade on the right. Make sure you have some change to tip the attendant. Your best bet may be to go to a nice-looking cafe (though you have to buy something, like a cup of coffee, to use the restroom).

Safety

Rome is a very safe city; however, petty theft is common. Pickpockets abound in tourist areas, on public transportation, and around crowded open-air markets like the Porta Portese. Observe common big-city caution: Keep your valuables in your hotel safe, don't be distracted, watch your belongings, don't count your money in public, and avoid displaying valuable jewelry and electronic equipment. Rome has some areas of poverty where a wealthy-looking tourist with an expensive camera may be mugged after dark, but those are way out on the outskirts of the city.

If you're a woman traveling alone, chances are that you'll attract young men's attention. Rome has become a cosmopolitan city, and the way you dress may offend some cultural segments. In general, the dress code is stricter in Rome than in North America, and although you'll see a lot of female skin displayed, you'll also notice that these women always move in company; if you're alone, you may want to cover up a bit. Also, it isn't a good idea to wander too far from the beaten path at night if you're alone; the area behind Termini station can be unsafe for women on their own, as can some deserted, dark, and narrow streets in the historical center. Just take it easy and, if you feel harassed, immediately speak up and don't hesitate to ask for help from a passerby or enter a cafe or shop and ask for the attendant's assistance.

Smoking

In 2005, Italy passed a law outlawing smoking in most public places. Smoking is allowed only where there is a separate, ventilated area for nonsmokers. If smoking at your table is important to you, call beforehand to make sure the restaurant or cafe you'll be visiting offers a smoking area.

Taxes

The value-added tax in Italy (called IVA) is a steep 19 percent and is already included in the sticker price of any item. Non-EU citizens who spend more than 155€ ($248) in a single store are entitled to a refund. (The store gives you an invoice that you can cash in for euros at the airport's Customs office as you leave Italy, or you can have the invoice stamped at the airport by Customs, and mail it back to the store, for a check or credit to your charge account.) Hotel taxes are 10 percent and are also usually included in quoted prices (except, oddly, in the most expensive luxury hotels).

Taxis

If you need a taxi, call ☎ 06-88177, 06-6645, 06-4994, 06-5551, or 06-6545 for radio-taxi service or walk to one of the many stations scattered around town at major squares and stations. You'll find taxi stands near major landmarks, including Piazza Barberini (at the foot of Via Veneto), Piazza San Silvestro, and Piazza SS. Apostoli (both not far from the Trevi Fountain).

Telephone

To call Italy from the U.S., dial the international access code, 011; then Italy's country code, 39; and then the local area code followed by the telephone number. Area codes have different numbers of digits — 06 for Rome, 055 for Florence, and so on — but always begin with 0; cellular lines instead always have three-digit area codes beginning with 3 (340, 338, and so on, depending on the company network). Toll-free numbers have an **800** or **888** area code, and some paying services use three-digit codes beginning with 9. Also, some companies have their own special numbers that don't conform to any of the preceding standards and that are local calls from anywhere in Italy, such as the railroad info line of Trenitalia, ☎ 892021.

To make a call within Italy, always dial the area code — including 0 if any — for both local and long distance. Public pay phones in Italy take a *carta telefonica* (telephone card), which you can buy at a *tabacchi* (tobacconist, marked by a sign with a white T on a black background), bar, or newsstand. The cards can be purchased in different denominations, from 2€ to 7.50€ ($3.20–$12). Tear off the perforated corner, stick the card in the phone, and you're ready to go. A local call in Italy costs 0.10€ (15¢).

To call abroad from Italy, dial the international access code, 00; then the country code of the country that you're calling (1 for the United States and Canada, 44 for the United Kingdom, 353 for Ireland, 61 for Australia, 64 for New Zealand); and then the phone number. Make sure that you have a

high-value *carta telefonica* before you start; your 5€ ($8) won't last long when you call San Diego at noon. Lower rates apply after 11 p.m., before 8 a.m., and on Sundays. Using your U.S. calling card may be cheaper: Some of them offer a toll-free access number in Italy, so check with your calling-card provider before leaving on your trip. You can also make collect calls. For AT&T, dial ☎ 800-172-4444; for MCI, dial ☎ 800-905825; and for Sprint, dial ☎ 800-172405 or 800-172406. To make a collect call to a country other than the United States, dial ☎ 170. For directory assistance, dial ☎ 12 for local (free within Italy) and ☎ 176 for international. Remember that calling from a hotel is convenient but usually expensive, because various surcharges apply.

Transit Info

The local public transportation authority (bus, tram, and Metro) is ATAC (☎ 800-431784 or 06-4695-2027; www.atac.roma.it). For railroad information, call Trenitalia (☎ 892021; www.trenitalia.it).

Chapter 20

Florence and Tuscany

• •

In This Chapter

⊙ Getting to and around Florence
⊙ Learning the lay of the land
⊙ Discovering the best hotels, restaurants, and attractions
⊙ Side-tripping to Pisa, Siena, and San Gimignano

• •

*I*f you're an art or history buff or enjoy your food and wine, Tuscany is a must-see destination on your trip to Europe. Your exploration of **Florence** may include Brunelleschi's ingenious cathedral dome and the Uffizi Galleries — the world's most esteemed collection of Renaissance artwork, from da Vinci's *Annunciation* to Botticelli's *Birth of Venus.* In **Siena,** you'll delight at the Duomo and at the magnificent frescoes inside the Libreria Piccolomini or in Santa Maria della Scala. The splendid Tuscan Gothic style dominates in **Pisa,** with its world-famous Leaning Tower, while **San Gimignano** remains a stronghold of medieval times, dominating the quaint hills of the Tuscany countryside with its towers. But Tuscany has much more to offer than just centuries-old art. You can enjoy a sumptuous Tuscan meal, with plenty of Chianti wine from the countryside, in each of these destinations.

Try to spend at least two days in Florence, three if you can swing it; the other destinations covered in this chapter are close enough for easy day trips from Florence, but they could also easily justify longer stays.

Getting There

Located in the heart of Italy, Tuscany and Florence are easy to get to.

Arriving by air

Both Florence's airport **Amerigo Vespucci** (☎ 055-306-1300; www. aeroporto.firenze.it) and Pisa's **Galileo Galilei** airport (☎ 050-849111; www.pisa-airport.com) receive flights from a number of European and Italian cities. Pisa's is the largest of the two airports, but both are easy to get around. You can find ATMs, currency exchange booths, and tourist information points at either airport in the arrivals concourse. Only flights from countries outside the European Union are subject to passport control. In most cases, you'll go directly to luggage delivery and then Customs. Here you'll find two gates: one for those who have something to declare (beyond allowance), and one for those who don't: this is where there may be random checks.

Locally called Peretola, from the name of the village nearby, the Amerigo Vespucci airport is only 4km (2½ miles) outside of Florence, a few minutes away by public transportation, which you'll find just outside the arrivals concourse. A taxi takes about ten minutes and costs about 20€ ($32). Otherwise, you can take the Volainbus shuttle bus for 4.50€ ($7.20); buses leave for the 20-minute trip every 20 minutes between 5:30 a.m. and 8:30 p.m., and hourly after that, and arrive at the Florence's SITA bus terminal (Via Santa Caterina 15r), just behind the central rail station of Santa Maria Novella. You can buy tickets onboard. You can also get into Florence by regular city bus (no. 62; 1.20€/$1.90), which takes about half an hour and also arrives at Santa Maria Novella.

The Galileo Galilei airport is only 3km (2 miles) south of Pisa — a ten-minute taxi ride — but 80km (50 miles) west of Florence. The easiest way to get from Pisa to Florence is to board the dedicated shuttle train (www.trenitalia.it) from the Pisa airport's terminal, which arrives into Florence inside Santa Maria Novella rail station; it makes ten runs a day, costs 5.20€ ($8.30), and takes about an hour.

Arriving by rail

Trains to Florence pull into **Stazione Santa Maria Novella** (☎ 055-288765), which is often abbreviated as **S.M.N.** You'll find a luggage check at the head of Track 16. A last-minute hotel reservations desk and a tourist information point can arrange for and distribute some information, such as the free city map; this is also where you can pick up your reserved tickets for the Uffizi or the Accademia (see "Exploring Florence," later in this chapter). Public transportation is just outside the station, where you'll find a taxi stand and a bus terminal with lines to basically anywhere in town. Located at the northwestern edge of the historic district, the station is also within walking distance of most attractions.

Street numbering Florence-style

Florence's tradition of independence is probably behind the towns' peculiar way of marking street addresses: Restaurant, office, and shop doors are numbered independently from residential and hotel doors. The first set of numbers is usually painted in red and always marked with the letter *r* appended to the number (for *rosso,* "red"); the second is painted in black or blue. Therefore it can easily happen that no. 1r (office or business) and no. 1 (private residence — or hotel, which is where it gets confusing) are in different buildings, and maybe a few door numbers apart.

Finding information after you arrive

The tourist office (APT, Via A. Manzoni 16, 50121 Firenze; ☎ 055-23320; Fax: 055-234-6286; www.firenzeturismo.it) maintains three tourist info points in town: at Via Cavour 1r (☎ 055-290832; open Mon–Sat 8:30 a.m.–6:30 p.m., Sun 8:30 a.m.–1:30 p.m.); at S.M.N. rail station, Piazza Stazione 4/a (☎ 055-212245; open Mon–Sat 9 a.m.–7 p.m., Sun 8:30 a.m.–2 p.m.); and at Borgo Santa Croce 29r (☎ 055-234-0444; open Mon–Sat 9 a.m.–7 p.m. [until 5 p.m. in winter], Sun 9 a.m.–2 p.m.).

Getting Around Florence

Florence is very safe; the major crime is pickpocketing, an activity that traditionally occurs in the crowded areas of the historic district.

The free **tourist office map** is completely adequate for most visitors, especially if you combine it with the free bus map you can get from ATAF (see the "By bus" section, later), but if you're an ambitious explorer and don't feel satisfied, you can buy a *cartina con stradario* (map with street directory) at any newsstand for about 6€ ($9.60).

On foot

Because the historic district is closed to all traffic except for public buses — no cars, no taxis, and no mopeds — and attractions lie relatively close to each other, walking is the best way to enjoy the town. The walk between the two farthest attractions in the historic center — Galleria dell'Accademia and Palazzo Pitti — takes only about one hour at an average pace, and you'd also pass most of the major sights in town.

By bus

Florence's bus system is well organized and easy to use. You'll probably most use the electric minibuses — identified by letters *A, B, C,* and *D* — which are allowed within the **centro storico.** They do come in handy when your feet ache after a long day at the Uffizi or shopping on Via Tornabuoni. Regular buses are great to move rapidly back and forth between **Oltrarno** and the center of town (lines 36 and 37), and to reach some out-of-the-way attractions such as **Fiesole** (Line 7).

You can buy bus tickets at the **ATAF** booth (☎ 800-424-500) across SMN train station, and at most bars, tobacconist shops (signed *tabacchi* or by a white *T* on a black background), and newsstands; a single ticket (a *biglietto*) costs 1.20€ ($1.90) in advance or 2€ ($3.20) onboard (exact fare only, bus drivers don't make change). It's valid for 70 minutes on as many buses as you want. You can save a bit if you get a **Carta Agile** — an electronic card worth ten single tickets for the price of eight (10€/$16), or 20 tickets for the price of 16 (20€/$32), which can be used by more than one person if you're traveling together: Just pass it in front of the magnetic eye of the machine onboard the bus as many times as you have passengers in your group; if you want to know how much money you have left on the card, press the button on the machine marked INFO and swipe your card. You can also get unlimited-ride passes: a **24-hour pass** costs 5€ ($8) and a **three-day pass** goes for 12€ ($19).

At press time, the municipality was about to launch a new 24-hour ticket: **Passpartour,** including all public transportation and City Sightseeing tours (see "Guided tours," later in this chapter) for 22€ ($35) adults, 11€ ($18) children 14 and under. They'll be sold onboard City Sightseeing buses, at hotels, and at all ATAF ticket vendors. Another option is the **Iris pass,** which gives access to all public transportation — including trains — within the province of Florence and Prato, plus a 20 percent discount on attractions. It's available for one day (8€/$13 adults, 5€/$8 children 14 and under) and three days (23€/$37 adults, 12€/$19 children 14 and under).

Remember that tickets need to be stamped upon boarding; unlimited-ride passes need to be stamped only once on your first trip.

Staying in Florence

Florence is a major tourist destination and the choice of accommodations is large and varied. Still, it may be hard to secure a nice room at a decent price during high season (May–June and Sept–Oct); depending on your budget, you may have to settle for a less central location, or else make sure you reserve well in advance (see Chapter 7 for more about hotel booking).

If you arrive in Florence without a hotel reservation, your best bet is the room-finding service run by the tourist info desk at the **Santa Maria Novella rail station.** If you're driving, there are similar services at the tourist info desks in the **Area di Servizio AGIP Peretola** (rest area) on Highway A11 (☎ 055-421-1800) and in the **Area di Servizio Chianti Est** on Highway A1 (☎ 055-621349).

The top hotels

Grand Hotel Villa Medici
$$$$ Teatro Comunale

This is the best of the luxury hotels if you're visiting Florence in summer: Although the beautiful 18th-century *palazzo* with its splendid salons is welcoming in any season, the large garden and swimming pool will feel absolutely heavenly in the town's heat — a unique plus for a centrally located hotel. The large, individually decorated guest rooms are tasteful, if a bit old-fashioned. All have beautiful bathrooms done in Carrara marble. Rooms on the higher floors have small private terraces and panoramic views of the city.

See map p. 426. Via il Prato 42, at Via Rucellai and Via Palestro. ☎ 800-273226 or 055-238-1331. Fax: 055-238-1336. Bus: D or 1. Rack rates: 539€–730€ ($862–$1,168) double. AE, DC, MC, V.

Accommodations, Dining, and Attractions in Florence

HOTELS ■

Grand Hotel Villa
Medici **24**
Hermitage Hotel **40**
Hotel Bellettini **25**
Hotel Calzaiuoli **6**
Hotel Casci **32**
Hotel Mario's **28**
Hotel Savoy **5**
Il Guelfo Bianco **29**
J. K. Place **22**
Monna Lisa **33**
Plaza Hotel
Lucchesi **41**
Relais Santa Croce **35**
Torre Guelfa **19**

RESTAURANTS ●

Buca Mario
dal 1886 **21**
Cantinetta Antinori
Tornabuoni **23**
Cantinetta del
Verrazzano **8**
Cavolo Nero **17**
Cibreo **34**
Consorzio Agrario
Pane and Co. **12**
Coronas Café **7**
Gelateria Carabè **30**
Gelateria Vivoli **37**

Mercato Centrale **27**
Narbone **28**
Osteria del Caffè
Italiano **38**
Osteria Ganino **10**
Pane e Vino **18**
Perchè No **9**
Trattoria Boboli **16**
Trattoria Garga **20**
Trattoria Le
Mossacce **11**

ATTRACTIONS ◆

Baptistery **4**
Bargello Museum **13**
Cappella de' Pazzi **36**
Duomo **2**
Galleria degli Uffizi **39**
Galleria dell'
Accademia **31**
Giardino di Boboli **14**
Giotto's Bell Tower **3**
Medici Chapels **26**
Museo dell'Opera
del Duomo **1**
Museo dell'Opera
di Santa Croce **36**
Palazzo Pitti **15**
Santa Croce **36**

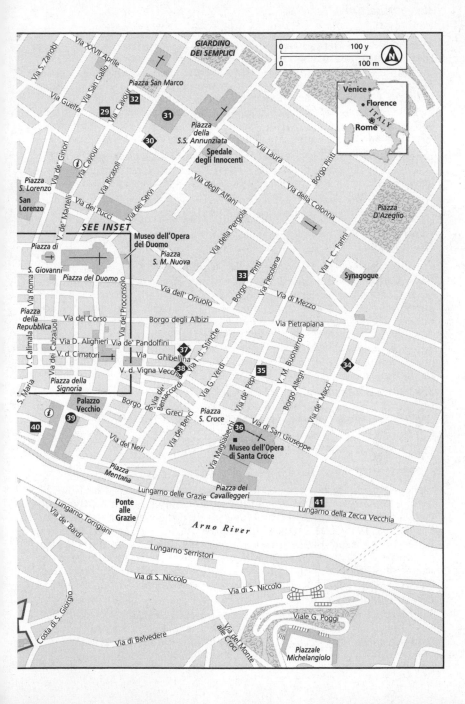

Hotel Bellettini
$ Duomo

This reliable, moderately priced hotel is run by two sisters who are very friendly and helpful. Housed in a 14th-century *palazzo* just steps from the Duomo, it is pleasantly old-fashioned and offers simple, clean guest rooms — some with fantastic views — and one of the best breakfasts in town for the price, with a buffet that includes ham and fresh fruit. You can get cheaper rates if you choose a shared bathroom, or you can splurge on one of the superior rooms in the annex. The latter are more spacious and come with Carrara marble bathrooms.

See map p. 426. Via de' Conti 7, steps from the Duomo. ☎ *055-213561. Fax: 055-283551.* www.hotelbellettini.com. *Bus: 1, 6, or 11 to Martelli; take Via de' Cerretani and turn right on Via de' Conti. Rack rates: 140€ ($224) double. Rates include buffet breakfast. AE, DC, MC, V.*

Hotel Calzaiuoli
$$$ Duomo

This centrally located hotel is a good moderate choice in an expensive town, with a pleasant hall, a nice restaurant, and excellent accommodations. Guest rooms are spacious and stylish, decorated with care and taste: pastel-colored walls, stucco moldings, carpeted or nicely tiled floors, and quality wooden furnishings. Some of the bathrooms are small, but nicely done in Carrara marble. If you like sleeping with an open window, make sure you reserve a room at the back; rooms overlooking Via dei Calzaiuoli get quite noisy with pedestrian traffic, and the double-pane windows won't help if you don't close them.

See map p. 426. Via dei Calzaiuoli 6. ☎ *055-212456. Fax: 055-268310.* www.calzaiuoli. it. *Bus: 22, 36, or 37. Parking: 23€–26€ ($37–$42) valet in garage. Rack rates: 300€–400€ ($480–$640) double. Rates include breakfast. AE, DC, MC, V.*

Hotel Casci
$ Accademia

We love this moderately priced hotel at a great location not far from the Accademia. Housed in a 15th-century *palazzo* once owned by the musician Gioacchino Rossini, and still family-run, it has charm and character. Public spaces include a pleasant room decorated with original frescoes, where the excellent buffet breakfast is served. Guest rooms differ in size, but all are done in similar style, with warm colors, pleasant colored-wood wainscoting, modern furnishings, tiled floors, and comfortable beds. Most bathrooms are small but functional and very well kept. The largest rooms are a good option for families.

See map p. 426. Via Cavour 13, off Piazza San Marco. ☎ *055-211686. Fax: 055-239-6461.* www.hotelcasci.com. *Bus: 1, 6, 7, 10, 11. Parking: 20€ ($32) in nearby garage. Rack rates: 150€ ($240) double. Rate includes buffet breakfast. AE, DC, MC, V.*

Hotel Savoy
$$$$ Piazza della Signoria

This is our favorite luxury hotel in Florence. In-depth renovations have brought modernity to this landmark hotel — which opened in 1896 — while respecting the original architecture. The splendid public spaces are completed by a small but state-of-the-art fitness room and a good restaurant-cum-bar. The spacious guest rooms are luxuriously appointed and done in a refined Italian style: clean and elegant, but also warm and welcoming. One of the Savoy's big draws is its special attention to children, with games, gifts, and child-sized everything, including slippers and bathrobes in the rooms.

See map p. 426. Piazza della Repubblica 7. ☎ ***055-27351.*** *Fax: 055-273-5888.* www.hotelsavoy.it. *Bus: 36 or 37. Rack rates: 510€–850€ ($816–$1,360) double. AE, DC, MC, V.*

J. K. Place
$$$$ Santa Maria Novella

A nice addition to the Florence hotel scene, this small lodging is a mix of charm and modernity. The public spaces are welcoming, with glowing fireplaces in winter and a pleasant rooftop terrace in good weather. Guest rooms are spacious and uniquely decorated: The four-poster beds, fireplaces, antiques, and stylish modern furniture make you feel like an aristocrat from this century — a rare opportunity. Bathrooms are modern and comfortable.

See map p. 426. Piazza Santa Maria Novella 7. ☎ ***055-264-5181.*** *Fax: 055-265-8387.* www.jkplace.com. *Bus: 14 or 23. Rack rates: 350€–500€ ($560–$800) double. Rates include buffet breakfast. AE, DC, MC, V.*

Plaza Hotel Lucchesi
$$$$ Santa Croce

This historic hotel — it opened in 1860 — was completely restored in 2001, with good taste and attention to detail that have brought it back to its splendor. We like the location at the eastern edge of the historic district. Guest rooms are spacious and bright, with parquet floors, elegant and comfortable wooden furnishings, and luxury fabrics that ensure a warm and welcoming feeling. Some rooms enjoy private balconies and all afford romantic views over the river or over Santa Croce. Bathrooms are modern and good-sized.

See map p. 426. Lungarno della Zecca Vecchia 38, east of Santa Croce. ☎ ***055-26236.*** *Fax: 055-2480921.* www.plazalucchesi.it. *Bus: B. Parking 20€ ($32). Rack rates: 360€–415€ ($576–$664) double. Rates include breakfast. AE, DC, MC, V.*

Runner-up hotels

Hermitage Hotel
$$$ Piazza della Signoria   This hotel is right off the Ponte Vecchio, nearer to the Uffizi, and has been recently renovated. Many guest rooms have beautiful views over the river and all have antique furniture and

premium bathrooms. The very pleasant rooftop garden/terrace is a real plus. *See map p. 426. Vicolo Marzio 1.* ☎ *055-287216.* www.hermitagehotel.com.

Hotel Mario's

$$ Fortezza da Basso   Recently renovated, this hotel offers bright, pleasant guest rooms with pastel walls and beamed ceilings. *See map p. 426. Via Faenza 89.* ☎ *055-218801.* www.hotelmarios.com.

Il Guelfo Bianco

$$ **Accademia** This hotel occupies 15th- and 17th-century adjacent *palazzi.* The guest rooms in the former are pleasantly furnished and come with beautiful bathrooms; many overlook the inner garden and courtyard. The rooms in the other building boast ceiling frescoes, and some have painted and carved wood ceilings. *See map p. 426. Via Cavour 57r, at Via Guelfa.* ☎ *055-288330.* www.ilguelfobianco.it.

Monna Lisa

$$$$ **Santa Croce** Yearning to be a private collector's home, this hotel is housed in a beautiful 14th-century *palazzo,* once home to the Neri family. Guest rooms vary in style and size. The antique furnishings, original coffered ceilings, inner garden and patio, modern bathrooms (some with Jacuzzis), and important artworks make this hotel very desirable. The hotel is accessible for people with disabilities. *See map p. 426. Borgo Pinti 27, off Via dell'Oriuolo.* ☎ *055-247-9751.* www.monnalisa.it.

Relais Santa Croce

$$$$ **Santa Croce** This small luxury hotel, housed in the 18th-century *palazzo* Ciofi-Jacometti, offers the comfort level of the top hotels in Florence, with a warm atmosphere and unique style. It combines antique furnishings and period architectural details — the original frescos are magnificent — with Italian contemporary design. Precious fabrics, elegant wood panels, and marble bathrooms — all with separate shower and tub — perfectly complete the picture. *See map p. 426. Via Ghibellina 87, at Via de' Pepi.* ☎ *055-234-2230.* www.relaissantacroce.it.

Torre Guelfa

$$$ **Piazza della Signoria** Near the Ponte Vecchio and the Uffizi, the Torre Guelfa offers pleasant and richly decorated guest rooms, good service, and a breathtaking view from its 13th-century tower. *See map p. 426. Borgo Santi Apostoli 8.* ☎ *055-239-6338.* www.hoteltorreguelfa.com.

Dining in Florence

If enjoyed in traditional fashion, a typical Tuscan meal can take a few hours to finish. The multiple courses begin with an appetizer, traditionally *affettati misti* (assorted cured meats) and *crostini misti* (round toast with assorted toppings such as liver pâté, mushrooms, tomatoes, and cheese). Your first course (called the *primo*) could be a soup — try the stewlike *ribollita* (vegetables, beans, and bread) — or pasta, such as

---

Fast food Florence-style

For a cheap but delicious meal that'll give your wallet a rest, drop by an *alimentari* (grocery shop) for the fixings for a picnic. You can buy some delicious Tuscan bread, local ham and cheese, fruit, mineral water, or wine. At **Consorzio Agrario Pane and Co.**, Piazza San Firenze 5r, at the corner of Via Condotta (☎ 055-213063; Bus: A to Condotta), you'll find a choice of local cheeses and cured meats, including the excellent *cinghiale* (wild boar), plus water, wine, and all the rest. You can also get a nice fruit tart or some *paste* (cream puffs and other small sweet pastries). Or head for the colorful and noisy **Mercato Centrale,** near Piazza San Lorenzo (entrance on Via dell'Ariento), where you'll find stalls selling all kinds of edibles, from fruit and vegetables to socks, passing by fragrant Tuscan bread and tasty local cheeses, and cured meats. For a quick bite Florentine-style, you can also try the centuries-old fare served at **Narbone** (stand no. 292 on the ground floor), a counter with a few tables. Among the offerings: the *panino col bollito* (boiled beef sandwich in its juice) and, if you're up to it, the *trippa alla Fiorentina* (tripe with tomato sauce and Parmesan). If tripe is your thing, try *lampredotto* (traditional boiled tripe sandwich) at the street stand in front of the American Express office on Piazza de' Cimatori. To the other end of the spectrum, the elegant **Cantinetta del Verrazzano,** Via dei Tavolini 18r (☎ 055-268590), sells focaccia hot from the oven and wine by the glass, and also has a small self-service lunch counter.

---

pappardelle al cinghiale (wide noodles in a wild boar sauce), or *crespelle Fiorentine* (crepes layered with cheese and béchamel sauce). The main course *(secondo)* could be stewed or grilled meat, such as the superb *bistecca Fiorentina* (steak of local Chianina cow, grilled and brushed with olive oil and herbs). Veggies *(contorno)* are ordered separately and could be anything from sautéed greens to *patate fritte* (french fries) to *fagioli all'uccelletto* (stewed white Tuscan cannellini beans) — a local specialty.

Tuscany is famous across the globe for its red wines, from its Chianti Classico — generally served as house wine at local restaurants — to Vino Nobile di Montepulciano and Brunello di Montalcino. Its whites include the Vernaccia di San Gimignano and the sweet dessert wine Vin Santo.

Buca Mario dal 1886
$$$ Santa Maria Novella   FLORENTINE

This historic restaurant serves traditional Tuscan cuisine in a friendly atmosphere. It's housed in a cellar (*buca* in Florentine), with vaulted and whitewashed dining rooms decorated with dark-wood paneling (the décor is original). Everything is well prepared, though it doesn't come cheap. We liked the classic *ribollita* and the *osso buco*, as well as the *coniglio fritto* (fried rabbit), a Tuscan delicacy.

See map p. 426. Piazza degli Ottaviani 16r, just south of Santa Maria Novella. ☎ *055-214179.* www.bucamario.it. *Reservations recommended. Bus: A, 36, or 37 to Piazza Santa Maria Novella. Main courses: 18€–28€ ($29–$45). AE, MC, V. Open: Thurs 7:30–10 p.m.; Fri–Tues 12:30–3 p.m. and 7:30–10 p.m. Closed Aug.*

432 Part V: Mediterranean Europe

Cantinetta Antinori Tornabuoni
$$$ Santa Maria Novella FLORENTINE/ITALIAN

Antinori is the family name of the oldest and one of the best producers of wine in Italy. In this restaurant, typical Tuscan dishes and many specialties from the Antinori farms are served to accompany the wine. The *cantinetta* (small wine cellar) occupies the 15th-century *palazzo* of this noble family and serves as their winery in town. You can sample the vintages at the counter or sit at a table and have a full meal. The *pappa al pomodoro* is delicious, as is the risotto with prawns.

See map p. 426. Piazza Antinori 3r, off the north end of Via de' Tornabuoni. ☎ *055-292234. Reservations recommended. Bus: A, 6, 11, 36, or 37 to Piazza Antinori. Main courses: 14€–25€ ($22–$40). AE, DC, MC, V. Open: Mon–Fri 12:30–3 p.m. and 7:30–10 p.m. Closed 1 week at Christmas and 1 week in Aug.*

Cavolo Nero
$$ Piazza del Carmine FLORENTINE

Cavolo Nero serves great food, prepared with enthusiasm and creativity. The name of the restaurant refers to the black cabbage (similar to kale) that is typical of Tuscan cooking. The menu isn't very extensive, but its offerings are delicious. We enjoyed the homemade gnocchi with broccoli and wild fennel, as well as the bass filet rolled in eggplant and served over a yellow-pepper purée.

See map p. 426. Via d'Ardiglione 22, off Via de' Serragli. ☎ *055-294744.* www.cavolonero.it. *Reservations recommended. Bus: D, 11, 36, or 37 to Via de' Serragli. Main courses: 10€–16€ ($16–$26). AE, DC, MC, V. Open: Mon–Sat 7:30–10 p.m. Closed 3 weeks in Aug.*

Cibreo
$$$ Santa Croce FLORENTINE

Renowned chef-owner Fabio Picchi changes his menu daily, depending on the market and his imagination. The backbone of the menu is historic Tuscan, with some recipes that go back to the Renaissance — but they're presented here in a modern way. One hallmark of the place is that you won't find pasta of any kind; the other is that dinner is at 7:30 or 9 p.m. If you choose the first service, you'll have to be out by 9 p.m. On the menu, you'll find soufflés; polenta; roasted and stuffed birds — such as the superb pigeon stuffed with a traditional fruit preparation — and the much imitated *pomodoro in gelatina* (tomato aspic). For a more informal atmosphere and lower prices, you can try the **trattoria** next door (Via de'Macci 122r) or the **Caffè Cibreo** across the street.

See map p. 426. Via Andrea del Verrocchio 8r. ☎ *055-234-1100. Reservations required for the restaurant; not accepted for the trattoria. Bus: A to Piazza Sant'Ambrogio (outdoor vegetable market). Main courses: 35€ ($56). AE, DC, MC, V. Open: Tues–Sat 7:30–9 p.m. Trattoria also open for lunch. Closed first week in Jan and Aug.*

Osteria del Caffè Italiano
$$ Santa Croce FLORENTINE

This is our favorite place in Florence: serving genuine Tuscan food all day long until late at night, with some of the best Tuscan wines by the glass. And it's no wonder: This *osteria* is the urban outpost of Tuscany's ten best vineyards, which send a selection of their finest products here regularly. Featuring a more formal dining room and a casual tavern, this place allows you to choose between a complete meal or light fare; lunch is also available in either room. *Ribollita, farinata al cavolo nero* (thick black cabbage soup), *cinghiale in salmì* (wild-boar stew), and a great choice of Tuscan cold cuts will more than satisfy.

See map p. 426. Via Isola delle Stinche 11r. ☎ *055-289020.* www.caffeitaliano. it. *Reservations recommended on Sat. Bus: A or 14 to Piazza Santa Croce. Main courses: 9€–19€ ($14–$30). AE, DC, MC, V. Open: Tues–Sun noon to 11 p.m.*

Osteria Ganino
$$ Piazza della Signoria FLORENTINE

At this cozy, centrally located trattoria, you'll find ubiquitous Florentine specialties, such as *bistecca alla fiorentina* and *tagliatelle* with truffle sauce, served on polished stone tables covered in paper. Though prices may seem a bit high for this simple setting, the food is nicely prepared and served by an attentive staff; you'll welcome the offering of *mortadella* before you order. Sit out on the small terrace in good weather.

See map p. 426. Piazza dei Cimatori 4r. ☎ *055-214125. Reservations recommended. Bus: A to Condotta or Cimatori; Via dei Cimatori is 2 short blocks north of Piazza della Signoria. Main courses: 9€–18€ ($14–$29). AE, DC, MC, V. Open: Mon–Sat 12:30– 3 p.m. and 7:30–10 p.m.*

Pane e Vino
$ Piazza della Signoria CREATIVE FLORENTINE

In the comfortably modern dining room of this trattoria, you'll find a wide choice of dishes, ranging from simple countryside "snacks" — such as a variety of rare local cheeses served with sweet fruit preparations — to elaborate main courses. We liked the pasta with a pork and wild-fennel *ragù*, as well as the *saltimbocca di rana pescatrice con ratatouille di zucchine* (sautéed fish and bacon bites with zucchini stew). The restaurant also offers a tasting menu (30€/$48) and many wines by the glass.

See map p. 426. Piazza di Cestello 3r. ☎ *055-247-6956. Reservations recommended. Bus: 14 or 23 to Proconsolo. Main courses: 7€–15€ ($11–$24). DC, MC, V. Open: Mon–Sat 7:30–10 p.m. Closed 2 weeks in Aug.*

Trattoria Boboli
$$ Piazza Santo Spirito FLORENTINE

Near the Palazzo Pitti and the entrance to Boboli Gardens, this unassuming small restaurant is a real mom-and-pop operation where you'll find a lot

Looking for a gelato break?

Ice cream is certainly one of the best treats in Italy, and Florence is famous for its gelato. Of a different school from the Venetian, the Roman, or the Sicilian gelati, Florentine ice cream was invented — as were many other Tuscan gastronomic specialties — to gratify the palates of the Medicis. Alas the Medici family had a very big sweet tooth, judging from the result: Florentine ice cream is extremely sugary. You'll find some of the best in Florence at **Gelateria Vivoli**, Via Isola delle Stinche 7r, between the Bargello and Santa Croce (☎ 055-292334; Bus: A to Piazza Santa Croce), which is truly a marvel for its zillions of flavors, but also at **Coronas Café**, Via Calzaiuoli 72r (☎ 055-239-6139; Bus: A to Orsanmichele); **Perchè No**, Via dei Tavolini 19r, just off Via Calzaiuoli (☎ 055-239-8969; Bus: A to Orsanmichele), one of the oldest Florentine *gelaterie;* and **Gelateria Carabè**, Via Ricasoli 60r, near the Accademia (☎ 055-289476; Bus: C or 6 to Santissima [SS] Annunziata), where you'll find excellent Sicilian gelato: The owner has the ingredients — lemons, almonds, pistachios — shipped from Sicily, and his ice cream has been rated among the best in Italy.

of warmth and all the specialties of Tuscan cuisine. The dining room is small, but the food is good. They make a good *ribollita* and *pappa al pomodoro*, as well as an excellent *osso buco*.

See map p. 426. Via Romana 45r. ☎ *055-233-6401.* www.paginegialle.it/bobolitratt. *Reservations recommended. Bus: D, 6, 11, 36, or 37 to Via Romana. Main courses: 8€–19€ ($13–$30). AE, MC, V. Open: Thurs–Tues 12:30–2:30 p.m. and 7:30–10:30 p.m.*

Trattoria Garga
$$$ Santa Maria Novella   TUSCAN/CREATIVE

The ebullient personality of the chef-owner, Garga, has overflowed onto the walls, which he has personally decorated with his own frescoes. Elegant yet laid-back, this restaurant isn't cheap. The extravagant atmosphere pairs perfectly with his interpretations of Tuscan fundamentals. Try the famous *taglierini alla Magnifico* (angel-hair pasta with a mint-cream sauce flavored with lemon and orange rind and Parmesan cheese). Or sign up for the great cooking classes.

See map p. 426. Via del Moro 50r. ☎ *055-239-8898.* www.garga.it. *Reservations required. Bus: A to Via del Moro. Main courses: 21€–23€ ($34–$37). AE, DC, MC, V. Open: Tues–Sun 7:30–10 p.m.*

Trattoria Le Mossacce
$ Duomo   FLORENTINE

This small, cheap, historic trattoria offers home-style Florentine food. Listen up to the daily offerings from the waiter and make your pick among the choice of Tuscan specialties such as *crespelle* (eggy crepes, served lasagna-style or rolled and filled) and *ribollita* as well as spaghetti with clams. Among the *secondi* (main courses), try the *involtini* (rolled and filled veal *scaloppini*, cooked in tomato sauce).

See map p. 426. Via del Proconsolo 55r, near the Duomo. ☎ *055-294361. Reservations recommended. Bus: 14 or 23 to Proconsolo. Main courses: 8€–12€ ($13–$19). AE, MC, V. Open: Mon–Fri 12:30–3 p.m. and 7:30–10 p.m.*

Exploring Florence

Florence offers precious little in the way of bargains. You might consider the **Iris pass** (see "Getting Around Florence," earlier in this chapter), which gives you a 20 percent discount on most attractions.

Reservations are not required but we highly recommend them to avoid the long lines at Florence's most sought-after attractions: **Uffizi** and **Accademia.** Call ☎ 055-294883 during office hours (Mon–Fri 8:30 a.m.–6:30 p.m., Sat 8:30 a.m.–12:30 p.m.) and pick a time slot (every 15 minutes during opening hours; see listing later in this chapter); the English-speaking operator will give you a confirmation number. Alternatively, make your reservation and buy your ticket online at www.polomuseale.firenze.it with a credit card. In either case, you can then get to the museum only a bit before your selected time to pay (cash only) for the ticket or pick it up. Make sure you don't line up in the wrong queue (you need the reserved tickets line, where at the most you'll find only the people in your time slot, which is 20; don't be shy to ask) and you'll breeze through. The 4€ ($6.40) per ticket reservation fee is well worth it. You can always make last-minute reservations, but you'll run the risk of all time slots being sold out.

Beware of the many tourist agencies that pose as an attraction's official site and charge high fees. Use only the official museum's call center or Polo Museale Web site (www.polomuseale.firenze.it).

Florence's top attractions

The compact medieval district of Florence is an attraction unto itself, developing around **Piazza del Duomo** with its stunning cathedral and, several blocks to the south, **Piazza della Signoria,** a statue-filled elegant square lined with cafes, the medieval Palazzo Vecchio, and the art-packed Galleria degli Uffizi. The long north–south stretch of **Via dei Calzaiuoli,** a wide, pedestrian-choked promenade, links the two *piazze* (squares), and leads to the River Arno, bisecting the historic district east–west. **Ponte Vecchio,** the only surviving medieval bridge in Florence, is the most picturesque way to **Oltrarno,** the neighborhood on the left bank of the river; included within the walls of Florence "only" in 1173, it has Palazzo Pitti and an artsy and active cultural life.

Bargello Museum

What the Uffizi is to Renaissance painting, the Bargello is to sculpture from the same period. You can spend 45 minutes here or, if you get really

---

A bit of Florentine history

The first town to develop in the area was not Florence but Fiesole, up the hill overlooking what was to become Florence. Fiesole began thriving in the ninth century B.C. and grew to become an important Etruscan center. During Roman rule, though, it lost importance, and Florence was born on its splendid location by the Arno River. A flourishing but small village until medieval times, Florence suddenly developed into a town when it grew to be a great banking center, dominating the European credit market. The town's wealth encouraged the development of the arts and of a lively culture: from Dante (born here in 1265) to Cimabue (Giotto's teacher), and more when the Renaissance blossomed in the 1300s, despite difficulties such as floods, the black plague, and political upheaval that deterred it elsewhere.

The 15th century brought the rule of Lorenzo the Magnificent, head of the powerful Medici clan, and the town reached its apogee. By this point, Florence had become the leading city-state in central Italy, overcoming the competition of nearby Siena and Pisa. Artists such as Leonardo, Michelangelo, and Raphael produced amazing works. After a brief restoration of the republic, in 1537, the Medici family returned to power in the person of Cosimo I, but it was the end of the Renaissance. The Inquisition began in 1542, suffocating cultural life, while Italy became the appetizing booty of the succession wars among royal families in Europe. Florence Gran Duchy resisted as such and passed to the Lorraine house, which maintained its power and independence through the 17th and 18th centuries, passing then to the Bourbon. In 1860, the population rebelled and was able to join the burgeoning Italian kingdom. Florence was then made the capital of Italy for five short years, from 1865 to 1870, when the capital finally moved to Rome.

---

engrossed, two hours. The collection includes works by Michelangelo, including his famous tipsy *Bacchus,* the *Madonna of the Stairs,* and a *Bust of Brutus* that may be a semi–self-portrait. Be sure to see the works by Donatello, the first great sculptor of the Renaissance. A huge second-floor room contains some of his masterpieces, including a mischievous bronze *Cupid* and two versions of a *David* — an early marble work and a bronze that depicts the biblical hero as a young boy.

See map p. 426. Via del Proconsolo 4, between Via Ghibellina and Via della Vigna Vecchia. ☎ *055-294833.* www.polomuseale.firenze.it. *Bus: A. Admission: 4€ ($6.40), 7€ ($11) for special exhibits. Open: Winter daily 8:15 a.m.–2 p.m.; summer daily 8:15 a.m.–6 p.m.; ticket booth closes 40 minutes earlier. Closed 2nd and 4th Mon each month; 1st, 3rd, and 5th Sun each month; and Jan 1, May 1, and Dec 25.*

Duomo (Basilica di Santa Maria del Fiore), Baptistery, Giotto's Bell Tower, and Museo dell'Opera

The **Duomo** of Florence is decorated in festive white, green, and pink marble, with an extravagant neo-Gothic facade from the 18th century, all capped by a huge brick-red dome that extends nobly into the skyline. The cathedral is joined on its bustling square by its bell tower, baptistery, and museum — a group of buildings that together take about four hours to see.

If you're pressed for time, limit your visit to the baptistery (only open in the afternoon) and the cathedral's outside. Climbing either Brunelleschi's dome (463 steps) or Giotto's bell tower (414 steps) takes about an hour.

The largest in the world at the time it was built, the Duomo's **dome** is 45m (150 ft.) wide and 104m (300 ft.) high from the drum to the distinctive lantern at the top of the cupola. Great Renaissance architect Brunelleschi had to take over the project where the previous builders left off, unsure of how to complete the building without having it collapse. His ingenious solution was constructing the dome of two layers enclosing a space inside, and having each layer become progressively thinner toward the top, thus reducing the weight. If you're up to it, climb the 463 spiraling steps hidden in the space between the layers to see this architectural marvel from the inside. In the crypt are the remains of Santa Reparata, the earlier Duomo, and archaeological excavations going back to ancient Roman times. Be sure to wander to the back-left corner of the cathedral to admire the bronze doors to the New Sacristy (by Luca della Robbia). Monday through Saturday you can enjoy free tours, given every 40 minutes from 10:30 a.m. to noon and 3 to 4:20 p.m.

To the right of the cathedral is what's known as Giotto's bell tower, even though that early Renaissance painter died after completing only the first two levels and other architects finished it. The tower became "The Lily of Florence," a 277-foot-high marble pillar with slender windows. If climbing the Duomo's dome didn't tire you out, try clambering up this monument, too — and without the crowds found at the dome. The view's not quite so sweeping, but you get a great close-up of the neighboring dome.

The baptistery, across from the Duomo, is the oldest building of the group, dating back to between the fourth and seventh centuries. Its north and east bronze doors, covered with relief panels, are the life's work of Lorenzo Ghiberti and considered one of the world's most important pieces of Renaissance sculpture; Michelangelo once called them "The Gates of Paradise," and the name stuck. These large panels show the artist's skill in using perspective and composition to tell complicated stories (these are replicas — the originals are in the Museo dell'Opera; see the following paragraph). Inside, glittering 13th-century mosaics cover the baptistery, and a cone-shaped ceiling contains a highly detailed Last Judgment scene presided over by an enormous Christ.

Definitely worth visiting is the **Museo dell'Opera del Duomo** (Museum of Cathedral Works), located right behind the cathedral at Piazza del Duomo 9. The museum holds all the works of art removed from the outside of the cathedral, baptistery, and bell tower in order to save them from the elements. You'll find Ghiberti's bronze Gates of Paradise panels from the baptistery and Donatello's highly realistic sculpture of Habbakuk and his *Mary Magdalene* in polychromed wood from Giotto's bell tower. You'll also see one of Michelangelo's *Pietà* and Luca della Robbia's *cantoria* (choir loft) facing a similar work by Donatello, offering an example of the diversity of Renaissance styles.

See map p. 426. Piazza Duomo/Piazza di San Giovanni. ☎ **055-230-2885.** www.operaduomo.firenze.it. Bus: A, 1, 6, 7, 10, 11, 36, or 37. Admissions: Duomo free, Santa Reparata excavations 3€ ($4.80), dome 6€ ($9.60), baptistery 3€ ($4.80), bell tower 6€ ($9.60), Museo dell'Opera 6€ ($9.60); children 5 and under free at all sites. Open: Duomo and Santa Reparata excavations Mon–Wed and Fri 10 a.m.–5 p.m., Thurs and first Sat of each month 10 a.m.–3:30 p.m., other Sat 10 a.m.–4:45 p.m., Sun and holidays 1:30–4:45 p.m. (open Sun morning for services only), closed Jan 6; dome Mon–Fri 8:30 a.m.–7 p.m., Sat 8:30 a.m.–5:40 p.m., except first Sat of month and May 1 8:30 a.m.–4 p.m. (last ascent 40 minutes earlier), closed all religious holidays; baptistery Mon–Sat noon to 7 p.m. and Sun, holidays, and first Sat of each month 8:30 a.m.–2 p.m. (last entry 30 minutes earlier), closed Jan 1, Easter, Sept 8, Dec 24 and 25; bell tower daily 8:30 a.m.–7:30 p.m. (last admission 20 minutes earlier), closed Jan 1, Easter, Sep 8, and Dec 25; Museo dell'Opera Mon–Sat 9 a.m.–7:30 p.m., and Sun 9 a.m.–1:45 p.m. (last admission 40 minutes earlier).

Galleria degli Uffizi

Housed in the administrative offices of the Tuscan Duchy (*uffizi* means "offices"), the gallery is a visual primer on the growth of the Renaissance from the 13th to the 18th centuries, and one of the world's best art galleries. You can easily spend all day here, finding room after room of recognized masterpieces, but you can see the highlights in two hours.

Your exploration of the Uffizi gets off to a fast start in the first room with a trio of giant *Maestà* paintings tracing the birth of the Renaissance — from the rigid, Byzantine style of Cimabue, through Gothic elements from Sienese great Duccio, to the innovative work by Giotto, who broke painting out of its static mold and gave it life, movement, depth, and emotion. From there, you move through rooms featuring the work of early Sienese masters, such as Pietro Lorenzetti and Simone Martini, and then continue on to Florentine and other Tuscan virtuosos such as Fra Angelico, Masaccio, Piero della Francesca, Paolo Uccello, and Filippo Lippi.

Next, you enter a huge room dedicated to Botticelli and focused on his two most famous works, *The Birth of Venus* (the woman rising out of a seashell) and *The Allegory of Spring,* and his contemporary Ghirlandaio, who taught a young Michelangelo how to fresco. After this, you can see works by Signorelli and Perugino; a young Leonardo da Vinci's *Annunciation;* and rooms filled with northern European art from the pre- and early Renaissance eras (Dürer, Cranach, Hans Holbein the Younger) and Venetian masters such as Correggio, Bellini, and Giorgione.

After you move to the second corridor, Michelangelo's colorful *Holy Family* signals your entry into the High Renaissance. Michelangelo's use of startling colors and his attention to detail in the twisting bodies influenced a generation of artists called *mannerists,* whose paintings are on display in the next few rooms. Works by mannerist artists (Rosso Fiorentino, Pontormo, Andrea del Sarto, and Parmigianino) are mixed with paintings by such famous names as Raphael, Titian, and Caravaggio. At press time, work was ongoing on the renovation for the upgrading of the exhibit space, but visits to the gallery were not affected.

See map p. 426. Piazzale degli Uffizi 6, off Piazza della Signoria. ☎ *055-294883.* www.polomuseale.firenze.it. *Bus: B. Admission: 6.50€ ($10), 4€ ($6.40) with advance reservation. Open: Tues–Sun 8:15 a.m.–6:50 p.m. Last admission 45 minutes earlier. Closed Jan 1, May 1, Dec 25.*

Galleria dell'Accademia (Michelangelo's David)

Many visitors come to Florence with one question on their lips: "Which way to the *David?*" and forget that the Accademia contains many other works of art, including magnificent paintings by Perugino, Botticelli, and Pontormo, among others.

In 1501, Michelangelo took a huge piece of marble that a previous sculptor had declared unusable and by 1504 had carved a Goliath-sized *David,* a masterpiece of the male nude. *David* stood in front of the Palazzo Vecchio until 1873 (a replica is there now); the location inside this gallery makes the sculpture look a little oversized, giving it an awkward feel. In 1991, *David* was attacked by a lunatic with a hammer, so you have to view him through a reinforced-glass shield (like the *Pietà* in Rome). The hall leading to the *David* is lined with other sculptures, including Michelangelo's unfinished *Slaves* — muscular figures which seem to be struggling to emerge from their stony prisons.

You can pop in and admire *David* in about 20 minutes, but it takes at least 45 minutes to wander through the rest of the Accademia's collection.

See map p. 426. Via Ricasoli 60, at Via Guelfa. ☎ *055-294883.* www.polomuseale. firenze.it. *Bus: 1, 6, 7, 10, or 11 to Via Guelfa, then walk 1 block east; C to Piazza San Marco, then walk 1 block south. Admission: 6.50€ ($10), 4€ ($6.40) with advance reservation, 9.50 € ($15) for special exhibits. Open: Tues–Sun 8:15 a.m.–6:50 p.m. Ticket booth closes 45 minutes earlier. Closed Jan 1, May 1, Dec 25.*

Palazzo Pitti and Giardino di Boboli

On the south side of the River Arno, this huge palace, once home to the Medici grand dukes, now houses several museums and an impressive painting gallery, the **Galleria Palatina.** These lavish rooms are appointed to look much the way they did in the 1700s, with works by a mind-boggling list of late-Renaissance and baroque geniuses such as Caravaggio, Rubens, Perugino, Giorgione, Guido Reni, Fra Bartolomeo, Tintoretto, Botticelli, and many more. The selection of works by Raphael, Titian, and Andrea del Sarto is particularly good. Your ticket to the Galleria Palatina also allows for admission to the **Royal Apartments,** the residence of three ruling families — Medici, Lorena, and finally Savoy during the brief time that Florence was the capital of Italy in the 1870s — a sight to behold with their rich fabrics, frescoes, and oil paintings.

As for other sites in the *palazzo,* the **Modern Art Gallery** has some good works by the *Macchiaioli* school, the Tuscan version of Impressionism. The **Galleria del Costume** (Costume Gallery) has some wonderful dresses that date back to the 1500s. The **Museo degli Argenti** (Silver Museum) is a decorative arts collection that shows off the grand duke's consistently bad taste but does have kitsch appeal.

Designed between 1549 and 1656, and located behind the Pitti Palace, the **Giardino di Boboli** is the world's most grandiose example of Italianate garden. This expanse of 4.5 hectares (11 acres) of gardens features statues, fountains, grottoes, a rococo *kaffehaus* for summer refreshment, and some nice wooded areas to walk in. Take the **Viottolone** — literally "large lane" — lined with laurels, cypresses, and pines and punctuated by statues to **Piazzale dell'Isolotto,** with the beautiful **Fontana dell'Oceano** (Ocean Fountain). In the park, you'll also find several pavilions, such as the 18th-century neoclassical **Palazzina della Meridiana,** and the elegant **Casino del Cavaliere** — built in the 17th century as a retreat for the Granduca and dominating the whole park from the top of the hill. It houses the **Porcelain Museum,** including Sèvres, Chantilly, and Meissen pieces as they were used at the tables of the three reigning families that resided in the palace.

You'd be hard-pressed to visit all the museums *and* the Giardino di Boboli in one day, but if you're short for time, take two hours to run through the Galleria Palatina and the Royal Apartments, and reserve an hour for the gardens.

See map p. 426. Piazza de' Pitti, steps from the Ponte Vecchio. ☎ *055-294883.* www.polomuseale.firenze.it. *Bus: D. Admission: Combination ticket valid 3 days for all the museums and gardens 11€ ($18), or 9€ ($14) for admission after 4 p.m.; Galleria Palatina, Royal Apartments, and Modern Art Gallery 8.50€ ($14); Museo degli Argenti, Porcelain Museum, Galleria del Costume, and Giardino di Boboli 6€ ($9.60). Open: Galleria Palatina, Royal Apartments, and Modern Art Gallery Tues–Sun 8:15 a.m.–6:50 p.m.; Museo degli Argenti, Porcelain Museum, Galleria del Costume, and Giardino di Boboli daily 8:15 a.m. to 1 hour before sunset (last admission 1 hour earlier, 30 minutes earlier for Museo degli Argenti). Galleria Palatina, Royal Apartments, and Modern Art Gallery closed Jan 1, May 1, and Dec 25. Royal Apartments closed Jan. Museo degli Argenti, Porcelain Museum, Galleria del Costume, and Giardino di Boboli closed Jan 1, May 1, and Dec 25.*

Santa Croce, Cappella de' Pazzi, and Museo dell'Opera di Santa Croce

This large Franciscan church on the city's western edge is the Westminster Abbey of the Renaissance. The church houses the tombs of several household names: Michelangelo, composer Rossini (*Barber of Seville* and the *William Tell Overture*), political thinker/writer Machiavelli, and astronomer and physicist Galileo. The church also has a monument to poetic giant Dante Alighieri, who was exiled from his beloved Florence on trumped-up charges during a period of political turmoil, and whose bones rest in the city of Ravenna, where he died just after completing his masterpiece, the *Divine Comedy* (of which the famed *Inferno* is but one-third).

Inside you can also see two chapels covered by the frescoes of Giotto, the ex-shepherd who became the forefather of the Renaissance in the early 14th century, but they are not well preserved. Near the chapels, a

The birth of opera

The story goes that, in 1589, the Medici organized a wedding reception in the Giardino di Boboli at the Palazzo Pitti and, of course, wanted something grand. They hired the best local composers of the time — Jacopo Peri and Ottavio Rinuccini — to provide musical entertainment. They came up with the idea of setting a classical story to music and having actors sing the whole thing, as in a modern musical. The show was a great success and the Medici added another feather at their caps: the birth of opera.

corridor leads through the gift shop to the famed leather school (pricey, but very high quality).

Admission to the church also gets you into the splendid 15th century **Cappella de' Pazzi,** designed by Brunelleschi, and the **Museo dell'Opera di Santa Croce.** This museum houses many of the artistic victims of the 1966 Arno flood, including Cimabue's *Crucifix,* as well as several art pieces taken from the church itself and the cloisters, such as the splendid sculpture of San Ludovico da Tolosa by Donatello. Enter through a door to the right of the church facade.

See map p. 426. Piazza Santa Croce. ☎ *055-246-6105.* www.santacroce. firenze.it. *Bus: C. Admission: 5€ ($8) includes admission to the Museo dell'Opera di Santa Croce. Open: Mon–Sat 9:30 a.m.–5:30 p.m.; Sun and holidays 1–5:30 p.m. Closed all religious holidays.*

More cool things to see and do

✔ If you're a fan of Michelangelo, you should not miss the **Medici Chapels,** Piazza Madonna degli Aldobrandini, behind the church of San Lorenzo (☎ **055-238-8602**), where his sculptures are lavishly distributed over the Medicis' monumental tombs in a space that is considered the founding work of the Mannerist style. Admission is 4€ ($6.40). It's open daily 8:15 a.m. to 5:50 p.m. (ticket booth closes 30 minutes earlier); closed second and fourth Sundays and first, third, and fifth Mondays of each month, as well as January 1, May 1, and December 25.

✔ How are your negotiation skills? Striking a bargain at the **outdoor leather market** by San Lorenzo church, with stalls peddling imitation Gucci merchandise, souvenir T-shirts, jewelry, wallets, and lots of leather might not be easy but could be fun. The carnival of colors and noise is a welcome, down-to-earth break from all that art, and you can buy interesting goods at a reasonable price. Just be alert to pickpockets. The stalls stay open from 8 a.m. to 6 p.m. (later if business is booming) daily March through October, and Tuesday through Saturday November through February.

✔ Florence shares the top spot on the hill of Italian high fashion with Milan, and **shopping** on **Via de' Tornabuoni** is a great experience, with the flagship stores of Pucci, Gucci, Beltrami, and Ferragamo for fashion and Buccellati for jewelry and silver. Other great names of Italian fashion and design line the nearby streets of **Via della Vigna Nuova** and **Via Strozzi,** from Italy's fashion guru Armani and Enrico Coveri for fashion, to Controluce for some beautifully designed light fixtures.

✔ You can experience a bit of Tuscan countryside with a ride on Florence's no. 7 bus to the village of **Fiesole.** Older than Florence and overlooking it from above, this hilltop Etruscan village has a few sights, cafes on the main square, and best of all, a cool mountain breeze on even the hottest summer days. The combination ticket *Biglietto Fiesole Musei* includes admission to all the local attractions for 10€ ($16). A tourist office (Piazza Mino 37; ☎ 055-598720; www.comune.fiesole.fi.it) is on your right as you step off the bus in Fiesole. Stop by the 11th-century cathedral, which contains some delicate Mino da Fiesole carvings, and then go up (*way* up) Via San Francesco to the panoramic gardens overlooking a picture-perfect view of Florence down in the valley. Perhaps the most popular sight in Fiesole is the ruins of the Roman theater and baths, **Teatro Romano and Museo Civico,** Via Partigiani 1 (☎ 055-59477; www.fiesolemusei.it), an excavation that has a temple from the fourth century B.C., a theater from the first century B.C. (which now hosts summertime concerts under the stars), and a few arches still standing from some first-century-A.D. baths. Admission is free, and it's open October through March Thursday through Monday 10 a.m. to 6 p.m., and April through September Wednesday through Monday 10 a.m. to 7 p.m.

Guided tours

We like the hop-on/hop-off bus tour run by **City Sightseeing** (☎ 800-424500; www.firenze.city-sightseeing.it); 24-hour tickets cost 20€ ($32) adults, 10€ ($16) children 5 to 15, and are valid on their two loop lines: **A,** making 15 stops between SMN train station and Piazzale Michelangelo (every 30 minutes daily), and **B,** making 24 stops between Porta San Frediano in Oltrarno and Fiesole (every hour daily). Tickets are for sale onboard or are included in the special bus ticket Passpartour (see "Getting Around Florence" earlier in this chapter).

Suggested itineraries

If you don't like tour buses and would prefer to discover Florence and the surrounding region on your own, this section provides some suggested plans of attack.

If you have one day

If you only have one day in Florence, you'll have to start bright and early. Head to the **Galleria dell'Accademia** (where you have made advance reservations), strolling on your way through Piazza Santissima Annunziata — one of Florence's nicest squares — and maybe stopping for a gelato at **Carabé.** If you're not keen on the *David,* head instead for the **Bargello Museum,** near Piazza della Signoria, Florence's best sculpture museum. Make your way then to the **Duomo,** enjoying the sight of the cathedral and of **Giotto's bell tower,** but linger only in the **baptistery,** since you're short on time. After your visit, lunch with a sample of cheeses and cured meats from the Tuscan countryside at **Consorzio Agrario Pane and Co.,** waiting for your set time for the **Galleria degli Uffizi,** where you also made advance reservations. Once you're saturated with Renaissance paintings, walk around **Piazza della Signoria,** taking in **Palazzo Vecchio,** and then head for **Ponte Vecchio** on Via Por Santa Maria, crossing over to **Oltrarno,** checking some of the shops on your way. After a nice stroll along the Arno, it's now time for *aperitivo,* and what best then to sample the Florentine invention *Negroni*? Try it at **Giacosa,** Via de' Tornabuoni 83r (☎ **055-239-6226;** Bus: 6, 11, 36, or 37 to Tornabuoni). For dinner, treat yourself at **Cibreo.**

If you have two days

Start **Day 1** as in the itinerary in the preceding section, visiting also the Bargello but reserving the Duomo for the next day. Have lunch at **Osteria Ganino.** Continue your day at the **Galleria degli Uffizidlis** where you've made an advance reservation. After your visit, spend the rest of your afternoon and evening exploring **Ponte Vecchio, Palazzo Vecchio,** and **Piazza della Signoria.**

On **Day 2,** start off with a visit to the church of **San Lorenzo** and the **Medici Chapels** behind it. You can also stroll through the **Mercato San Lorenzo** for some shopping. Have lunch at **Le Mossacce** before heading for the **Duomo,** with **Giotto's bell tower** and the **baptistery.** Continue with the **Museo dell'Opera del Duomo.** Finish your day with an *aperitivo* and dinner as in the preceding "If you have one day" itinerary.

If you have three days

Spend **Day 1** and **Day 2** as indicated in the preceding section. On the morning of **Day 3,** head for the **Basilica Santa Croce** and visit the **Cappella de' Pazzi** and the **Museo dell'Opera di Santa Croce.** Don't forget to have a look at the leather goods of the **Scuola del Cuoio di Santa Croce** in the convent compound. Have lunch at the **Osteria del Caffè Italiano.** In the afternoon, head for **Palazzo Pitti** and the **Giardino di Boboli.** End your day with a stroll and dinner in Oltrarno, maybe at **Cavolo Nero.**

Traveling Beyond Florence

Several worthwhile sites make easy day trips from Florence, including Pisa, Siena, and San Gimignano. Each stop has its own unique allure.

Pisa: The Leaning Tower and more

Pisa is much more than its famous Leaning Tower: Its medieval alleys and buildings overlooking the curving Arno are little visited yet offer some of Italy's nicest riverside views.

You won't need more than three or four hours to visit Pisa's most famous attractions, but you'd miss much: Pisa deserves being explored and knows how to reward its visitors. If you have the time, try to spend at least one night.

Getting there

Trains leave Florence for Pisa every half-hour; the trip takes an hour and costs about 5€ ($8). From the rail station, shuttle A (or a 15-minute walk) takes you across the Arno to the Leaning Tower.

A tiny tourism office sits to the left of the train station exit (☎ 050-42291), but the main **tourism office** is just outside the Porta Santa Maria gate on the west end of the Campo dei Miracoli at Via C. Cammeo 2 (☎ 050-560464; www.pisa.turismo.toscana.it).

Seeing the sights

You can get a cumulative ticket for your choice of two (6€/$9.60) or all five (10€/$16) of the attractions in Campo dei Miracoli (Duomo, Cemetery, Baptistery, Museo delle Sinopie, Museo dell'Opera del Duomo).

If you'd like to see Pisa via a guided tour from Florence, **American Express** (☎ 055-50981) and **SitaSightseeing** (☎ 055-214721) in Florence both offer tours of Pisa for about 26€ ($42).

The **Campo dei Miracoli** — also called Piazza del Duomo — is Pisa's monumental piazza and one of the most picturesque squares in Italy. Built in medieval times abutting the city walls, it's covered with shining green grass — a perfect background for the carved marble masterpieces in the monumental compound.

Pisa's **Duomo** (☎ 050-560-547; www.opapisa.it) is a magnificent cathedral from the 11th century, with a 13th-century facade of stacked colonnades. Make sure that you see the 12th-century **bronze doors** at the south entrance, the only set to survive a 1595 fire. The cathedral's interior was rebuilt after the fire, but some items from the earlier era remain — including the *Christ Pancrator* mosaic and Cimabue's St. John Evangelist in the apse, and one of Giovanni Pisano's greatest carved **pulpits** (1302–1311), a masterpiece of Gothic sculpture. Admission is 2€ ($3.20) adults, free for children 9 and under. The Duomo is open November through December 24 and January 8 through February 28 daily from 10 a.m. to 1 p.m. and 2 to 5 p.m.; December 25 through January 7 daily from 9 a.m. to 6 p.m.; March 1 through March 13 daily from 10 a.m. to 6 p.m.; March 14 through March 20 daily from 10 a.m. to 7 p.m.; March 21 through September daily from 10 a.m. to 8 p.m.; and in

Tuscany

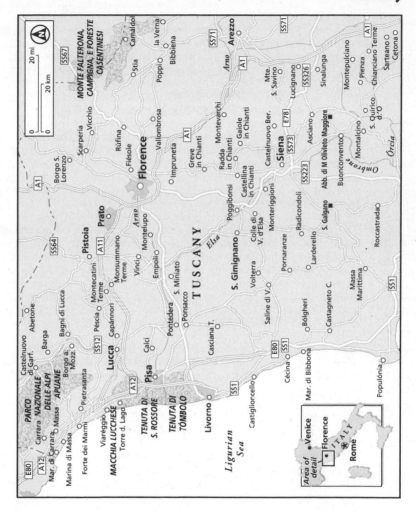

October daily from 10 a.m. to 7 p.m. (Sun and holidays open only after 1 p.m.). Last admission 30 minutes earlier.

The cathedral bell tower, better known as the **Leaning Tower,** is attractive enough to draw attention even if it didn't tilt so curiously. Threaded with colonnade arches, it is one of the prettiest towers you may ever see. Because all that marble is too heavy for the sandy soil to support, the tower started tilting right away in the 12th century. Builders tried to correct the tilt during construction, giving the tower a slight banana-like curve. In 1990, engineers determined that the tower's slant — 15 feet from center — made it too dangerous for visitors, and the tower was closed; it sat with steel bands belted around it and ugly lead weights stacked on one side until 70 tons of soil from the foundation's high side were removed so that the tower could gradually tip back. When, in December 2001, the tower was deemed safe (now only 13½ feet off-center), it was reopened to the public — but with a new and highly restricted admissions policy. Guided visits last 30 minutes and are limited to 20 people. Available slots sell fast, particularly in high season, so if you're keen on the climb make your reservations a minimum of two weeks in advance at ☎ 050-560547 or www.opapisa.it (with an additional reservation fee of 2€/$3.20). Admission is 15€ ($24). The tower is open November through December 24 and January 8 through February 28 daily from 10 a.m. to 5 p.m.; December 25 through January 7 daily from 9 a.m. to 6 p.m.; March 1 through March 13 daily from 9 a.m. to 6 p.m.; March 14 through March 20 daily from 9 a.m. to 7 p.m.; March 21 through June 13 and September 5 through September 30 daily from 8:30 a.m. to 8:30 p.m.; June 14 through September 4 daily from 8:30 a.m. to 11 p.m.; and in October daily from 9 a.m. to 7 p.m.

There are no elevators in the Leaning Tower, and access is through the original — and very narrow — staircase. It's 300 steps to the top — it's impossible to stop or turn around — and there are passages in the open making the climb physically and psychologically taxing. Anybody suffering from vertigo or claustrophobia or with a heart condition should not attempt it. Children 7 and under are not allowed in the tower, and children 17 and under are allowed only if accompanied by an adult. You'll need to hold the hand of your children ages 8 to 12 during the climb.

The other sites on the square are the **Camposanto,** the **Baptistery,** the **Museo delle Sinopie,** and the **Museo dell'Opera del Duomo.** The long wall of Gothic carved marble marks the **Camposanto,** the monumental cemetery filled with holy dirt from Golgotha (Calvary) in Palestine — where Christ was crucified — brought back by Pisan ships after a Crusade. It was the burial ground for Pisa's constables, who had their tombs richly decorated with sarcophagi, statues, and marble bas-reliefs. Allied firebombs in World War II destroyed most of the dazzling medieval frescoes that covered the walls, but the few that were salvaged — including the macabre *Triumph of Death* — are on display in a side room. Across the square from the Camposanto, obscured by souvenir stands,

A picnic in Pisa

Whether you want to buy food or not, the **food market** on **Piazza delle Vettovaglie,** a few steps north of Ponte di Mezzo, is a wonderful sight. Located here since the Middle Ages, it's a lively affair held Monday through Saturday from 7 a.m. to 1:30 p.m., where food producers from the countryside offer their specialties for sale. You can get the makings for a great picnic, to enjoy perhaps along the riverbanks: fresh produce, Tuscan bread and cured meats, fruit, and all the fixings.

is the **Museo delle Sinopie** (temporarily closed for restoration at press time), which contains the *sinopie,* or preparatory drawings, of the ill-fated frescoes. Behind the Leaning Tower is the **Museo dell'Opera del Duomo,** preserving many statues and other works that decorated the Duomo and Baptistery. Admission is 5€ ($8) adults, free for children 9 and under. It's open November through December 24 and January 8 through February 28 daily 10 a.m. to 5 p.m.; December 25 through January 7 daily 9 a.m. to 6 p.m.; March 1 through March 13 daily 9 a.m. to 6 p.m.; March 14 through March 20 daily 9 a.m. to 7 p.m.; March 21 through September daily 8 a.m. to 8 p.m.; and in October daily 9 a.m. to 7 p.m. Last admission 30 minutes earlier.

The monuments on Campo dei Miracoli steal the show in Pisa, but the **National Museum of San Matteo,** Lungarno Mediceo-Piazza San Matteo, near Piazza Mazzini (☎ 050-541865) should not be overlooked and will give you the opportunity for a stroll along Pisa's famed **Lungarni** (river promenades). The museum holds a stunning collection of Renaissance art (one of the best in the world). Important masterpieces include the 1426 painting *San Paolo* by Masaccio, two paintings of the *Madonna con i Santi* by Ghirlandaio, the sculpture of the *Madonna del Latte* by Andrea and Nino Pisano, and sculptures by Donatello. Consider one or two hours to visit this museum. Admission is 5€ ($8) adults, free for children 9 and under. The museum is open Tuesday through Saturday 9 a.m. to 7 p.m., Sunday 9 a.m. to 2 p.m. It's closed January 1, May 1, August 15, and December 25.

Where to stay and dine

The **Hotel Relais dell'Orologio,** Via della Faggiola 12–14 (☎ 050-830361; Fax: 050-551869; www.hotelrelaisorologio.com; rack rates: 350€–400€/$560–$640 double, including breakfast), is a historic medieval mansion only steps from Campo dei Miracoli, which opened as a hotel in 2004. You'll be comfortable and stay in style. For terrific Pisan cuisine in a traditional trattoria setting, head just north of the city walls to **Antica Trattoria Da Bruno,** Via Luigi Bianchi 12 (☎ 050-560818; www.pisaonline.it/trattoriadabruno; open Mon 12:15–2:30 p.m., Wed–Sun 12:15–2:30 p.m. and 7:15–10:30 p.m.).

Siena: A departure from the Renaissance

This lovely town in Tuscany is an overgrown medieval hill town, where you find brick-and-marble palaces and cafes, not museums and boutiques. Siena has its own proud artistic tradition, which relies on emotion, elegance of line, and rich color — a shift from Florence's precise, formula-driven, exacting classical painting.

Many people spend only half a day in Siena, but try to spend at least one night so that you have a good day and a half to absorb its medieval atmosphere and see its scattered sights.

Getting there

Siena lies 62km (37 miles) south of Florence. The newly introduced **Pisa Airport shuttle bus** from Pisa Airport takes you to Siena in about two hours. The bus is offered by **TRA-IN** (☎ **0577-204246;** www.trainspa.it), costs 14€ ($22), and can be reserved in advance at ☎ **800-905183** or through the Siena tourist office (see the following paragraph). Siena is also best reached by **bus** because the bus station in Piazza Gramsci (off the La Lizza pedestrian gallery) is only steps from the town center. **TRA-IN** and **SITA** (☎ **800-373760;** www.sita-on-line.it) offer regular service from Florence (from SITA bus station near SMN train station); the trip takes 75 minutes and costs about 5€ ($8), with buses leaving every half-hour. Siena's **rail** station (☎ **0577-280115**) is on Piazza Fratelli Rosselli, about 2.5km (1½ miles) downhill from the town center. The train trip from Florence takes about 90 minutes and costs about 6€ ($9.60). You then have to take a taxi or a minibus (Line C to Piazza Gramsci).

The **tourist office** (☎ **0577-280551;** www.terresiena.it) is at Piazza del Campo 56 in Siena.

Seeing the sights

The **Biglietto Unico Musei** covers the main museums in town (Museo Civico, Pinacoteca Nazionale, Santa Maria della Scala, Duomo and Piccolomini Library, and State Archives) for 14€ ($22). You can purchase it from the tourist office and from the travel agency **Vacanze Senesi** (www.bookingsiena.it).

If you're planning to see everything in town, the **Siena Itinerari d'Arte (SIA) Pass** (including Museo dell'Opera, Baptistery, Oratorio di San Bernardino and Museum, Palazzo delle Papesse, Santa Maria della Scala, Museo Civico, and Sant'Agostino) is the ticket for you: It exists in winter (Nov 2–Feb 28 for 13€/$21) and summer (Mar 1–Nov 1 for 16€/$26) versions and is valid for seven days.

Those who are less ambitious, or have less time, can take advantage of the **Biglietto Cumulativo Musei Comunali,** which includes entrance to Museo Civico, Palazzo delle Papesse, and Santa Maria della Scala for 10€ ($16) and is valid for two days, or the **Biglietto Cumulativo Opera Duomo,** which also costs 10€ ($16), is valid three days, and includes admission to the Duomo, Museo dell'Opera, Baptistery, Crypt, and Oratorio di San Bernardino with Museum.

American Express (☎ **055-50981**) teams with **CAF Tours,** Via Roma 4 (☎ **055-283200;** www.caftours.com), for an all-day excursion from Florence that includes both Siena and San Gimignano, described later in this chapter, for 60€ ($96).

At the center of the city is **Il Campo,** a beautiful, fan-shaped brick area that slopes down to the **Palazzo Pubblico** (1297–1310). You can climb the 503 steps of its bell tower, the **Torre di Mangia,** to get an unforgettable view over the city's burnt-sienna rooftops out to the green countryside beyond. You can also visit the **Museo Civico** (☎ 0577-292226), for a look at the *palazzo*'s beautiful frescoes, including the greatest secular fresco to survive from medieval Europe: Ambrogio Lorenzetti's *Allegory of Good and Bad Government and Its Effect on the Town and Countryside,* wrapping around three walls and depicting the medieval ideal of civic life. Admission is 7€ ($11) for the museum and 6€ ($9.60) for the tower; a combined ticket is 10€ ($16). The museum is open March 16 to October 31 daily 10 a.m. to 7 p.m. and November 1 to March 15 daily 10 a.m. to 5:30 p.m. (until 6:30 p.m. Dec 25–Jan 6). The tower is open March 16 to October 31 daily 10 a.m. to 7 p.m. and November 1 to March 15 daily 10 a.m. to 4 p.m. (closed Dec 25).

Siena's other grand sight, the **Duomo,** Piazza del Duomo (☎ 0577-283048; www.operaduomo.siena.it), is a huge zebra-striped Gothic structure with a facade by Giovanni Pisano and an interior with a floor that combines inlaid, carved, and mosaic marble panels (1372–1547). At the right transept is the Chigi Chapel, designed by the baroque master Bernini. Nicola Pisano's best pulpit is at the start of the left transept; the intricately carved Gothic panels (which his son, Giovanni, helped create) depict the life of Christ in great detail. Off the left aisle is the entrance to the **Libreria Piccolomini,** which Umbrian master Pinturicchio filled with frescoed scenes from the life of Pope Pius II. Just outside this room is a large marble altar that holds statuettes of Sts. Peter, Paul, and Gregory, carved by a 26-year-old Michelangelo. Admission to the Duomo is free; entry fee for the library is 3€ ($4.80) except during the exposure of the floor when admission for the Duomo plus the library is 6€ ($9.60). It's open March through May and September through October Monday through Saturday from 10:30 a.m. to 7:30 p.m. and Sunday and holidays from 1:30 to 5:30 p.m.; June through August Monday through Saturday from 10:30 a.m. to 8 p.m. and Sunday and holidays from 1:30 to 6 p.m.; and November through February Monday through Saturday from 10:30 a.m. to 6:30 p.m. and Sunday and holidays 1:30 to 5:30 p.m. Hours vary during the exposure of the floor.

If you walk down the steep stairs around the Duomo's right side and turn around at the bottom, you see the **Baptistery,** Piazza San Giovanni, behind the Duomo (☎ 0577-283048), which was built under the cathedral. Inside is a font with bronze panels by some of the early Renaissance's greatest sculptors: Donatello, Ghiberti, and Siena's Jacopo della Quercia. Creative frescoes from the 15th century (look for the alligator) cover the walls and ceiling. Admission is 3€ ($4.80), and it's open November through February daily from 10 a.m. to 5 p.m.; March through May and September through October daily from 9:30 a.m. to 7 p.m.; and June through August daily from 9:30 a.m. to 8 p.m. (closed Jan 1 and Dec 25).

About 700 years ago, Siena started building an ambitious expansion of its cathedral that would have turned the present Duomo into just a portion of the grand new structure, but the Black Death hit in 1348, killing 75 percent of the town's population. The **Museo dell'Opera Metropolitana,** Piazza Jacopo della Quercia, adjacent to Piazza del Duomo (☎ 0577-283048;

www.operaduomo.siena.it), now fills the structure and holds artwork removed from the Duomo for preservation, such as the splendid statues that Giovanni Pisano carved for the Duomo's facade, as well as Pietro Lorenzetti's beautiful triptych *The Birth of the Virgin*. In the museum, you can climb several worn staircases up onto the wall of the unfinished nave for great views across the city. Admission is 6€ ($9.60); the museum is open March through May and September through October daily from 9:30 a.m. to 7 p.m.; June through August daily from 9:30 a.m. to 8 p.m.; and November through February daily from 10 a.m. to 5 p.m. (closed Jan 1 and Dec 25).

For more art, head across the Duomo to the former hospital of **Santa Maria della Scala,** Piazza Duomo 2 (☎ 0577-224811; http://santamaria. comune.siena.it), to admire its lavishly frescoed rooms. Admission is 6€ ($9.60); it's open daily 10:30 a.m. to 6:30 p.m. (ticket booth closes 30 minutes earlier).

If you're eager for a respite from history and art, visit the **Enoteca Italiana Permanente,** Via Camollia 72 (☎ 0577-288811; www.enoteca-italiana.it), Italy's official wine-tasting bar, with over 700 labels in stock. Together with the newly opened restaurant **Millevini** (open Mon–Sat noon to 3 p.m. and 7–10 p.m.), it fills the echoing brick halls and cellars of the 16th-century **Fortezza Medicea** fortress in Siena's northwest corner. Glasses range from 2€ to 8€ ($3.20–$13), and it's open Monday noon to 8 p.m. and Tuesday through Saturday noon to 1 a.m.

Where to stay and dine

The recently opened **Grand Hotel Continental,** Banchi di Sopra 85 (☎ 0577-56011; Fax: 0577-560-1535; www.royaldemeure.com; Rack rates: 420€–560€/$672–$896 double), housed in a beautifully frescoed historic *palazzo,* is the best in town.

Another of our favorites is **Hotel Scacciapensieri,** Strada di Scacciapensieri 10 (☎ 0577-41441; Fax: 0577-270854; Rack rates: 195€–305€/$312–$488 double, including buffet breakfast), a 19th-century villa a short distance (2.4km/1½ miles) from the historic district, and great amenities: the swimming pool is heavenly if you're visiting in the hot season.

Good, solid Sienese food is available at **Antica Trattoria Papei,** Piazza del Mercato 6, behind the Palazzo Pubblico (☎ 0577-280894; open Tues–Sun 12:15–2:30 p.m. and 7:15–10 p.m.). For a truly special experience, though, head to **Le Logge,** Via del Porrione 33 (☎ 0577-48013; open Mon–Sat 12:30–2:30 p.m. and 7:30–10:30 p.m.), a celebrated gourmet restaurant where you can enjoy wonderful creative Sienese food.

San Gimignano: Hills and towers

Perhaps the most famous of Tuscany's hill towns, San Gimignano bristles with 14 medieval towers that are remnants of the days when tiny city-states such as this were full of feuding families that sometimes went to war right in the middle of town. Although no other city in Italy has saved so many of its towers, what you see today is only a fraction of what used to be there; San Gimignano sported at least 70 towers in the 13th and 14th centuries. Although this little town is often packed with day-trippers, you won't find any other spot with such a profound Middle Ages flavor.

You can see San Gimignano in two to three hours, but smart travelers know that all the day-trippers head for their tour buses at dusk, leaving wonderful medieval towns like this virtually untouched. Those who spend the night can absorb the ancient village atmosphere and get to know the locals.

Getting there

The easiest way to reach San Gimignano is by bus from Siena: **TRA-IN** (☎ **0577-204246;** www.trainspa.it) offers regular service; the trip takes about 50 minutes and costs 4€ ($6.40). From Florence, you need to first reach the town of Poggibonsi by train or bus (**SITA;** Via Santa Caterina 17, west of the SMN train station; ☎ **800-373760;** www.sita-on-line.it) and then switch to the local bus to San Gimignano — possible but laborious. You're better off joining a guided tour from Florence (see "Seeing the sights" in the Siena section, earlier in this chapter).

The **tourism office** (☎ **0577-940-008;** www.sangimignano.com) is at Piazza del Duomo 1.

Seeing the sights

The small town center consists of two interlocked, irregularly shaped squares, with a 13th-century well in the center of one and the Collegiata (main church) taking up one end of the other. If you can't resist climbing up one of the looming towers, go to the **Museo Civico/Torre Grossa** (☎ **0577-990312**). After you admire paintings in the gallery by artists such as Pinturicchio, Gozzoli, and Lippo Memmi (and secular 14th-century frescoes in an anteroom that show the racier side of medieval courtship), you can climb the tallest remaining tower in town (54m/178 ft.), which provides a 360-degree view of the town and the rolling green countryside just outside its walls. Admission is 4€ ($6.40), and the museum is open March through October daily 9:30 a.m. to 7 p.m. and November through February daily 10 a.m. to 5:30 p.m. (Dec 24 10 a.m.–1:30 p.m., Dec 25 and 31 10 a.m.–5 p.m., and Jan 1 12:30–5 p.m.; closed Jan 31).

The **Collegiata,** Piazza del Duomo (☎ **0577-940316**) has no bishop's seat and, therefore, technically, is no longer a *duomo* (cathedral), but it sure is decorated to look like one. The interior walls are completely covered with a colorful collage of 14th- and 15th-century frescoes. The ones down the left wall tell Old Testament stories; the right wall features the New Testament. A *St. Sebastian* thick with arrows is against the entrance wall, and near the entrance — high on the interior nave wall — spreads a gruesomely colorful *Last Judgment* scene. Off the right aisle is the tiny

Chapel of St. Fina, which Ghirlandaio frescoed with two scenes from the young saint's brief life. Admission is 3€ ($4.80). It's open November through January 20 and March Monday through Saturday from 9:30 a.m. to 4:40 p.m. and Sunday and holidays from 12:30 to 4:40 p.m.; April through October Monday through Friday from 9:30 a.m. to 7:10 p.m., Saturday from 9:30 a.m. to 5:10 p.m., and Sunday and holidays from 12:30 to 5:10 p.m. (closed Jan 21–Feb).

Where to stay and dine

L'Antico Pozzo, Via San Matteo 87 (☎ **0577-942014;** Fax: 0577-942117; www.anticopozzo.com; Rack rates: 140€–180€/$224–$288 double, including buffet breakfast), is our favorite hotel within the town walls. **La Mangiatoia,** Via Mainardi 5 (☎ **0577-941528;** open Wed–Mon 12:30–2:30 p.m. and 7:30–10 p.m.), has an intimate atmosphere and a hearty Tuscan menu, and its more imaginative dishes are the best.

Fast Facts: Florence

American Express

The Florence American Express office, Via Dante Alighieri 22r (☎ 055-50-981), is open Monday through Friday from 9 a.m. to 5:30 p.m., and Saturday from 9 a.m. to 12:30 p.m.

Area Code

The local area code is **055** (see "Telephone" under "Fast Facts: Rome" in Chapter 19 for more on calling to and from Italy).

Currency

In 2002, the euro became the legal tender in Italy, replacing the lira. The euro is divided into 100 cents, and there are coins of 0.01, 0.02, 0.05, 0.10, 0.20, 0.50, 1€, and 2€. Paper-note denominations are 5, 10, 20, 50, 100, 200, and 500 euros. The exchange rate used to calculate the dollar value given in this chapter is 1€ equals $1.60. Amounts over $10 are rounded to the nearest dollar.

Doctors and Dentists

Call your consulate or the American Express office for a current list of English-speaking doctors and dentists. The Tourist Medical Service, Via Lorenzo il Magnifico

59 (☎ 055-475-411), is open 24 hours and can be reached by bus nos. 8 and 80 (to Lavagnini) or bus no. 12 (to Poliziano).

Embassies and Consulates

United States: Lungarno Amerigo Vespucci 38, near the intersection with Via Palestro (☎ 055-239-8279). United Kingdom: Lungarno Corsini 2 (☎ 055-284123). For other embassies and consulates, see Chapter 19.

Emergency

Ambulance, ☎ **118;** police ☎ **113;** fire, ☎ **115;** road assistance, ☎ **116.**

Hospitals

First aid is available 24 hours a day in the *pronto soccorso* (emergency room) of Careggi in Viale Morgagni 85 (☎ 055-427-7247), and in the centrally located hospital Ospedale di Santa Maria Nuova, Piazza Santa Maria Nuova (☎ 055-27581), 1 block northeast from the Duomo.

Information

The tourist office, APT, Via A. Manzoni 16, 50121 Firenze (☎ 055-23320; Fax: 055-234-6286; www.firenzeturismo.it), maintains three tourist info points in town: at Via Cavour 1r (☎ 055-290832; open Mon–Sat 8:30 a.m.–6:30 p.m., Sun 8:30 a.m.–1:30 p.m.); at S.M.N. rail station, Piazza Stazione 4/a (☎ 055-212245; open Mon–Sat 9 a.m.–7 p.m., Sun 8:30 a.m.–2 p.m.); and at Borgo Santa Croce 29r (☎ 055-234-0444; open Mon–Sat 9 a.m.–7 p.m. [until 5 p.m. in winter], Sun 9 a.m.–2 p.m.).

Internet Access and Cybercafes

The Internet Train chain has several locations, the most convenient being Via Guelfa 24a, near the train station (☎ 055-214-794; open Mon–Fri 9 a.m.–11 p.m., Sat 10 a.m.–8 p.m., Sun noon to 9 p.m.); Via dell'Oriuolo 40r, near the Duomo (☎ 055-263-8968; open Mon–Sat 10 a.m.–10 p.m., Sun 3–9 p.m.); and Borgo San Jacopo 30r, near the Ponte Vecchio (☎ 055-265-7935; open Mon–Fri 10:30 a.m.–11 p.m., Sat–Sun 11 a.m.–11 p.m.). EasyEveryThing has a shop near the Duomo in Via Martelli 22 (open daily 9 a.m.–8 p.m.).

Maps

The tourist office hands out a free map. You can buy a more-detailed one at any newsstand or bookstore.

Pharmacies

The most centrally located 24-hour pharmacies are Farmacia Molteni, Via Calzaiuoli 7r (☎ 055-215472); Farmacia Comunale, inside S.M.N. train station (☎ 055-216761); and All'insegna del Moro, Piazza San Giovanni 28r (☎ 055-211343).

Police

Dial ☎ **113.**

Post Office

The main post office is the Ufficio Postale in Via Pellicceria 3, off Piazza della Repubblica, open Monday to Friday from 9 a.m. to 6 p.m., Saturday from 9 a.m. to 2 p.m.

Restrooms

Museums have public restrooms; otherwise, your best bet is to go to a cafe or the Rinascente Department store in Piazza della Repubblica.

Safety

The historic district is quite safe; your only major worries are pickpockets and purse snatchers because of the huge concentration of tourists. Avoid deserted areas after dark (such as behind the train station and the Cascine Park), and exercise normal urban caution.

Smoking

In 2005, Italy passed a law outlawing smoking in most public places. Smoking is allowed only where there is a separate, ventilated area for nonsmokers. If smoking at your table is important to you, call beforehand to make sure the restaurant or cafe you'll be visiting offers a smoking area.

Taxes

See "Fast Facts: Rome" in Chapter 19 for details.

Taxis

For radio taxi, call ☎ 055-4390, 055-4798, or 055-4242, or 055-4499.

Telephone

See "Fast Facts: Rome" in Chapter 19 for information on making calls and calling-card access codes.

Chapter 21

Venice and Environs

*B*uilt on water and marshland, Venice is not just an amazing city — it's also a feat of engineering and determination. The city's famous canals serve as its main streets, traveled by a variety of boats, including the famous *gondole.* Centuries of political stability and wealth allowed Venice to create a rich urban and cultural landscape (including hundreds of churches such as the Basilica de San Marco) and to nurture such great late-Renaissance artists as Titian and Tintoretto. Every year, more than 7 million tourists join the city's 70,000 residents, and in high season the crowds can be overwhelming. And yet . . . Canal Grande after sunset, Piazza San Marco early in the morning, the Gallerie dell'Accademia, the lagoon, the Canaletto skies, and the stillness beneath the hubbub are sights you just have to experience. And Venice's famous serenity (the republic was called *La Serenissima,* the "serene one") is as seductive as ever.

If you had the time to stay a week in Venice it would be well spent, but you can see the highlights in two days.

Getting There

Water surrounds Venice, threading its way through every neighborhood, so arriving in town without hopping on a boat of some sort is nearly impossible. While in the city, walking is the best way to get around.

Arriving by air

Flights land at the **Aeroporto Marco Polo,** 10.5km (6½ miles) north of the city on the mainland (☎ **041-260-9260;** www.veniceairport.it). You'll find ATMs and a tourist information desk on the ground floor in the arrivals hall.

Though fast and convenient, a **water taxi** (☎ 041-541-5084) costs between 98€ and 120€ ($157–$192) for two to four people depending on the distance. At **Motoscafi Venezia** (☎ 041-522-2303; www.motoscafi venezia.it) you can book a water taxi or the cheaper **water shuttle**, which takes up to ten passengers to drop-off points that are convenient to most destinations (you then have to walk to your hotel); they maintain a desk at the airport, inside the terminal at arrivals. Cheaper but longer are the larger water shuttles run by **Alilaguna** (☎ 041-240-1701; www. alilaguna.it): 12€ ($19) per person for the 50-minute ride to San Marco and other stops in the historic district. If you're on a budget, you can take the **ATVO shuttle bus** (☎ 041-520-5530; www.atvo.it), which runs hourly to Piazzale Roma, Venice's car terminal on the mainland, for 3€ ($4.80) per person. The trip takes about 20 minutes, and you can then take a *vaporetto* (the local water "bus"; see "Getting Around Venice," later in this chapter) or a water taxi to your hotel.

Arriving by rail

Trains pull in at **Santa Lucia**, Venice's historic district's rail station. Venice's mainland rail hub is **Mestre.** Choose a direct train to Santa Lucia if you don't want to switch in Mestre to a local shuttle train for the ten-minute trip to Santa Lucia. Just outside Santa Lucia rail station, you'll find the ticket booth for the *vaporetto*, as well as water taxis.

Finding information after you arrive

The APT (Fondamenta San Lorenzo, Castello 5050, 30122 Venezia; ☎ 041-529-8700; www.venicetouristboard.com and www.turismo venezia.it) maintains tourist info points at the airport, Piazzale Roma, and Santa Lucia train station, as well as other info centers in town; see "Information" under "Fast Facts: Venice" at the end of this chapter.

Getting Around Venice

Your only options for getting around in the historic district are by foot or by boat. No book-size map can give you full details of the narrow *calli* and bridges. If you're planning major exploring, get a **good map,** such as the smartly folded Falk map, available at most bookstores and newsstands.

By foot

We've seen many a tourist, unprepared for the rigors of walking Venice, slumped in dismay in front of the steps of yet another bridge. Yet, after having your own boat, walking is the best way to visit Venice, and you'll be doing a lot of it. You only need to remember to keep to your right — yes, even while walking — to avoid stopping on narrow bridges and blocking the circulation (a major breech to local etiquette), and to wear comfortable shoes (perhaps packing a good foot balm, an end-of-the-day treat for your faithful "wheels").

Although it may appear daunting and mazelike, you can't get lost in Venice as you would in a regular city. Venice has very few streets and a canal will always stop you — at worst, you'll have to backtrack and then try the next turn. So don't feel shy about exploring — no matter how deserted a *calle* may look — you're never very far from a crowded spot where you can ask for directions.

As you wander, look for the ubiquitous signs with arrows (sometimes a little old, but still readable) that, just like trailblazers, direct you toward major landmarks, such as FERROVIA (the train station), PIAZZALE ROMA (the car terminal), VAPORETTO (the nearest *vaporetto* stop), RIALTO (the bridge), PIAZZA SAN MARCO, ACCADEMIA (the bridge), and so on.

By vaporetto (water bus)

Public transportation in Venice (☎ 041-272-2111; www.actv.it) is by boat: The *vaporetto* is a water bus — something between a small barge and a ferry — and can be great fun. One must-do experience is the ride down the Canal Grande early in the day and by night (see "Exploring Venice," later in this chapter). With rush-hour crowds, remember to put your backpack down when standing; it'll be less exposed to pickpockets, and the locals will appreciate it. A one-hour ticket valid on all lines is 6.50€ ($15).

If you plan to use the *vaporetto* a lot, go for one of the many available passes, such as a **12-hour pass** for 14€ ($22), a **48-hour pass** for 26€ ($42), or a **72-hour pass** for 31€ ($50). These passes give you access to the whole public transportation system, including the lines crossing the lagoon to Murano, Burano, and Lido. Transportation passes are included with the **Venice Card** and discounted (a three-day transportation pass for 18€/$29) with the **Rolling Venice Card** (see "Exploring Venice," later in this chapter).

Street smarts: Venetian addresses

Venice doesn't label its streets and squares like the rest of Italy does. A *calle, ruga,* or *ramo* is a street; a *rio terrà* is a street made from a filled-in canal; and a *fondamenta* or *riva* is a sidewalk along the edge of a canal. A *canale* or *rio* is a canal. A *campo* or *campiello* is a square (but you see exceptions here, including Piazza San Marco, Piazzetta San Marco, and Piazzale Roma).

Although a street or *campo* name can be used only once within a Venetian neighborhood, no rule exists against another *sestiere* (neighborhood) using the exact same label. As a result, the most popular names (such as Calle della Madonna) are recycled three or four times in Venice, yet refer to streets half a city apart. Because of the confusing naming conventions, save yourself a headache and know the *sestiere* along with any address. (By the way, don't even try to figure out the street-numbering system in Venice — it's devoid of any logic whatsoever.)

Sinking beauty

Venice has weathered wars, dictators, and conspiracies, and enjoyed more than a thousand years of democracy. But its most treacherous foe may be the very sea it has relied on for centuries. The city is literally sinking into the muddy lagoon on which it was built. In spite of advice from experts all over the world, cement injections, and the ongoing work of restoration and solidification of the canals, the city continues to sink. The search for ways to save one of the most beautiful and extraordinary cities ever built continues, but the increase in the sea levels registered all over the planet in recent years because of global warming spells doom.

By traghetto (ferry skiff)

Just three bridges span the Grand Canal. To fill in the gaps, *traghetti* skiffs (oversize gondolas rowed by two standing gondoliers) cross the Grand Canal at eight intermediate points — **San Tomà, Santa Maria del Giglio, Dogana, Ferrovia, Rialto, San Marcuola, San Samuele,** and **Santa Sofia** — with boarding at the end of any street named Calle del Traghetto on your map and indicated by a yellow sign with the black gondola symbol. The fare is 0.50€ (80¢), which you hand to the gondolier when boarding.

By taxi

Though a little expensive, water taxis are the perfect way to get to and from your hotel with your luggage and to have a taste of luxury. You can get one by walking to a taxi stand — San Marco, rail station, Rialto — or calling for pickup (see "Fast Facts: Venice" at the end of this chapter for numbers). The meter starts at 8.70€ ($14) and adds 1.30€ ($2.10) every minute; you'll also have to pay a surcharge of 5.50€ ($8.80) for night hours, 5.90€ ($9.45) for holidays, plus 6€ ($9.60) if you call for service, and 1.50€ ($2.40) for each piece of luggage larger than 50 centimeters (20 inches) per side. Remember that even water taxis can't reach certain locations, in which case you'll have to walk the rest of the way.

Staying in Venice

With the euro climbing sky high and several million fellow tourists to compete against, landing a moderately priced accommodation in Venice is quite tricky. Low season is basically nonexistent, and you'll want to make your reservations well in advance (the best deals are booked up to a year early, particularly for Carnival). You'll get much better rates on the island of **Lido.** Another possibility is staying in nearby **Padova,** a charming town located a short 30-minute train ride from Venice (see "Traveling beyond Venice," later in this chapter). If you arrive without a reservation, the **Hotel Association of Venice** (AVA; ☎ 041-522-2264;

Accommodations, Dining, and Attractions in Venice

HOTELS ■
Antica Locanda Sturion **6**
Gritti Palace **30**
Hotel Colombina **10**
Hotel Do Pozzi **32**
Hotel Falier **23**
Hotel Metropole **33**
Hotel San Cassiano Ca' Favretto **2**
Hotel Santo Stefano **28**
Locanda ai Santi Apostoli **3**
Palazzo Sant'Angelo **19**
Pensione La Calcina **26**

RESTAURANTS ◆
Ae Oche **25**
A la Vecia Cavana **4**
Antico Martini **18**
Bar Pizzeria da Paolo **34**
Boutique del Gelato **9**
Da Raffaele **31**
Met de l'Hotel Metropole **33**
Osteria ai 4 Feri **24**
Osteria da Fiore **21**
Osteria di Santa Marina **8**
Trattoria alla Madonna **5**

ATTRACTIONS ●
Bridge of Sighs **13**
Correr Museum **17**
Galleria dell'Accademia **27**
Palazzo Ducale **14**
Peggy Guggenheim Collection **29**
Piazza San Marco **16**
Ponte di Rialto **7**
Santa Maria Gloriosa dei Frari **20**
Scuola Grande di San Rocco **22**
St. Mark's Basilica **12**
St. Mark's bell tower **15**
Torre dell'Orologio **11**
Venetian Ghetto **1**

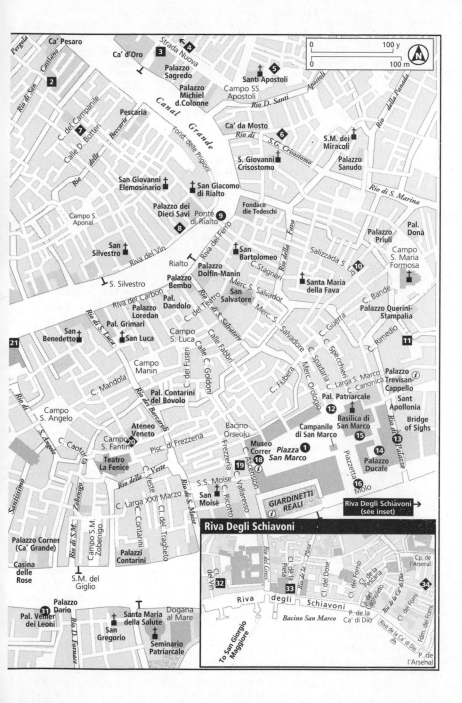

`www.veneziasi.it`) offers a free reservations service; it maintains booths at Santa Lucia train station, at Piazzale Roma, at the airport, and at the tourist info point by the Venice highway exit on the mainland. In choosing which hotels to list here, we considered accessibility (direct access by water or with a short walk with no bridges); we highly recommend you do the same.

Venice's top hotels

Cipriani
$$$$ Dorsoduro

At the tip of La Giudecca — a few minutes from San Marco by free shuttle boat — this hotel offers one of the most romantic experiences in Venice and some of the highest rates in Europe. Housed in a 16th-century monastery overlooking the water on three sides, and complete with cloisters, it offers individually decorated rooms that are sumptuous but not overly ornate. Even the simplest double rooms with garden views are palatial, with super-comfortable beds, quality linens, large bathrooms, and views. Public spaces include gardens and a heated Olympic-size swimming pool filled with filtered saltwater. With a ratio of two staff members for each room, the service here is perfect. The hotel's restaurant, **Fortuny,** is one of the best restaurants in Italy.

Isola della Giudecca 10. ☎ *041-520-7744. Fax: 041-520-7745.* www.hotelcipriani. com. *Vaporetto: 41, 42, or 82 to Zitelle. Rack rates: 870€–1,320€ ($1,392–$2,112) double. Rates include full American breakfast. Children 12 and under stay free in parent's room. AE, DC, MC, V. Closed Nov–Mar.*

Hotel Campiello
$$ Castello

This pink 15th-century building, once a convent, is a bargain for the area; run by two sisters, this hotel offers friendly and expert service. The location is nearly perfect, by Riva degli Schiavoni but somewhat quieter. Guest rooms are elegant and decorated in either Liberty (Art Nouveau) or 19th-century style, with carpet or wooden floors, comfortable beds, and new bathrooms. Their three apartments are great for families, decorated in elegant modern style, with comfortable beds and kitchenettes complete with microwave ovens; the modern bathrooms come with separate showers and Jacuzzi tubs. The substantial buffet breakfast is served in a rather glitzy hall.

Campiello del Vin, 4647 Castello. ☎ *041-239682. Fax: 041-520-5798.* www.hotel campiello.it. *Vaporetto: 1, 5, 41, 42, 51, 52, or 82 to San Zaccaria, and then walk up Calle del Vin. Rack rates: 250€ ($400) double, 120€–450€ ($192–$720) apartments. Rates include buffet breakfast. AE, MC, V.*

Hotel Colombina
$$$ Castello

This elegant hotel is a great addition to the Venice hotel scene, only steps away from St. Mark's Basilica. Once inside, you'll feel miles away from the crowds outside. Guest rooms are spacious and nicely done in Venetian style, with carpeted or wooden floors, comfortable beds, fine fabrics, and quality reproduction furniture. The staff is attentive and friendly. The hotel also includes an annex, the Locanda Remedio. Guest rooms there are somewhat smaller but perfectly adequate and well appointed, with wooden floors, period furnishings, and small but nice modern bathrooms. Rates are lower than in the main hotel (starting at 295€/$472). Note that Internet specials may bring rates down by as much as 40 percent.

See map p. 458 Calle del Remedio, 4416 Castello. ☎ *041-277-0525. Fax: 041-277-6044.* www.hotelcolombina.com. *Vaporetto: 82 to San Zaccaria, and then walk up Calle Rasse, take a quick jog left and immediately right onto Calle Sagrestia, turn left at Campo San Zani, and continue on to Calle Remedio to the left. Rack rates: 395€–460€ ($632–$736) double. Rates include buffet breakfast. AE, DC, MC, V.*

Hotel Metropole
$$$$ Castello

We love this hotel: It is one of the few posh hotels on Riva degli Schiavoni that's still family run (the others have been bought by American chains), and the family has managed to keep up the challenge by offering great service and quality for your money. This romantic property includes the chapel where Vivaldi composed the *Four Seasons;* from its opulent Venetian baroque interior to its peaceful courtyard garden, this hotel sets itself apart. Each guest room is spacious and individually furnished with brocades and luxury fabrics, carpeted or wood floors, comfortable beds, and period furniture that include original antiques; the good-size bathrooms (all with tubs) are done in marble or mosaic. The restaurant **Met** is one of the best in Italy; here, you can get heavenly creative Venetian cuisine in the cozy and luxurious dining room. The Internet rates are as much as 40 percent off.

See map p. 458. Riva degli Schiavoni, 4149 Castello. ☎ *041-520-5044. Fax: 041-522-3679.* www.hotelmetropole.com. *Vaporetto: 1, 5, 41, 42, 51, 52, or 82 to San Zaccaria, and then walk right. Rack rates: 500€–800€ ($800–$1,280) double. Rates include buffet breakfast. AE, DC, MC, V.*

Hotel San Cassiano Ca' Favretto
$$$ Santa Croce

This is your chance to stay in a gorgeous 14th-century *palazzo* on the Canal Grande without spending a fortune. Located across from the Ca' d'Oro and left of the Ca' Corner della Regina, this was a noble Venetian residence before being turned into a hotel after careful renovation. Guest rooms are spacious and bright, decorated with original tiled or wood floors, Venetian plaster on the walls, quality dark-wood or gilded period furniture with many antiques, some lovely carpets, and large windows. The best rooms face Canal Grande, others the smaller canal on the side or the courtyard. The hotel also has a beautiful terrace overlooking the canals.

See map p. 458. Calle della Rosa, 2232 Santa Croce. ☎ *041-524-1768. Fax: 041-721033.* www.sancassiano.it. *Vaporetto: 1 to San Stae, and then walk to the left of Campo San Stae, cross the canal, turn right on Fondamenta Rimpetto Mocenigo, turn* *left on Calle del Forner, cross the bridge, continue on Calle del Ravano, cross the bridge, and turn left on Calle della Rosa. Rack rates: 319€–439€ ($510–$702) double. Rates include breakfast. AE, V.*

Locanda ai Santi Apostoli
$$ Cannaregio

This small family-run hotel offers cozy accommodations and charming details. Set on the top floor of a 14th-century *palazzo* overlooking the Canal Grande, the guest rooms are quite large and individually decorated with a mix of modern furnishings and period reproductions, along with a few antiques. Bathrooms are small, but come with all the amenities. Two of the rooms have views of the canal.

See map p. 458. Strada Nuova, 4391a Cannaregio. ☎ *041-521-2612. Fax: 041-521-2611.* www.locandasantiapostoli.com. *Vaporetto: 1 to Ca' d'Oro, and then walk up Calle ca' d'Oro and turn right. Rack rates: 230€–330€ ($368–$528) double. Rates include buffet breakfast. AE, DC, MC, V.*

Venice's runner-up accommodations

Bauer Palladio

$$$$ Giudecca On quiet Giudecca Island and connected to San Marco by ultra-new and ecological electric/solar-powered shuttle launch, the newest of the Bauer family of hotels is a winner. The graceful renovation has enhanced the beauty of the original property, a residence for unmarried women designed by architect Andrea Palladio. Guest rooms are large, individually decorated in pastel colors, with elegant carpeting, fine brocade and fabrics, super-comfortable beds, and large bathrooms. *Giudecca 33.* ☎ *041-520-7022.* www.palladiohotelspa.com.

Hotel Falier

$ Santa Croce A great moderate choice, the Falier's rooms have been furnished with taste and care; they're decorated with lace curtains and bright bedspreads. *See map p. 458. Salizada S. Pantalon, 130 S. Croce.* ☎ *041-710882.* www.hotelfalier.com.

Locanda Novecento

$$ San Marco Only a few steps from St. Mark's and Accademia, this new family-run boutique hotel offers individual and attentive service. The décor of both the public spaces and the sumptuous guest rooms was inspired by the famous Spanish artist Mariano Fortuny, who worked and lived in Venice in the first half of the 20th century. The small garden — used for breakfast in good weather — is a delight. *Campo San Maurizio, Calle del Dose, 2694 San Marco.* ☎ *041-241-3765.* www.novecento.biz.

Luna Hotel Baglioni

$$$$ San Marco We love this hotel — at one of Venice's historic addresses — for its charm, the quality of its service, and its management skill in keeping up with modern standards. The hotel is housed in a 13th-century former convent and offers spacious and nicely appointed guest rooms; if a view and light are important to you, make sure you specify it in our reservation, because a number of rooms open onto airshafts and inner courtyards. The **restaurant** on the premises is quite good. The Internet rates can be more than 50 percent off. *See map p. 458. Calle di Ca'Vallaresso, San Marco 1243. Vaporetto: 1 to San Marco-Vallaresso.* ☎ *041-528-9840.* www.baglionihotels.com.

Palazzo Sant'Angelo

$$$$ **San Marco** The first hotel to open on Canal Grande in over a century, this addition to Venice luxury accommodations offers a perfect location, with its private entrance on Canal Grande and a *vaporetto* stop next door, in one of the few quieter corners of San Marco neighborhood. It offers gorgeous public spaces, a delightful courtyard garden, and sumptuous guest rooms. *See map p. 458. Ramo del Teatro, 3488 San Marco.* ☎ *041-241-1452.* www.palazzosantangelo.com.

Pensione La Calcina

$$ **Dorsoduro** Half the unfussy but luminous rooms at this three-star hotel overlook the sunny Zattere and Giudecca Canal toward architect Palladio's 16th-century Redentore. The outdoor floating terrace and the rooftop terrace are glorious places to begin or end any day. The apartments with small kitchens are excellent for families. *See map p. 458. Dorsoduro 780, on Zattere al Gesuati.* ☎ *041-520-6466.* www.lacalcina.com.

Dining in Venice

Venice is a tricky place to eat. Not because the local cuisine isn't good — it's delicious, especially if you like seafood — but because so many eateries in Venice are such tourist traps. When you find the right restaurant, though, it's heavenly: Fish and shellfish from the lagoon and the Adriatic served on rice, pasta, or *polenta* (cornmeal) are the staples of Venetian cuisine, and wine is an important part of the meal. Venice is small, and restaurants and *trattorie* are basically everywhere, but good ones are hard to find. Also, restaurants in Venice are rather expensive; all will add a *coperto* (cover) charge to your bill between 1.50€ and 5€ ($2.40–$8), and a 10 percent to 15 percent service charge.

There is no fishing on Sundays, so the fish market is closed on Mondays; the seafood you'll eat is from the Saturday before. On Mondays, have meat or a pizza instead.

Italy is famed for its wines, and the vineyards around Venice produce some great ones, including the white Soave and two reds, Bardolino and Valpolicella.

Venetian lunch on the go

Eating in Venice is very expensive, and your purse will welcome a little picnic now and then. You'll find many bars selling sandwiches, but you should consider making your own out of local specialties and freshly baked local bread. You'll find all the above in the many bakeries and grocery shops lining **Strada Nuova** in Cannaregio, together with some scrumptious sweets. Two other excellent places are **Via Garibaldi** in Castello — where you'll also find **Coop**, a supermarket with mainland prices — and around **Campo Rialto Nuovo** in San Polo, where you'll find the lively and colorful fish, produce, and flower markets. Another **Coop** supermarket is on Rio Terà Santi Apostoli (4612 Cannaregio), near Strada Nuova. Remember that Piazza San Marco is an open-air museum and, as such, eating on the premises is forbidden.

Ae Oche
$ Dorsoduro   PIZZA

This welcoming loftlike restaurant — housed in a former storage building — is the new branch of a local restaurant focusing on quality, speed of service, and sympathy (the logo goose is quite cute). The décor combines modernity with respect for ancient beauty, with beamed roof and Murano chandeliers, and the menu includes 100 different pizzas and a selection of beer on tap, plus an extensive salad selection and a few meat and pasta dishes. The original restaurant is at Campo San Giacomo dall'Orio, at Calle de le Oche (Santa Croce 1552; ☎ 041-524-1161); they also have one near the Santa Lucia train station (Rio Terra Lista Spagna, Cannaregio 158/A; ☎ 041-717879).

See map p. 458. Fondamenta Zattere, 1414 Dorsoduro ☎ *041-522-3812.* www. aeoche.it. *Reservations recommended. Vaporetto: 61 or 82 to San Basilio, and then walk right. Main courses: 8€–15€ ($13–$24); pizza 4.50€–9€ ($7.20–$14). AE, MC, V. Open: Daily noon to 3 p.m. and 6:30–11 p.m.*

A la Vecia Cavana
$$$ Cannaregio   VENETIAN

This justly renowned restaurant is housed in a picturesque 17th-century boathouse (*gondole* were repaired and stationed here), completely restored and decorated in bright colors. The cuisine is typically Venetian, with many "turf" options besides the "surf" ones. The *granchio al forno* (oven-roasted crab) is an excellent antipasto, as are the *baccalà mantecato* (creamed cod) and the *sarde in saôr* (savory sardines). Also very good are the *risotto al basilico con le capesante* (risotto with basil and scallops) and the *frittura mista* (fried calamari and small fish).

See map p. 458. Rio Terà Santi Apostoli, 4624 Cannaregio. ☎ *041-528-7106.* www. veciacavana.it. *Reservations recommended. Vaporetto: 1 to Ca' d'Oro, and then walk straight ahead to Strada Nuova, turn right, and bear left at Campo dei Apóstoli. Main courses: 13€–24€ ($21–$38). AE, DC, MC, V. Open: Tues–Sun noon to 2:30 p.m. and 7–10:30 p.m. Closed 2 weeks in July.*

Antico Martini
$$$$ San Marco VENETIAN/CREATIVE

This elegant restaurant on the site of an 18th-century cafe is one of the city's best and, as such, comes with a high price. Under gilded frames and chandeliers — and in the delightful terrace in the warmer weather — you can sample Venetian specialties (try the excellent *fegato alla veneziana* [veal liver with onions]), as well as other innovative dishes such as a wonderful *sformato di scampi e carciofi* (young artichokes and prawn torte). This gourmet spot is famous for its *involtini di salmone al caviale* (rolled salmon and caviar).

See map p. 458. Campo San Fantin, 1983 San Marco. ☎ *041-522-4121.* www.antico martini.com. *Reservations required. Vaporetto: 1 to Giglio, and then walk up Calle Gritti, turn right on Calle delle Ostreghe, continue into Calle Larga XXII Marzo, turn left on Calle delle Veste, and follow it to Campo San Fantin. Main courses: 25€–56€ ($40–$90). AE, DC, MC, V. Open: Daily noon to 2:30 p.m. and 7–11:30 p.m.*

Bar Pizzeria da Paolo
$ Castello PIZZA/VENETIAN

This local neighborhood hangout offers a good location across from the Arsenale, cozy dining rooms, and a pleasant décor. The pizza is good and you can get all the classics — *margherita, capricciosa,* and so on, plus a good selection of local dishes. If you dine outside, the small campo with the Arsenale and its canal in the background are especially quiet and picturesque at night.

See map p. 458. Campo Arsenale, 2389 Castello. ☎ *041-521-0660. Reservations not necessary. Vaporetto: 1, 41, or 42 to Arsenale, and then follow Calle dei Forni to its end, turn left on Calle di Pegola, and turn right into Campo Arsenale. Main courses: 8€–15€ ($13–$24). MC, V. Open: Tues–Sat noon to 3 p.m.; Mon–Sat 6–11 p.m.*

Osteria ai 4 Feri
$ Dorsoduro VENETIAN

This unassuming *osteria* is one of the traditional charming restaurants that are disappearing from Venice. It's a real local hangout where you'll eat simple food in an old-fashioned décor. The menu includes many traditional dishes, including the excellent *spaghetti alle vongole* (spaghetti with clams) and grilled fish sold by the weight — a tasty fare.

See map p. 458. Calle Lunga San Barnaba, 2754 Dorsoduro. ☎ *041-520-6978. Reservations recommended in the evening. Vaporetto: 1 to Ca' Rezzonico, and then follow Calle Traghetto and cross Campo San Barnaba. Main courses: 9€–17€ ($14–$27). MC, V. Open: Mon–Sat 12:30–3 p.m. and 7:30–11 p.m.*

Osteria da Fiore
$$$$ San Polo VENETIAN/SEAFOOD

One of the most exclusive restaurants in Venice, it's also the best. The menu is based on seafood, and the extremely well-prepared dishes are made with only the freshest ingredients and local fish, and are carefully served in the subdued elegance of the two dining rooms. Excellent are the *spaghetti al cartoccio* (cooked in a pouch), the *scampi al limone con sedano e pomodoro* (prawns with a lemon, tomato, and celery sauce), and the many seasonal seafood *antipasti*.

See map p. 458. Calle del Scaleter, 2202/A San Polo. ☎ 041-721308. Reservations required. Vaporetto: 1 or 82 to San Tomà, and then walk straight ahead to Campo San Tomà, continue straight on Calle larga Prima toward Santa Maria dei Frari and the Scuola di San Rocco, and 1 block before the Scuola and behind the Frari turn right on Calle del Scaleter. Main courses: 25€–43€ ($40–$69). AE, DC, MC, V. Open: Tues–Sat 12:30–2:30 p.m. and 7:30–10 p.m. Closed Dec 25–Jan 15 and 10 days around Aug 15.

Trattoria alla Madonna
$ San Polo   VENETIAN/SEAFOOD

Seafood and more seafood! In this local trattoria, celebrated by locals and tourists alike, you find all the bounty the Adriatic has to offer — including some existing only in the Venetian lagoon — masterfully prepared according to tradition. You'll find the market offerings grilled, roasted, fried, or served with pasta, risotto, or polenta. The moderate prices attract crowds, so be prepared for a long wait.

See map p. 458. Calle della Madonna, 594 San Polo. ☎ 041-522-3824. Reservations accepted only for large parties. Vaporetto: 1, 4, or 82 to Rialto, and then cross the bridge, turn left on Riva del Vin along the Canal Grande, and turn right onto Calle della Madonna. Main courses: 12€–18€ ($19–$29). AE, MC, V. Open: Thurs–Tues noon to 3 p.m. and 7:15–10 p.m. Closed Dec 24–Jan and 1 week around Aug 15.

Trattoria Tre Spiedi
$$ Cannaregio   VENETIAN

This friendly trattoria is a favorite with local families; it's also a convenient choice in the touristy area near Ponte di Rialto. The traditional

---

Taking a sweet break

Venetians definitely have a sweet tooth and make delicious pastries; you can sample several typical delights at **Pasticceria Tonolo**, San Pantalon, 3764 Dorsoduro (*Vaporetto:* San Tomà), or **Pasticceria Marchini**, Spadaria, 2769 San Marco (☎ 041-522-9109). Of course, Venice has many, many other pastry shops. Don't be afraid to stop and sample — you'll rarely find a bad one. Good *gelato* (ice cream) is more difficult to find: Industrial and pretend-homemade ice cream is sold at every corner, but it's a pale imitation of what you can have in Rome, Naples, or heavenly Sicily. One of the best places for gelato is the hole-in-the-wall **Boutique del Gelato**, Salizzada San Lio, 5727 Castello (☎ 041-522-3283), where everything is made fresh on the premises. Another good address is **Gelateria Paolin**, Campo Stefano Morosini (☎ 041-522-5576), Venice's oldest, dating from the 1930s.

cuisine features a lot of fresh fish. The many spaghetti *primi* are excellent; for *secondo*, try the veal liver sautéed with onions or the eel stew, both served with polenta.

See map p. 458. Salizada San Canciano, 5906 Cannaregio. ☎ *041-520-8035. Reservations not accepted. Vaporetto: 1, 4, or 82 to Rialto, and then walk up and turn left on Salizada S. Giovanni Grisostomo, cross the bridge, continue straight, and turn right on Salizada San Canciano. Main courses: 11€–18€ ($18–$29). AE, MC, V. Open: Tues–Sat 9 a.m.–2:45 p.m. and 6–9:45 p.m.; Sun 12:30–3:30 p.m.*

Vecio Fritolin
$$$ Santa Croce   CREATIVE VENETIAN/SEAFOOD

Hidden away in the heart of Santa Croce, this is one of the best addresses in Venice. We love this restaurant, where you can taste authentic food away from the tourist crowds. The small menu offers a few well-balanced choices, with a strong focus on seafood, and changes often. We loved the *frittura* (deep-fried fish), one of the best we ever had, as well as the perfect *sarde in saôr* (bluefish in a typical Venetian preparation with onions). The desserts are superb.

See map p. 458. Calle della Regina, 2262 Santa Croce. ☎ *041-522-2881.* www.vecio fritolin.it. *Reservations recommended. Vaporetto: 1 to S. Stae, and then, following signs for Rialto, cross the bridge to your left, turn right, and immediately turn left to the next bridge, cross and turn right, take the first left, and keep straight across a bridge and beyond, and then turn right and again right to the restaurant. Main courses: 21€–28€ ($34–$45). AE, DC, MC, V. Open: Tues–Sun noon to 2:30 p.m. and 7–10:30 p.m.*

Vini da Gigio
$$ Cannaregio   VENETIAN/WINE BAR

The restaurant attached to this traditional *enoteca* (wine bar) — still one of the best in town — has become a favorite for both the excellent service and the tasty food. The menu is based on traditional fare: We loved the pasta with squid and the grilled eel. Leave room for the homemade desserts.

See map p. 458. Fondamenta della Chiesa, 3628a Cannaregio. ☎ *041-528-5140.* www.vinidagigio.com. *Reservations recommended. Vaporetto: 1 to Ca d'Oro, and then walk up to Strada Nova and turn left, pass the bridge, and turn right. Main courses: 12€–18€ ($19–$29). DC, MC, V. Open: Wed–Sun 12:15–2:30 p.m. and 7:15–10:30 p.m. Closed 3 weeks Jan–Feb.*

Exploring Venice

To avoid the long lines at **Palazzo Ducale** and **Accademia Galleries,** purchase the appropriate pass, card, or cumulative ticket (see the next paragraph) at one of the less sought-after attractions (the best is Ca' Pesaro). Buying a pass or card in advance will also allow you to avoid the lines at the **Frari Basilica** (Santa Maria Gloriosa dei Frari).

The **Venice Card** (☎ 041-2424; www.venicecard.it) is a good deal, and though it's best to buy it online before hitting Venice (because you get an extra discount), it's also available for sale all over town: at the airport, Piazzale Roma, and train station, as well as at all the tourist information offices and most of the Hellovenezia ticket booths (*vaporetto* and public transportation). The basic **three-day transportation pass** costs 38€ ($61) at a ticket booth and 34€ ($54) online; the **three-day culture and transport pass** is 59€ ($94) at the ticket booth and 47€ ($75) online. Both passes get you a welcome kit including a good map, and they give you access to all public transportation, use of the public bathrooms, and a bunch of discounts; the culture card also includes a Museum Pass and a Chorus Card (see the following list). For an additional fee, you can include the airport shuttle boat **Alilaguna.**

If you're between the ages of 14 and 29, once you're in Venice you can purchase the **Rolling Venice Card,** which gives you substantial discounts on hotels, restaurants, museums, public transportation (see earlier in this chapter), and shops. You can get the card for 4€ ($6.40) by presenting a photo ID at one of the tourist information points in Venice or at one of the Hellovenezia ticket booths. You'll get a kit with a map of Venice charting the location of all the participating hotels, restaurants, clubs, and shops, as well as a special guidebook with interesting facts and smart itineraries.

Alternatively, here are the other deals:

- ✔ **Museum Pass:** Admission to each of the 12 Venice civic museums — Palazzo Ducale, Correr Museum, Libreria Marciana, Ca' Rezzonico, Clock Tower, Palazzo Mocenigo, Carlo Goldoni's house, Ca' Pesaro, Fortuny Museum, Natural History Museum (with Planetarium), Murano Glass Museum, and Burano Lace Museum — for 18€ ($29) (with Rolling Venice Card only 12€/$19). Children 4 and under are free. The pass is valid for six months, and you can purchase it at each of the participating museums.

- ✔ **Family ticket:** If you're a family group of two adults and at least two children, at all Venice civic museums (see the preceding bullet), you pay one regular admission and get reduced admission for all the others in your group. It works for the Museum Pass (you'll pay only 12€/$19) as well as for single admissions.

- ✔ **Chorus Card** (☎ 041-274-0462; www.chorusvenezia.org): Access to 16 churches in Venice — including Frari Basilica (see "Venice's top attractions," later in this chapter) — for 9€ ($14). A family version, for two adults and two children 11 to 18, goes for 18€ ($29). The pass is valid for one year and is for sale at all participating churches (avoid buying the pass at Frari, because lines there are always long) and at the **Venice Pavilion** tourist office.

- ✔ **Combination ticket:** A ticket for the Ca' d'Oro, Museo Orientale in Ca' Pesaro, and Accademia Galleries is available for 11€ ($18); you can purchase it at the ticket booth of any of the three museums.

As everywhere else in Italy, bare shoulders, halter tops, tank tops, and shorts or skirts above the knee will lead to your being turned away at churches' entrances — no kidding, and no matter your age or sex.

Venice's top attractions

Frari Basilica (Santa Maria Gloriosa dei Frari)
San Polo

This church is a magnificent example of the Venetian Gothic, built in the first half of the 14th century and enlarged in the 15th. Beside it is the original 14th-century **bell tower.** Its architecture singles out not only this church, but also the exquisite artworks it contains, none more so than Titian's *Pala Pesaro (Pesaro altarpiece)* and his *Assumption* over the main altar, a glorious composition that combines billowing forms with exquisite colors and a feeling of serenity. Other stars are Giovanni Bellini's triptych *Virgin and Child with Four Saints* and Donatello's *St. John the Baptist,* a rare sculpture in wood. Be sure to visit the original wooden choir, where monks participated in Mass — this is the only extant choir of its kind in Venice. The triangular marble monument dedicated to sculptor Antonio Canova was actually designed by Canova to be a monument to Titian (Canova's followers appropriated the design for their master after he died in 1822). A bit of trivia: If you look carefully at the walls near the monument, you see an **Austrian bomb** that was dropped on the church during World War I but miraculously failed to explode.

See map p. 458. Campo dei Frari. ☎ *041-522-2637.* www.basilicadeifrari.it. *Vaporetto: 1 or 82 to San Tomà, and then walk up to Calle Campaniel, turn right, turn left on Campo San Tomà, continue onto Calle larga Prima, and turn right. Admission: 3€ ($4.80). Admission includes audio guide. Open: Mon–Sat 9 a.m.–6 p.m.; Sun 1– 6 p.m. Closed Jan 1, Easter, Aug 15, and Dec 25.*

Gallerie dell'Accademia
Dorsoduro

If you have time for only one museum in Venice, take in the Accademia. Set aside a good 90 minutes to three hours to peruse the vast collections of masterpieces by Venice's color-loving artists. The museum covers the biggies in Venetian painting, from Paolo Veneziano's 14th-century *Coronation of the Virgin* altarpiece, and Giorgione's strange *The Tempest,* to Giovanni Bellini's numerous versions of *Madonna and Child,* and Paolo Veronese's *Last Supper,* retitled *Feast in the House of Levi* after the puritanical leaders of the Inquisition threatened the master with charges of blasphemy for depicting the holy meal as a drunken banquet.

See map p. 458. Campo della Carità, at the foot of the Accademia Bridge. ☎ *041-522-2247.* www.gallerieaccademia.org. *Vaporetto: 1 or 82 to Accademia. Admission: 6.50€ ($10). Open: Mon 8:15 a.m.–2 p.m.; Tues–Sun 8:15 a.m.–7:15 p.m.; ticket booth closes 45 minutes earlier. Closed Jan 1, May 1, and Dec 25.*

Palazzo Ducale and Bridge of Sighs
San Marco

Shimmering after a lengthy restoration, the pink-and-white facade of Venice's most beautiful *palazzo* has been returned to view. Pause to take in the delicate decorations, expressive carvings, and splendid bas-reliefs of its columns before entering. Once the private home of the doges (the *doge* was leader of the republic, elected for life), as well as the seat of the government and the court of law, the pink-and-white marble Palazzo Ducale was the Republic's heart. In Gothic-Renaissance style, it was begun in 1173, integrating the walls and towers of the previously existing A.D. 810 castle. The *palazzo* was enlarged in 1340 with the addition of the new wing housing the **Great Council Room,** a marvel of architecture for the size of the unsupported ceilings. Tintoretto's *Paradise* decorates that ceiling; said to be the largest oil painting in the world, it is not Tintoretto's best, however. On the left side of the courtyard is the **Staircase of the Giants,** guarded by two giant stone figures and a Renaissance masterpiece. At the top of these steps, you enter the loggia, from which departs the famous **Scala d'Oro** (Golden Staircase), leading to the **doge's apartments** and the **government chambers.** These were splendidly decorated by the major artists of the 16th century, including **Titian, Tintoretto, Veronese,** and **Tiepolo.** A little-known part of the palace's collection is a group of paintings bequeathed by a bishop, including interesting works by **Hieronymus Bosch.**

From the *palazzo,* continue your visit on the famous **Bridge of Sighs,** which didn't get its name from the lovers who met under it. The bridge was built in the 17th century to connect the *palazzo* — and the Courts of Justice — to the prisons, and those condemned to death passed over this bridge (supposedly sighing heavily) both on their way into the prison and eventually on their way out to be executed in Piazzetta San Marco. The two red columns on the facade of Palazzo Ducale mark the place where the death sentences were read out. You can visit both the 16th-century **New Prisons,** built when the palace's limited facilities became insufficient, and the **Old Prisons,** also called *pozzi,* literally "wells" but "pits" would be a better translation, as they were at and below the ground level, which, in Venice, means that they're flooded at high tide.

The Palazzo Ducale is huge, especially when you count the labyrinthine prison next door, through which you can wander (and shudder at the medieval conditions — the place was used into the 1920s). You can easily spend four hours inside, especially if you take one of the special tours.

See map p. 458. Piazza San Marco; the entrance to the palace is from the Porta del Frumento on the water side. ☎ *041-271-5911. Vaporetto: 1 or 82 to San Marco. Admission: Nov–Mar 12€ ($19), 6.50€ ($10) with Rolling Venice Card (ticket includes Correr Museum, Libreria Marciana, and National Archeological Museum); Apr–Oct 13€ ($21), 7.50€ ($12) with Rolling Venice Card (ticket includes Correr Museum, Libreria Marciana, National Archeological Museum, and one of the other Civic Museums of the Museum Pass). Open: Apr–Oct daily 9 a.m.–7 p.m.; Nov–Mar daily 9 a.m.–5 p.m.; ticket booth closes 1 hour earlier. Closed Jan 1 and Dec 25.*

Peggy Guggenheim Collection
Dorsoduro

Housed in the ground floor of a 1749 *palazzo* that was never completed, at the elegant Palazzo Venier dei Leoni opening on Canal Grande, this museum holds one of Italy's most important collections of avant-garde art. American expatriate collector Peggy Guggenheim lived here for 30 years; after her death in 1979, the building and collection became the property of New York's Guggenheim Foundation. Peggy G.'s protégés included Jackson Pollock, represented by ten paintings, and Max Ernst, whom she married. From dada and surrealism to expressionism and abstract expressionism, the collection is rich and diverse, with works by Klee, Magritte, Mondrian, De Chirico, Dalí, Kandinsky, Picasso, and others. The sculpture garden includes works by Giacometti.

See map p. 458. Calle San Cristoforo 701. ☎ *041-240-5411.* www.guggenheim-venice.it. *Vaporetto: 1 or 82 to Accademia, and then walk left past the Accademia, turn right on Rio Terà A. Foscarini, turn left on Calle Nuova Sant'Agnese, continue on Piscina Former, cross the bridge, continue on Calle della Chiesa and then Fondamenta Venier along the small canal, and turn left on Calle San Cristoforo. Admission: 10€ ($16). Open: Wed–Mon 10 a.m.–6 p.m. Closed Dec 25.*

Ponte di Rialto
San Marco/San Polo

The original wooden bridge here started rotting away, and the citizens of Venice couldn't decide what to do. Finally, in 1588, they decided to replace it with the current stone-and-brick, red-and-white marvel. The bridge opens onto the Rialto district in San Polo, Venice's main merchant area since the Middle Ages. Ships arrived here after stopping at the *dogana* (customhouse) at the tip of Dorsoduro and discharged their merchandise in the large warehouses here. Goods were then sold at the general market surrounding the warehouses. The fish and produce wholesale markets were moved to the new merchant and marine terminal across Santa Lucia rail station only in 1998, but the retail markets have survived with their picturesque flavor. Lined with shops and busy with crowds of tourists, it is difficult to truly enjoy this splendid bridge's architecture during the day: For the best view, try early in the morning or late in the evening, when shops are closed.

See map p. 458. Across the Canal Grande, between Riva del Vin and Riva del Carbon. Vaporetto: 1 or 82 to Rialto.

Piazza San Marco
San Marco

Maybe the world's most famous square, this uniquely beautiful space was created in the 11th century. Lined on one side by St. Mark's Basilica (see the following listing) and on the three others by the porticos and loggias of the **Procuratie** buildings, it was and is the heart of Venice, seat of ceremonies, celebrations, and once also tournaments. The buildings on the

Behave or be fined!

The whole historic district of Venice is considered a monument, so strict laws apply. It's forbidden to sit on a public walkway (sidewalk, bridge, piazza, and so on); have a picnic (sitting on a small wall, for example); swim in the canals; litter; use bikes or any other kind of transportation (including scooters and rollerblades); undress in public; and walk around underdressed (with no shirt or with beachwear). The fine is 50€ ($80) for any violation.

north side are the **Procuratie Vecchie,** built in the Renaissance as offices for the city's magistracy. Facing the piazza to the south are the **Procuratie Nuove,** built to house more offices and, after the fall of the Venetian Republic at the hands of Napoleon, turned into the Royal Palace. The wing closing the piazza to the west was added by Napoleon, after demolishing the church that was there. This last building houses today the **Correr Museum** (☎ 041-240-5211; www.museiciviciveneziani.it), with an interesting collection that includes some remarkable artworks, such as Canova's bas-reliefs; Cosmé Tura's *Pietà* from 1460 — a fanciful and in some ways surreal painting with a red Golgotha in the background — as well as the famous painting by Carpaccio *Two Venetian Ladies* (familiarly called *The Courtesans,* but now known to be a pair of respectable Venetian ladies, a fragment from a larger painting).

To the north of the piazza, adjacent to St. Mark's Basilica, is the **Torre dell'Orologio,** a clock tower built in 1496. The clock has two huge quadrants — one indicating phases of the moon and zodiac, the other the time with a complicated mechanism propelling wooden statues of the Magi (the three kings bringing offerings to Jesus) guided by an angel — and, above, two bronze Moors striking a bell on the hour. After a lengthy restoration, the tower is open to visitors (not recommended if you have a heart condition or are claustrophobic, pregnant, or otherwise movement-impaired, because the climb is steep and narrow) for a guided tour by reservation only. Tickets are 12€ ($19) or 7€ ($11) if you already have the Venice Card, Museum Pass, or Palazzo Ducale ticket.

To the south, **St. Mark's Bell Tower** (☎ 041-522-4064) dominates the piazza. Used as a lighthouse by approaching boats, this tall belfry — 97m (324 ft.) high — was originally built in the ninth century and was added to in the centuries that followed. It suddenly collapsed in 1902 but was faithfully — and solidly — rebuilt using much of the same materials. From atop, you can admire a 360-degree panorama of the city and the famous piazza below — and you can do so without climbing hundreds of steps: There's an elevator!

See map p. 458. Off Riva degli Schiavoni. Vaporetto: 1 or 82 to San Marco–Vallaresso. Admission: Correr Museum same as Palazzo Ducale (see listing earlier in this chapter); St. Mark's bell tower 6€ ($9.60). Open: Correr Museum same as Palazzo Ducale; St. Mark's Bell Tower Oct–Nov and Apr–June daily 9 a.m.–7 p.m., Nov–Apr daily 9:30 a.m.–3:45 p.m., July–Sept 9 a.m.–9 p.m.

St. Mark's Basilica
San Marco

The symbol of Venice, it was built in A.D. 829 to house the remains of San Marco, one of the four evangelists, martyred by the Turks in Alexandria of Egypt, and the city's patron saint. The original church was rebuilt after it burned down in 932, and again in 1063, taking its present shape. Five domes — originally gilded — top the five portals, while an elegant **loggia** opens in between: This is where the *doge* presided over the public functions held in the square; multilingual audio boxes here give a brief description of the sites you can see around the piazza. The rooms above the loggia contain the **Museo Marciano,** which holds the original horses of the *Triumphal Quadriga:* the famous gilded bronze horses (the ones outside gracing the loggia are copies) brought back from Constantinople in 1204 after the Fourth Crusade. Experts have estimated that the horses are Greek sculptures from the fourth century B.C. You can access the loggia, as well as the gallery and the museum from a long and steep flight of stone steps inside the basilica entrance on the right.

Due to the crowds, the visit to the basilica is limited to ten minutes (Pala d'Oro, Treasury, and Museum are separate); you can make a free reservation for your time slot at least 48 hours in advance at www.alata.it.

From April through October, Monday through Saturday, the parish offers free guided tours of the basilica, for which you need to make reservations in advance (at www.veneziaubc.org or ☎ 041-241-3817).

See map p. 458. Piazza San Marco. ☎ *041-522-5205.* www.veneziaubc.org. *Vaporetto: 1 or 82 to San Marco–Vallaresso. Admission: Basilica free; Pala d'Oro 1.50€ ($2.40); Treasury 2€ ($3.20); Museum 3€ ($4.80). Open: Basilica Mon–Sat 9:45 a.m.–5 p.m., Sun and religious holidays Nov–Mar 2–4 p.m., Apr–Oct 2–5 p.m.; Museum daily 9:45 a.m.–4:45 p.m.; Pala d'Oro and Treasury Nov–Mar Mon–Sat 9:45 a.m.– 4 p.m., Sun and religious holidays 2–4 p.m., Apr–Oct Mon–Sat 9:45 a.m.–5 p.m., Sun and religious holidays 2–5 p.m.*

Scuola Grande di San Rocco
San Polo

San Rocco is Jacopo Tintoretto's Sistine Chapel. From 1564 to 1587, Tintoretto, a brother of the school, decorated the **Sala dell'Albergo,** the **lower hall,** and the **upper hall** with a series of incredibly beautiful paintings depicting biblical and Christian subjects. The upper hall ceiling alone has 21 paintings (mirrors are available so that you don't have to strain your neck). The most impressive is his *Crucifixion,* a painting of almost overpowering emotion and incredible detail (the tools used to make the cross are strewn in the foreground); the painter shows the moment when one of the two thieves' crosses is raised. The upper hall is also decorated with a fascinating collection of **wood sculptures** carved by Francesco Pianta in the 17th century; some depict artisans and the tools of their trade with an amazing realism. Tintoretto was not the only artist who decorated this scuola: You'll see also works by Bellini, Titian, and Tiepolo.

See map p. 458. Campo San Rocco 3058. ☎ *041-523-4864.* www.scuolagrandesan rocco.it. *Vaporetto: 1 or 82 to San Tomà, and then walk up to Calle Campaniel, turn right, turn left on Campo San Tomà, continue onto Calle Larga Prima and Salizzada San Rocco, and turn left. Admission: 7€ ($11), free for children 17 and under. Open: Apr–Oct daily 9 a.m.–5:30 p.m.; Nov–Mar daily 10 a.m.–5 p.m. Closed Jan 1, Easter, and Dec 25.*

More cool things to see and do

✔ Yes, we know, gondolas are for, ahem, *tourists* . . . but really, what can be more romantic than being rowed in a gondola along off-the-beaten-path canals? Often dismissed as a tourist trap, a gondola ride is the best way to admire the city's architecture and experience Venice's unique serenity. It is a luxury that affords a glimpse into a little known universe: the Venetian sailors and fishermen community, people who make their living on the lagoon as they did centuries ago and are the keepers of many Venetian traditions. The tourist office organizes gondola tours, saving you the hassle of negotiating itinerary and prices with the gondola owner, but you can also organize your own by going to one of the many gondola stands in town.

The hiring of a gondola adheres to strict rules established by the local municipality to prevent abuses; the official rate (set by Ente Gondola; ☎ 041-528-5075; www.gondolavenezia.it) is 80€ ($128) for 40 minutes and a maximum of six people in the daytime and of 100€ ($160) for nighttime (7 p.m.–8 a.m.). Make sure you use only authorized gondolas from one of the official gondola stations, and establish the price, itinerary, and time in advance, before you get in the boat, to avoid unpleasant surprises. You'll find gondola stations at San Marco (☎ **041-520-0685**); San Tomà (☎ **041-520-5275**); Rialto (Riva del Carbon; ☎ **041-522-4904**); Santa Maria del Giglio (☎ **041-522-2073**); Campo San Moisé, off Calle Larga 22 Marzo (☎ **041-523-1837**); and Riva Schiavoni (across from Danieli; ☎ **041-522-2254**).

You may want to take your tour at high tide — to be more level with the pavement, instead of the interesting but rather scummy canal sidewalls. You'll also want to avoid the Canal Grande, except maybe in the wee hours: It is so large and busy that it gets very noisy and choppy and, therefore, can be quite unpleasant in a small boat.

✔ The word *ghetto* has been used to name the neighborhood once set apart for Jews in European cities, but the **Ghetto Novo** (Venetian Ghetto) was Europe's first. It was established in 1516 on a small island accessible by only one bridge that was closed at night (you can still see the grooves in the marble *sottoportico* [portico interior] where the iron bars fitted). In 1541, when groups of Jews from Germany, Poland, Spain, and Portugal fled to Venice, the government allowed the community to expand into the **Ghetto Vecchio** (Old Ghetto), the area between the Ghetto Novo and the Rio di Cannaregio, which has the two largest places of worship — the

Venezia and the gondola

This unique boat was developed to fit the local conditions and is a marvel of engineering: 11 meters (38 feet) long, it weighs up to 600kg (1,320 pounds), yet it is easily maneuvered by one person with only one oar. It is flat enough to float in a few inches of water. Its asymmetrical and curved design allows it to go straight under the push of one oar, and its curve is calculated based on the oarsman weight, so each gondola is built for its owner! Designed to transport people, it's decorated with elegance — gilded edgings, velvet and brocade over comfortable cushions, delicate carvings — while simpler boats were used for cargo. The gondola is traditionally built in wood, using eight different essences for the 280 parts that make it. No metal nails are used for its assembly and the only two pieces of iron are the characteristic *ferro,* decorating the bow — originally a balancing weight for the oarsman — and the *risso,* decorating the stern.

Levantine and Spanish synagogues (**Scola Levantina** and **Scola Spagnola**). To accommodate the growing population, buildings were made taller and taller, so that this area has some of the tallest buildings in Venice. The **Jewish Museum,** Museo Ebraico, Campo del Ghetto Novo, 2902/b Cannaregio (☎ 041-715359; www.museo ebraico.it; *Vaporetto:* 1 or 82 to San Marcuola; open Oct–May Sun–Fri 10 a.m.–6 p.m., June–Sept Sun–Fri 10 a.m.–7 p.m.; closed Jan 1, May 1, Dec 25, and Jewish holidays) offers guided tours of the synagogues in Italian or English every hour beginning at 10:30 a.m. on opening days. Admission is 3€ ($4.80) for the museum only, or 8.50€ ($14) with guided tour.

A visit to Venice isn't complete without a trip to the **lagoon. Murano** (*Vaporetto:* 41 or 42) is the closest island — actually a cluster of islands — and the largest. It feels like a small — and much quieter — replica of Venice (down to its main canal meandering across it) and is the island of the glassmakers. The industry that was created here centuries ago is still very active and as famous as ever for the unique quality of its artistic glasswork (some of the works allow you to sit and watch glass being blown, most only mornings). You'll find many shops selling glass of all kinds — from cheap trinkets and souvenirs to million-dollar chandeliers. At the **Glass Museum,** Fondamenta Giustinian (☎ 041-739586), you can see a number of splendid antique masterpieces. Admission is 5.50€ ($8.80), and the museum is open Thursday through Tuesday April through October 10 a.m. to 6 p.m., November through March 10 a.m. to 4:30 p.m. (ticket booth closes 30 minutes earlier). If you'd like to see more of the lagoon, head for **Burano,** the farthest of the islands and a picturesque fishing and — once upon the time — lace-making community. It's still the seat of the **Lace School/Museum,** Piazza Baldassarre Galuppi 187 (☎ 041-730034), a world-renowned center, and the repository of ancient and precious techniques and skills. Admission is 4€ ($6.40); the museum is open Wednesday through Monday April through October 10 a.m. to 5 p.m., November through March 10 a.m. to 4 p.m. Both museums are closed January 1, May 1, and December 25.

✔ **Shopping** for fine glass, lace, and Carnevale masks is a must in Venice, but be aware of quality: Many items are machine-produced elsewhere — sometimes Eastern Europe or Taiwan — even though they're presented as handmade. Your best guide is not to worry about pedigree and simply purchase things you like. However, if you're looking for the real deal or you're buying to build a formal collection, resign yourself to the fact that prices for quality items are high. For glass, visit **Venini,** Piazzetta dei Leoncini, just to the left of St. Mark's Basilica, 314 San Marco (☎ **041-522-4045**), or **Pauly & Co,** Palazzo Trevisan Cappello, Ponte dei Consorzi 4391/A San Marco, off Calle Larga San Marco (☎ **041-520-9899**), Piazza San Marco 73 (☎ **041-523-5484**), Piazza San Marco 77 (☎ **041-277-0279**), and Piazza San Marco 316 (☎ **041-523-5575**). For lace, go to **Jesurum,** Mercerie del Capitello, 4857 San Marco (☎ **041-520-6177**), or **Martinuzzi,** Piazza San Marco, 67/A San Marco (☎ **041-522-5068**). For masks, visit the **Laboratorio Artigiano Maschere,** Barbaria delle Tole, 6657 Castello (☎ **041-522310**), or **Mondonovo,** Rio Terà Canal, 3063 Dorsoduro (☎ **041-528-7344**).

Guided tours

The best traditional tours are offered by **American Express,** Salizzada San Moisè, 1471 San Marco (☎ **041-520-0844;** *Vaporetto:* 1 or 82 to San Marco–Vallaresso). A guide walks you around the sights and keeps you from getting lost for about 35€ ($56) for a two-hour tour.

We also love the special tours organized by the **Venice tourist office** (see "Fast Facts: Venice" at the end of this chapter for contact details), including such unusual offerings as a 20-minute helicopter tour for 220€ ($352) or an evening tour of the neighborhoods of Castello and Cannaregio to the discovery of Venetian legends and dark stories. Their guided tour of Canal Grande for 30€ ($48) is excellent (daily at 11:30 a.m. and 4:30 p.m.), but they require a minimum of four people.

Taking care of business

Standard business hours for shops in Venice are Monday through Saturday from 9 a.m. to 12:30 p.m. and 3:30 or 4 to 7:30 p.m.; shops close Monday mornings in summer and Saturday afternoons in winter. Most grocers close Wednesday afternoons year-round.

Suggested itineraries

Time in Venice always seems to fly. Here are a few suggestions on how to schedule your visits.

If you have one day

If you have only one day in Venice, you definitely want to make the most of it with an early start. Begin your day on **Piazza San Marco** with a visit to the **basilica,** including the climb to the **loggia** upstairs, where the light is at its most beautiful in the morning. You should then have a little time left for the **Doge's Palace.** Have a *caffè* or *cappuccino* at the terrace of one of the two historic cafes — **Caffè Florian** and **Caffè Quadri** — on the piazza: expensive, but oh so romantic. After, have a look at the beautiful Murano glass — and maybe even buy some — in **Venini** and **Pauly & Co.** Then walk toward the Accademia, taking the footbridge over the Canal Grande and having lunch in the lively area nearby at **Osteria da Fiore** or just a snack — for a sweet one, the **Pasticceria Tonolo** is wonderful. After lunch, visit the **Gallerie dell'Accademia** for a tour of several hundred years of Venetian art. Have a Venetian *aperitivo* — a *cicchetto* (a glass of dry wine accompanied by some savory tidbits) — in one of the small bars near the Accademia, or across the Canal Grande at the **Antico Martini.** Treat yourself for dinner at **Met** of the Hotel Metropole. After dinner, take a magical **gondola** ride if you want or settle for a slow ride down **Canal Grande** on *vaporetto* line no. 1 to take in its magical atmosphere, the glorious facades of the *palazzi* lining it, and the romantic **Ponte di Rialto** as you pass under it.

If you have two days

On **Day 1,** start as in the itinerary in the preceding section, but dedicate more time to **St. Mark's Basilica.** In the afternoon, take a tour of the **Palazzo Ducale** and the **Bridge of Sighs.** After your visits, head to **Antico Martini** for a well-deserved *aperitivo* and maybe dinner. Afterward, stroll to the **Ponte di Rialto.**

On **Day 2,** dedicate your morning to the **Gallerie dell'Accademia.** Have lunch at **Osteria da Fiore** and, after lunch, visit the **Santa Maria Gloriosa dei Frari** and the **Scuola Grande di San Rocco.** Follow the dinner and after-dinner recommendations in the preceding "If you have one day" itinerary.

If you have three days

On **Days 1 and 2,** follow the two-day itinerary in the preceding section. Dedicate **Day 3** to the lagoon, visiting first **Murano,** with its **Glass Museum** and the showrooms of the most famous glassmakers, and then **Burano,** with its **Lace Museum.** End the day visiting Venice's **Ghetto,** or just enjoy wandering the streets and shopping.

Traveling beyond Venice

For a change of pace, consider leaving Venice for a day in search of quieter (and less touristy) pleasures. A short train ride will lead you to **Padova,** a college town with stunning architecture and art galore; a slightly longer one to **Milan,** Italy's capital of fashion and shopping, which is also hiding some wonderful art.

Padova: Outstanding art and architecture

From its canals to its churches — including the **Cappella degli Scrovegni,** with Giotto's frescoes so breathtaking that they dwarf the other worthy attractions in town — Padova will not disappoint. You can easily see the highlights in one day, but spending the night will allow you to fully enjoy the town.

Getting there

Padova is only 30 minutes from Venice, with trains running as frequently as every few minutes during rush hours; the fare is about 4€ ($6.40).

The **tourist office** (☎ 049-875-2077; www.padovanet.it) is at the train station, as well as at Galleria Pedrocchi, off Piazza Cavour (☎ 049-876-7927; open Mon–Sat 9 a.m.–1:30 p.m. and 3–7 p.m.).

Seeing the sights

The **Padova Card** (☎ 049-876-7927; www.padovacard.it) is an excellent deal, granting one adult (and one child under 14) free public transportation, admission to the 12 major attractions in town (except the 1€/$1.60 reservation fee for the Scrovegni Chapel), and assorted discounts. It's available in several versions: the 48-hour card costs 15€ ($24), while the 72-hour card costs 20€ ($32); they're available from the tourist information desks, some hotels, and the Scrovegni Chapel (purchase online with reservation).

Walking distance from the rail station, or a short bus ride away, the **Cappella degli Scrovegni** (Arena Chapel), Piazza Eremitani 8 (☎ 049-201-0020; www.cappelladegliscrovegni.it), which Giotto, a master of emotion and artistic technique, adorned with gorgeous frescoes from 1303 to 1306, is the key attraction in town. Admission is 11€ ($18); free with Padova Card; children 5 and under are free. Mandatory reservations fees cost 1€ ($1.60) per person. It's open daily 9 a.m. to 7 p.m. (closed Jan 1, Dec 25, and Dec 26).

The chapel is accessible from the courtyard of the **Musei Civici di Eremitani** (☎ 049-820-4550), a museum housing an archaeological collection on the ground floor, a Giotto *Crucifix,* and minor works by major 14th-century Venetian painters (including Giorgione, Jacopo Bellini, Veronese, and Tintoretto).

Padova's other great sight is the eastern-looking **Basilica di Sant'Antonio,** Piazza del Santo 11 (☎ 049-878-9722). Admission is free, and the basilica is open daily 6:20 a.m. to 7:45 p.m. in summer, 6:20 a.m. to 7 p.m. in winter. Outside, the basilica is all domes and mini-minarets, while altars inside feature Donatello bronzes. Be sure to see the north transept for the tomb of St. Anthony and the south transept for a 14th-century fresco of the *Crucifixion.* A beautiful bronze sculpture of a man on horseback, called *Gattamelata,* also by Donatello, dominates the church's piazza.

The town has many other interesting attractions, including the extravagantly neoclassical **Caffè Pedrocchi,** Piazzetta Pedrocchi 15 (☎ 049-820-5007; www.caffepedrocchi.it), which has been the main intellectual gathering place since its opening in 1831, with its elegant 19th-century original furniture on the upper floor. Admission is 3€ ($4.80), and it's open daily 9:30 a.m. to 12:30 p.m. and 3:30 to 8 p.m. Also highly recommended is a **boat tour: Consorzio Battellieri di Padova e Riviera del Brenta,** Passeggio de Gasperi 3 (☎ 049-820-9825; www.padova navigazione.it), offers several itineraries, including a tour of the Venetian villas along the **Riviera del Brenta,** which starts in Padova and brings you to Venice (a great way to get into Venice). Boats run from March through October.

Where to stay and dine

The best hotel in town is the **Majestic Hotel Toscanelli,** Via dell'Arco 2 (☎ 049-663244; Fax: 049-876-0025; www.toscanelli.com; Rack rates: 178€/$285 double, including buffet breakfast). Another good hotel is the **Plaza,** Corso Milano 40 (☎ 049-656822; Fax: 049-661117; www.plaza padova.it; Rack rates: 220€/$352 double, including buffet breakfast).

A temple to good wine, **Per Bacco,** Piazzale Pontecorvo 10 (☎ 049-875-4664; www.per-bacco.it; open Tues–Sun noon to 2:30 p.m. and 7:30–11 p.m.), also offers wonderful, creative food. The **Osteria Speroni,** Via Speroni 36 (☎ 049-875-3370; open Mon–Sat 12:30–2:30 p.m. and 8–10:30 p.m.), has simpler but delicious, traditional local fare. And the Pedrocchi (see the preceding section) now offers an excellent lunch.

Milan: Art viewing and shopping

The fashion and economic heart of northern Italy, Milan is a city of art, with deep historical roots, and home to several gems — including one of the best art galleries in Italy — making it well worth a detour. You can see the highlights in a day, but spend the night if you can spare the time.

Getting there

Milan's international airport of **Malpensa** (☎ 02-7485-2200), 50km (31 miles) north of the city, is a large airport with all the conveniences — ATMs, tourist info point, hotel reservation service — in the arrival concourse. The **Malpensa Express train** takes you to **Cadorna** rail station at the west of Milan's historic district in 40 minutes; you can also take a **shuttle bus** (running every 40 minutes) for the 50-minute ride to **Milano**

Centrale rail station, at the north of Milan's historic district. Count on 70€ ($112) for the taxi ride, which, depending on the traffic, could take you over an hour.

The smaller **Linate Airport** (☎ 02-7485-2200) is only 10km (6¼ miles) east of the city and handles some European and most domestic flights. From there, it's a 15-minute taxi ride to the center of town; if you have no luggage, you can take the frequent (every ten minutes) **city bus** no. 73 to the M1 subway line.

From Venice, you can easily reach **Milano Centrale** rail station on Piazza Duca d'Aosta in a little over two hours by **train;** the trip costs about 18€ ($29).

Seeing the sights

Milan is a large city, but its historic district is manageable, dominated by the **Castello Sforzesco,** Porta Umberto (☎ 02-8846-3700; www.milano castello.it; Metro: M1 Cairoli or M2 Lanza/Cadorna), a real castle with crenellated walls, underground passages, and towers that you can visit because it houses a superb sculpture museum (Michelangelo's famous *Pietà Rondanini,* his last — and unfinished — work is here) and a picture gallery with artworks by such masters as Mantegna and Antonello da Messina. Admission to the castle is free; museum entry is 3€ ($4.80). The castle is open daily from 7 a.m. to 7 p.m. in summer, 7 a.m. to 6 p.m. in winter; the museum is open Tuesday through Sunday 9 a.m. to 5:30 p.m. (last admission at 5 p.m.; closed Jan 1, May 1, and Dec 25).

The **Duomo,** Piazza Duomo (☎ 02-8646-3456; Metro: M1 or M3 to Duomo), is Milan's grandiose Gothic cathedral, second in size in Italy only to St. Peter's. Admission to the cathedral is free; other entry fees include the baptistery of St. John at 2€ ($3.20), the treasure 1€ ($1.60), and the terraces 5€ ($8) to walk and 7€ ($11) to access via the elevator. Hours for the cathedral are daily 7 a.m. to 7 p.m.; for the treasure Monday through Friday 9:30 a.m. to 1:30 p.m. and 2 to 6 p.m., Saturday 9:30 a.m. to 1:30 p.m. and 2 to 5 p.m., and Sunday 1:30 to 4 p.m.; and for baptisteries and terraces daily 9 a.m. to 5:45 p.m. (until 4:45 p.m. Nov–Jan). Last admission is 30 minutes earlier.

Head inside Santa Maria delle Grazie, Piazza S. Maria delle Grazie 2, off Corso Magenta (☎ 02-8942-1146 for reservations; www.cenacolovinciano. it; Metro: M1 Conciliazione), to view **Leonardo's painting of the *Last Supper.*** Admission is 6.50€ ($10) plus a mandatory reservation fee of 1.50€ ($2.40). It's open Tuesday through Sunday 8:15 a.m. to 7 p.m. (last admission 6:45 p.m.).

Reservations are mandatory for *The Last Supper,* and you need to make them a minimum of 24 hours in advance.

The **Brera Picture Gallery,** Via Brera 28 (☎ 02-722631; www.brera. beniculturali.it; Metro: M2 to Lanza), is a stunning art collection attached to the Art Academy. Among the best paintings are Piero della Francesca's famous *Pala di Urbino,* Raffaello's *Sposalizio della Vergine,* Andrea Mantegna's *Cristo Morto,* and Caravaggio's *Cena di Emmaus.* Admission is 5€ ($8), and it's open Tuesday through Saturday 8:30 a.m. to 7:15 p.m. (last admission 6:30 p.m.).

But shopping is what drives many visitors to Milan, from the elegant boutiques lining **Via Montenapoleone** and nearby **Via della Spiga** and **Via Sant'Andrea,** to the many outlets selling discounted items, sometimes off the runways. Try **D Magazine Outlet,** Via Montenapoleone 26 (☎ 02-7600-6027), and **Biffi,** Corso Ganova 6 (☎ 02-831-1601; Metro: San Ambrogio), specializing in women's clothing in the main store and men's clothing across the street.

Where to stay and dine

Milan is very expensive. The best hotel in town is the **Four Seasons,** Via Gesù 8, off Via Montenapoleone (☎ 02-77088; Fax: 02-7708-5000; www. fourseasons.com; Rack rates: 730€–860€/$1,168–$1,376 double). A good moderate choice is the **Hotel Manzoni,** Via Santo Spirito 20 (☎ 02-7600-5700; Fax: 02-784212; www.hotelmanzoni.com; Rack rates: 350€–420€/$560–$672 double; closed Aug and Dec 25).

You can eat very well in Milan. Examples include the down-to-earth **Trattoria Milanese,** Via Santa Marta 11 (☎ 02-8645-1991; Metro: M1 to Cordusio; open Wed–Mon noon to 3 p.m. and 7 p.m.–1 a.m.; closed July 15–Aug 31 and Dec 24–Jan 10), and the upscale **CraccoPeck,** Via Victor Hugo 4 (☎ 02-876774; reservations required; open Mon–Fri 12:30–2 p.m., Mon–Sat 7:30–10 p.m., closed Sat June–Aug), the best restaurant in Milan.

Fast Facts: Venice

American Express

The office is at Salizzada San Moisè, 1471 San Marco (☎ 041-520-0844; *Vaporetto:* 1 or 82 to San Marco–Vallaresso). Summer hours are Monday through Saturday 8 a.m. to 8 p.m. (currency exchange) and 8 a.m. to 5:30 p.m. (everything else); winter hours are Monday through Friday 9 a.m. to 5:30 p.m. and Saturday 9 a.m. to 12:30 p.m.

Area Code

The local area code is **041** (see "Telephone" under "Fast Facts: Rome" in Chapter 19 for more on calling to and from Italy).

Currency

In 2002, the euro became the legal tender in Italy, replacing the lira. The euro is divided into 100 cents, and there are coins of 0.01, 0.02, 0.05, 0.10, 0.20, 0.50, 1€, and 2€. Paper-note denominations are 5, 10, 20, 50, 100, 200, and 500 euros. The exchange rate used to calculate the dollar values given in this chapter is 1€ equals $1.60. Amounts over $10 are rounded to the nearest dollar.

Doctors and Dentists

The American Express office keeps a list of English-speaking dentists and doctors.

Embassies and Consulates

The U.K. Consulate is at Piazzale Donatori di Sangue 2 in Mestre (☎ 041-505-5990). In Milan, you'll find the U.S. Consulate at Largo Donegani 1 (☎ 02-290351), the Australian consulate at Via Borgogna 2 (☎ 02-777-0421), the Canadian consulate at Via Pisani 19 (☎ 02-67581), and the New Zealand consulate at Via Guido d'Arezzo 6 (☎ 02-4801-2544). All others are in Rome (see Chapter 19).

Emergencies

Ambulance ☎ 118; fire ☎ 115; first aid (Pronto Soccorso) ☎ 041-520-3222.

Hospital

The Ospedali Civili Riuniti di Venezia (Campo SS. Giovanni e Paolo; ☎ 041-260711; *Vaporetto:* 41, 42, 51, or 52 to Ospedale) has English-speaking doctors.

Information

The APT (Fondamenta San Lorenzo, Castello 5050, 30122 Venezia; ☎ **041-529-8700;** www.turismovenezia.it) maintains tourist info points at the airport (☎ 041-529-8711; open daily 9:30 a.m.–7:30 p.m.), Piazzale Roma (☎ 041-529-8711; open daily 9:30 a.m.–6:30 p.m.), Santa Lucia rail station (☎ 041-529-8711; open daily 8 a.m.–6:30 p.m.), Lido (☎ 041-526-5711; open daily June–Sept 9 a.m.–12:30 p.m. and 3:30 p.m.–6 p.m.), San Marco all'Ascensione (☎ 041-529-8711; open daily 9 a.m.–3:30 p.m.), Venice Pavillion off the San Marco *vaporetto* stop (San Marco Ex Giardini Reali; ☎ 041-529-8711; open daily 10 a.m.–6 p.m.).

Internet Access

Venetian Navigator (Calle della Casselleria, 5300 Castello; ☎ 041-277-1056; www.venetiannavigator.com; open daily 10 a.m.–10 p.m. in summer and 10 a.m.–8.30 p.m. in winter) is only steps behind St. Mark's Basilica.

Maps

The tourist office's free map is good just to find *vaporetto* stops. They also sell a good map for 2.50€ ($4). Others are available at most bookstores and newsstands around town.

Newspapers and Magazines

Most newsstands in town sell English papers. One of the largest is in the Stazione Santa Lucia. A helpful small free publication, available in all major hotels, is *Un Ospite a Venezia,* a guide on everything useful, from public transportation to special events.

Pharmacies

A centrally located one is the International Pharmacy (Calle Larga XXII Marzo, 2067 San Marco; ☎ 041-522-2311; *Vaporetto:* 1 or 82 to San Marco–Vallaresso). If you need a pharmacy after-hours, ask your hotel or call ☎ 192 to get a list of those open near you.

Police

Call ☎ 113.

Post Office

The central one is the Ufficio Postale (Fontego dei Tedeschi, 5550 San Marco; ☎ 041-271-7111), near Ponte di Rialto.

Restrooms

The town maintains a number of well-kept public toilets in the historic district, well marked by signs on the walls; they're free for disabled people and for those with the Venice Card (see "Exploring Venice," earlier in this chapter), and otherwise available for a fee of 1€ ($1.60): San Leonardo in Cannaregio and Rialto Novo in S. Polo (open daily 7 a.m.–7 p.m.), Accademia in Dorsoduro (open daily 9 a.m.–8 p.m.), Calle Ascension in San Marco (open daily 9 a.m.–8 p.m.), San Bartolomeo in S. Marco (open daily 8 a.m.–8 p.m.), Giardini ex reali S. Marco (open daily 9 a.m.–7 p.m.), Bragora in Castello (open daily 9 a.m.–8 p.m.), and San Domenico, also in Castello (open daily 9 a.m.–6 p.m.); they also maintain one in each of the islands: Lido (S. Maria Elisabetta, in Via Isola di Cerigo; open daily 8 a.m.–7 p.m) Murano (Fondamenta Serenella; open daily 10 a.m.–7 p.m.); Burano (off Piazza Galluppi; open daily 9 a.m.–7 p.m.); and Torcello (near the museum; open daily 9 a.m.–7 p.m.).

Safety

Venice is very safe, even in the off-the-beaten-path solitary areas. The only real danger is pickpockets, always plentiful in areas with lots of tourists: Watch your bags and cameras, and don't display wads of money or jewelry.

Smoking

In 2005, Italy passed a law outlawing smoking in most public places. Smoking is allowed only where there is a separate, ventilated area for nonsmokers. If smoking at your table is important to you, call beforehand to make sure that the restaurant or cafe you'll be visiting offers a smoking area.

Taxes

See "Fast Facts: Rome" in Chapter 19 for details.

Taxis

Walk to one of the taxi stands around the city or call for pickup: San Marco (☎ 041-522-9750), Ferrovia (☎ 041-716286), Piazzale Roma (☎ 041-716922), Rialto (☎ 041-723112). You can also call one of the taxi firms: Cooperativa Veneziana (☎ 041-716124) in Cannaregio, Cooperativa Serenissima (☎ 041-522-1265) in Castello, or Cooperativa San Marco (☎ 041-522-2303).

Telephone

See "Fast Facts: Rome," in Chapter 19, for information on making calls and calling-card access codes.

Chapter 22

Madrid and the Best of Castile

*M*adrid is Spain's political and cultural, as well as geographic, center. With a splendid roster of museums, Madrid ranks as one of Europe's foremost art centers. And while it's the home of the Prado Museum, with its untold masterpieces by Velázquez and Goya, as well as Picasso's *Guernica,* it's also a city full of other, more down-to-earth images we've come to expect of Spain. Bulls still charge after matadors and red capes in the hot afternoon sun. Madrid nights still overflow with tapas joints, wine taverns, flamenco joints, and discos. Madrid thrives on its reputation as a place where you may find yourself going to bed at the time when you'd normally get up.

With less than 500 years under its belt, Madrid is one of Europe's youngest capital cities. It remained a small medieval town until the 16th and 17th centuries, Spain's Golden Age of exploration and wealth. In 1561, at the height of the era, Felipe II moved the court from Toledo to Madrid.

You can hit the major museums by day, embark upon an impromptu tapas crawl, and soak up theater, opera, and flamenco by night. The city's atmospheric *mesones* and *tascas* — cavelike restaurants and taverns — get the night started. When the sun goes down, you find that *Madrileños,* the people of Madrid, are among the most open and gregarious in Spain. And just beyond the city are the attractions El Escorial, Toledo, and Segovia, perfect for easy day trips.

Though serious art aficionados could easily spend a week in the capital, if you only want a taste of Madrid you'll still need at least a couple of days to see the Prado and some of Viejo (Old) Madrid and rest up enough to check out the city's dizzying nightlife.

Getting There

Madrid is a long, 12-hour train ride from Paris, the closest non-Spanish city in this book — so unless you're arriving in Madrid from elsewhere in Spain, flying here is probably a good idea. You can jump on a quick shuttle flight or the new, high-speed AVE train from Barcelona. After you arrive, you'll find that Madrid's local transportation system is efficient and relatively easy to use.

Arriving by air

Madrid's recently expanded airport, **Barajas** (☎ **902-40-47-04** or 91-305-83-43; www.aena.es), is about 16km (10 miles) outside town. In the arrivals hall, you'll find ATMs, banks at which you can change money, and a post office. High-tech Terminal 4 handles most international flights and is a shuttle bus away from the other terminals.

The airport's **tourist information office** (Oficina de Información Turística; ☎ **91-305-86-56**) is open daily from 8 a.m. to 8 p.m.

Line 8 of the **Metro,** or subway (www.metromadrid.es), runs from the airport to the Nuevos Ministerios stop (12 minutes), and then another 15 minutes from there to downtown (fare is 2€/$3.20). Or you can take a red **city bus** no. 200 (www.emtmadrid.es) to Avenida América in the city center for 1€ ($1.60), and then board the Metro for your destination from there. The ten-trip **Metrobus** ticket (see "Getting Around Madrid," later in this chapter) may be used for both the subway and the airport bus, although you'll pay a 1€ ($1.60) supplement. A **taxi** into town is about 25€ ($40), plus tip and airport and baggage-handling surcharges. Plan on 45 minutes to an hour of travel time from the airport to downtown.

Arriving by rail

If you take the train to Madrid, you'll most likely arrive at the city's main station, **Chamartín** (☎ **91-323-21-21**), the hub for trains coming from eastern Spain and France (international train routes come through the France–Spain border). From Chamartín, in Madrid's northern suburbs, you can get downtown quickly on Metro Line 10.

Madrid has two other train stations. Trains to and from southwest Spain and Portugal come into **Atocha** (☎ **91-563-02-02**). (Confusingly, two Metro stops also go by the name Atocha; the one marked ATOCHA RENFE is the one beneath Atocha train station; the Atocha Metro stop is one stop north of Atocha RENFE.) **Norte,** or Príncipe Pío, serves northwest Spain. **RENFE** is the name of the Spanish national train service; for information, call ☎ **902-24-02-02** or visit www.renfe.es.

Orienting Yourself in Madrid

Madrid has no natural landmarks useful for getting your bearings, though it does have several major *plazas* (squares) and elegant boulevards linking them, which will help you master the city's layout. Your best bet is to orient yourself using the Metro (subway) map, because most destinations are close to a Metro stop.

You want to spend most of your time in Old Madrid (near the Plaza Mayor) and Bourbon Madrid (including the Prado Museum and Retiro Park).

Introducing the neighborhoods

Plaza del Sol marks the very center of Madrid (and all of Spain, for that matter — all distances within the country are measured from a 0km mark in the plaza's southwest corner). The nearby **Plaza Mayor** is more scenic and is flanked by cafes and colonnades; in the center sits an equestrian statue of Felipe III. These two plazas constitute the heart of **Viejo Madrid** (Old Madrid), an area filled with authentic Spanish restaurants and nightlife hot spots. Madrid's 17th-century district lies south of **Plaza del Sol.**

The wide, modern **Plaza de España** marks the northwest corner of the city. Calle Bailén runs south from there, bordering the **Palacio Real** (royal palace) and marking the city's western edge. Madrid's main boulevard, **Gran Vía,** zigzags from Plaza de España across the northern Old City. Department stores, cafes, movie theaters, and office buildings line the grand boulevard. North of it are the **Malasana** and **Chueca** districts, both trendy nightlife zones. Chueca in particular has gone from being a little rough around the edges to becoming perhaps the coolest *barrio,* as well as the epicenter of gay life in the capital.

Old Madrid's east side is bordered by the tree-planted **Paseo del Prado,** which runs from north to south from **Plaza de la Cibeles** through **Plaza del Castillo** to the Atocha train station square. Hotels, cafes, and the city's major museums line the avenue. Vast **Retiro Park** lies on the east side of the Paseo.

Finding information after you arrive

Barajas Airport has an **Oficina de Información Turística** (☎ 91-305-86-56), open daily from 8 a.m. to 8 p.m. The municipal **Centro de Turismo de Madrid,** Plaza Mayor, 3 (☎ 91-588-16-36; www.munimadrid.es; Metro: Sol), is open Monday through Saturday from 10 a.m. to 8 p.m. and Sunday 10 a.m. to 3 p.m. The regional government's tourism office in Madrid is at Duque de Medinaceli, 2 (☎ 91-429-49-51 or 902-10-00-07; Metro: Banco de España), open Monday through Saturday from 9 a.m. to 7 p.m. and Sunday 9 a.m. to 3 p.m. The general tourist information numbers are ☎ 902-10-21-12 and ☎ 010.

Spain

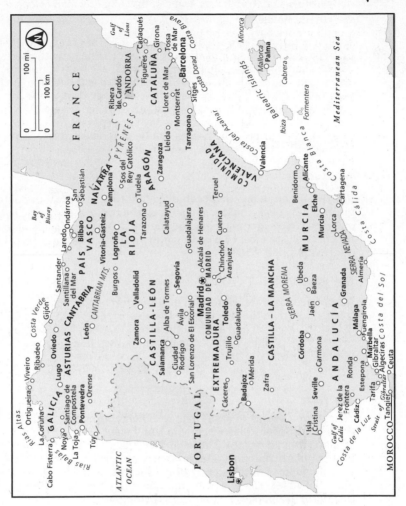

Getting Around Madrid

Madrid is large and sprawling, but the places that interest most visitors are in a fairly compact area. In fact, you can walk much of Madrid.

By subway

The **Metro** (☎ **012** or 902-444-403; www.metromadrid.es), marked by red and blue diamond-shaped signs, is Madrid's subway system, by far the fastest and easiest way to navigate the city. Stops are near almost everywhere you want to go. Single-ticket fares are 1€ ($1.60). Hours are daily from 6 a.m. to 1:30 a.m. You can find a handy map *(plano del metro)* at Metro stations.

A ten-trip ticket **(Metrobus)** is available for 6.70€ ($11), a nearly half-price bargain. It pays for itself after just six journeys on the Metro, and can be used by additional passengers. You'll use it up in no time, and it also works on the bus. Also worth considering is the **Abono Turístico,** a pass (available for one, two, three, five, or seven days) good for all public transportation within Madrid; prices range from 4€ ($6.40) for one day to 21€ ($34) for the seven-day pass (passes for children 10 and under are half-price). The passes can be purchased at any Metro station, Oficina de Turismo, or online (www.neoturismo.com).

By bus

The bus proves a bit complicated for first-time visitors. Conductors generally don't speak English, and with all the traffic on the wide avenues and tiny streets, getting a read on the city from the window of a bus is tough. Buses run from 6 a.m. to midnight daily; the fare is 1€ ($1.60). For information, call ☎ 012.

By taxi

Authorized taxis are white with diagonal red bands. Few taxi journeys in town, other than the ride in from the airport, cost more than 8€ to 10€ ($13–$16). You can hail a cab in the street (a green light on the roof means it's available) or pick one up where they line up (usually outside hotels). A slightly higher night rate is charged from 11 p.m. to 7 a.m. If you need to call a cab, call ☎ **91-447-32-32,** 91-405-55-00, or 91-371-21-31.

By foot

Except for a couple of easily managed neighborhoods, Madrid is one of the few European cities where you won't want to spend much time strolling around on foot. The wide boulevards are great for getting from place to place, but most offer relatively little in the way of character. With a couple of notable exceptions, such as the **Plaza Mayor** and other parts of Old Madrid, you won't miss much by traveling underground on the Metro or hopping a cab to your destination.

Staying in Madrid

Madrid offers three main types of sleeping accommodations: regular hotels, which can be anything from deluxe, elegant turn-of-the-last-century establishments to modern, moderately priced inns; *hostales,* bare-bones businesses where travelers usually get good value for their money; and *pensiones,* even simpler, less-expensive boardinghouses, often requiring half or full *board* (meals taken on premises).

Many hotels are scattered along the Gran Vía, which isn't the greatest of places to be walking after dark, and near Atocha Station. Old Madrid also has a good selection of accommodations ringing the central squares Plaza Mayor and Puerta del Sol. These areas attract their share of pick-pockets because they're popular travel destinations, but due to their proximity to prime dining and sightseeing, they're also among the most exciting places to be in Madrid.

The tourism office maintains a Hotel Tourist Line at ☎ 901-300-600.

Most hotel rates don't include breakfast or IVA, the 7 percent value-added tax. To ensure the bill doesn't shock you at the end of your stay, make sure you ask about these taxes when booking your room.

Madrid's top hotels

AC Palacio del Retiro
$$$$$ **Bourbon Madrid (near Retiro Park)**

It would be hard to improve upon the location of this midsize luxury hotel (50 rooms), which overlooks Retiro Park and is just a few short blocks from the Prado Museum. Inaugurated in 2004, it also has terrific bones, inhabiting a gorgeous, early-20th-century palace (a National Heritage–protected structure) that features a gorgeous central staircase, stained-glass windows, and marble columns. Rooms are sleek, respecting the original style of the building but adding some contemporary flair. The hotel has all the facilities, including a spa, that make it perfect for business and leisure travelers alike. Although the AC Palacio is definitely a high-end hotel and similar in character and luxury to Madrid's mega-splurge, grandaddy hotels, such as the Palace or the Ritz, it's quite a bit less expensive than those.

See map p. 490. Alfonso XII, 14. ☎ *902-29-22-93 or 91-523-74-60. Fax: 91-308-54-77.* www.ac-hoteles.com. *Metro: Plaza de la Cibeles. Rack rates: 236€–365€ ($378–$584) double. AE, DC, MC, V.*

Casa de Madrid
$$$$ **Viejo Madrid**

This intimate and refined residence, in a late-18th-century town house, takes the concept of B&B to a level rarely seen. In the center of old Hapsburg Madrid, near the Opera House and Royal Palace, it's a unique place to experience high style and luxury. It's on a par with Madrid's very finest hotels, and though it's not inexpensive, it is a relatively good deal given what you'd pay to stay at the Ritz or a super high-end boutique hotel. The sprawling second-floor apartment has seven rooms decorated with exquisite, old-world taste, featuring beautiful antiques and themes related to the owner's travels. Note that not all rooms have air-conditioning, though a couple feature kitchenettes. Shockingly, pets are permitted.

See map p. 490. Arrieta, 2–2. ☎ *91-559-57-91. Fax 91-540-11-00.* www.casade madrid.com. *Metro: Opera. Rack rates: 240€–275€ ($384–$440). AE, DC, MC, V.*

Accommodations, Dining, and Attractions in Madrid

HOTELS
AC Palacio del Retiro **26**
Casa de Madrid **2**
H10 Villa de la Reina **28**
Hotel de las Letras **29**
Hotel NH Nacional **18**
Hotel Plaza Mayor **5**
Petit Palace Posada del Peine **4**
Residencia Sud-Americana **25**
Room Mate Alicia **27**
Suite Prado Hotel **23**

RESTAURANTS ◆
Botín **8**
Casa Alberto **22**
Casa Antonio **9**
Casa Lucío **12**
Fast Good **31**
La Posada de la Villa **13**
Mesón de la Guitarra **7**
Mesón del Champigñon **7**
Samarkanda **17**
Taberna de Antonio Sánchez **15**
Taberna de Cien Vinos **11**
Taberna de Dolores **21**

ATTRACTIONS ●
CaixaForum Madrid **19**
El Rastro **14**
Monasterio de las
  Descalzas Reales **3**
Museo Nacional Centro de
  Arte Reina Sofía **16**
Museo Nacional del Prado **20**
Museo Thyssen-Bornemisza **24**
Palacio Real de Madrid **1**
Plaza de la Paja **10**
Plaza de la Villa **6**
Plaza de Toros de la Venta/
  Museo Taurino **30**

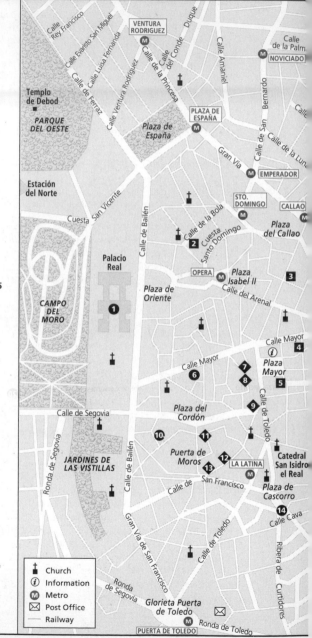

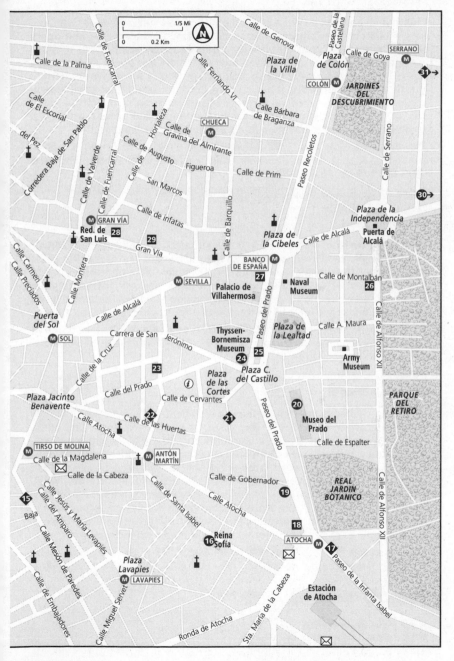

Calle de la Palma
Calle de Fuencarral
Calle de El Escorial
del Pez
Corredera Baja de San Pablo
Calle Baja de San Pablo
Calle de Valverde
Calle de Fuencarral
Hortaleza
Calle de Augusto Figueroa
San Marcos
Calle de Gravina del Almirante
Calle de infatas
Calle Montera
Calle Carmen
Calle Preciados
Puerta del Sol
SOL
Calle de la Cruz
Carrera de San Jerónimo
Calle del Prado
Plaza Jacinto Benavente
Calle Atocha
Calle de las Huertas
TIRSO DE MOLINA
Calle de la Magdalena
Calle de la Cabeza
ANTÓN MARTÍN
Calle Jesús y María Levapiés
Baja
Calle del Amparo
Calle Mesón de Paredes
Calle de Embajadores
Calle Miguel Servet
Plaza Lavapies
LAVAPIES
Calle de Santa Isabel
Reina Sofía
Calle de Gobernador
Calle Atocha
Sta. María de la Cabeza
Ronda de Atocha
GRAN VÍA
Red. de San Luis 28
Gran Via 29
SEVILLA
Palacio de Villahermosa
BANCO DE ESPAÑA 27
Thyssen-Bornemisza Museum 25
Plaza de las Cortes
Plaza C. del Castillo 24
23
21
19
18
ATOCHA
Estación de Atocha
Paseo del Prado
Plaza de la Lealtad
Naval Museum
Museo del Prado
Calle de Espalter
REAL JARDIN BOTANICO
Calle de la Cibeles
Calle de Alcalá
Calle de Alcalá
Plaza de la Independencia
Puerta de Alcalá
Calle de Montalbán 26
Calle A. Maura
Army Museum
PARQUE DEL RETIRO
Calle de Alfonso XII
Calle de Alfonso XII
Paseo de la Infanta Isabel
Calle de Genova
Paseo de la Castellana
Calle de Goya
SERRANO
31
Plaza de Colón
COLÓN
JARDINES DEL DESCUBRIMIENTO
Calle de Serrano
30
Plaza de la Villa
Calle Fernando VI
Calle Bárbara de Braganza
CHUECA
Calle de Prim
Paseo Recoletos
Calle de Barquillo
20

0 1/5 Mi
0 0.2 Km
N

Hotel de las Letras
$$$$–$$$$$ Gran Vía

This stylish hotel, in a 1917 Art Deco building on Madrid's famed Gran Vía, wears its literary ambitions in its name — "Hotel of Letters" — and on its walls. The modern, chic, and boldly colored rooms (each floor is a different color) feature inscriptions from famous writers and poets, and a library has comfy couches where guests can curl up with a work of great fiction. Yet it's anything but stuffy; it has a young and cool vibe. Other great amenities include a terrific rooftop terrace, with great views of the city; a small spa, with a steam room, workout space, and massage rooms; and a hip cocktail lounge. Good advance deals are available online.

See map p. 490. Gran Vía, 11. ☎ *902-42-24-82 or 91-523-79-80. Fax: 91-523-79-81.* www.hoteldelasletras.com. *Metro: Sevilla or Gran Vía. Rack rates: 275€–345€ ($440–$552) double. AE, DC, MC, V.*

Hotel Plaza Mayor
$$ Viejo Madrid

This small, well-located boutique hotel, situated right off the Plaza Mayor in the heart of Old Madrid, is a bargain hunter's dream, one of the best deals in the capital. Occupying an old church, the family-run hotel features bright and cheery, smartly outfitted rooms. Most have windows overlooking the street. You can even step it up a notch in the new Suite del Palomar, a huge, handsome loft space on the top floor with a rooftop terrace.

See map p. 490. Atocha, 2. ☎ *91-360-06-06. Fax: 91-360-06-10.* www.h-plaza mayor.com. *Metro: Sol. Rack rates: 85€–100€ ($136–$160) double. AE, DC, MC, V.*

Room Mate Alicia
$$$ Viejo Madrid

A design-oriented hotel that strikes an excellent balance between understated chic and affordable inn, this small, 34-room place, near Plaza Santa Ana, is hip and urban. Inside a landmark turn-of-the-20th-century industrial building, rooms have colorful accents and contemporary furnishings. Rooms are good-sized, with large windows, and bathrooms are stylish; many rooms feature coveted views of the square, and all have free Wi-Fi. The hotel's a definite bargain for anyone looking for copious style without a hefty price tag. The Room Mate Hoteles group has several other hotels, also given human first names, in central Madrid, including Mario, Oscar, and Laura — all excellent options for a reasonably priced stay.

See map p. 490. Prado, 2. ☎ *91-389-60-95. Fax: 91-369-47-95.* www.room-mate hoteles.com. *Metro: Sol. Rack rates: 118€–193€ ($189–$309) double. AE, DC, MC, V.*

Madrid's runner-up hotels

H10 Villa de la Reina
$$$$ Viejo Madrid/Gran Vía   A smart midsize hotel, the Villa de la Reina is good choice at the high end of midrange. It occupies a classic

early-20th-century building along the Gran Vía — a busy but central location. Rooms aren't huge, but they're finely detailed, with stylish furnishings and sleek bathrooms. *See map p. 490. Gran Vía, 22.* ☎ *91-523-91-01.*
www.h10hoteles.com.

Hotel NH Nacional

$$$ Bourbon Madrid   This hotel, designed for business travelers, fea-
tures spacious, well-decorated rooms with light woods and bold colors in
a historic 1920s building right on Paseo del Prado — smack in the middle
of the museum mile. Children 11 and under (one per couple) stay free in
their parents' room. *See map p. 490. Paseo del Prado, 48.* ☎ *91-429-66-29.*
www.nh-hoteles.es.

Petit Palace Posada del Peine

$$$$ Viejo Madrid   Sleek and modern, though in a historic building
dating to 1610, this midsize hotel is perfect for visitors who want stylish com-
fort, along with convenience and a historic location, virtually on top of the
Plaza Mayor. *See map p. 490. Postas, 17.* ☎ *91-523-81-51.* www.hthoteles.com.

Residencia Sud-Americana

$ Bourbon Madrid   If you don't mind sharing a bathroom, this is defi-
nitely a cut above most cheap hostels, though it's still decidedly basic and
strictly for budget travelers. It has whitewashed walls, high ceilings, well-
worn hardwood floors, vintage furniture and chandeliers, and above all, a
great location, across from the Prado Museum and with views over Paseo
del Prado. *See map p. 490. Paseo del Prado, 12.* ☎ *91-429-25-64.*

Suite Prado Hotel

$$$ Viejo Madrid/Puerta del Sol   With unexpectedly huge rooms, this
tiny hotel (just 18 rooms) is tucked away on a small street not far from
Plaza Santa Ana. It's perfect for families or groups of friends, with kitchenettes and comfortable salons for the price of a standard room. Rooms
are decorated with contemporary furniture in bright colors. *See map p. 490.
Manuel Fernández y González, 10 (around the corner from Teatro Español, off Calle
de las Huertas).* ☎ *91-420-23-18.* www.suiteprado.com.

Dining in Madrid

For years, dining in Madrid has meant either big, fancy restaurants where
elegant service is king, charming Viejo Madrileño taverns, or tapas,
which are really eating as an excuse for drinking. With a recently invigor-
ated dining scene, Madrid is trying to catch up to Bilbao, San Sebastián,
and Barcelona, where creativity has been more valued. As the capital, of
course, Madrid has all the regional specialties, a wide variety of international cuisines, and fresh seafood flown in from the coasts. While you can
easily find Spain's trademark dish, *paella* (a Mediterranean medley of
seafood and rice usually eaten at lunch), locals tend to go for roasted
meats, especially *cordero* (lamb) and *cochinillo* (suckling pig). Spain is the
place to be if you like pork; in many restaurants *chorizo* sausage and salty

jamón serrano ham hang from the ceiling and literally nearly hit patrons in the face.

Spaniards maintain a different eating schedule than the rest of the Continent, and Madrileños eat even later than the rest of their countrymen. Many still find time to eat their biggest meal between 1 and 4 p.m., while dinner is usually no earlier than 10 p.m. Some restaurants that try to attract international travelers serve dinner as early as 8 p.m. (which technically is still the *tarde,* or afternoon, in Spain), but Spaniards would never think of dining that early. Most good, authentic restaurants don't even open their doors until 9 or 9:30 p.m.

The city's *tascas* (tapas restaurants) and *mesones* (cavelike taverns) are ideal places to stop in for a *vinito* (bee-*nee*-toe; small glass of wine), *jerez* (hair-*eth;* dry sherry), and a smattering of tapas. *Tapas* are snacks eaten in small portions and can be as prosaic as olives or as elaborate as small meals. Spaniards spend late afternoons and evenings on the tapas prowl, or *tapeo* — strolling from *tasca* to *tasca* to drink, chat, and chomp. (You'll find descriptions of some of the better *tascas* and some typical tapas in "More cool things to see and do," later in this chapter.)

Botín
$$$ Viejo Madrid   CASTILIAN

You want classic Madrid? Botín can serve up the stalwarts of Castilian cooking: roast suckling pig and roast leg of lamb prepared in ancient wood ovens. Prepare to meet your neighbors from back home in this crowded spot, though. Everyone seems to know that Botín has the reputation of being the oldest continuously operating restaurant in the world (it hasn't closed its doors since 1725). A favorite with families who don't mind the bustling nature of the place, Botín doubles as a history lesson for kids. How's this for pedigree? Francisco de Goya, the legendary painter, was once a dishwasher at the restaurant Botín. Not good enough? Okay, how about the fact that Hemingway set a scene in *The Sun Also Rises* in this famed restaurant?

See map p. 490. Calle de Cuchilleros, 17. ☎ *91-366-42-17. Reservations required. Metro: Ópera or Sol. Main courses: 14€–32€ ($22–$51), fixed-price menu 35€ ($56). AE, DC, MC, V. Open: Daily 1–4 p.m. and 8 p.m. to midnight.*

Casa Lucío
$$$ Viejo Madrid   CASTILIAN

A historic tavern on one of Madrid's famous night-crawler streets, the Casa Lucío is a favorite spot for locals to take their foreign visitors. With its cinematic, cavelike ambience and hanging forest of cured hams, it's the kind of place that has you considering a sabbatical in Spain before you finish the first bottle of wine. The famous faces and sharply dressed crowd only add to the buzz. The food is top-quality comfort food — like the house *merluza* (hake, a white fish similar to cod), shrimp in garlic sauce, roasted lamb, and scrambled potatoes and eggs (now there's a dish even a finicky child will love).

See map p. 490. Cava Baja, 35. ☎ 91-365-82-17. Reservations recommended. Metro: La Latina. Main courses: 16€–30€ ($26–$48). AE, DC, MC, V. Open: Sun–Fri 1–4 p.m. and 9 p.m. to midnight; Sat 9 p.m. to midnight. Closed Aug.

Fast Good
$ Barrio de Salamanca/Modern Madrid FAST FOOD

If you're on the go and want a quick bite, how about a Spanish take on fast food that aims high, created by the world-famous chef of El Bulli, Ferrán Adrià (he of the foams and lab experiments), and the NH hotel chain? It serves inexpensive hamburgers with olive tapenade, fries cooked in Spanish olive oil, creative panini, spicy versions of roast chicken, and salads, all in a playfully hip, colorful environment. Additional locations are at Calle Padre Damián, 23, and Calle Orense, 11.

See map p. 490. Juan Bravo, 3 (corner of Lagasca). ☎ 91-577-41-51. Reservations not accepted. Metro: Rubén Dario. Main courses: 3.50€–6€ ($5.60–$9.60). AE, DC, MC, V. Open: Daily noon to midnight.

La Posada de la Villa
$$$–$$$$ Viejo Madrid SPANISH/STEAK

Here's a way not only to see Old Madrid, but to feel it in your bones. This inn, founded in 1642 in the heart of the tapas district, is famed for its Castilian roasts. Come for the historical ambience, and while you're at it, dig into the exquisite roast lamb (a classic dish in these parts) and cured pork.

See map p. 490. Cava Baja, 9. ☎ 91-366-18-60. Reservations required. Metro: La Latina. Main courses: 14€–39€ ($22–$62), fixed-price menu 38€ ($61). Open: Mon–Sat 1– 4 p.m. and 8 p.m. to midnight; Sun 1–4 p.m. Closed Aug.

Samarkanda
$$$ Bourbon Madrid CREATIVE INTERNATIONAL

Perched like a tree fort in the mini-botanical gardens of the Atocha train station, but looking more like an antique railway dining car, this great-looking restaurant serves a reasonably priced, well-prepared, and creative menu. Excellent main courses include beef tenderloin, squid in its ink, and ravioli stuffed with asparagus. The dark rattan chairs, peaked wooden ceiling and fans, long wall of red banquets, and tropical greenery flooding your view evoke a colonial outpost — and may be enough to trick you into believing that the train you're about to board is an old steamer rather than a high-speed rail to Seville.

See map p. 490. Estación de Atocha (Terminal AVE), Gta. de Carlos V. ☎ 91-530-97-46. Reservations recommended. Metro: Atocha. Main courses: 14€–24€ ($22–$38). AE, DC, MC, V. Open: Daily 1:30–4 p.m. and 9 p.m. to midnight.

Exploring Madrid

Madrid has the greatest concentration of important museums in Spain — and more first-class works by Spanish masters including El Greco, Velázquez, Goya, and Picasso (among others) than anywhere else. If you can hit only the top two or three, begin with the newly expanded Prado and the Royal Palace (which qualifies as a museum of sorts). Allow a full morning or afternoon for the Prado and a couple of hours for the Royal Palace. In Viejo Madrid, around the Plaza Mayor, spend a couple of hours (preferably in the early evening, when tapas crawlers are out and about) and discover the city's soul in its cinematic *mesones* and *tascas*.

If you're a serious art lover and are banking on hitting the Madrid's Big Three — the Prado, the Thyssen-Bornemisza, and the Reina Sofía museums, all along a stretch of the Paseo del Prado — within hours of landing in Madrid, make sure that your visit isn't on a Monday or Tuesday. The first two museums are closed on Monday, and the Reina Sofía collection shuts its doors on Tuesday. None of them closes for lunch, though, and occasionally, lunchtime is the best time to visit (when everyone else takes a break, from 1–4 p.m. or so). Architecture and art fans should also check out the newest addition to Paseo del Prado, the brand-new **CaixaForum Madrid,** Paseo del Prado, 36 (☎ **91-330-73-00;** www.fundacio.lacaixa.es/centros/caixaforummadrid_ca.html), a spectacular arts and cultural center designed by the Swiss team Herzog & de Meuron, that opened in February 2008. The redesigned building, which was once a power plant, houses three floors of galleries and a cool restaurant, and it has spurred some interesting development in the neighborhood Barrio de las Letras, once famed for its literary connections.

The **Madrid Card** Billete Turístico — available in one-, two-, and three-day versions — allows for unlimited travel on the subway (in Zone A), unlimited travel on the Madrid Visión tour bus, as well as free entry to more than 40 museums (including the Prado, Thyssen, Reina Sofía, Palacio Real, Aranjuez, and El Escorial) and a host of additional discounts at restaurants and other places of interest. Tickets, though, aren't cheap: 42€ ($67) for the one-day ticket; 55€ ($88) for the two-day; and 68€ ($109) for the three-day. You can purchase them online, at the Plaza Mayor and Duque de Medinaceli Oficinas de Turismo, or airport and train stations. For more information, call ☎ **91-360-47-72** or 902-088-908, or go to www.madridcard.com (discounts available for online purchase).

Be extremely careful around the Prado and other museum tourist haunts, where thieves artfully prey upon unsuspecting tourists. If someone offers to clean mustard or some other substance off your clothing, recognize it as a trick and refuse assistance: The thief is the one who put the mustard there, and he (or an accomplice) will proceed to rob you after distracting you.

Madrid's top sights

Museo Nacional del Prado
Bourbon Madrid

Many experts consider the Prado, with more than a dozen of the world's most famous paintings in its vast holdings, to rank just behind the Louvre in Paris among the greatest art museums in Europe. The Prado boasts the world's richest and most complete collection of Spanish Old Masters, easily making the museum one of the top attractions in Spain (in fact, it's the most-visited site in the country). Don't miss it — unless the thought of classical painting makes your skin crawl. The museum has finally completed a massive expansion and renovation project, by the celebrated Spanish architect Rafael Moneo, which doubled the Prado's exhibition space. The Prado's 12th- through 19th-century collection of the Spanish school includes masterpieces by Velázquez, Goya, El Greco, Murillo, Ribera, and Zurbarán. The Velázquez and Goya collections are the star draws; so go directly to the galleries featuring their works if your time or interest is limited. Expect crowds there, though; as you approach the room where Velázquez's masterpiece, *Las Meninas* (The Ladies-in-Waiting), hangs, you can hear the growing rumble of guides and groups. The Prado also has extraordinary works by Italian masters — including Titian, Fra Angelico, Raphael, Caravaggio, and Botticelli — and Flemish greats Hieronymus Bosch, Peter Paul Rubens, and Breughel the Elder. The lineup of masterpieces includes Fra Angelico's *Annunciation* (1430); El Greco's eerie *Adoration of the Shepherds* (1614); José de Ribera's *The Martyrdom of St. Philip* (1630); Rubens's fleshy *Three Graces* (1739); the freaky triptych *The Garden of Earthly Delights,* painted by ierony-mus Bosch ("El Bosco" to the Spanish) in 1516; and Goya's *Naked Maja* and *Clothed Maja,* as well as his "Black Paintings," the most disturbing and famous of which is *Saturn Devouring One of His Sons* (1823).

To try to beat the crowds at the Prado, enter through the Velázquez door (facing Pasco del Prado), and go early (9 a.m.) or during the Spanish lunch hour (2–4 p.m.). To save on admission, go in the evening, when the museum is free. If you're an art aficionado, purchasing a room-by-room guide is a good idea.

See map p. 490. Paseo del Prado. ☎ *91-330-28-00 or 902-10-70-77 (for advance bookings).* www.museodelprado.es. *Metro: Banco de España or Atocha. Admission: 9€ ($14) adults, 3€ ($4.80) non-EU students, free for EU-resident seniors and students, free for all Tues–Sat 6–8 p.m. and Sun 5–8 p.m. Audio guides: 3€ ($4.80). Open: Tues–Sun 9 a.m.–8 p.m.; Dec 24, Dec 31, and Jan 6 9 a.m.–2 p.m. Closed Jan 1, Good Friday, May 1, and Dec 25.*

Palacio Real de Madrid
Viejo Madrid

Occupying the site of a ninth-century Moorish *alcázar* (fortress), the Royal Palace built by Spain's Bourbon monarchs makes a grandiose statement about Madrid's place in the world, around 1750. Each room is an exercise in megawatt wealth, and taste flies out the window. The huge neoclassical palace — it has 2,000 rooms — incorporated the lavish tastes of both Carlos III and Carlos IV. The official residence of the royal family until 1931, it's now used only for state functions, because King Juan Carlos and Queen Sofía live in more modest digs, the Zarzuela Palace just beyond Madrid. Allow two to three hours to visit the palace; guided tours are optional but not really necessary or particularly worthwhile.

Of special note are the **Throne Room,** with its scarlet wall coverings, baroque gilded mirrors, and a Tiepolo fresco on the ceiling; the regal **Gala Dining Room,** which shows off a spectacular dining table and jaw-dropping tapestries; and the **Porcelain Room,** covered floor to ceiling in a garish display of green, white, and purple porcelain. Check out the old **Royal Pharmacy** (near the ticket office), which has Talavera pottery jars and old recipe books of medications. In the **Real Armería** is a fine display of arms and armor. Wander to the edge of the large Plaza de la Armería (Royal Armory Square) that faces the palace, and you see how abruptly Madrid ends and the plains begin. Look also for the new temporary exhibits hall, part of what will eventually become the **Museum of Royal Collections** (with a permanent display of carriages, tapestries, paintings, silver, and crystal belonging to Spain's long lines of monarchs).

If you visit the Royal Palace on the first Wednesday of the month, you have a chance to see the ceremonial changing of the guards (at noon for free). And if you're carrying a European Union passport, you can get into the Royal Palace for free on Wednesdays, too.

See map p. 490. Bailén, 2. ☎ *91-542-00-59.* www.patrimonionacional.es. *Metro: Ópera. Admission: 10€ ($16) adults, 3.50€ ($5.60) students and EU-resident seniors. Open: Summer Mon–Sat 9 a.m.–6 p.m., Sun and holidays 9 a.m.–3 p.m.; winter Mon–Sat 9:30 a.m.–5 p.m., Sun and holidays 9 a.m.–2 p.m.*

Museo Nacional Centro de Arte Reina Sofía
Bourbon Madrid

The third address on Madrid's celebrated Art Avenue — the Paseo del Prado — is the Queen Sofía contemporary art museum. It boasts major works from Spain's 20th-century greats, such as Picasso, Miró, Dalí, and Julio González, but it's Pablo Picasso's dramatic *Guernica,* the most famous painting of the 20th century, that dwarfs them all. The massive canvas in gray, black, and white is a moving antiwar protest. (Picasso painted it after the Nationalist bombing of a small Basque town during the Civil War.)

The Reina Sofía is especially strong in early-20th-century works by Spanish artists as well as contemporary international movements such as abstract art, pop art, and minimalism. The museum underwent a spectacular renovation and amplification, adding three new buildings by the French architect Jean Nouvel, in 2004. If you're a contemporary art lover, you'll want to spend almost as much time here as at the Prado; allow a couple of hours at a minimum for your visit.

See map p. 490. Calle Santa Isabel, 52 (at Paseo del Prado, opposite the Atocha train station). ☎ *91-774-10-00.* www.museoreinasofia.es. *Metro: Atocha. Admission: 6€ ($9.60) adults, 3€ ($4.80) students, free for seniors and children 17 and under, free* *for all Sat 2:30–9 p.m. and Sun 10 a.m.–2:30 p.m. Open: Mon and Wed–Sat 10 a.m.–9 p.m.; Sun 10 a.m.–2:30 p.m.*

Museo Thyssen-Bornemisza
Bourbon Madrid

Across the street from the Prado, the museum with a decidedly un-Spanish, tongue-twister of a name has quickly become a premier attraction in Madrid. In 1993, the Spanish government acquired the spectacular private collection amassed by the Baron Thyssen-Bornemisza and his son, two generations of German industrial magnates.

The Spanish government renovated the early-19th-century pink Villahermosa palace to show its new bounty. Begun in the 1920s, the Thyssen collection comprises 800 stylistically diverse works and aims to be no less than a survey of Western art, from primitives and medieval art to 20th-century avant-garde and pop art. Displayed chronologically (starting from the top floor) and heavy on Impressionism and German Expressionism, the collection reads like a roster of the greatest names in classical and modern art: Caravaggio, Rafael, Titian, El Greco, Goya, Rubens, Degas, Gauguin, Cézanne, Manet, van Gogh, Picasso, Chagall, Miró, and Pollock. Some observers tout it as the greatest private collection ever assembled, while others criticize it as a showy collection of minor works by major artists. In 2004, the museum doubled in size, to accommodate 700 works on long-term loan from the Carmen Thyssen-Bornemisza Collection. By almost any standard, the museum is a worthwhile complement to the great Prado, a must-see for fans of classical painting.

See map p. 490. Paseo del Prado, 8 (Palacio de Villahermosa). ☎ *91-369-01-51.* www.museothyssen.org. *Metro: Banco de España. Admission: 6€ ($9.60) adults, 4€ ($6.40) seniors and students, free for children 11 and under; temporary exhibits 5€ ($8) adults, 3€ ($4.80) seniors and students. Open: Tues–Sun 10 a.m.–7 p.m.*

Monasterio de las Descalzas Reales
Viejo Madrid

A visit to this former royal palace — and splendid example of Renaissance architecture — is a retreat from Madrid's modern madness. Converted into a convent for women in the mid-16th century, it's anything but plain. A grand, fresco-lined staircase takes visitors to an upper cloister gallery with a series of extravagant chapels. The convent's collection of religious art by the Old Masters is exceptional. The highlights are Breughel's *Adoration of the Magi,* Zurbarán's *Saint Francis,* Titian's *Caesar's Coin,* and a priceless collection of 16th-century tapestries. Visitation hours at the convent, where a small group of cloistered nuns still live, are peculiar and not always adhered to.

This small museum has a past as fascinating as its name (Monastery of the Royal Barefoot Franciscans). The daughter of the Emperor Carlos V, Juana of Austria, founded the convent of Poor Clares in a noble palace. The women of noble families that entered the nunnery brought sizable dowries, mostly great works of art. Nobles also squirreled away their young, illegitimate daughters here to be reared by the nuns.

Admission to the convent is by 45-minute guided tour (in Spanish) only; note that hours are rather limited.

See map p. 490. Plaza de las Descalzas, 3. ☎ *91-542-69-47 or 91-521-27-79.* www. patrimonionacional.es. *Metro: Sol or Opera. Admission: 5€ ($8) adults, 2.50€ ($4) students and EU-resident seniors and children 5–16, free on Wed for EU members; joint admission with Real Monasterio de la Encarnación 6€ ($9.60) adults, 3.40€ ($5.45) students and EU-resident seniors and children 5–16. Open: Tues–Thurs and Sat 10:30 a.m.–12:45 p.m. and 4–5:45 p.m.; Fri 10:30 a.m.–12:45 p.m.; Sun 11 a.m.–1:45 p.m. Closed Jan 1; Easter week (Wed–Sat); May 1, 2, 11, and 15; Aug 11; Nov 9; Dec 25.*

More cool things to see and do

✔ **Milling around Viejo Madrid:** One of the best ways to absorb the flavor of Madrid is to stroll the atmospheric streets of the Old City, where you uncover remnants of medieval Madrid and the city later built by the Hapsburgs. A good place to start is in the Plaza Mayor. Along Calle Mayor is Plaza de la Villa, Madrid's old town square; the cluster of handsome buildings dates to the 15th and 16th centuries. The oldest structure is the Torre de los Lujanes, a *mudéjar* (Moorish and Christian architectural mix) construction with a tall, minaret-like structure. Casa de la Villa, on the opposite side of the plaza, was built in 1640 and once housed both the town hall and city jail. Casa de Cisneros is a reconstructed 16th-century palace with a splendid Plateresque facade. South of the Plaza Mayor, beyond Calle Segovia, is Plaza de la Paja, a pretty and quiet space that was medieval Madrid's commercial center. On this plaza is Madrid's only Gothic building, the Capilla del Obispo (Bishop's Chapel). Nearby is the Moorish-looking 14th-century San Pedro church. Just east is a jumble of some of Madrid's most animated streets, full of tapas bars: Cava Baja, Cava Alta, Almendro, and Calle del Nuncio.

✔ **Sifting through the hidden treasures of the El Rastro flea market:** This busy flea market, a Madrid institution, is one of the biggest in Europe. Although it's less full of good and interesting items like antiques than it once was, you can find almost anything — including used car parts, paintings, secondhand clothes, and more. Stalls are open Sunday from dawn to 2 p.m. Take the Metro to La Latina; the market fills the streets around Ribera de Curtidores and Plaza Cascorro. Get ready to haggle over prices, and beware of pickpockets.

✔ **Seeing the spectacle of a bullfight:** Mixing barbarism with ballet and viewed as a cross between sport and art form, bullfighting draws the best and bravest young men (and even a few women) from all corners of Spain. In Spain, top bullfighters are awarded the celebrity of movie stars or sports heroes, but their fame can be even more fleeting. One misjudgment, one stray move into the bull's charge, and their midsections can literally take the bull by the horns.

If the sight of blood or the thought of animal cruelty sickens you, don't even think of attending one, but for the less squeamish or conflicted, the spectacle of the *corridas* (bullfights) offers a uniquely Spanish slice of life.

If you can't stomach a *corrida* or you land in Madrid out of season, you can visit the Museo Taurino (Bullfighting Museum; free admission), a modest place with portraits of famous matadors, jewel-encrusted capes and jackets, stuffed bull heads, and Goya etchings. Don't miss the bloody *traje de luces* (suit of lights) that the legendary Manolete was wearing when he was gored to death.

To see the bullring, visit during the bullfighting season (May–Oct) and choose either a *sol* (sun) or *sombra* (shadows) seat. A word of advice: Spring for the more expensive sombra seat. You can roast like a suckling pig in the *sol.* For tickets to bullfights (4€–115€/$6.40–$184), visit the ticket booth at the Plaza de Toros de la Venta, call ☎ 91-356-22-00 for information, or visit www.las-ventas.com.

✔ **Sampling wines and snacks during** *paseo:* From about 5 to 8 p.m., Spaniards young and old participate in a time-honored ritual, the evening *paseo,* tiding themselves over until the late 10 p.m. dinner hour by visiting tapas bars. Just saddle up to the bar and snack on such Spanish specialties as *chorizo* (sausage), *jamón serrano* (salty ham), *tortilla española* (wedges of onion and potato omelet), *albondigas* (meatballs), *calamares fritos* (fried squid), *gambas al la plancha* (grilled shrimp), and *queso manchego* (sheep's milk cheese). Eating at the bar is cheaper than grabbing a table. The best areas are around the **Plaza de Santa Ana, Plaza Mayor,** and the **Latina/Lavapies** neighborhoods, especially the Cava Baja and Cava Alta streets.

- **Latina/Lavapies** (Metro: La Latina): More than 200 years old, and a classic of bullfighting ambience, **Taberna de Antonio Sánchez,** Mesón de Paredes, 13 (☎ 91-539-78-26), is as authentic as they come. It may be the oldest tavern in Madrid. The name **Taberna de Cien Vinos,** Calle del Nuncio, 17 (☎ 91-365-47-04), means "Tavern of 100 Wines," but it offers much more than that, including some great tapas, such as roast beef and salt cod. **Casa Antonio,** Latoneros, 10 (☎ 91-429-93-56), is a Madrid classic with a zinc bar, Moorish tiles, and bright red doors.

- **Santa Ana/Huertas** (Metro: Sol/Antón Martín): You find an excellent assortment of tapas, such as anchovies and home-made canapés, at the very traditional, tile-lined **Taberna de Dolores,** Plaza Jesús, 4 (☎ 91-429-22-43; Metro: Banco de Sevilla). **Casa Alberto,** Calle de las Huertas, 18 (☎ 91-429-93-56; Metro: Antón Martín), an 1827 *taberna* with a front tapas bar and charming little restaurant in back, is a classic: Don Quixote's creator, Cervantes, once lived at this address.

- **Plaza Mayor** (Metro: Sol): The house specialty at **Mesón del Champiñon,** Cava de San Miguel, 17 (☎ 91-559-67-90), is as the name implies: garlicky mushrooms that are stuffed, grilled, salted, you name it. **Mesón de la Guitarra,** Cava de San Miguel, 13 (☎ 91-559-95-31; Metro: Sol), is what you expect to find in Madrid; it's almost always hopping with boisterous patrons, and wine and song flow freely.

✔ **Rocking to flamenco rhythms:** Flamenco is one of Spain's most treasured cultural expressions, a hypnotic and rhythmic music of suffering and eroticism. It evolved in Spain's unwanted classes of Jews and Moors during the Middle Ages, and was later appropriated and interpreted through the Gypsy culture of Andalusia. The finest and most authentic flamenco music and dancing breaks out spontaneously in bars in the wee hours of the morning, when revelers strum guitars, clap their hands, play castanets, and begin moving gracefully to the rhythm.

Although lacking in spontaneity, flamenco club performances can be just as much of a spectacle. Shows usually start at 10:30 or 11 p.m. and last until 2 or 3 a.m., but many clubs open around 9 p.m. to serve (a rather expensive) dinner before the show. (A better idea is to eat at a regular restaurant and then head to the club just for the performance.) Among the more reliable clubs (performances range from 25€–35€/ $40–$56, usually include one drink, and can be booked online) are **Casa Patas,** Cañizares, 10 (☎ 91-369-04-96; www.casapatas.com; Metro: Tirso de Molina); **Corral de la Morería,** Morería, 7 (☎ 91-365-84-46; www.corraldelamoreria.com; Metro: La Latina), one of the liveliest places in town and around since 1956; and the slightly less authentic **Café de Chinitas,** Torija, 7 (☎ 91-559-51-35; www.chinitas.com; Metro: Santo Domingo).

✔ **Dancing the night away — literally:** It may not have earned the nickname of the city that never sleeps, but Madrid is the town that parties determinedly until sunrise. Most Madrileños head to the clubs and discos around 11 p.m. or midnight, but most don't really heat up until 2 or 3 a.m. They don't empty out until the break of dawn. Most clubs have an admission charge that ranges from 10€ to 20€ ($16–$32), which includes your first drink.

The most popular nightclubs and discos change faster than a supermodel's wardrobe, but some of the current hot spots include the sprawling, anything-goes, cross-cultural **Kapital,** Atocha, 125 (☎ 91-420-29-06); the loud **Joy,** in the historic Teatro Eclava, Arenal, 11 (☎ 91-366-37-33; Metro: Sol), **Palacio Gaviria,** a wildly baroque place, Arenal, 9 (☎ 91-526-60-69; Metro: Puerta del Sol); and **Pachá,** Barceló, 11 (☎ 91-447-01-28; Metro: Tribunal), the stylish Madrid incarnation of the national chain that first struck a chord in Ibiza.

Guided tours

Madrid Visión operates multilanguage city bus tours (with headsets) of historic Madrid and modern Madrid. Lasting about 75 minutes, they depart from Gran Vía, 32, but you can get on or hop off anywhere along their route. The cost for one day is 16€ ($26) adults, 8.50€ ($14) seniors and children 7 to 16, 57€ ($91) families (two adults, three children); a two-day ticket is 20€ ($32) adults, 11€ ($18) seniors and children 7 to 16. Admission is free with purchase of the Madrid Card. For more information, call ☎ 91-779-18-88 or visit www.madridvision.es (discounts available for online purchase).

The **Patronato Municipal de Turismo** (City Tourism Office) offers an extensive series of **Descubre Madrid** (Discover Madrid) walks — guided historical and cultural tours of the city — throughout the year, though the schedule is heaviest in summer months. Tours depart from the main tourism office at Plaza Mayor, 3. Inquire at any tourism office about the program and scheduled visits, or call ☎ 91-588-16-36 or visit www.descubremadrid.com. Advance booking (a good idea in summer months, and discounts available) is possible by calling ☎ 902-22-16-22. Most tours cost 4€ ($6.40) adults, 3€ ($4.80) children 4 to 12.

Suggested itineraries

If you'd rather organize your own tours, this section offers some tips for building your own Madrid itineraries.

If you have one day

Begin your day exploring the artistic treasures of the **Prado Museum** — which should hold you for several hours, at least until lunchtime. Eat a light lunch at the **Museo del Jamón** on Paseo del Prado before jogging around the corner to pay homage to Picasso's *Guernica* in the **Centro de Arte Reina Sofía.** That and the other modern masters will keep your attention for a couple hours more, after which it's time to head back to your hotel for a well-earned siesta.

Make sure you take the time to walk through the **Plaza Mayor** at the heart of town, perhaps just before setting off on your *tapeo* in the early evening. This stroll through the heart of Old Madrid — from tapas bar to tapas bar, nibbling and imbibing along the way — should last from around 6 to 8 p.m. Head back to your hotel to rest up until 9:30 p.m. or so, when you can safely venture out for dinner at **Botín.**

If you have two days

Spend **Day 1** pretty much as outlined above. Start off **Day 2** touring the **Palacio Royal.** Afterward, head to the **Museo Nacional Centro de Arte Reina Sofía** to see Picasso's legendary, antiwar epic painting *Guernica,* as well as other Spanish and international modern masters. Afterwards, you might pop into the nearby Atocha train station for dinner at **Samarkanda.**

If these two days in Madrid represent the full extent of your time in Spain — and if it's the proper season — try to take in a bullfight at 5 p.m. If it's not bullfighting season, *tapeo* again in the evening. Either way, catch a flamenco show in the later evening (after dinner).

If you have three days

Spend **Day 1** and **Day 2** as outlined in the preceding sections, and then head off on **Day 3** for a day trip to Toledo, a commanding hilltop town that was once the capital of Spain, home to Christians, Moors, and Jews, and also the adopted city of the Renaissance master El Greco. Find out more about Toledo in the next section.

Traveling beyond Madrid: Three Day Trips

One of the highlights of visiting Madrid — oddly enough — is getting out of town. Just outside the capital are some of Spain's greatest hits, equal as a trio to the drawing power of the capital. Each of the following is an easy day trip from Madrid: **Toledo,** the one-time Spanish capital; the imposing 16th-century palace/monastery **El Escorial;** and **Segovia,** an easygoing town that features a castle that's like something out of a fairy tale and a gorgeous cathedral.

If you don't feel like doing the minimal planning (or driving) yourself, and you don't mind sticking to a group's timetable, three major players operate **no-hassle day trips** to the major sights outside of Madrid (El Escorial, Aranjuez, and the Valley of the Fallen), as well as to Toledo, Ávila, and Segovia. Prices for day tours range from 30€ to about 70€ ($48–$112). Prices generally include round-trip transportation, some museum admissions, and a guided tour. Contact **Juliatur,** Gran Vía, 68 (☎ 91-571-53-00; http://netdial.caribe.net/~juliatur; Metro: Plaza de España); **Pullmantur,** Plaza de Oriente, 8 (☎ 91-541-18-07; www.pullmantur spain.com; Metro: Ópera); or **Trapsatur,** San Bernardo, 5 (☎ 91-542-66-66; www.trapsatur.com; Metro: Santo Domingo).

Holy Toledo! Religious art and architecture

For most visitors interested in art and history, Toledo is probably the best day trip from Madrid. The town and the surrounding area are designated as a national landmark, with good reason. Toledo, the capital of Castile until the 1500s, was home to the painter El Greco and has always been the religious center of Spain — home to the Primate of Spain and a one-time host to a thriving Jewish community. You'll find Toledo worth the visit for its stunning Gothic cathedral, warren of medieval streets, and the famous views of the city from across the river (captured on canvas by none other than El Greco himself).

If you kick into high gear, you can tour Toledo in just a few hours, making it a long half-day trip from Madrid. You can also spend the whole day there and return to Madrid in the evening. But your best bet is to spend the night in Toledo; that enables you to explore the city at a leisurely pace after the day-tripping crowds and large buses leave.

Don't plan to visit Toledo on a Monday, when half the sights are closed.

Getting there

Ten trains (☎ 902-24-02-02; www.renfe.es) make the journey from Madrid's Atocha Station to Toledo every day. The trip takes just 30 minutes one-way. When you're in the station just outside Toledo, bus no. 5 takes you to Plaza de Zocodover in the heart of the old city (a visitor information kiosk is there).

The Toledo **tourist office** (☎ 925-22-08-43) is at Puerta de Bisagra, on the north end of town (turn right out of the station, go over the bridge, and walk along the city walls).

Seeing the sights

The immense Gothic **Catedral** (☎ 925-22-22-41) is in the center of Toledo, on Cardenal Cisneros, s/n. Built from 1226 to 1493, the cathedral features a gigantic carved and painted wooden *reredos* (screen) on the high altar, and behind it — illuminated by a skylight — the alabaster and marble baroque altar. Admission to the church is free, but entry to the treasury — with its 3m-high (10-ft.), 227kg (500-lb.) gilded 16th-century monstrance (made from gold brought back by Christopher Columbus) — costs 6€ ($9.60) adults, 4.50€ ($7.20) seniors and students. Summer hours are Monday through Saturday from 10:30 a.m. to 6:30 p.m. and Sunday and holidays from 2 to 6 p.m.; the cathedral closes an hour later in winter.

Although the cathedral contains works by El Greco, fans of the Greek painter's work won't want to miss **Iglesia de Santo Tomé**, Plaza del Conde, 2 (☎ 925-21-60-98). The small chapel is unremarkable, which is not a term that could be used to describe El Greco's masterpiece, the majestic *Burial of Count Orgaz* (1586). It is a breathtaking work of art; see if you can spot the painter himself among the figures. Admission is 1.90€ ($3.05), free on Wednesdays after 4 p.m.; summer hours are daily from 10 a.m. to 6:45 p.m. (until 5:45 p.m. the rest of the year).

El Greco left his imprint on Toledo to an extent that dwarfs almost any other painter's association with a city. Temporarily closed for restoration is what is touted as his Toledo home, **Casa y Museo de El Greco**, Samuel Leví, s/n (☎ 925-22-40-46), though the artist's house and studio were certainly in another location in the old Jewish quarter. For the sake of tourism, this is the place set up as an El Greco museum. Nobody pretends that the works in the museum are his best stuff; the collection is primarily small portrait-style paintings of Christ and the apostles, along with one of his famous views of Toledo. When it reopens, admission will be 2.40€ ($3.85), and hours will be Tuesday through Saturday from 10 a.m. to 2 p.m. and 4 to 6 p.m. (until 7 p.m. in summer), Sunday from 10 a.m. to 2 p.m.

Many visitors are more impressed by the Renaissance-style entrance and stairs of the **Museo de Santa Cruz**, Miguel de Cervantes, 3 (☎ 925-22-14-02) than by the works inside this former 16th-century hospice. Amid 15th-century tapestries, jewelry, artifacts, and swords and armor made from Toledo's famous damascene steel (blackened and traced with gold wire), you find lesser works by Goya, Ribera, and the omnipresent El Greco — who's represented by the 1613 *Assumption,* one of his last paintings. Admission is free. The museum is open Monday through Saturday from 10 a.m. to 6 p.m., Sunday from 10 a.m. to 2 p.m.

What do you get when a thriving Jewish community is crushed by the Catholic Inquisition and the local diocese takes over the temples? The answer: a synagogue named for the Virgin Mary. The **Sinagoga de Santa María La Blanca,** Reyes Católicos, 4 (☎ 925-22-72-57), has been restored to its Hebrew origins, which were heavily influenced by Islamic architecture. Built in the 1100s, it is the oldest of Toledo's eight remaining synagogues and features Moorish horseshoe arches atop the squat columns of the spare interior. Admission is 1.90€ ($3.05), and it's open daily from 10 a.m. to 6 p.m. (until 7 p.m. in summer).

The 14th-century **Sinagoga del Tránsito,** Samuel Leví, s/n (☎ 925-22-36-65), also blends Gothic, Islamic, and traditional Hebrew motifs. This synagogue contains a frieze inscribed with Hebrew script and set with a coffered ceiling. The **Museo Sefardí,** connected to the synagogue, preserves ancient tombs, manuscripts, and sacred objects of Toledo's Sephardic (Spanish Jewish) community. Admission (temple and museum together) is 2.40€ ($3.85). Hours are Tuesday through Saturday from 10 a.m. to 2 p.m. and 4 to 6 p.m. (until 9 p.m. in summer), and Sunday from 10 a.m. to 2 p.m.

The rebuilt **Alcázar,** Cuesta de Carlos V (☎ 925-22-16-73), dominates the town's skyline. It may not be much to look at now, but this fortress withstood many a siege. In 1936, it held up during 70 days of bombing during Spain's Civil War. It remains closed while awaiting the installation of the Museo del Ejército (Army Museum). When it reopens, admission will be 2€ ($3.20) adults, free for children 9 and under. Hours are likely to remain Tuesday through Sunday from 9:30 a.m. to 2:30 p.m.

Where to stay and dine

The **Hostal del Cardenal,** Paseo de Recaredo, 24 (☎ 925-22-49-00; Fax: 925-22-29-91; www.hostaldelcardenal.com), has a very good and reasonably priced Spanish cuisine, such as roast suckling pig. But it's better known as one of the most appealing and affordable small hotels in town. Doubles range from 116€ to 150€ ($186–$240), with free parking. Another excellent small inn in the thick of things, right by the cathedral, is **Hostal Casa de Cisneros,** Cardenal de Cisneros, 1 (☎ 925-22-88-28; Fax: 925-22-31-73; www.hostal-casa-de-cisneros.com), which has uniquely attractive double rooms for 70€ to 80€ ($112–$128). For an excellent meal with stunning views of Toledo from across the river, drop in on **La Ermita,** Ctra. de Circunvalación, s/n (☎ 925-25-31-93). The open-air bar next door is a great spot for a predinner drink.

El Escorial: A king-size monastery

King Felipe II was nothing if not creative — and zealous. When he needed a new royal residence in the late 16th century, instead of following in the footsteps of his European peers and building a palace, he built himself a live-in monastery. But not your run-of-the-mill monastery. Fortress-thick walls enclose San Lorenzo de El Escorial, a frescoed and tapestried complex of royal apartments, with a giant basilica, terrific art gallery, opulent library, and Spain's royal tombs.

Other than the huge monastery, you won't find much else in the town of El Escorial; allow two to three hours to tour the monastery.

Getting there

From Madrid, the bus and train trips to El Escorial both take about an hour. Buses from Madrid's Moncha Metro station (you can buy tickets at a kiosk in the station) drop you off right in front of the monastery. About 25 trains leave Madrid's Atocha Station daily for El Escorial; buses meet incoming trains to shuttle visitors the remaining mile to Plaza Virgen de Gracia, a block east of the monastery.

The **tourist office** (☎ 918-90-53-13) is at Grimaldi, 2, north of the visitor entrance to the complex.

Seeing the monastery

Felipe II's royal apartments in the monastery/fortress of San Lorenzo de El Escorial (☎ 91-890-78-19; www.patrimonionacional.es) are as stark and monastic as a king could get. He was such a devout Christian that he had his bedroom built to overlook the high altar of the impressive basilica, which has four organs and a dome based on Michelangelo's plans for St. Peter's in Rome. The basilica is also home to Cellini's *Crucifix*. Under the altar is the Royal Pantheon, a mausoleum containing the remains of every Spanish king from Charles I to Alfonso XII. The tapestried apartments of the Bourbon kings, Carlos III and Carlos IV, are more elaborate and in keeping with the tastes of most monarchs.

Paintings such as Titian's *Last Supper,* Velázquez's *The Tunic of Joseph,* El Greco's *Martyrdom of St. Maurice,* and works by Dürer, Van Dyck, Tintoretto, and Rubens are the source of the New Museum's popularity. The Royal Library houses more than 40,000 antique volumes under a barrel-vaulted ceiling frescoed by Tibaldi in the 16th century.

El Escorial is open Tuesday through Sunday and holidays from 10 a.m. to 5 p.m. (until 6 p.m. in summer). Admission is 10€ ($16) adults, 6€ ($9.60) seniors and students.

Where to dine

Even though El Escorial is an easy half-day trip from Madrid, you may want to eat lunch before you return, so try the suitably named **Mesón la Cueva,** San Antón, 4 (☎ **91-890-1516;** www.mesonlacueva.com).

Segovia: A tour of Spanish history

Segovia brings to life a cross section of Spain's history. Still standing are a 2,000-year-old Roman aqueduct, a Moorish palace, and a Gothic cathedral. With its medieval streets, Romanesque churches, and 15th-century palaces, Segovia is an enjoyable place to stroll and get a sense of what it was like to live in a small Castilian city.

You can easily see Segovia in three to four hours, but if you're in need of a break from the capital, it makes a nice place to hang around for an overnight escape.

Getting there

Trains (☎ 902-24-02-02; www.renfe.es) leave Madrid for Segovia every other hour (they depart Madrid from Atocha Station but also pause at Chamartín en route). The regular regional train takes two hours. From Segovia's train station, bus no. 3 runs to Plaza Mayor in the center of town. The new high-speed AVE train makes the trip in just 30 minutes, arriving in a new station, Segovia-Guiomar.

The **tourist office** (☎ 921-46-03-34) is at Plaza Mayor, 10.

Seeing the sights

The majestic **Roman aqueduct** runs 818m (2,685 ft.) along the Plaza del Azoguejo on the east side of town. The aqueduct, much of it two tiers high, contains 118 arches and is 29m (96 ft.) at its highest point. Built in the first century A.D. using stone blocks with no mortar, the aqueduct was one of the city's major water sources all the way until the 19th century.

The **Catedral de Segovia** (☎ 921-46-22-05), Marqués del Arco, s/n, dominates the city's old quarter. Isabella I (of Ferdinand and Isabella fame) was named queen on this very spot in 1474. Built from 1515 to 1558, Spain's last great Gothic cathedral is all buttresses and pinnacles. Inside, it overflows with riches, including beautiful stained-glass windows, which light the carved choir stalls, the 16th- and 17th-century paintings, and the grille-fronted chapels inside. The attached cloisters were originally part of an earlier church at the same location. The 17th-century Capilla de la Concepción is spectacular. The small museum holds paintings by Ribera, Flemish tapestries, jewelry, and manuscripts. Admission is 3€ ($4.80) adults, free for children 13 and under. April through October hours are daily from 9:30 a.m. to 6:30 p.m. (until 5:30 p.m. the rest of the year).

Segovia's commanding **Alcázar** (☎ 921-46-07-59; www.alcazarde segovia.com), a fairy tale of a fortress, anchors the west end of town. Originally raised between the 12th and 15th centuries, it was largely rebuilt after a disastrous 1862 fire destroyed many of its Moorish embellishments. Behind the formidable exterior are some sumptuous rooms, from the Gothic King's Room to the stuccoed Throne Room. Clamber up the Torre de Juan II, built as a dungeon, for panoramic views. Admission is 4€ ($6.40) adults, 3€ ($4.80) children 8 to 14; tower access is an additional 2€ ($3.20). Hours are daily from 10 a.m. to 7 p.m. (until 6 p.m. Oct–Mar).

Where to stay and dine

The tavernlike **Mesón de Cándido,** Plaza de Azoguejo, 5, right next to the Aqueduct (☎ 921-42-59-11), serves hearty Castilian specialties and is pretty much an obligatory stop in Segovia. You can get an inexpensive double room for 64€ to 75€ ($102–$120) in the **Hostal Residencia Las Sirenas,** Juan Bravo, 30 (☎ **921-46-26-63;** Fax: 92-146-2657; www.hotel sirenas.com), though a considerable step up is the classic **Hotel Infanta Isabel,** Calle Isabel la Católica, 1 (Plaza Mayor; ☎ **921-46-13-00;** Fax: 921-46-22-17; www.hotelinfantaisabel.com), right across from the cathedral. Doubles run 84€ to 214€ ($134–$342), and many have views of the Plaza Mayor. The modern **Parador de Segovia,** Carretera de Valladolid, s/n (☎ **921-44-37-37;** Fax: 921-43-73-62; www.parador.es), is a couple of kilometers north of town, but it has a large outdoor swimming pool and splendid distant views of Segovia. Doubles run 148€ to 224€ ($237–$358).

Fast Facts: Madrid

American Express

The American Express office is at Barajas airport and Plaza de las Cortes, 2 (☎ 91-743-77-55; Metro: Banco de España); it's open Monday through Friday from 9 a.m. to 7:30 p.m., Saturday from 9 a.m. to 2 p.m.

Area Code

The country code for Spain is **34** and the city code for Madrid is **91.**

ATMs

ATMs are widely available throughout Madrid; most banks have 24-hour ATMs. You can find such branches along Gran Vía and Calle Serrano in the Salamanca neighborhood.

Currency

The currency in Spain, like all of Western Europe, is the euro. The euro is divided into 100 cents, and there are coins of 0.01, 0.02, 0.05, 0.10, 0.20, 0.50, 1€, and 2€. Paper-note denominations are 5, 10, 20, 50, 100, 200, and 500 euros. The exchange rate used to calculate the dollar values given in this chapter is 1€ = $1.60. Amounts over $10 are rounded to the nearest dollar.

Currency Exchange

You can find currency exchange offices at the Chamartín rail station and Barajas airport. Major Spanish banks include La Caixa,

BBV, and Banco Central Hispano; most have branches on Gran Vía and/or Alcalá.

Doctors

To locate an English-speaking doctor or report a medical emergency, dial ☎ **112** or **061** (Insalud, Public Medical Care).

Embassies and Consulates

The U.S. Embassy, located at Calle Serrano, 75 (☎ 91-587-22-00; Metro: Núñez de Balboa), is open Monday through Friday from 9 a.m. to 6 p.m., except for U.S. and local holidays. The Canadian Embassy, Núñez de Balboa, 35 (☎ 91-423-32-50; Metro: Velázquez), is open Monday through Friday 8:30 a.m. to 5:30 p.m. The United Kingdom Embassy, Calle Fernando el Santo, 16 (☎ 91-319-02-00; Metro: Colón), is open Monday through Friday 9 a.m. to 1:30 p.m. and 3 to 6 p.m. The Republic of Ireland has an embassy at Claudio Coello, 73 (☎ 91-576-35-00; Metro: Serrano); it's open Monday through Friday 9 a.m. to 2 p.m. The Australian Embassy, Plaza Diego de Ordas, 3, Edificio Santa Engracia, 120 (☎ 91-441-93-00; Metro: Ríos Rosas), is open Monday though Thursday 8:30 a.m. to 5 p.m. and Friday 8:30 a.m. to 2:15 p.m. Citizens of New Zealand have an embassy at Plaza de la Lealtad, 2 (☎ 91-523-02-26; Metro: Banco de España); it's open Monday through Friday 9 a.m. to 1:30 p.m. and 2:30 to 5:30 p.m.

Emergencies

For street emergencies, call ☎ **061**. For an ambulance, call ☎ **112** or **092**.

Hospitals

To locate a hospital, dial ☎ 112. For medical emergencies, visit or call a 24-hour first-aid station (see "Emergencies," earlier in this section). For help finding an English-speaking doctor, call the Anglo-American Medical Unit, Calle Conde de Aranda, 1 (☎ 91-435-1823). All insurance is recognized, and emergencies will be seen to without bureaucratic red tape.

Information

Municipal Tourism Offices are located at Plaza Mayor, 3 (☎ 91-588-16-36), open Monday through Saturday from 10 a.m. to 8 p.m. and Sunday and holidays from 10 a.m. to 3 p.m.; Duque de Medinaceli, 2 (☎ 91-429-49-51), open Monday though Saturday from 9 a.m. to 7 p.m. and Sunday from 9 a.m. to 3 p.m.; Puerta de Toledo Market, 1 (☎ 91-364-18-76), open Monday through Saturday from 8 a.m. to 8 p.m. and Sunday from 8 a.m. to 2 p.m.; Barajas Airport (International Arrivals Terminal; ☎ 902-10-00-07), open daily from 8 a.m. to 8 p.m. Also look for tourist information offices at Atocha train station (☎ 902-10-00-07), open daily from 9 a.m. to 9 p.m., and Chamartín (☎ 91-315-99-76), open Monday through Saturday from 8 a.m. to 8 p.m. and Sunday 8 a.m. to 2 p.m. In summer months, yellow tourist information kiosks are set up near the Prado Museum, the Palacio Real, and Puerta del Sol. You can also call ☎ 902-10-00-07 to get tourism information by phone, or visit www.munimadrid.es. For general information, call ☎ 010.

For bus information, call ☎ 91-53-048-00 or 91-468-42-00. For train information, call ☎ 902-24-02-02 or 902-24-34-02 or log on to www.renfe.es. For flight information, dial ☎ 91-305-83-44 or 902-40-47-04.

Internet Access and Cybercafes

If you want to Net-surf or need to send an e-mail, try one of the following cafes or computer centers (though it's wise to check with the tourism office, because these tend to come and go with regularity): Interpublic, Carrera de San Jerónimo, 18, 1st floor (☎ 91-523-15-50; Metro: Sol); and easyEverything, Calle Montera, 10–12 (☎ 91-523-55-63; www.easyevery thing.com), open 24/7, with more than 200 computers. Prices range from 1€ to 3€ ($1.60–$4.80) per hour.

Maps

A free street map, covering the whole of Madrid, is available at tourist information offices at the airport, train stations, and in the city. The map is sufficient for virtually all city travel. You should also pick up the pocket-size map of the Metro subway system, available free at any Metro station.

Newspapers and Magazines

Most European newspapers are sold on the day of publication, as are the Paris-based *International Herald Tribune* and European edition of the *Wall Street Journal. USA Today* is also widely available, as are principal European and American magazines. You can find them at the many kiosks along Gran Vía or near Puerta del Sol. Spanish-speakers should check out the weekly entertainment information magazine *Guía del Ocio* (Leisure Guide), which lists bars, restaurants, cinema, theater, and concerts.

Pharmacies

Pharmacies (*farmacias,* indicated by neon-green crosses) operate during normal business hours, but one in every neighborhood remains open all night and on holidays. The location and phone number of this *farmacia de guardia* is posted on the door of all the other pharmacies. You can call ☎ 098 to contact all-night pharmacies.

Police

Call ☎ 112 or 092.

Post Office

The Central Post Office is located at Palacio de Comunicaciones, Plaza de la Cibeles, s/n (☎ 91-396-24-43). It's open Monday through Friday from 8:30 a.m. to 9 p.m., Saturday from 8 a.m. to 8 p.m., and Sundays and holidays from 8:30 a.m. to 2 p.m. The yellow sign CORREOS identifies branches of the post office. Stamps are also sold at *estancos* (tobacco sellers). An airmail letter or post-card to the United States is 0.75€ ($1.20).

Safety

Madrid has a reputation of having one of the highest crime rates in Spain, though street crime is normally limited to pickpocketing and breaking into cars with items left in the seats. Exercise extra care along Gran Vía, Puerta del Sol, Calle Montera (known as a heavy red-light district), the Rastro flea market, and areas with lots of bars (and rowdy drunks), such as Huertas and Latina. The presence of so many people out at all

hours of the night is generally cause for reassurance rather than fear. Also, be especially careful of tourist scams near the art museums on Paseo del Prado.

Taxes

The government sales tax, known as IVA (value-added tax), is levied nationwide on all goods and services, and ranges from 7 percent to 33 percent.

Taxis

If you need to call a cab, taxi companies include Tele-Taxi (☎ 91-371-21-31), Radio Taxi (☎ 91-447-32-32), and Radio Taxi Independiente (☎ 91-405-55-00).

Telephone

For general telephone information, call ☎ 010. For national telephone information, dial ☎ 009. Madrid's area code is 91, and you must dial it before all numbers. International call centers are located at the main post office, Plaza de la Cibeles, s/n; Gran Vía, 30; and Paseo de Recoletos, 41 (Plaza de colón).

Chapter 23

The Best of Barcelona

● ●

In This Chapter

▶ Getting to Barcelona

▶ Discovering the neighborhoods

▶ Visiting Barcelona's best restaurants and hotels

▶ Seeing Barcelona's top sights

● ●

*B*arcelona has been around since the Romans dubbed it *Barcino* and built a sturdy wall around it 2,000 years ago, but it was the 1992 Summer Olympic Games that really thrust this self-assured and cosmopolitan city onto the world stage. In a flash, Barcelona became one of Europe's hottest destinations. And it hasn't cooled off one bit.

Barcelona is as intoxicating a city as they come. Las Ramblas boulevard is a pulsating parade of locals, tourists, and cheery hucksters, dressed up in face paint and costumes like historical statues. The Gothic Quarter's narrow, dark alleys resonate with romance and history, as well as chic restaurants and shops. The Eixample district is a sparkling grid of Barcelona's signature *modernista* apartment buildings. With its palm trees, sparkling urban beaches, and outdoor cafes, Barcelona has the languid air of a sultry Mediterranean capital, while its commitment to eye-popping style and design give it the air of a progressive northern European city.

Barcelona has a long tradition of embracing visionary artists such as Pablo Picasso, Joan Miró, and Salvador Dalí, but the city's favorite eccentric son is Antoni Gaudí, whose wildly imaginative architecture is an appropriate symbol for this ancient yet cutting-edge city.

Barcelona is the capital of the fiercely independent-minded region of prosperous Catalonia, which recently was granted more autonomy than ever before by the central Spanish government. The people of Spain's second-largest city are ambitious, pragmatic, and serious about their Catalan identity, with its unique language and strong ties to the countryside. Citizens of Barcelona are fluent in both Catalan and Spanish, and although you'll likely hear more of the former, you shouldn't hesitate to use any Spanish that you know.

Getting There

Getting into the city from the airport is fairly simple, and the train station is connected to a subway line. When you're in town, getting around by public transportation is also easy.

Arriving by air

Barcelona's **El Prat** airport (☎ 93-478-50-00; www.aena.es) is 12km (7 miles) southeast of the city. In the arrivals hall are several ATMs and an information desk. For flight information, call ☎ 93-298-38-38. Most flights from North America still fly direct to the capital, Madrid, before continuing on to Barcelona, but **American Airlines** (☎ 800-443-7300; www.aa.com) recently introduced direct flights from New York to Barcelona.

Trains (www.renfe.es) run every 30 minutes from the airport to Estació Sants, Plaça Catalunya, and Arc de Triomf; they cost 1.25€ ($2). Even more convenient is the **Aerobús** (www.grupsarbusb.com), which departs every 6 to 15 minutes to Plaça de Catalunya, Passeig de Gràcia, or Plaça Espanya. The trip takes 30 minutes and costs 3.90€ ($6.25); there is a 20 percent discount with the Barcelona Card (see "Exploring Barcelona," later in this chapter). Tickets are sold on the bus. A **taxi** into town is about 17€ to 20€ ($27–$32), plus tip and supplements for luggage.

Arriving by train

Most trains bound for Barcelona arrive either at the **Estació Sants** on the western edge of the Eixample, or at the **Estació de França,** near the harbor at the base of the Ciutadella park. Both stations link to the Metro network. A recently inaugurated (Dec 2007) high-speed AVE train travels to Barcelona from Madrid in three hours (and will cut the trip to two-and-a-half hours as soon as the latest version of the European Train Control System [ETCS] is in place).

Orienting Yourself in Barcelona

A split personality of the city is evident in the contrast between the old city and the new city. The **Ciutat Vella** (Old City) is a hexagon of narrow streets nudged up against the harbor. The massive grid of streets that makes up the new city, known as the **Eixample** (occasionally called El Ensanche in Spanish), surrounds the old one.

The famed street **Las Ramblas** (Les Rambles in Catalan, but also referred to in the singular, La Rambla) bisects the Ciutat Vella and runs from the harbor north to Plaça de Catalunya. Las Ramblas is a wide, tree-shaded boulevard with street entertainers, flower stalls, cafes, and the bustle of the city. (The street runs northwest, but all city maps are oriented with this street pointing straight up and down.) The street degenerated during the fascist Franco era early in the 20th century, as did much of old Barcelona, but it has mostly regained its footing and respectability as new businesses revive the Ciutat Vella.

Introducing the neighborhoods

Barri Gòtic, the medieval heart of town around the cathedral, lies to the east of Las Ramblas. Site of the original Roman city, this is, along with the Ramblas, the most appetizing area for wandering. Lots of shops, museums, and restaurants fill its narrow streets with old buildings. The Barri Gòtic's eastern edge is Via Laietana, and from this wide street over to the Carrer Montcada is **La Ribera** and its vibrant adjunct **El Born,** site of innumerable bars, restaurants, and chic shops. South of these two districts is the scenic, lake-spotted **Parc de la Ciutadella.** On a triangular peninsula jutting into the harbor just south of that, the former fishing village of **Barceloneta** teems with activity, seafood restaurants, and tapas bars. To the east are the **Vila Olímpica,** an upscale neighborhood created to house the Olympic athletes in 1992, and the most fashionable beaches.

The **Barri Xinés** (officially know as the **Raval**), a historically seedy neighborhood of prostitutes, beggars, and thieves, is to the west of Las Ramblas. Though much improved and an area of large gentrification projects, led by the Barcelona Museum of Contemporary Art (MACBA), it remains a ramshackle neighborhood characterized by populations of newly arrived immigrants. Only the more adventurous visitors will want to venture there after dark. Well beyond this, to the city's west, rises the hill of **Montjuïc,** site of the World's Fair and Olympic parks.

Dividing the old city from the new, the **Plaça de Catalunya,** at Las Ramblas's north end, is the center of Barcelona. The grid of streets spreading north from this plaza is known as the **Eixample,** and its chic shopping boulevard **Passeig de Gràcia,** home to several of *modernisme*'s greatest hits. The main thoroughfare is logically, if prosaically, named Avinguda Diagonal, as it crosses the grid diagonally. Beyond this, the largely working-class neighborhood of **Gràcia** expands to the north, where Castilian Spanish is heard much less than Catalan.

Finding information after you arrive

The most central and helpful of the several information offices is the subterranean **Turisme de Barcelona,** Plaça de Catalunya, 17 underground (☎ 93-285-38-34; www.barcelonaturisme.com; Metro: Catalunya), open daily from 9 a.m. to 9 p.m. The multilingual attendants can provide street maps, answer questions, change money, and make hotel reservations. Other city information bureaus are located on Plaça Sant Jaume, at the airport, and the Sants train station.

Informació Turística de Catalunya, which provides information on Barcelona and the entire autonomous region, is located in Palau Robert, Passeig de Gràcia, 107 (☎ 93-238-40-00). It's open Monday through Saturday from 10 a.m. to 7 p.m., Sunday 10 a.m. to 2 p.m.

Getting Around Barcelona

For transit info, call ☎ **010** or check online at www.tmb.net for city public transport.

By public transportation

Barcelona's **Metro** (subway; ☎ **010** or 93-298-70-00; www.tmb.net) covers the city pretty well. Line 3 runs down Las Ramblas (and to the Sants-Estació train station), and Line 4 follows Via Laietana, bordering the eastern edge of the Ciutat Vella. Plaça de Catalunya is one of the main Metro junctions, with nearby Passeig de Gràcia as another main transfer station. You can hoof it from most Metro stations to wherever you're headed, but occasionally you may find that taking a bus is easier.

Tickets for both the Metro and bus cost 1.30€ ($2.10). A one-day Metro and bus pass costs 5.50€ ($8.80), and a T-10 ticket, good for ten rides on either, is 7.20€ ($12). You can also get free rides on all public transport with purchase of the Barcelona Card (see "Exploring Barcelona," later in this chapter).

By taxi

Black-and-yellow taxis are affordable and everywhere. Few journeys cost more than 7€ ($11). In addition to the numerous taxi stands located throughout the city, cabs cruise the streets looking for fares. Available cars advertise with LIBRE or LLIURE signs or with an illuminated green sign. Reliable taxi companies include **FonoTaxi** (☎ **93-330-11-00**), **Barna Taxi** (☎ **93-357-77-55**), and **Radio Taxi** (☎ **93-303-30-33**); the latter accepts credit cards.

By funicular and cable car

Funiculars (trams) and cable cars run up some of the hills around the city, including Montjuïc and Tibidabo. The **Funicular de Montjuïc**, which departs from the Paral.lel Metro station, is included in the T-10 multi-journey ticket. The Montjuïc cable car, which runs from the waterfront to the top of Montjuïc, costs 5.50€ ($8.80) adults one-way, 7.50€ ($12) adults round-trip, and 4.25€ ($6.80) children 4 to 12 one-way, 5.75€ ($9.20) children 4 to 12 round-trip.

By foot

Unlike Madrid, Barcelona is a joy to wander — especially the medieval alleys of the Barri Gòtic, along the wide pedestrian sidewalk that runs down the middle of Las Ramblas, and the elegant boulevard Passeig de Gràcia. To get back and forth between the Ciutat Vella or the waterfront and the newer part of town, the Eixample, you'll want to take public transportation or a taxi.

Staying in Barcelona

Barcelona's hotels have risen with the city's popularity and are now comparably priced to other large European cities. Barcelona went nuts building and refurbishing hotels in time for the 1992 Olympics, and, more than a decade later, new hotels are still sprouting up all over the city to meet the city's ever-growing demand. Many cheaper places are mostly located in areas that are not the most desirable.

Barcelona no longer really has high and low travel seasons; hotel rates remain relatively constant throughout the year, though some hotels offer slightly lower prices when Barcelonans escape the city in droves (Easter, the month of Aug, and Christmas).

Turisme de Barcelona operates a hotel-booking service online and at its office in Plaça de Catalunya (☎ 93-285-38-32; www.barcelonaturisme. com/hotelsbcn). The service concentrates on last-minute (same-day) bookings.

The top hotels

Duquesa de Cardona
$$$$ Ciutat Vella (Barri Gòtic)

At the edge of the Gothic Quarter and just across the street from the waterfront, this handsome, sedate boutique hotel is a great all-around place to stay. The location is perfect for walks along the Moll de la Fusta promenade and is walking distance from restaurants in the port and La Rambla. Housed in a meticulously restored 19th-century palace, it's elegant and intimate but also welcoming and relaxed. It boasts a bonus feature that few Barcelona hotels can lay claim to: a large rooftop solarium terrace with an attractive little pool and commanding views of the waterfront and port. It also has a very nice full restaurant, another surprise for a small hotel. Accommodations are luxurious and warm, chic but not coldly "drunk on design," as many aspiring design hotels tend to be in Barcelona. Rooms with sea views are more expensive, while interior rooms are quieter. Check online for packages and special deals.

See map p. 518. Passeig Colom, 12. ☎ *93-268-90-90. Fax: 93-268-29-31.* www.hduquesa decardona.com. *Metro: Drassanes. Rack rates: 185€–285€ ($296–$456) double. AE, DC, MC, V.*

Hispanos Siete Suiza
$$$ Eixample

An aparthotel with the comforts of a top-flight hotel, the Suiza is perfect for families and long-term stays. The location, out near the Sagrada Família, is not as convenient as others in the Eixample, but the amenities and comfort more than make up for it, especially for families or anyone needing a little space to stretch out. Apartments in the historic house are two-bedroom, two-bath, with living rooms and full kitchens; continental breakfast is included in the price. Incredibly, for a place of this size, the sophisticated in-house La Cúpula restaurant is overseen by the famed Catalan chef, Carles Gaig. But best of all, some of the hotel's profits go toward a cancer foundation established by the original owner of the house. *Sicilia, 255.* ☎ *93-208-20-51. Fax: 93-208-20-52.* www.hispanos7suiza.com. *Metro: Sagrada Família. Rack rates: 140€–195€ ($224–$312). AE, DC, MC, V.*

Hotel Banys Orientals
$$ Ciutat Vella (La Ribera)

An exciting option in a lively location, near the Born and Santa María del Mar — and not so far from the waterfront — is this inexpensive but hugely hip little hotel. Managed by the same people who run the excellent Senyor Parellada restaurant next door (see "Dining in Barcelona," later in this chapter), this place is perfect for people with tons of style but not a huge budget. Rooms are small but very cool, with a chic monochromatic design. The suites, located in two nearby buildings, are more independent but more spacious, and also an equally good deal at 130€ ($208). Though the hotel is very convenient for sightseeing and dining, it's probably best for young people and not ideal for anyone who's averse to crowds and a bit of noise; particularly on weekend nights, this area is overrun with revelers spilling out of bars and restaurants.

See map p. 518. Argenteria, 37. ☎ *93-268-84-60. Fax: 93-268-84-61.* www.hotel banysorientals.com. *Metro: Sant Jaume. Rack rates: 100€ ($160) double. AE, DC, MC, V.*

Hotel Constanza
$$$ Eixample

If you're looking for a dose of Barcelona's legendary style but at an affordable price, this boutique hotel may be the answer. It has just 20 rooms; although they're not huge, they're fashionably sleek and very comfortable, with leather trim, plush pillows, and sparkling bathrooms. The hotel's very nicely located (a short walking distance from Plaça de Catalunya) for the bargain rates. In essence, it's like the excellent Prestige Paseo de Gracia (see the upcoming listing), but on a much tighter budget.

See map p. 518. Bruc 33. ☎ *93-270-19-10. Fax: 93-317-40-24.* www.hotel constanza.com. *Metro: Urquinaona. Rack rates: 120€ ($192) double. AE, DC, MC, V.*

Hotel Pulitzer
$$$ Eixample

Sleek and trendy, but rather affordable for a boutique hotel of its considerable comfort, design, and amenities, this relative newcomer to the Barcelona hotel scene has quickly become very popular. It occupies a beautifully renovated, historic building with great flair. The design focus was on creating a hotel that feels more like an urbane apartment building than an anonymous hotel. Rooms feature warmly modern lighting, woods

Accommodations, Dining, and Attractions in Barcelona

HOTELS ■
Duquesa de Cardona **6**
H10 Montcada **25**
H10 Racó del Pi **19**
Hotel Banys Orientals **10**
Hotel Colón **22**
Hotel España **14**
Hotel Gótico **12**
Hotel Granvía **28**
Hotel Jardí **18**
Prestige Paseo de Gracia **30**

RESTAURANTS ◆
Agua **3**
Agut d'Avignon **13**
Cal Pep **7**
Casa Calvet **27**
Principal **31**
Restaurante 7 Portes **5**
Senyor Parellada **9**
Talaia Mar **4**

ATTRACTIONS ●
Catedral de Barcelona **23**
Els Quatre Gats **21**
La Boquería **15**
La Pedrera (Casa Milà) **32**
La Rambla **16**
La Sagrada Familia **34**
Manzana de la Discòrdia **29**
Monument à Colom **2**
Museu Nacional d'Art de
    Catalunya (MNAC) **1**
Museu Picasso **8**
Palau de la Música Catalana **26**
Parc Güell **33**
Plaça del Pi **17**
Plaça del Rei **24**
Plaça de Sant Jaume **11**
Plaça Sant Felip de Neri **20**

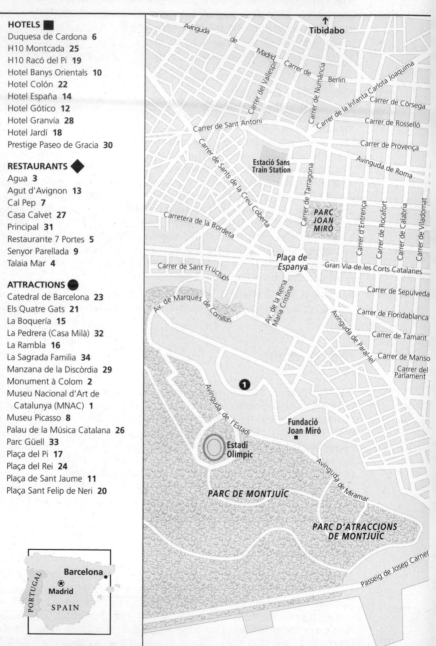

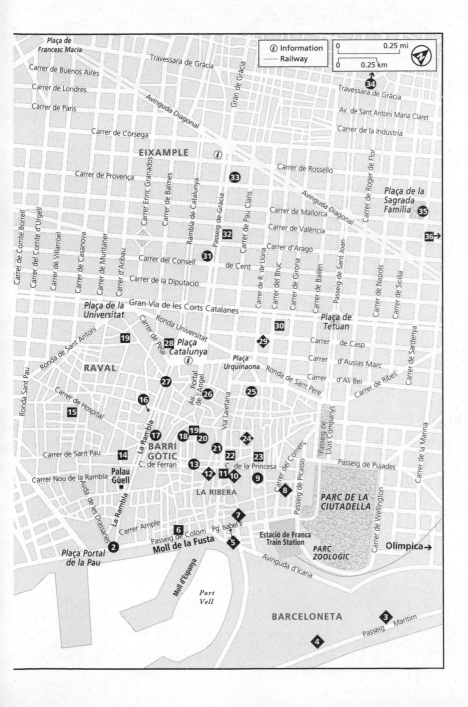

Plaça de Francesc Macia
Carrer de Buenos Aires
Carrer de Londres
Carrer de Paris
Travessara de Gràcia
Gran de Gràcia
Avinguda Diagonal
Carrer de Còrsega

(i) Information
— Railway

0   0.25 mi
0   0.25 km

Travessara de Gràcia
Av. de Sant Antoni Maria Claret
Carrer de la Industria

EIXAMPLE (i)

Carrer de Provença
Carrer Enric Granados
Carrer de Balmes
Rambla de Catalunya
Passeig de Gràcia
Carrer de Pau Claris

Carrer de Rosselló
Avinguda Diagonal
Carrer de Mallorca
Carrer de València
Carrer d'Aragó
Carrer de R. de Llúria
Carrer del Bruc
Carrer de Girona
Carrer de Bailèn
Passeig de Sant Joan

Carrer de Roger de Flor

Plaça de la Sagrada Família 35

36→

33
32
31
30
29

Carrer de Comte Borrell
Carrer del Comte d'Urgell
Carrer de Villarroel
Carrer de Casanova
Carrer de Muntaner
Carrer d'Aribau
Carrer del Consell
Carrer de la Diputació
de Cent
Gran Via de les Corts Catalanes

Carrer de Napols
Carrer de Sicilia

Plaça de Tetuan

Carrer   de Casp
Carrer   d'Ausias Marc
Carrer   d'Ali Bei
Carrer de Ribes

Carrer de Sardenya

Plaça de la Universitat
Ronda Universitat
Ronda de Sant Antoni
Carrer de Pelai
19
28 **Plaça Catalunya** (i)

Plaça Urquinaona
Ronda de Sant Pere

RAVAL

Ronda Sant Pau
Carrer de Hospital
15
27
16
Av. Portal de l'Angel
26
Via Laietana
25

Passeig de Lluís Companys

Carrer de la Marina

17
18 19 20
BARRI GÒTIC
La Rambla
C. de Ferran
13
21
22
24
23
C. de la Princesa
Carrer del Comerç
Passeig de Picasso

Carrer de Sant Pau
14

Palau Güell
12 11 10
9
8

LA RIBERA

Passeig de Pujades

PARC DE LA CIUTADELLA

Carrer de Wellington

Carrer Nou de la Rambla
Avda. de les Drassanes
La Rambla
Carrer Ample
7
6
5
Passeig de Colom
Moll de la Fusta
Pg. Isabel II
Estació de Franca Train Station

PARC ZOOLOGIC

Olímpica→

2
Plaça Portal de la Pau
Avinguda d'Icaria

Moll d'Espanya
Port Vell

BARCELONETA
3
Passeig Marítim
4

and textiles, and sleek slate or marble bathrooms. With a stylish cocktail bar, chic white restaurant, and alluring candlelit rooftop terrace, this hotel is bound to win a design prize or two.

Bergara, 8. ☎ *93-481-67-67. Fax: 93-481-64-64.* www.hotelpulitzer.es. *Metro: Catalunya. Rack rates: 165€–250€ ($264–$400). AE, DC, MC, V.*

Prestige Paseo de Gracia
$$$$ Eixample

An exquisite new small hotel (45 rooms) smack on Barcelona's swankest boulevard, Paseo de Gracia, this chic place exudes cool. The minimalist rooms have a Zen-like tranquility, and some have their own quiet and beautiful garden bamboo terraces. The hotel plays the by-now-expected Barcelona design card but does it better than almost any other hotel. It has soothing bathrooms and a well-thought-out, detail-oriented design scheme — everything from flowers to intelligent lighting. Extras include an extremely helpful "Ask Me" information attendant, a hip Zeroom lounge for listening to music and reading, free wireless Internet in the entire hotel, and Bang & Olufsen TVs. For this level of style and comfort, the hotel is a good value, especially given its pricey location.

See map p. 518. Paseo de Gracia, 62. ☎ *902-20-04-14 or 972-25-21-00. Fax: 972-25-21-01.* www.prestigepaseodegracia.com. *Metro: Passeig de Gràcia. Rack rates: 170€–360€ ($272–$576) double. AE, DC, MC, V.*

Runner-up hotels

Ciutat Barcelona Hotel
$$ Ciutat Vella (La Ribera)   A bargain hotel that offers a lot of cool design and comfort for a bargain price, this recent addition to the neighborhood, just steps from the Picasso Museum, is a winner for folks on a budget. Rooms are crisp contemporary and clean, and there's a nice rooftop pool and deck. *See map p. 518. Carrer de la Princesa, 35.* ☎ *93-269-74-75.* www.ciutatbarcelona.com.

H10 Montcada
$$$ Ciutat Vella (Barri Gòtic)   This centrally located, midsize hotel — part of the growing H10 chain of fairly priced and very smart hotels — is right across from Plaça de l'Angel, within walking distance of the Ramblas, port, Gothic Quarter, and *modernista* buildings of the Eixample. Rooms feature very warm tones and wood and are comfortable for the price. *See map p. 518. Vía Laeitana, 24.* ☎ *902-100-906 or 93-268-85-70.* www.h10.es.

Hostal Gat Xino
$$ Ciutat Vella (Raval)   This place counts with bargain design for travelers with a sense of style and adventure but not deep pockets. Rooms are spare, with a bright green, white, and black aesthetic, and there are hip photographs and flat-screen TVs. Also noteworthy is the surprisingly bountiful breakfast. The open-air deck is a good spot to soak up some sun

and meet up with fellow travelers from around the globe. *Carrer Hospital, 155.* ☎ *93-324-88-33.* www.gataccommodation.com.

Hotel Barcelona Catedral
$$ Ciutat Vella (Barri Gòtic) One of Barcelona's newer hotels is in the oldest part of town, right across from the Cathedral. It's stylishly modern but affordably priced, with unexpected bonuses including a pool, terrace, and wireless Internet access, as well as cooking lessons, wine tastings, and guided tours around the old city. *See map p. 518. Capellans, 4.* ☎ *93-304-22-55.* www.barcelonacatedral.com.

Hotel España
$$ Ciutat Vella (La Rambla) Anything but homogenous, the Hotel España, off the lower part of La Rambla, was decorated by one of *modernisme*'s star architects, Domènech i Montaner. His colorful stamp in the terrific public rooms is what makes this place special. Guest rooms, on the other hand, are simple but attractive enough. They're clean and large, but the neighborhood may give some visitors pause. *See map p. 518. Sant Pau, 9–11.* ☎ *93-318-17-58.* www.hotelespanya.com.

Dining in Barcelona

Catalans love to eat and love to eat out, and they enjoy one of the best and most imaginative cuisines in Spain. Barcelona's stature as a dining capital has really exploded in the past few years, as a number of highly creative young chefs have made the city second only to San Sebastián for fine dining. Expect market-fresh ingredients and Mediterranean dishes with a flourish. In addition to haute cuisine, you'll also find the traditional rustic dishes that have nourished Catalans for centuries. Most restaurants are in the Ciutat Vella and Eixample, though the most popular new dining area is along the Waterfront and in the new port.

Although Barcelona natives aren't quite as addicted to tapas as their brethren in the Basque country and Madrid, you should spend at least one evening doing a *tapeo,* or tapas-bar crawl (see "More cool things to see and do," later in this chapter). The best picnic pickings by far are at the excellent La Boquería market on Las Ramblas — it's loaded with produce, meats, fish, and cheeses.

A handful of restaurants feature menus printed only in Catalan, but increasingly, English-language menus are widely available.

Agua
$$–$$$ Waterfront (Port Marítim) MEDITERRANEAN
A bright and informally hip place overlooking the beach, Agua is appropriately named. It's an excellent spot for simply prepared, and inexpensive, fresh fish and shellfish, as well as rice dishes (such as risottos) and vegetarian preparations. It has a great outdoor terrace with ocean views

that are perfect for people-watching. Easygoing and often boisterous — not to mention right on the beach — it's a great spot to take the kids.

See map p. 518. Passeig Marítim de la Barceloneta, 30. ☎ *93-225-12-72.* www. aguadeltragaluz.com. *Metro: Ciutadella. Reservations recommended. Main courses: 11€–23€ ($18–$37). MC, V. Open: Daily 1:30–4 p.m. (until 5 p.m. Sat–Sun) and 8:30 p.m. to midnight (until 1 a.m. Fri–Sat). Closed last 3 weeks in Aug.*

Café de L'Academia
$$ Ciutat Vella (Barri Gòtic) CATALAN

It would be easy to overlook this dark, ancient-looking little restaurant, which sits tucked away on a lovely medieval square, but locals don't. They pack it for lunch, when it offers a superb fixed-price menu. In warm weather, tables are set out on the terrace, a perfect place to drink in this quintessential Barri Gòtic corner.

Lledó, 1 ☎ *93-315-00-26. Metro: Jaume I. Reservations recommended. Main courses: 10€–18€ ($16–$29). AE, MC, V. Open: Daily 1:30–4 p.m. (until 5 p.m. Sat–Sun); Mon–Sat 8 p.m. to midnight.*

Cal Pep
$$$–$$$$ Barri Gòtic/Waterfront SEAFOOD

This tiny, bustling, and even magical seafood restaurant is a classic Barcelona dining experience. It serves the freshest specials of the day anywhere. The restaurant has no menu, and virtually no tables (just four in back); everyone sits at the long bar and waits for Pep, the gravelly voiced owner, to recommend whatever's fresh off the boats and out of the markets. Wait patiently for a table and let Pep guide you (something he's eminently capable of, even if shared language amounts to hand signals). Though you may be in for a long wait — the place just gets more and more popular — you won't be sorry, and prices are pretty reasonable given the phenomenal quality.

See map p. 518. Plaça de les Olles, 8. ☎ *93-310-79-61. Metro: Barceloneta. Reservations not accepted. Main courses: 13€–29€ ($21–$46). MC, V. Open: Mon 8:30–11:30 p.m.; Tues–Sat 1–4:30 p.m. and 8:30–11:30 p.m.*

Can Majó
$$$ Waterfront/Port Vell SEAFOOD

Insiders, including many Barcelonans who venture down to the waterfront for lunch on weekends, know that this tavern-style, harborfront restaurant is one of the top seafood places in Barcelona. The fish is fresh, bought each morning, and a table on the terrace is coveted in warm weather. Try the excellent *sopa de pescado y marisco* (fish and shellfish soup), sautéed squid, or paellas.

See map p. 518. Almirall Aixada, 23. ☎ *93-221-58-18. Metro: Barceloneta. Reservations recommended. Main courses: 14€–28€ ($22–$45). AE, DC, MC, V. Open: Tues–Sat 1–4:30 p.m. and 8:30–11:30 p.m.; Sun 1–5 p.m.*

Casa Calvet
$$$$ Eixample Catalan

Housed on the first floor of one of Antoni Gaudí's earliest but still emblematic apartment buildings (with the oldest elevator in Barcelona), this restaurant's sumptuous white-brick and stained-glass *modernista* décor alone is enough to recommend a visit. The welcome surprise is that it's an excellent and fairly priced restaurant serving creative Catalan cuisine. Give the Galician oyster raviolis in champagne a whirl. Dining at Casa Calvet is a great, nontouristy way to get up close and personal with a *modernista* classic.

See map p. 518. Casp, 48. ☎ *93-412-40-12. Metro: Jaume I. Reservations recommended. Main courses: 19€–32€ ($30–$51). AE, MC, V. Open: Mon–Sat 1–3:30 p.m. and 8:30–11 p.m. Closed holidays and last 2 weeks in Aug.*

Comerç 24
$$$$ Ciutat Vella (Barri Gòtic) CREATIVE CATALAN/TAPAS

The Born district has exploded with trendy restaurants and bars, but this spot, which puts creativity and elegance into that Spanish staple, tapas, continues to be one of the city's coolest places to dine. The kitchen is the work of Carles Abellán, who has quickly become one of Barcelona's hottest young chefs. Here he's essentially created *tapas de autor,* and there's a great bit of theater in his preparations. The bold colors and chic stylings of the restaurant, which feels like an industrial-flavored club (it's in an old salting house), lend the perfect backdrop. The theater begins with a series of "snacks" served in sardine tins. Everything here is worthy of recommendation. Some dishes are playful; others, more traditional.

Carrer Comerç 24. ☎ *93-319-21-02. Reservations required. Metro: Jaume I. Main courses: 9€–21€ ($14–$34); tasting menus 48€ ($77) and 68€ ($109). AE, DC, MC, V. Open: Tues–Sat 1–4:30 p.m. and 8:30 p.m.–12:30 a.m.*

Cuines Santa Caterina
$$ Ciutat Vella (La Ribera) MEDITERRANEAN/ASIAN

Inside the recently renovated, wildly colorful and cool Mercat Santa Caterina (it of the undulating tiled roof), a produce, flowers, and fresh-fish-and-meat market, is this informal place that feels very much a part of its surroundings. With soaring beamed ceilings, ficus trees, and long bars and communal tables, it has just the right amount of commotion. It's perfect for an easygoing lunch, late-night snacks, or even breakfast, and there's something to please everyone. The menu careens all over the place, but in a good and fun way, featuring everything from tapas, Thai curries and sushi to great salads, fresh pastas, vegetarian and Mediterranean dishes, and, of course, fresh seafood — all at very fair prices. The breakfast and tapas bar is open daily from 9 a.m. to 11:30 p.m. (until 12:30 a.m. Thurs–Sat), and you even get food to go.

Av. Francesc Cambó, 16 (La Ribera). ☎ *93-268-99-18. Reservations not accepted. Metro: Jaume I. Main courses: 7€–20€ ($11–$32). AE, DC, MC, V. Open: Daily 1–4 p.m. and 8–11:30 p.m. (until 12:30 a.m. Thurs–Sat).*

Restaurante 7 Portes
$$$–$$$$ Waterfront (Port Vell)   SEAFOOD/CATALAN

This Barcelona institution and national monument, which has seven doors facing the street (hence the name), has been hosting large dining parties since 1836. (It was the first place in Barcelona with running water.) Barcelonans drop in to celebrate special occasions. *Set Portes,* as it is also known, is famous for its rice dishes; one favorite is the black rice with squid in its own ink. All the paellas are tremendous. Portions are huge and very reasonably priced. The dining rooms — some semiprivate — are classically elegant, with beamed ceilings, checkerboard marble floors, antique mirrors and posters, and plenty of room between tables. The place is hugely popular with families (those small dining rooms are great if your kids tend to get rambunctious at dinnertime) and young people on dates.

See map p. 518. Passeig d'Isabel II, 14. ☎ *93-319-30-33. Metro: Drassanes. Reservations recommended. Main courses: 14€–32€ ($22–$51). AE, DC, MC, V. Open: Daily 1 p.m.–1 a.m.*

Senyor Parellada
$$ Ciutat Vella (Barri Gòtic)   MEDITERRANEAN/CATALAN

This hip and handsomely decorated two-story restaurant is in a renovated old building just up the street from Santa Mará del Mar. It feels like someone's stylish house, with lamps on the tables and contemporary art on the lemon yellow and deep red walls. The menu holds its own against the décor, as do the extremely fair prices for such fresh preparations — all reasons the restaurant continues to be so popular among both locals and visitors to Barcelona. The authentic Catalan fare features excellent salads and fish, and a few adventurous choices, such as pig's trotters in garlic sauce.

See map p. 518. Argentaria, 37. ☎ *93-310-50-94. Metro: Jaume I. Reservations recommended. Main courses: 9€–19€ ($14–$30). MC, V. Open: Daily 1–4 p.m. and 8:30 p.m. to midnight.*

Exploring Barcelona

Barcelona has a greater diversity of things to see and do than any other city in Spain (something folks from Madrid may be loath to admit). When visiting, concentrate your time on distinct neighborhoods, which is how we lay out the attractions in this section. The works of Gaudí and his imaginative *modernista* cohorts and the lively Ramblas boulevard are perhaps the city's most obvious highlights, but the rich medieval Gothic Quarter, with its Picasso Museum and enticing little corners, and the newly dynamic waterfront are also huge draws. Apart from those sites, Barcelona ranks among Europe's great strolling cities, with secluded plazas, open-air cafes, tree-lined boulevards, and an inexhaustible supply of nooks where you can stop and have coffee, a beer, or tapas during your meanderings.

The **Barcelona Card** (☎ 93-285-38-32; www.barcelonaturisme.com), available at tourist offices and online (which nets you a 10 percent discount), grants free rides on all public transportation, plus 30 percent to 50 percent off on admission to most sights in town and 12 percent to 25 percent off at more than 80 shops, tours, and entertainment venues. The card costs 25€ ($40) for two days and 30€ ($48) for three days. Rates for children 4 to 12 are 4€ ($6.40) less at each level. Another bargain card, the **ArTicket** (www.articket.com; 20€/$32), gets you admission to seven museums: the Picasso Museum, the National Museum of Catalan Art (MNAC), La Pedrera, the Barcelona Museum of Contemporary Art (MACBA), the Joan Miró Foundation, the Barcelona Museum of Contemporary Culture (CCCB), and the Antoni Tàpies Foundation.

You can purchase the Barcelona Card and ArTicket at **Turisme de Barcelona** information offices in Plaça de Catalunya, Plaça de Sant Jaume, and Estació de Sants (Sants Railway Station), as well as at Corte Inglés stores, Casa Battló, and the Barcelona Nord bus station, and online with 5 percent or 10 percent discounts.

The top attractions

La Pedrera (Casa Milà)
Eixample

Gaudí's unfinished church, La Sagrada Família, leaves jaws agape, but the architect's most fascinating and inspired civic work — and perhaps the crowning glory of *modernisme* — is Casa Milà, named after the patrons who allowed him to carry through with such an avant-garde apartment building back in 1910. The masterpiece is known to almost all as La Pedrera, which means "stone quarry" — a reference to its immense limestone facade.

The massive exterior undulates like ocean waves on Passeig de Gràcia and around the corner onto Provença; on the roof are a set of chimneys that look like the inspiration for Darth Vader. On the first floor (near the entrance on Provença) is a great exhibition space for temporary art shows. The building received a head-to-toe face-lift in the mid-1990s. The apartments inside had suffered unspeakable horrors, and Gaudí's beautiful arched attics had been sealed up, but the painstaking restoration has revealed its author's genius in new ways. The attic floor is now a high-tech Gaudí museum (Espai Gaudí), with cool interactive exhibits, terrific slide shows, and access to the roof, where you can hang out with the warrior chimneys (which, according to some, represent Christians and Moors battling for Spanish turf). Both the kid-friendly, fast-paced museum and the rooftop will be unqualified hits with children.

One of the original Gaudí apartments — all with odd shapes, handcrafted doorknobs, and idiosyncratic details — has now been opened to the public. The apartment, called El Pis in Catalan, is meticulously outfitted with period furniture, including many pieces of Gaudí's design. For the entire visit, which includes museum, apartment, and rooftop, allow at least a minimum of two hours.

See map p. 518. Passeig de Gràcia, 92 (at Provença 261–265). ☎ *902-40-09-73.* www.lapedreraeducacio.org. *Metro: Diagonal or Provença. Admission: 8€ ($13) adults, 4.50€ ($7.20) students. Part of ArTicket joint admission. Open: Nov–Feb daily 9 a.m.–6 p.m.; Mar–Oct, daily 9 a.m.–8 p.m. Closed Dec 25–26, Jan 1, Jan 6. Tours available in English, Spanish, and Catalan. Audio guides available in 7 languages.*

La Sagrada Família
Eixample

Barcelona's landmark is Antoni Gaudí's unfinished legacy and testament to his singular vision, the art of the impossible. Hordes of people come to gawk at this mind-altering creation, and it's not anywhere near completion. Begun in 1884 after Gaudí took over from another architect — who was making an ordinary Gothic cathedral — the father of *modernisme* transformed the project with his fertile imagination. Even though Gaudí abandoned all other works to devote his life to this cathedral, which would be the world's largest if completed, he knew he could never finish it in his lifetime. Although he surely intended for future generations to add their signatures (he left only general plans), he probably didn't plan on resigning from the project when he did: Gaudí was run over by a tram in 1926.

The eight bejeweled spires (plans called for 12, one for each of Jesus's disciples) drip like melting candlesticks. Virtually every square inch of the surface explodes with intricate spiritual symbols. Love it or hate it, you can't deny that the church is the work of a unique visionary. A private foundation works furiously to finish the church, and though a debate once raged whether it should be completed or left unfinished as a monument to Gaudí, construction has progressed over the last two decades at a rate few could have predicted. By 2010 the cathedral will receive a full roof for the first time, allowing cultural events and religious observations to be held inside. Completion is now projected for 2025, when the central tower, the 550-foot Tower of Jesus, will be finished. Not everyone is pleased, of course — in particular, the Barcelona sculptor Josep María Subirachs's additions on the west side depicting the life of Christ have been derided as disastrous kitsch — but even the staunchest detractors have little choice now but to live with the notion of a Sagrada Família considerably changed.

The best stuff at La Sagrada Família is what you see on the outside. If you skip going in and save your 10€ ($6), you miss an elevator to the top for the (admittedly excellent) views and a fairly skimpy museum.

See map p. 518. Mallorca, 401. ☎ *93-207-30-31.* www.sagradafamilia.org. *Metro: Sagrada Família. Admission: 10€ ($6) adults, 8€ ($13) students. Open: Oct–Mar daily 9 a.m.–6 p.m.; Apr–Sept daily 9 a.m.–8 p.m.*

Gaudí or gaudy?

Around the turn of the 20th century, Art Nouveau arrived in Barcelona in the form of *modernisme,* a particularly fluid and idiosyncratic Catalan version of a larger architectural revolution. The high priest of *modernisme,* Antoni Gaudí, apprenticed as a blacksmith before taking up architecture. Creative wrought-iron patterns became just one of the many signature details that Gaudí incorporated into his flowing, organic structures; he was especially fond of creating colorful mosaics out of pieces of ceramic and mirror.

If you see only a handful of *modernisme* buildings, make them Gaudí's most famous trio: the **Sagrada Família** (see listing earlier in this chapter); **Casa Milà** (see listing earlier in this chapter), usually called La Pedrera ("the quarry") for its undulating rocky shape; and the colorful **Casa Batlló,** Passeig de Gràcia 43 (☎ **93-416-03-06;** www.casabatllo.es; Admission: 17€/$27, including audio guide; Open: Daily 9 a.m.–8 p.m.), with a roof shaped like a dragon's back and theater-mask balconies.

Two other *modernisme* architects of note were Domènech i Montaner and Puig i Cadafalch. To compare them, and to get a handle on Gaudí, walk down the Manzana de la Discòrdia ("the block of discord") on Passeig de Gràcia between Carrer del Consell de Cent and Carrer d'Arago. Here, their interpretations of *modernisme* compete in the form of apartment buildings. At no. 35 is Montaner's **Casa Lleo Morera,** at no. 41 is Cadafalch's **Casa Amatller,** and at no. 43 is Gaudí's **Casa Batlló.** (For these and Casa Milà, take the Metro to Passeig de Gràcia or Diagonal, which is closer to Casa Milà.)

Montaner also designed the gorgeous venue **Palau de la Música Catalana,** Carrer de Sant Francesc de Paula, 2 (☎ **93-295-72-00;** www.palaumusica.org), now a UNESCO World Heritage Site. It's surely the trippiest music hall you'll ever see, with a sky-lit stained glass of the inverse dome in the auditorium; 50-minute guided tours depart Wednesdays and weekends every half-hour from 10 a.m. to 3:30 p.m. for 9€ ($14). One of Cadafalch's other major works is **Els Quatre Gats,** a restaurant where Picasso and other artists used to hang out (Montsió, 3, in the Barri Gòtic).

Strolling La Rambla

Victor Hugo extolled Barcelona's La Rambla as "the most beautiful street in the world," and the Spanish poet García Lorca said it was the "only street he wished would never end." La Rambla (also referred to as Las Ramblas) is much more than an attractive street; it's an interminable street parade. Many locals practice the fine art of the *paseo* (stroll) every day of their lives along this mile-long pedestrian avenue.

Subdivided into five separate *ramblas,* each of different character and attractions, are a succession of newspaper kiosks, fresh flower stands, bird sellers, and mimes (or human statues) in elaborately conceived costumes and face paint hoping for a few stray euros. La Rambla may turn out to be the highlight of your trip to Barcelona (to ensure that it is, keep a keen eye on your bag and camera). You can walk the length of La Rambla in 30 minutes, but allow a couple hours if you want to make pit stops for refreshments, shopping, and exploring along the way.

About midway down is one of the highlights of La Rambla, the famous **La Boquería** food market. If you aren't already suffering from sensory overload, take a detour in here to see and smell an amazingly lively scene: the selling, slicing, and dicing of fresh fish, meats, produce, and just about everything your tummy wants.

At the bottom, facing the waterfront, is the **Monument à Colom** (Columbus Monument). Visitors can take the elevator up to Columbus's head for good views of the waterfront.

Exploring the Gothic Quarter

Barcelona's Barri Gòtic (or Barrio Gótico, the Gothic Quarter) — below Plaça de Catalunya and between La Rambla and Vía Laietana — is the oldest part of the city. Segments of the original Roman walls that once contained the whole of the city still survive. The district today is an intricate maze of palaces and treasures from the 11th through 15th centuries. One of Barcelona's greatest pleasures is an idle wander among the Quarter's narrow streets, along alleys filled with hanging laundry and shouting neighbors, past shops of antiques dealers, and onto stunning little squares.

The cathedral and Picasso Museum (covered later in this section) are the district's major sights, but also worth a visit is the noble **Plaça del Rei,** the courtyard of the 14th-century palace of the kings of Aragón. (The Catholic monarchs received Columbus here after his successful voyage to the Americas.) On your strolls through the Gothic Quarter, don't miss the **Roman walls** at **Plaça Nova; Plaça de Sant Jaume,** the heart of the Roman city and today the site of the municipal and regional governments; **Plaça del Pi,** the district's liveliest square, teeming with outdoor cafes and a weekend art market; peaceful **Plaça Sant Felip de Neri** (though walls ravaged by Spanish Civil War shrapnel indicate it wasn't always so quiet); and the lovely winding streets **Carrer de la Palla** and **Carrer Banys Nous,** known for their antiques dealers.

Catedral de Barcelona
Barri Gòtic

This Catalonian Gothic cathedral, the focal point of the Old City, is actually a mix of architectural styles. Though construction began in 1298, most of the structure dates from the 14th and 15th centuries. The facade was added in the 19th century. Even with that lengthy birth process, the cathedral is a splendid example of Gothic architecture. Inside, check out the handsome carved choir and surprisingly lush cloister. With its magnolias, palm trees, pond, and white geese, the cathedral is a lovely oasis in the midst of the Medieval Quarter. (In the Middle Ages, geese functioned as guard dogs, their squawks alerting priests to intruders.) Try to visit at least once at night, when the cathedral is illuminated and birds soar in the floodlights, or head to the rooftop for a view of the surrounding Gothic Quarter. A half-hour or an hour is sufficient to see the cathedral.

See map p. 518. Plaça de la Seu, s/n. ☎ *93-315-51-54.* www.website.es/ catedralbcn. *Metro: Jaume I. Admission: Cathedral free, cloister museum and tour 4€ ($6.40). Open: Daily 8 a.m.–1 p.m. and 4:30–7:30 p.m.*

Museu Nacional d'Art de Catalunya (MNAC)

If you want to get a sense of Catalonia's unique history, this splendid medieval art museum — one of the world's finest, and Barcelona's preeminent art collection — is a vital stop, presenting more than 1,000 years of art history. (Sadly, many rushed visitors unjustly overlook it). At the top of the stairs and fountains leading up to Montjuïc, housed in the domed **Palau Nacional** (National Palace), the museum is anything but a stale repository of religious art. The collection of Romanesque works, salvaged from churches all over Catalonia, is unequaled. Here you can view superb altarpieces, polychromatic icons, and treasured frescoes displayed in apses, just as they were in the country churches in which they were found. The museum also holds paintings by some of Spain's most celebrated painters, including Velázquez, Ribera, and Zurbarán. Plan on spending a couple of hours at the MNAC.

See map p. 518. Mirador del Palau, 6 (Palau Nacional, Parc de Montjuïc). ☎ *93-622-03-60.* www.mnac.cat. *Metro: Espanya. Admission: 8.50€ ($14), free for children 7 and under, free first Sun of month. Part of ArTicket joint admission. Open: Tues–Sat 10 a.m.–7 p.m., Sun 10 a.m.–2:30 p.m.*

Museu Picasso
Ciutat Vella

Pablo Picasso, though born in Málaga in southern Spain, spent much of his youth and early creative years in Barcelona before making the requisite artistic pilgrimage to Paris, where he soon became the most famous artist of the 20th century. Barcelona's Picasso museum, the second-most-visited museum in Spain (after the Prado in Madrid), can't compete with the superior collection in Paris, but it's the largest collection of his works in his native country. Picasso (1881–1973) donated 2,500 paintings and sculptures to the museum, many of them early (and more traditional figurative) pieces, including several from his blue period. If you're already a fan, you're likely to love the museum, even though few works are considered among Picasso's masterpieces; individuals looking for a comprehensive career-spanning collection may be disappointed. The artist's loopy series based on Velázquez's renowned painting *Las Meninas* is unusual but it's also evidence of Picasso's playful genius. The Picasso Museum currently occupies several exquisite 15th-century palaces on a pedestrian-only street lined with medieval mansions. It's one of the city's loveliest streets, and the museum's administrators are continuing their expansionist craze, with plans to take over yet more buildings along Carrer Montcada in the next several years. Plan on spending at least a couple of hours here.

See map p. 518. Montcada, 15–23 (Ribera). ☎ *93-256-30-00.* www.museu picasso.bcn.es. *Metro: Jaume I. Admission: 9€ ($14), free for children 12 and under, free first Sun of month. Open: Tues–Sun 10 a.m.–8 p.m.*

More cool things to see and do

✔ **Traipsing along on a** *tapeo:* When in Spain, do as the Spanish do: Indulge in an early evening *tapeo* (tapas-bar crawl). (For more details on this most Spanish of activities — tapas rank somewhere between a snack and a passion — see "Dining in Madrid" in Chapter 22.) Barcelona may not have the reputation for tapas-grazing that Madrid has, but it's a wonderful city in which to eat on the run — or tide yourself over until those late mealtimes at most restaurants. Among the best spots are **Irati,** Cardenal Casanyes, 17 (Barri Gòtic; ☎ 93-302-30-84), a bustling Basque tapas tavern just off La Rambla that's always at standing-room-only capacity; **Tapaç 24,** Diputació, 269 (Eixample; ☎ 93-488-09-77), an offshoot of the wonderfully creative upscale restaurant Comerç 24; **La Bodegueta,** Rambla de Catalunya, 100 (Eixample; ☎ 93-215-48-94), an easy-to-miss, simple step-down bar that's ideal for a small snack and a glass of wine or cava; and **Inopia,** Tamarit, 104 (☎ 93-424-52-31), a classic tapas bar with a boisterous vibe, owned by the brother of the legendary experimental chef Ferran Adrià. A Catalan specialty is the champagne bar, called a *xampanyería.* These bars serve cava (sparkling wine) as well as a selection of tapas. Not to be missed is the bustling, nearly always SRO **El Xampanyet,** Montcada, 22 (☎ 93-319-70-03; Metro: Jaume I).

✔ **Wading in at the waterfront:** Check out **Vila Olímpica,** an award-winning neighborhood and medley of conceptual architecture, where swimmers, baseball players, weightlifters, and other Olympic athletes were the first to inhabit the apartments, later sold and rented to the public. **Port Olímpic** (the new harbor) swims with bars and restaurants and **Port Vell** (the old port) is a hyper-developed entertainment and shopping area, with attractions like the IMAX Port Vell cinema, Maremágnum mall, and L'Aquarium. The pedestrian boulevard along the old harbor, called the **Moll de la Fusta,** makes for a very enjoyable *paseo* (stroll); it stretches from the Columbus statue at the bottom of La Rambla to a giant Liechtenstein sculpture (Metro: Drassanes, Barceloneta, or Ciutadella–Vila Olímpica).

✔ **Putting the pieces together at Parc Güell:** The whimsical open-air Parc Güell, Ctra. del Carmel, 23 (☎ 93-213-04-88; Metro: Lesseps), another of Gaudí's signature creations, is north of the Eixample district, but still relatively easy to reach (you can take the bus, but visiting by taxi is easiest and quickest). Envisioned as a housing development, the garden city was never fully realized. Gaudí originally planned to design every detail of the 60 houses; however, only one was finished, and Gaudí lived in it as he struggled to complete the project (it now houses the small Casa-Museu Gaudí). The parts that Gaudí did finish — in fact, his talented disciple, Josep María Jujol, executed most of what you see — resemble an idiosyncratic theme park, with a mosaic-covered lizard fountain, Hansel and Gretel pagodas, and magically undulating park benches swathed in broken pieces of ceramics, called *trencadís.* Gaudí was so intent on the community's total integration into nature that he inserted part of it into a hill, constructing a forest of columns that look remarkably like tree trunks. On clear days, you can see much of Barcelona, making out the spires of Gaudí's La Sagrada Família and the twin towers on the beach. Allow at least an hour to take in the full flavor of the park. It's probably best to grab a cab, because it's a 6-block walk uphill from the nearest subway stop. Admission to the park itself is free, though the Casa-Museu Gaudí charges 4€ ($6.40). The Casa-Museu Gaudí is open daily from 10 a.m. to 6 p.m.; the park is open daily March through April and September through October from 10 a.m. to 7 p.m., May through August from 10 a.m. to 9 p.m., November through February from 10 a.m. to 6 p.m.

✔ **Partying 'til dawn with Barcelona's pulsing nightlife:** Like most of Spain, Barcelona loves late-night action, be it bar-hopping, dancing, or just general partying until the wee hours. The most traditional evening — if you can call it that, given the surroundings — can be had in the *modernisme* architectural triumph of the **Palau de la Música Catalana,** San Francesc de Paula, 2 (☎ **93-295-72-00;** www. palaumusica.org), which features year-round classical, jazz, and pop concerts as well as recitals. Or check out a flamenco bar such as **Tablao Flamenco Cordobés,** Las Ramblas, 35 (☎ **93-317-57-11**), or **El Tablao de Carmen** in the Poble Espanyol (☎ **93-325-68-95**), or a jazz club, such as **Jamboree** (☎ **93-301-75-64**), a soul-oriented basement venue at Plaça Reial, 17. The historic **Sala Apolo,** Nou de la Rambla, 113 (☎ **93-441-40-01**), perpetually "in" **City Hall,** Rambla Catalunya, 2–4 (☎ **93-317-2177**); sleek-chic **Baja Beach Club,** Passeig Marítim, 34 (☎ **93-225-91-0**); and the fashionable Latin-flavored dance-club **Mojito Club,** Roselló, 217 (☎ **93-352-87-46**) are all good night spots. Or hang out at the outdoor cafes and bars that keep the neighbors awake in the El Born district. The **El Born,** Passeig del Born, 26 (☎ **93-310-37-27**), is just one of many happening spots in this ultracool neighborhood.

Guided tours

Hop aboard one of **Barcelona Bus Turístic's** buses for a tour of 27 city sights. You can take either the Red or the Blue route (or both), and get on and off at any of the 44 stops as you please. Both depart from Plaça de Catalunya at 9:30 a.m. daily; all stops have full timetables. Complete journey time is about three-and-a-half hours. The bus runs daily throughout the year, except December 25 and January 1. The cost of a one-day ticket is 20€ ($32) adults, 12€ ($19) children 4 though 12. A two-day ticket costs 26€ ($42) adults, 16€ ($26) children. Purchase tickets onboard or in advance at **Turisme de Barcelona,** Plaça de Catalunya, 17 (☎ **93-285-38-32;** www.barcelonaturisme.com).

You can join English-language, guided tours of the Gothic Quarter, as well as *modernista,* Picasso, and gourmet routes, year-round with **Barcelona Walking Tours.** Walks (90 minutes to 2 hours) begin at **Turisme de Barcelona,** Plaça de Catalunya, 17. For information, call ☎ **93-285-38-32.** Prices are 11€ to 15€ ($18–$24) adults, 4.50€ to 6.50€ ($7.20–$10) children 4 through 12.

Suggested itineraries

If you're the type who'd rather organize your own tours, this section offers some tips for building your own Barcelona itineraries. Two full days will give you a good taste of what the city has to offer.

If you have one day

Begin early in the morning at the only grand cathedral of Europe still in the midst of being built, Gaudí's **Sagrada Família.** Take an hour or so to clamber around its spires and admire the whimsical sculpture adorning its odd hidden corners. Then take the Metro to Avinguda Diagonal for more *modernisme* masterpieces in Gaudí's **Casa Milà** and the famed **Manzana de la Discòrdia** along Passeig de Gràcia.

Hop back on the Metro at the Passeig de Gràcia stop to transfer to the Jaume I stop so that, after grabbing some lunch at **Cuines Santa Caterina,** you can pop into the **Museu Picasso,** a museum honoring Barcelona's other artistic giant of the 20th century. Backtrack along Carrer de la Princesa, and cross Via Laietana to the square in front of Barcelona's massive Gothic **Catedral.**

As evening draws near, make your way over to the grand promenade of **La Rambla** to watch the street performers and the locals out for their *paseo* (evening walk) and to simply stroll one of the greatest pedestrian boulevards in Europe. Cut out by 6 p.m. or so for the evening *tapeo,* before heading back to your hotel to rest up from your full day; get back out there at 10 p.m. for dinner at **Restaurant 7 Portes** or **Cal Pep** in the old quarter.

If you have two days

Begin **Day 1** seeing perhaps Barcelona's greatest sight: **La Rambla,** the long, wide, pedestrian boulevard that glides right through the heart of the old city, from Plaça de Catalunya to the port. Start at the port end, at the Drassanes Metro stop. Stop into **La Boquería** market. Pause at the twittering, tweeting cages of the tiny portable bird market; toss coins to the performers who pose as statues and only move when a clink of change hits their plates. Follow Las Ramblas all the way to Carrer de Portaferrisa and turn right until you get to the **Catedral.**

After lunch, work your way south through the back streets of the medieval Barri Gòtic and head over to the **Museu Picasso** and then stroll the atmospheric neighborhoods of **La Ribera** and **El Born,** a great place to stop for a glass of wine or cava.

Day 2 is the day for *modernisme.* Start it off by proceeding to **Sagrada Família** and the Art Nouveau wonderland of **Passeig de Gràcia,** where you'll find the **Manzana de la Discòrdia.** Don't miss a visit to see Antoni Gaudí's masterpiece, **Casa Milà.**

Now, because the last day-and-a-half have been pretty packed (and you've done lots of walking), take the afternoon to relax while still sightseeing. Either head up (by taxi) to the Gaudí-designed **Parc Güell,** a wonderful place to wander, full of whimsical architectural accents, or take the Metro down to the **waterfront,** new port, and revitalized beaches. Have an easygoing dinner at **Agua,** which overlooks the beach, or head back to the Gothic Quarter and perhaps dine at **Senyor Parellada.**

Fast Facts: Barcelona

Area Code

The country code in Spain is **34.** The Barcelona city code of **93** is incorporated into the full number, which means you must always dial it (no matter where you're calling from). To call Barcelona from the United States, dial ☎ **011-34** followed by the number.

Currency

The currency in Spain, like all of Western Europe, is the euro. The euro is divided into 100 cents, and there are coins of 0.01, 0.02, 0.05, 0.10, 0.20, 0.50, 1€, and 2€. Paper-note denominations are 5, 10, 20, 50, 100, 200, and 500 euros. The exchange rate used to calculate the dollar values given in this chapter is 1€ equals $1.60. Amounts greater than $10 are rounded to the nearest dollar.

Doctors and Dentists

Dial ☎ 061 to find a doctor. The U.S. Consulate has a list of English-speaking physicians. For a dentist, call ☎ 93-415-99-22.

Embassies and Consulates

The U.S. Consulate is located at Paseo Reina Elisenda, 23, in Sarrià (☎ 93-280-22-27).

Emergencies

For general emergencies, call ☎ **112.** Medical emergencies, dial ☎ **061.** For the police, call ☎ **092.**

Hospitals

For a medical emergency, dial ☎ **061.** To locate a hospital, dial ☎ 93-427-20-20. Barcelona Centro Médico, Avenida Diagonal, 612 (☎ 93-414-06-43), dispenses information about hospitals and medical specialists to

foreigners. Three main hospitals have *urgéncias* (emergency departments): Hospital Clínic, Villarroel, 170 (☎ 93-227-54-00; Metro: Hospital Clínic); Hospital Creu Roja de Barcelona, Dos de Maig, 301 (☎ 93-507-2700; Metro: Hospital de Sant Pau); and Hospital de la Santa Creu I Sant Pau, Sant Antoni Maria Claret, 167 (☎ 93-291-9000; Metro: Hospital de Sant Pau).

Information

Call ☎ 010 for general visitor information. Turisme de Barcelona, Plaça de Catalunya, 17 (underground) (☎ 93-285-38-34; www. barcelonaturisme.com; Metro: Catalunya), is open daily from 9 a.m. to 9 p.m. For details on it and other tourist offices in Barcelona, see "Finding information after you arrive," near the beginning of this chapter.

Internet Access and Cybercafes

Many Internet cafes and *cabinas* have sprung up across the city. The Internet Gallery Cafe is down the street from the Picasso Museum, Barra de Ferro, 3 (☎ 93-268-15-07). Another excellent center is EasyEverything, La Rambla dels Caputxins, 29 (☎ 93-318-2435; Metro: Liceu or Drassenes), open daily from 7 a.m. to 2 a.m. Acoma Cafe-Bar, on c/Boquería, 21, offers free Internet access (☎ 93-301-75-97; Metro: Liceu); it's open Monday through Saturday from 10 a.m. to midnight.

Maps

Get free maps at Turisme de Barcelona, Plaça de Catalunya, 17 (underground), or purchase city, regional, and country maps at any kiosk along La Rambla.

Newspapers and Magazines

The best sources for national and international press are the kiosks along La Rambla, which are open virtually round-the-clock. The most useful weekly guide is the *Guía del Ocio,* available at any newsstand for 1€ ($1.60), which includes an English-language section at the back; but there are also a host of English-language freebies to be found lying around in every shop, restaurant, and bar. The monthly *Metropolitan* provides a local's-eye view of Barcelona.

Pharmacies

Farmàcies (pharmacies) operate during normal business hours, and one in every district remains open all night and on holidays. The location and phone number of this *farmacia de guardia* is posted on the door of all the other pharmacies. You can also call ☎ 010 or 93-481-00-60 to contact all-night pharmacies. A very central pharmacy is open 24/7, Farmàcia Álvarez, at Passeig de Gràcia, 26 (☎ 93-302-11-24).

Police

For municipal police, dial ☎ 092; for national police, ☎ 091. The main police station is at Vía Laietana, 43 (☎ 93-290-30-00). The Tourist Police are located at La Rambla, 43 (☎ 93-301-90-60).

Post Office

The Central Post Office is at Plaça de Antoni López, s/n, at the end of Via Laietana (☎ 902-19-71-97). It's open Monday through Saturday from 8:30 a.m. to 9:30 p.m. The yellow sign marked CORREOS identifies branches of the post office. Those at Aragó, 282, and Ronda Universitat, 23, are open from 8:30 a.m. to 8:30 p.m.

Safety

The street crime for which Barcelona once drew unwanted attention has diminished, due in part to an increased police presence and new lighting on dark streets in the Old Town. But with Barcelona's surging popularity, there are pockets of the city where thieves prey on tourists. Be careful around any major tourist sight, but especially: La Rambla (especially the section closest to the sea); Barri Gòtic; Raval neighborhood; and La Sagrada Família. Much of the crime on La Rambla has moved, with greater police presence there, to side streets in the Gothic Quarter and the Raval district, and you shouldn't walk alone at night in either place. Your primary danger is from pickpockets and purse snatchers, and all these areas have earned reputations for frequent robberies directed at tourists.

Turisme Atenció (Tourist Attention Service), La Rambla, 43 (☎ 93-256-24-30; Metro: Liceu), has English-speaking attendants who can aid crime victims in reporting losses and obtaining new documents. The office is open 24/7.

Taxes

The government sales tax, known as IVA (value-added tax), is levied nationwide on all goods and services, and ranges from 7 percent to 33 percent.

Telephone

For national telephone information, dial ☎ 1003. For international telephone information, dial ☎ 025.

Phone cards worth 12€ ($19) are good for 150 minutes. Use them to make international calls from properly equipped booths, which are clearly identified. Phone cards are available at *estancos* (tobacco shops) and post offices.

To make an international call, dial ☎ 00, wait for the tone, and dial the country code, the area code, and the number.

Transit Info

See "Getting Around Barcelona," earlier in this chapter.

Chapter 24

Athens and the Greek Islands

● ●

In This Chapter

▶ Getting to Athens and the Greek islands
▶ Learning the lay of the land
▶ Locating the best hotels, restaurants, and historical sights
▶ Side-tripping to the best beaches outside the big city

● ●

*B*y the fifth century B.C., when the rest of Western civilization was still in its infancy, Athens was already a thriving metropolis, the site of the world's first successful democracy. The city gave birth to influential schools of art, architecture, literature, drama, and philosophy that continue to be the touchstones of modern culture.

Four magnificent sights from antiquity are preserved in Athens: the world's most famous ancient temple, the Parthenon, perched atop Acropolis Hill; two outstanding archaeological museums; and the sprawling Ancient Agorá, the civic laboratory in which contemporary democracy was first developed and tested.

Athens has one of the most important cultural heritages in Europe, but first impressions are colored by where you stay and go. Athens may be a study in overdevelopment and chaos (which also has its charms), but the city also has also pockets of green areas, and long and wide, car-free streets are located throughout the historic center.

A project completed by the 2004 Olympic Games to unify Athens's archaeological sites (Temple of Olympian Zeus, Hadrian's Arch, the Acropolis, Filopáppou Monument, the Ancient Agorá, and Ancient Kerameikós cemetery) on a traffic-free, cobblestone promenade included upgrading the surrounding areas. Buildings were restored, and new pockets of activity sprang up along the route. With ever more sidewalk cafes and places to enjoy the atmosphere, the view, visual arts, and free music performances, the effect has been enchanting, for Athenians and visitors alike.

Having said that, because Athens is farther from the heart of Europe than most people realize, first-time visitors to the Continent and those on a whirlwind trip should consider whether to invest the time it takes to visit Greece overland. It's worth the effort, especially if you can fly from another European city (luckily, new no-frills airlines — see Chapter 6 — now make this affordable for many travelers). Otherwise, be prepared to spend a full six days on a train and a ferry just to get from Rome to Athens and back.

Getting There

In addition to the usual options for getting to a major European city — plane, train, bus, and (for adventuresome travelers) automobile — Athens offers another mode of entry: ferry. But the marine journey is long. Flying is still the best alternative.

After you get to Athens, your feet and the Metro are likely to be your best transportation bets.

Arriving by air

The **Athens International Airport Eleftherios Venizelos** (☎ 210-353-0000; www.aia.gr), 27km (17 miles) east of the city at Spata, opened in March 2001. As the main southeastern Europe transport hub, it's functional but faceless, given its history- and character-rich location. Check out the on-site museum if you have time to kill.

In the arrivals hall are two airport information desks, three ATMs, a currency exchange machine (a staffed bureau is at departure level), two free Internet kiosks, a pharmacy, and a post office. The Greek National Tourism Organization (GNTO — often abbreviated to the Greek acronym EOT) has a desk in the arrivals hall, where you can ask about hotels and transportation into Athens and pick up a map, while the adjacent travel agencies provide similar info, plus a hotel booking service.

A **taxi** into central Athens costs about 30€ to 50€ ($48–$80); not metered is a 3.40€ ($5.45) surcharge for trips to or from the airport, road tolls, and baggage charges. Drivers may not pick up bags weighing more than 15kg (33 pounds).

If you decide to take a taxi, ask the driver for an estimate of how much the journey should cost, and get in or not based on the answer. If the driver tries to overcharge, do not pay or get out of the car unless you're in front of your hotel (despite being in pedestrian areas, all the hotels listed are accessible by car), and either ask a clerk there for assistance or ask to be driven to a police station, which should be effective enough. If you're taking a taxi to the airport, ask the hotel desk clerk to order it for you in advance.

The airport is linked to central Athens by both the Metro system (Line 3), which goes through Sýntagma Square to Egaleo station in western

Greece

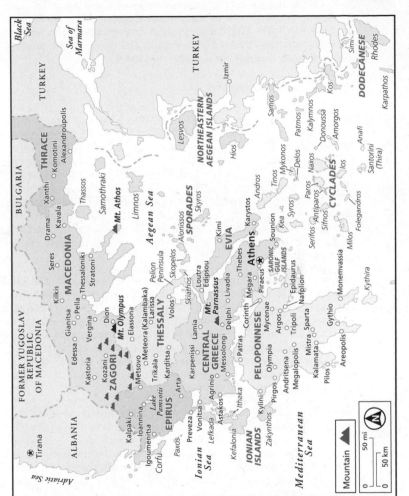

Athens, and the Suburban Rail, which goes to Larissa (railway) Station and out of the city to Corinth or Kiato, where you change trains if you're heading to Patras for a ferry to Italy. Change to Line 1 at Monastiraki station for domestic ferries at the port of Piraeus. The suburban rail also goes to the port, changing at Ano Liosia. Travel time into town is about 45 minutes. One-way tickets on either cost 6€ ($9.60); validate (cancel) the ticket before going to the shared platform.

Buses (☎ 185; www.oasa.gr**)** from the airport into the center of town cost 3.20€ ($5.10); purchase tickets at the booth in front of the bus stop;

from the driver only when the bus is en route. Both the X94 and X95 run to the Ethniki Amyna Metro station on Line 3, but X95 continues on to Sýntagma Square in the heart of Athens, about a 70-minute trip. Bus X96 stops at the Faliro Metro station (and connects with the tram) before continuing on to Piraeus Metro station at Athens's port, southwest of the city; both those stops are also on Line 1.

Arriving by ferry

Hordes of travelers take the ferry to Greece from Italy. You can leave from Venice, Bari, Ancona, and Brindisi in Italy, and Igoumenitsa, Corfu, Cephalonia, Zakynthos, Paxi, and Patras in Greece. Most ferries leave in the afternoon or evening and take from 10 to 17 hours to Patras on the mainland. Schedules, ports of departure, and prices change seasonally, with tickets ranging from 18€ ($29) for deck/economy class to 255€ ($408) for a luxury cabin in August. Eurail pass holders should check their booklet to determine which operators honor their passes, and then depart from the relevant port; however, expect to pay port taxes and/or fuel fees and a season surcharge (20€–30€/$32–$48). Schedules, rates, and special offers for small groups are all linked through www.greek ferries.gr.

 To get to Athens from Patras, you can take the bus (☎ 210-514-7310 in Athens, 2610-623-887 in Patras) that leaves every 30 to 45 minutes; the trip takes two-and-a-half hours and costs 16€ ($26). You can also take one of six daily trains that make the trek in three-and-a-half to four hours and cost 8.80€ ($14) or 12€ ($19) for the Intercity, with a change at Kiato to the Suburban Rail (Proastiakos). Or you can catch a bus to Delphi or to ancient Olympia via Pirgos. Make your connections as quickly as possible, because the last train and bus of the day usually pull out soon after the ferry arrives.

Getting from Rome to Athens by ferry takes about three full days. Flying is likely the easiest and cheapest alternative when you tally all the rail, ferry, meal, and accommodations costs. Check www.skyscanner.net or www.flyairone.it/en for e-booking cheap flights from various Italian cities to Athens, which may not be much more than a deck-class ticket to Patras; or check at the Rome airport (☎ 06-65951; www.adr.it) for some dozen daily flights. You can also find cheap flights in and out of Athens at www.airtickets.gr.

Arriving by rail

Trains (☎ 1110; www.ose.gr) arrive at **Larissa Station,** Athens's main train station. A Metro stop (also called Larissa Station) is just out front, or take Trolley 1 (4:25 a.m.–11:35 p.m.) to Sýntagma Square, Makriyánni, or Koukáki districts.

Arriving by bus

Regional (KTEL) buses pull into Athens at one of two bus terminals. **Terminal A** (for buses from Patras; northern, southern, and western

Greece; and the Peloponnese) is at 100 Kifissoú St. (☎ 210-512-4910); from there, city bus no. 051 runs to Menándrou Street, west of Omónia Square. **Terminal B** (for buses from central Greece, including Delphi and Metéora) is at 260 Liossíon St. (☎ 210-831-7153; www.ktel.org); from this terminal, a dozen city buses go to Attiki Metro station, from which you can catch lines 1 or 2, but the driver usually drops passengers off near Line 1, before reaching the terminal. Buses to sights in Attica (Cape Soúnion, Marathon) leave from **Aigýptou Square** on Patissíon Street (☎ 210-822-5148), just past the National Archaeological Museum. A Soúnion-bound bus stop is at central Klafthmónos Square on Stadíou Street. Buses leave every hour until 5:30 p.m.; the fare is 5.40€ ($8.65). The last bus returns at 7 p.m., so check the time of the renowned sunset beforehand.

Orienting Yourself in Athens

Athens is a sprawling metropolis with an insatiable appetite for expansion, bordering low mountains and the sea. The center has largely been redeveloped into one big pedestrian zone, and the main sites are located here, including the **Acropolis.** Use a map to navigate narrow streets and get your bearings. Streets can change names blocks apart, and spellings rendered in English vary widely. The political and geographical hub is **Sýntagma** (Constitution) **Square,** but the always-lit hill of the Acropolis is Athens's "true North."

Introducing the neighborhoods

From **Sýntagma Square,** pedestrian- and tourist-friendly **Pláka** is to the southwest, one of the most colorful old sections of town.

Pláka's southwest is bounded by the **Acropolis Hill,** perched by the **Parthenon.** The **Monastiráki** area, which features cafes along the train line and a flea market at Avyssinias (Abyssinian) Square, lies north of the Acropolis and west of Pláka, next to the **Ancient Agorá.** The neighborhood of **Makriyánni,** south of the Acropolis, is a tourist bedroom and residential area.

North of Pláka and Sýntagma, arterial roads lead to **Omónia Square,** once the commercial heart of the city. The square still bustles with activity by day, but at night it becomes grittier.

Northeast of Sýntagma is **Kolonáki,** the chichi shopping and residential district. The area around **Exárcheia Square,** east of Omónia, has hip shops and is quite lively, given the student (and infamously anarchist) population living there.

 North of Ermoú Street at Monastiráki is **Psirrí,** with its tanners, shoemakers, and tinsmiths by day, a prime dining and entertainment area at night. More Old Athens craft shops with real experts in their field are across Athinás Street north of Ermoú, particularly Polyklítou Street.

Pedestrian **Ermoú** (Hermes) **Street,** up to Sýntagma Square, is the city's shoe-mad "mall." The area of **Thissío,** bordering the Ancient Agorá's west side, has superb views of the Acropolis and **Lykavittós Hill** (reachable on foot or by cog railway), and overflows with cafes and bars, particularly along Iráklidon Street.

Finding information after you arrive

The **Greek National Tourism Organization** (often shortened to the Greek acronym EOT) offers maps and information. The **Information desk** is at 26 Amalías St., at Sýntagma (☎ 210-331-0392; www.gnto.gr), and is open Monday through Friday 9 a.m. to 7 p.m., weekends and holidays 10 a.m. to 4 p.m.

Getting Around Athens

The best way to sightsee around town is on foot, by Metro, and by hailing the occasional taxi. Except for a visit to the city's main museum, you'll likely spend most of your time in or near pedestrian-friendly Pláka, Monastiráki, Thissío, and Psirrí.

Drivers are erratic and impatient, rarely heeding right of way at pedestrian crossings. Look both ways. Sidewalks are slippery, uneven, and usually blocked, which is why most people prefer to use the roads. Rent a car only if you're planning trips out of Athens.

By Metro (subway)

The **Metro** (☎ 210-679-2399; www.ametro.gr) system in Athens is clean and efficient. Line 1 begins at Piraeus, Athens's seaport, and runs through central Athens before terminating north of the city at Kifissiá, an upscale suburb. Lines 2 and 3 make a large X across the city, meeting at Sýntagma Square. For tourists, the most useful stops are Akropoli, Thissío, Sýntagma, and Monastiráki, the latter two of which are centrally located and offer access to two of the Metro lines.

A **single ticket** costs 0.80€ ($1.30) and is valid for 90 minutes; a 24-hour **day pass** is 3€ ($4.80); and a **weekly ticket** is 10€ ($16). The tickets are valid on all modes of public transport within the city. Children 5 and under ride free. Buy tickets at machines and booths inside the stations, and cancel them in the validation machines before you reach the platform. Keep your ticket with you — it's an honor system, but it's subject to random checks.

By bus and trolley

Athens has several overlapping bus and bus-trolley networks. Bus no. 200 makes a circle, and can be taken from Kolokotroni Street in Monastiráki or in Sýntagma, west of Stadíou Street. It's useful for reaching the National Archaeological Museum, Exárcheia, and Kolonáki districts.

Bus and trolley tickets, which are sold in the Metro stations, bus ticket booths, and some kiosks, cost 0.80€ ($1.30) and are good on all modes of public transport for 90 minutes. Make sure you cancel (validate) the ticket in the machines on the buses (public transport uses the honor system); otherwise you face a fine.

By tram

You can get from Amalías Street at Sýntagma to the shopping and nightlife area of coastal **Glyfáda** and nearby **beaches** (destination: Voula) by tram (☎ 210-997-8000; www.tramsa.gr), or to Flisvos Marina and the port of Piraeus (destination: SEF). Tickets are 0.80€ ($1.30) for all modes of public transport and valid for 90 minutes. You can also purchase tickets at machines or booths at certain stations, as well as Metro stations and bus ticket booths. Trams run from 5 a.m. to midnight (24 hours Fri–Sat).

Upon arrival in the city, and if you want to go beyond the sightseeing center, pick up transportation maps to help you sort out the routes, or look online at www.oasa.gr.

By taxi

Taxis are yellow and cheap — if you can avoid getting overcharged. The rates, normally posted on the dashboard, are 1.05€ ($1.70) to start, with a minimum charge of 2.80€ ($4.50), and then 0.36€ (60¢) per kilometer (tariff 1, which shows up on the meter), rising to 0.68€ ($1.10; tariff 2) if you leave the city limits (except the airport), or travel between midnight and 5 a.m. Other small-change add-ons include going to the airport or being picked up from a port or bus station.

The meter should be running once you're in the car, and the driver normally puts his photo ID in full view on the dashboard. Taxis also regularly pick up other passengers to destinations that are on the way, but everyone pays separately. This tacit sharing arrangement between drivers and passengers helps to keep the rates down. Check the amount on the meter when you climb in and pay the difference when you get out, including the minimum or pickup charge. Taxis can also be difficult to find around 3 p.m. (shift change) and 11:30 p.m. (waiting till the night tariff kicks in).

You can hail a taxi on the street or call ☎ 210-341-0553, 210-994-3000, or 210-222-1623, but you pay a surcharge of 3€ to 6€ ($4.80–$9.60), depending on the company, for a rendezvous. For airport pickup and tours, try George the Famous Taxi Driver (☎ 210-963-7030).

By foot

Most of Athens's main attractions are in the city center, and districts such as Pláka, Psirrí, and Thissío are pedestrianized, so expect to see much on foot. But watch your step, and beware of impatient drivers.

Staying in Athens

Most Athens hotels were overhauled for the 2004 Games — a bonus for post-Olympics visitors, so things such as air-conditioning and televisions are standard issue in budget hotels. If you want to stay near the sightseeing and nightlife, the areas around Pláka, Monastiráki, and Makriyánni are your best bets. The **Hellenic Chamber of Hotels,** 24 Stadíou St. (☎ 210-323-7193; www.grhotels.gr), has hotel information for all of Greece, but you must book yourself or through a travel agency.

The downtrodden **Omónia Square** zone, including southwest to Sofokléous Street and Theátrou Square, near the Central Market, is still a haven for shabby budget inns interspersed with a few good hotels, but most people find the area too seedy.

Note: Hotels can request a deposit of up to 25 percent of the total for a multiple-night stay, or not less than one night's rate. Hotels also offer considerable discounts: in the off-season, which can be July and August in Athens; for multiple-night stays; for cash payment; for e-booking; and so on. The rates quoted in this section are based on rack rates, so by all means ask.

Athens's top hotels

Acropolis View Hotel
$$ Makriyánni

This friendly hotel, on a quiet side street just near the entrance to the Acropolis at the edge of Filopáppou Hill, has small but modern rooms, and a few even have a view of the Parthenon. If your room lacks one, head up to the roof terrace, where you can get outstanding Acropolis vistas, especially at sunset.

See map p. 544. 10 Webster (also known as Wemster, Gouempster) St. (off Rovértou Gálli, 2 blocks down from its intersection with Dionysíou Aeropagítou). ☎ *210-921-7303. Fax: 210-923-0705.* www.acropolisview.gr. *Metro: Akropoli. Rack rates: 80€–100€ ($128–$160) double. Rates include breakfast. MC, V.*

Athens Cypria
$$ Sýntagma Square

The street where this close-to-everything (and hence, busy) business hotel is located is small and quiet, as are most of the pleasantly modernized rooms. But book early so that you can snag one (room nos. 603–607) with a view of the Acropolis. The Cypria's low season is July and August.

See map p. 544. 5 Diomías St. (3 blocks from Sýntagma Square, down Ermoú Street and right). ☎ *210-323-8034 or 210-323-0470. Fax: 210-324-8792.* www.athens cypria.com. *Metro: Sýntagma. Rack rates: 119€–129€ ($190–$206) double. Rates include breakfast. AE, MC, V.*

Attalos Hotel
$ Monastiráki

On busy Athinás Street, plain-but-nice rooms and cheerful service make the Attalos popular, as does its Metro location, close to Pláka and the Central Market *(agorá)*. The roof terrace has a snack bar and view to the Acropolis, as do 37 of the upper-floor rooms, many with balconies. A 2004 renovation brought soundproof windows, hair dryers, in-room safes, and a Wi-Fi–equipped Internet corner.

See map p. 544. 29 Athinás St. (1½ blocks from Monastiráki Square). ☎ *210-321-2801. Fax: 210-324-3124.* www.attaloshotel.com. *Metro: Monastiráki. Rack rates: 60€–94€ ($96–$150) double. Rates include breakfast. AE, MC, V.*

Electra Palace
$$$ Pláka

For the price — and do ask about discounts — you can't beat this luxury-category hotel's prime spot. On higher floors the rooms are smaller but have bigger balconies, and about 20 of them, including suites, have an Acropolis view. Rooftop pool, Jacuzzi, and bar are open May to September, or use the indoor pool, sauna, steam room, Jacuzzi, and gym.

See map p. 544. 18 N. Nikodímou St. (2 streets south of Sýntagma Square and west 3 short blocks). ☎ *210-324-1401 or 210-337-0000. Fax: 210-324-1875.* www.electra hotels.gr. *Metro: Sýntagma. Rack rates: 180€–360€ ($288–$576) double. Rates include breakfast. AE, DC, MC, V.*

G. R. Louis Athens Hotel
$$ Embassy District

This boutique hotel is suited for those who want to stay "uptown," where the Athens Tower, concert hall, and many embassies, museums, hospitals, and businesses are based. Just east of upmarket Kolonáki and Lykavittós Hill, a lively bar and restaurant zone is at nearby Ambelokipi Metro station, and more intimate cafe/bars are at Mavili Square just around the corner.

See map p. 544. 22 Timoleontos Vassou St., Ambelokipi. ☎ *210-641-5000. Fax: 210-646-6361.* www.grlouis.gr. *Metro: Ambelokipi. Rack rates: 130€ ($208) double. Breakfast 18€ ($29). AE, DC, MC, V.*

Hotel Grande Bretagne
$$$$$ Sýntagma Square

This opulent, 160-year-old landmark hotel, part of the Starwood Luxury Collection, is on the main square, and anyone who's anyone stays here. Business rater *Forbes* has listed Alexander's Bar as one of the world's best, and its three restaurants are also meeting places for corporate and political heavyweights. An Acropolis-view rooftop bar/restaurant, the city's best spa, and indoor and outdoor rooftop pools are also here.

See map p. 544. Sýntagma Square. ☎ *210-333-0000. Fax: 210-333-0400.* www.grande bretagne.gr. *Metro: Sýntagma. Rack rates: 317€–611€ ($507–$978) double. AE, DC, MC, V.*

Accommodations, Dining, and Attractions in Athens

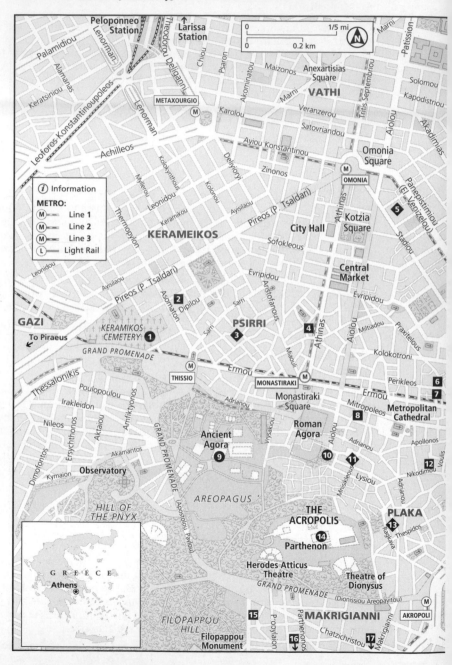

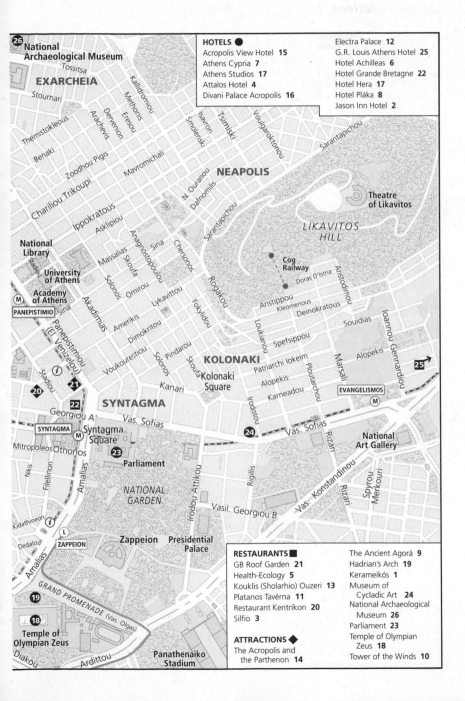

26 National Archaeological Museum

Tossitsa

EXARCHEIA

Stournari

HOTELS ●
Acropolis View Hotel **15**
Athens Cypria **7**
Athens Studios **17**
Attalos Hotel **4**
Divani Palace Acropolis **16**

Electra Palace **12**
G.R. Louis Athens Hotel **25**
Hotel Achilleas **6**
Hotel Grande Bretagne **22**
Hotel Hera **17**
Hotel Pláka **8**
Jason Inn Hotel **2**

Themistokleous
Benaki
Zoodhou Pigis
Chariliou Trikoupi
Ippokratous
Asklipiou
Kallidromiou
Methonis
Eresou
Dervenion
Arachevis
Mavromichali
N. Ouranou
Dafnomilis
Isavron
Smolenski
Tsimiski
Voulgaroktonou
Sarantapichou

NEAPOLIS

Theatre of Likavitos

LIKAVITOS HILL

National Library

University of Athens

Academy of Athens

M PANEPISTIMIO

Massalias
Skoufa
Solonos
Omirou
Akadimias
Amerikis
Dimokritou
Solonos
Pindarou
Skoufa
Anagnostopoulou
Sina
Chersonos
Rogakou
Fokylidou
Lykavittou
Sarantapichou
Sina

Cog Railway
Doras D'Istria
Aristippou
Kleomenous
Deinokratous
Aristodimou
Loukianou
Spefsippou
Souidias
Ioannou Gennadiou

KOLONAKI
Kolonaki Square
Patriarchi Iokeim
Alopekis
Karneadou
Ploutarchou
Marsali
Alopekis

25

EVANGELISMOS **M**

Panepistimiou (El. Venizelou)
Voukourestiou
Kanari
Irodotou

i

Stadiou

20

21

22

SYNTAGMA

Georgiou A'
Vas. Sofias

SYNTAGMA **M**
Syntagma Square

24 Vas. Sofias

National Art Gallery

Mitropoleos Othonos
23
Parliament

Rizari

Nikis
Filellinon
Amalias
NATIONAL GARDEN
Irodou Attikou
Rigillis
Vas. Konstandinou
Rizari
Spyrou Merkouri

Vasil. Georgiou B

Kidathineon **i**
Dedalou **L** ZAPPEION
Zappeion
Presidential Palace

RESTAURANTS ■
GB Roof Garden **21**
Health-Ecology **5**
Kouklis (Sholarhio) Ouzeri **13**
Platanos Tavérna **11**
Restaurant Kentrikon **20**
Silfio **3**

The Ancient Agorá **9**
Hadrian's Arch **19**
Kerameikós **1**
Museum of Cycladic Art **24**
National Archaeological Museum **26**
Parliament **23**
Temple of Olympian Zeus **18**
Tower of the Winds **10**

Amalias
GRAND PROMENADE (Vas. Olgas)

19

18
Temple of Olympian Zeus

Diakou
Ardittou

Panathenaiko Stadium

ATTRACTIONS ◆
The Acropolis and the Parthenon **14**

Hotel Hera
$$ Makriyánni

This A-category boutique hotel has a wonderful Acropolis view from the roof-garden bar and restaurant. Rooms are small but modern and plush, with balconies and plenty of cupboards. The location is convenient and close to the New Acropolis Museum on a busy street south of Pláka, across the pedestrian promenade to the Acropolis.

See map p. 544. 9 Falírou St. (extension of Makriyánni Street, just past Hatzichristou Street). ☎ *210-923-6682. Fax: 210-923-8269.* www.herahotel.gr. *Metro: Akropoli. Rack rates: 120€–170€ ($192–$272) double. Rates include breakfast. AE, D, MC, V.*

Athens's runner-up accommodations

Athens Studios

$$ Makriyánni Backpackers often upgrade to these IKEA-fitted, self-catering apartments that are also ideal for families. Downstairs are a self-service laundry and a sports bar, which also serves as reception when it's open during games; otherwise call the sister Backpackers hostel: ☎ **210-922-4044.** *See map p. 544. 3A Veikou St.* ☎ **210-923-5811** *(9 a.m.–1 p.m.).* www.athensstudios.gr.

Divani Palace Acropolis

$$$$ Makriyánni Three blocks south of the promenade to the Acropolis in a residential neighborhood, this luxury-class hotel caters mainly to tour groups. Rooms are large with private balconies, but the staff can be inattentive. *See map p. 544. 19–25 Parthenonos St., Makriyánni.* ☎ **210-928-0100.** www.divanis.gr.

Hotel Achilleas

$$ Sýntagma The renovated Achilleas is a nice three-star property with modern, minimalist lines, and friendly, helpful staff. Located on a quiet street, it's in the main shopping area and near Pláka. *See map p. 544. 21 Lekka St.* ☎ **210-323-3197.** www.achilleashotel.gr.

Hotel Pláka

$$ Pláka This place near Monastiráki and the main pedestrian shopping street, Ermoú, is in a great location and has comfy amenities and balconies, but it may feel a bit cramped. Get a room on the fifth or sixth floor, facing the back, for a great view of the Acropolis. *See map p. 544. 7 Kapnikaréas St. (at Mitropóleos).* ☎ **210-322-2096.** www.plakahotel.gr.

Jason Inn Hotel

$ Psirrí/Thissío/Kerameikós On the north side of the Ancient Agorá, this hotel is clean, comfortable, relatively quiet, and cheap. It's close to cafe and nightlife areas, the Metro, and sites. Rates include breakfast, served in the rooftop garden. *See map p. 544. 12 Asomaton St. (2 blocks off Ermoú).* ☎ **210-325-1106.** www.douros-hotels.com.

Dining in Athens

Greeks are more concerned about the quality and freshness of food than the appearance of where it's served. Fruits and vegetables still taste of what they look like, and portions are generous. Look for places that are full at 10 p.m. — the Greek dinner hour — if you want to eat where the locals do. *Tavérnas* (typical Greek restaurants that serve barrel wine) that cater to tourists are open earlier than the usual 7 p.m. You'll find scores of them in Pláka.

Mezédes or *mezé,* appetizers served before the main course or on their own, are a key part of the Greek diet, as is the ubiquitous *horiátiki saláta,* or village salad, known to you and me as Greek salad. Greeks eat *mezédes* with wine at a laid-back *tavérna,* or with *oúzo* (a popular anise-flavored spirit) at an *oúzerie* (a *tavérna* where you find *oúzo,* beer, wine, and *mezédes*). The tastiest are *tzatzíki* (a yogurt, cucumber, and garlic dip), *melitzanosaláta* (puréed eggplant), grilled *kalamári* (squid), *oktapódi* (octopus), *loukánika* (sausage), and *krokétes* (croquettes), usually made with potato, cheese, zucchini, or tomato.

Other outstanding dishes served as *mezédes* are *dolmádes* (grapevine leaves stuffed with rice and sometimes minced meat), *keftédes* (spicy meatballs), and *moussaká* (an eggplant, potato, and minced-meat casserole with a béchamel and cheese crust), which might also be listed as an entree. Other entrees are *souvláki* — shish kebabs of *hirinó* (pork) or *kotópoulo* (chicken) — and dishes made with pork and chicken, as well as *arní* (lamb), *psária* (fish), *moskári* (beef), and *katsíki* (goat).

Greek *yiaoúrti* (yogurt) is creamy and delicious, served as dessert drizzled with *méli* (honey). *Baklavá* is flaky, thin *phyllo* pastry layered with walnuts and soaked in honey; variations include a syrupy fruit or chocolate center.

Athens's port city of Piraeus, 10km (6 miles) away, boasts the best seafood restaurants; freshness is a concern in non-seafood restaurants in Athens due to overfishing and high prices.

You'll rarely find pine-resin-flavored *retsína* (a table wine) these days. *Krasí* (barrel wine) is served at most *tavérnas* and restaurants. Although most Greeks now prefer whiskey, the national distilled drink is *oúzo,* a clear, anise-flavored liqueur that turns milky white when you add water.

For lunch on the run, eat a *gýro* (pita bread filled with strips of grilled spiced lamb, pork, or chicken), a sandwich, or a crepe from one of the many sandwich shops, or a *tirópita* (cheese pie) or sweet *bougátsa* (a warm, creamy semolina-filled pie) from one of countless holes in the wall. At a cafe, try a *frappé* (iced coffee) in summer.

GB Roof Garden
$$$$ Sýntagma MEDITERRANEAN

This destination restaurant and bar on the eighth floor of the city's most prestigious hotel has an amazing panoramic view, which includes the Acropolis. Get good grilled fish, steaks, and pastas, or just a sunset drink at the bar, which is open-air in summer. Also open for breakfast.

See map p. 544. Grande Bretagne Hotel, Syntagma Sq. ☎ 210-333-0000. www. grandebretagne.gr. *Reservations recommended. Metro: Sýntagma. Main courses: 25€–40€ ($40–$64). AE, DC, MC, V. Open: Daily 6:30 a.m.–11 a.m. and 1 p.m.–1:15 a.m.; New Year's Eve 8 p.m.–3:30 a.m.; New Year's Day 1–4 p.m. Reduced holiday hours.*

Health-Ecology
$ Omónia VEGETARIAN

On the circuit of locals and organic-food enthusiasts, this dryly named cafeteria serves organic vegetarian food, Greek style. Always busy at lunch for takeout, there's also space upstairs to sit and eat. You can get fresh juices at the bar near the entrance. A health store is attached.

See map p. 544. 57 Panepistimíou St. ☎ 210-321-0966. Metro: Omónia. Main courses: 4€–6€ ($6.40–$9.60). No credit cards. Open: Mon–Fri 8 a.m.–9:30 p.m.; Sat 8 a.m.–8 p.m.; Sun 10 a.m.–4 p.m. Closed holidays.

Kouklis (Sholarhio) Ouzeri
$$ Pláka GREEK

Kouklis is the best, and perhaps only, "tray *tavérna*" for *mezédes* of all kinds in Pláka. No entrees here; instead you choose from a selection of appetizers brought to your table. Ten dishes, a liter of wine (or a substitute), mineral water, and dessert goes for 12€ ($19) per person for a group of four or more.

See map p. 544. 14 Tripódon St. (between Fléssa and Théspidos). ☎ 210-324-7605. www.sholarhio.gr. *Metro: Sýntagma. Appetizers: 2.50€–5€ ($4–$8). MC, V. Open: Daily 11 a.m.–2 a.m.*

Platanos Tavérna
$$ Pláka GREEK

This classic Greek *tavérna* is located on a tree-shaded, residential street near the Tower of the Winds and has sheltered tables outside. Inside it has an old-fashioned Greek ambience. Platanos serves hearty mainstays cooked with a keen eye for freshness and quality.

See map p. 544. 4 Dioyénous St. (end of Aiólou, adjacent to Adrianoú). ☎ 210-322-0666. Metro: Monastiráki. Main courses: 8€–9€ ($13–$14). No credit cards. Open: Mon–Sat noon to 4:30 p.m. and 7:30 p.m. to midnight. Closed 1 week either side of Aug 15 holiday.

Restaurant Kentrikon
$$ Near Sýntagma Square   INTERNATIONAL

This retro institution of the Athens restaurant scene is an oasis in the hectic shopping district. With hall-like high ceilings and good air-conditioning, it has an enormous menu, excellent food, and top-notch service (waiters in bow ties; cloth napkins), but it's in no way pretentious.

See map p. 544. 3 Kolokotróni St. (just west of Stadíou, in the arcade). ☎ *210-323-2482. Metro: Sýntagma. Main courses: 11€–19€ ($18–$30). AE, DC, MC, V. Open: Mon–Sat noon to 6 p.m.*

Silfio
$$ Psirrí   GREEK

Quality, service, and many restaurants may come and go, but Silfio is a stalwart in the Psirrí maze, noted for its reliability: big portions, tasty food, and good service. Live music keeps patrons entertained in winter, and the charming space next door is set out with tables in summer.

See map p. 544. 24 Táki and Lepeniótou sts., Psirrí. ☎ *210-324-7028. Metro: Thissío. Main courses: 14€ ($22). AE, DC, MC, V. Open: Mon 5:30 p.m. till late, Tues–Sun noon to 2 a.m. Closed Orthodox Easter weekend.*

Exploring Athens

The sprawling appearance of Athens today can't hide the fact that it was once the center of Western civilization. The world-class sites located here are a testament to the city's history, and they mustn't be missed.

Athens's top sights

The Acropolis and the Parthenon

The Acropolis Hill in Athens's heart is where, mythology tells us, the gods Athena and Poseidon squared off to see who could take better care of the citizens and, thus, become the city's guardian and namesake. (Poseidon produced a saltwater spring from the rock of the Acropolis; Athena produced the versatile olive tree.)

The Sacred Rock of the Acropolis, topped by the **Parthenon** temple to Athena, the *parthéna* (virgin) goddess, is part of Greece's identity, a landmark that symbolizes the country itself. It is a constant reminder of the modern city's ancient heritage.

It is not as difficult a climb as it appears. You enter beside the Beulé Gate, built by Roman Emperor Valerian in A.D. 267. The attractive Ionic temple of Athena Nike (built 424 B.C., rebuilt A.D. 1940, and again in progress) is on your right.

The world has bigger and better-preserved ancient shrines, but even with the seemingly permanent scaffolding for restoration, the Parthenon remains the poster child of Greek temples. Between 447 and 438 B.C., the Athenians spent lavishly to build this shrine to their patron. A 40-foot statue of Athena (a small Roman copy is in the National Archaeological Museum) once graced this all-marble temple. The structure is perfectly proportioned, and a few architectural tricks make it appear flawless to the naked eye. To compensate for the eye's natural tendency to create illusions, the horizontal surfaces are bowed slightly upward in the middle to appear perfectly level, the columns lean slightly inward to appear parallel, and each is thicker in the middle so it looks like a typical cylinder.

The Parthenon remained virtually intact through the Middle Ages. It became an Orthodox church in the sixth century, a Catholic church during the Crusades, and an Islamic mosque when the Ottoman Turks occupied the region, an occupation that lasted some 400 years. But in 1687 Venetians attacked the Turkish-ruled city, and lobbed a cannonball at the temple where ammunition was stored. The explosion blew up the heart of the building. They left town (along with some major antiquities), within six months.

Although the Parthenon was once covered almost entirely with sculptures and ornamental carvings, little remains on the temple today. Covetous travelers and diplomats helped themselves from the rubble in the late 18th century during Turkish rule, famously (or infamously, depending on your viewpoint), Britain's Lord Elgin. After gaining access to the military-controlled Acropolis armed with a permit only to draw Athens's ancient buildings, his foreman and workers hastily set about chiseling out what they could from the remaining sculpted friezes and pediments on the facade. Some were destroyed in the process, and the temple was left severely damaged. The Elgin (or Parthenon) marbles were shipped to England from 1801 to 1811 and are now housed in the British Museum. Greece has long campaigned for their return, but the museum has refused, despite increasing international pressure. Confident of their eventual return, Athens constructed the massive and impressive **New Acropolis Museum,** 2–4 Makriyanni St. (☎ **210-924-1043** [info only]; www.newacropolis museum.gr), near the south slope to house the friezes, as well as display some ten times more than the collection at the old museum on the hill. Built on stilts over an archaeological site (you can see it floodlit through the floor), it will fully open by the end of 2008 or early 2009. Some exhibits can be sneak-previewed before then.

If you look down the Acropolis's south side, you see the half-moon shapes of two theaters. The huge one to the east that is mostly in ruins is the **Theater of Dionysos,** built in 330 B.C. (entrance on Dionysíou Areopagítou; ☎ **210-322-4625**). Near the entrance to the Acropolis is the **Odeum of Heródes Átticus,** built in A.D. 161 and restored in recent decades to stage concerts during the Athens Epidaurus Festival from June to October. For information, visit the festival office, 39 Panepistimíou St. (also known as El. Venizelou; ☎ **210-327-2000** or 210-928-2900; www.greekfestival.gr), or the Odeum (also known as Iródion; ☎ **210-324-2121** or 210-323-2771).

The admission ticket is valid for four days and includes admission to the Acropolis and north slope, Ancient Agorá museum and site, Theater of Dionysus and south slope, Temple of Olympian Zeus, Kerameikós museum and site, and Roman Agorá (Tower of the Winds). You can also buy individual, reduced-rate tickets at all these sites, except the Acropolis. Also, check the Web site for free admission days.

See map p. 544. The Acropolis entrance is on the west side of the hill. ☎ *210-321-0219.* www.culture.gr. *Metro: Akropoli. Bus: 230. Admission: 12€ ($19). Open: May–Oct daily 8 a.m.–6 p.m.; Nov–Apr hours change yearly, usually closing between 3 and 5 p.m. Closed Dec 25–26, Jan 1, Mar 25, Easter (Orthodox) Sun, Ayiou Pnévmatos (Whit Mon, in May or June), and May 1.*

The Ancient Agorá (Market)

The everyday life of ancient Athenians revolved around the *agorá* (marketplace). You have to use your imagination to reconstruct the historic site today, which extends as an enclosed park from Areopagus (Mars Hill) into Monastiráki. Broken columns are strewn among ancient foundations interspersed with olive, pink oleander, cypress, and palm trees. It takes time to really study the lay of the land, but it's also a pleasant place just to sit under a tree and read after a hectic day. Otherwise, you can breeze through in an hour.

The **Hephaisteíon,** better known as the **Thisseíon,** built between 449 and 447 B.C. (and one of the world's best-preserved Greek temples), and the reconstructed **Stoa of Attalos** are the two most remarkable remains. A *stoa* was a series of columns spaced evenly apart supporting a long roof under which shopkeepers set up business, people met, and philosophers held court in the shade. Stoics were followers of a school of thought that developed at a *stoa.*

The Agorá's museum is in the circa-1950s Stoa of Attalos, the second-century-B.C. version rebuilt by the Rockefeller-funded American School of Classical Studies. The Agorá holds fascinating artifacts that show how the ancients carried out early democratic processes. Check out the bronze jury ballots — where jurors voted with a bronze wheel with a solid axle if they felt the man on trial was innocent and with an empty axle if they found the defendant's story as hollow as the rod — and the marble *kleroterion* (allotment machine), an early version of our modern lotto machines, used for selecting citizens for jury duty.

See map p. 544. Entrances on Adrianoú Street and Ay. Philipou in Monastiráki; west end of Polignótou Street, Pláka; and Thissío Square, Thissío. Metro: Thissío or Monastiráki. ☎ *210-321-0185.* www.culture.gr. *Admission: 4€ ($6.40) adults. Open: May–Oct Mon 11 a.m.–7 p.m., Tues–Sun 8 a.m.–7 p.m.; Nov–Apr hours change yearly, usually closing between 3 and 5 p.m. Closed Dec 25–26, Jan 1, Mar 25, Easter (Orthodox) Sun, Ayiou Pnévmatos (Whit Mon, in May or June), and May 1.*

Museum of Cycladic Art
Kolonáki

If you have an hour to spare, this private collection of the Nicholas P. Goulandris Foundation highlights the art and simple sculpture of the Cycladic tradition, which began in about 3000 B.C. Famed 20th-century artists such as Brancusi, Henry Moore, Modigliani, and Picasso were all inspired by these sculptures. The museum's second floor houses ancient Greek pieces from the fifth century B.C.

See map p. 544. 4 Neophytou Douká, Kolonáki. ☎ **210-722-8321** *or 210-722-8323.* www.cycladic.gr. *Metro: Evangelismos. Admission: 3.50€ ($5.60) adults, 1.80€ ($2.90) Sat. Open: Mon and Wed–Fri 10 a.m.–4 p.m.; Sat 10 a.m.–3 p.m. Closed Dec 25–26, Jan 1, Mar 25, Ayiou Pnévmatos (Whit Mon, in May or June), May 1, Aug 15, and Oct 28.*

National Archaeological Museum
Museío/Polytechnío

This museum is one of the greatest archaeological museums in the world — a testament to Greece's eminence and beauty hundreds of years before the rise of Rome, and thousands of years before Columbus set sail for the New World.

You need two hours for the most perfunctory run-through, and much longer to fully appreciate the staggering collection. A guide would be ideal, but a printed catalog is also helpful.

Life-size and oversize bronze statues from Athens's Golden Age (400s B.C.) are the most striking artifacts, including Poseidon about to throw his (now missing) trident, and a tiny child jockey atop a galloping horse. Most of these bronzes were found at the bottom of the sea by divers in the late 19th and 20th centuries, except for the draped and scarved "Lady of Kalymnos." Found by a fisherman in 1994, she looks an awful lot like the Virgin Mary, but is believed to date from the second century B.C.

Representing the sixth and seventh centuries B.C., the museum has statues of *kouri* — attractive young men with cornrow hair, taking one step forward with their arms rigidly at their sides. These figures, adapted from Egyptian models, set the standard in Greek art until the Classical period ushered in more lifelike sculpture.

There is also delicate jewelry and pottery, drama masks, and a good collection of what could be contemporary Cycladic figurines dating from 2800 B.C., highlighted in the opening ceremony of the 2004 Olympics.

See map p. 544. 44 Patissíon (28th Octovriou St.; several blocks north of Omónia Square). ☎ **210-821-7717** *or 210-821-7724.* www.culture.gr. *Bus/trolley: A5, A8, 2, 3, 4, 5, 6, 7, 8, 9, 11, 13, 15, 22, 60, or 200. Admission: 7€ ($11) adults, 3€ ($4.80) students; check the Web site for free admission days. Open: Mon 1–7:30 p.m.; Tues–Sun and holidays 8:30 a.m.–3 p.m. (until 7:30 p.m. June–Sept.); Good Friday (Orthodox) open noon to 5 p.m. Closed Dec 25–26, Jan 1, Mar 25, Easter (Orthodox) Sun, Ayiou Pnévmatos (Whit Mon, in May or June), and May 1. No admittance 15 minutes before closing.*

More cool things to see and do

✔ **Wandering the city in search of less touristy sites:** Apart from the ancient ruins, there is an enormous legacy from other eras, including Byzantine, Ottoman, and the 1821 War of Independence that attracted romantics throughout the Continent, the most celebrated being the English poet, Byron. Scores of museums and galleries hold beautifully displayed relics of this vast cultural heritage.

For more antiquities, walk past **Hadrian's Arch** (on Amalías Avenue), through which the Roman emperor marched in A.D. 132 to dedicate the gigantic **Temple of Olympian Zeus** (☎ 210-922-6330). Built at a snail's pace between 515 B.C. and A.D. 132, Greece's one-time largest temple measures 110m × 44m (360 × 143 ft.). Fifteen of the original 104 columns are still standing, each 17m (56 ft.) high. The site is open May through October daily from 8 a.m. to 7:30 p.m., November through April daily from 8:30 a.m. to 5 p.m. It's closed December 25 and 26, January 1, March 25, Easter (Orthodox) Sunday, *Ayiou Pnévmatos* (Whit Mon, in May or June), and May 1. Admission is 2€ ($3.20).

The octagonal **Tower of the Winds,** also known as *Aérides,* in the **Roman Agorá** (☎ 210-324-5220 or 210-321-0185) was built in the first century B.C. by astronomer Andronikos. Now missing its bronze weather vane, it shows the eight wind deities and once held a mechanized water clock. In the 18th century, whirling dervishes did their religious spinning dance here. The site also has a 15th-century mosque. It's open May through October daily from 8 a.m. to 7 p.m., November through April daily from 8:30 a.m. to 3 p.m. It's closed December 25 and 26, January 1, March 25, Easter (Orthodox) Sunday, *Ayiou Pnévmatos* (Whit Mon, in May or June), and May 1. Admission is 2€ ($3.20).

An ancient cemetery, **Kerameikós** (☎ 210-346-3552), at the west end of Ermoú Street, was outside the walls of the ancient city. You can see some of the old walls here, as well as the ancient city gates. The site has roads lined with tombs and includes a section of the *Iera Odos* (Sacred Way), which still exists just outside the cemetery and reaches Elefsína (Eleusis), 23km (14 miles) west, where the ancients worshipped Demeter. Hours are November through April daily from 8:30 a.m. to 3 p.m., May through October daily from 8 a.m. to 7 p.m. It's closed December 25 and 26, January 1, March 25, Easter (Orthodox) Sunday, *Ayiou Pnévmatos* (Whit Mon, in May or June), and May 1. Admission is 2€ ($3.20).

✔ **Seeing the changing of the guard:** Two guards wearing traditional costume at the Tomb of the Unknown Soldier in front of Parliament at Sýntagma Square, ceremoniously march back and forth at the top of the hour, every hour. The more elaborate duty-rotation ceremony is each Sunday at 11 a.m.

✔ **Enjoying some Greek nightlife:** Apart from *tavérnas* offering live *bouzoúki* music (you'll find many of these in Psirrí), *bouzoúki* clubs — named after the mandolin-type instrument played in them — can give you a taste of traditional folk music and dancing. The musical styles include the *rebétika* and *laiká* tunes of the urban lower class, or *dimotiká,* upbeat country folk music. Don't expect to smash plates, however. The practice disappeared as people prospered, and however fun it was as entertainment, it has also gone the way of the contrived village party. You can throw flowers instead.

As you get farther from touristy Pláka, the clubs get more authentically Greek, but deep pockets are needed, such as to share a bottle of whiskey over a long night with friends. Some clubs are used to seeing tourists, and the waiters may teach you some simple dances. Things really kick off around 11 p.m., but if you want a good seat, the earlier you arrive, the better.

For good *rebétika* music, try **Rebétiki Istorías,** 181 Ippokrátous St., Neapoli (☎ 210-642-4937). From September through Easter, it's open Tuesday through Sunday; from Easter through June, it's only open on Friday and Saturday; and it's closed July and August. Cover with a drink is 6€ ($9.60). (Bus no. 230 runs up here; take a taxi home.) **Taverna Mostroú,** 22 Mnissikléos St., in Pláka (☎ 210-323-5558 or 210-322-5337), is a small *dimotiká* club (most are huge halls). It's open daily from 6 p.m. to 2 a.m. (Nov–Apr Fri–Sun only). A bottle of wine and *mezé* (to share) will set you back 75€ ($120); a seat at the bar starts at 10€ ($16).

You can see folk-dancing in costume at the **Dora Stratou Greek Dance Theater,** 8 Scholíou St., Pláka (☎ 210-324-4395 office, or 210-921-4650 theater; www.grdance.org). Shows take place May through September Tuesday through Saturday at 9:30 p.m., Sunday at 8:15 p.m. Sunday (closed Mon) performances are at the open-air theater on Filopáppou Hill. Tickets cost 15€ ($24).

Cinephiles shouldn't miss a screening at an **open-air cinema** in a garden or on a rooftop during the summer. One is the **Cine Paris,** 22 Kydathinéon St., Pláka (☎ 210-322-2071).

Guided tours

Key Tours (☎ 210-923-3166; www.keytours.com) offers morning tours of Athens that include the Acropolis for 52€ ($83), afternoon tours to coastal Cape Soúnion (Temple of Poseidon) for 40€ ($64), and day trips to Delphi or Mycenae and Epidaurus, site of the acoustically perfect ancient theater, for 86€ ($138). A night tour that includes dinner in Pláka with *bouzoúki* and Greek dancing runs 60€ ($96).

For organized walking tours, try **Athens Walking Tours** (☎ 210-884-7269; www.athenswalkingtours.gr). The tours, including customized ones, take three hours, and cost 29€ ($46) adults, 19€ ($30) students; they're free for children 12 and under. Note that you'll need to pay for admission to the various archaeological sites on top of the cost of the tour.

For organized bicycle tours or long-term bicycle rentals (7 days or more), try **Pame Volta** (☎ 210-675-2886; www.pamevolta.gr). They mainly do group tours, but from May through November, two-hour city tours leave on Wednesdays and Saturdays and cost 40€ ($64), including a coffee break in Thissío. Advance reservations (two to three weeks) are needed for May, September, and October tours.

Following an itinerary

If you'd rather organize your own tour, this section offers some tips for building your own Athens itineraries.

If you have one day

If you see only one sight in Athens, it has to be the **Acropolis,** with its imposing **Parthenon.** Spend the morning here admiring the work of the ancients, their temple, and their theaters. Then visit the **New Acropolis Museum** near the hill's south slope, if it's open by the time of your visit.

After lunch (grab a *souvláki* or *gýros* to go), and trolley up from Panepistimíou Street to the incredible **National Archaeological Museum,** which houses one of the richest collections of antiquities in the world.

In the late afternoon, go to **Pláka** to explore the alleyways and have dinner. If you're there between May and September, make your way to Filopáppou Hill to take in a performance of the **Dora Stratou Greek Dance Theater,** or see a film at an **open-air cinema.** Then head to a **Thissío** cafe/bar for a nightcap and to gaze at the Acropolis and Lykavittós Hill.

If you have two days

Spend **Day 1** as described in the previous section. On **Day 2,** start off at the **Ancient Agorá,** exploring its ruins and visiting the museum inside the Stoa of Attalos to see, literally, the machinery of the world's first democracy. Then make your way through Monastiráki for an early lunch at one of its sidewalk *tavérnas* (**Thanasis** at Monastiráki station is excellent). Take bus no. 200 at Kolokotroni Street to the **Museum of Cycladic Art** in Kolonáki to peruse Cycladic sculptures, and then take bus no. 060 from there to the *teleferíque* (cog railway) up **Lykavittós Hill** to admire the view over the city.

In the late afternoon, go through the **National Gardens** and **Záppeion** en route to the marble **Panathinaikó** (also known as Panathenian, Kalimármara) **Stadium,** site of the first modern Olympics in 1896.

Walk past the **Temple of Olympian Zeus** and **Hadrian's Arch** on your way to dinner in **Pláka** (try **Platanos Tavérna**), or find either a *bouzoúki* restaurant in **Psirrí** or a real *bouzoúki* club to plant yourself in for an evening of *oúzo* and song. Otherwise, head to upmarket **Thissío** for a lively or laid-back evening under the stars, or to student-zone **Exárcheia** to mingle with Athenian youth at a thumping bar.

If you have three days

Spend **Day 3** shopping and exploring Old Athens on both sides of **Athinás Street,** between Ermoú and Evrípídou (Euripides). Tinware, shoes, gloves, and bags are still made to order in **Psirrí,** but this won't last for long.

Have lunch at a *souvláki* joint on Athinás Street opposite the **Central Market,** and buy dried herbs to take home. Then go down to **Kerameikós** ancient cemetery, ogle at the **flea market** just across Ermoú Street if it's Sunday (before 3 p.m.), and go across Pireós Street to the fascinating old gasworks at **Gázi,** now called the Technopolis, to see what's on exhibit, or to see if a music festival is taking place.

Late afternoon, come back through **Thissío** and have a *frappé* at the square, with its superb view. If you aren't tired yet, head up **Ermoú Street** toward Sýntagma Square to buy a beautiful pair of leather shoes, or go into **Pláka** for souvenirs or intricate gold jewelry at great prices. Or take a break from shopping and take the bus to **Cape Soúnion** to see the sunset at the **Temple of Poseidon.**

At night, take up what you missed from the evenings on **Days 1** and **2,** or head down to the lively small port of **Mikrolimáni** (Faliro Metro station or tram) in **Piráeus** for a seafood blowout.

Traveling beyond Athens

Most visitors come to Greece to see the remains of an ancient culture or relax on a sun-drenched island. Indeed, archaeology buffs and island-hoppers alike have seemingly endless choices to consider. Delphi's interesting artifacts and beautiful mountain setting is a top contender, and the most visually spectacular island is Santoríni. (Its Greek name is Thira, but everyone recognizes it by its Venetian moniker.) Even though Santoríni is the farthest Cycladic island from Athens, its tourist infrastructure makes it easy for first-time visitors to see. It has interesting ancient sites, a stunning cliff-top view, as well as quaint seaside villages and a hopping nightlife — and don't forget the beaches.

Delphi: The center of the ancient world

If you only have time to visit one archaeological site in Greece, it would be a hard choice between Ancient Olympia near Patras, site of one of the Seven Wonders of the Ancient World, with its unique, Games-related antiquities; Delphi, the site of oracle Apollo, with its amazing setting; Alexander the Great's stomping grounds at the foot of Mount Olympus, Dion, the most enchanting; and, lest we forget, the tombs at Vergina. But the ancients chose well for the place they considered the center of the world, and you won't be disappointed if you choose it, too. Delphi lies halfway up a mountainside, with the impressive Mount Parnassós surrounding the site and a lush, narrow valley of olive trees stretching down to the Gulf of Corinth.

You can do Delphi in one long day trip from Athens, but staying the night will make the trip less hectic. After spending time in the city, you may welcome Delphi's small-town beauty and pace.

Getting there

Buses (☎ **210-831-7096** or 210-880-8080 in Athens, 22650-82-317 or 22650-82-880 in Delphi) make the three-hour trip from Athens six times a day; the fare is 14€ ($22). If you're taking the ferry to Greece, you can bus directly from Patras, or else from the northern port city of Thessaloniki if you're arriving by train. Both make the journey once a day and arrive via Amfissa, a well-connected town 20km (12 miles) from Delphi.

Tourist information is available at the town hall, 11 Apóllonos St. (☎ **22650-82-900**), usually open Monday through Friday from 7:30 a.m. to 2:30 p.m. The office of the **Tourist Police,** which also provides information, is at 3 Angelos Sikelianoú St. (☎ **22650-82-220**).

Seeing the sights

Delphi is a small town with little side streets connecting the arterial roads. The bus can drop you off in the town center near the archaeological site, or at the west end of town, where it's then a five- to ten-minute walk. Many visitors start at the museum on the way to the ruins, but if you want to beat the heat and the crowds, go straight to the ruins first thing in the morning, which will also set the stage for the more intellectual experience of examining the museum's treasures.

The main ruins area is the **Sanctuary of Apollo** (☎ 22650-82-312 or 22650-82-346), which extends up the lower slopes of Mount Parnassós. You follow the **Sacred Way,** a marble path lined with the ruined treasuries of Greek city-states that tried to outdo each other in their efforts to offer the greatest riches to the sanctuary. The Athenian Treasury, located just past the first bend in the Sacred Way, looks remarkably well-preserved because it was rebuilt in 1906.

The Sacred Way hits a plateau at what was once the inner sanctum of the **Temple of Apollo.** Pilgrims from all over the Western world came here to seek advice or have their fortunes told by a seer, the Oracle of Delphi, who spoke the wisdom of Apollo. Earthquakes, looting, and landslides have pretty much destroyed the temple's partially underground chambers.

The fourth-century-B.C. **theater** at the top of the sanctuary is the best preserved of its kind in Greece. (The Romans helped, rebuilding it about 2,000 years ago.) Musicians and performers competed here in the Pythian Games, which emphasized culture more than the Olympic Games, as they were held in honor of Apollo, god of poets and inventor of the lyre. The view of the whole archaeological site is fantastic from the theater, but you can climb even farther up to the long, tree-lined stadium, which dates to the sixth century B.C. and is where the Pythian Games' athletic contests took place.

After you leave the Sanctuary of Apollo, if you keep walking down the main road, you see Delphi's most beautiful ruins below you. These ruins are in the **Marmaria** — so named because later Greeks used the area as a marble quarry. The most striking sight is the remains of the small, round temple called **Tholos,** built in 380 B.C. In the 1930s, three of the original 20 columns in the temple's outer shell were re-erected and a section of the *lintel* (the horizontal connecting span) was replaced on top. The temple is at its most beautiful when the sun sets behind it.

Admission to the ruins is 6€ ($9.60), 9€ ($14) for both the site and the museum. The ruins are open in summer daily from 8 a.m. to 7:15 p.m. In winter (Nov–May), hours are usually from 8:30 a.m. to 3 p.m. The site is closed December 25 to 26, January 1, March 25, Easter (Orthodox) Sunday, *Ayiou Pnévmatos* (Whit Mon, in May or June), and May 1.

Delphi's **Archaeological Museum (☎ 22650-82-312;** www.culture.gr) has *kouri* (stylized statues of youths) from the seventh century B.C. and gifts that were once part of the Sacred Way's treasuries, among other artifacts. Don't miss the winged sphinx of the Naxians or the bronze charioteer from 474 B.C. The museum also houses the **Omphalós,** or Navel Stone, a piece of rock that marked the spot that the ancient Greeks believed was the center (belly button) of the world, under the Temple of Apollo. God of gods Zeus was believed to have released two eagles simultaneously at opposite ends of the earth (which was thought to be flat), and the point where they crashed into each other and fell to the ground marked the world's midpoint.

Admission is 6€ ($9.60), 9€ ($14) for both the museum and the site. The museum is open in summer Tuesday through Sunday from 8 a.m. to 7:15 p.m. and Monday noon to 6:30 p.m. In winter (Nov–May), hours are usually from 8:30 a.m. to 3 p.m. The museum and site are closed December 25 to 26, January 1, March 25, Easter (Orthodox) Sunday, *Ayiou Pnévmatos* (Whit Mon, in May or June), and May 1. *Note:* The ruins normally close slightly earlier than the museum.

Where to stay and dine

Spend the night at the **Hotel Varonos,** 25 Pavlou and Frederíkis St., Delphi's main street (☎/Fax **22650-82-345;** www.hotel-varonos.gr), where the rooms have spectacular views and doubles run 80€ ($128) with breakfast and air-conditioning in summer. **Taverna Vakhos,** 31 Apóllonos St. (☎ **22650-83-186**), is a simple but delicious and inexpensive restaurant with great views.

Santoríni: Sun, sea, and . . . black sand

Santoríni (*Thíra* in Greek) is the farthest in the Cyclades, a "circle" of isles skirting once-sacred Delos islet in the Aegean Sea. The group of islands is most famous for the cubic, whitewashed houses. Crescent-shaped Santoríni's main attraction is its steep black and red cliffs that curve around a *caldera* (volcanic crater) of water and a still-active

Santoríni

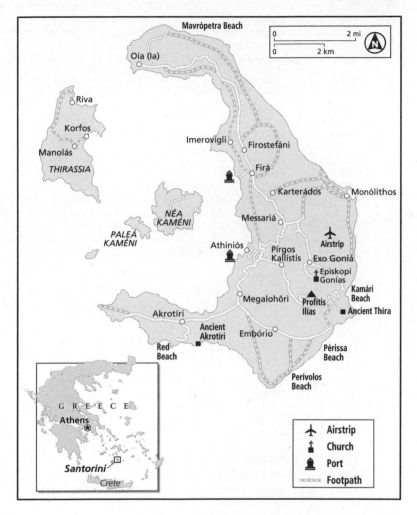

volcano; the views from here are sublime. Black-sand beaches, vineyards, whitewashed villages, and ancient cities combine to make it a must-see.

Santoríni's charms are not a secret; it's one of the most heavily visited Greek islands and can seem like one big disco in July and August, a modern symbol of mythical hedonism. Regardless, it remains well worth a visit whenever possible.

Some people actually make Santoríni a day trip by plane from Athens, and passengers stopping for an afternoon cruise break make noon the most crowded time. Santoríni is worth a two- to four-day stay if you can swing it, though life winds down considerably from late October through Easter.

Getting there and getting around

Several flights make the easy 50-minute trip from Athens daily. Call **Olympic Airways** (☎ 210-966-6666; www.olympicairlines.com) or **Aegean Air** (☎ 210-626-1000; www.aegeanair.com). Fares are based on availability and cost from 50€ ($80) one-way. Flying even one-way saves time, especially if you also want to island-hop in the area.

Two to five boats depart daily to Santoríni from Athens's Piraeus port for around 35€ ($56) one-way in the summer. For information on the ferry companies and their schedules, visit a travel agent (central Athens has many), or call the **Port Authority** in Piraeus (schedules for one week only, changing on Wed) at ☎ **1441** (English-speaking; phone charges apply), or 210-414-7800 (recording in Greek), or in Santoríni's main town of Fira at ☎ 22860-23-702 or 22860-22-239. The trip takes 5 to 14 hours, depending on how many stops the ferry makes at other islands along the way.

Buses (☎ 22860-25-462; www.ktel-santorini.gr) on the island connect Athinios ferry port with Fira a few miles north; there are travel agencies for booking private transport and accommodations at the port but not much else.

Buses also connect Fira with the airport, the ruins of Akrotíri, and most villages and popular beaches. Tickets cost from 1.40€ to 2€ ($2.25–$3.20), paid on the bus, and most buses leave every 30 to 60 minutes (schedules are posted at the depot in Fira). **Taxis** (☎ **22860-22-555** or 22860-23-951) from the airport to Fira should cost around 12€ ($19).

Santoríni has no official tourist office, but dozens of private travel agents distribute free info, including **Kamari Tours** (☎ **22860-31-390** or 22860-22-666 in Fira), opposite the landmark Museum of Prehistoric Thira, and **Dakoutros Travel** (☎ **22860-22-958**) on the main square. They can help you get a hotel or book a ferry or plane ticket, and they also offer tours. For additional information about the island, visit www.santorini.com or the municipality Web site at www.thira.gr.

Seeing the sights

If you don't want to make the sightseeing connections yourself, stop by one of Fira's travel agencies, which make their living selling half- and full-day excursions to all the island's sights, including boat trips to the volcano and hot springs for 18€ ($29), and sunset cruises on a schooner for 40€ ($64).

A very long set of steps connects Fira to the old port that's used for excursions; walk, take a mule, or the cable car that runs every 20 to 30 minutes for 4€ ($6.40).

The island's best waterfront is **Kamári Beach,** a 7.25km-long (4½-mile) stretch of black pebbles and sand on the southeast shore. It gets very crowded in July and August.

The romantic should go straight to picture-perfect **Oía** (Ia), 12km (7½ miles) north of Fira by bus or 8km (5 miles) on the clifftop road, but be warned: The shops and prices are high-end, although rooms can be reasonable.

Other popular activities include shopping at Santoríni's many boutiques, renting scooters to explore the island, and sampling the tasty wine produced with the help of mineral-rich volcanic soil. There are many wineries; **Boutari winery** (☎ 22860-81-011; www.boutari.gr) has wine-tasting tours running from March through November and costing from 5€ ($8). Ask the driver of the bus from Fira to Akrotíri to let you off at the winery, 100m (328 feet) from Megalohori bus stop.

The impressive ruins of the Minoan city of **Ancient Akrotíri** (☎ 22860-81-366), also referred to as Greece's Pompeii, are a must-see, if the site is open. Archaeologists have conducted covered excavations of this 3,700-year-old town near popular Red Beach, but it's been closed since 2005 when part of the roof collapsed.

After most of the island was destroyed in a volcanic explosion in the mid-1600s B.C., a second civilization began. The capital was **Ancient Thíra** (900 B.C.–A.D. 150), which lies 1,200 feet above Kamári Beach. Considerably less is left standing than at Akrotíri, but the site itself, perched up on a headland, is very impressive. Ancient Thíra is open Tuesday through Sunday from 9 a.m. to 2:30 p.m. There is no entrance fee when archaeologists are excavating, but take a little cash with you in case this changes when you visit, and to buy refreshments or snacks from the canteen at the top of the paved road. From here, it's a short but sharp climb to the ruins.

Get there by taking the bus to Kamári, which lets you off at the bottom of the steep 4km (2½-mile) switchback road; give yourself an hour to walk up. If you have your own wheels, a scooter will make it. **Kamari Tours** (☎ 22860-31-390 or 22860-22-666 in Fira) does excursions to the site for 10€ ($16) round-trip by minibus from Kamári. Or take a taxi for 50€ ($80) an hour from Fira; expect to spend about an hour there.

Fira's small but outstanding **Archaeological Museum** (☎ 22860-22-217) near the cable-car terminus, contains artifacts from Ancient Thíra; the superb **Museum of Prehistoric Thíra** (☎ 22860-23-217) holds objects from Ancient Akrotíri, including Cycladic figurines and beautifully designed 3,700-year-old pottery. Admission is 3€ ($4.80) at each museum. Both are open Tuesday through Sunday from 8:30 a.m. to 3 p.m. (to 7:30 p.m. July and Aug). Closed December 25 to 26, January 1, March 25, Easter (Orthodox) Sunday, *Ayiou Pnévmatos* (Whit Mon, in May or June), and May 1.

The island that blew its top

Santoríni was a circular volcano until an eruption in the 1600s B.C. blew half the island into the air. This created massive tidal waves, spewed ash all over the region, and sparked earthquakes that swept the Aegean — an event that may have helped destroy the Minoan civilization, which was centered on Crete. A wealthy Minoan city called Akrotíri was on Santoríni, and some historians think that this city's volcanic destruction, just at the dawn of recorded history, fueled the mythology about a "lost continent." In other words, it could be the basis of the myth of Atlantis.

Where to stay

Most hotels are in Fira — but you also hear the most noise and run into the most tourists. Try to get a room with a view of the caldera, which is what you get in the 95€ to 175€ ($152–$280) doubles at **Loucas Hotel** (☎ **22860-22-480** or 22860-22-680; Fax: 22860-24-882; www.loucashotel. com). Go left at the FRANGO's sign on the way to the old port to reach it.

If you want to stay on the beach at Kamári, try the **Kamári Beach Hotel** (☎ **22860-31-216** or 22860-31-243; Fax: 2286-32-120; www.kamari beach.gr). Many of the 100€ to 160€ ($160–$256) doubles — including breakfast — have balconies for enjoying the beach and sea view.

In Oía, most studios and hotels are built right into the cliff. Try the **Chelidonia** (☎ **22860-71-287;** www.chelidonia.com), which has villas and studios from 140€ to 155€ ($224–$248) for a studio.

As on most Greek islands, people who want to rent you a room in their house greet most ferries. Ask questions, especially about location, before you head off, and don't commit until you've seen the place. These private rooms can be your only option if you arrive late and without reservations in July or August. Most rooms cost from 30€ ($48) off-season, to 80€ ($128) or 100€ ($160) in summer.

Many hotels on Santoríni are open only from Easter (Orthodox) to late October. In the off-season, the demand for hotel rooms nose-dives, so you can get a good deal on a private room.

Where to dine

For light dining in Fira, try **Kástro** (☎ **22860-22-503**), which attracts scads of day-trippers because of its location across from the cable-car terminal, but the beautiful views of the volcanic crater are worth the hassle. For one of the best meals in Greece, hit much-reviewed **Selene** (☎ **22860-22-249;** www.selene.gr) in Fira, known for dishes such as sliced octopus with white eggplant salad, and baked sea bass with tomatoes and capers wrapped in fava beans. It opens at 7 p.m. from April through October.

If you're at Kamári Beach, most restaurants cater to foreign palates from the influx of package tourists. Head for *tavérnas* along the beachfront, such as **Skaramagas** (☎ 22860-32-771), for typical Greek fare and seafood.

In Oía, best-value meals are at cliffside **Skala** (☎ 22860-71-362) and **Thalami taverna** (☎ 22860-71-009), on the main pedestrian road (Nik. Nomikou) south of the church square.

Fast Facts: Athens

American Express

The American Express office is at 318 Messogíon Ave., Agia Paraskeví (☎ 210-659-0700). It's open Monday through Friday from 8:30 a.m. to 7:30 p.m. The travel and mail desks are open Monday through Friday from 8:30 a.m. to 7:30 p.m., Saturday from 9:30 a.m. to 1:30 p.m. Get there by taking the Metro to Ethniki Amyna station, and then bus no. A5 or B5.

A bank at 43 Academias St. (☎ 210-363-5960) is open Monday through Thursday from 8 a.m. to 2:30 p.m., Friday 8 a.m. to 2 p.m.

Area Code

The country code for Greece is **30**. All phone numbers in Greece require dialing ten digits that includes the area code, beginning with **2** and normally ending with **0**. Athens is **210** or **211** plus seven digits; Thessaloniki is **2310** plus six digits, as is Patras (**2610**) and other urban areas. A five-digit area code is used elsewhere in the country. Cellphones in Greece do not follow the area-code rule but require ten digits and begin with **6**.

Currency

In 2002, the monetary unit in Greece became the euro (€). The euro is divided into 100 cents, and there are coins of 0.01, 0.02, 0.05, 0.10, 0.20, 0.50, 1€, and 2€. Paper-note denominations are 5, 10, 20, 50, 100, 200, and 500 euros. The rate of exchange used to calculate the dollar values given in this chapter is 1€ equals $1.60. Amounts over $10 are rounded to the nearest dollar.

Doctors and Dentists

Most doctors speak English, but you can call your embassy for lists of English-speaking doctors and dentists, or call the 24-hour SOS Doctors (☎ 1016; www.sosiatroi.gr), who make house calls. Most of the larger hotels have doctors whom they can call for you in an emergency.

Embassies and Consulates

The U.S. Embassy (☎ 210-721-2951; http://athens.usembassy.gov) is at 91 Vassilíssis Sofías Ave. If you need emergency help after the embassy has closed for the day, call ☎ 210-729-4301 or 210-729-4444.

Emergency

In an emergency, dial ☎ 100 for fast police assistance and ☎ 171 for the Tourist Police (see "Police," later for a description of the Tourist Police). Dial ☎ 199 to report a fire and ☎ 166 for an ambulance or a hospital. Dial ☎ 112 for the multilingual European Union emergency hot line.

Hospitals

A first-aid clinic is on the corner of P. Tsaldari (Piraeós) and Socrátous streets near Omónia Square. One private hospital is

Euroclinic, 9 Athanasiádou St., off Soutsou Street, Ambelókipi (☎ 210-641-6600; www.euroclinic.gr).

Information

The Greek National Tourism Organization Information desk is at 26 Amalías St., Sμntagma (☎ 210-331-0392; www.gnto.gr). For details on it, see "Finding information after you arrive," near the beginning of this chapter. Two good online resources are the privately maintained www.greecetravel.com, and for sites of interest, the Hellenic Ministry of Culture's www.culture.gr.

Another handy resource is the Tourist Police, 43 Veíkou St., Koukáki (☎ 171 or 210-920-0724), south of the Acropolis. This service offers round-the-clock visitor support in English and is the place to turn if you encounter any problems. Hotel and patron regulations are online at www.grhotels.gr.

Internet Access and Cybercafes

Most hotels provide Internet access; however, you can find a few places around town to get online. At Sμntagma Square try Arcade, 5 Stadíou St. (☎ 210-322-1808), which can also burn CDs and DVDs. It's open daily 9 a.m. to 11 p.m. C@fe 4U, 44 Ippokrátous St. (☎ 210-361-1981), is a 24-hour cafe and bar in Exárcheia that also sells food and drinks.

Maps

The GNTO provides free maps to tourists (see "Finding information after you arrive," near the beginning of this chapter), or you can purchase them at most foreign-press newsstands.

Newspapers and Magazines

English-language newspapers are found at foreign-press newsstands around the country, including all the kiosks at the top of Ermoú Street at Sμntagma Square. The

Athens News (www.athensnews.gr) is a weekly English-language newspaper, and *Kathimerini* (www.ekathimerini.com) is a daily, which includes translations from the Greek press and is found inside the *International Herald Tribune.* There are also the monthly *Insider* and *Odyssey* magazines. The most complete listings to find a bar/club, restaurant, exhibition, or to see who's in town, are only available in Greek, such as the weekly *Athinorama* or *TimeOut* listings magazines, available at all newsstands. Get assistance from your hotel or at a tourist information desk to find what you want.

Pharmacies

Pharmakía are marked by green and sometimes red crosses. They're usually open from 8 a.m. to 2 p.m., but the location of the nearest after-hours pharmacy is posted on all pharmacies' doors. You can also find a round-the-clock pharmacy by dialing ☎ 1434 (in Greek), by picking up a copy of the *Athens News* or *Kathimerini (IHT),* or by looking online (www.ekathimerini.com).

Police

In an emergency, dial ☎ **100.** For help dealing with a troublesome taxi driver or hotel, restaurant, or shop owner, call the Tourist Police at ☎ 171; they're on call 24 hours and speak English, as well as other foreign languages.

Post Office

Athens's main post office is on Sμntagma Square at Mitropóleos Street (☎ 210-331-9500). It's open Monday through Friday from 7:30 a.m. to 8 p.m., Saturday from 7:30 a.m. to 2 p.m. and Sunday from 9 a.m. to 1:30 p.m. The parcel post office (for packages weighing more than 2kg/4.4 pounds), 60 Mitropóleos St. (☎ 210-321-8156 or 210-321-8143), is open Monday through Friday from 7:30 a.m. to 8 p.m. Parcels must be open for inspection before you seal them (bring your own tape and string) at the post office.

Safety

Apart from averting a fall on an uneven sidewalk and giving selfish drivers the right of way, visitors have only a few minor concerns. Young women may get propositioned by shopkeepers in tourist areas, and touts often try to lure single men to unscrupulous bars with beautiful women or to hotel room "parties." The visitor is then forced to pay the bill for all. Don't accept offers of food or water, which may be drugged, from "friendly locals" at tourist sites, and put your hand over the keypad at ATMs when you enter your PIN to avoid "card theft." Although Greece has a low crime rate and you can safely walk the streets well into the night, pickpocketing, mostly on public transport during busy times, is a problem. Motorcycle thieves have also targeted mainly seniors by pulling up alongside and pulling off shoulder bags, and often, the victim. Keep your valuables out of reach and out of sight.

Taxes

A value-added tax (VAT), normally 19 percent, is included in the price of all goods and services in Greece, with reduced rates for items like books and food. Non–European Union residents can get VAT refunds at the airport with a form obtained at shops with TAX FREE or DUTY FREE signs, if they've spent a minimum of 120€ ($192). Look for the Tax Refund booth (☎ 210-353-2216) at the Departures level. For more on the VAT, see Chapter 4.

Taxis

See "Getting Around Athens," earlier in this chapter.

Telephone

Many of the city's public phones only accept phone cards, available at newsstands in several denominations starting at 3€ ($4.80). The card works for 100 short local calls (fewer long-distance or international calls). Widely available prepaid calling cards (kiosks, exchange bureaus, and so on) start at 5€ ($8) and work out cheaper. Some kiosks still have metered phones; you pay what the meter records. Local phone calls cost 0.03€ (5¢) for the first two minutes or part thereof, and a similar rate for each additional minute. You can phone home directly by contacting AT&T (☎ 00-800-1311), MCI (☎ 00-800-1211), or Sprint (☎ 00-800-1411).

For telephone assistance in English, dial ☎ 139.

Transit Info

For local bus schedules, dial ☎ 185; for bus schedules in the rest of Greece, call ☎ 210-512-4910 or 210-831-7153. For train info, call ☎ 1110. For flight info, call the airport at ☎ 210-353-0000. For domestic ship info, call ☎ 1441 or 210-414-7800 (recording in Greek). For more information, see "Getting Around Athens," earlier in this chapter.

Part VI
The Part of Tens

The 5th Wave   By Rich Tennant

"It's the room next door. They suggest you deflate your souvenir bagpipes before trying to pack them in your luggage."

In this part . . .

The final three chapters are *For Dummies* top-ten lists of Europe's bests, worsts, and little-known wonders. We want you to be better prepared than the travelers next to you on the plane, the ones who bought one of those densely written guides that lists dozens of hotels (usually without saying anything useful about them) and explains the history of every painting in the museum.

Chapter 25

The Ten Most Overrated Sights and Attractions in Europe

· ·

In This Chapter

▶ Taking a pass on London's Changing of the Guard and Madame Tussaud's

▶ Recognizing the fakery in many of Madrid's flamenco shows

▶ Skipping the city of Athens

▶ Foregoing famed boulevards and beaches

▶ Bypassing the big-name shopping locales

· ·

The sights listed in this chapter don't always live up to their hype. Nevertheless, we still include some of them in this book, because they're too popular to ignore. Plus, this list is subjective. We think these places and activities are overrated — but you may enjoy the heck out of them, and that's okay, too.

Some of the sights listed in this chapter are so unjustly famous that we simply didn't include them in the book at all. So if you're wondering why the French Riviera is missing, read on and find out.

London's Changing of the Guard at Buckingham Palace

On the yawn scale, we give it about an eight out of ten. The changing of the guard features diffident pomp, halfhearted ceremony, and a clearly bored marching band. And it's crowded, too.

If you absolutely must take part in this tourist tradition, see Chapter 10 for the details.

London's Madame Tussaud's Wax Museum

Pay $42 to ogle wax portraits (albeit expertly executed) of famous dead people? Kitschy, maybe. A must-see? Never. This place is only famous because it has been franchised around the world — sort of a fast-food approach to culture for a museum that's only of marginal historical interest in the first place.

If you want to judge for yourself, see Chapter 10 for the details.

Paris's Champs-Elysées and Rome's Via Veneto

These boulevards — world-class public living rooms where the rich and famous went to sip coffee at a sidewalk cafe, to see and be seen — were the talk of the town into the 1960s.

Now the Champs-Elysées that once welcomed the carriage of Catherine de' Medici has become Paris's main drag for fast-food chains and movie multiplexes. The Via Veneto of Fellini's *La Dolce Vita* (the film that coined the term *paparazzi*) has gone from glitterati ground zero to a string of overpriced, internationally affiliated hotels booked only by tour-bus companies.

The French Riviera

From a beachgoing point of view, the French Riviera is a disappointment. Americans are used to vast expanses of glittering sand. In Europe, sand is a precious commodity, and the beaches — sand, shingle, pebbles, or outright rocks — are mostly private, crowded, narrow strips of shoreline with tightly packed regiments of umbrellas and changing cabins. Come to the Riviera for the casinos or nightlife, if that's your sort of thing. But don't come for the beaches.

Madrid's Flamenco Shows

The shows given for tourists are often of poor quality and overpriced. In Chapter 22, you find my recommendations for some of the more authentic flamenco shows, but remember that the real thing (a spontaneous nighttime ritual) is in Andalusia.

Athens, Greece

Yes, you definitely want to see the Acropolis and the Parthenon, the Ancient Agorá, and the National Archaeological Museum if you visit Athens (see Chapter 24), but be forewarned that the city itself is dirty, crowded, and boring. And getting there is no easy task — you must spend three days of your trip traveling by train or ferry if you choose not to fly. Exploring Greece's fascinating interior is a much better use of your time. Or you can island-hop for loads of fun.

Four Shopping Disappointments: The "Big Names" in London, Paris, Rome, and Florence

Harrods was an incredible, almost unbelievable institution when it first opened — a block-long, multilevel building packed to the gills with every imaginable item that you may want to buy (and many that you never thought of), all in one place. We have a term for that today: *department store*. Sure, Harrods is still extraordinarily classy when compared to even top-end chains such as Macy's, and it has a nifty food section, but you can actually find more variety (if not quality) these days at the Mall of America in Minnesota.

Paris's **rue du Faubourg St-Honoré** is, indeed, lined with remarkable shops and high-end boutiques. But one of the cardinal rules of elite shopping in Europe is that high fashion costs no less in its country of origin (France or Italy) than it does in a New York boutique or upscale factory outlet in the United States. This applies to the other streets mentioned in this section, as well as any other street and city in Europe. Yes, buying that little black dress in Paris or leather shoes in Florence has cachet, but don't make the mistake of thinking that you're coming here for a bargain — those are found in stock shops and Europe's outdoor markets.

Via Condotti, the main shopping drag that shoots like an arrow from the base of Rome's Spanish Steps, is now home to a Foot Locker and a Disney Store. The big names of Italian fashion (not to mention the small "Made in Italy" boutiques) have slipped around the corners onto the side streets and parallels of Via Condotti.

Via de' Tornabuoni in Florence has similar problems (though Florence's new Foot Locker and Disney Store are actually located a couple of blocks over on Via de' Calzaiuoli). Aside from Ferragamo's massive medieval palace/flagship anchoring one end, and the original Gucci store in the middle of it, most of the best shops — big-name or not — are not on Via de' Tornabuoni. Instead, they reside on tributaries and side streets such as Via della Vigna Vecchia.

Fair warning.

Chapter 26

Ten Overlooked Gems

*T*his chapter lists ten unforgettable places where you can avoid the tourists and see some cool sights to boot. Some of these recommendations don't appear elsewhere in this book, but all are within easy striking distance from the major cities, and we let you know where to begin your journey in each case.

Avebury, England

Okay, so it's not entirely unknown, but compared to Stonehenge, just 20 miles to the north, Avebury (☎ 01672-539-250; www.nationaltrust. org.uk) receives perhaps 5 percent the number of visitors. Believe us, a prehistoric circle of stones feels much more mystical without throngs of camera-toting tourists posing around it.

But the relative lack of crowds is not the only thing that makes Avebury so special. The Avebury circle is absolutely huge; you even find a small village built halfway into it, with a pub, restaurant, and fine little archaeology museum. And unlike at Stonehenge, you can actually wander around amid the stones.

Buses leave regularly from Salisbury station for Avebury. For details on getting to Salisbury (and Stonehenge), see Chapter 10.

Dingle Peninsula, Ireland

Almost everyone flocking to southeastern Ireland heads out of the main town of Killarney to ride around the famed Ring of Kerry. Far fewer know that, just one inlet to the north, the road looping around the Dingle Peninsula has the same sort of fishing hamlets, village pubs, ancient ruins, and stunning vistas as the Ring of Kerry, but with almost none of the crowds.

Getting to Killarney from Ireland's big cities is easy. For details on visiting Dingle Peninsula, see Chapter 12.

Paris's Lesser-Known Museums

Everyone piles into Paris's Louvre and Musée d'Orsay — and with good reason. But Paris has more than 145 other museums, many of them unknown to the average tourist. At the beautiful little **Musée Rodin,** 77 rue de Varenne (☎ **01-44-18-61-10;** www.musee-rodin.fr), castings of Rodin's greatest works fill the rooms, while his *Thinker* ponders in the lush garden. Or you can search out the **Musée National du Moyen Age** (Museum of the Middle Ages), 6 place Paul Painlevé (☎ **01-53-73-78-00;** www.musee-moyenage.fr), installed in the remains of a bathhouse built almost 2,000 years ago during the city's Roman era.

The Marais's **Musée Carnavalet,** 23 rue de Sévigné (☎ **01-44-59-58-58;** www.carnavalet.paris.fr), is dedicated to the history of Paris. The **Musée Marmottan Monet,** 2 rue Louis-Boilly (☎ **01-44-96-50-33;** www.marmottan.com), on the edge of the Bois de Boulogne woods, houses Monet's *Impression, Sol Levant,* the painting the title of which was taken to coin the term *Impressionism.* And don't leave out the **Musée Picasso,** 5 rue de Thorigny (☎ **01-42-71-25-21;** www.musee-picasso.fr), or the **Musée de l'Orangerie,** just off place de la Concorde (☎ **01-44-77-80-07;** www.musee-orangerie.fr), with its 360-degree painting of *Waterlilies* by Monet. For more about the Musée Rodin and Musée Picasso, see Chapter 13.

Hoge Veluwe Park, Netherlands

At this large national park outside Arnhem, you can borrow a bike for free and ride around the park's many roads and trails, exploring a microcosm of the many environments of the Netherlands, from sand dunes to forests to meadows to formal gardens. Make sure that you stop into the Kröller-Müller Museum, a fantastic and underrated gallery of modern art in the middle of the park. It features more than 270 works by van Gogh and hundreds of other works by 20th-century and contemporary artists, plus one of the most beautiful outdoor sculpture gardens in the world. For more about the park, see Chapter 14.

The Heuriger of Grinzig, Austria

If you ride Vienna's no. 38 trolley out to the end of the line, you arrive at the edge of the fabled Vienna Woods in the wine hamlet of Grinzig. Here, almost every block is home to a different *heurige,* a small vineyard that produces limited quantities of white wine and will serve some to you, along with platters of roast sausages, dumplings, goulash, pastries, and other hearty Austrian dishes. You can enjoy your feast under aged, wood-beamed ceilings or, in warm weather, in wine gardens crowded by locals. For more about Austria, see Chapter 16.

Ostia Antica, Italy

At the crack of dawn each morning in Rome, lines of tour buses set out for a long day trip to Pompeii. Take our advice and sleep late, and then take the B metro line for a less-than-an-hour trip to another excavated ancient city called Ostia Antica, near the Italian shore.

In Ostia Antica, the cracked mosaic pavements and crumbling brick walls of 1,800-year-old houses, shops, and public buildings flutter with wildflowers; weeds grow in the flagstone roads; and the headless statues lean nonchalantly amid tall grasses as if simply forgotten. And that's what the town was — forgotten — as the empire fell, the coast receded, and malaria infested the area. Explore it all here: abandoned temples, an empty theater and amphitheater, windswept streets, and the broken remains of wealthy villas, simple flour mills, and public bathhouses. For more about day trips from Rome, see Chapter 19.

Venetian Islands, Italy

Glorious St. Mark's Basilica, the pink-and-white Doge's Palace, the Carnival mask makers — the touristy side of Venice is all fine and well, but for a more authentic experience — and a slower pace — head to a series of smaller islands strung throughout the vast Venetian lagoon.

Hop a *vaporetto* (one of the ferries that serve as Venice's public buses) and in half an hour you can chug out to bustling **Murano,** where the art of Venetian glass-blowing was born and its main factories still reside. After wandering its canals and poking into its marvelous Byzantine/Renaissance churches, continue on to the islet of **Burano,** a fishing village of brightly colored houses and tiny boats bobbing in the little canals, where lace making is the local specialty.

Another *vaporetto* leaves from here to carry you to isolated **Torcello,** where the earliest lagoon settlement was established (older than Venice itself). Now all that's left are a few houses, a scraggly vineyard, and a Byzantine cathedral with a tipsy bell tower and gorgeous, glittering mosaics carpeting the apse and the entrance wall. The island is also the improbable home to Locanda Cipriani, a refined restaurant (same owners as Venice's Harry's Bar) that Hemingway used to frequent. Headed back to Venice proper on the last *vaporetto,* the sun setting over the lagoon, you now know how Venice lives outside the tourist trade.

For more on visiting the islands of Venice, see Chapter 21.

Arena Chapel, Padova, Italy

At the start of the 14th century, Giotto, a shepherd turned Gothic painter, kick-started the artistic revolution that would eventually flower into the Renaissance. His famous frescoes in Assisi attract plenty of visitors, but few people visit this beautiful chapel, covered almost from floor to ceiling with the master's vibrant painting, in Padova, just a 20-minute train ride from Venice. For details on visiting Padova, see Chapter 21.

Spain — All of It

Spain spent much of the last century under a dictatorship, so it didn't end up on most tourist itineraries. Although the backpackers are slowly rediscovering it, and in summer the Brits flock to the coastal resorts, Spain is still woefully overlooked by most travelers — their loss.

This country's rich history and heritage of Celtic, Roman, Moorish, Basque, and other influences make it one of the most diverse and culturally dense nations in Europe. **Madrid** is stuffed with museums, and **Barcelona** is an eminently livable city where life centers on a parklike pedestrian boulevard that runs through the very heart of town.

But if you have to pick one region to explore, choose the southlands of **Andalusia** (www.andalucia.org), full of genteel Moorish castles, Christian cathedrals, medieval quarters, Renaissance and baroque palaces and churches, and whitewashed villages. Bullfights, flamenco dancing, and fine sherries all hail originally from Andalusia, and there's nowhere better to experience life *a l'Española* than in the cities of Seville, Granada, and Córdoba; the hill towns northeast of Jerez (home of sherry); and the beaches of the Costa del Sol around Málaga.

For details on Madrid and Barcelona, see Chapters 22 and 23, respectively.

Medieval Hamlets and Hill Towns

If you want to turn back the clock and see villages and small towns where the leisurely pace of life has helped keep the winding stone streets in a veritable time capsule, Europe is the place to go. And many of these, dare we call them "quaint," old villages are just a short bus or train ride outside major cities.

San Gimignano, in Tuscany, bristles with 14 medieval stone towers just a hop, skip, and a jump from Florence (see Chapter 20). **Chartres,** with its glorious Gothic cathedral, is just an hour from Paris on the train (see Chapter 13). **Salisbury** and its massive Gothic cathedral is a similar easy day trip from London (see Chapter 10). **Toledo** once the capital of Castille, is today a bright, oversize village full of El Greco paintings that's an easy day's jaunt out from Madrid (see Chapter 22).

The hamlets high in the **Lauterbrunnen Valley** of the Swiss Alps are centuries away in attitude from the grand business-capital cities of Switzerland, and even from the busy and modernized resort town of **Interlaken** at the valley's mouth (see Chapter 17). And the tidy Tyrolean town of **Innsbruck** nestles its medieval alleyways and baroque facades amid the Austrian Alps, halfway between Vienna and Munich, making for a perfect stop between the two cities (see Chapter 16).

Chapter 27

Ten Ways to Break Out of the Tourist Mold

- -

In This Chapter

▶ Doing as the locals do

▶ Going to a soccer match

▶ Tuning into local TV

▶ Leaving this book behind (we mean it!)

- -

Sometimes it pays to be less touristy when you travel to foreign countries. We take our inspiration from Michael Palin in his BBC series *Around the World in 80 Days;* when he arrived in Venice, he decided to cruise the canals . . . in a Venetian garbage scow.

To enjoy the "real" Europe, do something other than what all the other travel books recommend. You'll be rewarded with a unique experience that travelers who stick solely to the major sights never have. Here are our suggestions for finding the road less traveled.

Do as the Locals Do

Find out how the locals live by exploring their neighborhoods. Be the first on your block to discover the upscale but thoroughly untouristy **17th arrondissement in Paris.** Regale your friends back home with tales from **London's Clerkenwell,** where you can still have beer with breakfast and see the spot where Braveheart was executed outside Smithfield meat market; or **London's East End,** where amid the immigrant families working to achieve the good life, you can still find pockets of proud working-class Londoners speaking genuine Cockney. Or wander **Rome's Parioli district,** where you can admire the funky architecture and join the well-heeled matrons strolling down to the cafe in their de rigueur fur coats.

Drink coffee (or something stronger) with the regulars in the corner bar. Sit on the edge of one of those seemingly endless daily games of cards, backgammon, or bocce ball, watching carefully to get an idea of how the game is played. One of the grizzled old men may eventually gesture you over, and everyone will get a kick out of trying to pantomime to the foreigner the rules of the game as you proceed to lose spectacularly.

Find that local version of Wal-Mart or Target and just wander the aisles, checking out the daily essentials of the French or the Austrians, for example; as a souvenir, pick up a brand of toothpaste you've never heard of. If you're a music fan, wander into a European music store, most of which have listening stations. Pick up a CD by what seems to be the hottest native pop group.

Take a Dip in Bern's Aare River

Few capital cities in the world have river water that's actually clean enough for swimming; Bern (see Chapter 17) is proud to be one of them. On warm summer days, the locals troop partway upstream, jump in, and let the surprisingly swift current float them downriver into the heart of town, where a public bathing complex awaits. Upon arrival, they clamber out and relax poolside or hike 20 minutes back up the tree-shaded path to jump back in the river.

Rent an Apartment or Villa

Instead of staying at several hotels in different cities or towns, pick a city or region to explore more fully and rent an apartment or villa. If you choose a small town or a place in the country, rent a car and settle down to life, European-style. Not only can you save money, but you'll also become a temporary native of sorts. Become a "regular" at the cafe on the corner and the little grocery store down the street. Get to know your neighbors; maybe they'll share a family recipe with you. You may enjoy the lifestyle so much that you find yourself pausing at the windows of local real estate agents to peruse the offerings and check on property values.

Visit a Small Private Museum

You wouldn't believe the places you can find where wealthy collectors left behind dusty old mansions jumbled with valuable bric-a-brac ranging from Ming vases and Roman reliefs to medieval suits of armor and occasional paintings by Renaissance masters. Although few of the individual pieces, or the collections as a whole, tend to be first rate, they offer fascinating insights into one man's or one family's tastes and styles — and as often as not these places are preserved exactly as the collector left them in 1754 or 1892 or whenever, and as such offer a glimpse into the lives and times of a different era.

And before you pooh-pooh the idea of a private collection, remember the names of a few larger ones installed in the personal residences of Europe's richest past collectors: the Louvre (the French monarchs' collection in their city palace), the Uffizi (the Medicis' artwork installed in their old office building), and the Vatican (the pope's best heirlooms in his private digs).

Jog with the Locals

Europeans may not be as exercise-driven as your modern North American (they walk more and get their exercise as part of their daily lives), but the concept of a good cardio workout seems to be catching on here. Find out where the locals jog, and join them for a morning (or evening) run. You can clear your head, explore a city park or two, and maybe make some new friends.

Hike in the Countryside

Leave the crowds of the big city behind, and explore the country on foot. Buy the best, most detailed, small-scale map you can find that shows all the unpaved roads and trails (if any). The tourist offices of most smaller towns can help you out with maps, and sometimes even itineraries, or they can point you toward the local trekking group. A few cities are so small (Florence comes to mind) that you can start many country walks right outside your doorstep — or from the end of a local bus line.

Catch a Football (Soccer) Match

In Europe, football (known as soccer in the U.S.) is like packing all the cheers, joys, agonies, and devoted fandom of American baseball, football, basketball, and hockey into one sport and one season. Except for a few oddball games — cricket in England or hurling in Ireland — this is the only sport that most Europeans follow, making it a close second to Christianity as the national religion in each country.

Find out when the big match takes place (often Sun) and where the die-hard fans of the home team sit in the stadium. Then get a seat near them and root, root, root for the home team (unless you seem to be seated amid fans of the opposing team, in which case scream your bloody lungs out for the visitors). Just avoid any obvious hooligans and any sign that a brawl's about to break out.

Pick Grapes or Olives

During harvest seasons, you're bound to see people out working their fields or small plots. Often, they're more than happy to accept any help you offer, and you can spend a day picking grapes or olives — both of which are a lot harder on your fingers and, in the case of grapes, your back, than you may imagine. But the experience can be fun, and you may even get to pass around the wine bottle with the farmers during breaks.

Watch Some Local Television Programs

Watching TV in Europe doesn't make you a couch potato. Tell your friends that you're having a cultural experience! You may be amazed by what they put on TV in other countries — a whole lot more nudity, for one thing. Plus, you get awful slapstick comedies (which are pretty easy to follow in any language), oddball game shows, and commercials for chewing gum or spring water — and you can discover that Bart Simpson is a beloved bad boy in just about every country.

Liberate Yourself from Your Guidebook

Once in a while, stow away this and any other guidebooks you may have. Check out sights and restaurants without following our advice. If the bistro is cheap and full of French patrons, chances are, it's good. Wander into a church without even checking to see if it's listed in your book and admire the baroque altarpiece and paintings for their aesthetic value alone, not because you know someone famous made them.

Try a dish that your menu translator doesn't cover. (Okay, that can be risky, but if the locals are willing to eat it, it probably isn't poison — just don't hold us responsible if it involves more tentacles than you're comfortable with.) Enjoy the thrill of discovery! Turn tourism into travel and your vacation into an adventure. The memories will be more than worth it.

Appendix

Quick Concierge

●●

Average Travel Times by Rail

Amsterdam to
Munich   8½ hours
Paris   4¼ hours
Zurich   10 hours

Athens to
Munich   42½ hours
Vienna   43 hours

Barcelona to
Madrid   7 hours
Paris   11½ hours

Bath to
London   1¼ hours

Bern to
Interlaken   1 hour
Paris   4½ hours
Zurich   1½ hours

Edinburgh to
London   4 hours

Florence to
Paris   12½ hours
Rome   1½ hours
Venice   3 hours
Zurich   8 hours

Glasgow to
London   5 hours

Innsbruck to
Munich   3 hours
Vienna   8 hours
Zurich   5 hours

Interlaken to
Bern   1 hour

London to
Bath   1¼ hours
Edinburgh   4 hours
Glasgow   5 hours
Paris   3 hours

Madrid to
Barcelona   7 hours

Munich to
Amsterdam   8½ hours
Athens   42½ hours
Innsbruck   3 hours
Paris   8½ hours
Prague   7½ hours
Rome   11 hours
Venice   9 hours
Vienna   4¾ hours
Zurich   5 hours

Paris to
Amsterdam   4¼ hours
Bern   4½ hours
Barcelona   11½ hours
Florence   12½ hours
London   3 hours

Munich   8½ hours
Rome   15 hours
Venice   12¼ hours
Vienna   13½ hours
Zurich   6 hours

Pisa to

Rome   4 hours

Prague to

Munich   7½ hours
Vienna   5 hours

Rome to

Florence   1½ hours
Munich   11 hours
Paris   15 hours
Pisa   4 hours
Siena   3 hours
Venice   4½ hours
Zurich   8½ hours

Siena to

Rome   3 hours

Venice to

Florence   3 hours
Munich   9 hours
Paris   12¼ hours
Rome   4½ hours
Vienna   8 hours

Vienna to

Athens   43 hours
Innsbruck   8 hours
Munich   4¾ hours
Paris   13½ hours
Prague   5 hours
Zurich   12 hours

Zurich to

Amsterdam   10 hours
Bern   1½ hours
Florence   8 hours
Innsbruck   5 hours
Munich   5 hours
Paris   6 hours
Rome   8½ hours
Vienna   12 hours

Metric Conversions

Liquid Volume

To convert	Multiply by
U.S. gallons to liters	3.8
Liters to U.S. gallons	0.26
U.S. gallons to imperial gallons	0.83
Imperial gallons to U.S. gallons	1.20
Imperial gallons to liters	4.55
Liters to imperial gallons	0.22

Distance

To convert	Multiply by
Inches to centimeters	2.54
Centimeters to inches	0.39
Feet to meters	0.30
Meters to feet	3.28
Yards to meters	0.91
Meters to yards	1.09
Miles to kilometers	1.61
Kilometers to miles	0.62

Weight

To convert	Multiply by
Ounces to grams	28.35
Grams to ounces	0.035
Pounds to kilograms	0.45
Kilograms to pounds	2.20

Temperature

To **convert °F to °C,** subtract 32 and multiply by $\frac{5}{9}$ (0.555).

To **convert °C to °F,** multiply by 1.8 and add 32.

32°F = 0°C

Clothing Size Conversions

Women's Clothing

American	Continental	British
6	36	8
8	38	10

(continued)

Women's Clothing *(continued)*

American	Continental	British
10	40	12
12	42	14
14	44	16
16	46	18

Women's Shoes

American	Continental	British
5	36	4
6	37	5
7	38	6
8	39	7
9	40	8
10	41	9

Children's Clothing

American	Continental	British
3	98	18
4	104	20
5	110	22
6	116	24
6X	122	26

Children's Shoes

American	Continental	British
8	24	7
9	25	8
10	27	9

American	Continental	British
11	28	10
12	29	11
13	30	12
1	32	13
2	33	1
3	34	2

Men's Suits

American	Continental	British
34	44	34
36	46	36
38	48	38
40	50	40
42	52	42
44	54	44
46	56	46
48	58	48

Men's Shirts

American	Continental	British
14½	37	14½
15	38	15
15½	39	15½
16	41	16
16½	42	16½
17	43	17
17½	44	17½
18	45	18

Men's Shoes

American	Continental	British
7	39½	6
8	41	7
9	42	8
10	43	9
11	44½	10
12	46	11
13	47	12

Toll-Free Numbers and Web Sites

Major North American airlines

Air Canada
☎ 888-247-2262
www.aircanada.com

American Airlines
☎ 800-433-7300
www.aa.com

Continental Airlines
☎ 800-231-0856
www.continental.com

Delta Air Lines
☎ 800-241-4141
www.delta.com

Northwest/KLM Airlines
☎ 800-447-4747
www.nwa.com

United Air Lines
☎ 800-538-2929
www.united.com

US Airways
☎ 800-622-1015
www.usairways.com

Major European airlines

Aer Lingus (Ireland)
☎ 800-474-7424 (U.S. and Canada)
☎ 0870-876-5000 (U.K.)
☎ 0818-365-000 (Ireland)
www.aerlingus.com

Air France
☎ 800-237-2747 (U.S.)
☎ 800-667-2747 (Canada)
☎ 0870-142-4343 (U.K.)
☎ 1300-390-190 (Australia)
☎ 0820-820-820 (France)
www.airfrance.com

Alitalia (Italy)
☎ 800-223-5730 (U.S.)
☎ 800-361-8336 (Canada)
☎ 0870-544-8259 (U.K.)
☎ 06-2222 (Italy)
www.alitalia.com

Austrian Airlines
☎ 800-843-0002 (U.S.)
☎ 888-817-4444 (Canada)
☎ 0870-124-2625 (U.K.)
☎ 800-642-438 (Australia)
☎ 05-1789 (Austria)
www.aua.com

British Airways (U.K.)
☎ 800-247-9297 (U.S. and Canada)
☎ 0870-850-9850 (U.K.)
☎ 1300-767-177 (Australia)
www.ba.com

CSA Czech Airlines
☎ 800-223-2365 (U.S.)
☎ 800-641-0641 (Canada)
☎ 870-444-3747 (U.K.)
☎ 420-239-007-007 (Czech Republic)
www.czechairlines.com

EasyJet (U.K.)
☎ 0870-6000-000 (overseas)
☎ 0871-244-2366 (U.K.)
www.easyjet.com

Iberia (Spain)
☎ 800-772-4642 (U.S. and Canada)
☎ 0870-609-0500 (U.K.)
☎ 902-400-500 (Spain)
www.iberia.com

KLM Royal Dutch Airlines/Northwest (The Netherlands)
☎ 800-447-4747 (U.S. and Canada)
☎ 0870-507-4074 (U.K.)
☎ 1-300-392-192 (Australia)
☎ 0800-800-316 (N.Z.)
☎ 020-4-747-747 (The Netherlands)
www.klm.com or www.nwa.com

Lufthansa (Germany)
☎ 800-645-3880 (U.S.)
☎ 800-563-5954 (Canada)
☎ 0870-837-7747 (U.K.)
☎ 1-300-655-727 (Australia)
☎ 0-800-945-200 (N.Z.)
☎ 01-803-803-803 (Germany)
www.lufthansa.com

Olympic Airways (Greece)
☎ 800-223-1226 (U.S.)
☎ 416-964-2720 or 514-878-9691 (Canada)
☎ 0870-606-0460 (U.K.)
☎ 612-9251-2044 (Australia)
☎ 80-111-44444 (Greece)
www.olympic-airways.com

Ryanair (U.K. and Ireland)
☎ 353-1-249-7851 (U.S., Canada, and Australia)
☎ 0871-246-0000 (U.K.) 10p/minute
☎ 0818-303-030 (Ireland)
www.ryanair.com

Swiss (Switzerland)
☎ 877-359-7947 (U.S. and Canada)
☎ 0845-601-0956 (U.K.)
☎ 1-300-724-666 (Australia)
☎ 0848-700-700 (Switzerland)
www.swiss.com

Virgin Atlantic (U.K.)
☎ 800-821-5438 (U.S. and Canada)
☎ 0870-574-7747 (U.K.)
☎ 1-300-727-340 (Australia)
www.virgin-atlantic.com

Major Pacific Rim airlines

Air New Zealand
☎ 800-262-1234 (U.S.)
☎ 800-663-5494 (Canada)
☎ 0800-028-4149 (U.K.)
☎ 132-476 (Australia)
☎ 0800-737-000 (N.Z.)
www.airnewzealand.com

Qantas (Australia)
☎ 800-227-4500 (U.S. and Canada)
☎ 0845-774-7767
☎ 0800-808-767 (N.Z.)
☎ 131-313 (Australia)
www.qantas.com

Car-rental agencies

Advantage
☎ 800-777-5500 (U.S. and Canada)
www.advantagerentacar.com

Alamo
☎ 800-462-5266 (U.S. and Canada)
www.alamo.com

Auto Europe
☎ 888-223-5555 (U.S. and Canada)
www.autoeurope.com

Avis
☎ 800-331-1212 (U.S. and Canada)
www.avis.com

Budget
☎ 800-527-0700 (U.S.)
☎ 800-268-8900 (Canada)
www.budget.com

Enterprise
☎ 800-261-7331 (U.S. and Canada)
☎ 0870-350-3000 (U.K.)
www.enterprise.com

Europe by Car
☎ 800-223-1516 (U.S. and Canada)
www.europebycar.com

Hertz
☎ 800-654-3001 (U.S. and Canada)
www.hertz.com

Kemwel Holiday Auto (KHA)
☎ 877-820-0668 (U.S. and Canada)
www.kemwel.com

National
☎ 800-227-7368 (U.S. and Canada)
www.nationalcar.com

Sixt
☎ 888-749-8227 (U.S. and Canada)
www.sixt-europe.com

Thrifty
☎ 800-847-4389 (U.S. and Canada)
www.thrifty.com

Where to Get More Information

National tourist boards exist to help you plan a trip to their country. If you e-mail or call, they'll gladly send you a big envelope stuffed with brochures and information packets. Many of them are helpful enough to address specific questions and concerns you may have. Even more useful are their Web sites, which are loaded with country-specific information and links to other sites.

That said, take any mailing from a tourist office with a grain of salt. Most of the material is promotional literature and always puts the best spin possible on every aspect of the country. Read between the lines and rely on a quality, impartial, third-party guidebook (like this one!) for the real, opinionated scoop on the local scene.

For local tourist boards, see the "Fast Facts" sections of Chapters 10 through 24. These offices can also send you tons of useful information — but again, view these materials with a critical eye.

International tourist office

European Travel Commission
www.visiteurope.com

National tourism offices

Austrian National Tourist Office
In the U.S.: P.O. Box 1142, New York, NY 10108-1142 (☎ 212-944-6880); 6520 Platt Ave., PMB 561, West Hills, CA 91307-3218 (☎ 818-999-4030).

In Canada: 2 Bloor St. W., Suite 400, Toronto, ON M4W 3E2 (☎ 416-967-4867).

In the U.K.: P.O. Box 2363, London W1A 2QB; 3rd Floor, 9–11 Richmond Buildings, London W1D 3HF (☎ 020-7440-3830).

www.austriatourism.com

Visit Britain (formerly the British Tourist Authority)
In the U.S.: ☎ 800-462-2748. 551 Fifth Ave., Suite 701, New York, NY 10176 (☎ 212-986-2200); 625 N. Michigan Ave., Suite 1001, Chicago, IL 60611 (☎ 312-787-0464).

In Canada: ☎ 888-847-4885. 5915 Airport Rd., Suite 120, Mississauga, ON L4V 1T1 (☎ 905-405-1720).

In the U.K.: 1 Lower Regent St., Piccadilly Circus, London SW1Y 4XT (☎ 020-7808-3864).

In Australia: Level 2, 15 Blue St., North Sydney, NSW 2060 (☎ 02-9021-4400 or 1-300-858-589).

In New Zealand: 151 Queen St., 17th Floor, Auckland 1 (☎ 09-309-1899).

www.visitbritain.com

Czech Tourist Authority
In the U.S.: 1109 Madison Ave., New York, NY 10028 (☎ 212-288-0830).

In Canada: 401 Bay St., Suite 1510, Toronto, ON M5H 2Y4 (☎ 416-363-9928).

In the U.K.: 13 Harley St., London W1M 5RA (☎ 020-7307-5180).

www.czechtourism.com or www.czechcenter.com

French Government Tourist Office
In the U.S.: 444 Madison Ave., 16th Floor, New York, NY 10022 (☎ 212-838-7800); 205 N. Michigan Ave., Suite 3770, Chicago, IL 60601 (☎ 312-751-7800); 9454 Wilshire Blvd., Suite 715, Beverly Hills, CA 90212 (☎ 310-271-6665). To request information at any of these offices, call ☎ 410-286-8310.

In Canada: Maison de la France/French Government Tourist Office, 1981 av. McGill College, Suite 490, Montreal, PQ H3A 2W9 (☎ 514-288-2026).

In the U.K.: Maison de la France/French Tourist Office, 178 Piccadilly, London, W1J 9AL (☎ 09068-244-123, 60p/minute).

In Australia: French Tourist Bureau, Level 20, 25 Bligh St., Sydney, NSW 2000 (☎ 02-9231-5244).

www.franceguide.com or www.francetourism.com

German National Tourist Office
In the U.S.: 122 E. 42nd St., 52nd Floor, New York, NY 10168 (☎ 212-661-7200); P.O. Box 59594, Chicago, IL 60659-9594 (☎ 773-539-6303); 1334 Parkview Ave., Suite 300, Manhattan Beach, CA 90266 (☎ 310-545-1350).

In Canada: 480 University Ave., Suite 1410, Toronto, ON M5G 1V2 (☎ 416-968-1685).

In the U.K.: Nightingale House, 65 Curzon St., London, W1Y 8NE (☎ 020-7371-0908).

In Australia: Lufthansa House, 143 Macquarie St., 12th Floor, Sydney, NSW 2000 (☎ 02-8296-0488).

www.germany-tourism.de or www.cometogermany.com

Greek National Tourist Organization
In the U.S.: Olympic Tower, 645 Fifth Ave., Suite 903, New York, NY 10022 (☎ 212-421-5777).

In Canada: 1500 Don Mills Rd., Suite 102, Toronto, ON M3B 3K4 (☎ 416-968-2220).

In the U.K.: 4 Conduit St., London W1S 2DJ (☎ 020-7495-9300).

In Australia: 37–49 Pitt St., Sydney, NWS 2000 (☎ 02-9241-1663 or 02-9252-1441).

www.greektourism.com

Irish Tourist Board
In the U.S.: 345 Park Ave., New York, NY 10154 (☎ 800-223-6470 or 212-418-0800).

In Canada: 2 Bloor St. W., Suite 3403, Toronto, ON M4W 3E2 (☎ 416-925-6368).

In the U.K.: Nations House, 103 Wigmore St., London W1U 1QS (☎ 020-7518-0800).

In Australia: 36 Carrington St., 5th Level, Sydney, NSW 2000 (☎ 02-9299-6177).

In New Zealand: 18 Shortland St., 6th Floor, Private Bag 92136, Auckland 1 (☎ 09-977-2255).

www.tourismireland.com or www.discoverireland.ie

Italian Government Tourist Board
In the U.S.: 630 Fifth Ave., Suite 1565, New York, NY 10111 (☎ 212-245-5618 or 212-245-4822); 500 N. Michigan Ave., Suite 2240, Chicago, IL 60611 (☎ 312-644-0996); 12400 Wilshire Blvd., Suite 550, Beverly Hills, CA 90025 (☎ 310-820-1898).

In Canada: 175 Bloor St. E., Suite 907, South Tower, Toronto, ON M4W 3R8 (☎ 416-925-4882).

In the U.K.: 1 Princes St., London W1B 2AY (☎ 020-7408-1254).

In Australia: 46 Market St., Level 4, Sydney, NSW 2000 (☎ 02-9262-1666).

www.italiantourism.com or www.enit.it

The Netherlands Board of Tourism
In the U.S.: ☎ 212-557-3500; 355 Lexington Ave., 21st Floor, New York, NY 10017 (☎ 212-370-7360).

In Canada: 14 Glenmount Ct., Whitby, ON L1N 5MB (☎ 905-666-5960).

In the U.K.: P.O. Box 30783, London, WC 2B 6DH (☎ 020-7539-7950 or 0906-871-7777, 60p/minute).

www.holland.com

Scottish Tourist Board
Outside the U.K., the Scottish Tourist Board falls under Visit Britain (formerly the British Tourist Authority; see listing earlier in this section).

www.visitscotland.com

Tourist Office of Spain
In the U.S.: 666 Fifth Ave., 35th Floor, New York, NY 10103 (☎ 212-265-8822); 845 N. Michigan Ave., Suite 915E, Chicago, IL 60611 (☎ 312-642-1992); 8383 Wilshire Blvd., Suite 956, Beverly Hills, CA 90211 (☎ 323-658-7195); 1395 Brickell Ave., Suite 1130, Miami, FL 33131 (☎ 305-358-1992).

In Canada: 2 Bloor St. W., Suite 3402, Toronto, ON M4W 3E2 (☎ 416-961-3131).

In the U.K.: 79 New Cavendish St., 2nd Floor, London W1W 6XB (☎ 020-7486-8077).

www.okspain.org

Switzerland Tourism
In the U.S.: ☎ 877-794-8037. Swiss Center, 608 Fifth Ave., New York, NY 10020 (☎ 212-757-5944); 222 N. Sepulveda Blvd., Suite 1570, El Segundo, CA 90245 (☎ 310-335-5980).

In the U.K.: Swiss Centre, 30 Bedford St., London WC2E 9ED (☎ 0800-1002-0030 or 020-7420-4900).

www.myswitzerland.com

Index

Accommodations Index

Restaurant Index

BUSINESS, CAREERS & PERSONAL FINANCE

Accounting For Dummies, 4th Edition*
978-0-470-24600-9

Bookkeeping Workbook For Dummies†
978-0-470-16983-4

Commodities For Dummies
978-0-470-04928-0

Doing Business in China For Dummies
978-0-470-04929-7

E-Mail Marketing For Dummies
978-0-470-19087-6

Job Interviews For Dummies, 3rd Edition*†
978-0-470-17748-8

Personal Finance Workbook For Dummies*†
978-0-470-09933-9

Real Estate License Exams For Dummies
978-0-7645-7623-2

Six Sigma For Dummies
978-0-7645-6798-8

Small Business Kit For Dummies,
2nd Edition*†
978-0-7645-5984-6

Telephone Sales For Dummies
978-0-470-16836-3

BUSINESS PRODUCTIVITY & MICROSOFT OFFICE

Access 2007 For Dummies
978-0-470-03649-5

Excel 2007 For Dummies
978-0-470-03737-9

Office 2007 For Dummies
978-0-470-00923-9

Outlook 2007 For Dummies
978-0-470-03830-7

PowerPoint 2007 For Dummies
978-0-470-04059-1

Project 2007 For Dummies
978-0-470-03651-8

QuickBooks 2008 For Dummies
978-0-470-18470-7

Quicken 2008 For Dummies
978-0-470-17473-9

Salesforce.com For Dummies,
2nd Edition
978-0-470-04893-1

Word 2007 For Dummies
978-0-470-03658-7

EDUCATION, HISTORY, REFERENCE & TEST PREPARATION

African American History For Dummies
978-0-7645-5469-8

Algebra For Dummies
978-0-7645-5325-7

Algebra Workbook For Dummies
978-0-7645-8467-1

Art History For Dummies
978-0-470-09910-0

ASVAB For Dummies, 2nd Edition
978-0-470-10671-6

British Military History For Dummies
978-0-470-03213-8

Calculus For Dummies
978-0-7645-2498-1

Canadian History For Dummies, 2nd Edition
978-0-470-83656-9

Geometry Workbook For Dummies
978-0-471-79940-5

The SAT I For Dummies, 6th Edition
978-0-7645-7193-0

Series 7 Exam For Dummies
978-0-470-09932-2

World History For Dummies
978-0-7645-5242-7

FOOD, GARDEN, HOBBIES & HOME

Bridge For Dummies, 2nd Edition
978-0-471-92426-5

Coin Collecting For Dummies, 2nd Edition
978-0-470-22275-1

Cooking Basics For Dummies, 3rd Edition
978-0-7645-7206-7

Drawing For Dummies
978-0-7645-5476-0

Etiquette For Dummies, 2nd Edition
978-0-470-10672-3

Gardening Basics For Dummies*†
978-0-470-03749-2

Knitting Patterns For Dummies
978-0-470-04556-5

Living Gluten-Free For Dummies†
978-0-471-77383-2

Painting Do-It-Yourself For Dummies
978-0-470-17533-0

HEALTH, SELF HELP, PARENTING & PETS

Anger Management For Dummies
978-0-470-03715-7

Anxiety & Depression Workbook
For Dummies
978-0-7645-9793-0

Dieting For Dummies, 2nd Edition
978-0-7645-4149-0

Dog Training For Dummies, 2nd Edition
978-0-7645-8418-3

Horseback Riding For Dummies
978-0-470-09719-9

Infertility For Dummies†
978-0-470-11518-3

Meditation For Dummies with CD-ROM,
2nd Edition
978-0-471-77774-8

Post-Traumatic Stress Disorder For Dummies
978-0-470-04922-8

Puppies For Dummies, 2nd Edition
978-0-470-03717-1

Thyroid For Dummies, 2nd Edition†
978-0-471-78755-6

Type 1 Diabetes For Dummies*†
978-0-470-17811-9

INTERNET & DIGITAL MEDIA

AdWords For Dummies
978-0-470-15252-2

Blogging For Dummies, 2nd Edition
978-0-470-23017-6

**Digital Photography All-in-One
Desk Reference For Dummies, 3rd Edition**
978-0-470-03743-0

Digital Photography For Dummies, 5th Edition
978-0-470-9802-9

**Digital SLR Cameras & Photography
For Dummies, 2nd Edition**
978-0-470-14927-0

**eBay Business All-in-One Desk Reference
For Dummies**
978-0-7645-8438-1

eBay For Dummies, 5th Edition*
978-0-470-04529-9

eBay Listings That Sell For Dummies
978-0-471-78912-3

Facebook For Dummies
978-0-470-26273-3

The Internet For Dummies, 11th Edition
978-0-470-12174-0

Investing Online For Dummies, 5th Edition
978-0-7645-8456-5

iPod & iTunes For Dummies, 5th Edition
978-0-470-17474-6

MySpace For Dummies
978-0-470-09529-4

Podcasting For Dummies
978-0-471-74898-4

**Search Engine Optimization
For Dummies, 2nd Edition**
978-0-471-97998-2

Second Life For Dummies
978-0-470-18025-9

**Starting an eBay Business For Dummies,
3rd Edition†**
978-0-470-14924-9

GRAPHICS, DESIGN & WEB DEVELOPMENT

**Adobe Creative Suite 3 Design Premium
All-in-One Desk Reference For Dummies**
978-0-470-11724-8

**Adobe Web Suite CS3 All-in-One Desk
Reference For Dummies**
978-0-470-12099-6

AutoCAD 2008 For Dummies
978-0-470-11650-0

**Building a Web Site For Dummies,
3rd Edition**
978-0-470-14928-7

**Creating Web Pages All-in-One Desk
Reference For Dummies, 3rd Edition**
978-0-470-09629-1

**Creating Web Pages For Dummies,
8th Edition**
978-0-470-08030-6

Dreamweaver CS3 For Dummies
978-0-470-11490-2

Flash CS3 For Dummies
978-0-470-12100-9

Google SketchUp For Dummies
978-0-470-13744-4

InDesign CS3 For Dummies
978-0-470-11865-8

**Photoshop CS3 All-in-One
Desk Reference For Dummies**
978-0-470-11195-6

Photoshop CS3 For Dummies
978-0-470-11193-2

Photoshop Elements 5 For Dummies
978-0-470-09810-3

SolidWorks For Dummies
978-0-7645-9555-4

Visio 2007 For Dummies
978-0-470-08983-5

Web Design For Dummies, 2nd Edition
978-0-471-78117-2

Web Sites Do-It-Yourself For Dummies
978-0-470-16903-2

Web Stores Do-It-Yourself For Dummies
978-0-470-17443-2

LANGUAGES, RELIGION & SPIRITUALITY

Arabic For Dummies
978-0-471-77270-5

Chinese For Dummies, Audio Set
978-0-470-12766-7

French For Dummies
978-0-7645-5193-2

German For Dummies
978-0-7645-5195-6

Hebrew For Dummies
978-0-7645-5489-6

Ingles Para Dummies
978-0-7645-5427-8

Italian For Dummies, Audio Set
978-0-470-09586-7

Italian Verbs For Dummies
978-0-471-77389-4

Japanese For Dummies
978-0-7645-5429-2

Latin For Dummies
978-0-7645-5431-5

Portuguese For Dummies
978-0-471-78738-9

Russian For Dummies
978-0-471-78001-4

Spanish Phrases For Dummies
978-0-7645-7204-3

Spanish For Dummies
978-0-7645-5194-9

Spanish For Dummies, Audio Set
978-0-470-09585-0

The Bible For Dummies
978-0-7645-5296-0

Catholicism For Dummies
978-0-7645-5391-2

The Historical Jesus For Dummies
978-0-470-16785-4

Islam For Dummies
978-0-7645-5503-9

**Spirituality For Dummies,
2nd Edition**
978-0-470-19142-2

NETWORKING AND PROGRAMMING

ASP.NET 3.5 For Dummies
978-0-470-19592-5

C# 2008 For Dummies
978-0-470-19109-5

Hacking For Dummies, 2nd Edition
978-0-470-05235-8

Home Networking For Dummies, 4th Edition
978-0-470-11806-1

Java For Dummies, 4th Edition
978-0-470-08716-9

**Microsoft® SQL Server™ 2008 All-in-One
Desk Reference For Dummies**
978-0-470-17954-3

**Networking All-in-One Desk Reference
For Dummies, 2nd Edition**
978-0-7645-9939-2

**Networking For Dummies,
8th Edition**
978-0-470-05620-2

SharePoint 2007 For Dummies
978-0-470-09941-4

**Wireless Home Networking
For Dummies, 2nd Edition**
978-0-471-74940-0